Handbook of
Eating Disorders

HANDBOOK OF EATING DISORDERS

Physiology, Psychology, and Treatment of Obesity, Anorexia, and Bulimia

EDITED BY

Kelly D. Brownell and John P. Foreyt

Basic Books, Inc., Publishers   *New York*

Library of Congress Cataloging-in-Publication Data

Handbook of eating disorders.

Includes bibliographies and index.
1. Appetite disorders. I. Brownell, Kelly D.
II. Foreyt, John Paul. [DNLM: 1. Appetite Disorders.
WM 175 H2355]
RC552.A72H36 1986 616.85′2 85–48021
ISBN 0–465–02862–4

CONTENTS

PART II

ANOREXIA NERVOSA

PART III

BULIMIA

EDITORS

Kelly D. Brownell, Ph.D.
*Associate Professor, Department of Psychiatry, University of Pennsylvania
School of Medicine, Philadelphia.*

John P. Foreyt, Ph.D.
*Director, Diet Modification Clinic, and Associate Professor, Department
of Medicine, Baylor College of Medicine, Houston.*

CONTRIBUTORS

W. Stewart Agras, M.D.
Professor of Psychiatry and Director, Behavioral Medicine Program, Stanford University School of Medicine, Stanford, California.

Arnold E. Andersen, M.D.
Associate Professor, Department of Psychiatry and Behavioral Sciences, The Johns Hopkins University School of Medicine, Baltimore.

Per Björntorp, M.D., Ph.D.
Professor of Medicine and Head, Department of Medicine I, University of Göteborg, Sweden.

George L. Blackburn, M.D., Ph.D.
Associate Professor of Surgery, Harvard Medical School, Boston, and Chief, Nutrition / Metabolism Laboratory, New England Deaconess Hospital, Boston.

Marlene Boskind-White, Ph.D.
Codirector, Outpatient Services, Saint Albans Psychiatric Associates, Roanoke, Virginia, and Saint Albans Psychiatric Hospital, Radford, Virginia.

George A. Bray, M.D.
Professor of Medicine, University of Southern California, and Chief, Section of Diabetes and Clinical Nutrition, Los Angeles County-University of Southern California Medical Center, Los Angeles.

Kelly D. Brownell, Ph.D.
Associate Professor, Department of Psychiatry, University of Pennsylvania School of Medicine, Philadelphia.

Hilde Bruch, M.D.
Dr. Bruch died on December 15, 1984. She was Professor Emeritus, Department of Psychiatry, Baylor College of Medicine, Houston.

Peter J. Cooper, D.Phil., Dip.Psych.
Lecturer in Psychopathology, Department of Psychiatry, University of Cambridge, Addenbrookes Hospital, Cambridge, England.

Zafra Cooper, D.Phil.
Clinical Psychologist, Department of Clinical Psychology, Oxford University, Warneford Hospital, Oxford, England.

Johanna T. Dwyer, D.Sc., R.D.
Professor of Medicine, Tufts Medical School, and Director, Francis Stern Nutrition Center, New England Medical Center Hospitals, Boston.

Leonard H. Epstein, Ph.D.
Professor of Psychiatry, University of Pittsburgh School of Medicine.

Christopher Fairburn, M.Phil., M.R.C.Psych.
Wellcome Trust Senior Lecturer, Department of Psychiatry, Oxford University, Warneford Hospital, Oxford, England.

John P. Foreyt, Ph.D.
Associate Professor, Department of Medicine, Baylor College of Medicine, Houston.

Paul E. Garfinkel, M.D., M.Sc., F.R.C.P.(C)
Psychiatrist-in-Chief, Toronto General Hospital, and Professor and Vice-Chairman, Department of Psychiatry, University of Toronto.

David Garner, Ph.D.
Professor of Psychiatry, University of Toronto, and Department of Psychiatry, Toronto General Hospital.

John S. Garrow, M.D., Ph.D.
Head, Nutrition Research Group, Clinical Research Centre, Division of Clinical Sciences, Harrow, Middlesex, England.

Craig Johnson, Ph.D.
Associate Professor of Psychiatry, Northwestern University Medical School, Chicago.

Allan S. Kaplan, M.D., F.R.C.P.(C)
Medical Director, Eating Disorders Center, Toronto General Hospital, and Assistant Professor, Department of Psychiatry, University of Toronto.

Ann Kearney-Cooke, Ph.D.
Assistant Clinical Director, Eating Disorders Clinic, Psychiatry Department, University of Cincinnati Medical College.

Richard E. Keesey, Ph.D.
Professor of Psychology, University of Wisconsin, Madison.

Betty G. Kirkley, Ph.D.
Assistant Professor, Department of Nutrition, University of North Carolina, Chapel Hill, North Carolina.

Patricia Lowney, B.A.
Graduate Fellow, Food Intake Laboratory, Department of Nutrition, University of California at Davis.

Margaret E. Lynch, B.A.
Research Assistant, Nutrition / Metabolism Laboratory, New England Deaconess Hospital, Boston.

James E. Mitchell, M.D.
Associate Professor of Psychiatry, Department of Psychiatry, University of Minnesota, Minneapolis.

Patricia Nicholas, M.S., R.D.
Frances Stern Nutrition Center, Department of Medicine, New England Medical Center Hospitals, and Department of Medicine, Tufts Medical School, Boston.

Darryl L. Pure, Ph.D.
Research Associate, Department of Psychiatry, Northwestern University Medical School, Chicago.

Judith Rodin, Ph.D.
Philip R. Allen Professor of Psychology and Professor of Psychiatry, Yale University, New Haven, Connecticut.

Gerald F. M. Russell, M.D., F.R.C.P., F.R.C.P.(E.D.), F.R.C.Psych.
Professor of Psychiatry, Institute of Psychiatry and the Maudsley Hospital, London.

Judith S. Stern, Sc.D.
Professor of Nutrition and Director, Food Intake Laboratory, Department of Nutrition, University of California at Davis.

Ruth H. Striegel-Moore, Ph.D.
Associate in Research, Department of Psychology, Yale University, and Clinical Director, Yale Eating Disorders Clinic, New Haven, Connecticut.

Michael Strober, Ph.D.
Associate Professor of Psychiatry and Biobehavioral Sciences and Director, Teenage Eating Disorders Program, Neuropsychiatric Institute, School of Medicine, University of California at Los Angeles.

Albert Stunkard, M.D.
Professor of Psychiatry, University of Pennsylvania, Philadelphia.

George I. Szmukler, M.D., D.P.M., M.R.C.Psych.
Consultant Psychiatrist, Crisis Intervention Service, The Royal Melbourne Hospital, Victoria, Australia.

Thomas A. Wadden, Ph.D.
Assistant Professor, Department of Psychiatry, University of Pennsylvania School of Medicine, Philadelphia.

William C. White, Jr., Ph.D.
Codirector, Outpatient Services, Saint Albans Psychiatric Associates, Roanoke, Virginia, and Saint Albans Psychiatric Hospital, Radford, Virginia.

G. Terence Wilson, Ph.D.
Oscar K. Buros Professor of Psychology, Graduate School of Applied and Professional Psychology, Rutgers University, Piscataway, New Jersey.

Stacie L. Wong, B.A.
Research Assistant, Nutrition / Metabolism Laboratory, New England Deaconess Hospital, Boston.

Susan C. Wooley, Ph.D.
Director, Eating Disorders Clinic, Psychiatry Department, and Associate Professor of Psychiatry, University of Cincinnati Medical College.

A Tribute to Hilde Bruch

Hilde Bruch was to have written the other foreword to this volume. Her recent death, in an old age filled with honors, has deprived us of this commentary, and of so much else. I know of no one who could have commented more wisely on this rich and varied volume. For she could bring to the task the perspective of half a century of work in the eating disorders. And she did more than simply watch the field evolve; more than anyone else, Hilde Bruch was responsible for its creation.

It is often difficult to look back in time and recognize what were the significant contributions to the development of a discipline, to understand what things made the difference, what changed the paradigms. Two sources of change are certainly new ideas and new observations, and Hilde Bruch contributed significantly to both. Her concept of "preferred weight" foreshadowed currently popular notions of a body weight set point, and her description of the problems of reduced obese persons— "thin fat people"—astutely recognized the physiological pressures resulting from weight loss in some persons—perhaps those who reduce below a body weight set point. She soon recognized the heterogeneity of obesity and her early attempts at a clinical classification of the disorder preceded later (and still continuing) efforts to this end. It was Bruch who described the "family frame" of children with obesity and set the stage for the development of family therapy.

But new ideas and new observations play only a part in the creation of new paradigms—in this case, in our understanding of the eating disorders. More important is the questioning of the old ways. As long as we look at things in the old ways, it is often difficult to see what is in front of us. Once the blinders are removed, it is often striking how much we can see. Hilde Bruch's main contribution may well have been to remove the blinders.

I remember a gourmet meal that she cooked for me in the summer of 1953 when I was embarking on full-time research on obesity, and the impression that she made at the time. I had been listening to other experts' bland assurances that we knew just about everything that could be learned about obesity. No doubt there were a few rough edges that could be polished, but there really wasn't very much left to find out. What a contrast it was to listen to Hilde Bruch!

Angry, questioning, probing, she scorned the certainties of both the endocrinologists and the psychoanalysts (who weren't talking to one another). She was adamant: If we knew so much about eating disorders, why couldn't we treat them? It was immoral to be satisfied with what we were doing; we were shortchanging our patients if we stopped here. She was particularly incensed over the established views on anorexia nervosa. At that time the dominant view was that anorexia nervosa was caused by unconscious fears of oral impregnation, a theory that was proving better suited to explain therapeutic failure than to contribute to successful treatment. Bruch dismissed it as "gobbledygook," and wasn't afraid to say so. Perhaps it was this lack of reverence for the established views that enabled her to see for the first time what has now become so obvious: the critical role of what she was the first to call "the relentless pursuit of thinness."

This volume is a celebration of what Hilde Bruch began. Its twenty-five chapters include contributions by most of the leaders in the field, including Hilde Bruch. As she would have liked, it deals largely with clinical concerns and with treatment. And, though this treatment may not yet be as effective as we would like, the contributors show none of the complacency that pervaded the field when Hilde Bruch began and against which she struggled so long and so effectively. Each chapter is an unfinished story, a snapshot of work in progress, a question as well as an answer. Perhaps that is why they are so good.

—ALBERT J. STUNKARD

PART I

OBESITY

1

Effects of Obesity on Health and Happiness

George A. Bray

Leave gourmandizing; Know the grave doth gape
For thee thrice wider than for other men.
—SHAKESPEARE, *Henry IV*, Part II

The medical and social problems identified with obesity can be manifested in many ways. Obesity may decrease longevity, aggravate the onset and clinical progression of maladies, and modify the social or economic quality of life. On the positive side, weight loss can reverse all or most of the disadvantages of obesity.

Most of the data relating health and obesity have been collected and analyzed in terms of overweight. Overweight refers to deviations in body weight from some "standard weight" related to height. Being overweight, however, does not necessarily mean being obese. This distinction is most obvious in athletes but may also apply to other groups and individuals with body weights only slightly above the upper limits of normal. The correlation between measures of body weight such as weight divided by height, percentage overweight, or body mass index (wt/ht^2), have a correlation of between 0.7 and 0.8 with body fat measured by other more precise laboratory methods. Of these indices, the body mass or Quetelet index has the highest correlation with body fat. In this chapter the following definitions will be used.

FIGURE 1.1

Nomogram for body mass index (BMI). To determine BMI, place a ruler or other straight edge between the body weight column on the left and the height column on the right and read the BMI from the point where it crosses the center.

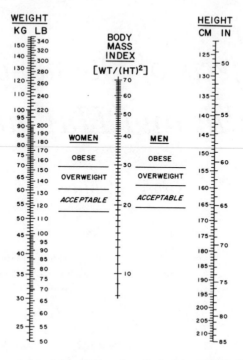

NOTE: Reprinted, by permission of the publisher, from G. A. Bray, 1978, Definitions, measurements and classification of the syndromes of obesity, *International Journal of Obesity* 2:99–112.

Overweight:

1. Body mass index (BMI) of 25 to 30 kg/m² (see figure 1.1 for nomogram to determine BMI).
2. Body weight between the upper limit of normal and 20 percent above that limit (see table 1.1 for weight ranges).

Obesity:

1. BMI above 30 kg/m².
2. Triceps plus subscapular skin fold (mm): 45 mm for males and 69 mm for females.
3. Body weight more than 20 percent above the upper limit for height.
4. Body fat 25 percent of body weight in males or 30 percent in females.

When the BMI (kg/m²) is between 25 and 30, some individuals will not meet the criteria for "obesity" using skin folds. However, when the BMI is above 30, the skin-fold measures almost always confirm the presence of obesity.[2]

TABLE 1.1
Fogarty Table of Desirable Weights

Height (cm)[a]	Men Average Weight (kg)[a]	Men Acceptable Weight Range[a]	Women Average Weight (kg)[a]	Women Acceptable Weight Range[a]
	Metric			
145			46.0	42–53
148			46.5	42–54
150			47.0	43–55
152			48.5	44–57
154			49.5	44–58
156			50.4	45–58
158	55.8	51–64	51.3	46–59
160	57.6	52–65	52.6	48–61
162	58.6	53–66	54.0	49–62
164	59.6	54–67	55.4	50–64
166	60.6	55–69	56.8	51–65
168	61.7	56–71	58.1	52–66
170	63.5	58–73	60.0	53–67
172	65.0	59–74	61.3	55–69
174	66.5	60–75	62.6	56–70
176	68.0	62–77	64.0	58–72
178	69.4	64–79	65.3	59–74
180	71.0	65–80		
182	72.6	66–82		
184	74.2	67–84		
186	75.8	69–86		
188	77.6	71–88		
190	79.3	73–90		
192	81.0	75–93		
	Nonmetric			
4'10"			102	92–119
4'11"			104	94–122
5'0"			107	96–125
5'1"			110	99–128
5'2"	123	112–141	113	102–131
5'3"	127	115–144	116	105–134
5'4"	130	118–148	120	108–138
5'5"	133	121–152	123	111–142
5'6"	136	124–156	128	114–146
5'7"	140	128–161	132	118–150
5'8"	145	132–166	136	122–154
5'9"	149	136–170	140	126–158
5'10"	153	140–174	144	130–163
5'11"	158	144–179	148	134–168
6'0"	166	152–189		
6'1"	166	152–189		
6'2"	171	156–194		
6'3"	176	160–199		
6'4"	181	164–204		

SOURCE: G. A. Bray, ed., *Obesity in Perspective*, vol. 2, part 1, DHEW Publication no. (NIH) 75–708. Washington, D.C.: U.S. Government Printing Office, p. 72.
[a] Height without shoes, weight without clothes.

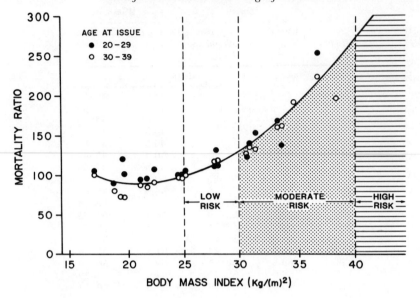

FIGURE 1.2

Relation of body mass index (BMI) to excess mortality. The u- or j-shaped relationship between the mortality ratio and BMI is apparent. The dashed lines indicate the various levels of risk associated with ranges from BMI.

Overweight and Life Expectancy

RETROSPECTIVE LIFE INSURANCE STUDIES

Applicants for life insurance usually undergo a medical examination. In the Build Study of 1979,[136] weight was measured in 86.1 to 88.5 percent of the 3,997,650 men and 592,509 women on whom policies were taken out. The analysis of such data, with all of its limitations, provides the major retrospective studies on the effects of body weight on mortality and morbidity. One limitation is that persons who buy life insurance may not represent the American population. They earn above-average income, are Caucasian, are free of serious medical diseases, and are usually engaged in "safe" occupations. The mortality rate among insured individuals is only about 90 percent of the rate for the entire population at all ages between 15 and 70.[17]

The information obtained from analysis of the life insurance experience is valuable for two reasons. The sample size is large, comprising several million individuals. Second, the individuals are continually followed until death, an event in which the life insurance companies have a financial interest. Figure 1.2 shows the relation between excess mortality and deviations in body weight. The overall mortality rate—that is, the ratio of deaths to the total population of insured lives—was taken as 100. The insured individuals were subdivided into subgroups based on the percentage deviation from the mean for the entire group. The death rate in each subgroup was then compared to the population as a whole and expressed as deviation from the overall mortality of 100. The minimum death rate occurred at a body weight that was slightly less than the average weight for the entire population. As body weight, expressed as the BMI (kg/m^2), increased, there was a progressive increase in "excess mortality." There was also a small increase in excess mortality with very low body weight. This was more pronounced in the younger age group than in the older one and may reflect a higher number of smokers. The excess mortality among those with life insurance was due to diabetes mellitus, digestive diseases, hypertension, cardiovascular diseases, and cancer.

Comparison of the Build and Blood Pressure Study of 1959[135] with the Build Study of 1979[136] reveals several facts. Body weights of insured Americans were higher in the recent study. However, the curvilinear relation of excess mortality to BMI was evident for all age groups in both studies. Unfortunately, few grossly obese individuals were insured in either study. The implications from the life insurance studies is that obesity is hazardous.

Drenick and associates[36] provided a clear insight into the effects of gross obesity on life expectancy. They reviewed two hundred morbidly obese men whose average weight was 143.5 kg, who were admitted for a weight-control program and followed for an average period for seven and a half years. Of these men, 185 were followed until death or termination of the study. The age range was 23 to 70 years with a mean of 42.7 years. The mortality rate was higher at all ages when compared with the mortality expected for the general population of U.S. males (see figure 1.3). In men aged 25 to 34, the excess mortality was 1,200 percent! In those aged 35 to 44, the excess mortality had declined to 550 percent, and in men 45 to 54, it was 300 percent. In men aged 55 to 64, the excess mortality was only double that of the normal U.S. population. This study showed that the excess mortality associated with obesity is greatly increased in the younger age groups and that excess mortality is substantially higher in grossly obese persons.

PROSPECTIVE STUDIES OF OVERWEIGHT AND LONGEVITY

The mortality experience of insured lives has served as an impetus for a number of prospective studies that have examined the relationship of overweight and obesity to the development of cardiovascular disease.[29,68,81,85] Table 1.2 summarizes the findings in some of the studies that will be reviewed.

The Framingham Study. One of the most widely quoted studies on the risk factors related to coronary artery disease was conducted on 2,252 men and 2,818 women living in Framingham, Massachusetts.[29] Initial examinations were performed between 1948 and 1950 and participants

FIGURE 1.3

*Excess probability of dying among morbidly obese men relative to
the mortality of U.S. men as a whole.*

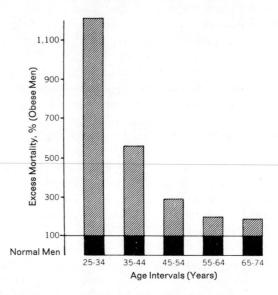

NOTE: Reprinted, by permission of the publisher, from E. J. Drenick, S. B. Gurunanjappa, F. S. A.
Seltzer, and D. G. Johnson, 1980, Excessive mortality and causes of death in morbidly obese men, *Journal
of the American Medical Association* **243**:443–445.

were examined at two-year intervals thereafter. Two criteria were used
for body weight. The first, called "Framingham relative weight," was
based on the median body weights for height obtained from the initial
examination. The median body weights of subjects living in Framingham
were almost identical with the upper limits for individuals with heavy
frames in the life insurance tables published in 1959 by the Metropolitan
Life Insurance Company. In other studies the midpoint of the medium
frame in the Metropolitan Life Insurance table was used to define a Metropolitan Relative Weight. Using the Metropolitan Relative Weight, 15
percent of the men and 18.9 percent of the women were 20 percent
overweight. Three percent of the men and 9 percent of the women were
more than 50 percent overweight.

Weight gain was associated with increases in serum lipids, blood pressure, and uric acid, and impairment in glucose tolerance.[6] After twenty-
six years there were 870 deaths among the men and 688 among the
women.[58] Relative weight at entry into the study was an independent
predictor for development of cardiovascular disease, particularly in
women. The twenty-six year incidence of coronary disease (including angina pectoris and coronary disease other than angina), death from coronary disease, and the likelihood of developing congestive heart failure in
men was predicted from the initial degree of overweight using multiple
logistic regression analysis. The predictive power for the relative degree

TABLE 1.2

Associations Between Body Weight and Mortality

Author	Year	Number Subjects	Sex	Follow-up Years	Type of Study	Criterion for Overweight of Obesity	Associated Risks
Society of Actuaries	1980	3,700,000 500,000	M F	6.6	Retrospective mortality	Relative weight	Heart diseases, digestive diseases, diabetes mellitus
Rabkin	1977	3983	M	26	Retrospective morbidity	$Wt/(ht)^2 (kg/m^2)$	Ischemic heart disease—mainly in men under 40
Drenick	1980	200 (massive obesity)	M	2–8	Retrospective mortality	Weight for height and frame size	Deaths increased up to twelvefold in men 25–34: heart diseases, hypertension, diabetes mellitus, arthritis, and gout
Hubert	1983	2252 2818	M F	26	Prospective morbidity	Relative weight (actual/desirable wt)	Coronary heart disease and death; congestive heart failure—men and women
Keys	1980	2571 (U.S.) 2555 (N. Europe) 5205 (S. Europe)	M M	10	Prospective morbidity and mortality	Relative weight; subscapular plus triceps; skin folds > 37 mm $wt/ht^2 > 27\ kg/m^2$	Overweight and obesity associated with coronary heart disease in U.S. and S. European men. Effect mainly through association of overweight and hypertension
Lew	1979	336,442 419,060	M F	12	Prospective mortality	Wt (lb) average wt for height and age	Coronary heart disease, diabetes mellitus, digestive diseases, cancer all sites, cerebrovascular disease
Rimm	1975	73,532	F		Retrospective morbidity	Wt (lb) ht (in) in quintiles	Diabetes mellitus, hypertension, gallbladder disease, gout, hypothyroidism, heart disease, arthritis, jaundice

of overweight was independent of age, cholesterol, systolic blood pressure, cigarette smoking, or glucose intolerance. Relative body weight in women also positively and independently predicted the likelihood for developing coronary disease, stroke, congestive failure, and death from coronary heart disease. Weight gain after the young-adult years increased the risk of cardiovascular disease in both sexes. There was, however, no effect of excess weight on the frequency of intermittent claudication. One conclusion from this study is that obesity is an important long-term predictor of cardiovascular disease particularly among younger individuals. In women only age and blood pressure were more powerful predictors.[58] The importance of long-term follow-up has also been noted in the Manitoba study.[116] The observation of greater impact of obesity on younger individuals was noted by Drenick (see figure 1.3) and again in the Manitoba study.[116] From the data collected in the Framingham study, it can be estimated that "if everyone were at optimal weight, there would be 25 percent less coronary heart disease, and 35 percent less congestive heart failure and brain infarction" (p. 143).[63]

The International Cooperative Study of Cardiovascular Epidemiology. This prospective study involved an international collaborative examination of risk factors for development of coronary heart disease in fourteen cohorts of men in Holland and Finland (2,349 men, called the Northern European group); in Italy, Greece, and Yugoslavia (6,519 men, called the Southern European group); and in railway workers in the United States (2,442 men).[68] Men at entry into the study were between 40 and 59 years old. Overweight was defined as a BMI greater than 27 kg/m², and obesity as the sum of the triceps and subscapular skin folds greater than 37 mm. Using these criteria, over half (52.3 percent) of the United States railway workers were obese. This is a substantially higher fraction of obese men than in the Northern European group but comparable to that in the Southern European group.

Coronary events were divided into two subgroups: The "hard" events were those associated with death from coronary heart disease or definite myocardial infarction; and the "soft" events included classical angina pectoris and clinical judgment of possible heart disease. The data were similar for BMI in U.S. railwaymen and in the population in Southern Europe; both were much different from that observed in the men from Northern European countries. Among the men from the United States and Southern Europe, there were few, if any, significant relationships between body weight and "hard" events of coronary heart disease, but overweight was correlated with the "soft" criteria for coronary artery disease. Among the men from Northern Europe, the relationship was nearly reversed. There were statistically significant correlations between all measures of body weight and "hard" criteria but no significant association with body weight and "soft" diagnostic criteria for coronary artery disease.

The study's authors used a multivariate analysis to assign the relative risk for each factor. Relative weight and blood pressure were highly correlated. This finding has been observed in almost all studies in which body weight and blood pressure have been measured.[26,69,85] Keys and associates[69] concluded that neither relative weight nor fatness was an independent value in predicting the risk of developing coronary heart disease, but excess weight *was* important because of its association with high blood pressure. In addition, they[69] studied men aged 40 to 59 at the time of entry into the study. The effects of overweight on mortality diminish with age.[36,116] This suggests that overweight may have its major influences on mortality in men under age 40 and might not be detected in studies of older men.

American Cancer Society Study. In 1978 Lew and Garfinkel[85] reported on one portion of a prospective study on mortality in relation to body weight of more than 750,000 individuals studied between 1959 and 1972. In the fall of 1959 more than 1 million volunteers completed a detailed four-page questionnaire. The families who participated came from twenty-six states and included at least one individual over 45 years of age. The survival status of all individuals was reported annually, and death certificates were obtained for those who died. Through 1971, 98.4 percent of the participants were successfully traced. Height and weight were self-reported, and data were included for only those individuals who said they were not sick, had not lost 10 pounds or more in the past year, and who did not have cardiovascular disease, cancer, or stroke.

Seven weight categories were established, from those less than 80 percent of average weight to those above 140 percent of average weight. Body weights for women were more variable than were those reported by men. Socioeconomic influences were reported for both sexes; those with less schooling were more overweight. Relative death rates for the eight subgroups were compared to the death rate of the group whose weight was between 90 to 109 percent of average. As the BMI increased, the overall mortality rate increased. The data for men and women have been plotted after converting the data to BMI (kg/m^2). The j or u shape of the curves is readily apparent (see figure 1.4) and is similar to the life insurance data (see figure 1.2) and other prospective studies.[67] The American Cancer Society Study is one of the few prospective studies that allows for a separation of smokers and nonsmokers. The data for men and women are shown in figure 1.4. Note that a smoker of normal body weight has an increased mortality comparable to a nonsmoker with a BMI of 30 to 35.

The major factor in this extra mortality is cardiovascular disease. When the data for cardiovascular disease are plotted using the format just given, there is no increase in mortality if the BMI is below 25 kg/m^2. Above this point, the increase in excess mortality is almost linear for both sexes. These findings are similar to those of the Build study[136] and the Framingham study.[29]

The effects of excess weight on death from diabetes mellitus was particularly apparent in this study. There was no increase in mortality until the BMI exceeded 25 kg/m^2. Above this point, the effect of increasing weight was much more profound than for heart disease. In the highest

FIGURE 1.4

*The relation of body mass index to mortality from all causes for smokers and nonsmokers.
The j curves are evident for both smokers and nonsmokers,
but the smokers are at much higher risks for both sexes.*

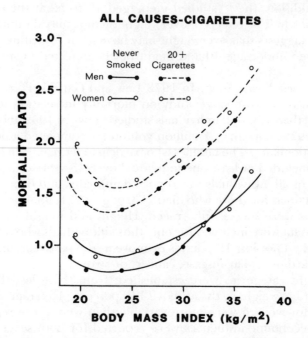

SOURCE: E. A. Lew and L. Garfinkel, 1979, Variations in mortality by weight among 750,000 men and women, *Journal of Chronic Diseases* 32:563–576.

weight groups, the extra mortality was increased by 800 percent! Digestive disease, primarily gallbladder disease, was second in importance to diabetes. Death from cancer also rises with excess weight. There were higher rates of prostatic and colo-rectal cancer in males and of cancers of the gallbladder, breast, cervix, endometrium, uterus, and ovary in women.

The Gothenburg Study. A prospective study from Gothenburg, Sweden, provided additional information about the health consequences of moderate obesity.[81] A sample of 855 men were randomly selected from the general population in 1963 and were evaluated for initial degree of obesity and various health indicators. Of these men, 787 (84 percent) were reexamined at age 60, ten years following the initial examination. A second group of 226 50-year-old men were examined at the same time. Obesity was determined from anthropomorphic measures and from total body fat determined by total body potassium (^{40}K). About one-third of the study population were using prescribed drugs. These were more frequently used among obese than among normal-weight men. The main cause for increased drug use in the overweight men was for hypertension. Subjective indicators of illness, on the other hand, were not related to the degree of fatness. In the longitudinal analysis, men who developed kidney stones, gallstones, and diabetes were significantly more obese at the initial examination than those who did not. An increase in BMI or body fatness was weakly associated with increased risk for stroke. Those who developed angina pectoris, intermittent claudication, or peptic ulcer, however, did not differ in their initial weight status. Obesity was related to myocardial infarction or death. Larsson and his colleagues concluded "that even moderate obesity increases the risk for hypertension, diabetes mellitus, gallstone disease, kidney-stone disease and cerebrovascular disease" (p. 115).

These authors have recently reexamined the data on these men using tertiles based on BMI and the ratio of waist circumference to hip circumference. These two measures were positively correlated in those who developed strokes. That is, men with a higher waist/hip ratio and higher BMI had the higher risk for developing strokes. The highest risk of stroke was in the group with both a high BMI and a high ratio of hips to waist. For cardiovascular disease, the highest risk was in the group with the highest hips to waist ratio and the lowest BMI (kg/m^2). Carrying extra fat around the waist is particularly risky for individuals who are not very much overweight.[82] The effects of excess weight may be more important in younger people than in those who develop obesity later in life. In the men who are overweight early in life, early death may reduce the at-risk population by the time they reach the age of 50 to 60. The most convincing evidence for this proposition comes from Drenick and associates[36] (see figure 1.3) and from Abraham, Collins, and Nordsieck.[1] This latter study related the changes in weight status between childhood and adult life to the incidence of hypertensive and cardiovascular renal disease in 715 males (see figure 1.5). Childhood weight status was determined from school records when these men were aged 9 to 13. Follow-up weights were taken at an average age of 48. The highest prevalence for both hypertension and cardiovascular renal disease occurred in the men with the lowest childhood weight who became overweight as adults. It may well be that changing weight categories during adolescence and the early-adult years has more impact on the development of subsequent risk than maintaining a higher weight throughout life. Such a hypothesis awaits further research.

If significant degrees of "overweight" are "hazardous to your health," does weight reduction improve longevity? Few data are available to help answer this question.[6,97,136] The life insurance industry has provided data on individuals who had initially received substandard insurance because they were overweight but who subsequently were issued other policies at a lower weight. Among policyholders who lost weight and maintained the loss, life expectancy improved to that of insured people with "standard" risk. Data from the Framingham study buttresses this argument by showing the correlation of changes in glucose, blood pressure, cholesterol, and uric acid to changes in body weight.[6] From this data it was

FIGURE 1.5

Relation of weight gain to hypertension and cardiovascular renal disease. The individuals who gained weight in adult life and who had a normal (95–104) or low (<95) weight status as children showed the highest incidence of both diseases as adults.

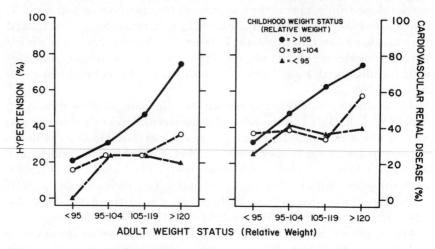

SOURCE: S. Abraham, G. Collins, and M. Nordsieck, 1971, Relationship of childhood weight status to morbidity in adults, *HSMHA Health Reports* 86:273–284.

estimated that a 10-percent reduction in body weight for men would translate into a 20-percent reduction in the risk of developing coronary artery disease.

Overweight and Morbidity

CARDIOVASCULAR FUNCTION AND OBESITY

The relationship between obesity and cardiovascular disease has been studied extensively.[147] Total blood volume increases linearly with excess weight[3] but is normal when expressed per unit body weight. Cardiac output is also increased in relation to the higher oxygen consumption associated with obesity.[3] The increased output is produced primarily by increased stroke volume of the heart, since a major reason for the increased cardiac output is the increased blood flow to the splanchnic bed and adipose tissue. When the blood volume and cardiac output are expressed per kilogram of body weight, they are only about 60 percent of the predicted value. However, the use of gross body weight does not make any correction for differences in the composition of the extra weight. Surface area probably provides the most appropriate basis for this comparison. Estimates of blood flow through various peripheral tissues of obese patients

TABLE 1.3

Effect of Weight Loss on Cardiovascular Function

	Before	*After*
Weight (kg)	112 to 218 kg	53 kg loss
Heart rate (min^{-1})	73 ± 10	68 ± 8
Stroke volume (ml)	107 ± 15	92 ± 17
Left ventricular stroke work (g-m)	150 ± 29	110 ± 29
Left ventricular work (kg-m/min)	11.1 ± 3.9	7.4 ± 2.0
VO$_2$ (ml/min)	360 ± 82	247 ± 43
Cardiac output (l/min)	7.9 ± 1.8	6.2 ± 1.2
Systemic arterial pressure (mm Hg)	102 ± 16	87 ± 12
Blood volume (l)	7.8 ±	6.1 ± 1.4

SOURCE: Adapted, by permission of the American Heart Association, Inc., from J. K. Alexander and K. L. Peterson, 1972, Cardiovascular effects of weight reduction, *Circulation* 45:310–318.

indicate that it is essentially normal, although renal blood flow tends to be high. Radiographic studies of the heart show that the transverse diameter has a positive correlation with body weight. Echocardiographic studies show increased thickness of the posterior wall and interventricular septum.[38] These studies are buttressed by the demonstration of myocardial hypertrophy in the Framingham study.[62] Because the circulation may be overtaxed as body weight increases, congestive heart failure may occur in grossly obese individuals.[3]

Essentially all of the abnormalities in cardiac function return toward normal with weight loss.[3] The heart rate, stroke volume, cardiac work, and oxygen uptake are all reduced (see table 1.3). When the cardiovascular findings before and after weight loss in nine grossly obese patients were compared, every parameter improved.[3] It thus appears that most of the cardiovascular changes observed in obese patients are a consequence of the obesity and are ameliorated by weight reduction.

OBESITY AND BLOOD PRESSURE

Hypertension can be defined as a sustained blood pressure with the systolic readings above 140 mm Hg or diastolic readings above 90 mm Hg. The range of diastolic pressures between 90 to 95 is considered borderline, and only those consistently below 90 mm Hg are considered normal. Systolic pressures of 140 to 160 mm Hg are borderline, and those above 160 are abnormally high.

Technical problems in the measurement of blood pressure in obese subjects have proved troublesome. It is widely believed that the indirect auscultatory method of obtaining blood pressure with an inflatable cuff produces higher readings in obese individuals than does direct intraarterial measurement. This may not be true, however, because in measuring arterial blood pressure, the length of the cuff bladder for the manometer is of prime importance. When the cuff is short, there are great differences between systolic and diastolic pressures measured by direct intraarterial

TABLE 1.4

Guidelines for Selection of Blood
Pressure Cuff Size in Relation
to Arm Circumference

Arm Circumference	Calf Size
<33 cm	Regular
33–41 cm	Large
>41 cm	Thigh

SOURCE: M. H. Maxwell et al., 1982,
Error in blood pressure due to incorrect
cuff size in obese patients, *Lancet* 2:
33–36.

methods as compared to indirect measurements. However, the more nearly the inflatable bladder of the cuff surrounds the arm, the more reliable the indirect measurements become. To test these ideas, Maxwell and associates[100] compared 84,000 measurements of blood pressure in 1,240 obese subjects using cuffs of three different sizes. Arm circumference was correlated with standard body weight in both males ($r = 0.79$) and females ($r = 0.84$). The values for both diastolic and systolic blood pressure were highest with the regular cuff and lowest with the large cuff or the thigh cuff. As arm circumference increases, the comparative blood pressure also rises with decreasing cuff size. The authors estimate that nearly 37 percent of subjects with arm circumferences between 33 and 41 cm (large arms) found to be hypertensive with normal cuffs may actually be normotensive. (See table 1.4.)

Even with the limitations in the techniques of measuring blood pressure by indirect auscultation, the available data almost uniformly indicate the important relationship between body weight and blood pressure.[26] The increased blood pressure probably results from increased peripheral arteriolar resistance. The increase in peripheral resistance may in turn be due to the increased secretion of catecholamines from an hyperactive sympathetic nervous system.[137]

Several points emerge from a review of the relationship between obesity and hypertension.[26,102] First, obesity has a striking correlation not only with body weight but with lateral body build. Individuals with a large chest circumference relative to their height and weight have higher blood pressure than slender individuals. Hypertension was present in 37 percent of the broad-chested men but in only three percent of the slender men. Body build exerted an almost proportional effect on systolic and diastolic blood pressure. Second, when blood pressure was compared in groups with constant body build, there was no significant correlation between obesity and hypertension. The greatest correlation of blood pressure with obesity was observed in men with a slender build. A much smaller correlation was found in broad-chested men. From these data it would appear that body build is more important than obesity per se in the positive correlation between blood pressure and body weight.

TABLE 1.5

Effects of Weight Loss on "Atherogenic Traits"

Atherogenic Trait	Mean Decrease with 10% Reduction in Body Weight in Males
Cholesterol	11 mg/dl
Systolic blood pressure	5 mm/Hg
Blood glucose	2 mg/dl
Uric acid	0.4 mg/dl

SOURCE: F. W. Ashley and W. B. Kannel, 1974, Relation of weight change to changes in atherogenic traits: The Framingham study, *Journal of Chronic Diseases* 27:103–114.

A reduction in blood pressure usually follows weight loss.[26] During periods of caloric deprivation during World War II, hypertension was almost nonexistent. A number of clinical studies correlating changes in blood pressure with weight reduction have shown that 50 to 70 percent of those who lose weight show a fall in blood pressure. One explanation might be the reduced intake of salt that is associated with reduced caloric intake. However, Reisin and Frohlich[119] and Tuck and associates[143] showed that the reduction in blood pressure occurred even when salt intake was held constant. The latter group suggested that the lower caloric intake reduced sympathetic activity and thus blood pressure.

The beneficial effects of weight loss on blood pressure, cholesterol, and uric acid are shown in table 1.5, derived from the Framingham study. Weight reduction is more effective in lowering systolic than in lowering diastolic pressure. Whether the therapeutic effect of weight reduction is related to the magnitude of the decline in body weight or to other environmental factors is still not entirely settled. However, weight reduction can produce significant reduction in blood pressure in more than half of the hypertensive patients.

DIABETES MELLITUS AND OBESITY

Although there is a large literature on the relationships of obesity and diabetes, the basis for this interrelation is still unclear. Two assessments of this literature can be gleaned from two recent reviews of this field. Berger and colleagues[12] state that "Although textbooks of medicine often refer to 'ample epidemiological evidence' linking the incidence rates of diabetes and obesity, critical evaluation reveals that adequately controlled quantitative data are available to a limited extent only" (p. 213). In a second review, Keen and associates[66] pointed out that "despite strong and frequent assertions of the importance of obesity in the pathogenesis of diabetes, sound evidence of the frequency of obesity in established diabetes is scanty and contradictory" (p. 94).

Retrospective studies provide some evidence of a link between diabetes and obesity. Life insurance data were among the first to suggest an association between diabetes and increased mortality. Excess mortality is increased to 125 percent of expected in individuals who are 5 to 15 percent overweight and rises to over 500 percent of the expected level in those individuals who are 25 percent or more overweight.[136]

There have been a number of studies on the prevalence of coincident diabetes and obesity. During a retrospective analysis of patient charts, Joslin, Dublin, and Marks[59] found that 51 percent of diabetic males and 59.3 percent of diabetic females were at least 20 percent overweight and that 16.5 percent males and 25.9 percent of females were actually 40 percent or more above average weight. Those patients whose diabetes began between ages 20 and 35 showed appreciably lower proportions of excess body weight than those in older age groups. In an epidemiological study of 10,000 Israeli civil servants,[101] those destined to develop diabetes were significantly fatter. In a study of the Pima Indians,[72] the incidence of diabetes was strongly related to preceding obesity. When the BMI was below 20 kg/m^2, the incidence of diabetes was 0.8 cases per 1,000 person years, rising steadily to 72.2 cases per 1,000 when the BMI was above 40 kg/m^2. This effect remained when subjects were classified according to the diabetic status of their parents.

It is clear from a variety of studies that adiposity predicts diabetes mellitus. The United States National Diabetes Commission[120] reported that the chance of becoming diabetic more than doubles for every 20 percent of excess body weight. Pyke and Please[114] extended these studies by comparing the body weights of 946 patients. In those patients below 30 years of age, there was little difference between normal subjects and diabetic patients in their weight distribution. In individuals over 30, the number of diabetic patients who were overweight exceeded the normal group. Between 43 and 55 percent of older diabetic men and 51 and 55 percent of older diabetic women exceeded 110 percent of the mean normal weight. Among nondiabetic patients, only 21 to 27 percent are more than 110 percent of normal weight. Moreover, a significantly larger percentage of older diabetic patients were also above the ninety-fifth percentile in body weight as compared to normal subjects.

Rimm and associates[122] have investigated the relationship of diabetes and obesity in a retrospective analysis of more than 73,000 responses to a questionnaire submitted to members of a voluntary weight-loss group. Both increasing body weight and age are associated with a rising frequency of diabetes mellitus (see figure 1.6). Less than 1 percent of normal-weight women aged 25 to 44 reported diabetes mellitus, whereas 7 percent of those of the same age who were 100 percent overweight reported this disease. The Framingham study has also shown that obesity has an important relation to diabetes. Only glucose was a better predictor than body weight for the risk of developing glucose intolerance over a fourteen-year period.[64] The percentage of increase in body weight for males and females that occurs between age 25 and 60 in four different countries is also related to the frequency of diabetes. The mortality from diabetes mellitus was highest among females who had the greatest gain in weight

FIGURE 1.6

Obesity and diabetes mellitus. The percentage of women in various age groups with a history of diabetes mellitus rises with groups according to percentage above ideal weight.

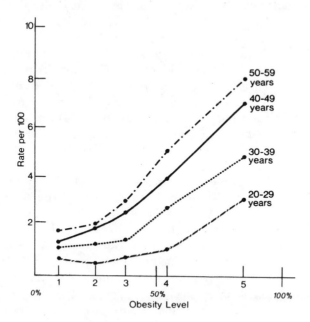

SOURCE: A. A. Rimm, L. H. Werner, B. Van Iserloo, and R. A. Bernstein, 1975, Relationship of obesity and disease in 73,532 weight-conscious women, *Public Health Reports* 90:44–54.

between ages 25 and 60. Canada and United States, whose population had the greatest percentage increase in body weight between these ages, thus had the highest mortality from diabetes. The epidemiological data is buttressed by the cross-cultural studies of West and Kalbfleisch.[152] These investigators examined the prevalence of diabetes in twelve age-matched populations from eleven countries. There was a correlation ($r = 0.89$) between the prevalence of diabetes and standard weight in these populations. More recently, Larsson and his colleagues[81] have demonstrated a correlation between obesity and the development of diabetes over a ten-year period in a longitudinal study of nearly 900 middle-aged men.

Early studies demonstrated that impairment in glucose tolerance is related to the duration of obesity,[109] but not all obese subjects develop diabetes. Indeed, the prevalence of carbohydrate intolerance in grossly obese subjects has been repeatedly found to be around 50 percent, varying somewhat with age, sex, and race. The question of why only one grossly obese patient in two develops an impairment in carbohydrate intolerance is intriguing. In a ten-year follow-up of sixty-three massively obese patients, eleven of fourteen who did not lose weight developed diabetes but only nine of twenty-three who did lose weight developed diabetes.[141]

In 1956 Vague[146] suggested that increased body fat in the upper region of the body as opposed to the lower region was more likely to be associated with the onset of diabetes mellitus. The female, or gynoid, type of body fat distribution, with fat deposited primarily on the hips and thighs, was found to have a lower association with diabetes than the male, or android, type of obesity where fat is deposited predominantly in the abdomen and upper body. Subsequently Feldman, Sender, and Sieglaub[41] and more recently Hartz, Rupley, and Rimm[54] confirmed this association by demonstrating that diabetic subjects (especially diabetic women) showed a significant shift toward an android or centripetal distribution of fat. Kissebah and his colleagues[70] have extended these observations using the circumference of the waist to the circumference of the hips as a measure of upper- versus lower-body fatness. With this measure, they found a greater rise in glucose and insulin following a glucose tolerance test in subjects with upper-body obesity as compared to lower-body obesity when both groups had comparable amounts of total body fat. Krotkiewski and associates[78] used a similar measure for regional fat distribution and found that both total fat and upper-body fat distribution are associated with higher blood pressure as well as greater rise in glucose and insulin during a glucose tolerance test. These differences in fat distribution may be associated with differences in fat cell sizes. Subjects with large fat cells, which tend to be distributed over the abdomen, were more likely to have impaired glucose tolerance and higher insulin values than those with smaller fat cells.[14] Finally the android, or upper-body, obesity is associated with higher androgen levels in women than is lower-body obesity.[40]

It has been recognized since the work of Newberg[107] that weight loss in obese subjects could improve glucose tolerance and that weight gain could worsen it. Glucose rises when normal-weight subjects gain weight[6,134] and declines when they lose.[6] This relationship was demonstrated most elegantly by Drenick, Brickman, and Gold,[35] who showed the marked amelioration in glucose tolerance and insulin secretion with weight loss. In a group of five obese males whose glucose tolerance was normal, the insulin levels required to maintain normal glucose levels declined when weight declined from 270 lb (122 kg) to 196 lb (89 kg). In another group of subjects with abnormal glucose tolerance and high insulin secretion, there was improvement in both insulin secretion and glucose concentrations after weight loss (291 lb to 207 lb [132 kg to 94 kg]). After a modest regain in weight to 227 lb (103 kg), glucose tolerance deteriorated significantly and insulin secretion had failed to rise.

With weight gain in normal subjects, not only is there a small but significant increase in plasma glucose but there is a rise in the concentration of insulin.[6,117,134] Basal levels of insulin increase linearly with the degree of overweight.[10] The elevation in basal insulin represents increased secretion and may also represent reduced metabolic clearance by the liver.

The increased basal level of insulin is associated with increased release of insulin in response to the administration of such secretagogues as glucose, arginine, glucagon, L-leucine and tolbutamide.[16] Both insulin and the connecting peptide (c-peptide) produced when proinsulin is cleaved to form insulin are secreted in increased amounts in obesity. Conversely, the level of c-peptide is suppressed in both normal and obese subjects by infusing exogenous insulin, but the relative differences in concentration of insulin remain.

The mechanism for the hyperinsulinemia in obesity is only partly understood. Both humoral and neural mechanisms may play a role. The raised levels of several amino acids could act synergistically with glucose to enhance the secretion of insulin. Increased vagal tone or reduced sympathetic tone could also augment the release of insulin.

Obese persons also have a reduced response to the infusion of exogenous insulin, which indicates insulin resistance. This has been shown when the human forearm is perfused *in vivo*[115] and when various tissues are studied *in vitro.*[5] One mechanism for the resistance to insulin may be a reduction in the number of receptor sites on fat cells and other tissue cells.[5] A second mechanism that exists in some obese people is a postreceptor disturbance whose nature has yet to be clearly defined.[73,110]

OBESITY AND PULMONARY FUNCTION

Measurement of pulmonary function in the obese individual shows a number of abnormalities.[88,118,123,128] At one extreme are the patients with the pickwickian syndrome, named after Joe, the fat boy in Dickens's *Pickwick Papers.*[22] The pickwickian or obesity-hypoventilation syndrome is characterized by somnolence, obesity, and hypoventilation. At the other extreme are the impairments in work capacity and pulmonary function due to obesity itself. There is a fairly uniform decrease in expiratory reserve volume in obesity (i.e., that volume of air which can be blown out after normal ventilation). There is also a low maximum rate of voluntary ventilation as well as a tendency toward a general reduction in lung volumes.

Studies on airway resistance, on the compliance of the lung, and on the oxygen cost of breathing have also revealed abnormalities. Lung compliance appears to be normal, but studies on the mechanics of breathing show increased oxygen consumption associated with breathing since more work is required to move the mass of the obese chest. Finally, there appears to be some element of venous admixture; segments of the lung that are not well perfused but are ventilated and other regions that are perfused but not adequately ventilated lead to the consistent but modest decrease in arterial oxygenation without a corresponding increase in arterial carbon dioxide content.[34]

Some obese patients show a diminished sensitivity of the respiratory center to the stimulatory effects of carbon dioxide. When breathing 5 percent carbon dioxide, these patients do not show the expected increase in the rate of respiration. This may play a role in the development of pulmonary abnormalities observed with the pickwickian syndrome.[128]

Significant alterations in pulmonary function in obesity are observed primarily in the massively obese or in those with obesity and some other

FIGURE 1.7

Mean vital capacity (VC; solid circles), total lung capacity (TLC; open circles), residual volume (RV; open squares), and functional residual capacity (FRC; solid squares) as a percent of predicted for subjects grouped by weight/height ratio (kg/cm).

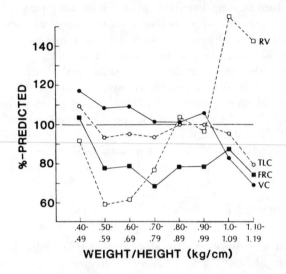

SOURCE: C. S. Ray et al., 1983, Effects of obesity on respiratory function, *American Review of Respiratory Disease* 128:501–506.

respiratory or cardiovascular problem. In a careful study of twenty-nine obese women and fourteen obese men, we noted a progressive decrease in expiratory reserve volume as the weight/height (cm/kg) ratio increased (see figure 1.7). On the other hand, vital capacity, inspiratory capacity, residual volume, and diffusion capacity remained fairly constant until the weight/height ratio exceeded 1.0 (i.e., massive obesity).

The higher metabolism of obese subjects at rest and during exercise increased the uptake of oxygen and the output of carbon dioxide. This demand is met by increased minute ventilation.[31] The extra weight on the chest and abdomen of subjects weighing, on average, 114 kg (251 lb) was associated with a two- to fourfold increase in the mechanical work required to passively ventilate the lungs.[128] The compliance of the chest wall—that is, the force required to move it—is thus decreased in obesity, a finding consistent with the increased work of breathing.[105] Sharp[129] has also reported that in otherwise normal obese subjects the characteristics of chest expansion could be mimicked by placing bags filled with shot on the chest or abdomen or by binding the chest of normal subjects. Thus in obesity the efficiency of respiratory work was reduced when measured as the ratio of the mechanical work divided by the oxygen costs of breathing.

Respiratory muscles may also function abnormally in obese patients. The electrical response of the diaphragmatic nerves to breathing carbon dioxide is similar in normal and obese patients without the pickwickian syndrome, but is reduced by 75 percent in those with the syndrome of alveolar hypoventilation.[83] Rochester and Enson[123] also report differences in diaphragmatic electromyograms between obese subjects with and without the obesity-hypoventilation syndrome. A five- to tenfold increase in electrical activity of the diaphragm was noted during respiration in normal obese subjects but not in the obese subjects with this syndrome. The authors suggested that part of this difference might lie in a small diaphragmatic muscle mass in those suffering from alveolar hypoventilation. Using the technique of diaphragm electromyography coupled with measurements of airway closing pressure, it was possible to distinguish two types of patients with the obesity-hypoventilation syndrome. In one group patients had a low closing pressure relative to electromyographic activity, suggesting the presence of a neuromuscular defect. Patients in the other group had a normal relationship of closing pressure to diaphragmatic electromyogram.[87]

A disturbance in ventilation-perfusion is the most common abnormality in gas exchange associated with obesity. There are varying degrees of hypoxemia, which is worse in the supine position.[144] Using the radioactive gas xenon, Holley and associates[57] showed that the lower portions of the lungs in obese patients were relatively underventilated and overperfused. In subjects weighing 95 to 140 kg (209 to 308 lb), the distribution of tidal respiration was predominantly to the upper lobes with perfusion mainly to the bases.

The most significant pulmonary problem in the obese patient is the pickwickian syndrome, or the obesity-hypoventilation syndrome. Although obesity is common, the obesity-hypoventilation syndrome is not. The obesity-hypoventilation syndrome is worsened by sleep apnea, of which there are two types. The first type is central and is associated with transient cessation of neural impulses from the central nervous system to the lung muscles. The second type is obstructive apnea and occurs when the tongue obstructs the glottis, preventing entry of air into the trachea. Most patients with sleep apnea are of normal weight, and only 5 percent of sleep-apnea patients have the obesity-hypoventilation syndrome. However, the symptoms of the obesity-hypoventilation syndrome may result largely from sleep apnea. Sharp, Barrocas, and Chokroverty[128] believe that the hypoxemia and hypercapnia that occur during part of the day may eventually adversely affect the control of ventilation during the rest of the day. Patients with the obesity-hypoventilation syndrome have markedly impaired ventilatory responses to breathing carbon dioxide. Sharp and associates[128] have proposed that obstructive or mixed sleep apnea produces hypoxia, which worsens as the obesity progresses. The hypoxia in turn blunts the hypoxemic drive. Sleep is disturbed and compensatory sleep occurs during the day (diurnal hypersomnolence). With time, the hypoxemia is followed by hypercapnia, which eventually leads to cor pulmonale.

In its full-blown clinical form the obesity-hypoventilation syndrome represents a medical emergency. Hospitalization, preferably in a respiratory unit, may be needed to maintain life. These patients may have lower thoracic compliance and higher mechanical work of breathing than other obese patients.[128] They may also be breathing more rapidly.[65] Tracheostomy may be needed since hypoxic drives may be reduced by 80 percent or more and the hypercapnic drive by 60 percent or more.[154] Once the acute emergency has passed, progestational agents may help. In seven of eight patients studied by Lyons and Huang,[89] the arterial pCO_2 returned to normal. Similarly, Sutton and associates[140] found that 90 percent of their patients normalized their arterial pCO_2 when treated with 20 mg medroxyprogesterone per day sublingually. Stohl and co-workers[138] also reported significant improvement in sleep apnea in five of nine patients using oral medroxyprogesterone. A tricyclic antidepressant, protriptyline, has also been reported to reduce the number and duration of apneic episodes in these patients.[153] The finding of elevated beta-endorphin in the cerebrospinal fluid of a child with this syndrome prompted the use of naloxone with dramatic, but transient, improvement.[112] Weight loss is clearly important in these patients and warrants aggressive therapy to reduce the mass of fat.

OBESITY AND DIGESTIVE DISEASES

The association of obesity with gallbladder disease has been documented in several studies.[84] The life insurance statistics show that obesity increases the risk of dying from gallbladder disease.[136] Digestive diseases were 140 percent of expected among those 15 to 35 percent overweight and nearly 250 percent among those who were 25 percent or more overweight. Increased mortality from digestive diseases is also evident in the American Cancer Society study.[85] In one autopsy study in which 612 gallbladder specimens were examined, 377 had gross disease, with 44 of the diseased gallbladders coming from subjects weighing over 95 kg (210 lb). In another autopsy study, Sturdevant, Pearce, and Dayton[139] found that body weight of the men without gallstones was significantly less than that of men with gallstones. The incidence of gallstones at autopsy was 16 percent (25 of 156) in men who were more than 9.1 kg (20 lb) overweight. In a cross-sectional study of 62,739 respondents to a questionnaire developed by the self-help group called Take Off Pounds Sensibly (TOPS), Bernstein and associates[13] found that the risk of gallbladder disease increases with age, body weight, and parity. Within any age group, the frequency of gallbladder disease increases with the level of body weight (see figure 1.8). For women aged 25 to 34 years who are 100 percent or more overweight, 18 percent had gallbladder disease compared to nearly 35 percent of the women aged 45 to 55 who were 100 percent or more overweight. In this study 88 percent of the variation in frequency of gallbladder disease was accounted for by weight, age, and parity, with weight being the most important variable. Obese women between 20 and 30 years of age had a sixfold increase in the risk of developing gallbladder disease compared to normal-weight women. By age 60 nearly one-third

FIGURE 1.8

Obesity and gallbladder disease. The percentage of women in various age groups with a history of gallbladder disease rises with body weight. The weight categories divide the patients into ten groups. Group X was 100 percent overweight. Group VII was 50 percent overweight.

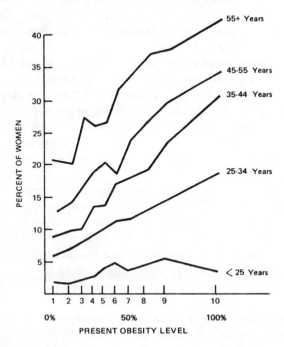

SOURCE: R. A. Bernstein et al., 1977, Gallbladder disease—II. Utilization of the life table method in obtaining clinically useful information. TOPS, *Journal of Chronic Diseases* 30:529–541.

of obese women can expect to develop gallbladder disease. In the Framingham study individuals who were at least 20 percent above the median weight for their height had about twice the risk of developing gallbladder disease as those who were less than 90 percent of the median weight for height.[42]

Increased cholesterol production and secretion provides one explanation for the increased risk of gallbladder disease. Garn, Bailey, and Block[47] used the data from the National Collaborative Perinatal Project to assess the effects of weight status on cholesterol levels. There was a significant correlation between the degree of fatness and cholesterol. Nestel, Ishikawa, and Goldrick[106] showed that cholesterol production rate was correlated with body weight. For each extra kilogram of excess body weight, cholesterol production increased 22 mg per day. Miettinen[103] estimated that an additional 20 mg per day of cholesterol was produced for each additional kilogram of adipose tissue. Bennion and Grundy[11] found that bile was more saturated with cholesterol in twenty-three obese subjects than in a like number of nonobese controls. The hepatic secretion of cholesterol was higher before weight loss in eleven subjects than afterward but neither phospholipids nor bile salt secretion changed.

Changes in gastric pressure might be expected from the increased size of the abdominal panniculus of morbidly obese subjects. However, in one study of massively obese middle-aged women, the mean esophageal sphincter pressure was within the normal range in twenty-two of the twenty-five subjects. Moreover, reflux of gastric juices into the lower esophagus as determined by a pH electrode was demonstrable in only four of twenty-one patients.[108] In a second study Backman and associates[9] measured the lower esophageal sphincter pressure in forty obese subjects before gastric bypass surgery. Fourteen of the subjects were reexamined after weight reduction. Normal levels for gastrointestinal sphincter pressures ranged between 13.3 and 25 mm Hg in several series of patients. In this study the mean figure for esophageal pressure was 20 ± 2.2 mm Hg. The fourteen subjects measured before surgery and after a loss of weight that averaged 37 kg (81 lb) showed no significant change in their lower esophageal sphincter pressures.

Abnormalities in hepatic function have been commonly noted in obesity. Steatosis occurs with a reported frequency ranging from 68 to 94 percent of cases.[15] Fatty infiltration involving more than half of the hepatocytes was present in 25 and 35 percent of the cases. Inflammatory lesions, on the other hand, were much less frequent, varying from a high of 8.7 percent of biopsies to no detectable lesions.[15]

Whether fibrosis or cirrhosis is present varies with the type of patients being evaluated.[15] To study the nature of the fatty infiltration, liver biopsies from five controls were compared with eighteen obese patients and thirty-one patients with alcoholic liver disease.[15] Fat was present in 88.9 percent of the liver biopsies and fibrosis in 44.4 percent but was absent in all of the control biopsies. None of the liver function tests, which included measurement of serum glutamic-oxaloacetic transaminase, alkaline phosphatase, bilirubin, and serum albumin, were abnormal in the obese patients. However, there were differences in the concentrations of various lipid components (see table 1.6). The concentrations of fatty acids, diglycerides, and triglycerides were significantly higher in the obese patients compared to the controls. The alcoholic group had even higher levels of fatty acids, diglycerides, and cholesterol than the obese group. In both the alcoholic and the obese group, the distribution of fatty acids between free fatty acids and those in triglycerides differed, indicating a preferential incorporation of unsaturated fatty acids into triglycerides.[99]

OBESITY AND THE SKIN, BONES, AND JOINTS

Two cutaneous abnormalities have been associated with obesity. The first is fragilitas cutis inguinalis. Ganor and Even-Paz[43] examined the resistance to stretching of the inguinal skin in two hundred patients. In sixty-three of the patients the inguinal skin ruptured in a linear fashion at right angles to the applied force. This phenomenon was restricted to

TABLE 1.6

Hepatic Lipids in Obesity and Alcoholic Liver Disease

Lipids (μmoles/gm wet weight)	Controls (N = 5)	Obesity (N = 18)	Alcoholic Liver Diseases[a]
Fatty acids	1.6 ± 0.7[b]	13.7 ± 1.6[c]	19.9 ± 2.4[c,d]
Monoglycerides	1.3 ± 1.2	3.1 ± 1.0	6.0 ± 1.4
Diglycerides	0.6 ± 0.2	5.9 ± 1.1[c,e]	15.5 ± 3.6[c,d]
Triglycerides	14.1 ± 2.4	228.4 ± 43.2[c,e]	164.5 ± 24.6[c]
Cholesterol	5.0 ± 1.3	5.3 ± 0.2	7.5 ± 0.6[f]

SOURCE: P. G. Mavrelis et al., 1983, Hepatic free fatty acids in alcoholic liver disease and morbid obesity, *Hepatology* 3:226–231.
[a] AH-0, ALD without hepatitis; AH-1 to AH-4, alcoholic hepatitis Grades 1 to 4.
[b] Values are mean ± S.E. Classification of patients corresponds to that in table 1.1. Phospholipids and cholesterolesters were not analyzed.
[c] $p < 0.01$ vs. control.
[d] $p < 0.05$ vs. obesity.
[e] $p < 0.05$ vs. control.
[f] $p < 0.01$ vs. obesity.

the groin and was unrelated to the sex or age of the patient. But it was clearly associated with obesity. Nearly 70 percent of the fat patients as compared to 20 to 25 percent of the medium-weight patients showed this phenomenon. These authors also noted a positive relationship between the presence of stria and obesity but not between the presence of stria and the tendency of the inguinal skin to rupture under stretching. The meaning of the relationship between the sensitivity to rupture of the inguinal skin in obese subjects during stretching is unclear.

Acanthosis nigricans is a second dermal abnormality having a significant association with obesity. Darkening of the skin in the creases of the neck, in the axillary region, and over the knuckles is important because it is sometimes associated with highly malignant cancers, usually an intraabdominal adenocarcinoma occurring in middle-aged and elderly patients. In a study of one hundred patients by Brown and Winklemann,[21] seventeen had the malignant form and seventy-three the benign form of acanthosis nigricans. In the patients with obesity and benign acanthosis nigricans, most had stigmata of other endocrine diseases. These included hirsutism, acne, amenorrhea, abdominal striae, and moon facies. The relationship of acanthosis nigricans to insulin resistance has been described in several patients who have circulating antibodies to the insulin receptor.[61] In contrast to the type of insulin resistance associated with obesity, the patients with circulating antireceptor antibodies are usually thin. Whether the obese patients with acanthosis nigricans have a more severe form of insulin resistance than those without acanthosis nigricans remains to be answered.[60]

Increasing body weight might be expected to add additional trauma to the weight-carrying joints and thus accelerate the development of osteoarthritis, which is an age-related, noninflammatory disease of the diarthrodial joints with degeneration and overgrowth of the cartilage and with overgrowth and sclerosis of the bone. The literature on this issue is contradictory. The weight distribution of people with primary and secondary osteoarthritis of the hip is similar to that of persons with normal hip joints. Surprisingly, in one study where individuals were more than 100 percent overweight, the incidence of osteoarthritis by x-ray was only 12 percent.[125] Other authors[39,49,55,150] report an increased prevalence of osteoarthritis in obese individuals. An increased mean weight for those with osteoarthritis has been reported in other studies.[39,49,55,150] The knee joint seems to be most frequently involved. Engel's study[39] of the prevalence of osteoarthritis of the hands, a non-weight-bearing set of joints, and the ankle, a weight-bearing joint, is of particular interest. The population included 2,548 individuals who were divided into four age groups. There was an age-related increase in the prevalence of osteoarthritis. Within each age group there was a clear increase in the prevalence of osteoarthritis and body weight for all groups of women over 35 years of age. The slope of the increase with weight was sharpest below 90 kg (200 lb), suggesting that weight is only one of the factors involved. Silberberg[132] found that differences in lipid concentrations may be another such factor.

RENAL FUNCTION AND OBESITY

Description of the nephrotic syndrome in four patients with massive obesity has reawakened interest in the interrelation between obesity and renal function.[151] These patients had proteinuria, which ranged between 3.1 and 19.2 g per day. However, hematuria was absent and x-rays of the kidney in three patients showed a normal pattern in two and a horseshoe kidney in one. Renal biopsies in two patients showed minimal abnormalities and no definable pathologic cause for the nephrotic syndrome. Of particular importance was the relationship between the proteinuria and body weight. In all four patients, there was a significant decline in protein excretion as the patients lost weight.

OBSTETRICS AND THE OVERWEIGHT PATIENT

Body weight before pregnancy and the weight gain during pregnancy both influence the course of labor and its outcome. Peckham and Christianson[113] performed a careful analysis of 3,939 white females who delivered babies between 1963 and 1965. At each height the lowest 10 percent, the middle 10 percent, and the highest 10 percent in body weight were selected for review. The "heavy" women averaged 77 kg (169 lb). They were older than the lightest women (29 vs. 25 years). Nearly 22 percent of the heavy women were over 35 years old; only 7.4 percent of the light women were this old. Moreover, 40 percent of the women in the "light" weight group were having their first pregnancy, but this percentage was much smaller in the heavy group. Menarche occurred at a younger age in the heavy women and was somewhat delayed in the light-weight women, confirming other data. By age 11, 27.5 percent of the heavy women had begun menstruating compared to 16.5 percent of the light ones. Menstruation began after age 14 in 28 percent of the light women but in only 13.7 percent of the heavy women. Among the heavy women the frequency of toxemia and hypertension were significantly increased, and the duration of labor was longer. In over 7 percent of the heavy women labor lasted more than twenty-four hours. This occurred in only 0.8 percent of the light women. Caesarean section was performed in 5.5 percent of the heavy patients but in only 0.7 percent of the light ones. Thus more obstetrical complications were present in the heavy group than in the light one.

Gross, Sokol, and King[52] reviewed data on 2,746 consecutive deliveries of whom there were 279 obese women weighing more than 90 kg (198 lb). The obese women were older and had a higher parity and an increased frequency of hypertension, diabetes mellitus, and twin gestation. The frequency of abnormal labor, including oxytocin infusion and caesarean section, was also higher in the obese women.[56,131]

The heavy women had significantly heavier infants than did the light women. In an analysis of data from the National Collaborative Perinatal Project, Garn[44] compared the relationship between placental weight, birth weight, and weights of the children at 7 years of age. He demonstrated a direct relationship between placental weight and prepregnancy body weight. Birth weight and maternal prepregnancy weight were also related. If infants were compared at age 7, approximately 50 percent of the incremental weight gain could be accounted for by the differences in placental weight at birth. The remaining 50 percent of the difference was accounted for by the postnatal environment. Similar observations have also been made by McKeown and Record.[91] The mean birth weight of the infants increased with maternal height and increasing maternal weight. However, McKeown and Record failed to observe any relationship between the duration of labor and the effect of body weight or body build. Naeye[104] found that the fewest fetal and neonatal deaths occurred when mothers who were overweight at the beginning of the pregnancy gained an average of 7.3 kg (16 lb). The optimal weight gain during pregnancy was 9.1 kg (20 lb) for normal-weight women and 13.6 kg (30 lb) for underweight women.

OBESITY, HEMATOLOGY, IMMUNOLOGY, AND CANCER

A significant difference in the level of hemoglobin has been reported in lean and obese subjects. Scheer and Guthrie[126] evaluated the data from the National Health and Nutrition Examinations Survey (NHANES 1) and divided the subjects into two groups (ages 6 to 9 and 10 to 14). Although the differences between lean and obese subjects in the concentration of hemoglobin were not significant, the concentrations in obese subjects were consistently 0.1 to 0.3 g per dl higher. Using the same data Garn and Ryan[46] found a significant increase in the hemoglobin of obese subjects as compared to lean subjects when four age groups were examined (infants aged 1 to 3; children aged 4 to 11; adolescents aged 12 to 17; and adults aged 18–74). The difference between the obese and lean subjects was approximately 0.2 g per dl. The difference between the conclusion arrived at by these two groups may be based in the criteria by which the triceps skin folds were used to define obesity. Scheer and Guthrie[126] used the standards developed by Seltzer and Mayer,[127] while Garn and Ryan[46] used the upper and lower 15 percent according to triceps skin fold. In a further analysis using the same criteria, Garn and Petzold[45] demonstrated a similar 0.2 g-per-dl increase in hemoglobin concentrations in obese subjects compared to lean ones regardless of racial background.

Nutritional factors influence immune response in many conditions, including obesity. In a study on the maturation of monocytes, Krisnen and associates[77] showed that the number of monocytes that matured into macrophages when monocytes were incubated in vitro was significantly less in obese than in lean subjects. The generation of migration inhibiting factor by lymphocytes from obese subjects with normal glucose levels was also significantly less in the presence of purified protein derivative (PPD) than in normal controls.[74] In a study of obese and nonobese children,[25] the levels of serum immunoglobulins, the complement components C3 and C4, and the numbers of T and B lymphocytes were similar in the two groups. However, 38 percent of the obese children and adolescents showed a variable impairment in cell-mediated immune response and a reduction in the intracellular bacterial killing by polymorphonuclear leukocytes. In the search for an explanation the authors examined the serum copper and zinc levels and observed that both micronutrients showed subclinical deficiency. It is well known that zinc deficiency can impair immune functions. Therapy with zinc and copper for four weeks resulted in improved immunologic function. These data suggest that immunologic responses may be impaired in obese subjects, in part because of other nutritional deficiencies.

Obesity has been implicated in several types of cancer.[85] Obese males have a higher rate of prostate and colo-rectal cancer, and obese females have increased gallbladder, breast, cervix, endometrial, uterine, and ovarian cancer. Endometrial cancer has been shown to be two to three times more common in obese women as compared to normal-weight ones.[93] Endometrial tumors also occur more frequently in menopausal women at the time when endogenous estrogen levels are falling. One explanation for this increased risk might be the production of estrogen in fat tissue. Urinary estrone production rates are increased in obese postmenopausal women; normal women show values of 20 to 40 mc g per day, while obese women exhibit values of 50 to 120 mc g per day.[76,86,133] In postmenopausal women the source of increased estrogen production appears to be the conversion of the adrenal steroid androstenedione to estrone by the stromal elements of adipose tissue.[90] Estrone production rates also increase in young women as body weight rises.

Obesity is related to the risk for developing breast cancer and perhaps also for its recurrence.[32,93] Donegen, Johnstone, and Biedrzycki[33] found a correlation between the degree of obesity in postmenopausal women and the presence of estrogen receptors in women treated with mastectomy. They concluded that the excess estrogen production may play a role in the poor prognosis of these tumors by promoting tumor growth. Sherman, Wallace, and Bean[130] examined the relationships between patterns of menstrual cycles in women aged 24 and 43 and during the seven years before menopause. They found no relationship between relative weight and menstrual cycles, nor could they identify abnormalities in the menstrual cycle in patients who developed breast cancer. In another effort to relate breast cancer and obesity, Trichophoulos, Polychronopoulou, and Brown[142] examined the relationship of estrogen to height, weight, obesity index, and serum cholesterol in a group of women living in rural Greece. They found no consistent relationship between these variables and urinary estrogen excretion. Their data did not support the hypothesis of a relationship in body weight and breast cancer mediated through the effects of body weight on estrogen levels. These data contrast with the numerous earlier studies suggesting a relationship between estrogen production and body weight and point up the difficulties of epidemiological studies of urinary sampling in a complex question of this type. At this writing the preponderance of data appears to suggest that obesity may influence the development and progression of both endometrial and breast cancer through influences on estrogen production.

LIPOPROTEINS AND OBESITY

There is a consistent correlation between the concentration of very-low-density lipoproteins (VLDL) and obesity.[148] Moreover, weight reduction is the best treatment for hypertriglyceridemia resulting from increased levels of VLDL.[111] This increase probably reflects increased hepatic synthesis of VLDL since peripheral removal of triglyceride is normal.

In contrast with VLDL, which is increased in obesity, the high-density lipoproteins (HDL cholesterol) are consistently reduced in obese males and females.[51] The concentration of HDL cholesterol bears an inverse relationship to the risk of developing coronary artery disease,[51] so that high levels of HDL are related to lower risk. The low levels of HDL may be one mechanism by which obesity is associated with an increased risk of developing cardiovascular disease.

The concentration of free fatty acids (FFA) and their turnover are increased in obese subjects. There is enhanced basal lipolysis in large fat cells[20] and increased response of large fat cells to lipolytic agents. The increased release of free fatty acids and glycerol from the enlarged fat cells is responsible for the supply of free fatty acids to the liver, which may be used for the synthesis of VLDLs that enter the circulation to produce hypertriglyceridemia. The production rate of fatty acids released by adipose tissue has been documented by metabolic clearance studies.[106]

The removal role of FFA is also enhanced in obesity, reflecting the increased oxidation of fatty acids as detected by the lower respiratory quotient.

ENDOCRINE AND METABOLIC CHANGES IN OBESITY

Pituitary Hormones. It has been recognized for twenty years that the release of growth hormone (GH) is impaired in obese subjects.[48] The expected rises in GH with sleep and four to five hours after a meal are blunted as is the rise after administering arginine, levodopa, or inducing hypoglycemia with insulin.[16] This impairment is reversible after weight loss. Moreover, normal subjects who overeat show a reduction in their responsiveness of GH release to a variety of stimuli, which indicates the role nutrition plays in this adaptive response.[134] In contrast to GH, somatomedin C, a peptide thought to mediate the effects of GH at the cellular level, is usually normal in obesity.[48] Prolactin secretion may be impaired in some obese humans. This has been proposed as a way of separating two groups of obese subjects, those who release prolactin normally and those who do not.[75]

Thyroid Hormones. Nutrition appears to be more important than body weight per se in determining the circulating concentration of triiodothyronine (T_3). Regardless of initial body weight, predictable changes in the pathways of thyroxine (T_4) metabolism will occur if calorie or carbohydrate intake changes. Both total calories and the relative proportion of carbohydrate, protein, and fat are important parameters in the thyroidal adaptation to food.

During fasting, total T_4 levels remain normal but the serum concentration of total T_3 falls. After three weeks of fasting, serum concentrations of total T_3 declined from 145 ng per dl to 66 ng per dl. There is a concurrent increase in total reverse triioidothyronine (rT_3), which increased from 36 ng per dl to 54 ng per dl.[145] Fasting also changes the responsiveness of pituitary thyrotrophs to release of thyrotropin (TSH) after injection of thyrotropin-releasing hormone (TRH).[48]

In contrast to starvation, overnutrition is associated with a rise in serum T_3 and a fall in rT_3 values. T_3 levels increased in both obese and lean subjects during overfeeding.[19,27] Danforth and coworkers[27] studied both short- and long-term overfeeding and found a significant increase in serum T_3 concentration from 136 ng per dl prior to overfeeding to 152 ng per dl after seven months of increased caloric intake. Short-term overfeeding also resulted in an increase in T_3 levels. Davidson and Chopra[28] noted a similar increase in T_3 in their subjects who ate more than 4,000 calories per day for one week. After seven months of long-term overfeeding, Danforth and associates[27] did not find any difference in rT_3 levels.

Adrenal Corticosteroids. In obese subjects at their usual weight, the plasma level of cortisol and the urinary concentration of free cortisol are

FIGURE 1.9

Effect of obesity on plasma testosterone. Note that as the ideal body weight increases the concentration of testosterone falls, becoming significantly different from normal as the body weight approaches 150 percent of ideal body weight.

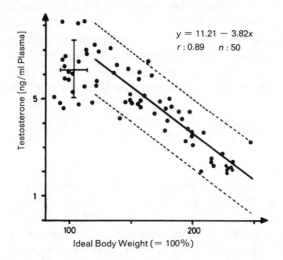

NOTE: Reprinted, by permission of the publisher, from H. K. Kley, H. G. Solbach, J. C. McKinnan, and H. L. Kruskemper, 1979, Testosterone decrease and estrogen increase in male patients with obesity, *Acta Endocrinologica* 91:553–563.

normal.[48] The circadian rhythm of cortisol in plasma and urine is also normal. However, the adrenal secretion of cortisol and the excretion of urinary metabolites of cortisol are significantly increased. The secondary nature of this effect can be discerned in the overfeeding studies of Sims and coworkers.[134] During the high-caloric diet, plasma cortisol showed a small but significant decline, probably reflecting increased hepatic uptake and metabolism. In response to this lower cortisol concentration the pituitary gland is activated with increased adrenal production. The release of adrenocorticotrophic hormone (ACTH) from the pituitary after inducing hypoglycemia with insulin, and the rise in plasma or urinary 11-deoxycorticosteroids after metyrapone, a drug that blocks 11-beta-hydroxylase, appear to be normal whether measured as changes in plasma concentrations of the appropriate steroid or in the urinary concentrations of these substances.[16,48] However, these results are obtained from groups and might be different if individual subjects were considered. The suppression of cortisol by exogenous administration of dexamethasone is normal in obese subjects providing plasma dexamethasone attains normal levels.

Reproductive Hormones. There is a consistent reduction in the concentration of total serum testosterone in obesity.[48] The decline in testosterone is directly related to the degree of overweight (see figure 1.9). There is also a weight-related rise in both estradiol and estrone in males. The decline in testosterone is probably the result of a reduction in the concentration of sex hormone binding globulin (SHBG), which transports testosterone in the serum. The mechanism for the reduction in SHBG is currently unknown. The concentration of free testosterone remains essentially normal except in massively obese individuals, where free testosterone is also low. Testicular size and the basal concentration of the pituitary gonadotropins, follicle-stimulating hormone (FSH) and luteinizing hormone (LH), are normal. Similarly, the pituitary release of LH and FSH in response to an injection of luteinizing hormone-releasing hormone (LHRH) (gonadotrophin-releasing hormone [GnRH]) is normal as is the concentration of these pituitary peptides during treatment with chlomiphene.

In contrast to the normal anatomy of the testis in obese males, the ovary in obese women often shows an increase in hyalinization and an increased frequency of atretic follicles.[48] In obese women there is a reduction in the concentration of SHBG just as there is in males. The metabolism of androstenedione in peripheral tissues with the production of estrone increases with the degree of obesity, but in premenopausal women this is not associated with higher plasma levels of estrogens. Similarly, the secretion of the adrenal androgen dehydroepiandosterone (DHEA) and its metabolism to, and excretion as, urinary-17-ketosteroid (17-KS) are increased in many obese women. The basal concentrations of LH and FSH, on the other hand, are normal in obese women. The response of these circulating pituitary gonadotrophins to the administration of LHRH is also normal. In contrast to the increased secretion of adrenal androgens and enhanced conversion of androstenedione to estrone in fibroblasts from adipose tissue of obese subjects, the turnover of estradiol in obese women appears to be reduced. These defects might enhance the risk of developing endometrial cancer and might reduce fertility. Menstrual irregularities are common in obese women. With weight loss, even the more severe abnormalities revert to normal.[48]

Miscellaneous Hormones. Gastrin, a peptide that stimulates hydrogen release by parietal cells in the stomach, is normal in obesity.[8] Gastric inhibitory polypeptide or GIP (also called glucose insulin polypeptide) is known to stimulate the release of insulin. Release of this hormone in response to an oral glucose load appears to be normal in obese subjects. Endorphin and lipotropin, two components of the larger pro-opiomelanocortin molecule present in the anterior pituitary, have been measured and are increased in obesity. Vasopressin from the posterior pituitary is normal, as is the renal hormone renin. The concentrations of parathyroid hormone may be significantly increased in obese subjects and may be reduced following intestinal bypass surgery.[7]

This brief review of metabolic and hormonal changes in obesity indicates a wide-ranging series of alterations.[16,48,148] Some of these alterations, such as hyperinsulinemia, impaired GH response, reduction in SHBG, and the enhanced conversion of androstenedione to estrone by the stromal elements in adipose tissue, are reversed with weight loss. However, other alterations, such as the function of the adrenal or thyroid system, may not change after weight loss.

Social Disadvantages of Obesity

SOCIAL ATTITUDES TOWARD THE OBESE

Obesity carries a social stigma.[4,23,121] This was most clearly shown by studies with children and adults who were asked to express a preference for various forms of disability, including obesity. Children and adults were shown six pictures. These included: (1) a child with no disability; (2) a child with crutches and a brace on the left leg; (3) a child in a wheelchair with a blanket over the legs; (4) a child with a left hand missing; (5) a child who was disfigured around the left side of the mouth; and (6) an obese child. The sex of the drawings corresponded with that of the person who was shown the pictures. In the first study,[121] groups of schoolboys and girls aged 10 to 11 from New York City, from Montana, and from northern California were asked to rate the pictures by selecting the child they would find most easy to like. The picture they chose was removed, and they were then asked to select the child they would find next most easy to like until all six pictures had been rated. The order of the rating was the same for all groups of children regardless of their sex, socioeconomic status, racial background, and whether they came from rural or urban communities. In all cases, the obese child was liked least. The numbers of children studied by Richardson and associates[121] left little doubt about the social stigma of being an obese child. In an extension of this study, Goodman and coworkers[50] showed that the ratings for the same six pictures by a group of adults including physical therapists, occupational therapists, nurses, physicians, and social workers were similar to the ratings of the children from rural and urban America. Maddox, Back, and Liederman[96] provided confirmation of these data. They used the same group of pictures with patients from an outpatient clinic. As a whole the clinic population ordered the six pictures in almost the same rank order as did the children and adults. Disabled adults and children did not like the obese child. These authors were surprised by the observation that black females, who often value obesity, rated the obese child as fourth from the top—not much improvement. When asked why the obese child was ranked at the bottom, many respondents indicated that the other disabled children were the unfortunate victims of the environment. By implication the obese child was frequently thought to be "responsible" for his or her plight. This hypothesis that dislike for the obese stemmed from perceived responsibility for their condition was tested by asking adolescent girls to provide opinions of an obese peer. When the obese peer could provide an excuse for her obesity, such as a glandular disorder, or could document a successful weight loss, the evaluation was more positive than when these excuses or weight loss were absent.[30] In addition, many obese patients disliked the drawings of the obese child because it reminded them of themselves. When a series of twelve line drawings of lean normal and fat people were shown to 447 adults and children, the normal-weight figures were viewed as more desirable as friends and were viewed as happier, smarter, and better looking. A similar stigmatization of the obese stereotypes was reflected in the fact that fat nicknames were given primarily to fat stimuli.[53]

The potential disadvantages of obesity have been emphasized again in studies on social mobility and dating behavior. Elder[37] indicated that physical appearance was the most important factor for women in attracting upwardly mobile men for marriage. Physical attractiveness was again the single most important factor in dating behavior among college-age students.[149] Because of the importance of attitudes about physical attractiveness in our society and the relatively unattractive view of obesity held by many children and adults, it is easy to understand the relative social positions and feelings of many obese individuals. Because a "lean" figure is so valued in women, Krupka and Vener[79] have examined the responses of a group of college-age students to a questionnaire to learn their approaches to weight control. Exercise and diet were the preferred methods of weight loss, but the authors learned that in the past twelve months 27.3 percent of 115 women used over-the-counter agents for weight loss. Obese people were stigmatized to the same degree as prostitutes and embezzlers. College students would prefer to marry cocaine users, ex-mental patients, and divorcees rather than obese individuals.

Obesity as a social disability has been examined further by Maddox and his collaborators.[94,95] In a study in the outpatient clinic at Duke University, the concordance between entries in the physician's chart concerning overweight and the actual degrees of overweight in the sample were compared. There was only about one chance in four that a patient who was more than 20 percent overweight would encounter a physician who would note in the medical record that body weight was significantly increased and who would propose a program for management of this problem. The average weight of those whose weight was not mentioned was 88 kg (193 lb) and those whose weight was mentioned in the chart but for whom no proposal for management was made was 92 kg (202 lb)! Those patients for whom a program of management was suggested weighed on average 97 kg (212 lb). An elevation in blood pressure or the presence of hypertension or coronary artery disease made it more likely that the weight problem would be noted and that a proposal for action would be initiated.[95] In an evaluation of the basis for medical referral to an endocrine consultant, forty-five physicians were asked to evaluate twenty-four clinical cases for possible referral.[124] The major reason for referral was the patient's desire to be referred, not the weight or medical status of the patient.

To explore the problem further, Maddox and Liederman[94] submitted a questionnaire to 197 senior physicians, house officers, and medical student clerks who were working in an outpatient clinic. Only 51 percent of the questionnaires were returned. Among the responding physicians, 93 percent said that their major source of knowledge about obesity was from personal experience. Sixty-six percent indicated that personal research had contributed to their understanding of obesity; 50 percent had learned about obesity in medical conferences; a bare 22 percent stated that their sources of information included medical school lectures. More than half of the physicians admitted that they were usually unsuccessful in treating obesity. But 40 percent indicated that careful management was the preferred approach in spite of its relatively low success rate. Despite this, less than half the physicians actually made proposals for treatment of patients who were more than 20 percent overweight.

EDUCATIONAL DISADVANTAGES OF OBESITY

The low esteem with which obese people are viewed by many might prejudice their educational opportunities. Obesity and intelligence were not correlated among a group of obese and nonobese teenagers where mean IQ values were 112 and 114.[24] Similarly, the Scholastic Aptitude Test scores were similar for both groups. However, there were significantly fewer obese males in the top third of the high school class than there were lean males (21 versus 26 percent). Suggestive differences were also present for females but were not statistically significant (41 versus 32 percent for nonobese versus obese girls). Finally, the mean high school grade-point average was lower for obese than for nonobese students, but this was also not statistically significant. In this study there were no differences in school attendance records nor in plans for jobs or education following graduation from high school. Yet when Canning and Mayer[24] examined the frequency of obese and nonobese individuals in Ivy League colleges, they found a significantly lower number of obese females than of nonobese females. These data suggest that there might be a prejudicial admission policy toward the obese high school students. These authors noted that obese and nonobese students were equally interested in attending high-ranking colleges and that evaluation of their capacities by objective data such as school standing and IQ showed no significant differences.

OBESITY AND EMPLOYMENT

In a survey of public opinion in southern California, one television station found that nearly two-thirds of the five hundred respondents felt that employers were reluctant to hire fat people. Documentation of this, however, is difficult to obtain. In a study to examine overweight job applicants, Larkin and Pines[80] reported "overweight persons are seen as significantly . . . less desirable employees who, compared with others, are less competent, less productive, not industrious, disorganized, indecisive, inactive and less successful" (p. 315). Another study suggests that fat bosses get lower salaries than their lean counterparts.[92] This study was conducted among 15,000 men who were known to an employment agency. Among the men who were greater than 10 percent overweight, only 9 percent were earning $25,000 to $40,000 per year. However, 40 percent of the men earning between $10,000 and $20,000 per year were more than 10 percent overweight. This employment agency had had only one job request for an obese man and that was to fill a job as an executive for a clothing company making clothes for overweight men. On the other hand, McLean and Moon[92] could find no negative effects of obesity on earning power of 2,456 men aged 51 to 65 using data obtained from responses to the National Longitudinal Survey for mature men.

Further observations on the economic difficulties associated with overweight have appeared in newspaper articles. A federal judge recently ordered a major airline to pay back salary and interest to stewardesses who were dismissed because of overweight. This ended the dismissal of stewardesses because they did not meet weight limits. A candidate scoring near the top in her civil service examination was fired for being 50 pounds overweight. This patent discrimination in employment practices is being ended by action in the federal courts. These instances serve to illustrate the significant economic and social hurdles that obese individuals must overcome in American society today. However, the concept that obesity is a "handicap"[98] may provide one approach to dealing with this stigmatized disability within the governmental framework.

Concluding Remarks

The focus of this chapter has been the role of weight control in promoting good health. Several types of evidence have been marshalled to show that excess weight is detrimental to longevity, to health while living, and to some social interactions. Equally important, most of these detrimental effects can be reversed by weight reduction. In conclusion, the motto from this chapter might appropriately be: "Overweight is risking fate."

REFERENCES

1. Abraham, S., Collins, G., and Nordsieck, M. 1971. Relationship of childhood weight status to morbidity in adults. *HSMHA Health Reports* 86:273–284.

2. Abraham, S., Carrol, M. D., Najjar, M. F., and Fulwood, R. 1983. *Obese and overweight adults in the United States, vital and health statistics.* U.S. DHHS Publication no. (PHS) 83-1680, PHS NCHS, series 11, no. 230.

3. Alexander, J. K. 1973. Effects of weight reduction on the cardiovascular system. In *Obesity in perspective*, ed. G. A. Bray, vol. 2, pp. 233–236. DHEW Publication no. (NIH) 75-708. Washington, D.C.: U.S. Government Printing Office.

4. Allon, N. 1973. The stigma of overweight in everyday life. In *Obesity in perspective*, ed. G. A. Bray, vol. 2, pp. 83–102. DHEW Publication no. (NIH) 75-708. Washington, D.C.: U.S. Government Printing Office.

5. Archer, J. A., Gorden, P., and Roth, J. 1975. Defect in insulin binding to receptors in obese man. Amelioration with calorie restriction. *Journal of Clinical Investigation* 55: 166–174.

6. Ashley, F. W., and Kannel, W. B. 1974. Relation of weight change to changes in atherogenic traits: The Framingham study. *Journal of Chronic Diseases* 27:103–114.

7. Atkinson, R. L., Dahms, W. T., Bray, G. A., and Schwartz, A. 1978. Parathyroid hormone levels in obesity: Effects of intestinal bypass surgery. *Mineral and Electrolyte Metabolism* 1:315–320.

8. Atkinson, R. L., et al. Gastrin secretion after weight loss by dieting and intestinal bypass surgery. *Gastroenterology* 77:696–699.

9. Backman, L., Granstrom, L., Lindahl, J., and Melcher, A. 1983. Manometric studies of lower esophageal sphincter in extreme obesity. *Acta Chirurgica Scandinavica* 149: 193–197.

10. Bagdade, J. D., Porte, D., Jr., and Bierman, E. L. 1969. The interaction of diabetes and obesity on the regulation of fat mobilization in man. *Diabetes* 18:759–772.

11. Bennion, L. T., and Grundy, S. M. 1978. Risk factors for the development of cholelithiasis in man (part 2). *New England Journal of Medicine* 229:1221–1227.

12. Berger, M., Muller, W. A., and Renold, A. E. 1978. Relationship of obesity to diabetes: Some facts, many questions. In *Diabetes, obesity and vascular disease*, ed. H. M. Katzen and R. J. Mahler, pp. 211–228. Washington, D.C.: Hemisphere Publishing.

13. Bernstein, R. A., et al. 1977. Gallbladder disease—II. Utilization of the life table method in obtaining clinically useful information. TOPS. *Journal of Chronic Diseases* 30: 529–541.

14. Björntorp, P., and Sjöström, L. 1971. Number and size of adipose tissue fat cells in relation to metabolism in human obesity. *Metabolism* 20:703–713.

15. Braillon, A., and Capron, J. P. 1983. Foie et l'obesite. *Gastroenterologie Clinique et Biologique* 7:627–634.

16. Bray, G. A. 1975. Metabolic effects of corpulence. In *Recent advances in obesity research I*, ed. A. Howard, pp. 56–65. London: Newman Publishing.

17. ———. 1976. *The obese patient*. Philadelphia: W. B. Saunders.

18. ———. 1978. Definitions, measurements and classification of the syndromes of obesity. *International Journal of Obesity* 2:99–112.

19. Bray, G. A., Chopra, I. J., and Fisher, D. A. 1976. Relation of thyroid hormones to body weight. *Lancet* 1:1206–1208.

20. Bray, G. A., et al. 1977. Spontaneous and experimental human obesity: Effect of diet and adipose cell size on lipolysis and lipogenesis. *Metabolism* 26:739–747.

21. Brown, J., and Winkelmann, R. K. 1968. Acanthosis nigricans: A study of 90 cases. *Medicine* 47:33–51.

22. Burwell, C. S., Robin, E. D., Whaley, R. D., and Bickelman, A. G. 1956. Extreme obesity associated with alveolar hypoventilation—a Pickwickian syndrome. *American Journal of Medicine* 21:811–818.

23. Cahnman, W. J. 1968. The stigma of obesity. *Social Quarterly* 9:283–299.

24. Canning, H., and Mayer, J. 1966. Obesity—its possible effect on college acceptance. *New England Journal of Medicine* 275:1172–1174.

25. Chandra, R. K., and Kutty, K. M. 1980. Immunocompetence in obesity. *Acta Paediatrica Scandinavica* 69:25–30.

26. Chiang, B. N., Perlman, L. V., and Epstein, F. H. 1969. Overweight and hypertension: A review. *Circulation* 39:403–421.

27. Danforth, E., et al. 1979. Dietary-induced alterations in thyroid hormone metabolism during overnutrition. *Journal of Clinical Investigation* 64:1336–1347.

28. Davidson, M. B., and Chopra, I. J. 1979. Effect of carbohydrate and non-carbohydrate sources on plasma 3,5,3′ triiodothyronine concentrations in man. *Journal of Clinical Endocrinology and Metabolism* 48:577–581.

29. Dawber, T. B. 1980. *The Framingham study. The epidemiology of atherosclerotic disease.* Cambridge, Mass.: Harvard University Press.

30. DeJong, W. 1980. The stigma of obesity: The consequences of naive assumptions concerning the causes of physical deviance. *Journal of Health and Social Behavior* 21:75–87.

31. Dempsey, J. A., Reddan, W., Balke, B., and Rankin, J. 1966. Work capacity determinants and physiologic cost of weight-supported breathing in obesity. *Journal of Applied Physiology* 21:815–820.

32. de Waard, F. W. 1975. Breast cancer incidence and nutritional status with particular reference to body weight and height. *Cancer Research* 35:3351–3356.

33. Donegan, W. L., Johnstone, M. F., and Biedrzycki, L. 1983. Obesity, estrogen production, and tumor estrogen receptors in women with carcinoma of the breast. *American Journal of Clinical Oncology* 6:19–24.

34. Douglas, F. G., and Chang, P. Y. 1972. Influence of obesity on peripheral airways patency. *Journal of Applied Physiology* 33:559–563.

35. Drenick, E. J., Brickman, A. S., and Gold, E. M. 1972. Dissociation of the obesity-hyperinsulinism relationship following dietary restriction and hyperalimentation. *American Journal of Clinical Nutrition* 25:746–755.

36. Drenick, E. J., Gurunanjappa, S. B., Seltzer, F. S. A., and Johnson, D. G. 1980. Excessive mortality and causes of death in morbidly obese men. *Journal of the American Medical Association* 243:443–445.

37. Elder, G. H., Jr. 1969. Appearance and education in marriage mobility. *American Sociological Review* 34:519–533.

38. Elmesallamy, F. H., and Rubal, B. J. 1982. Echocardiographic evaluation of a group of obese women. *Federation Proceedings* 41:713.

39. Engel, A. 1968. Osteoarthritis and body measurements. *Vital Health Statistics* 11:1–37.

40. Evans, D. J., Hoffmann, R. G., Kalkhoff, R. K., and Kissebah, A. H. 1983. Relationship of androgenic activity to body fat topography, fat cell morphology, and metabolic aberrations in premenopausal women. *Journal of Clinical Endocrinology and Metabolism* 57:304–310.

41. Feldman, R., Sender, A. J., and Sieglaub, A. B. 1969. Difference in diabetic and non-diabetic fat distribution patterned by skin-fold measurements. *Diabetes* 18:478–486.

42. Friedman, G. D., Kannel, W. B., and Dawber, J. R. 1966. The epidemiology of gallbladder disease: Observations in the Framingham study. *Journal of Chronic Diseases* 19:273–393.

43. Ganor, S., and Even-Paz, Z. 1967. Fragilitas cutis inguinalis. A phenomenon associated with obesity. *Dermatologia* 134:113–124.

44. Garn, S. M. 1983. Some consequences of being obese. In *Controversies in obesity*, ed. B. C. Hansen, pp. 287–300. New York: Praeger.

45. Garn, S. M., and Petzold, A. S. 1982. Fatness and hematological levels during pregnancy. *American Journal of Clinical Nutrition* 36:729–730.

46. Garn, S. M., and Ryan, A. S. 1982. Relationship between fatness and hemoglobin levels in the national health and nutrition examinations of the USA. *Ecology of Food and Nutrition* 12:211–215.

47. Garn, S. M., Bailey, S. M., and Block, W. D. 1979. Relationship between fatness and lipid levels in adults. *American Journal of Clinical Nutrition* 32:733–735.

48. Glass, A. R., Burman, K. D., Dahms, W. T., and Boehm, T. M. 1981. Endocrine function in human obesity. *Metabolism* 30:89–103.

49. Goldin, R. H., et al. 1976. Clinical and radiological survey of the incidence of osteoarthrosis among obese patients. *Annals of the Rheumatic Diseases* 35:349–353.

50. Goodman, J. I., Richardson, S. A., Dornbusch, S. M., and Hastorf, A. H. 1963. Varient reactions to physical disabilities. *American Sociological Review* 28:429–435.

51. Gordon, T., et al. 1977. High density lipoprotein as a protective factor against coronary heart disease. *American Journal of Medicine* 62:707–714.

52. Gross, T., Sokol, R. J., and King, K. C. 1980. Obesity in pregnancy: Risks and outcome. *Obstetrics and Gynecology* 56:446–450.

53. Harris, M. B., and Smith, S. D. 1983. The relationships of age, sex, ethnicity, and weight to stereotypes of obesity and self perception. *International Journal of Obesity* 7: 361–371.

54. Hartz, A. J., Rupley, D. C., and Rimm, A. A. 1984. The association of girth measurements with disease in 32,856 women. *Journal of Epidemiology* 119:71–80.

55. Herrell, W. E. 1961. Osteoarthritis and symptomatic arthritis. *Journal of the Kentucky Medical Association* 59:241–245.

56. Hodgkinson, R., and Husain, F. J. 1980. Caesarean section associated with gross obesity. *British Journal of Anaesthesia* 52:919–923.

57. Holley, H. S., Milic-Emili, J., Becklake, M. R., and Bates, D. V. 1967. Regional distribution, pulmonary ventilation and perfusion in obesity. *Journal of Clinical Investigation* 46:475–481.

58. Hubert, H. B., Feinleib, M., McNamara, P. M., and Castelli, W. P. 1983. Obesity as an independent risk factor for cardiovascular disease: A 26-year follow-up of participants in Framingham heart study. *Circulation* 67:968–977.

59. Joslin, E. P., Dublin, L. I., and Marks, H. H. 1936. Studies in diabetes mellitus. IV. Etiology, part II. *American Journal of Medical Science* 192:9–23.

60. Kahn, C. R., et al. 1976. The syndromes of insulin resistance and acanthosis nigricans: Insulin-receptor disorders in man. *New England Journal of Medicine* 294:739–745.

61. Kahn, R. C., et al. 1981. Insulin receptors, receptor antibodies, and the mechanism of insulin action. *Recent Progress in Hormone Research* 37:377–533.

62. Kannel, W. B., and Gordon, T. 1976. Physiological and medical concomitants of obesity: The Framingham study. *Clinics in Endrocrinology & Metabolism* 5:125–163.

63. ———. 1979. Obesity and some physiological and medical concomitants: The Framingham study. In *Obesity in America*, ed. G. A. Bray, pp. 125–163. NIH Publication no. 79-359. Washington, D.C.: U.S. Government Printing Office.

64. Kannel, W. B., Gordon, T., and Castelli, W. P. 1979. Obesity, lipids, and glucose intolerance. The Framingham study. *American Journal of Clinical Nutrition* 32:1238–1246.

65. Kaufman, B. J., Ferguson, M. H., and Cherniack, R. M. 1956. Hypoventilation in obesity. *Journal of Clinical Investigation* 21:811–818.

66. Keen, H., Jarrett, R. J., Thomas, B. J., and Fuller, J. H. 1979. Diabetes, obesity and nutrition: Epidemiological aspects. In *Diabetes and obesity*, ed. J. Vague and F. J. G. Ebling, pp. 91–103. International Congress Series no. 454. Amsterdam: Excerpta Medica.

67. Keys, A. 1980. Overweight, obesity, coronary heart disease and mortality. *Nutrition Review* 38:297–307.

68. ———. 1980. *Seven countries. A multivariate analysis of death and coronary heart disease.* Cambridge, Mass.: Harvard University Press.

69. Keys, A., et al. 1973. Coronary heart disease: Overweight and obesity as risk factors. *Annals of Internal Medicine* 77:15–27.

70. Kissebah, A. H., et al. 1982. Relation of body fat distribution to metabolic complications of obesity. *Journal of Clinical Endocrinology and Metabolism* 54:254–260.

71. Kley, H. K., Solbach, H. G., McKinnan, J. C., and Kruskemper, H. L. 1979. Testosterone decrease and estrogen increase in male patients with obesity. *Acta Endocrinologica* 91:553–563.

72. Knowler, W. C., Pettitt, D. J., Savage, P. J., and Bennett, P. H. 1981. Diabetes incidence in Pima Indians: Contributions of obesity and parental diabetes. *American Journal of Epidemiology* 113:144–156.

73. Kolterman, O. G., Insel, J., Saekow, M., and Olefsky, J. M. 1980. Mechanisms of insulin resistance in human obesity: Evidence for receptor and postreceptor defects. *Journal of Clinical Investigation* 65:1272–1284.

74. Kolterman, O. G., Olefsky, J. M., Kurahara, C., and Taylor, K. 1980. A defect in cell-mediated immune function in insulin-resistant diabetic and obese subjects. *Journal of Laboratory and Clinical Medicine* 96:535–543.

75. Kopelman, P. G., Pilkington, T. R. E., White, N., and Jeffcoate, S. L. 1979. Impaired hypothalamic control of prolactin secretion in massive obesity. *Lancet* 1:747–750.

76. Krisnen, M. A., Ertel, N., and Schneider, G. 1981. Obesity, hormones, and cancer. *Cancer Research* 41:3711–3717.

77. Krisnen, E. C., Trost, L., Arons, S., and Jewell, W. R. 1982. Study of function and maturation of monocytes in morbidly obese individuals. *Journal of Surgical Research* 33: 89–97.

78. Krotkiewski, M., Björntorp, P., Sjöström, L., and Smith, U. 1983. Impact of obesity on metabolism in men and women. Importance of regional adipose tissue distribution. *Journal of Clinical Investigation* 72:1150–1162.

79. Krupka, L. R., and Vener, A. M. In press. Patterns of use and perceptions of users of over-the-counter anorectics. In *Phenylpropanolamine: Examining the benefits and risks,* ed. D. Morgan and J. Kagan. New York: Praeger.

80. Larkin, J. C., and Pines, H. A. 1979. No fat persons need apply: Experimental studies of the overweight stereotype and hiring preference. *Sociology of Work and Occupations* (August):315–316.

81. Larsson, B., Björntorp, P., and Tibblin, G. 1981. The health consequences of moderate obesity. *International Journal of Obesity* 5:97–116.

82. Larsson, B., et al. 1984. Abdominal adipose tissue distribution, obesity, and risk of cardiovascular disease and death: 13-year follow-up of participants in the study of men born in 1913. *British Medical Journal* 288:1401–1404.

83. Laurenco, R. V. 1969. Diaphragm activity in obesity. *Journal of Clinical Investigation* 48:1609–1614.

84. Leijd, B. 1980. Cholesterol and bile acid metabolism in obesity. *Clinical Science* 59: 203–206.

85. Lew, E. A., and Garfinkel, L. 1979. Variations in mortality by weight among 750,000 men and women. *Journal of Chronic Diseases* 32:563–576.

86. Longcope, C. 1974. Steroid production in pre-menopausal and post-menopausal women. In *The menopausal syndrome,* ed. R. B. Greenblatt, V. B. Mahesh, and P. C. MacDonald, p. 6. Baltimore: Williams & Wilkins.

87. Lopata, M., and Onal, E. 1982. Mass loading, sleep apnea, and the pathogenesis of obesity hypoventilation. *American Review of Respiratory Disease* 126:640–645.

88. Luce, J. M. 1980. Respiratory complications of obesity. *Chest* 78:626–631.

89. Lyons, H. H., and Huang, C. T. 1968. Therapeutic use of progesterone in alveolar hypoventilation associated with obesity. *American Journal of Medicine* 44:881–888.

90. MacDonald, P. C., et al. 1976. Origin of estrogen in a post-menopausal woman with a non-endocrine tumor of the ovary and endometrial hyperplasia. *Obstetrics and Gynecology* 47:644–650.

91. McKeown, T., and Record, R. G. 1957. The influence of body weight on reproductive function in women. *Journal of Endocrinology* 15:410–422.

92. McLean, R. A., and Moon, M. 1980. Health, obesity and earnings. *American Journal of Public Health* 70:1006–1009.

93. MacMahon, D. P., Cole, P., and Brown, J. 1973. Etiology of human breast cancer: A review. *Journal of the National Cancer Institute* 50:21–42.

94. Maddox, G. L., and Liederman, W. 1969. Overweight as a social disability with medical implications. *Journal of Medical Education* 44:214–220.

95. Maddox, G. L., Anderson, C. F., and Bogdonoff, M. D. 1966. Overweight as a problem of medical management in a public outpatient clinic. *American Journal of Medical Science* 252:394–402.

96. Maddox, G. L., Back, K. W., and Liederman, V. R. 1968. Overweight and social deviance and disability. *Journal of Health and Social Behavior* 9:287–298.

97. Marks, H. H. 1960. Influence of obesity in morbidity and mortality. *Bulletin of the New York Academy of Science* 36:296–312.

98. Matusewitch, E. 1983. Labor relations: Employment discrimination against the overweight. *Personnel Journal* (June):446–450.

99. Mavrelis, P. G., et al. 1983. Hepatic free fatty acids in alcoholic liver disease and morbid obesity. *Hepatology* 3:226–231.

100. Maxwell, M. H., et al. 1982. Error in blood pressure due to incorrect cuff size in obese patients. *Lancet* 2:33–36.

101. Medalie, J. H., Papier, C. M., Goldbourg, N., and Herman, J. D. 1975. Major factors in the development of diabetes mellitus in 10,000 men. *Archives of Internal Medicine* 135:811–817.

102. Messerli, F. H., et al. 1983. Disparate cardiovascular effects of obesity and arterial-hypertension. *American Journal of Medicine* 74:808–812.

103. Miettinen, T. A. 1971. Cholesterol production in obesity. *Circulation* 44:842–850.

104. Naeye, R. L. 1979. Weight gain and the outcome of pregnancy. *American Journal of Obstetrics and Gynecology* 135:3–9.

105. Naimark, A., and Cherniack, R. M. 1960. Compliance of the respiratory system and its components in health and obesity. *Journal of Applied Physiology* 15:377–382.

106. Nestel, P., Ishikawa, T., and Goldrick, B. 1978. Diminished plasma free fatty acid clearance in obese subjects. *Metabolism* 27:589–597.

107. Newberg, L. H. 1942. Control of hyperglycemia of the obese diabetics by weight reduction. *Annals of Internal Medicine* 17:935–942.

108. O'Brien, T. F. 1980. Lower esophageal sphincter pressure (LESP) and esophageal function in obese humans. *Journal of Clinical Gastroenterology* 2:145–148.

109. Ogilvie, R. F. 1935. Sugar tolerance in obese subjects: A review of 65 cases. *Journal of Medicine* 16:345–358.

110. Olefsky, J. M., Kolterman, O. G., and Scarlett, J. A. 1982. Insulin action and resistance in obesity and noninsulin-dependent type II diabetes mellitus. *American Journal of Physiology* 243:E15–E30.

111. Olefsky, J., Reaven, G. M., and Farquhar, J. W. 1974. Effects of weight reduction on obesity: Studies of lipid and carbohydrate metabolism in normal and hyperlipoproteinemic subjects. *Journal of Clinical Investigation* 53:64–76.

112. Orlowski, J. P., Herrell, D. W., and Moodie, D. S. 1982. Narcotic antagonist therapy of the obesity hypoventilation syndrome. *Critical Care Medicine* 10:604–607.

113. Peckham, C. H., and Christianson, R. E. 1971. The relationship between pre-pregnancy weight and certain obstetric factors. *American Journal of Obstetrics and Gynecology* 111:1–7.

114. Pyke, D. A., and Please, N. W. 1957. Obesity, parity and diabetes. *Journal of Endocrinology* 15:26–33.

115. Rabinowitz, D., and Zierler, K. L. 1962. Forearm metabolism in obesity and its response to intra-arterial insulin. Characterization of insulin resistance and evidence for adaptive hyperinsulinism. *Journal of Clinical Investigation* 41:2173–2181.

116. Rabkin, S. W., Mathewson, F. A., and Hus, P. H. 1977. Relation of body weight to development of ischemic heart disease in a cohort of young North American men after a 26-year observation period. The Manitoba study. *American Journal of Cardiology* 39:452–458.

117. Ratzmann, K. P., et al. 1981. Changes of early insulin response to glucose in obese subjects with normal and impaired carbohydrate tolerance. *Endokrinologie* 78:89–98.

118. Ray, C. S., et al. 1983. Effects of obesity on respiratory function. *American Review of Respiratory Disease* 128:501–506.

119. Reisin, E., and Frohlich, E. D. 1978. Effects of weight without salt restriction on the reduction of blood pressure in overweight hypertensive patients. *New England Journal of Medicine* 298:1–5.

120. Report of the National Commission on Diabetes to the Congress of the United States. 1976. DHEW Publication no. 76-1019. Washington, D.C.: U.S. Government Printing Office, p. 1.

121. Richardson, S. A., Hastorf, A. H., Goodman, N., and Dornbusch, S. M. 1961. Cultural uniformity in reaction to physical disabilities. *American Sociological Review* 90:44–51.

122. Rimm, A. A., Werner, L. H., Van Iserloo, B., and Bernstein, R. A. 1975. Relationship of obesity and disease in 73,532 weight-conscious women. *Public Health Reports* 90:44–54.

123. Rochester, D. F., and Enson, Y. 1974. Current concepts in the pathogenesis of the obesity-hypoventilation syndrome, mechanical and circulatory factors. *American Journal of Medicine* 57:402–420.

124. Rothert, M. L., et al. 1984. Differences in medical referral decisions for obesity among family practitioners, general internists, and gynecologists. *Medical Care* 22:42–55.

125. Saville, P. D., and Dickson, J. 1968. Age and weight in osteoarthritis of the hip. *Arthritis and Rheumatism* 11:635–643.

126. Scheer, J. C., and Guthrie, H. A. 1981. Hemoglobin criteria with respect to obesity. *American Journal of Clinical Nutrition* 34:2748–2751.

127. Seltzer, C. C., and Mayer, J. A. 1965. A simple criterion of obesity. *Postgraduate Medicine* 38A:101–107.

128. Sharp, J. T., Barrocas, M., and Chokroverty, S. 1980. The cardiorespiratory effects of obesity. *Clinics in Chest Medicine* 1:103–118.

129. Sharp, J. T., et al. 1965. Effects of mass loading the respiratory systems in man. *Journal of Applied Physiology* 19:959–966.

130. Sherman, B. M., Wallace, R. B., and Bean, J. A. 1982. Cyclic ovarian function and breast cancer. *Cancer Research* 42(Suppl.):3286–3288.

131. Sicuranza, B. J., and Tisdall, L. H. 1975. Caesarean section in the massively obese. *Journal of Reproductive Medicine* 14:10–11.

132. Silberberg, R. 1979. Obesity and osteoarthritis. In *Medical complications of obesity*, ed. M. Mancini, B. Lewis, and F. Contaldo, pp. 301–315. London: Academic Press.

133. Silteri, P. K., and MacDonald, P. C. 1973. The role of extraglandular estrogens in human endocrinology. In *Handbook of physiology*, ed. S. R. Geiger, E. B. Astwood, and R. O. Greep, pp. 615–629. New York: American Physiological Society.

134. Sims, E. A. H., et al. 1973. Endocrine and metabolic effects of experimental obesity in man. *Recent Progress in Hormone Research* 29:457–487.

135. Society of Actuaries. 1960. *Build and blood pressure study, 1959.* Chicago: Society of Actuaries.

136. Society of Actuaries and Association of Life Insurance Medical Directors of America. *Build study, 1979.* Chicago: Society of Actuaries.

137. Sowers, J. R., et al. 1982. Role of the sympathetic nervous system in blood pressure maintenance in obesity. *Journal of Clinical Endocrinology & Metabolism* 54:1181–1186.

138. Stohl, K. P., Saunders, N. A., Feldman, N. T., and Hallett, M. 1978. Obstructive sleep apnea in family members. *New England Journal of Medicine* 299:969–973.

139. Sturdevant, R. A. L., Pearce, M. L., and Dayton, S. 1973. Increased prevalence of cholelithiasis in men ingesting a serum cholesterol-lowering diet. *New England Journal of Medicine* 288:24–27.

140. Sutton, F. D., et al. 1975. Progesterone for outpatient treatment of Pickwickian syndrome. *Annals of Internal Medicine* 83:476–479.

141. Toeller, M., et al. 1979. Massive adipositas mit gestorter glucosetoleranz. *Deutsche Medizinische Wochenschrift* 104:1513–1517.

142. Trichophoulos, D., Polychronopoulou, A., Brown, J., and MacMahon, B. 1983. Obesity, serum cholesterol, and estrogens in premenopausal women. *Oncology* 40:227–231.

143. Tuck, M. L., et al. 1981. The effect of weight reduction on blood pressure, plasma renin activity, and plasma aldosterone levels in obese patients. *New England Journal of Medicine* 304:930–933.

144. Tucker, D. H., and Sieker, H. O. 1960. The effects of change in body position on lung volumes and intrapulmonary gas mixing in patients with obesity, heart failure and emphysema. *Journal of Clinical Investigation* 39:787–791.

145. Vagenakis, A. G., et al. 1975. Diversion of peripheral thyroxine metabolism from activating to inactivating pathways during complete fasting. *Journal of Clinical Endocrinology & Metabolism* 41:191–194.

146. Vague, J. 1956. The degree of masculine differentiation of obesities: Factor for determining pre-disposition to diabetes, atherosclerosis, gout and uric calculous disease. *American Journal of Clinical Nutrition* 4:20–34.

147. Vaughan, R. W., and Conahan, T. J. 1980. Part I: Cardiopulmonary consequences of morbid obesity. *Life Sciences* 26:2119–2127.

148. Vaughan, R. W., Gandolfi, A. J., and Bentley, J. B. 1980. Part II: Biochemical considerations of morbid obesity. *Life Sciences* 26:2215–2221.

149. Walster, E., Aronson, V., Abrahams, D., and Ratlmann, L. 1966. Importance of physical attractiveness in dating behavior. *Journal of Personality and Social Psychology* 4:508–516.

150. Weber, M. L. 1939. Clinical and roentgenological analysis of 150 cases of chronic nonspecific arthritis. *Medical Bulletin of the Veterans Administration* 2:43–60.

151. Weisinger, J. R., Kempson, R. L., Eldridge, F. L., and Swenson, R. S. 1974. The nephrotic syndrome: A complication of massive obesity. *Annals of Internal Medicine* 81:440–447.

152. West, K. M., and Kalbfleisch, J. M. 1971. Influence of nutritional factors on prevalence of diabetes. *Diabetes* 20:99–108.

153. Whitcomb, M. E., Altman, N., Clark, R. W., and Ralstin, J. H. 1978. Central and obstructive sleep apnea. *Chest* 73:857–860.

154. Zwillich, C. W., et al. 1975. Progesterone for outpatient treatment of Pickwickian syndrome. *Annals of Internal Medicine* 83:476–479.

2

Physiological Aspects of Obesity

John S. Garrow

Regulation of Energy Balance

At the end of the last century, W. O. Atwater and F. C. Benedict performed a beautiful series of experiments in a basement room of the Orange Judd Hall of the Wesleyan University in Middletown, Connecticut.[4] Their laboratory assistant and janitor, a Mr. E. Osterberg, permitted himself to be sealed into a well-insulated box for periods of four days at a time while exact measurements were made of the food he ate, the amount of heat he produced, and the change in his body stores of protein and fat. Over a series of six four-day experiments, the difference between the observed heat generated by Mr. Osterberg and that which would have been predicted from the energy content of the diet which he ate was −1.6 ± 2.2 percent. For sheer technical virtuosity these experiments have not been excelled by any recent investigators, although we now have computer-controlled calorimeters that do the same work with much less arduous labor. The pioneering work of Atwater and Benedict, and all subsequent investigations, confirmed beyond doubt that the laws of thermodynamics apply to man as well as to the rest of nature. The energy stores in the human body accurately reflect the balance between energy input (from food and drink) and energy expenditure.

This is the physiological basis of obesity. Obesity is a condition in which the energy stores of the body (mainly fat) are excessively large. If a normal person weighs 70 kg, and an obese person of similar height, age, and sex weighs 110 kg, we can be fairly sure that the obese person has energy stores that contain 280,000 kcal (1,170 megajoules) more than those of the normal person. The uncertainty arises because the ratio of fat to lean tissue in excess weight varies somewhat (see the next section). However, if we knew the energy value of the excess weight, we could be quite sure that the obese person had eaten or drunk that amount in excess of expenditure, and we could be equally sure that to return to the normal body composition the obese person would have to expend the same quantity of energy in excess of intake.

The mechanism by which energy balance is regulated in man is a subject of lively, and often confused, debate. Physiologists who are interested in the regulation of eating and drinking have used as their model the laboratory rat fed on a monotonous chow diet. Adolph[2] offered rats a diet of chow in which the energy per unit weight was increased by adding fat or decreased by adding inert filler. Within a range of about 50 percent change in energy density the rats compensated after a few days and ate less or more chow so their energy intake was the same as before. This capacity to regulate intake was disturbed when nuclei in the hypothalamus were damaged. It is rather difficult to do similar tests on human subjects, so for want of better information textbooks state quite firmly that energy balance in man is regulated by controlling food intake, and this is supervised by the hypothalamic nuclei. If this view is true then all of us who manage to retain a fairly steady and normal body weight must regulate energy intake with amazing precision.

Consider these lines from a recent nutrition textbook: "If a healthy man or woman eats only an extra slice of bread (20 g) at breakfast, this provides a surplus of 200 kJ or 48 kcal of energy, which is stored as triglyceride. If he continues with this as a daily habit, after 20 years the store has grown by 20 kg and he has become very obese"[9] (p. 246).

This statement cannot be true. The arithmetic is correct: $20 \times 365 \times 48$ kcal is roughly the energy value of 20 kg triglyceride. However, the physiology is wrong, since it assumes that the increase in food intake will have no effect on energy expenditure, which it does. Farmers would very much like to have a breed of animal that had 100 percent food conversion efficiency—that is, one that stored 100 percent of the extra food given to it—but for all their efforts at selective breeding, no such productive paragon has been, or ever will be, achieved. Our own species, which has not been selectively bred for efficient fattening, does not have 100 percent food conversion efficiency either.

To understand the physiology of obesity in man we need to understand the three components of the energy balance equation: energy stores, energy intake, and energy expenditure, and how each affects the other two. These aspects will now be considered in turn.

FIGURE 2.1
Diagrammatic representation of the components of body weight
in a normal 70-kg male adult. For energy equivalence see table 2.1.

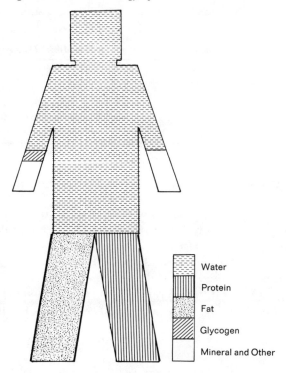

SOURCE: J. S. Garrow, 1981, *Treat obesity seriously: A clinical manual*, Edinburgh: Churchill Livingstone.

Body Composition in Obesity

Figure 2.1 shows a simplified version of the body composition of a normal adult male.[14] The energy value for each component is shown in table 2.1. A detailed justification for this scheme is given elsewhere.[14] For purposes of energy balance the only components that concern us are protein, fat, and glycogen, but it is important to note that by far the largest component of body weight is water. Overweight patients are concerned about their weight and tend to regard weight loss as a desirable aim. In fact, as the following discussion will show, weight loss may not be a good indicator of success in dealing with the problem of obesity. If the weight lost is not fat but water or, worse still, protein, then it is usually undesirable.

Unfortunately, it is not easy for the obese patient—or for the therapist—to know the composition of excess weight or of weight that is lost. In a well-equipped metabolic laboratory, this can be measured by the following techniques.

TABLE 2.1

*The Approximate Energy Stores
of a Normal Adult Male*

Component	Weight (kg)	Energy Equivalent	
		(Mcal)	(Megajoules)
Water	42.0	0	0
Protein	12.0	48	200
Fat	12.0	108	450
Glycogen	0.5	2	8
Mineral, etc.	3.5	0	0
Total	70.0	158	658

ESTIMATION OF FAT FROM BODY DENSITY

Fat has a density (at body temperature) of 0.90 g per cc; protein is 1.34 g per cc; water, 0.99 g per cc; and bone mineral, 3.00 g per cc. The fat-free body is a mixture of protein, water, and mineral that has a density of about 1.10 g per cc. If the simplifying assumption is made that any person is composed of fat (density 0.90 g/cc) and fat-free tissue (density 1.10 g/cc), and if the average density of a person (d) is determined, then the percentage fat in the body ($\%F$) is given by the following formula:

$$\%F = \frac{495}{d} - 450$$

The technical problem is to determine the average density of the tissues of a living subject. Behnke, Feen, and Welham[5] pioneered the technique of underwater weighing to determine the volume of the subject. If weight and volume are known then density is easily calculated. However, not all subjects are willing and able to submerge completely and calmly while an accurate measurement of weight is made, so new methods have been developed that permit the accurate measurement of body volume without requiring the subject to submerge completely in water.[17]

ESTIMATION OF FAT FROM TOTAL BODY WATER

Pace and Rathbun[23] showed that the fat-extracted eviscerated carcasses of guinea pigs contained about 73 percent water, however much fat they had contained. If fat-free tissue always contains 73 percent water, and total body water is known, the amount of fat-free tissue in the body and, by subtraction from body weight, the total amount of fat could be calculated. The water content of the fat-free component of six cadavers of adult human subjects has been measured, and the proportion was 72.4 ± 3.4 percent.[14] This agrees reasonably well with the figure found in animals. Total body water can be measured in living subjects by giving a known tracer dose of water labeled with an isotope of hydrogen or oxygen and taking a sample of blood after an equilibration period of three to four hours. The dilution of the concentration of the isotope label in the blood sample indicates the dilution of the tracer dose in total body water. Since the volume of the dose is known, total body water (TBW kg) can be calculated. From this the fat content of the body (*F* kg) can be calculated using the formula:

$$F = \text{Body weight} - \frac{\text{TBW}}{0.73}$$

ESTIMATION OF FAT FROM TOTAL BODY POTASSIUM

Fat-free tissue in men contains about 66 mmol potassium per kg, and in women the value is about 60 mmol potassium per kg. The potassium content of the body can be estimated, since potassium contains a natural radioactive isotope, ^{40}K, which emits a high-energy gamma ray. With suitable equipment (which is very expensive) the amount of this radiation can be measured, and hence the total body potassium (TBK mmol) can be calculated. The fat content of the body (*F* kg) can then be calculated from these formulas:

$$F = \text{Body weight} - \frac{\text{TBK}}{66} \quad \text{(for men)}$$

$$F = \text{Body weight} - \frac{\text{TBK}}{60} \quad \text{(for women)}$$

THE COMPOSITION OF EXCESS WEIGHT IN OBESE WOMEN

The quotation cited earlier from a nutrition textbook implies that excess energy is stored as triglyceride, but that is not quite true. Unlike the genetically obese mouse,[13] obese people have increased lean mass as well as increased fat mass. Figure 2.2 shows the relation of body weight to weight of fat in 104 women ranging in fatness from 6 to 60 percent of body weight.[32] The values for body fat are based on all three of the methods described earlier. The linear correlation coefficient between weight and fat in this series of women is 0.955, indicating that over the whole range, from very lean women to very obese women, increments of weight are made up of material with a similar proportion of fat. The slope of the line shows that about 75 percent of the weight difference is fat and 25 percent is nonfat tissue. This estimate agrees well with studies in which the composition of weight changes has been studied longitudinally.[13]

An important inference from this calculation is that changes in weight will normally have an energy value of about 7,000 kcal per kg (29

FIGURE 2.2

The relation of body weight to body fat in a series of 104 women varying from 6 to 60 percent body fat.

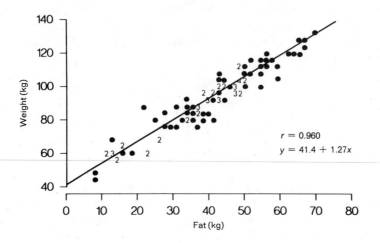

SOURCE: J. D. Webster, R. Hesp, and J. S. Garrow, 1984, The composition of excess weight in obese women estimated by body density, total body water and total body potassium, *Human Nutrition: Clinical Nutrition* 38(clinical ser.):299–306.

MJ/kg). This is because each kilogram will contain about 750 g fat (energy value 6,750 kcal, or 28 MJ) and 250 g lean tissue (energy value 250 kcal, or 1 MJ).[14]

QUETELET'S INDEX AS A MEASURE OF OBESITY

More than one hundred years ago Quetelet[26] observed that the weight of adults of normal build was proportional to the square of their height. This fact has been rediscovered several times, notably by Keys and associates,[20] who renamed Quetelet's index W/H^2 the "body mass index." However, it has recently been suggested that "efforts should be made to develop uncomplicated indices that correlate better with the body fat content than body mass index does" (p. 294).[29] This criticism is not quite fair, since Quetelet's index has been compared unfavorably with, for example, skin-fold measurements in its ability to predict *percentage* body fat.[15] It will be evident from fig 2.2 that Quetelet's index does relate linearly over a large range of fatness with the *weight* of fat in the body. However, if increments of weight are 75 percent fat and 25 percent lean, then anyone who is already nearly 75 percent fat cannot greatly increase his percentage of fat however much weight he may gain.

For practical purposes, Quetelet's index is very useful. It is easy to measure accurately, and the range W/H^2 20–25 (where W is measured in kg and H in meters) corresponds with the desirable range for longevity and physical fitness.[15]

Control of Energy Intake

It is common experience that when people miss a meal they feel hungry, and it is reasonable to suppose that some internal signal indicates a state of energy deficit. However, the experiments of Wooley et al.[35] show that both lean and obese subjects are unable to detect the energy content of a meal if they are given no cognitive clues. Volunteers were provided with a liquid meal of the same energy content as their normal meal for a period of five to ten days. Over the next ten to fourteen days the subjects were given meals of similar taste and texture, but with either half or double the normal energy content, and were asked each day if the meal had been higher or lower than usual in energy content. Over a series of 262 meals neither lean nor obese subjects were significantly better than chance at guessing correctly.

Other experiments lead to similar conclusions. Porikos and associates[25,26] observed the intake of lean and obese subjects when sucrose in the diet was replaced by the synthetic sweetener aspartame. After three days there was a partial compensation for the decrease in energy density of the diet, but both lean and obese subjects failed to achieve the accurate compensation Adolph[2] observed in rats.

In another experiment lean and obese subjects were given milkshakes of disguised energy content on several days and their spontaneous food intake was monitored for the remainder of the day.[11] Neither lean nor obese subjects accurately adjusted their spontaneous intake to compensate for the differences in the energy content of the milkshakes.

This chapter is concerned with physiological aspects of obesity, so it is not within its scope to consider what psychological and cognitive factors influence food intake. The preceding studies are cited to show that short-term physiological control of energy intake is very unreliable on its own. If we achieve a reasonably constant energy intake that matches energy expenditure (as we must do to achieve constant body weight over many years), then this must be by some mechanism other than the purely physiological controls of hunger and satiety.

Measurement of Energy Expenditure

In recent years there have been considerable advances in the techniques for studying the various aspects of energy output, so we now have a clearer picture of the contribution of energy output to the general regulation of energy balance. Because some of the confusion in the literature is attributable to poor technique in measuring metabolic rate, a few of the technical pitfalls will be briefly reviewed here.

DIRECT CALORIMETRY

The most fundamental measurement of energy expenditure by a person (or any organism) is to observe the heat generated over a period of time. The energy involved in all physiological reactions—contraction of muscles, pumping of sodium across cell walls, formation of peptide bonds to assemble amino acids into proteins, and every other type of synthesis or transport—eventually is degraded to heat. There is some dispute among experts in thermodynamics about exactly how these processes should be treated mathematically,[34] but for the purpose of this chapter we can regard heat production as the absolute standard for measurement of metabolic rate.

If we put our subject in a box with walls constructed of material that measures the passage of heat (a "gradient layer" calorimeter), or a box with some device by which we can extract heat to prevent the subject from heating the inside of the box above the temperature of the surroundings (a "heat sink" calorimeter), we can measure the amount of heat emitted by the subject. Over a period of many days we can safely assume that the heat emitted must be very similar to the heat generated, otherwise the subject's body temperature would become intolerably high or low. The classical studies of Atwater and Benedict,[4] which were mentioned at the beginning of this chapter, were conducted on the tolerant Mr. Osterberg, who was prepared to spend several days in such a box. However, most subjects, and certainly most patients in whom we suspect disorders of energy metabolism, are not so cooperative. Even if we did persuade patients to spend many days in a calorimeter, we would be hardly justified in assuming that their metabolic state was the same as it would have been if they had been going about their ordinary business.

In summary, then, direct calorimeters are the "gold standard" against which other methods for measuring energy expenditure are measured. A properly calibrated calorimeter will measure heat loss with an accuracy of 1 percent from an inanimate source such as an alcohol lamp.[14] The limitation in practice of direct calorimetry is that it is only suitable for long-term measurement, otherwise errors arise from heat storage in the body of the subject and the method is no longer very accurate. Since the procedure involves prolonged cooperation from the subject in an unusual environment, it may be argued that the measurement, although technically precise, is not a valid measurement of the energy expenditure of a free-living subject. This criticism applies to a greater or lesser extent to every method for measuring energy output (or intake). However, there are techniques by which the "stress" of being in a calorimeter can be measured,[6] so corrections can be made for this type of error.

INDIRECT CALORIMETRY

All physiological energy-producing reactions eventually result in the oxidation of substrate (carbohydrate, fat, protein, or alcohol) to carbon dioxide and water; "eventually" because brief periods of intense muscular activity (e.g., weightlifting) do not involve uptake of oxygen and production of carbon dioxide in the muscle during contraction, but the oxygen debt incurred during anaerobic work must eventually be paid. Therefore, a measurement of oxygen uptake and carbon dioxide production is the basis of indirect calorimetry. Modern physical gas analyzers have made the measurement of expired gas concentrations much easier and more accurate than the older manometric techniques.

The advantage of indirect calorimetry over direct calorimetry is that changes in metabolic rate are reflected in immediate changes in oxygen uptake, so it is possible to monitor minute-to-minute changes. The main disadvantage is that the relation of gas exchange to energy production is different according to the substrate oxidized: One liter of oxygen used to oxidize starch yields 5.047 kcal (21.13 kJ); from fat it yields 4.868 kcal (19.62 kJ); and from protein, 4.600 kcal (19.26 kJ). It is rarely possible to know accurately the mixture of substrate being oxidized in a living person, and there may be times when, for example, glucose is being oxidized and fat is being synthesized simultaneously. Another pitfall in indirect calorimetry is that expired carbon dioxide does not necessarily reflect the carbon dioxide being produced in the body at that time. The bicarbonate buffer in the plasma is in dynamic equilibrium with the body pool of carbon dioxide, so changes in the acid-base status of the subject, or in the ventilation rate, can cause discrepancies between carbon dioxide exhaled and carbon dioxide produced, particularly over a brief period of measurement.

Respiration Chamber. The method of collecting expired air that involves the least inconvenience to the subject is a respiration chamber. This is an airtight room with controlled ventilation at a rate sufficient to prevent the buildup of excessive quantities of carbon dioxide. If a level of 0.5 percent carbon dioxide is acceptable, and if the rate of production of carbon dioxide is 250 ml per minute, then a flow-rate of 50 l per min through the chamber is required. Because the change in gas concentration of effluent air with respect to ingoing air is small (about 0.5 percent), it is necessary to use very accurate and well-calibrated analyzers to obtain accurate estimates of metabolic rate. The disadvantages of a respiration chamber include those of the direct calorimeter—that the subject is confined in an unaccustomed environment. However, a respiration chamber is less expensive to construct than a direct calorimeter.

Ventilated Hood. Still less expensive is an arrangement by which the head of the subject is in an enclosure through which air is drawn at a known rate, and the effluent air is analyzed. For a resting subject a flow-rate of about 20 l per min is usually adequate in a ventilated hood, since the flow of air over the face can be arranged to reduce the likelihood that expired air will be rebreathed. Because the flow-rate is slower than in the respiration chamber, the change in gas concentration for a given metabolic rate is larger and hence easier to measure accurately. It does not matter if there are small leaks between the subject and the hood provided the flow of air through these leaks is inward, as it will be if the pressure within the hood is kept slightly below ambient pressure.

Facemask and Douglas Bag. About twenty years ago the standard technique for measuring metabolic rate was to fit the subject with an airtight facemask, or a nose-clip and mouthpiece, and by a system of tubes and valves to collect expired air in a large plastic bag. This technique is not acceptable except for rather crude measurements. The main objection is that observations cannot be made over a period of more than a few minutes: If the subject's resting ventilation rate is 5 liters per minute, he will fill a 100-liter Douglas bag in twenty minutes, and it is hardly practicable to use bags larger than these. Even if a series of bags is used the technique is marred by the discomfort of wearing an airtight mask or mouthpiece over a long period, especially when the intention is to measure "resting" metabolic rate. Anyone who has tried wearing such a mask for a long period will know that the experience is not conducive to restfulness.

Portable Respirometers. These also use tight-fitting facemasks, but collect a sample of expired air for analysis. They are useful in applications where fairly high rates of energy expenditure are being used in the field[18] but are not suitable for measurement of resting metabolism for the reasons just given.

INDIRECT INDIRECT CALORIMETRY

The term indirect indirect calorimetry may be used to describe methods for estimating energy expenditure that measure neither heat production nor gaseous exchange, but other factors that are related to energy expenditure. These methods interfere less with the activity and normal life style of the subject, but are inherently less accurate than the methods just described.

Heart Rate Monitoring. During physical exercise there is, for any individual, a close relation between energy expenditure and heart rate. The exercise increases the requirement for oxygen transport above resting level, so there must be an increase in cardiac output, and since there is little scope for increase in the stroke-volume of the heart, the increased cardiac output is achieved mainly by increasing the heart rate. Modern portable electronic devices will record heart rate with minimal inconvenience to the subject, so this is an attractive measure of energy expenditure in the field.[1] The disadvantages are, first, that the relation of heart rate to oxygen consumption varies between individuals and within the same individual with changes in posture and, second, that the close relation between heart rate and energy expenditure holds only at fairly high rates of energy expenditure. At-rest heart rate fluctuates over the range of about sixty to eighty beats per minute in a manner unrelated to oxygen uptake. Thus heart rate monitoring is a possible method for estimating the energy expenditure of such people as workers in heavy industry or endurance athletes (provided it is suitably calibrated for each individual), but not for people in sedentary occupations.

Doubly-Labeled Water. A normal adult contains about 42 l of water, and each day takes in about 2 l in food and drink. If total body water is labeled with deuterium hydroxide, the concentration of the deuterium label will therefore decrease by about 5 percent per day. The 42 l of body water contain about 30 kg oxygen, and this oxygen equilibrates with the oxygen in expired carbon dioxide. A production rate of 250 ml per minute of carbon dioxide incorporates about 500 g oxygen per day. Therefore, if total body water is labeled with an isotope of oxygen, the oxygen label will decrease by about 1.7 percent faster than the decrease of the deuterium, and the difference between the decay rate of the hydrogen and oxygen labels is an indication of the production rate of carbon dioxide.

In principle this is a most attractive way to measure energy expenditure in free-living man. All that is required is to give a dose of water labeled with an isotope of both hydrogen and oxygen, and a week or two later to take a sample of blood and measure the abundance of these two labels relative to that in the initial tracer dose. From this the mean production rate of carbon dioxide can be calculated over the period since the tracer dose was given. Assuming that oxygen consumption is 20 percent greater than carbon dioxide production (as it is in normal circumstances), the energy expenditure can be calculated.

It is still too early to know how reliable this method will be in practice.[21] The technique is expensive, since doubly-labeled water is expensive (but will no doubt become cheaper if the technique is widely used), and the isotope-ratio mass spectrometer needed to do the analysis is also expensive. The method assumes that the subject loses a constant proportion of water by evaporative routes and drinks water with a constant deuterium concentration. If either assumption is not true there will be an error in the answer, but the magnitude of the potential error is not yet known.

Pedometers. Various mechanical devices that record movement such as walking can be worn on the body. They may be useful in comparing the level of activity in a subject at different times, but the variation in pattern of movement between subjects is such that it is quite difficult to obtain an accurate estimate of the relative activity of different subjects by this method. Since such a small fraction of total energy expenditure is related to physical activity, these devices are not useful in measuring total daily energy expenditure.

Activity Diary. The classical studies of energy balance in military cadets were conducted using an activity diary as a measure of energy expenditure.[12] Each subject has the energy cost of a repertoire of activities measured by indirect calorimetry. The number of minutes in each day spent in each activity is recorded by the subject, or an observer, in an activity diary. Total daily energy expenditure is then calculated by multiplying the cost per minute of the activity by the minutes spent in that activity and summing the total for the day.

The weaknesses of this method are that the result depends on the accurate recording of time spent in each activity and that it is assumed that the energy cost of the activity is constant and at the level when the sample measurement was made. The first requirement is very difficult to meet, and the second is not possible. For example, the same activity before or after a meal will probably be associated with different levels of metabolic rate. The best that can be achieved is an average value with which, over a fairly long period of observation, the errors tend to cancel out.

Control of Energy Expenditure

Many texts on energy balance have implicitly assumed that energy *intake* is controlled, but that for a given person and life style energy output is virtually fixed. This is not so. Energy expenditure may be considered under four headings: resting metabolism, the thermic effect of food, the thermic effect of exercise, and other thermogenesis. Each of these components of energy expenditure may show regulatory changes if a person is not in energy balance.

RESTING METABOLIC RATE

The pioneers in clinical calorimetry were concerned to diagnose thyroid disease, so they tried to obtain the most reproducible and standardized measurements of "basal metabolic rate" (BMR). It was stipulated that the subject should be bodily and mentally at rest, in a neutral thermal environment, and twelve to eighteen hours after taking any food. By the end of 1926 this measurement had been made on over 60,000 individuals at the Mayo Clinic, of whom 6,888 were selected "who, on careful physical examination revealed no abnormality which would influence their rate of heat production" (p. 290).[8] It was upon this selected group that the "normal" values were based: When standardized for age, sex, and surface area, the coefficient of variation was 9 percent.

By the time most people have fasted eighteen hours they tend not to be mentally at rest, so the conditions for measurement of BMR are unnecessarily stringent. The modern practice is to measure resting metabolic rate (RMR) under defined conditions: For the purpose of this chapter these conditions are that the subject is at rest in bed in a neutral thermal environment, before breakfast, between 8 and 9 A.M. The measurement technique is by ventilated hood over a period of one hour.

A multiple regression analysis in our series of 140 women with varying degrees of obesity showed that RMR (ml oxygen/min) was best predicted by weight (W kg), age (A yr) and total body potassium (TBK mmol) as a measure of fat-free mass.[10] The regression formula is:

$$RMR = 99.8 + (1.155W) + (0.02227TBK) - (0.456A)$$

with a multiple correlation coefficient of 0.833 (i.e., these factors explained 69 percent of the observed variability in resting metabolic rate).

It should be noted that both weight and potassium (i.e., fat-free weight) contribute positively to the prediction of RMR, while age contributes negatively. This means that in our series the more obese women tended to have a higher metabolic rate than women of similar age and fat-free weight who were less obese. It can be seen from figure 2.2 that increasing fatness is very closely associated with increasing fat-free weight also, so it is dangerous to try to extract contributions of different fractions of body weight that are themselves highly correlated. However, these data do not at all suggest that more obese women have lower metabolic rates.

It might be that our series of women was a mixture of two populations: One had "metabolic" obesity associated with a low energy requirement, while others were obese purely because they had a high energy intake. To test this hypothesis we assumed that patients with a metabolic predisposition to obesity would be more likely to have become obese in early life and would be more likely to have a family history of obesity than those with no such predisposition. However, when we examined the RMR of sixty-five women in relation to their age of onset of obesity, or family history of obesity, there was no evidence that those with the postulated markers of "metabolic" obesity had any lower RMR than those who did not.[16]

THE THERMIC EFFECT OF FOOD

If the metabolic rate of a resting fasting subject is continuously monitored by means of indirect calorimetry in order to obtain a baseline, and then after about an hour food is given with minimal physical disturbance (e.g., by nasogastric tube), the metabolic rate will start to increase within about twenty minutes of the meal and will not return to baseline levels for several hours. Rubner,[27] who worked on dogs, was impressed with the fact that the increase in metabolic rate was greater after a protein meal (meat) than after a meal of sugar or lard. He named the effect "specific dynamic action," and for many years it was thought to be an effect related to the protein content of the meal. It has now been shown that the effect also occurs after meals that contain no protein, so the term thermic effect of food or diet-induced thermogenesis is more appropriate.

The relevance of this to the physiology of obesity is that it has been reported that obese people show a smaller thermic response to food than lean people. The first technically satisfactory and well-controlled study that supported this conclusion was from Lausanne:[24] Obese women showed an increase in metabolic rate of only 5.2 percent during 150 minutes after an oral dose of 50 g glucose, compared with 13.0 percent among lean controls. Workers in Cambridge, England, reported that obese subjects showed a reduced thermic response to a mixed meal,[29] but not to protein.[36] Later there were reports of a greatly reduced thermic response to fat overfeeding in obese people compared with controls.[31,37] We have been unable to show a decreased thermic response to carbohydrate, protein, or fat meals in obese subjects compared with controls,[22] and other laboratories have reported similar findings.[33]

These discrepant findings need some explanation. On some points there is agreement among all laboratories. The magnitude of the thermic effect is larger and more prolonged for a protein meal than for an isoenergetic meal of carbohydrate, while the response to a fat meal is very slow. This is in accord with the known rates of assimilation of these nutrients. It is also agreed that the baseline before the meal is significantly higher in the obese group than in the lean group of subjects. When the thermic responses of obese subjects are compared between laboratories, the results are similar, but some laboratories have responses for "control" subjects that are very large, and it is these laboratories that report a difference between lean and obese subjects. The best that can be done to reconcile all the findings is to say that there are some lean subjects who seem to have a very large thermic response to food, but these people have a particularly low baseline before the meal. The results cannot be interpreted to show that the reduced thermic response in obese people (if it exists) enables them to maintain weight on a lower energy intake than the lean controls.

THERMIC RESPONSE TO EXERCISE

Athletes are selected and trained to maintain high rates of energy output, and in this they differ from the ordinary person. The highest average rate of work output that can be sustained over a period of hours by nonathletes is about 5 kcal per min (20 kJ/min). This is equivalent to the uptake of about 1 liter of oxygen per min. Thus people who jog for two hours will use about 600 kcal (2.5 MJ). If they had remained at some sedentary occupation they would have used about 180 kcal (0.75 MJ) in the two-hour period, so the net cost of the exercise is about 420 kcal (1.75 MJ). It has been argued that this calculation greatly underestimates the energy cost of exercise, because the metabolic rate remains elevated for many hours after the exercise ceases.[3] However, there is no evidence that this is true for the relatively modest levels of exercise nonathletes can achieve,[14] and there is evidence from twenty-four-hour direct calorimetry that moderate exercise does not cause a prolonged elevation of metabolic rate.[7] This point will be discussed further in the next section.

There is ample evidence that the exercise tolerance of obese people

TABLE 2.2

The Effect of Four Thermogenic Stimuli on Mean 24-hour Heat Loss of Lean and Obese Women Measured by Direct Calorimetry

Thermogenic Stimulus	Lean Subjects		Obese Subjects	
	Heat Loss (Watts)	Difference from Control (Watts)	Heat Loss (Watts)	Difference from Control (Watts)
Warm	62.1	+0.4	99.9	+3.8
Cool	66.5	+4.8	94.1	−2.0
Exercise	72.0	+10.3	106.2	+10.1
Food	64.7	+3.0	99.5	+3.4
Control	61.7	—	96.1	—

SOURCE: S. E. Blaza and J. S. Garrow, 1983, Thermogenic response to temperature, exercise and food stimuli in lean and obese women, studied by 24 h direct calorimetry, *British Journal of Nutrition* 49:171–180.

is less than normal, but a given amount of activity costs them more energy. It is hard to sustain the view that inactivity is an important cause of obesity, since so many lean people are also inactive.[14] However, there are both physical and psychological benefits to be derived from exercise, so it is reasonable to promote exercise in any health education program. The place of exercise in obesity is discussed elsewhere in this book.

OTHER THERMOGENIC RESPONSES

In genetically obese mice the capacity to generate heat in response to cold stress is impaired. It has been shown that this thermogenesis depends on the metabolic activity of brown adipose tissue, which is defective in obese mice. There has been speculation that a similar thermogenic defect may help to explain obesity in man.[19] To investigate this possibility we have compared the twenty-four-hour heat loss of lean and obese subjects in a direct calorimeter under various conditions, such as might be encountered in real life, in which a thermogenic defect might be expected to reveal itself. Each subject was measured on five occasions: a control day on which no thermogenic stimulus was applied, a day in which the calorimeter was at the upper limit of the thermal comfort zone for that subject, a day at the lower limit of thermal comfort, a day with exercise on a bicycle ergometer, and a day with an extra 800 kcal (3.4 MJ) of food. The observed heat losses from the lean and obese subjects are shown in table 2.2.

The table shows some interesting differences between the lean and obese groups. In warm conditions the lean subjects hardly altered their metabolic rate while the obese subjects showed an increase of 3.8 watts. In cool conditions the lean subjects showed an increase in metabolism while the obese subjects showed a small decrease. The response of both groups to food and exercise was very similar. However, the striking difference between the two groups was the much greater overall energy expenditure of the obese group. In only two of the twenty-five pairs of lean/obese comparisons did a member of the lean group of subjects achieve a higher rate of energy expenditure than the lowest of the obese group of subjects. In terms of energy balance, therefore, small differences in thermogenic responsiveness of lean and obese subjects are of negligible importance compared with the large differences in baseline energy expenditure.

Conclusion

Recent improvements in techniques for measuring body composition and energy expenditure have greatly strengthened our understanding of the physiology of obesity. The composition of excess weight gained by obese women is about 75 percent fat and 25 percent lean tissue, and this has the effect of increasing resting metabolic rate and thus limiting the amount of weight gained for a given increase in energy intake. The thermic effect of excess energy intake also increases metabolic rate. These two effects combine to ensure that the observed storage of energy is always much less than the increase in intake.

Within any group of lean or obese individuals there is quite a wide range of energy requirements: The coefficient of variation among subjects matched for age, sex, and body composition, and without any evident metabolic abnormality, is about 10 percent, so the normal range extends from 80 to 120 percent of the mean. However, when the energy requirements of groups of lean and obese subjects are compared by twenty-four-hour direct calorimetry, the obese group has significantly higher requirements than the lean group. Even if obese subjects are selected who have a family history of obesity, or early-onset obesity, they do not have low energy requirements compared with lean people of similar age and sex.

It has been shown that a defect in brown adipose tissue of genetically obese mice accounts for their inability to increase metabolism in response to cold stress, and this defect is an important factor in the etiology of genetic obesity in mice. In man, however, the evidence of thermogenic defects is equivocal, and in any case would be inadequate to explain the etiology or persistence of obesity.

REFERENCES

1. Acheson, K. J., et al. 1980. The measurement of daily energy expenditure—an evaluation of some techniques. *American Journal of Clinical Nutrition* 33:1155–1164.

2. Adolph, E. F. 1947. Urges to eat and drink in rats. *American Journal of Physiology* 151: 110–125.

3. Allen, D. W., and Quigley, B. M. 1977. The role of physical activity in the control of obesity. *Medical Journal of Australia* 2:434–438.

4. Atwater, W. O., and Benedict, F. G. 1899. Experiments in the metabolism of matter and energy in the human body. *Bulletin of the U.S. Department of Agriculture* 69:112.

5. Behnke, A. R., Feen, B. G., and Welham, W. C. 1942. The specific gravity of healthy men: Body weight and volume as an index of obesity. *Journal of the American Medical Association* 118:495–498.

6. Blaza, S. E., and Garrow, J. S. 1980. The effect of anxiety on metabolic rate. *Proceedings of the Nutrition Society* 39:13 (abstract).

7. ———. 1983. Thermogenic response to temperature, exercise and food stimuli in lean and obese women, studied by 24 h direct calorimetry. *British Journal of Nutrition* 49: 171–180.

8. Boothby, W. M., and Sandiford, I. 1929. Normal values for standard metabolism. *American Journal of Physiology* 90:290–291.

9. Davidson, S., Passmore, R., Brock, J. F., and Truswell, A. S. 1979. *Human nutrition and dietetics,* 7th ed. Edinburgh: Churchill Livingstone.

10. Dore, C., Hesp, R., Wilkins, D., and Garrow, J. S. 1982. Prediction of energy requirements of obese patients after massive weight loss. *Human Nutrition: Clinical Nutrition* 36(clinical ser.):41–48.

11. Durrant, M. L., Royston, J. P., Wloch, R. T., and Garrow, J. S. 1982. The effect of covert changes in energy density of preloads on subsequent ad libitum intake in lean and obese human subjects. *Human Nutrition: Clinical Nutrition* 36(clinical ser.):297–306.

12. Edholm, O. G., Fletcher, J. G., Widdowson, E. M., and McCance, R. A. 1955. The energy expenditure and food intake of individual men. *British Journal of Nutrition* 9: 286–300.

13. Forbes, G. B., and Welle, S. L. 1983. Lean body mass in obesity. *International Journal of Obesity* 7:99–107.

14. Garrow, J. S. 1981. *Treat obesity seriously: A clinical manual.* Edinburgh: Churchill Livingstone.

15. ———. 1983. Indices of adiposity. *Reviews in Clinical Nutrition* 53:697–708.

16. Garrow, J. S., Blaza, S. E., Warwick, P. M., and Ashwell, M. A. 1980. Predisposition to obesity. *Lancet* 1:1103–1104.

17. Garrow, J. S., et al. 1979. A new method for measuring the body density of obese adults. *British Journal of Nutrition* 42:173–183.

18. Humphrey, S. J. E., and Wolff, H. S. 1977. The oxylog. *Journal of Physiology* (London) 267:12 (proceedings).

19. James, W. P. T., and Trayhurn, P. 1981. Thermogenesis and obesity. *British Medical Bulletin* 37:43–48.

20. Keys, A., et al. 1972. Indices of relative weight and obesity. *Journal of Chronic Diseases* 25:329–343.

21. Klein, P. D., et al. 1984. Calorimetric validation of the doubly-labelled water method for determination of energy expenditure in man. *Human Nutrition: Clinical Nutrition* 38(clinical ser.):95–106.

22. Nair, K. S., Halliday, D., and Garrow, J. S. 1983. Thermic response to isoenergetic protein, carbohydrate or fat meals in lean and obese subjects. *Clinical Science* 65:307–312.

23. Pace, N., and Rathbun, E. N. 1945. Studies on body composition: Water and chemically combined nitrogen content in relation to fat content. *Journal of Biological Chemistry* 158:685–691.

24. Pittet, P. H., et al. 1976. Thermic effect of glucose in obese subjects studied by direct and indirect calorimetry. *British Journal of Nutrition* 35:281–292.

25. Porikos, K. P., Booth, G., and Van Itallie, T. B. 1977. Effect of covert nutritive dilution on the spontaneous food intake of obese individuals: A pilot study. *American Journal of Clinical Nutrition* 30:1638–1644.

26. Porikos, K. P., Hesser, M. F., and Van Itallie, T. B. 1982. Caloric regulation in normal-weight men maintained on a palatable diet of conventional foods. *Physiology and Behavior* 29:293–300.

27. Quetelet, L. A. J. 1869. *Physique sociale*, vol. 2. Brussels: C. Muquardt.

28. Rubner, M. 1902. *Die gesetze des energieverbrauchs bie der Ernährung.* Leipzig: Deuticke.

29. Shetty, P. S., et al. 1981. Postprandial thermogenesis in obesity. *Clinical Science* 60: 519–525.

30. Simopolous, A. P., and Van Itallie, T. B. 1984. Body weight, health and longevity. *Annals of Internal Medicine* 100:285–295.

31. Swaminathan, R., King, R. F. J., Holmfield, J., and Wales, J. K. 1982. Dietary fat induced thermogenesis in obesity. *Clinical Science* 62:16 (proceedings).

32. Webster, J. D., Hesp, R., and Garrow, J. S. 1984. The composition of excess weight in obese women estimated by body density, total body water and total body potassium. *Human Nutrition: Clinical Nutrition* 38 (clinical ser.):299–306.

33. Welle, S. L., and Campbell, R. J. 1983. Normal thermic effect of glucose in obese women. *American Journal of Clinical Nutrition* 37:87–92.

34. Wilkie, D. R. 1974. Second law of thermodynamics. *Nature* (London) 251: 601–602.

35. Wooley, O. W., Wooley, S. C., and Dunham, R. B. 1972. Can calories be perceived, and do they affect hunger in obese and non-obese humans? *Journal of Comparative and Physiological Psychology* 80:250–258.

36. Zed, C. A., and James, W. P. T. 1980. Postprandial thermogenesis (PPT) in obese subjects after either protein or carbohydrate. *Alimentazione Nutrizione Metabolismo* 1:385 (abstract).

37. ———. 1982. Thermic response to fat feeding in lean and obese subjects. *Proceedings of the Nutrition Society* 41:32 (abstract).

3

A Set-point Theory
of Obesity

Richard E. Keesey

Obesity is regarded by many as a behavioral problem, stemming principally from disordered eating habits. Behavioral therapy, with the goal of modifying maladaptive eating patterns, thus constitutes the most common form of treatment. But the resistance of obesity to such treatment raises concern that its origins may not be behavioral.

This chapter explicates a "set-point" model of energy regulation in contrast to the more traditional behavioral perspective. Body weight (BW) is treated as a physiological variable regulated at a specified level, or "set point." The adjustments in energy flux stabilizing weight at this level, the physiological mechanisms determining set point, and possible ways of changing the set point value are discussed. The proposal that obesity represents a condition of regulation at an elevated set point is then considered. Three animal forms of obesity are examined, and each is evaluated with respect to whether it is physiologically regulated or the product of regulatory failure. This line of inquiry is extended to obese humans where proposals are made both for diagnosing the etiology of each patient's obesity and for selecting appropriate treatment.

This research was supported in part by National Institutes of Health grant AM 19944. The author gratefully acknowledges the many helpful suggestions and criticisms of this manuscript contributed by Dr. S. W. Corbett and Dr. T. R. Vilberg.

Energy Regulation

BODY-WEIGHT STABILITY

Though body weight seems susceptible to wide fluctuation, the adult weights of most animals and humans are actually quite stable. When one considers that many animals and people must contend with seasonal fluctuations in food availability ranging from scarcity to abundance, or with temperature variations ranging from severe cold (requiring the expenditure of considerable energy to maintain body temperature) to very hot, their changes in weight are remarkably small. People in technologically advanced societies face different, but likewise challenging, circumstances. They are confronted with highly palatable, calorically dense foods, available at all times in practically unlimited quantities. They lead sedentary lives in well-heated homes and offices, expending little energy either on activity or thermoregulation. Yet their weights are usually little different from those of others living under far more austere circumstances.

It is also known that body weight, if displaced from the normally maintained level, is subsequently restored to the initial level. Adult rats whose weight has been experimentally reduced quickly regain their lost weight and return precisely to the level appropriate for their age and sex.[50] The same result is observed when the weight of rats is experimentally elevated by force-feeding[11] or lateral hypothalamic stimulation.[72]

Adult humans respond similarly to weight displacements. Shortage of food during wars, famines, and other calamities can lead to weight loss in whole populations. Yet the weights generally return to prior levels once adequate food is available. During World War II, a group of conscientious objectors submitted to a semistarvation diet.[46] Though their body weight was reduced by approximately 25 percent, most restored weight to its former level within months of having food restrictions removed.

Harder to find are instances of an individual's body weight being displaced upward. In one experiment, however, Vermont prisoners increased their caloric intake markedly for over half a year and achieved weight gains of 15 to 25 percent.[71] When the experiment terminated, the weight of these subjects typically returned to its former level.

CONTROL OF ENERGY INTAKE

This stable maintenance of body weight requires that energy intake and expenditure be balanced. We must thus ask whether it is through the active control of intake or expenditure that weight stability is achieved.

Traditionally, adjustments in food intake have been regarded as fundamental to our maintenance of energy balance. Innumerable reports demonstrate that adjustments in food intake compensate for perturbations

FIGURE 3.1

The caloric intake and body weight of a Vermont prisoner. For more than half a year, this man's daily caloric intake greatly exceeded his initial basal requirements. Yet his maximum weight gain during this period was approximately 13 kg. Note also that body weight has begun to decline by the end of this experiment despite the fact that intake is still approximately 50 percent above initial levels.

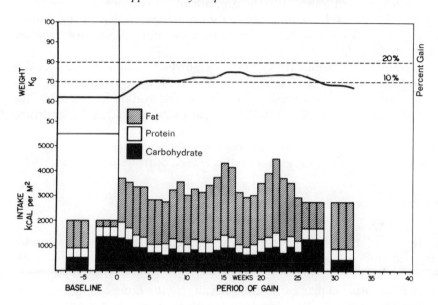

NOTE: Reprinted, by permission of the publisher, from E. A. H. Sims, 1976, Experimental obesity, dietary-induced thermogenesis, and their clinical implications, *Clinics in Endocrinology and Metabolism* 5: 381.

in energy balance. The rats whose weights were elevated by lateral hypothalamic stimulation[72] ceased eating entirely (except for the periods of stimulation). Even after hypothalamic stimulation ceased, their intake remained very low. Only when body weight finally declined to the level of nonstimulated rats did their intake return to prestimulation levels.

One cannot account fully for the stability in body weight by food intake alone. In fact, variation in food intake often fails to produce the expected changes in body weight. When the food intake of a rat is restricted, the actual weight lost is almost invariably substantially smaller than would be expected from the apparent caloric debt.[71] Nor does over consumption yield weight gains as large as would be expected from the apparent caloric excess. Prior to the experiment on Vermont prisoners who voluntarily overconsumed,[71] one individual, whose body weight and daily caloric intake is depicted in figure 3.1, was maintaining his body weight (about 62 kg) with a daily intake of 2,000 kcal. He then increased his daily intake to approximately 3,500 kcal for over half a year. Initially his weight increased by about 10 kg. Thereafter, further changes in weight were unexpectedly small despite continued high intake. By the end of the experiment this person was actually losing weight, though still consuming close to 3,000 kcal per day (which was 50 percent more than was necessary to maintain his initial weight).

Not only does body weight fail to faithfully follow changes in intake, but weight changes can occur when intake remains constant. A rat whose weight has been reduced by caloric restriction can restore weight to the former level when given only the amount of food it normally ate prior to restriction.[38,51] It has likewise been shown in humans that weight gained through overeating can be lost even though intake never drops below the normal level.[57]

Weight gain without overeating, weight loss without dieting, and a general failure of body weight to track increases and decreases in food intake could not occur were the rate of energy utilization and expenditure constant. Only by changing an individual's rate of energy expenditure could they occur. But, if rate of energy expenditure does vary, is it a controlled component in the process of energy regulation? And, if so, what components of energy expenditure are controlled?

CONTROL OF ENERGY EXPENDITURE

In considering the control of energy expenditure, it will be useful first to identify the fate of ingested energy and to specify how it is normally partitioned and expended. Ingested energy first passes through the digestion and absorption process to arrive in a form the body can utilize ("metabolizable energy"). Three major categories of energy expenditure are then identified: (1) resting or "basal" energy expenditure, (2) diet-induced thermogenesis or energy expenditure thought to be associated with the ingestion and processing of food, and (3) activity or energy expended by the somatic musculature. In a recent study on the rat,[12] the largest portion of energy (72.5 percent of metabolizable energy) was spent meeting resting or basal metabolic needs. Approximately 11 percent of the rat's metabolizable energy was associated with the processing of ingested energy ("SDA"), and 16.5 percent was given over to somatic activity.

Assuming that adjustments in energy expenditure participate in maintaining energy balance, which categories of expenditure participate in this process? If, as historically assumed, expenditure or "basal" metabolism represents the amount of energy necessary to maintain basic bodily functions, and the SDA represents the energetic cost of processing a meal, neither would seem to be likely candidates. Yet both resting metabolism and SDA have been shown to vary according to an organism's nutritional status. Consider first what happens to the resting metabolic rate of rats when intake is restricted and weight declines. Corbett and I[40] subjected rats to a mild caloric restriction for two weeks. Their weights declined by 9 percent (compared to nonrestricted rats of the same age), but their resting metabolic rate declined by 17 percent compared to nonrestricted rats. Some decline in energy expenditure is to be expected since there is less tissue to maintain. However, the decline in resting metabolism was

FIGURE 3.2

Oxygen consumption of normal-weight and weight-reduced rats first under postabsorptive conditions and then following an intragastric meal. Note how the usual increment in oxygen consumption following a meal is sharply attenuated in the weight-reduced rats.

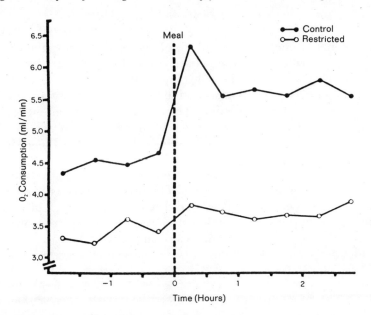

SOURCE: P. C. Boyle, L. H. Storlien, A. E. Harper, and R. E. Keesey, 1981, Oxygen consumption and spontaneous locomotor activity in rats during restricted feeding and controlled realimentation, *American Journal of Physiology* 241:R395.

nearly double that predicted by the tissue loss. Similar changes in basal metabolism were observed in the previously discussed conscientious objectors who submitted to a semistarvation diet.[46] After adjusting for the metabolically active tissue they had lost, their resting metabolism was still 16 percent below the expected level.

The SDA or increase in heat production associated with the ingestion of food also varies with nutritional status. The resting oxygen consumption of normal-weight and weight-reduced rats can be seen in figure 3.2.[4] Note first that resting oxygen consumption is markedly lower in the weight-reduced rat. Next observe the large increment in oxygen consumption following a meal in the normal-weight rats. The increment in the weight-reduced rats following the same meal is only a fraction as large. Clearly, the increase in heat production that follows a meal must reflect more than just the energetic cost of processing the ingested nutrients.

Energy expenditure is also adjusted during periods of overconsumption and weight increase. Animals and humans expend energy at higher than expected rates when food intake increases and body weight rises above the normally maintained level. Overconsumption stimulated by palatable "cafeteria" diets causes resting metabolism in rats to increase more than expected from their increase in body mass.[62] This "luxuskon-sumption," or elevated rate of heat production in response to increased caloric intake, also occurs in man.[53]

ENERGY EXPENDITURE AND BODY-WEIGHT REGULATION

Adjustments in energy expenditure of the sort just described make an important contribution to the maintenance of stable body weight. By elevating or lowering the rate at which ingested energy is expended, one can blunt the effects of overconsumption in times of plenty and of un-derconsumption in times of famine. The sharp reduction in energy ex-penditure with weight loss likewise suggests an explanation of why most dieters lose only limited amounts of weight before even the reduced amount their diet allows is sufficient to maintain their weight. Or why, after giving up on the diet they believe is no longer working, they quickly regain their lost weight though eating only normal amounts. An expla-nation of why the Vermont prisoners did not gain more weight despite enormous consumptions, or why they then required such large amounts just to maintain their added weight, is also suggested by an appreciation of these metabolic responses to deviation from the body-weight set point.

What Determines the Set Point?

Though individual body weights ordinarily do not vary greatly, variation in body weight between different members of a species can be consider-able. Two individuals of the same age, sex, and height may each maintain their weight with little fluctuation for years; yet their weights may differ by 100 pounds or more. What determines or sets the body weight each individual maintains and defends?

It is believed that the lateral hypothalamus (LH) plays a primary role in determining the body-weight set point. Lesions of the LH in rats pro-duce aphagia and anorexia, a result leading to the historic designation of this hypothalamic region as a "feeding center."[1] After a time, intake returns and the LH-lesioned rat again ingests food in sufficient amounts to maintain its body weight.[77] More recent work has shown, however, that the weight lost during the postlesion period of aphagia and anorexia is not restored upon the return of food intake. Instead, LH-lesioned rats chronically maintain body weight at some reduced percentage of normal.[60] Furthermore, they defend these reduced body weights when attempts are made to displace them.[42] It can be seen in figure 3.3 that just as nonlesioned rats quickly restore body weight to its proper level following a period of food restriction and weight loss, LH-lesioned rats quickly

FIGURE 3.3

Recovery of body weight by control and LH-lesioned rats following a period of food restriction. The body weights of the control-deprived and LH-deprived groups were first reduced to 80 percent the weight maintained by nondeprived control and LH-lesioned animals, respectively. Both deprived groups were then returned to an ad libitum *feeding schedule.*

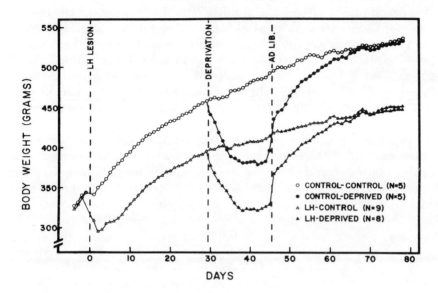

NOTE: Reprinted, by permission of the publisher, from J. S. Mitchel and R. E. Keesey, 1977, Defense of a lowered weight maintenance level by lateral hypothalamically lesioned rats: Evidence from a restriction-refeeding regimen, *Physiology and Behavior* 18:1123.

restore weight to their reduced level of postlesion maintenance.[54] And, just as nonlesioned rats reduce body weight to the normal level after it has been elevated by force-feeding, so do LH-lesioned rats quickly return to the reduced level they maintain if they have been force-fed to normal weight levels.[42] It has also been demonstrated that lowering body weight prior to an LH lesion not only eliminates the aphagia and anorexia but, in some cases, leads to a postlesion hyperphagia.[77] This stands in marked contrast to the aphagia and anorexia normally seen following LH lesions and indicates that the postlesion feeding behavior of LH rats can be viewed as appropriate to the reduced body weight they then maintain. If above their new (reduced) level of weight maintenance, they display aphagia and/or anorexia; if below it, they respond by increasing intake.

Recent work[41] demonstrates that the metabolic adjustments that stabilize body weight at a normal level in animals and man act to maintain the body weight of LH-lesioned rats at a reduced level. In one experiment[15] LH-lesioned rats were stimulated by a highly palatable diet to overconsume and restore their body weight to the level of nonlesioned but chow-fed rats. Though at the same weight as the nonlesioned rats, the LH rats were hardly normal metabolically. Their resting metabolic rate was 30 percent higher than that of nonlesioned rats of the same weight. This is similar to the condition of LH rats immediately after lesioning when their body weight is still at the level of controls but their resting metabolism is also sharply elevated.[13] But just as LH-lesion–induced aphagia and anorexia can be eliminated by reducing body weight prior to lesioning, so can this hypermetabolic response to lesioning.[43]

When at the lower body weight they chronically maintain, the resting metabolic rate of LH-lesioned rats is normal in that it is appropriate for their reduced metabolic mass. Expressed in terms of their metabolic body size (MBS) ($BW^{.75}$),[47] the resting heat production of LH-lesioned rats is at the expected level.[15] This would not be the case were the weight of nonlesioned rats lowered to the levels maintained by LH-lesioned rats. As noted earlier, weight-reduced nonlesioned rats are hypometabolic, displaying a reduction in resting energy expenditure greatly exceeding that expected on the basis of their reduced metabolic mass. Just as do nonlesioned rats, LH-lesioned rats display the appropriate decline in resting metabolism when their intake is restricted and they lose weight.[15] But this metabolic adjustment is seen in response to a decline from the reduced weight level they maintain, not a normal weight.

In their normal expenditure of energy at a reduced body weight, in their increased energy metabolism following overconsumption and weight gain from this level, and in their lowered energy expenditure following restriction and weight loss, LH-lesioned rats metabolically defend a reduced body weight. From these and earlier observations[42] it appears that the LH plays a primary role in determining set point for regulated body weight. Conceivably, it is also through this LH mechanism that the known genetic and developmental influences upon body weight are expressed, thus yielding the large individual differences in body weight between adult members of the same species.

Can Body-weight Set Points Be Changed?

Though as a rule adult body weights are stable, changes do occur. Such changes have been cited as evidence against the set-point regulation of body weight,[27] but just as stability is not sufficient to establish that weight is regulated,[22] neither is its change proof that it is not. It is necessary in either case to determine whether a prevailing body weight, stable or otherwise, is actively defended by appropriate behavioral and physiological adjustments.

Applying these criteria, there is little question that the set point for many physiologically regulated variables can be shifted. Body core temperature is under the control of a set-point regulator,[30] but it is not always the same and many of the changes appear to be regulated. Temperature changes associated with fever, for example, occur not because of a failure in regulation, or because the mechanisms for heat dissipation are overwhelmed by the increased heat produced by the body combating infection. Instead, the higher body core temperature is physiologically defended, suggesting that the set point itself has been elevated.[31] Just as we maintain a normal body temperature by vasoconstriction and shivering when core temperature drops below 37° C, and perspire and vasodilate when it rises above this level, so does the individual with a fever defend a core temperature several degrees higher when ill. There is evidence that both the circadian variation in core temperature[9] and the core temperature changes that occur during the menstrual cycle[18] may also represent set-point alterations.

Certain changes in body weight might also be traced to an altered set point. A compelling example is the weight change seen in hibernating rodents. Ground squirrels display a prolonged phase of weight gain preceding hibernation. Weight then declines until the squirrel emerges from hibernation and the cycle is repeated. Mrosovsky and Fisher[55] have demonstrated that this annual cycle of weight change is regulated. If weight is caused to deviate from this expected level, either by the restriction of food intake before hibernation or by arousing the squirrel to accelerate weight loss during hibernation, adjustments in food intake are made until body weight is restored to the appropriate level. Thus even though it is *never* stable, the ground squirrel's body weight is closely and continuously regulated, apparently following the dictate of a constantly changing or "sliding" set point.[55]

Though hibernators present an interesting example of body-weight set-point change, few mammals hibernate. Nor is it likely that lesions to the LH account for many cases of weight change. By what other means can the body-weight set point be changed? Recent evidence suggests several distinct possibilities.

DIET-INDUCED SET-POINT CHANGES

It appears that the body-weight set point can be elevated by long-term exposure to weight-promoting diets. We know that the initial response to diet-induced weight gain is a marked increase in the rate of heat production.[53] Yet when my associates and I studied rats that had grown obese during six months on a high-fat diet, their heat production was not elevated.[14] Though their actual rate of oxygen consumption was higher than that of rats fed a regular diet, it was normal considering their increased body size. If the oxygen consumption scores of the *ad libitum*-fed high and low rats (shown in figure 3.4) are expressed relative to their metabolic mass ($BW^{.75}$), the consumption rates of the obese and normal-weight rats are virtually identical (9.15 vs. 9.27 m/O_2/min/MBS).

The intakes of some obese (high-fat-fed) rats and a group of normal-

FIGURE 3.4

Body weight and resting oxygen consumption of rats fed a high- or low-fat diet for six months. High-fat feeding caused a significant elevation in body weight. Some high- and low-fat-fed rats were then food restricted to produce a decline in weight from the maintained level. In both groups, weight reduction caused resting oxygen consumption to decline. Note in particular that, though the food-restricted high-fat-fed rats still weigh more than ad libitum-*fed low-fat rats, their resting oxygen consumption is considerably lower.*

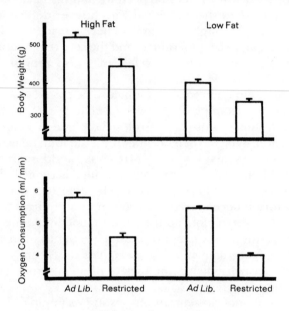

Source: S. W. Corbett, J. S. Stern, and R. E. Keesey, in press, Energy expenditure of rats with diet-induced obesity, *American Journal of Clinical Nutrition.*

weight rats (fed the regular low-fat diet) were then restricted. The ensuing weight reduction caused a sharp decline in the resting metabolism of both groups (see figure 3.4). Note in particular, however, that restriction caused the resting oxygen consumption of the high-fat-fed rats to drop significantly below that of *ad libitum*-fed low-fat rats, though they still weighed 53 g more!

These observations provide two indications that the weight changes on the high-fat diet elevated the body-weight set point. First, after six months' time, the high-fat-fed rats display resting levels of heat production appropriate to their body size, not the "luxuskonsumption," or elevated levels initially seen following overfeeding and weight gain. Second, the adjustments in energy expenditure these rats display to caloric privation indicate that their obesity is physiologically regulated.

One can only speculate as to the mechanism underlying this apparent shift in set point following long-term exposure to a high-fat diet. With the assistance of Dr. Judith Stern's laboratory, Corbett and I learned that the rats fed the high-fat diet had increased fat cell size and number.[14]

Other work indicates that increases in fat cell number tend to occur following several months on such diets; increased body lipids prior to that time occur largely through fat cell hypertrophy.[23] We also know that, while dietary obese rats ordinarily return to normal weight when restored to a regular diet, they often fail to do so when maintained on the diet for a matter of months.[61] All these observations are consistent with the view that long-term maintenance on high-fat diets produces anatomic and/or physiological changes which cause body energy to be regulated at a higher set point.

DRUG-INDUCED WEIGHT REDUCTIONS

It is possible that anorectic drugs may also alter the body-weight set point.[75] Though it is generally assumed that anorectic drugs act by suppressing appetite, several observations are not easily reconciled with this view. Anorectic drugs are effective in suppressing food intake only until body weight drops to a lower level. Intake then returns to essentially normal levels and body weight is maintained at this reduced level. Tolerance to the anorectic agent has traditionally been offered as the explanation for its failure to continue suppressing food intake. Stunkard, however, proposes that the primary effect of anorectic drugs is to lower the body-weight set point.[75] According to this view, the suppression in food intake is secondary to lowering body weight to the new (drug-altered) set point. The observation that fenfluramine in rats does not suppress food intake if body weight has been reduced prior to drug administration[52] certainly favors Stunkard's interpretation.

Weight Changes Induced by Toxic Agents

It now appears that certain toxic agents lower the body-weight set point. TCDD (2,3,7,8-tetrachlorodibenzo-p-dioxin) administered to rats at sublethal doses reduces the level of maintained body weight.[69] Furthermore, these rats display an unimpaired capacity to defend this reduced weight. If challenged by changes in the caloric density of a diet, TCDD-treated rats display the same adjustments in intake as control rats.[68] If their weight is experimentally displaced by underfeeding, they restore weight to its former level as quickly and precisely as do normal-weight rats (see figure 3.5). Also like normal rats, TCDD-treated rats stimulated to overconsume a highly palatable diet deposit the excess calories as fat. As a result, the body composition of TCDD-treated rats whose weights have been restored to control levels are not normal; instead, such rats are obese.[68] It thus appears that TCDD reduces the body-weight set point.

FIGURE 3.5

Recovery of body weight to maintenance levels in control and TCDD-treated rats following weight loss produced by food restriction (left figure) or weight gain stimulated by a palatable eggnog diet (right figure). On day 0, rats were treated with TCDD (15 μg/kg) or vehicle alone. Restriction was begun on day 23 and continued until ad libitum *feeding was reinstated on day 33. The eggnog diet was first provided on day 21 and was available continuously until day 51 when the regular chow diet was returned.*

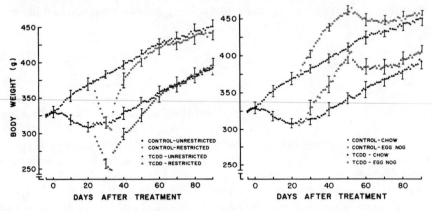

NOTE: Reprinted, by permission of the publisher, from M. D. Seefeld, R. E. Keesey, and R. E. Peterson, 1984, Body weight regulation in rats treated with 2,3,7,8-tetrachlorodibenzo-p-dioxin, *Toxicology and Applied Pharmacology* 76:531–552.

Exercise-induced Weight Reduction

Exercise-induced weight reductions may also involve a set-point shift. The increased energy associated with exercise is apparently not compensated for by increased food intake until body weight declines to a lower maintenance level. Exercising individuals then display a level of resting metabolism appropriate for the lower body weight, not the hypometabolic condition created by dieting alone (see figure 3.6).[19] Cessation of regular exercise results in the return of body weight to the preexercise level. Each of these observations suggests that the weight reduction associated with exercise is secondary to a shift in the level of regulation, not the direct consequence of increased expenditure.

OTHER FACTORS POSSIBLY ALTERING SET POINT

The changes in body weight that accompany shifts in the ovarian hormones,[81] the onset or cessation of smoking,[10] as well as the metabolic and body compositional changes associated with aging[25,45] appear in many ways to involve shifts in set point. However, until more is known con-

FIGURE 3.6

*Adjusted resting metabolic rate (RMR) and body weight in eight overweight women
undergoing treatment. Resting metabolism declines at approximately twice the rate of
weight loss during the diet phase of the treatment. When an exercise regimen is combined
with the diet, body weight continues to decline, but resting metabolism is restored to the
level appropriate to the prevailing body weight.*

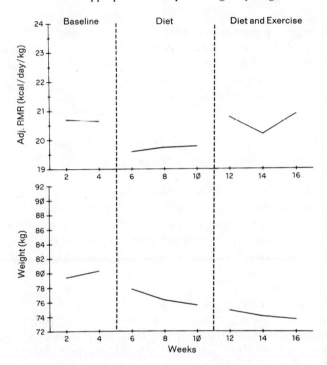

NOTE: Reprinted, by permission of the publisher, from C. P. Donahoe, D. H. Lin, D. S. Kirschenbaum,
and R. E. Keesey, 1984, Metabolic consequences of dieting and exercise in the behavioral treatment of
obesity, *Journal of Consulting and Clinical Psychology* 52:830.

cerning the weight changes associated with these factors, it remains uncertain whether they occur because energy intake and/or expenditure
are directly influenced or because the set point has been changed.

Obesity: Regulatory Failure or Elevated Set Point?

We come now to the central issue of this chapter—the causes of obesity.
Do obese individuals lack appropriate control over food intake, as the
view of obesity as an eating disorder suggests? Do the regulatory mech-

anisms responsible for controlling the expenditure of energy fail to restrain weight gain in obese persons, as others have suggested?[36,70] Or is body weight regulated in obesity though at an elevated set point?[39,41]

ANIMAL OBESITIES

We will begin by examining three forms of animal obesities—genetically transmitted obesity, dietary obesity, and ventromedial hypothalamic obesity. All three have been studied extensively, and each is potentially useful to a better understanding of human obesity.

Genetically Transmitted Obesity. In 1961 Dr. L. M. Zucker and Dr. T. F. Zucker[85] described a form of obesity in rats inherited as a single Mendelian recessive gene (fa/fa) from the mating of two heterozygous lean rats. The "fatty" rat of this strain, which often weighs 50 percent more than its lean littermates, has since become the object of considerable attention.[6]

Overconsumption plays an important role in the development of the Zucker's obesity. Its increased intake can be detected as early as seventeen days after birth.[73] At the same time, an enhanced energetic efficiency also contributes to this obesity. Increased body fat can be detected both in week-old suckling fatties (i.e., before hyperphagia is evident) and in fatties pair-fed to lean littermates.[3,84] This increased efficiency of energy utilization can be traced, in part, to a reduced rate of resting metabolism, which is seen within seven days after birth.[58]

The adult fatty defends its obesity, exercising appropriate control over both energy intake and expenditure. If its diet is rendered unpalatable with quinine, the fatty continues to ingest sufficient quantities to maintain a high body weight.[17] Unlike the ventromedial hypothalamus (VMH)–lesioned rat, the obesity of the fatty is not diet-dependent.

Fatties also defend their obesity metabolically by adjusting resting metabolism during caloric privation and weight loss.[40] As can be seen in figure 3.7, lean Zucker rats whose weights were reduced by 27 g (9 percent of initial level) displayed a 17 percent reduction in resting metabolic rate. This decline in resting metabolism, being substantially greater than expected from the loss of metabolically active tissue, is evidence of an active metabolic adjustment that serves to blunt further weight loss. It can be seen in the figure that an identical adjustment is seen in the Zucker fatty. For a weight decline of 27 g (4.5 percent of initial weight), resting metabolism declines by 17 percent.

To gain an appreciation of this metabolic adjustment in maintaining the fatty's obesity, consider the following. Figure 3.7 shows the unrestricted fatty rats' resting oxygen consumption to be 26 percent higher than that of lean littermates. But, with only a modest reduction in body weight (from 610 g to 583 g), the fatty's resting oxygen consumption falls to approximately the level of nonrestricted lean rats that weigh only 285 g. Thus a weight loss of only 4.5 percent caused the fatties' daily energy

FIGURE 3.7

Body weight and resting oxygen consumption of normal and weight-reduced Zucker fatty and lean rats. Both fatty and lean rats show a decline in resting metabolism following a period of caloric restriction and weight loss. Note that the resting oxygen consumption of weight-reduced fatty rats is very nearly the same as that of normal-weight lean rats even though the fatties still weigh more than twice as much as the leans.

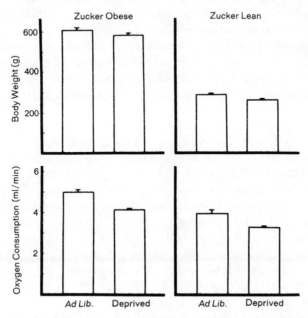

NOTE: Reproduced, by permission of R. E. Keesey and S. W. Corbett, 1985, unpublished observations.

requirements to decline to hardly more than those of lean rats weighing only half as much. For the fatties to lose more weight, their intake would have to be further restricted, probably to levels below those of their lean littermates. Such observations should lend credence to the claim of many obese individuals that they eat no more, or even less, than many of their lean friends.

While these observations suggest that Zucker fatties regulate their body weight, albeit at a markedly elevated set point, there are reports of certain irregularities in their energy utilization. A failure to display the expected increase in heat production to cold stress[28] or to a meal[63] points to a thermogenic thriftiness that could contribute to the fatties' obesity. Even so, the fatties clearly protect their elevated weight from decline and can be said to defend an elevated set point.

Diet-induced Obesity. If offered certain highly palatable diets or a cafeteria selection of "junk foods," the normal resistance of rats to weight gain can be overcome and obesity results.[66] Some rat strains are more susceptible than others,[65] and some diets produce greater weight gains than others,[66] but, given the appropriate conditions, considerable weight gain can occur.

Though inadequate to compensate for the high levels of intake these diets stimulate, rats exposed to these diets display the increased rates of heat production that typically accompany overconsumption. Curiously, this metabolic resistance diminishes over time. As was seen in figure 3.4, rats maintained on a high-fat diet for six months are not hypermetabolic. Instead, their resting heat production is normal for the body weight they maintain. These rats also show a metabolic defense of their obesity by reducing energy expenditure when their weight declines. With only mild caloric restriction, the resting metabolic rate of the dietary obese rats in figure 3.4 fell to that of normal-weight rats weighing 53 g less. This metabolic response to weight loss may help explain why dietary obese rats sometimes fail to return to normal body weights when restored to a regular diet.[61]

The specific physiological or anatomical changes underlying these diet-induced shifts in set point remain unspecified. The possibility that the changes in adipocyte number may play a role in this adjustment was raised earlier in this chapter. Another possibility is suggested by the observation that norepinephrine (NE) turnover rates in the tissues of rats fed palatable diets display a corresponding pattern of change. NE turnover is initially elevated in rats fed weight-promoting diets.[49] Thereafter, however, NE turnover declines until, after several months, it is at near-normal levels. Thus NE turnover rates and whole-body metabolism display roughly parallel patterns of change in rats exposed to weight-enhancing diets. Further study will be required to determine whether the link suggested by these observations is causal.

Hypothalamic Obesity. Destruction of the VMH, an area of the brain lying immediately above the pituitary gland, induces voracious eating and obesity both in animals and man.[6,7] Experimental studies on laboratory animals have characterized two stages to this syndrome. Soon after the lesion, animals are markedly hyperphagic, eating as much as two to three times normal amounts. Rapid weight gain, essentially all in the form of carcass fat, marks this "dynamic" stage. Like genetically and dietary obese rats, the increased adiposity of VMH-lesioned rats involves a proliferation of fat cell number as well as increased cell size.[74] This is usually followed by a "static" phase when food intake returns to near-normal levels and body-weight gains remain roughly parallel to those of nonlesioned rats.

Kennedy[44] first proposed that VMH obesity stems from a lesion-induced elevation in the body's lipostat. Supporting this view are the observations that static obese VMH rats not only maintain a stable body weight but restore weight to this level when forced to still higher levels (by insulin injections) or to lower levels (by food restriction).[33] However, other features of this syndrome are inconsistent with this interpretation. Most notable is the failure of static obese VMH rats to defend their body weight against dietary challenges. If their normal diet is rendered un-palatable by quinine, obese VMH rats curtail their intake until their weight returns to the level of nonlesioned controls.[82] In fact, if quinine-adulterated diets are given immediately after the lesion, weight gain is blocked and VMH rats remain at the weight of nonlesioned rats.[24,67] VMH rats also display hyperresponsivity to nonaversive dietary properties. Their usual hyperphagia and obesity can be further enhanced by increasing diet palatability.[16] This is unlike nonlesioned rats, where the effects of palatability shifts are normally blunted by their nutritional consequences. Powley[59] has suggested that this diet-dependent obesity of VMH rats is due to an exaggerated cephalic response to palatable diets. To the extent that the food intake of VMH rats is driven by diet taste or texture, rather than nutritional features, VMH obesity represents a form of regulatory failure.

Other evidence of regulatory dysfunction in VMH rats derives from studies of their energy utilization and expenditure. The set point of normal-weight rats is maintained by appropriate adjustments in energy expenditure. When stimulated to overeat, nonlesioned rats display an increase in resting metabolism that blunts weight gain. Increased brown fat thermogenesis appears to be the source of this caloric wasting.[62] This thermogenic response, however, appears to be absent in VMH-lesioned rats. Though their response to cold is normal,[34] they fail to increase brown fat thermogenesis when stimulated to overeat cafeteria diets.[32] Not surprisingly, sympathetic nervous activity, which initiates brown fat thermogenesis, is reduced in rats with VMH lesions.[78]

Immediately following surgery, the VMH-lesioned rat is far below the terminal weight it will eventually attain if provided a suitable diet. Were the static obese weight to be regulated, one would expect just-lesioned VMH rats to have markedly reduced metabolic rates, similar to nonlesioned rats whose weight is below their set point. Early reports did indicate that resting metabolism was attenuated in postlesion VMH rats;[8,29] but other studies suggest that this decline in energy expenditure occurs subsequent to changes in carcass composition[35,80] and is probably of little regulatory significance.

Few other tests of the ability of the VMH to adjust metabolic rate in response to shifts in weight and/or nutritional status have been reported. Preliminary work[79] suggests that static obese VMH rats have lower resting metabolic rates than normal rats made equally obese. Similarly, static obese VMH rats do not appear to reduce resting metabolism in response to deprivation. Thus, while more work is needed to delineate the deficit, it appears that many of the characteristic metabolic adjustments a normal rat displays in response to weight change are lacking or blunted in VMH rats.

In summary, VMH-lesioned rats appear to become obese primarily because of an eating disorder—an exaggerated response to palatable diets. In addition, the metabolic responses that normally serve to stabilize body weight at some particular level appear to be impaired in VMH animals. It thus appears that this obesity is due to a failure in regulation rather than to an elevated set point.

Animal Obesities: An Assessment. We conclude from the animal models that obesity can stem from different causes and involve different mechanisms. In two instances (the Zucker fatty and the dietary obese rat) it appears that the obesity is physiologically regulated. The Zucker fatty rat defends both behaviorally and metabolically its adiposity against decline. The dietary obese rat initially resists weight gain by elevating its rate of energy expenditure. But adaptations then occur to the higher weight, and the dietary obese rat subsequently displays the characteristics of one regulating at an elevated set point. In VMH-lesioned rats, however, neither energy intake nor expenditure appear to be controlled in a manner consistent with the normal regulation of body weight. When stimulated to overconsume by palatable diets, VMH-lesioned rats appear not to display the normal metabolic resistance to weight gain. Though they do display stable body weights, they fail, when challenged by changes in diet, to defend these levels either by adjusting intake or expenditure. A set point for body weight thus appears to be lacking in the VMH-lesioned rat.

Human Obesity: Regulatory Failure or Elevated Set Point?

Each of the rat preparations just discussed has been cited as an appropriate model for human obesity. The VMH-lesioned rat has received particular attention, owing to the writings of Schachter and his students.[56,64] Yet these rat forms of obesity have different origins, so we must assume either that human obesity also has differing etiologies or that certain rat preparations are inappropriate for modeling human obesity. It should be possible to resolve this issue by comparing the critical characteristics of these animal preparations to those seen in humans. Unfortunately, the critical observations for such comparisons are rarely part of the clinical record. Nor are the data necessary to answer questions as to whether obese individuals fail to regulate energy normally, or do regulate normally but at an elevated set point, readily found in the clinical literature. Still, enough is known to make an effort at such a classification.

It is clear that the body weight of obese persons, like individuals of normal weight, is maintained at a rather stable level. Given the pressure on obese people to lose weight, it would be surprising were their weight not somewhat more variable. Even when they are successful in shedding weight, they tend subsequently to regain that which was lost.[37,76]

However, evidence of a stable body weight, even the tendency to restore body weight to a particular level when displaced, is not sufficient to establish that obese individuals are regulating at a high set point. What is also required is evidence of an active physiological defense of their obesity.

Though not extensive, there is evidence that weight is closely regulated in many obese humans. Obese individuals undergoing weight loss often

FIGURE 3.8

Oxygen consumption in six obese patients during caloric restriction. After seven days on a 3,500 calorie diet, intake was restricted to 450 calories and maintained for an additional twenty-four days. By the end of this period, the decline in oxygen consumption approximated 17 percent of the prerestriction values, while body weight had declined by less than 3 percent.

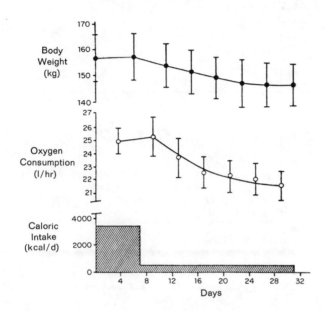

NOTE: Reprinted, by permission of the publisher, from G. A. Bray, 1969, Effect of caloric restriction on energy expenditure in obese patients, *Lancet* 2:397–398.

display adjustments in resting metabolism consistent with active regulation of weight at an obese level. Such a response by obese patients can be seen in figure 3.8. After dieting for four weeks, these patients showed a 3-percent weight loss.[5] Their resting rate of oxygen consumption, however, declined by 17 percent. This large a decline in metabolic rate with so modest a weight loss suggests the participation of a physiological process actively resisting weight change. This is not an isolated observation. A decline in resting metabolism substantially in excess of what would be expected on the basis of tissue loss is now well documented.[2,21,46] Furthermore, these adjustments persist over time. Obese patients maintaining reduced weight for four to six years still display reduced metabolic rates.[48]

Obese patients likewise appear to be in energy balance only at the high body weight that they ordinarily maintain. In terms of calories required for weight maintenance, they require approximately the same or only slightly more than normal-weight people.[48] This is an important observation since, were a nonobese person's weight somehow elevated to that of an obese individual, the former would not show normal resting metabolism. Such a person would be hypermetabolic and would display

FIGURE 3.9

Resting metabolic rate and body weight in twenty-seven obese women before (open circles)
and after (closed circles) three weeks on a diet supplying 3.4 MJ (800 kcal) daily.
The dashed line is a best fit to the open circles and represents the relation between
resting metabolic rate and body weight prior to weight loss.

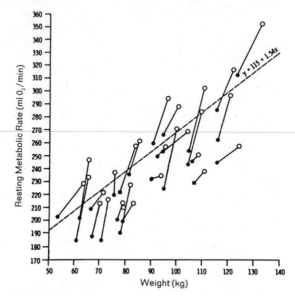

SOURCE: J. S. Garrow, 1978, *Energy balance and obesity in man*, Amsterdam: Elsevier/North Holland
Biomedical Press, p. 91.

elevated rates of thermogenesis. Conversely, the obese person would be
hypometabolic were his weight to be lowered to normal.

While these observations indicate that obese humans regulate body
weight normally (albeit at an elevated set point), other reports suggest
certain irregularities in their energy regulation. Like the Zucker fatty rat,
obese humans display reduced diet-induced thermogenesis that may contribute to their obesity.[36,70] Likewise, some obese patients who lose weight
fail to display the adaptive adjustments in resting metabolism just discussed.
One study reports that changes in the resting metabolism of nineteen
obese women patients undergoing weight loss matched but did not exceed
their decline in body weight.[20] This seemingly passive decline in resting
metabolism in response to weight loss is similar to that seen in static obese
VMH-lesioned rats.

It may be possible to reconcile these differences by considering the
individual observations on the resting metabolism of twenty-seven obese
women before and after weight loss (see figure 3.9).[26] Using the resting
metabolic rates before weight loss (open circles), these investigators derived a function describing the relationship between the obese weight of
the twenty-seven women and their resting metabolism. They then used
this relationship (represented by the dashed line) to assess the effects of
weight loss on resting metabolism. If changes in resting metabolism pas-

sively followed the decline in body weight (as appears to be the case in VMH-lesioned rats), the relationship between resting metabolism and body weight should remain unchanged with weight loss. That is, a line connecting the value of each patient's resting metabolic rate before and after weight loss should track or parallel the dashed line representing this relationship. If the loss of weight is actively resisted by adjusting energy expenditure (as with Zucker fatty and some dietary obese rats), resting metabolism should decline at a greater rate than the relationship between resting metabolism and body weight predicts. The line connecting the resting metabolic value for each patient before and after weight loss would then have a steeper slope than the dashed line.

Most dieting women (eighteen to twenty of the twenty-seven) reduced their resting metabolism faster than was expected on the basis of their weight loss. The remaining seven to nine did not. This suggests the need to recognize at least two types of obese individuals: those who display a normal capacity to regulate and defend body weight, though at an elevated set point, and those who do not and whose obesity is a result of regulatory failure. Until further observations of this type are made, we can only assume that the proportion of each type in a population of obese individuals is approximated by the sample represented in figure 3.9.

Clinical Implications and Future Directions

If there are two distinct populations of obese humans, how might they be identified and treated? An answer to this question will require a determination of whether individuals display evidence of regulating body weight at their obese level. Observing the effects of weight change (gain or reduction) on resting metabolic rate or the heat increment to a meal (SDA) should reveal the presence or absence of physiological adjustments resisting those weight changes. Changes in metabolism that passively follow weight change would suggest that obesity results from a regulatory dysfunction. Such a finding would also indicate a treatment strategy. It is likely that conventional therapies such as dieting, behavioral modification of eating habits, increased expenditure through exercise, and so forth, might well be effective in the absence of physiological resistance to weight loss.

Conversely, evidence that an individual's obesity was physiologically regulated would indicate a different approach. The previously discussed energy-conserving metabolic adaptations resisting weight change will, in all likelihood, greatly diminish the chances of achieving significant weight loss or of sustaining losses that do occur. In these patients, sustained weight loss requires a lifelong commitment to diets providing a daily caloric intake that is certainly less than that which satisfies and probably less than that consumed by normal-weight individuals. Inasmuch as current treatment focuses primarily on the control of intake, Wooley and Wooley[83] raise a serious issue when they ask whether the disordered eating and life-style patterns often created by chronic dieting as well as the inadequate nutrition and metabolic depression this constricted intake produces may not be too great a price to pay for the modest weight losses obese patients are able to achieve.

Although the current prospects for patients with regulated obesity are not attractive, basic research may eventually reveal means of altering the body-weight set point. Safe and effective means for accomplishing substantial reductions in set point do not currently exist. But the growing evidence that set points can be altered by various neuroanatomical, physiological, and pharmacological manipulations should serve to intensify the search for procedures capable of reducing an obese individual's regulated level of body weight, possibly to normal levels. If this were accomplished, the patients with regulated obesity might actually have the best prognosis for treatment!

REFERENCES

1. Anand, B. K., and Brobeck, J. R. 1951. Localization of a "feeding center" in the hypothalamus of the rat. *Proceedings of the Society for Experimental Biology and Medicine* 77: 323–324.
2. Apfelbaum, M., Bostsarron, J., and Lacatis, D. 1971. Effect of caloric restriction and excessive caloric intake on energy expenditure. *American Journal of Clinical Nutrition* 24: 1405–1410.
3. Boulange, A., Planche, E., and de Gasquet, P. 1979. Onset of genetic obesity in the absence of hyperphagia during the first week of life in the Zucker rat (fa/fa). *Journal of Lipid Research* 20:857–864.
4. Boyle, P. C., Storlien, L. H., Harper, A. E., and Keesey, R. E. 1981. Oxygen consumption and spontaneous locomotor activity in rats during restricted feeding and controlled realimentation. *American Journal of Physiology* 241:R392–R397.
5. Bray, G. A. 1969. Effect of caloric restriction on energy expenditure in obese patients. *Lancet* 2:397–398.
6. Bray, G. A., and York, D. A. 1979. Hypothalamic and genetic obesity in experimental animals: An autonomic and endocrine hypothesis. *Physiological Reviews* 59:719–809.
7. Brobeck, J. R. 1946. Mechanisms of the development of obesity in animals with hypothalamic lesions. *American Journal of Physiology* 26:541–559.
8. Brooks, C. M., Marine, D. N., and Lambert, E. F. 1946. A study of the oxygen consumption of albino rats during various phases of experimentally produced obesity. *American Journal of Physiology* 147:717–726.
9. Cabanac, M., Hildebrandt, G., Massonnet, B., and Strempel, H. 1976. A study of the nycthemeral cycle of behavioral temperature regulation in man. *Journal of Physiology* (London) 257:275–291.
10. Carney, R. M., and Goldberg, A. P. 1984. Weight gain after cessation of cigarette smoking. *New England Journal of Medicine* 310:614–616.
11. Cohn, C., and Joseph, D. 1962. Influence of body weight and body fat on appetite of "normal" lean and obese rats. *Yale Journal of Biology* 34:598–607.

12. Corbett, S. W., and Keesey, R. E. 1982. Energy balance of rats with lateral hypothalamic lesions. *American Journal of Physiology* 242:E273–E279.

13. Corbett, S. W., Kaufman, L. N., and Keesey, R. E. 1983. The effects of β-adrenergic blockade on lateral hypothalamic lesion-induced thermogenesis. *American Journal of Physiology* 245:E535–E541.

14. Corbett, S. W., Stern, J. S., and Keesey, R. E. 1986. Energy expenditure of rats with diet-induced obesity. *American Journal of Clinical Nutrition.* In press.

15. Corbett, S. W., Wilterdink, E. J., and Keesey, R. E. 1986. Resting oxygen consumption in over- and underfed rats with lateral hypothalamic lesions. *Physiology and Behavior.* In press.

16. Corbit, J. D., and Stellar, E. 1964. Palatability, food intake and obesity in normal and hyperphagic rats. *Journal of Comparative and Physiological Psychology* 58:63–67.

17. Cruce, J. A. F., Greenwood, M. R. C., Johnson, P. R., and Quartermain, D. 1974. Genetic versus hypothalamic obesity: Studies of intake and dietary manipulations in rats. *Journal of Comparative and Physiological Psychology* 87:295–301.

18. Cunningham, D. J., and Cabanac, M. 1971. Evidence from behavioral thermoregulatory response of a shift in setpoint temperature related to the menstrual cycle. *Journal of Physiology* (Paris) 63:236–238.

19. Donahoe, C. P., Lin, D. H., Kirschenbaum, D. S., and Keesey, R. E. 1984. Metabolic consequences of dieting and exercise in the behavioral treatment of obesity. *Journal of Consulting and Clinical Psychology* 52:827–836.

20. Dore, C., Hesp, R., Wilkins, D., and Garrow, J. B. 1982. Prediction of energy requirements of obese patients after massive weight loss. *Human Nutrition: Clinical Nutrition* 366:41–48.

21. Drenick, E. J., and Dennin, H. F. 1973. Energy expenditure in fasting obese men. *Journal of Laboratory and Clinical Medicine* 81:421–430.

22. Engelberg, J. 1966. Physiological regulation: The steady state. *Physiologist* 9:69–88.

23. Faust, I. M., Johnson, P. R., Stern, J. S., and Hirsch, J. 1978. Diet-induced adipocyte number increase in adult rats: A new model of obesity. *American Journal of Physiology* 235:E279–E286.

24. Ferguson, N. B. L., and Keesey, R. E. 1975. Effect of a quinine-adulterated diet upon body weight maintenance in male rats with ventromedial hypothalamic lesions. *Journal of Comparative and Physiological Psychology* 89:478–488.

25. Forbes, G. B., and Reina, J. S. 1970. Adult lean body mass declines with age: Some longitudinal observations. *Metabolism* 19:653–663.

26. Garrow, J. S. 1978. *Energy balance and obesity in man.* Amsterdam: Elsevier/North Holland Biomedical Press.

27. Garrow, J. S., and Stalley, S. 1975. Is there a "set-point" for human body-weight? *Proceedings of the Nutrition Society* 34:84–85.

28. Godbole, V., York, D. A., and Bloxam, D. P. 1978. Developmental changes in the fatty (fa/fa) rat: Evidence for defective thermogenesis preceding hyperlipogenesis and hyperinsulinemia. *Diabetologia* 15:41–44.

29. Han, P. W. 1968. Energy metabolism of tube-fed hypophysectomized rats bearing hypothalamic lesions. *American Journal of Physiology* 215:1343–1350.

30. Hardy, J. D. 1965. The "set-point" concept in physiological temperature regulation. In *Physiological controls and regulations,* ed. W. S. Yamamoto and J. R. Brobeck, pp. 98–116. Philadelphia: W. B. Saunders.

31. Hensel, H. 1981. Displacement of set point. In *Thermoregulation and temperature regulation,* by H. Hensel, pp. 199–218. London: Academic Press.

32. Himms-Hagen, J., Hogan, S., and Coscina, D. V. 1982. Cafeteria (CAFE) diet does not activate brown adipose tissue (BAT) thermogenesis or growth in rats with medial hypothalamic (MH) lesions. *North American Association for the Study of Obesity* (Abstract):33.

33. Hoebel, B. G., and Teitelbaum, P. 1966. Weight regulation in normal and hypothalamic hyperphagic rats. *Journal of Comparative and Physiological Psychology* 61:189–193.

34. Hogan, S., Coscina, D. V., and Himms-Hagen, J. 1982. Brown adipose tissue of rats with obesity-inducing ventromedial hypothalamic lesions. *American Journal of Physiology* 243:E338–E344.

35. Hustvedt, B., Jeszka, J., Christophersen, A., and Lovo, A. 1984. Energy metabolism in rats with ventromedial hypothalamic lesions. *Physiological Reviews* 246:E319–E326.

36. James, W. P. T., and Trayhurn, P. 1981. Thermogenesis and obesity. *British Medical Bulletin* 37:43–48.

37. Johnson, D., and Drenick, E. J. 1977. Therapeutic fasting in morbid obesity. *Archives of Internal Medicine* 137:1381–1382.

38. Kaunitz, H., Slanetz, D. A., and Johnson, R. E. 1957. Utilization of food for weight maintenance and growth. *Journal of Nutrition* 62:551–559.

39. Keesey, R. E. 1980. The regulation of body weight: A set-point analysis. In *Obesity*, ed. A. J. Stunkard, pp. 144–165. Philadelphia: W. B. Saunders.

40. Keesey, R. E., and Corbett, S. W. 1985. Unpublished observations.

41. ———. 1984. Metabolic defense of the body weight set-point. In *Eating and its disorders*, ed. A. J. Stunkard, pp. 87–96. New York: Raven Press.

42. Keesey, R. E., Boyle, P. D., Kemnitz, J. W., and Mitchel, J. S. 1976. The role of the lateral hypothalamus in determining the body weight set-point. In *Hunger: Basic mechanisms and clinical implications*, ed. D. Novin, W. Wyrwicka, and G. A. Bray, pp. 243–255. New York: Raven Press.

43. Keesey, R. E., Corbett, S. W., Hirvonen, M. D., and Kaufman, L. N. 1984. Heat production and body weight changes following lateral hypothalamic lesions. *Physiology and Behavior* 32:309–317.

44. Kennedy, G. C. 1953. The role of depot fat in the hypothalamic control of food intake in the rat. *Proceedings of the Royal Society*, series B. 140:578–592.

45. Keys, A., Taylor, H. L., and Grande, F. 1973. Basal metabolism and age of adult man. *Metabolism* 22:579–587.

46. Keys, A., et al. 1950. *The biology of human starvation*. Minneapolis: University of Minnesota Press.

47. Kleiber, M. 1975. *The fire of life*. Huntington, N.Y.: Robert E. Krieger.

48. Leibel, R. L., and Hirsch, J. 1984. Diminished energy requirements in reduced-obese patients. *Metabolism* 33:164–179.

49. Levin, B. E., Triscari, J., and Sullivan, A. C. 1983. Altered sympathetic activity during development of diet-induced obesity in the rat. *American Journal of Physiology* 244:R347–R355.

50. Levitsky, D. A. 1970. Feeding patterns of rats in response to fasts and changes in environmental conditions. *Physiology and Behavior* 5:291–300.

51. Levitsky, D. A., Faust, I., and Glassman, M. 1976. The ingestion of food and the recovery of body weight following fasting in the naive rat. *Physiology and Behavior* 17:575–580.

52. Levitsky, D. A., Strupp, B. J., and Lupoli, J. 1981. Tolerance to anorectic drugs: Pharmacological or artifactual. *Pharm Biochem Behav* 14:661–667.

53. Miller, D. S., Mumford, P., and Stock, M. J. 1967. Gluttony: II. Thermogenesis in overeating man. *American Journal of Clinical Nutrition* 20:1223–1229.

54. Mitchel, J. S., and Keesey, R. E. 1977. Defense of a lowered weight maintenance level by lateral hypothalamically lesioned rats: Evidence from a restriction-refeeding regimen. *Physiology and Behavior* 18:1121–1125.

55. Mrosovsky, N., and Fisher, K. C. 1970. Sliding set points for body weight in ground squirrels during the hibernation season. *Canadian Journal of Zoology* 48:241–247.

56. Nisbett, R. E. 1972. Hunger, obesity and the ventromedial hypothalamus. *Psychological Review* 79:433–453.

57. Obersanik, E., and Levitsky, D. A. 1984. Weight gain through overeating and return to normal without undereating. *Federation Proceedings* 43:1057.

58. Planche, E., Joliff, M., de Gasquet, P., and Leliepure, X. 1983. Evidence of a defect in energy expenditure in 7-day-old Zucker rat (fa/fa). *American Journal of Physiology* 245:E107–E113.

59. Powley, T. L. 1977. The ventromedial hypothalamic syndrome, satiety, and a cephalic phase hypothesis. *Psychological Review* 84:89–126.

60. Powley, T. L., and Keesey, R. E. 1970. Relationship of body weight to the lateral hypothalamic feeding syndrome. *Journal of Comparative and Physiological Psychology* 70:25–36.

61. Rolls, B. J., Rowe, E. A., and Turner, R. C. 1980. Persistent obesity in rats following a period of consumption of a mixed high energy diet. *Journal of Physiology* (London) 298:415–427.

62. Rothwell, N. J., and Stock, M. J. 1979. A role for brown adipose tissue in diet-induced thermogenesis. *Nature* 281:31–35.

63. Rothwell, N. J., Saville, M. E., and Stock, M. J. 1981. Acute effects of food, 2-deoxy-D-glucose and noradrenaline on metabolic rate and brown adipose tissue in normal and atrophinised lean and obese (fa/fa) Zucker rats. *Pfluegers Archives* 392:172–177.

64. Schachter, S. 1971. Some extraordinary facts about obese humans and rats. *American Psychologist* 26:129–144.

65. Schemmel, R., Mickelson, O., and Gill, J. L. 1970. Dietary obesity in rats: Body weight and fat accretion in seven strains of rat. *Journal of Nutrition* 100:1941–1948.

66. Sclafani, A., and Springer, D. 1976. Dietary obesity in adult rats: Similarities to hypothalamic and human obesity syndromes. *Physiology and Behavior* 17:461–471.

67. Sclafani, A., Springer, D., and Kluge, L. 1976. Effects of quinine-adulterated diets on the food intake and body weight of obese and non-obese hypothalamic hyperphagic rats. *Physiology and Behavior* 16:631–640.

68. Seefeld, M. D., Keesey, R. E., and Peterson, R. E. 1984. Body weight regulation in rats treated with 2,3,7,8-tetrachlorodibenzo-p-dioxin. *Toxicology and Applied Pharmacology* 76:526–536.

69. Seefeld, M. D., Corbett, S. W., Keesey, R. E., and Peterson, R. E. 1984. Characterization of the wasting syndrome in rats treated with 2,3,7,8-tetrachlorodibenzo-p-dioxin. *Toxicology and Applied Pharmacology* 73:311–322.

70. Shetty, P. S., et al. 1981. Postprandial thermogenesis in obesity. *Clinical Science* 60:519–525.

71. Sims, E. A. H. 1976. Experimental obesity, dietary-induced thermogenesis, and their clinical implications. *Clinics in Endocrinology and Metabolism* 5:377–395.

72. Steffans, A. B. 1975. Influence of reversible obesity on eating behavior, blood glucose, and insulin in the rat. *American Journal of Physiology* 228:1738–1744.

73. Stern, J. S., and Johnson, P. R. 1977. Spontaneous activity and adipose cellularity in the genetically obese Zucker rats (fa/fa). *Metabolism* 26:371–380.

74. Stern, J. S., and Keesey, R. E. 1981. The effect of ventromedial hypothalamic lesions on adipose cell number in the rat. *Nutrition Reports International* 23:295–301.

75. Stunkard, A. J. 1982. Anorectic agents lower a body weight set point. *Life Sciences* 30:2043–2055.

76. Stunkard, A. J., and Penick, S. B. 1979. Behavior modification in the treatment of obesity. *Archives of General Psychiatry* 36:801–806.

77. Teitelbaum, P., and Epstein, A. N. 1962. The lateral hypothalamic syndrome: Recovery of feeding and drinking after lateral hypothalamic lesions. *Psychological Review* 69:74–94.

78. Vander Tuig, J. G., Knehaus, A. W., and Romsos, D. R. 1982. Reduced sympathetic nervous system activity in rats with ventromedial hypothalamic lesions. *Life Sciences* 30:913–920.

79. Vilberg, T. R., and Keesey, R. E. 1982. Metabolic contributions to VMH obesity. *North American Association for the Study of Obesity* (Abstract): 1982.

80. ———. 1984. Reduced energy expenditure after ventromedial hypothalamic lesions in female rats. *American Journal of Physiology* 247:R183–R188.

81. Wade, G. N. 1975. Some effects of ovarian hormones on food intake and body weight in female rats. *Journal of Comparative and Physiological Psychology* 88:183–193.

82. Weingarten, H. P., Chang, P., and Jarvie, K. R. 1983. Reactivity of normal and VMH-lesion rats to quinine-adulterated foods: Negative evidence for negative finickiness. *Behavioral Neuropsychiatry* 97:221–233.

83. Wooley, S. C., and Wooley, O. W. 1984. Should obesity be treated at all? In *Eating and its disorders*, ed. A. J. Stunkard and E. Stellar, pp. 185–192. New York: Raven Press.

84. Zucker, L. M. 1967. Some effects of caloric restriction and deprivation on the obese hyperlipemic rat. *Journal of Nutrition* 91:247–254.

85. Zucker, L. M., and Zucker, T. F. 1961. Fatty, a new mutation in the rat. *Journal of Heredity* 52:275–279.

4

Fat Cells and Obesity

Per Björntorp

The fat cell, the adipocyte, is the cellular unit that accumulates and stores excess energy in the form of triglycerides, which are a characteristic of obesity. The adipocyte is the main functional entity of the enlarged adipose tissue in obesity. This tissue also contains other cellular and structural units that serve the adipocytes with nutrients, transport fat to and from the fat cells, and furnish a stroma to support the tissue and keep its structure. These parts of adipose tissue are also enlarged in obesity.

Topographical differences in adipose tissue distribution in obesity are well known. Some of these can be recognized as exaggerations or even caricatures of the normal difference in fat distribution between men and women. Vague[35] started to systematize such differences in adipose tissue distribution by first describing the differences between nonobese men and women and then finding the same kind of adipose tissue distribution in obese subjects. Obese men typically had enlarged fat depots, located mainly on the upper part of the body, while most obese women had accumulated their excess fat in the lower part of the body, where nonobese women have a typical female fat depot. There were exceptions, some obese men having the female type and some obese women the male type of fat distribution. Vague called obesity with the male type of fat distribution android obesity, and gynoid obesity when the female type of fat distribution was found, irrespective of the sex of the patient. In further extensive studies it was found that obesity complications of a metabolic type were mainly associated with the android type of obesity. Although Vague is the pioneer in this field, several reports have more recently verified and extended his original findings, often by including other more easily applicable measurements of the fat distribution.*

Although the fat distribution characteristics have been long known, only recently has the functional significance of regional differences in fat

* See references 1, 8, 13, 16, and 24.

storage been revealed. Thanks to modern methodology, morphological and functional studies of the fat cell in different adipose tissue regions in humans have now been performed, and the results indicate statistical associations between adipocyte morphology and function in different regions, on one hand, and complications of obesity, on the other. This has also suggested several new ways to understand the etiology of the obesity complications. It should be stated at the outset that there is little or no evidence of primary malfunction of the adipocyte in obesity, but that adaptive changes in adipocyte metabolism, resulting from the excess of stored triglycerides, might be responsible for many of the regulatory aberrations seen in central energy metabolism in human obesity.

Adaptations of Adipocytes to Triglyceride Storage

Excessive energy in the form of triglycerides is transported after gastrointestinal absorption to adipose tissue for storage mainly as chylomicra, which are triglyceride-rich particles packed in a hydrophilic, protein-containing outer layer to allow transport in a water solution, the blood plasma. Their adipose tissue destination is most likely determined by the regional activity of the rate-limiting enzyme for triglyceride uptake in the adipocyte, lipoprotein lipase. This enzyme is produced in the adipocyte but exerts its action bound to the surface area of adjacent capillary endothelium. When chylomicra are transported through such lipoprotein lipase–active areas of adipose tissue capillaries, they are trapped and their triglycerides are hydrolyzed and transported into the adipocyte. The activity of this enzyme in different adipose tissue regions is thus of fundamental importance for the regional deposition of circulating fat. The balance between this activity and the subsequent regulation of the mobilization of fat are the factors determining the regional accumulation of depot fat. There is now considerable evidence in humans that such regulation occurs.

Before we examine such regional regulation of adipose tissue fat storage, however, let us first see what consequences extra triglycerides will have on the adipocytes of a certain region. There seems to be a generally applicable chain of events for different adipose tissue regions. Two events take place very early after induction of positive energy balance and subsequent net uptake of triglycerides in adipose tissue. The triglycerides captured from circulation are stored in the adipocytes in the central lipid droplet, which then is expanding. This further stretches the enclosing cell membrane over the enlarging central fat vacuole; the whole adipocyte is enlarged and shows hypertrophy. This has metabolic consequences. The machinery for both lipid uptake and mobilization now becomes livelier and shows enlarged capacity (for review, see Björntorp and Smith[4]).

Another early event occurring in adipose tissue with overfeeding is increased formation of new cells. These cells are both adipocyte precursor cells and cells belonging to the system of supply and support of the adipocytes, for example, capillary endothelium. This might be considered an adaptation of adipose tissue toward an increased readiness to accumulate more triglycerides. For example, an enlarged capillary surface area will have an increased capacity to catch circulating lipid via the lipoprotein lipase trap just described. Available evidence suggests that the new adipose precursor cells formed in this situation remain nondetermined until needed. They are needed when the available adipocytes have reached a certain critical size, indicating that their storage capacity has been fully utilized. At this point the newly formed adipose precursor cells seem to be determined and are irreversibly committed to be adipocytes. They assist efficiently in the triglyceride-accumulating process, and the storage capacity of adipose tissue has now been enlarged by adipocyte hyperplasia. This information is obtained mainly from studies in the rat, but it seems likely, and is partially demonstrated, that the same regulatory changes occur in humans (for review, Björntorp[2]).

This chain of events seems generally applicable to all regions of adipose tissue. This probably means that the regional activity of lipoprotein lipase would be the primary regulating factor that is trapping circulating triglycerides in a certain adipose tissue region. The secondary adaptations of the storage capacity of that region then follow: first adipocyte hypertrophy with metabolic consequences, then, if needed, adipocyte hyperplasia. There might also be regional differences in critical size of adipocytes at which point new adipocytes are recruited, or in control of cell hyperplasia. However, there is transsectional evidence in obese subjects that there are no regional differences in critical adipocyte size. My associates and I have observed that when a certain adipocyte size has been reached, the regional number of adipocytes is elevated irrespective of region, sex, or severity of obesity (see figure 4.1). There might well be interindividual differences, however.

Researchers have suggested an abnormal rate of replication of adipose precursor cells in severely obese subjects,[29] but this has not been possible to confirm.[26] Important information is missing on several points in this area.

The main factor known to determine regional adipose tissue fat accumulation is thus the regional lipoprotein lipase activity. Regional differences in this activity have now been established. Since they seem to be followed by differences in other metabolic pathways, mainly in lipolysis variations, the whole metabolic pattern in different regions of adipose tissue will be reviewed in the next section.

FIGURE 4.1

Regional Growth of Adipose Tissue with Increasing Obesity
(Contribution of Enlargement and Multiplication of Cells)

The relationship between adipocyte size and number in different adipose tissue regions in women and men. Nonobese and obese men and women are divided into different groups of body fat (abscissa, kg). Fat cell size in these regions denoted in shaded areas. Local fat cell number was obtained by ultrasound thickness and fat cell size measurements.[30] An increase over the fat cell number found in subjects with 10-kg body fat is denoted with open areas. Note the apparent appearance of new fat cells at approximately the same fat cell expansion (0.6–0.8 µg). The figures on top of each panel denote the maximal increase in regional fat cell number obtained in relation to controls. Note the seemingly even distribution of excess fat cell number in women and the preferential accumulation in the abdominal regions in men.

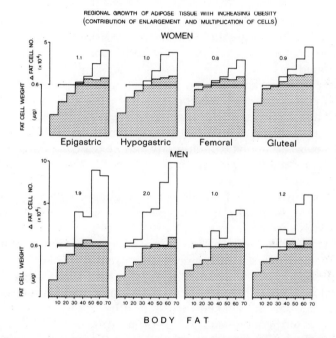

SOURCE: M. Krotkiewski, P. Björntorp, L. Sjöström, and U. Smith, 1983, Impact of obesity on metabolism in men and women—importance of regional adipose tissue distribution, *Journal of Clinical Investigation* 72:1150–1162; M. Krotkiewski, L. Sjöström, P. Björntorp, and U. Smith, 1975, Regional adipose tissue cellularity in relation to metabolism in young and middle-aged women, *Metabolism* 24:703–710; and L. Sjöström, U. Smith, M. Krotkiewski, and P. Björntorp, 1972, Cellularity in different regions of adipose tissue in young men and women, *Metabolism* 21:1143–1153.

Regulation of Regional Adipocyte Metabolism

The current knowledge of regional differences in adipocyte metabolism was preceded by information obtained from morphological studies. Such studies had shown that adipocytes in the gluteal and femoral regions in women were larger than those in the abdominal regions.[18,30] This specific fat-cell enlargement was found also in obese women, even in extreme obesity.[16]

Regional differences in fat-cell size indicated changes in the regulation of triglyceride storage and mobilization in such cells. Morphological studies suggested that the metabolism of femoral and gluteal fat cells in women is different from that in abdominal fat cells. The fact that this was a specific sex difference suggested that sex hormones were involved in the regulation of metabolism of these adipocytes. This was supported by other observations that steroid hormones exerted regional effects on adipocyte size; the gluteal region seemed most sensitive.[15,17]

Recent functional studies have now demonstrated differences in adipocyte metabolism in different adipose tissue regions. In comparison with adipocytes from the abdominal subcutaneous site, adipocytes from the femoral region have higher lipoprotein lipase activity and lower lipolytic responsiveness.* In these studies, however, no distinct separation was performed between sexes, and the exact endocrine status of the subjects was not defined.

Recent studies have attempted to resolve these uncertainties by examining only women in defined endocrine situations, namely in the follicular and luteal phases of the menstrual cycle, during early and late pregnancy, and during lactation.[28] These studies have shown that the previously described lipolytic insensitivity and increased lipoprotein lipase activity of femoral adipocytes are indeed found in women during both the follicular and luteal phases of the menstrual cycle. These adaptations are even more pronounced during early pregnancy, when the lipolytic sensitivity of the femoral region is severely depressed and lipoprotein lipase activity is very high.

This situation changes at the end of pregnancy, when lipid mobilization from the femoral region is no longer different from that of the abdominal adipocytes. During lactation this is again the case; lipoprotein lipase is similar and low in both abdominal and femoral adipocytes, which suggests that triglycerides are now taken up also in other locations than adipose tissue, perhaps in the mammary gland for lactation purposes.[28]

This picture can be interpreted to mean that femoral adipocytes ordinarily tend to accumulate triglycerides by an increased lipoprotein lipase activity combined with a low lipolytic activity. This probably explains why these adipocytes are larger. The picture is more accentuated during pregnancy. The extra lipid accumulated in the femoral adipocytes is then mobilizable during late pregnancy and lactation, and might well be specifically stored in the femoral region to be reserved for the purpose of providing reserve energy for pregnancy and lactation. In postmenopausal women these female functions of femoral adipocytes disappear, lipoprotein lipase activity is no longer elevated, and these adipocytes are no longer enlarged in comparison with abdominal adipocytes.†

This morphological evidence and the more recent functional studies

* See references 10, 12, 20, 25, and 32.
† M. Rebuffé-Scrive, personal communication, 30 April 1985.

strongly indicate that the specific metabolic pattern of femoral adipocytes is regulated by female sex hormones. It is known, for example, from studies in the rat that progesterone exerts regionally specific effects on fat-cell size[14] and on lipoprotein lipase activity,[33] and that prolactin is lipolytic.[31] It might be speculated that femoral adipocytes in women are specifically sensitive to these hormonal regulations. The sluggish lipid mobilization from the femoral region in nonpregnant, nonlactating women is associated with elevated alpha-adrenergic activity that inhibits lipolysis[12,20] and whose endocrine background is not known.

It has now been shown that the adipocytes in the femoral region, and presumably also in the gluteal region, has a specific metabolic regulation. They have increased lipoprotein lipase activity and mobilize fat less effectively than abdominal adipocytes. These cells therefore are enlarged. With excess lipid energy to be stored, such as in overfeeding resulting in obesity, the increased flow of fat transported in circulation is taken up primarily in the femoral-gluteal regions. The fat cells become increasingly enlarged, and, eventually when full, new adipocytes are formed. In this way the femoral-gluteal fat depot tends to be enlarged prior to other depots. It seems logical that this should occur mainly in women with intact ovarian functions. In men, who essentially lack this depot, excess fat is instead localized in the abdominal regions. It also seems logical that in postmenopausal women obesity would be localized more to the abdominal regions. The sex differences have been documented,[16] but the differences between pre- and postmenopausal women still remain hypothetical.

Regional Fat Distribution and Complications of Obesity

Obese men have more pronounced hyperinsulinemia, decreased glucose tolerance, overt diabetes mellitus, hypertriglyceridemia, and hypertension than obese women at comparable degrees of moderate obesity. Women have to be much more severely obese to reach the degree of complicating disorders that obese men suffer at a moderate increase of total body fat. These sex differences are at least partly associated with the distribution of body fat, because obese women with the male type of adipose tissue distribution (much abdominal fat) are more prone to complications than obese women with the female type of adipose tissue distribution.[16]

These are statistical associations. If we now integrate these interpretations with the functional characteristics of the adipocytes in the enlarged adipose tissue regions, the following picture will emerge.

The female type of fat distribution (enlargement of the femoral-gluteal regions) is only weakly associated with obesity complications. Since adipocytes here store the lipid in a stable way, it is comparatively difficult to mobilize. The male type of fat distribution, with enlarged abdominal fat depots, involves fat that is easier to mobilize.

Adipocyte morphology has been used as a basis for subdividing human obesity. Obese subjects with increased body fat due to enlarged fat cells could be separated from those with an increased number of fat cells. These subgroups were called hypertrophic and hyperplastic obesity respectively. The first was associated with complications, the latter was more difficult to treat.[3,19]

One disadvantage of this attempt to subdivide human obesity is the lack of precision in estimating fat-cell hyperplasia. Utilizing regional adipose cellularity and function to subdivide human obesity is more precise, and also brings adipocyte function into the picture. Obesity characterized by female fat distribution corresponds to hyperplastic obesity. In this type there are more fat cells in the large femoral-gluteal fat depot, cells not present in the male type of distribution. The male distribution corresponds to the hypertrophic obesity previously suggested to be associated with complicating disorders. The new subdivision then should replace the old one because it is more precise and because it includes not only morphological but functional aspects of the adipocytes. In addition, this framework has greater potential for explaining the etiology of the complications of obesity.

Causative Links Between Adipose Tissue Distribution and Complications

The important question of why the complications of obesity are clustered mainly in the male type of obesity cannot yet be answered, but several interesting possibilities exist. The male type of adipose tissue distribution is associated with a specific endocrine profile including an increase in free testosterone.[9] Such changes might provide a background to explain both the distribution of adipose tissue and the obesity complications. It is also possible, of course, that the specific functional differences of the enlarged adipose tissue in these two types of obesity are causing the complications.

With an enlarged lipolytically sensitive adipose depot there would be a risk for excessive concentrations of circulating free fatty acids (FFA). This might have consequences for insulin sensitivity and glucose transport in the periphery, as suggested by Randle and associates[27] and as indicated in recent studies.[7] When the enlarged and lipolytically sensitive depot is localized intraabdominally, the FFA would reach the liver in increased concentrations. This would cause hypertriglyceridemia.[5] Recent studies also suggest the interesting possibility that portal FFA might inhibit insulin uptake in the liver.[34] In this way peripheral hyperinsulinemia, insulin resistance, decreased glucose tolerance, and diabetes mellitus might be triggered. In the long term, hypertension might also result from increased sodium reabsorption in the tubuli, caused by the hyperinsulinemia.[6]

Prospective Epidemiological Studies

It is a well-known fact that obesity is associated with a number of established risk factors for ischemic heart disease (IHD) and related conditions. These include hyperinsulinemia, diabetes mellitus, hyperlipidemia, and hypertension. Nevertheless, obesity by itself has often not been found to be a risk factor for IHD. This is particularly the case with population studies of limited magnitude and duration (for review, see Larsson, Björntorp, and Tibblin[23]). In order to precipitate IHD, a long duration of severe obesity seems to be necessary. This could be detected only in long-term studies, such as the Framingham study, which has data over 26.5 years.[11]

The discrepancy between the consistent findings of associations between obesity and risk factors for IHD but the lack of statistical connection between obesity itself and IHD has been puzzling. One way to explain this might be that the risk associated with obesity is found only in a subgroup. This possibility has recently been tested.

In a prospective study of men born in 1913 in Göteborg, Sweden, no increased risk for IHD was found in obese men when obesity was expressed in terms of body weight, body mass index (BMI), or similar general measures of obesity. Obese men were, however, glucose intolerant, hyperinsulinemic, and had high blood lipids and blood pressure, all risk factors for IHD.[22,23] Recently this population study has been reexamined and regional obesity factors have been brought into the analyses. By measuring the circumference of the waist, standardizing this for the skeletal frame by dividing with hip circumference, a measure of abdominal obesity is obtained. In transsectional analyses among obese subjects, this ratio shows a strong association with the complications of obesity, including several risk factors for IHD.[16] When used for reanalyses of the prospective study, this simple ratio predicted IHD independent of general measures of obesity such as BMI. In multivariate analyses, it was actually the men who were leanest in terms of BMI but who had the highest waist/hip circumference ratio who were at greatest risk for IHD. The magnitude of this risk appeared to be comparable to that of established strong risk factors such as smoking and hypertension.[24] Similar results have also been reported from the Paris prospective study, where abdominal obesity has been found to predict IHD.[8] Furthermore, another prospective population study in

Göteborg, examining women, shows the same result, that waist/hip circumference ratio strongly predicts IHD.[21]

In summary, then, prospective studies have now shown that abdominal obesity is a risk factor for IHD, independent of other measurements of obesity. This indicates that the risk for IHD is found only in a subgroup of obese persons characterized by location of excess fat in the abdominal region.

Concluding Remarks and Outlook for the Future

Recent research has reestablished the validity of Vague's pioneering work and has also brought adipocyte localization, morphology, and function into the picture. This has provided a seemingly understandable way in which obesity causes adipose tissue to be localized to different regions rather than distributed in the normal manner. It appears that the differences in function of the adipocytes in these enlarged regions are of importance in explaining the complications of obesity. In the future, it is necessary to explore these possibilities to understand how the complications of obesity are triggered. These complications include a number of prevalent diseases with cardiovascular catastrophies as endpoints such as hyperinsulinemia, diabetes mellitus, hyperlipidemia, and hypertension. When the mechanisms at work are understood more precisely, therapeutic approaches may follow.

It seems, however, that the available knowledge is strong enough to justify conclusions for practical, clinical applications. The evidence reviewed here consistently points in the same direction: Abdominal obesity is more dangerous than gluteal-femoral obesity. This evidence comes from transsectional examinations in large populations of obese persons studied by different research groups, from experimental work, and from the unanimous results of three independent prospective epidemiological studies in both men and women.

Several practical conclusions seem justified. First, it seems more urgent to treat moderate obesity in men than in women. Unfortunately, today it is probably moderately obese women who are more concerned about their condition than are men. It seems advisable to prevent the emerging male obesity, which often starts at the beginning of middle age. A practical rule for an upper limit of allowable abdominal obesity seems to be when the abdominal circumference starts to exceed that of the hip region.[24] The risk for cerebrovascular and cardiovascular disease then increases ten- to twentyfold within the next ten to fifteen years. These measurements can be performed when the fasting subject is standing, at the level of the umbilicus at normal respiratory position, and over the largest circumference of the hip region. In women, the corresponding ratio of abdomen to hip circumference is not 1 to 1 as in men, but approximately 0.8 to 1.[21] When abdominal obesity is present according to these definitions, it is advisable to check not only blood pressure but also to take a fasting venous blood sample for determination of glucose, lipids, and insulin.

The future may bring more precise measurements of abdominal obesity. Computerized tomography seems very promising for this purpose both because of its precision and its ability to measure selectively extra-abdominal, subcutaneous, and intraabdominal fat. On the other hand, the circumference measurements are so simple that they can be used by anyone and are very useful for self-screening in the free-living population.

REFERENCES

1. Albrink, M. J., and Meigs, J. W. 1964. Interrelationship between skinfold thickness, serum lipids and blood sugar in normal men. *American Journal of Clinical Nutrition* 15: 255–261.

2. Björntorp, P. 1981. Adipocyte development. In *Proceedings from the third international congress on obesity, Rome 1980*, ed. P. Björntorp, M. Cairella, and H. A. Howard, pp. 58–69. London: Libbey.

3. Björntorp, P., and Sjöström, L. 1971. Number and size of adipose tissue fat cells in relation to metabolism in human obesity. *Metabolism* 20:703–713.

4. Björntorp, P., and Smith, U. 1976. The effect of fat cell size on subcutaneous adipose tissue metabolism. *Frontier of Matrix Biology* 2:37–61.

5. Carlson, L. A., Boberg, J., and Högstedt, B. 1965. Some physiological and clinical implications of lipid mobilization from adipose tissue. In *Handbook of physiology. Adipose tissue*, ed. A. E. Renold and G. F. Cahill, Jr., pp. 625–644. Baltimore: Williams & Wilkins.

6. De Fronzo, R. A., et al. 1975. The effect of insulin on renal handling of sodium, potassium, calcium and phosphate in man. *Journal of Clinical Investigation* 55:845–855.

7. Deibert, D. C., and De Fronzo, R. A.. 1980. Epinephrine induced insulin resistance in man. *Journal of Clinical Investigation* 65:717–721.

8. Ducimetiere, P., Avons, P., Cambien, F., and Richard, J. L. 1983. Corpulence history and fat distribution in CHD etiology—the Paris prospective study. *European Heart Journal* 4(Supplement E):8.

9. Evans, P. J., Hoffman, R. G., Kalkhoff, R. K., and Kissebah, A. H. 1983. Relationship of androgenic activity to body fat topography, fat cell morphology and metabolic aberrations in premenopausal women. *Journal of Clinical Endocrinology and Metabolism* 57:304–310.

10. Guy-Grand, B., and Rebuffé-Scrive, M. 1980. Anatomical and nutritional correlates of lipoprotein lipase of human adipose tissue: Third International Congress on obesity. *Alimentazione Nutrizione Metabolismo* 1:273.

11. Hubert, H. B., Feinleib, M., and McNamara, P. M. 1983. Obesity as an independent risk factor for cardiovascular disease: A twenty-six year follow-up of Framingham heart study participants. *Circulation* 67:968–977.

12. Kather, H., Schröder, F., Simon, B., and Schlierf, G. 1977. Human fat cell adenylate cyclase: Regional differences in hormone-sensitivity. *European Journal of Clinical Investigation* 7:595–599.

13. Kissebah, A. H., et al. 1982. Relation of body fat distribution to metabolic complications of obesity. *Journal of Clinical Endocrinology and Metabolism* 54:254–260.

14. Krotkiewski, M., and Björntorp, P. 1976. The effect of progesterone and insulin administration on regional adipose tissue cellularity in the rat. *Acta Physiologica Scandinavica* 96:122–127.

15. ———. 1978. The effects of estrogen treatment of carcinoma of the prostate on

regional adipocyte size. *Journal of Endocrinological Investigation* 1:365–366.

16. Krotkiewski, M., Björntorp, P., Sjöström, L., and Smith, U. 1983. Impact of obesity on metabolism in men and women—importance of regional adipose tissue distribution. *Journal of Clinical Investigation* 72:1150–1162.

17. Krotkiewski, M., Blohmé, B., Lindholm, N., and Björntorp, P. 1976. The effects of adrenal corticosteroids on regional adipocyte size in man. *Journal of Clinical Endocrinology and Metabolism* 42:91–97.

18. Krotkiewski, M., Sjöström, L., Björntorp, P., and Smith, U. 1975. Regional adipose tissue cellularity in relation to metabolism in young and middle-aged women. *Metabolism* 24:703–710.

19. Krotkiewski, M., et al. 1977. Adipose tissue cellularity in relation to prognosis for weight reduction. *International Journal of Obesity* 1:395–416.

20. La Fontan, M., Dang-Tran, L., and Berlan, M. 1979. Alpha-adrenergic antilipocyte effect of adrenaline in human fat cells of the thigh: Comparison with adrenaline responsiveness of different fat depots. *European Journal of Clinical Investigation* 9:261–266.

21. Lapidus, L., et al. 1984. Adipose tissue distribution and risk of cardiovascular disease and death—a 12-year follow-up of participants in the population study of women in Gothenburg, Sweden. *British Medical Journal* 289:1257–1261.

22. Larsson, B. 1978. Obesity—a population study of men, with special reference to development and consequences for the health. Thesis, University of Göteborg, Sweden, Kungälv, Sweden, Gotab.

23. Larsson, B., Björntorp, P., and Tibblin, G. 1981. The health consequences of moderate obesity. *International Journal of Obesity* 5:97–116.

24. Larsson, B., et al. 1984. Abdominal adipose tissue distribution, obesity and risk of cardiovascular disease and death. A 13-year follow-up of the study of men born in 1913. *British Medical Journal* 288:1401–1404.

25. Lithell, H., and Boberg, J. 1978. The lipoprotein-lipase activity of adipose tissue from different sites in obese women and relationship to cell size. *International Journal of Obesity* 2:47–52.

26. Pettersson, P., Van, R., Karlsson, M., and Björntorp, P. 1986. Adipocyte precursor cells in obese and non-obese humans. *Acta Medica Scandinavica*. In press.

27. Randle, P. J., Garland, P. B., Hales, C. N., and Newsholme, E. A. 1963. The glucose-fatty acid cycle. Its role in insulin sensitivity and the metabolic disturbances of diabetes mellitus. *Lancet* 2:785–789.

28. Rebuffé-Scrive, M., et al. 1985. Regulation of human adipose tissue metabolism during the menstrual cycle, pregnancy and lactation. *Journal of Clinical Investigation* 75:1973–1976.

29. Roncari, D. A. K., Lau, D. C. W., and Kindler, S. 1981. Exaggerated replication in culture of adipocyte precursors from massively obese persons. *Metabolism* 30:425–427.

30. Sjöström, L., Smith, U., Krotkiewski, M., and Björntorp, P. 1972. Cellularity in different regions of adipose tissue in young men and women. *Metabolism* 21:1143–1153.

31. Smith, R. W., and Walsh, A. 1976. Effect of lactation on lipolysis in rat tissue. *Lipids* 11:418–420.

32. Smith, U., Hammarsten, J., Björntorp, P., and Kral, J. 1979. Regional differences and effect of weight reduction of human fat cell metabolism. *European Journal of Clinical Investigation* 9:327–332.

33. Steingrimmsdottir, L., Brasel, J., and Greenwood, M. R. C. 1980. Hormone modulation of adipose tissue lipoprotein lipase may alter food intake in rats. *American Journal of Physiology* 239:E162–E167.

34. Strömblad, G., et al. Inhibition of hepatic insulin uptake by portal fatty acids. Manuscript.

35. Vague, J. 1947. La differenciation sexuelle—facteur determinant des formes de l'obésité. *La Presse Médicale* 30:339–340.

5

The Influence of Psychological Variables in Obesity

Ruth Striegel-Moore and Judith Rodin

Numerous attempts have been made to understand obesity from a psychological perspective, but recently the focus has shifted away from unitary explanations (e.g., the "obese personality") to models viewing obesity as multiply determined.[150] In this chapter we will review the contribution of psychological research to our understanding of these multiple determinants of obesity. Among the most widely considered are studies evaluating personality factors that may lead to or maintain obesity. Implicit in such approaches is the assumption that overeating is the primary mediating variable in the development of obesity, that is, that psychological variables cause excessive food intake. We will consider evidence on this issue later, but it appears that obese people do not eat more and often eat less than lean persons.[199]

Isolating the effects of food intake depends, in part, on how overeating is defined. We have argued that overeating is best defined as the degree of food intake that brings in more energy than is needed for an individual.[151] This makes overeating a descriptive term, but one that is not definable operationally without characterizing the person's unique genetic, physiological, conditioned, and environmental response to food. Indeed it is difficult to separate the effects of psychological and physiological factors on both the cause and maintenance of obesity precisely because they interact so greatly. In evaluating causal factors, it is often unclear whether obese persons overate to create their obesity initially. But there is convincing evidence that numerous morphologic and metabolic changes which occur as a result of obesity or cycles of dieting and regaining make it easier to *maintain* obesity even on relatively low caloric intake.[7,36,40]

Personality and Psychopathology of Obese Individuals

PSYCHODYNAMIC EXPLANATIONS

Psychoanalytic theories lead to two global predictions about obese individuals. First, unconscious conflicts lead to overeating; these conflicts arise from disruptions in personality development. Such disturbances occur with a specific pattern of personality traits. As McReynolds[100] summarizes, the psychoanalytic description of an obese person includes "passive dependence, emotional frustration, a strong desire to be loved, and poor coping abilities" (p. 38). Second, overeating is a response to emotional distress such as anxiety or depression. According to Slochower's review,[191] current psychoanalytic theorists consider personality pathology and emotional conflicts as central, but they focus primarily on the link between emotional distress and overeating. For example, Kornhaber[82] attributes overeating to a response to depression. Garetz[39] describes overeating as a means of coping with a wide range of distressing feelings.

Three lines of evidence have been cited to suggest that obesity is a defense against depression or anxiety. Weight loss has been found to be accompanied by depression and anxiety and, in some cases, by extreme disruptions of psychological functioning bordering on psychotic episodes.* Furthermore, several studies reported that obese subjects scored lower on measures of anxiety and depression than normal-weight controls.[28,80,184] Several experiments found that obese subjects ate significantly more than normal-weight subjects when exposed to anxiety-arousing conditions.[3,99,108] Similarly, an association between dysphoria and food intake has been reported in both male and female patients seeking help in losing weight.†

There are, however, several convincing arguments to reject the psychodynamic hypothesis of obesity. Depressed affect during weight loss is transient for most individuals and may be secondary to dieting. Emotionality, including irritability, anxiety, and depression, was reported in the classic study by Keys and colleagues of starvation in normal-weight subjects.[76] One need not be obese to suffer from the effects of severe food restriction.[17,76] Incidentally, not all studies find depression or anxiety with dieting,[94,217] and there is some evidence that depression at pretreatment

* See references 44, 47, 81, 137, 209, and 211.
† See references 8, 19, 66, 87, 90, and 184.

is positively correlated with success in a weight-loss program.[119]

The negative states that do occur during weight loss may be transient[50] and may reflect the aversive experience of food deprivation, especially for people who love to eat.[141] This hypothesis is supported by research on psychological changes in patients who have undergone jejunoileal or gastric bypass surgery. Unlike patients on diets, these individuals can experience oral gratification while losing weight rapidly. Several studies found significant improvements in self-concept and mood in bypass patients.*

While it is possible that psychodynamic mechanisms are important for some individuals,[19] more parsimonious and scientific hypotheses have been proposed to explain why eating may occur as a response to arousal.[141,142] As we discuss later, increased food intake may be induced by physiological arousal per se, rather than by a need to ward off negative feelings. Also, food intake does not appear to reduce anxiety in obese individuals.[90,99]

PERSONALITY TRAITS

There is an extensive clinical literature on the personality traits and psychological functioning of obese persons.[73,77,98,100] These clinical accounts portray obese patients as neurotic, sometimes even psychotic, as experiencing overpowering dependency needs, and as engaged in a relentless pursuit of oral gratification.[100] However, research with nonpatient samples and studies in which appropriate control subjects were included have shown with remarkable consistency that obese and nonobese individuals do not differ on a wide variety of global measures of personality traits and mental health.

In a sample of almost 2,300 Danish school children, ranging in age from 6 to 15 years, Quaade[132] found no differences in psychological functioning between obese and normal-weight children. Examining extensively a subsample of 36 obese children, Quaade[132] failed to find evidence for immaturity, dependency, or lack of assertiveness. Similar results were reported from a study in the United States.[20] In a carefully designed study Sallade[173] recruited 120 obese boys and girls from a total of 1,310 students (grades three through ten) and randomly selected 120 control subjects matched for age, sex, and school membership. On a battery of widely used measures of psychological adjustment, obese children's test profiles were similar to those obtained from their normal-weight peers in the domains of social and emotional adjustment. The only comparison that yielded a significant group difference involved self-concept; normal-weight children had a more positive self-concept than the obese children. This finding is not surprising when we consider that stigmatization and rejection of overweight individuals begins at an early age.[154]

Similar to the studies with children, studies with adults have failed to

* See references 1, 30, 51, 52, 55, 84, 85, 93, 129, 135, 144, 174, 193, 194, and 218.

show psychological disturbance in obese persons.* A large study investigating male Belgian post office employees found no differences on depression and anxiety measures when comparing 184 obese, 1,271 normal-weight, and 239 lean subjects aged 20 to 60 years.[180] Similarly, a later study of obese, normal-weight, and underweight Belgian workers showed no significant group differences on the Eysenck Personality Inventory. Instead the analyses revealed that the heavy subjects smoked fewer cigarettes and were less neurotic, more extroverted, and of a lower occupational class than lighter subjects.[80]

Just as there are normal-weight persons with poor and good psychological adjustment, obese individuals may or may not have psychiatric problems. Current evidence suggests that obese persons do not as a group differ from normal-weight individuals on measures of global psychological adjustment and on standard measures of personality. Therefore, reporting personality and psychopathology data collected from obese patients without comparing these results with a matched control group[24] or generalizing from such patient samples to the obese population in general fosters the already negative stereotype of obese people held by both laymen and health professionals.†

LOCUS OF CONTROL AND DELAY OF GRATIFICATION

Locus of control (LOC) has been of interest in obesity research because of its postulated link with dependency and self-regulation skills. Individuals with external LOC[133,166] are more dependent and less effective in their use of self-reinforcement than persons with internal LOC.[9,10] Internal LOC may be associated with greater control over impulses, including the desire to eat.[67]

One study that evaluated LOC in male adolescents[195] and another with male and female adults[69] found no differences between normal-weight and obese subjects. Using the Reid-Ware three-factor internality-externality scale,[133] a multidimensional measure of LOC, Thomason[212] found that obese college students obtained significantly higher externality scores on the self-control subscale and on the social system control scale than their normal-weight peers, whereas no group differences were identified on the fatalism subscale. While obese subjects were as likely to perceive fate or luck as controlling life events (fatalism scale), they felt less personal control over their social environment and over their impulses and desires. Developmental studies are needed to examine when differences in perceived LOC emerge. It is likely that obese children are told by others that they lack the ability to control themselves, so they may learn to accept externality as part of their self-image. Furthermore, obese children who face discrimination may have less control over their environment than their normal-weight peers.

* See references 8, 28, 66, 72, 92, 181, 184, and 220.
† See references 54, 56, 75, 101, 154, and 227.

Several studies have investigated delay of gratification, and mixed results have been reported. Two studies[71,183] found that obese children chose both edible and nonedible immediate rewards more frequently than normal-weight children. Bonato and Boland[13] reported that overweight children preferred the immediate incentive only when it was a food item, but not when it was a toy pen. On the other hand, Geller, Keane, and Scheirer[43] found no differences between obese and control subjects for either edible or nonedible rewards. In yet another study, overweight girls did not differ from normal-weight girls in their ability to delay gratification or their preference for delayed rewards, though the self-control strategies employed by the overweight girls were considered less effective by the authors than those of the control subjects.[16]

Several methodological issues may explain these contradictory findings. Bourget and White[16] studied relatively young children (5 to 9 years), and at this age, group differences may be small. Several studies did not actually present the incentives but had the children respond to hypothetical rewards.[43,71] Furthermore, some studies used only males[183] while others used only females.[16] Also, the time period children had to wait for their delayed reward varied greatly. Finally, only one study assessed whether obese children preferred the immediate food reward because they could not delay gratification when faced with a food stimulus in their immediate environment. In fact, Bonato and Boland[13] found that for obese children the food reward was more highly valued than the nonfood reward. Studies are needed in which the incentive value of both the food and nonfood rewards are equally high in both groups of subjects.

The literature on personality traits as measured by conventional inventories does not show a distinct obese personality or a close link with psychopathology.[91,142] Though obese persons do not have characteristic personality traits or psychiatric status, other psychological or behavioral variables might differentiate between obese and nonobese groups. Abnormal patterns of eating are one possibility.

Eating Styles of Obese Individuals

AMOUNT OF FOOD EATEN

Several investigators have examined the belief that obese persons overeat. The ability to draw clear inferences has been hampered by methodological problems, intrinsic to both laboratory and field studies. In field studies, measuring food intake accurately is complicated because subjects have access to many foods, and the experimenter must remain inconspicuous. Since the subjects' body weight cannot be concealed from the observer, observational data on food intake are vulnerable to bias. In most laboratory studies, amount eaten is assessed objectively, but subjects usually have fewer food choices and less control over when, where, and how they eat. Furthermore, being observed may influence the subject's eating behavior. Recent efforts to make observation less obvious in the laboratory, however, have been promising.[78,198] Perhaps because of these difficulties, studies in both laboratory and field have produced weak and conflicting data.

Of twenty-nine laboratory studies reviewed by Spitzer and Rodin,[199] nine found obese persons to have a higher food intake* whereas twenty found no group differences.† One might argue that obese subjects are self-conscious and curtailed their food intake even under deception. However, as we will see later, strong weight differences for amount eaten do emerge in interaction with other variables such as palatability. This suggests that concerns over self-presentation do not sufficiently explain the failure to find reliable effects of body weight on amount eaten.

In contrast to experimental studies, field studies provide some evidence that obese individuals eat more than nonobese persons, although the number of naturalistic studies is relatively small. More food was consumed by obese compared to nonobese subjects in several studies,‡ whereas no group differences were found in others.[26,35,128]

Field studies may include different types of subjects than do laboratory studies. Certain types of overweight people may be overrepresented in some of the naturalistic settings chosen for field research. Stunkard and Mazer[207] observed attendance at several restaurants when food was served in a smorgasbord and compared it to nights when food was served in the traditional manner. With a few exceptions, attendance increased sharply among obese persons on smorgasbord nights. Such differences in sample composition—as a function of setting selection—obviously may affect experimental outcomes.

Obese and normal-weight subjects in field studies may also differ with regard to the types of foods chosen for consumption.[41,83,221] If overweight and normal-weight groups tend to choose different foods, there is a possibility that apparent differences in amount eaten are due to the type of food chosen.

It is important to emphasize that differences in amount eaten, if they can be found at all, do not correlate with degree of overweight or level of weight gain. As Rose and Williams[161] documented, subjects of identical weight and activity level, matched for age and sex, may all maintain their body weight with twice the intake of other subjects.

* See references 2, 99, 114, 115, 127, 148, 149, 155, and 215.
† See references 4, 25, 27, 59, 63, 65, 117, 120, 122, 134, 162, 164, 171, 176, 179, 186, 187, 190, 192, and 196.
‡ See references 31, 41, 83, 107, and 221.

TOPOGRAPHY OF EATING

Behavior therapists have targeted eating style as potentially significant in the etiology and treatment of obesity. For example, Ferster, Nurnberger, and Levitt[37] had obese subjects consume smaller amounts of food, eat their meals more slowly by taking smaller bites, chew bites longer, and take breaks between bites.[103,204,205] Empirical studies have evaluated duration of a meal, rate of eating, and a variety of microelements of eating style such as choice of eating utensils[178] and number of chews during a meal.

DURATION OF A MEAL

Laboratory studies have failed to find reliable effects of weight on meal duration.* To keep the subjects unaware that their eating is observed, these studies usually engage subjects in some parallel activity during eating. It is unclear whether group differences would emerge if subjects are not distracted during their meal. However, even in more naturalistic studies without distraction, meal duration of obese and nonobese subjects does not differ, when all subjects are served identical meals.[102,106]

RATE OF EATING

Rate of eating has been studied with other measures of appetite (e.g., perceived hunger) and as an aspect of a stable eating style. Presumably eating faster permits a greater intake before postingestive satiety cues occur. Wooley, Wooley, and Turner[224] found that rate of eating at one meal has a positive influence on salivation, a putative measure of appetite, at a subsequent meal.

Laboratory studies on rate of eating produce conflicting findings (for a review see Stunkard and Kaplan).[206] When analyzing amount of food eaten per time period, Hill and McCutcheon[65] found that the obese subjects ate more quickly. On the other hand, when measuring number of bites per time period, nonsignificant differences were observed between obese and normal-weight subjects by Mahoney[102] and Warner and Balagura.[219] Interestingly, Dodd, Birkey, and Stalling[31] replicated both sets of findings within one study.

A frequently overlooked fact is that rate of eating changes over the course of a meal, presumably as a function of satiety.[4,64,79,111] Several studies measured rates during only part of the meal and found significant weight group differences.[42,86,106,107] However, studies measuring rate of eating continuously throughout the meal did not find significant differences between overweight and normal-weight individuals.[31,102,219]

In summary, the current data provide an inconsistent picture of dif-

* See references 4, 65, 102, 162, 163, 186, 187, and 219.

ferences in eating style or amount eaten between overweight and normal-weight subjects. Differences that do emerge may not be causally related to obesity since efforts to modify eating style in behavioral treatment programs have not shown substantial effects on weight loss for all over-weight clients.[33,38] Rather eating style appears to be learned, and many normal-weight as well as overweight people eat too quickly, take large bites, and so forth. Interestingly, Epstein and associates[35] found that both obese and nonobese subjects reduced intake when they followed a pro-cedure (placing utensils down after eating) that was aimed at increasing interbite interval. Thus, despite substantial research interest in this area, studies have not shown stable differences between overweight and normal-weight people in either amount eaten or eating style.

The Externality Hypothesis

Stimulated by Bruch's suggestion[18] that obese individuals are unable to differentiate among internal arousal states and frequently interpret such states as hunger, Schachter and his colleagues[114,115,175,177] studied whether people at different weights used different cues to stimulate eating. The resultant internality-externality hypothesis[175] proposed that the eating of normal-weight individuals was influenced by internal signals such as gastric motility and other peripheral and central physiological cues signaling hunger and satiety.[179] The eating behavior of obese persons, on the other hand, was thought to be influenced largely by external cues, including time, the taste and sight of food, and the number of highly palatable food cues present.[2,122,155,215] This hypothesis spawned a great number of sub-sequent studies, which ultimately led to a reformulation of Schachter's[175] early hypotheses.[116,141,146]

Rodin[141,146] proposed that an external food cue has two effects: a spe-cific one that elicits an anticipatory digestive response and a nonspecific one that arouses the organism and thereby increases the likelihood that behavioral responses, including eating, will occur.[202] For example, the sight and smell of food can cause salivation and a rise in immunoreactive insulin.[143,172,189,223] Other external cues that have been associated with food also come to elicit conditioned physiological responses (such as insulin release) associated with the actual state of hunger. One example is the time of day.[114,115,176] Due to culturally determined work schedules and rules about eating, most people eat at relatively fixed times. Therefore, regardless of physiological requirements, people must learn to be hungry at appropriate times. Certain times, as well as visual, olfactory, gustatory, and cognitive cues, predict food availability and so come to elicit responses that characterize caloric depletion.[14] According to Booth,[14] meal onset and termination are largely determined by conditioned responses learned through prior experience in which the postingestive effects of food serve as unconditioned stimuli.

During the 1970s many studies examined the effects of external and cognitive cues on the food intake of overweight and normal-weight people. There were reports of significant interactions of body weight with variations of the visual salience of food cues,* the cognitive salience of food cues,[164] and the perceived passage of time.[176] More striking, however, is the number of nonsignificant interactions with body weight that have been found.†

As discussed in detail elsewhere,[141,145,146,199] the simple internality-externality hypothesis demanded reconsideration on several grounds. Given the commonly found morphological and endocrine abnormalities associated with obesity,[185] one does not need a psychological construct (i.e., internality) to explain differences in responsiveness to internal hunger or satiety cues.[114,115,121,179] More significant, normal-weight subjects too are often inaccurate in their perceptions of internal hunger and satiety cues, as reflected, for example, in their sluggish and incomplete compensation for changes in the caloric density of experimental meals.‡

The concepts "external cue" and "external responsiveness" were often operationalized poorly, leading to further confusion. Manipulations of putative external cues have ranged from variations of granulated sugar glaze on cookies[25] to whether the experimenter was dressed in a lab coat.[201] External responsiveness should be defined as the extent to which a greater magnitude response (e.g., increased eating, increased emotionality, increased attention) is evoked by highly salient cues in the external environment, as compared to cues of low salience.[145] Using this definition, external responsiveness is calculated as the difference score for each subject between his or her response to a high- versus a low-intensity cue, with intensity determined on the basis of independent criteria (e.g., number of food cues, decibels of noise, degree of proximity of food) and not the subject's response. Comparing responses when there are no cues versus when there are some cues would not be a reasonable test in this case. Furthermore, external cues need to be considered against a background of physiological conditions,[21,22] as we will exemplify in our discussion on the influence of palatability on food intake.

In conclusion, overweight people are not necessarily more "external" than leaner controls. On the other hand, there is considerable evidence that external responsiveness is an individual difference variable that can be identified at birth,[110] although presumably there may be a learned component as well,[147] and it does have the potential to produce weight gain. In a study to consider how external responsiveness might relate to weight gain when external food cues were abundant, Rodin and Slochower[152] observed normal-weight children at an eight-week summer

* See references 114, 138, 139, 155, 164, and 215.
† See references 27, 117, 122, 127, 128, 130, 162, 171, 196, and 225.
‡ See references 23, 34, 74, 109, 126, 131, 197, and 222.

camp. Those children who showed the greatest external responsivity, measured at the start of the summer, gained the most weight. The degree of external responsiveness did not change as a function of the weight gain, suggesting that externality is an individual difference variable that may lead to overweight but is not caused by being heavy. Further support comes from the finding that external responsiveness does not decrease with substantial weight loss.[155]

Palatability

Palatability was originally considered an external food-related cue[115] and was frequently studied in experiments on external responsiveness. However, psychophysiological experiments have shown that palatability is not simply an intrinsic property of food. Hedonic judgments are strongly influenced by physiological variables such as the individual's acute state of energy deficit or surfeit, amount of fat stored, and metabolic status.[15,21,68,213] Even changes in peripheral mechanisms such as changing the anatomy of the intestine appear to alter taste preferences, as has been reported in studies of intestinal bypass patients.[153] Palatability is also related to the nutrient value of food,[53] and it reflects the learning history of the person rating the food.[169]

Virtually all studies on palatability show that both normal-weight and overweight individuals consume more when food is palatable.* However, palatability has a greater effect on the food intake of overweight subjects compared to normal-weight subjects.† In general, findings that overweight individuals ingest more highly palatable food (than normal-weight people) are stronger than findings of reduced intake of overweight subjects with low palatability.[199] These studies leave unexplained why overweight people eat more under conditions of high palatability. Weight history and chronic energy deficit due to dieting have generally been overlooked and yet, if overweight subjects in these studies were currently dieting or had recently done so, differential consumption in response to palatable food would, in fact, be expected.[116,125,155] Furthermore, it is unclear whether obese subjects eat more because they perceive foods as more palatable than normal-weight subjects or whether they consume more of food perceived by both groups to be equally palatable.

We need to learn more about how heightened taste responsiveness relates to the development and maintenance of obesity. If differences between overweight and normal-weight persons exist after controlling

---

* See references 64, 65, 99, 114, 115, 138, 155, and 169.
† See references 65, 114, 115, 127, 139, 215, and 226.

for diet history and level of chronic energy deficit, and if increased responsiveness precedes obesity in some individuals, this variable may be of etiological significance. If increased responsiveness is determined only by factors such as dieting and energy deficit, it may play a role in the maintenance of obesity by providing a mechanism that guards against weight loss. Finally, these two possibilities may not be mutually exclusive. There may be individual differences in responsiveness;[110] factors such as deprivation may produce transient changes, and responsiveness to palatability may interact with deprivation.

A number of experiments examined differences between obese and normal-weight individuals in how they perceive tastes, sweet tastes in particular. If sweet tastes more intense, this may lead to overeating. However, subjects of different body weights do not differ in perceptions of intensity.* Weight loss achieved by dieting has been shown both to increase the perceived intensity of sweet-tasting solutions[49] and to leave it unchanged.[152]

Since the sensory properties of food play an important role in feeding behavior,[228] greater appreciation of the gustatory properties of food may contribute to obesity, but certainly not in all cases. Even if procedural variables were constant across studies, the evidence suggests no systematic variation between obese and average-weight subjects in their evaluations of sweet stimuli.

VARIETY

Presentation of a variety of palatable foods augments food intake. For example, subjects ate a third more when offered sandwiches with four different fillings than when offered four sandwiches with similar fillings.[160]

The variety effect may be mediated by perceived changes in palatability. Reduction in palatability has been attributed to sensory-specific satiation, a mechanism first postulated by LeMagnen.[88] He suggested that an oral satiety mechanism, which is sensory-specific, operates through stimulation (i.e., flavor, texture, shape) of food passing through the mouth. Several studies show that pleasantness ratings for foods eaten during a meal decline more than the pleasantness ratings of foods not eaten.[123,158,160,182] Rolls, Rolls, and Rowe[157] argued that satiety relies on an interaction between internal satiety signals and sensory food cues such as texture, shape, smell, taste, and temperature. While sensory-specific satiety serves the adaptive function of ensuring a balanced intake of nutrients, it may promote overeating if a wide variety of foods are available. Both animals and humans eat more when offered a variety of foods simultaneously† or in succession.[113,157,159]

* See references 48, 112, 139, 152, 213, and 214.
† See references 11, 123, 156, 157, 165, and 167.

Restrained Eating

Herman, Polivy, and their coworkers[59,62,63] first suggested that the obesity-externality correlation was an epiphenomenon of the fact that obese persons were always dieting. They asserted that conscious restraint was responsible for externality.

Laboratory studies suggest that overeating can result from manipulations that "break" the dietary restriction of the restrained person. The classical design involves serving subjects a preload and then measuring their subsequent food intake. Early experiments found that restrained subjects, compared to unrestrained subjects, tended to overeat after a preload, whereas in no-preload conditions restrained subjects ate less than their unrestrained counterparts.[59,63,124] This phenomenon, which occurred from disruption of the cognitive control dieters usually exert over their food intake, was called counterregulation. Disruption was observed by inducing arousal,[60] administering alcohol,[58] or manipulating cognitive variables such as knowledge of the caloric content of the preload. For example, restrained subjects who were told they had received a high-calorie, rich pudding ate 61 percent more food at a subsequent tasting experiment than restrained subjects who were told that they had eaten a low-calorie diet pudding.[124]

Several studies have reported that restraint, as measured with the restraint scale (or Eating Habits Questionnaire) developed by Herman and Mack,[59] is more common among obese individuals than among normal-weight persons. Hibscher and Herman[63] reported that 28 percent of underweight subjects, 57 percent of normal-weight subjects, and 73 percent of overweight subjects (defined as 15 percent or more above normal weight) scored high on restraint. Using slightly different criteria (overweight was defined as 25 percent or more above normal weight), Drewnowski, Riskey, and Desor[32] identified 30 percent of normal-weight subjects as restrained eaters, compared to 90 percent of overweight subjects. However, the high number of obese persons who are identified as restrained eaters may be related to the properties of the restraint scale. In three studies, factor analyses yielded two main factors: a weight fluctuation factor and a dietary concern factor.[12,32,170] Hence, loading high on the weight factor reflects weight fluctuation and discrepancy between actual weight and ideal weight. Obese subjects score higher almost by definition on these items, a finding confirmed by the high correlation between actual overweight and the factor scores on weight fluctuation in all three studies.

Drewnowski, Riskey, and Desor[32] argued convincingly that the restraint scale should be divided into two subscales, each yielding a separate score. Whereas weight fluctuation scores increased with overweight in all studies, dietary concern scores did not vary with body weight. Drewnowski and associates[32] suggested that the latter subscale may be a more appropriate measure of the theoretical construct of restraint. Interestingly, in this study[32] overweight subjects actually scored lower on dietary concern than the normal-weight subjects. Consistent with these methodological considerations, Ruderman and Wilson[171] argued that restraint may be more characteristic of normal-weight individuals than obese persons.

In a reanalysis of two earlier studies[63,196] and in their own experiment, Ruderman and Wilson[171] found that obese restrained eaters ate considerably less than normal-weight restrained eaters after a preload aimed at inducing counterregulation. These three studies suggest that counterregulation may be most typical for normal-weight restrained eaters. Given this finding it is not surprising that research on restrained eaters has generated more interesting findings on normal-weight individuals. For example, some aspects of restraint correlate with binge-eating tendencies,[57,61] and dieting and cognitive restriction have been implicated as risk factors for bulimia.[77,203] More discrete factors of the global construct of restraint have recently been proposed,[208] which should help determine how various aspects of restraint relate to binge eating, obesity, and other eating disorders.

Arousal-induced Eating

Another major theoretical approach to explain the inconsistent findings of the externality studies has focused on arousal. As described earlier, one property of an external stimulus is its nonspecific arousing effect, which permits certain responses to occur.[202] Herman and Polivy[60] described arousal as resulting in increased food intake due to a disruption of cognitive regulation of eating. A different explanation was offered by Robbins and Fray,[136] who argued that large stimulus changes induce arousal, which the organism may not be able to differentiate from hunger; therefore the organism overeats. Finally, Rodin[140,141,146] proposed that arousal from both positive and negative states increases consumption by increasing responsiveness to salient environmental stimuli. The neurochemical link between external responsivity, arousal, and feeding has been investigated for animals,[6,105] but more work is needed before drawing conclusions regarding humans.

While laboratory studies have not supported the hypothesis that arousal leads to overeating, most have induced fleeting anxiety in subjects in relatively artificial ways.* The degree and type of arousal in the laboratory may be quite different from the distress that many overweight people report leads to overeating. In fact, Slochower[190] and Slochower and Kaplan[192] showed that even in a laboratory context, unexplained arousal (arousal for which there was no salient environmental label pro-

* See references 3, 99, 134, 179, and 208.

vided in the experimental context) was related to overeating in obese subjects and labeled arousal was not (see also Slochower[191]).

The relationship between arousal and overeating merits further investigation, especially in light of recent demonstrations in animals that several forms of arousal produce overeating.[5,104,168] Moreover, clinical accounts continue to suggest a strong relationship between arousal and overeating.[89,118,188]

Again we point out that while some data suggest a link between arousal and overeating in overweight individuals,[136] the association between arousal and obesity is far less clear. Even if we assume that arousal induces overeating, the amount of food consumed in a brief laboratory observation cannot be presumed to be an important determinant of the levels of body weight maintained over the long term without data that specifically address that point.[216] Nonetheless, the relevance of arousal theory to eating behavior seems clear. An optimal level of arousal is thought to increase the probability of a prepotent response in a given situation, so individuals might eat more under optimal arousal than when less aroused. Despite the apparent simplicity of this formulation, however, most experiments on arousal and eating behavior have not provided data that could be used to evaluate this hypothesis.

We have further suggested that arousal plays a role in determining how eating becomes a prepotent response.[200] Arousal may influence the conditioning process itself, enhancing and strengthening the condition of responses to particular environmental stimuli. If so, food consumption in a given situation would be dependent not only on the person's present state of arousal but on arousal levels present in similar past situations.

Conclusions

Human eating behavior has been studied extensively. The search for psychological, social, and environmental variables related to overeating continues, and many questions remain unanswered. Obesity is not a homogeneous disorder,* and even the same types of obesity may be multiply determined.[29,142] Thus, whether one finds differences between weight groups may depend on the type of overweight or normal-weight subjects included in the sample. Describing subjects in terms of such variables as weight history, age of onset, and fat-cell size and number may help us explain the amount of variance accounted for by psychological factors.[147] Furthermore, few studies have evaluated whether subjects are currently maintaining their weight or are in a dynamic phase of losing or gaining weight. Such distinctions are crucial.

* See references 70, 140, 141, 142, 145, and 210.

Thus far most studies have tried to elucidate the etiology of obesity by studying overweight people. Incidentally, many studies must have included obese subjects with a history of repeated dieting. Since being fat or dieting may influence the behaviors under study, such persons, with appropriate control groups, are of interest if we wish to understand the consequences of dieting for the regulation of weight and food intake. Many recent studies have focused on newborn infants and young children.* Such studies bring a developmental perspective to the study of obesity and may provide a better understanding of etiological factors by studying subjects prospectively.

Finally, we are struck by the research emphasis on determining the psychological and behavioral factors that relate to eating. By contrast, there is a paucity of data with regard to factors that relate to exercise. Since obesity is determined by both energy output and energy input, such studies might be fruitful in helping us to understand the role of psychosocial variables in the development and maintenance of obesity.

REFERENCES

1. Abram, H. S., Meixel, S. A., Webb, W. W., and Scott, H. W. 1976. Psychological adaptation to jejunoileal bypass for morbid obesity. *Journal of Nervous and Mental Disease* 162:151–157.
2. Abramson, E. E., and Stinson, S. G. 1977. Boredom and eating in obese and nonobese individuals. *Addictive Behaviors* 2:181–185.
3. Abramson, E. E., and Wunderlich, R. A. 1972. Anxiety, fear and eating: A test of the psychosomatic concept of obesity. *Journal of Abnormal Psychology* 79:317–321.
4. Adams, N., Ferguson, J., Stunkard, A. J., and Agras, S. 1978. The eating behavior of obese and nonobese women. *Behaviour Research and Therapy* 16:225–232.
5. Antelman, S. M., Rowland, N. E., and Fisher, A. E. 1976. Stress-related recovery from lateral hypothalamic hyperphagia. *Brain Research* 102:346–350.
6. Antelman, S. M., Szechtman, H., Chin, P., and Fisher, A. E. 1975. Tail pinch-induced eating, gnawing and licking behavior in rats: Dependence on the nigrostriatal dopamine system. *Brain Research* 99:319–337.
7. Apfelbaum, M. 1975. Influence of level of energy intake on energy expenditure in man: Effects of spontaneous intake, experimental starvation, and experimental overeating. In *Obesity in perspective*, ed. G. A. Bray, vol. 2, pp. 145–155. Washington, D.C.: U.S. Government Printing Office.
8. Atkinson, R. M., and Rinquette, E. L. 1967. A survey of biographical psychological features in extraordinary fatness. *Psychological Medicine* 29:121–133.
9. Bellack, A. S., and Tillman, W. 1974. The effects of task and experimenter feedback on the self-reinforcement behavior of internals and externals. *Journal of Consulting and Clinical Psychology* 42:330–336.
10. Bellack, A. S., Schwartz, J., and Rozensky, R. H. 1974. The contribution of external control to self-control in a weight reduction program. *Journal of Behavior Therapy and Experimental Psychiatry* 5:245–250.
11. Bellisle, F., and Lemagnen, J. 1981. The structure of meals in humans: Eating and drinking patterns in lean and obese subjects. *Physiology and Behavior* 27:649–658.
12. Blanchard, F. A., and Frost, R. O. 1983. Two factors of restraint: Concern for

* See references 46, 95, 96, 97, and 110.

dieting and weight fluctuation. *Behaviour Research and Therapy* 21:259–267.

13. Bonato, D. P., and Boland, F. J. 1983. Delay of gratification in obese children. *Addictive Behaviors* 8:71–74.

14. Booth, D. A. 1977. Satiety and appetite are conditioned responses. *Psychosomatic Medicine* 39:76–81.

15. ———. 1978. Acquired behavior controlling energy intake and output. *Psychiatric Clinics of North America* 1:547–579.

16. Bourget, M. A., and White, D. R. 1984. Performance of overweight and normal-weight girls on delay of gratification tasks. *International Journal of Eating Disorders* 3:63–71.

17. Brown, J. D., and Pulsifier, D. H. 1965. Clinical problems in aviation medicine: Outpatient starvation in normal obese subjects. *Aerospace Medicine* 36:267–268.

18. Bruch, H. 1961. Transformation of oral impulses in eating disorders: A conceptual approach. *Psychiatric Quarterly* 35:458–481.

19. ———. 1973. *Eating disorders: Obesity, anorexia nervosa, and the person within.* New York: Basic Books.

20. Burchinal, L. G., and Eppright, E. S. 1959. Test of the psychogenic theory of obesity for a sample of rural girls. *American Journal of Clinical Nutrition* 7:288–294.

21. Cabanac, M. 1971. Physiological role of pleasure. *Science* 173:1103–1107.

22. Cabanac, M., and Duclaux, R. 1970. Specificity of internal signals in producing satiety for taste stimuli. *Nature* 227:966–967.

23. Campbell, R. G., Hashim, S. A., and Van Itallie, T. B. 1971. Studies of food-intake regulation in man: Responses to variations in nutritive density in lean and obese subjects. *New England Journal of Medicine* 285:1402–1407.

24. Castelnuovo-Tedesco, P., and Schiebel, D. 1975. Studies of superobesity: I. Psychological characteristics of superobese patients. *International Journal of Psychiatry in Medicine* 4:465–480.

25. Cheung, R. C., Barnes, T. R., and Barnes, M. J. 1980. Relationship between visually based food preference and amount eaten. *Perceptual and Motor Skills* 50:780–782.

26. Coll, M., Meyer, A., and Stunkard, A. 1979. Obesity and food choices in public places. *Archives of General Psychiatry* 36:795–797.

27. Costanzo, P. R., and Woody, E. Z. 1979. Externality as a function of obesity in children: Pervasive style or eating-specific attribute. *Journal of Personality and Social Psychology* 37:2286–2296.

28. Crisp, A. H., and McGuiness, B. 1976. Jolly fat: Relation between obesity and psychoneurosis in general population. *British Medical Journal* 1:7–9.

29. Daniels, J. S. 1984. The pathogenesis of obesity. *Psychiatric Clinics of North America* 7:335–347.

30. Dano, P., and Hahn-Pedersen, J. 1977. Improvement in quality of life following jejunoileal bypass surgery for obesity. *Scandinavian Journal of Gastroenterology* 12:769–774.

31. Dodd, D. K., Birky, H. J., and Stalling, R. B. 1976. Eating behavior of obese and nonobese females in a normal setting. *Addictive Behaviors* 1:321–325.

32. Drewnowski, A., Riskey, D., and Desor, J. A. 1982. Feeling fat yet unconcerned: Self-reported overweight and the restraint scale. *Appetite* 3:273–279.

33. Dubbert, P. M., and Wilson, G. T. 1983. Failures in behavior therapy for obesity: Causes, correlates, and consequences. In *Failures in Behavior Therapy,* ed. E. B. Foa and P. M. G. Emmelkamp, pp. 263–288. New York: John Wiley & Sons.

34. Duncan, K. M., Bacon, J. A., and Weinsier, R. L. 1983. The effects of high and low energy density diets on satiety, energy intake, and eating time of obese and nonobese subjects. *American Journal of Clinical Nutrition* 37:763–767.

35. Epstein, L., Parker, L., McCoy, J., and McGee, G. 1976. Descriptive analysis of eating regulation in obese and nonobese children. *Journal of Applied Behavior Analysis* 9:407–415.

36. Even, P., Nicolaidis, S., and Meile, M. J. 1981. Changes in efficiency of ingestants are a major factor of regulation of energy balance. In *The body weight regulatory system: Normal and disturbed mechanisms,* ed. L. A. Cioffi, W. P. T. James, and T. B. Van Itallie, pp. 115–123. New York: Raven Press.

37. Ferster, C. B., Nurnberger, J. I., and Levitt, E. B. 1962. The control of eating. *Journal of Mathetics* 1:87–109.

38. Foreyt, J. P., Goodrick, G. K., and Gotto, A. M. 1981. Limitations of behavioral treatment of obesity: Review and analysis. *Journal of Behaviorial Medicine* 4:159–174.

39. Garetz, F. K. 1973. Socio-psychological factors in overeating and dieting with comments on popular reducing methods. *Practitioner* 210:671–686.

40. Garrow, J. 1978. *Energy balance and obesity in man.* Amsterdam: Elsevier/North Holland Biomedical Press.

41. Gates, J. C., Huenemann, R. L., and Brand, R. J. 1975. Food choices of obese and nonobese persons. *Journal of the American Dietetic Association* 67:339–343.

42. Gaul, D. J., Craighead, W. E., and Mahoney, M. J. 1975. Relation between eating rates and obesity. *Journal of Consulting and Clinical Psychology* 43:123–125.

43. Geller, S., Keane, T., and Scheirer, J. 1981. Delay of gratification, locus of control, and eating patterns in obese and non-obese children. *Addictive Behaviors* 6:9–14.

44. Glucksman, M. L., Hirsch, J., and Levin, B. 1973. The affective response of obese patients to weight reduction: A differentiation based on age at onset of obesity. *Psychosomatic Medicine* 35:57–63.

45. Grinker, J. A. 1975. Obesity and taste: Sensory and cognitive factors in food intake. In *Obesity in perspective,* ed. G. A. Bray, vol. 2, part 2, pp. 73–80. Washington, D.C.: U.S. Government Printing Office.

46. ———. 1978. Infant taste responses are correlated with birthweight and unrelated to indices of obesity. *Pediatric Research* 12:371.

47. Grinker, J. A., Hirsch, J., and Levin, B. 1973. The affective response of obese patients to weight reduction: A differentiation based on age at onset of obesity. *Psychosomatic Medicine* 35:57–63.

48. Grinker, J. A., Hirsch, J., and Smith, D. V. 1972. Taste sensitivity and susceptibility to external influence in obese and normal weight subjects. *Journal of Personality and Social Psychology* 22:320–325.

49. Grinker, J. A., Price, J. M., and Greenwood, M. R. C. 1976. Studies in childhood obesity. In *Hunger: Basic mechanisms and clinical implications,* ed. D. Novin, W. Wywricka, and G. Bray, pp. 441–457. New York: Raven Press.

50. Hall, J. C., Veale, B., Horne, K., and Watts, J. M. 1984. The nutritional knowledge scores of morbidly obese patients selected for gastric bypass surgery. *International Journal of Obesity* 8:123–128.

51. Halmi, K., Long, M., Stunkard, A. J., and Mason, E. 1980. Psychiatric diagnosis of morbidly obese gastric by-pass patients. *American Journal of Psychiatry* 137:470–472.

52. Halverson, J. D., Wise, L., Wazna, R. F., and Ballinger, W. F. 1978. Jejunoileal bypass for morbid obesity. A critical appraisal. *American Journal of Medicine* 64:461–475.

53. Harper, A. E., and Boyle, P. C. 1976. Nutrients and food intake. In *Appetite and food intake,* ed. T. Silverstone, pp. 177–206. Berlin: Abakon.

54. Harris, M. B. 1983. Eating habits, restraint, knowledge and attitudes toward obesity. *International Journal of Obesity* 7:271–286.

55. Harris, M. B., and Green, D. 1982. Psychosocial effects of gastric reduction surgery for obesity. *International Journal of Obesity* 6:527–539.

56. Harris, M. B., and Smith, S. D. 1983. The relationship of age, sex, ethnicity and weight to stereotypes of obesity and self-perception. *International Journal of Obesity* 7: 361–371.

57. Hawkins, R. C., and Clement, P. F. 1984. Binge eating: Measurement problems and a conceptual model. In *The binge-purge syndrome,* ed. R. C. Hawkins, W. J. Fremouw, and P. F. Clement, pp. 229–253. New York: Springer.

58. Herman, C. P. 1978. Restrained eating. *Psychiatric Clinics of North America* 1: 593–607.

59. Herman, C. P., and Mack, D. 1975. Restrained and unrestrained eating. *Journal of Personality* 43:647–660.

60. Herman, C. P., and Polivy, J. 1975. Anxiety, restraint, and eating behavior. *Journal of Abnormal Psychology* 84:666–672.

61. ———. 1984. A boundary model for the regulation of eating. In *Eating and its disorders,* ed. A. J. Stunkard and E. Stellar, pp. 141–156. New York: Raven Press.

62. Herman, C. P., Polivy, J., and Silver, R. 1979. Effects of an observer on eating behavior. The induction of "sensible" eating. *Journal of Personality* 47:85–99.

63. Hibscher, J. A., and Herman, C. P. 1977. Obesity, dieting and the expression of "obese" characteristics. *Journal of Comparative and Physiological Psychology* 91:374–380.

64. Hill, S. W. 1974. Eating responses of humans during dinner meals. *Journal of Comparative and Physiological Psychology* 86:652–657.

65. Hill, S., and McCutcheon, N. 1975. Eating responses of obese and nonobese humans during dinner meals. *Psychological Medicine* 37:395–401.

66. Holland, J., Masling, J., and Copley, D. 1970. Mental illness in lower class normal, obese, and hyper-obese women. *Psychosomatic Medicine* 2:351–357.

67. Hood, J., Moore, T. E., and Garner, D. 1982. Locus of control as a measure of ineffectiveness in anorexia nervosa. *Journal of Consulting and Clinical Psychology* 50:3–14.

68. Jacobs, H. L., and Sharma, K. N. 1969. Taste versus calories: Sensory and metabolic signals in the control of food intake. *Annals of the New York Academy of Science* 157:1084–1125.

69. Jacobs, S. B., and Wagner, M. K. 1984. Obese and nonobese individuals: Behavioral and personality characteristics. *Addictive Behaviors* 9:223–226.

70. Jeanrenaud, B. 1977. An overview of experimental models of obesity. In *Advances in obesity research: II,* ed. G. Bray, pp. 111–122. London: Newman.

71. Johnson, W., Parry, W., and Drabman, R. 1978. The performance of obese and normal size children on a delay of gratification task. *Addictive Behaviors* 3:205–208.

72. Johnson, S. F., Swenson, W. M., and Gastineau, C. F. 1976. Personality characteristics in obesity: Relation to MMPI profile and age of onset of obesity to success in weight reduction. *American Journal of Clinical Nutrition* 29:626–632.

73. Jordan, H. A. 1969. Voluntary intragastric feeding: Oral and gastric contributions to food intake and hunger in man. *Journal of Comparative and Physiological Psychology* 68:498–506.

74. Kaplan, H. I., and Kaplan, W. S. 1957. The psychosomatic concept of obesity. *Journal of Nervous and Mental Disease* 125:181–201.

75. Kaplan, S. P. 1984. Rehabilitation counseling students' perception of obese male and female clients. *Rehabilitation Counseling Bulletin* 27:172–181.

76. Keys, A., et al. 1950. *The biology of human starvation.* Minneapolis: University of Minnesota Press.

77. Kiell, R. 1973. *The psychology of obesity.* Springfield, Ill.: Charles C Thomas.

78. Kissileff, H. R. 1980. Universal eating monitor for continuous recording solid and liquid consumption in man. *American Journal of Physiology* 238:R14–R22.

79. Kissileff, H. R., Klingsberg, G., and Van Itallie, T. B. 1980. Universal eating monitor for continuous recording of solid or liquid consumption in man. *American Journal of Physiology* 238:14–22.

80. Kittel, F., et al. 1978. Psycho-socio-biological correlates of moderate overweight in an industrial population. *Journal of Psychosomatic Research* 22:145–158.

81. Kollar, E., and Atkinson, R. 1966. Responses of extremely obese patients to starvation. *Psychosomatic Medicine* 28:229–245.

82. Kornhaber, A. 1970. The stuffing syndrome. *Psychosomatics* 11:580–584.

83. Krantz, D. 1979. A naturalistic study of social influences on meal size among moderately obese and nonobese subjects. *Psychosomatic Medicine* 41:19–27.

84. Kuldau, J. M., and Rand, C. S. W. 1980. Jejunoileal bypass: General and psychiatric outcome after one year. *Psychosomatics* 21:534–539.

85. Kuldau, J. M., Barnard, G., Kreutziger, S., and Rand, C. S. W. 1979. Psychosocial effects of jejunoileal bypass for obesity: Six month follow-up. *Psychosomatics* 20:462–472.

86. Lebow, M. D., Goldberg, P., and Collins, A. 1977. A methodology for investigating differences in eating behavior between obese and nonobese persons. *Behavior Therapy* 5:707–709.

87. Lecke, E. V., and Withers, R. F. J. 1967. Obesity and depression. *Journal of Psychosomatic Research* 11:107–115.

88. Lemagnen, J. 1971. Advances in studies on the physiological control and regulation of food intake. In *Progress in physiological psychology,* ed. E. Stellar and J. M. Sprague, vol. 4, pp. 203–261. New York: Academic Press.

89. Leon, G. R. 1975. Personality, body image, and eating patterns in overweight persons after weight loss. In *Recent advances in obesity research, I,* ed. A. Howard, pp. 228–231. London: Newman.

90. Leon, G. R., and Chamberlain, K. 1973. Emotional arousal, eating patterns and body image as differential factors associated with varying success in maintaining weight loss. *Journal of Consulting and Clinical Psychology* 40:474–480.

91. Leon, G. R., and Roth, L. 1977. Obesity: Psychological causes, correlations, and speculations. *Psychological Bulletin* 84:117–139.

92. Leon, G. R., Kolotkin, R., and Korgeski, G. 1979. MacAndrew addiction scale and other MMPI characteristics associated with obesity, anorexia, and smoking behavior. *Addictive Behaviors* 4:401–407.

93. Leon, G. R., Eckert, E. D., Teed, D., and Buchwald, H. 1979. Changes in body image and other psychological factors after intestinal bypass surgery for massive obesity. *Journal of Behavioral Medicine* 2:39–55.

94. Ley, P. 1984. Some tests of the hypothesis that obesity is a defense against depression. *Behaviour Research and Therapy* 22:197–199.

95. Lipps-Birch, L. 1980. Effects of peer models' food choices and eating behaviors on preschoolers' food preferences. *Child Development* 51:489–496.

96. Lipps-Birch, L., and Marlin, D. W. 1982. I don't like it; I never tried it: Effects of exposure on two-year-old children's food preferences. *Appetite* 3:353–360.

97. Lipps-Birch, L., Zimmerman, S., and Hind, H. 1981. The influence of social-affective context on the formation of children's food preferences. *Child Development* 51:856–861.

98. Louderback, L. 1970. *Fat power; whatever you weigh is right.* New York: Hawthorn Books.

99. McKenna, R. J. 1972. Some effects of anxiety level and food cues in the behavior of obese and normal subjects. *Journal of Personality and Social Psychology* 221:331–319.

100. McReynolds, W. T. 1982. Toward a psychology of obesity: Review of research on the role of personality and level of adjustments. *International Journal of Eating Disorders* 2:37–57.

101. Maddox, G. L., and Liederman, V. 1969. Overweight as a social disability with medical implications. *Journal of Medical Education* 44:214–220.

102. Mahoney, M. J. 1975. The obese eating style: Bites, beliefs, and behavioral modification. *Addictive Behaviors* 3:129–134.

103. Mahoney, M. J., and Mahoney, K. 1976. *Permanent weight control.* New York: W. W. Norton.

104. Marques, D. N., Fisher, A. E., Okrutny, M. S., and Rowland, N. E. 1979. Tailpinch induced fluid ingestion: Interactions of taste and deprivation. *Physiology and Behavior* 22:37–41.

105. Marshall, J. 1976. Neurochemistry of central monoamine systems as related to food intake. In *Appetite and food intake,* ed. T. Silverstone, pp. 43–63. Berlin: Abakon.

106. Marston, A. R., London, P., and Cooper, L. M. 1976. A note on the eating behavior of children varying in weight. *Journal of Child Psychology and Psychiatry* 17: 221–224.

107. Marston, A. R., London, P., Cooper, L. M., and Cohen, N. 1975. In vivo observation of the eating behavior of obese and nonobese subjects. In *Recent advances in obesity research, I,* ed. A. Howard, pp. 207–210. London: Newman.

108. Meyer, J. E., and Pudel, V. 1972. Experimental studies on food intake in obese and normal weight subjects. *Journal of Psychosomatic Research* 16:305–308.

109. ———. 1977. Experimental feeding in man: A behavioral approach to obesity. *Psychosomatic Medicine* 39:153–157.

110. Milstein, R. M. 1980. Responsiveness in newborn infants of overweight and normal weight parents. *Appetite* 1:65–74.

111. Moon, R. D. 1979. Monitoring human eating patterns during the ingestion of non-liquid foods. *International Journal of Obesity* 3:281–288.

112. Moskowitz, H., et al. 1976. The effects of hunger, satiety and glucose loads on taste intensity and hedonics. *Physiology and Behavior* 16:471–475.

113. Mugford, R. A. 1977. External influences on the eating of carnivores. In *The chemical senses and nutrition,* ed. M. R. Kare and O. Maller, pp. 25–48. New York: Academic Press.

114. Nisbett, R. E. 1968. Determinants of food intake in obesity. *Science* 159:1254–1255.

115. ———. 1968. Taste, deprivation and weight determinants of eating behavior. *Journal of Personality and Social Psychology* 10:107–116.

116. ———. 1972. Hunger, obesity and the ventromedial hypothalamus. *Psychological Review* 79:433–453.

117. Nisbett, R. E., and Storms, M. D. 1974. Cognitive and social determinants of food intake. In *Thought and feeling,* ed. H. London and R. E. Nisbett, pp. 190–208. Chicago: Aldine.

118. Pines, A., and Gal, R. 1977. The effect of food on test anxiety. *Journal of Applied Social Psychology* 4:348–358.

119. Pitta, P., Alpert, M., and Perelle, I. 1980. Cognitive stimulus-control program for obesity with emphasis on anxiety and depression reduction. *International Journal of Obesity* 4:227–233.

120. Pliner, P. 1973. Effect of liquid and solid preloads on eating behavior of obese and normal persons. *Physiology and Behavior* 11:285–290.

121. ———. 1974. On the generalizability of the externality hypothesis. In *Obese humans*

and rats, ed. S. Schachter and J. Rodin, pp. 111–129. Washington, D.C.: Erlbaum/Wiley.

122. Pliner, P., and Iuppa, G. 1978. Effects of increasing awareness on food consumption in obese and normal weight subjects. *Addictive Behaviors* 3:19–24.

123. Pliner, P., Polivy, J., Herman, C. P., and Zakalusny, I. 1980. Short-term intake of overweight individuals and normal weight dieters and nondieters with and without choice among a variety of foods. *Appetite* 1:203–214.

124. Polivy, J. 1976. Perception of calories and regulation of intake in restrained and unrestrained subjects. *Addictive Behaviors* 1:237–244.

125. Polivy, J., Herman, C. P., Olmstead, M. P., and Jazwinski, C. 1984. Restraint and binge eating. In *The binge-purge syndrome,* ed. R. C. Hawkins, N. J. Fremouw, and P. H. Clement, pp. 104–122. New York: Springer.

126. Porikos, K. P., Messer, M. F., and Van Itallie, T. B. 1982. Caloric regulation in normal-weight men maintained on a palatable diet of conventional foods. *Physiology and Behavior* 29:293–300.

127. Price, J., and Grinker, J. 1973. The effects of degree of obesity, food deprivation and palatability on eating behavior of humans. *Journal of Comparative and Physiological Psychology* 85:265–271.

128. Price, J. M., Sheposh, J. P., and Tiano, F. E. 1975. A direct test of Schachter's internal-external theory of obesity in a naturalistic setting. In *Recent advances in obesity research, I,* ed. A. Howard, pp. 204–207. London: Newman.

129. Printen, K. J., and Mason, E. E. 1973. Gastric bypass for relief of morbid obesity. *Archives of Surgery* 106:428–431.

130. Pudel, V. E. 1975. Psychological observations on experimental feeding in the obese. In *Recent advances in obesity research, I,* ed. A. Howard, pp. 217–220. London: Newman.

131. ———. 1977. Human feeding in the laboratory. In *Recent advances in obesity research, II,* ed. G. Bray, pp. 66–74. London: Newman.

132. Quaade, F. 195?. *Obese children: Anthropology and environment.* Copenhagen: Dansk Videnskabs Forlag.

133. Reid, D. W., and Ware, E. E. 1973. Multidimensionality of internal-external control. Implications for past and future research. *Canadian Journal of Behavioural Science* 5: 264–271.

134. Reznick, H., and Balch, P. 1977. The effects of anxiety and response cost manipulations on the eating behavior of obese and normal-weight subjects. *Addictive Behaviors* 2: 219–225.

135. Ridgen, S. R., and Hagen, D. Q. 1976. Psychiatric aspects of intestinal bypass surgery for obesity. *American Family Physician* 13:68–71.

136. Robbins, T. W., and Fray, P. J. 1980. Stress-induced eating: Fact, fiction or misunderstanding? *Appetite* 1:103–133.

137. Robinson, S., and Winnik, H. 1973. Psychotic disturbances following crash diet weight loss. *Archives of General Psychiatry* 29:559–562.

138. Rodin, J. 1975. The effects of obesity and set point on taste responsiveness and intake in humans. *Journal of Comparative and Physiological Psychology* 89:1003–1009.

139. ———. 1975. Human obesity and external behavior. In *Recent advances in obesity research,* ed. A. Howard, pp. 191–193. London: Newman.

140. ———. 1977. Bidirectional influences of emotionality, stimulus responsivity and metabolic events in obesity. In *Psychopathology: Experimental models,* ed. J. Maser and M. Seligman, pp. 27–65. San Francisco: Freeman.

141. ———. 1977. Obesity: Why the losing battle? *McMaster Lecture Series.* Washington, D.C.: American Psychological Association.

142. ———. 1977. Research on eating behavior and obesity: Where does it fit in personality and social psychology? *Personality and Social Psychology Bulletin* 3:333–355.

143. ———. 1978. Stimulus-bound behavior and biological self-regulation: Feeding, obesity, and external control. In *Consciousness and self-regulation,* ed. G. Schwartz and D. Shapiro, vol. 2, pp. 215–239. New York: Plenum Press.

144. ———. 1980. Changes in perceptual responsiveness following jejunoileostomy: Their potential role in reducing food intake. *American Journal of Clinical Nutrition* 33: 457–464.

145. ———. 1980. The externality theory today. In *Obesity,* ed. A. J. Stunkard, pp. 226–239. Philadelphia: W. B. Saunders.

146. ———. 1981. The current status of the internal-external obesity hypothesis: What went wrong. *American Psychologist* 36:361–372.

147. ———. 1981. Psychological factors in obesity. In *Recent advances in obesity research, III*, ed. P. Björntorp, pp. 106–123. London: Libbey.

148. ———. 1981. Understanding obesity: Defining the samples. *Personality and Social Psychology Bulletin* 7:147–151.

149. ———. 1982. *Exploding the weight myths.* London: Century Press.

150. ———. 1982. Obesity: Why the losing battle? In *Psychological aspects of obesity*, ed. B. Wolman, pp. 30–87. New York: Van Nostrand Reinhold.

151. ———. 1985. Insulin levels, hunger and food intake: An example of feedback loops in body weight regulation. *Health Psychology* 4:1–18.

152. Rodin, J., and Slochower, J. 1976. Externality in the nonobese: The effects of environmental responsiveness on weight. *Journal of Personality and Social Psychology* 33: 338–344.

153. Rodin, J., Moskowitz, H. R., and Bray, G. A. 1976. Relationship between obesity, weight loss and taste responsiveness. *Physiology and Behavior* 17:591–597.

154. Rodin, J., Silberstein, L., and Striegel-Moore, R. 1985. Women and weight: A normative discontent. In *Nebraska Symposium on Motivation, 1984: Psychology and gender*, ed. T. B. Sonderegger, pp. 267–307. Lincoln: University of Nebraska Press.

155. Rodin, J., Slochower, J., and Fleming, B. 1977. The effects of degree of obesity, age of onset, and energy deficit on external responsiveness. *Journal of Comparative and Physiological Psychology* 91:586–597.

156. Rogers, P. J., and Blundell, J. E. 1980. Investigation of food selection and meal parameters during the development of dietary induced obesity (Abstract). *Appetite* 1:85.

157. Rolls, B. J., Rolls, E. T., and Rowe, E. A. 1980. Specific satiety and its influence on feeding (Abstract). *Appetite* 1:85–86.

158. Rolls, B. J., Rowe, E. A., and Rolls, E. T. 1982. The influence of variety on human food selection and intake. In *The psychobiology of human food selection*, ed. L. M. Barker, pp 101–122. Westport, Conn.: Avi Publishing.

159. Rolls, B. J., Van Duijenvoorde, P. M., and Rolls, E. T. 1984. Pleasantness changes and food intake in a variety four-course meal. *Appetite* 5:337–348.

160. Rolls, B. J., et al. 1981. Variety in a meal enhances food intake in man. *Physiology and Behavior* 27:137–142.

161. Rose, G. A., and Williams, R. T. 1961. Metabolic studies on large and small eaters. *British Journal of Nutrition* 15:1–9.

162. Rosenthal, B. S., and McSweeney, F. 1979. Modeling influences on eating behavior. *Addictive Behaviors* 4:205–214.

163. Rosenthal, B. S., and Marx, R. D. 1978. Differences in eating, patterns of successful and unsuccessful dieters, untreated overweight and normal weight individuals. *Addictive Behaviors* 3:129–134.

164. Ross, L. D. 1974. Effects of manipulating the salience of food upon consumption by obese and normal eaters. In *Obese humans and rats*, ed. S. Schachter and J. Rodin, pp. 43–51. Washington, D.C.: Erlbaum/Wiley.

165. Rothwell, N. J. 1980. Reversible obesity induced by "cafeteria" diets (Abstract). *Appetite* 1:87.

166. Rotter, J. B. 1966. Generalized expectancies for internal versus external control of reinforcment. *Psychological Monographs* 80:1–28.

167. Rowe, E. A., and Rolls, B. J. 1980. Persistent dietary obesity and regulatory challenges (Abstract). *Appetite* 1:86–87.

168. Rowland, N., and Antelman, S. M. 1976. Stress-induced hyperphagia and obesity in rats: A possible model for understanding human obesity. *Science* 191:310–311.

169. Rozin, P. 1976. Psychobiological and cultural determinants of food choice. In *Appetite and food intake*, ed. T. Silverstone, pp. 285–312. Berlin: Abakon.

170. Ruderman, A. J. 1983. The restraint scale: A psychometric investigation. *Behaviour Research and Therapy* 21:253–258.

171. Ruderman, A. A., and Wilson, G. T. 1979. Weight, restraint, cognitions and counterregulation. *Behaviour Research and Therapy* 17:581–590.

172. Sahakian, B. J., Lean, M. E. J., Robbins, T. W., and James, W. P. T. 1981. Salivation and insulin secretion in response to food in nonobese men and women. *Appetite* 2:209–216.

173. Sallade, J. 1973. A comparison of the psychological adjustment of obese vs. nonobese children. *Journal of Psychosomatic Research* 7:89–96.

174. Saltzstein, E. C., and Gutmann, M. C. 1980. Gastric bypass for morbid obesity: Preoperative and postoperative psychological evaluation of patients. *Archives of Surgery* 115: 21–28.

175. Schachter, S. 1971. *Emotion, obesity, and crime.* New York: Academic Press.

176. Schachter, S., and Gross, L. 1968. Manipulated time and eating behavior. *Journal of Personality and Social Psychology* 10:98–106.

177. Schachter, S., and Rodin, J. 1974. *Obese humans and rats.* Washington, D.C.: Erlbaum/Wiley.

178. Schachter, S., Friedman, L., and Handler, J. 1974. Who eats with chopsticks? In *Obese humans and rats,* ed. S. Schachter and J. Rodin, pp. 61–64. Washington, D.C.: Erlbaum/Wiley.

179. Schachter, S., Goldman, R., and Gordon, A. 1979. Effects of fear, food deprivation and obesity on eating. *Behaviour Research and Therapy* 17:581–590.

180. Segers, M. J., and Mertens, C. 1974. Psychological and bioclinical CHD risk factors: Quantitative differences between obese, normal and thin subjects. *Journal of Psychosomatic Research* 18:403–411.

181. Shipman, W. G., and Plesset, M. R. 1963. Anxiety and depression in obese dieters. *Archives of General Psychiatry* 8:530–535.

182. Siegel, P. S., and Pilgram, F. J. 1958. The effect of monotony on the acceptance of food. *American Journal of Psychology* 71:756–759.

183. Sigal, J., and Adler, L. 1976. Motivational effects of hunger on time estimation and delay of gratification in obese and non-obese boys. *Journal of General Psychology* 128:7–16.

184. Silverstone, J. T. 1968. Psychosocial aspects of obesity. *Proceedings of the Royal Society of Medicine* 61:371–375.

185. Sims, E. A. H., et al. 1973. Endocrine and metabolic effects of experimental obesity in man. *Recent Progress in Hormone Research* 29:457–496.

186. Singh, D. 1973. Role of response habits and cognitive factors in determination of behavior of obese humans. *Journal of Personality and Social Psychology* 27:220–238.

187. Singh, D., and Sikes, S. 1974. Role of past experience of food-motivated behavior of obese humans. *Journal of Comparative and Physiological Psychology* 86:503–508.

188. Sjoberg, L., and Persson, L. 1979. A study of attempts by obese patients to regulate eating. *Addictive Behaviors* 4:349–359.

189. Sjöström, L., Garellick, G., Krotkiewski, M., and Luyckx, A. 1980. Peripheral insulin in response to the sight and smell of food. *Metabolism* 29:901–909.

190. Slochower, J. 1976. Emotional labeling and overeating in obese and normal weight individuals. *Psychosomatic Medicine* 38:131–139.

191. ———. 1983. *Excessive eating: The role of emotions and environment.* New York: Human Sciences Press.

192. Slochower, J., and Kaplan, S. P. 1980. Anxiety, perceived control, and eating in obese and normal weight persons. *Appetite* 1:75–83.

193. Solow, C. 1977. Psychosocial aspects of intestinal bypass surgery for massive obesity: Current status. *American Journal of Clinical Nutrition* 30:103–108.

194. Solow, C., Silberfarb, P. M., and Swift, K. 1974. Psychosocial effects of intestinal bypass surgery for severe obesity. *New England Journal of Medicine* 290:300–304.

195. Speaker, J. G., Schultz, C., Grinker, J. A., and Stern, J. S. 1983. Body size estimation and locus of control in obese adolescent boys undergoing weight reduction. *International Journal of Obesity* 7:73–83.

196. Spencer, J. A., and Fremouw, W. J. 1979. Binge eating as a function of restraint and weight classification. *Journal of Abnormal Psychology* 88:262–267.

197. Spiegel, T. A. 1973. Caloric regulation of food intake in man. *Journal of Comparative and Physiological Psychology* 84:24–37.

198. Spitzer, L. B. 1983. The effects of type of sugar ingested on subsequent eating behavior. Ph.D. diss., Yale University, New Haven.

199. Spitzer, L., and Rodin, J. 1981. Human eating behavior: A critical review of studies in normal weight and overweight individuals. *Appetite* 2:293–329.

200. ———. 1983. Arousal-induced eating: Conventional wisdom or empirical findings. In *Social psychophysiology,* ed. J. Cappioco and R. Petty, pp. 565–591. New York: Guilford Press.

201. Stalling, R. B., and Friedman, L. 1976. Effect of experimenter's attire and fictitious food ratings on eating. In *Eating behavior of obese and non-obese females in a natural setting,* ed. D. K. Dodd, H. J. Birky, and R. B. Stalling. *Addictive Behaviors* 1:321–325.

202. Stricker, E., and Zigmond, M. 1976. Brain catecholamines and the lateral hypothalamic syndrome. In *Hunger: Basic mechanisms and clinical implications,* ed. D. Novin, pp. 19–32. New York: Raven Press.

203. Striegel-Moore, R., Silberstein, L., and Rodin, J. Toward a risk factor model of bulimia. Submitted for publication.

204. Stuart, R. B. 1967. Behavioral control of overeating. *Behaviour Research and Therapy* 5:357–365.

205. Stuart, R. B., and Davis, B. 1972. *Slim chance in a fat world.* Champaign, Ill.: Research Press.

206. Stunkard, A. J., and Kaplan, D. 1977. Eating in public places: A review of reports of the direct observation of eating behavior. *International Journal of Obesity* 1:89–101.

207. Stunkard, A. J., and Mazer, A. 1978. Smorgasbord and obesity. *Psychosomatic Medicine* 40:173–175.

208. Stunkard, A. J., and Messick, S. 1985. The three-factor eating questionnaire to measure dietary restraint, disinhibition and hunger. *Journal of Psychosomatic Research* 29: 71–83.

209. Stunkard, A. J., and Rush, A. J. 1974. Dieting and depression reexamined: A critical review of reports of untoward responses during weight reduction for obesity. *Annals of Internal Medicine* 81:526–533.

210. Stunkard, A. J., and Stellar, E. 1984. *Eating and its disorders.* New York: Raven Press.

211. Swanson, D. W., and Dinello, F. A. 1970. Follow-up of patients starved for obesity. *Psychosomatic Medicine* 32:209–214.

212. Thomason, J. A. 1983. Multidimensional assessment of locus of control and obesity. *Psychological Reports* 53(3):1083–1086.

213. Thompson, D. A., Moskowitz, H. R., and Campbell, R. G. 1976. Effects of body weight and food intake on pleasantness ratings for a sweet stimulus. *Journal of Applied Psychology* 41:77–83.

214. ———. 1977. Brief communication: Taste and olfaction in human obesity. *Physiological Behavior* 19:335–337.

215. Tom, G., and Rucker, M. 1975. Fat, full and happy: Effects of food deprivation, external cues and obesity on preference ratings, consumption and buying intentions. *Journal of Personality and Social Psychology* 32:761–766.

216. Van Itallie, T. B., Smith, N. S., and Quartermain, D. 1977. Short-term and long-term components in the regulation of food intake: Evidence for a modulatory role of carbohydrate status. *American Journal of Clinical Nutrition* 30:742–757.

217. Wadden, T. A., Stunkard, A. J., Brownell, K. D., and Day, S. C. 1984. Treatment of obesity by behavior therapy and very low calorie diet: A pilot investigation. *Journal of Consulting and Clinical Psychology* 52:692–694.

218. Wampler, R. S., et al. 1980. Psychological effects of intestinal bypass surgery. *Journal of Counseling Psychology* 27:492–499.

219. Warner, K. E., and Balagura, S. 1975. Intrameal eating patterns of obese and nonobese humans. *Journal of Comparative and Physiological Psychology* 89:778–783.

220. Weinberg, N., Mendelson, M., and Stunkard, A. 1961. Failure to find distinctive personality features in a group of obese men. *American Journal of Psychiatry* 117:1035–1037.

221. Wing, R. R., Carrol, C., and Jeffery, R. W. 1978. Repeated observation of obese and normal subjects eating in the natural environment. *Addictive Behaviors* 3:191–196.

222. Wooley, O. W. 1971. Long-term food regulation in the obese and nonobese. *Psychosomatic Medicine* 33:436–444.

223. Wooley, O. W., and Wooley, S. C. 1981. Relationship of salivation in humans to deprivation, inhibition and the encephalization of hunger. *Appetite* 2:231–350.

224. Wooley, O. W., Wooley, S. C., and Turner, K. 1975. The effects of rate of consumption on appetite in the obese and nonobese. In *Recent advances in obesity research, I,* ed. A. Howard, pp. 212–215. Proceedings of the First International Congress on Obesity. London: Newman Publishing.

225. Wooley, S. C. 1972. Physiologic versus cognitive factors in short-term food regulation in the obese and nonobese. *Psychosomatic Medicine* 34:62–68.

226. Wooley, S. C., Tennenbaum, P., and Wooley, O. W. 1985. A naturalistic observation on the influence of palatability of food choice of obese and nonobese. Unpublished manuscript.

227. Wooley, S. C., Wooley, O. W., and Dyrenforth, S. 1979. Theoretical, practical, and the social issues in behavioral treatment of obesity. *Journal of Applied Behavioral Analysis* 12:3–25.

228. Young, P. T. 1967. Palatability: The hedonic response to foodstuffs. *Handbook of Physiology* 1:353–366.

6

Diets for Weight Reduction: Nutritional Considerations

Patricia Nicholas and Johanna Dwyer

Introduction

Obesity increases the risk for several chronic degenerative diseases, so weight loss in those at risk should be encouraged. The method chosen should be intelligent, rational, and nutritionally sound.

The purpose of this chapter is to review the nutritional factors in weight reduction. We will examine one popular form of dieting that can be fraught with nutritional problems: the use of popular diet books. We will analyze several popular diets based on their caloric, other nutritional, and consumer-related characteristics. The turnover of popular diet books is extremely rapid, so most of the books we have chosen for analysis are likely to be off the shelves shortly. However, our analysis highlights some general rules that can also be used in critiquing new contenders.

Those who have existing health problems or conditions requiring chronic use of medication; those who have emotional problems; those who are pregnant, lactating, in a period of rapid growth; or those who have experienced serious difficulties in previous weight loss efforts should not follow self-prescribed diets. They should consult their physicians and dietitians for a more highly individualized nutrition plan. This chapter describes the general principles governing medically and nutritionally sound weight reduction plans. It is hoped that the developers of diet books and programs will adopt these criteria.

We thank the Culpepper Foundation for partial support provided to Dr. Dwyer for the completion of this manuscript, and Ms. Susan Hill for editorial assistance.

Why Nutrition Is Important to Consider in Weight Reduction

Five compelling reasons exist for ensuring that nutrition is considered in choosing an approach to weight reduction. First, it is important to ensure that a hypocaloric diet is nutritionally adequate. Protein is particularly important because it is both an energy-yielding constituent of foods and a nutrient that has other essential functions, among them the maintenance of lean tissues. When energy intake falls below the level needed for energy balance, the requirement for protein rises since some amino acids that could have been used for other functions are diverted into energy-yielding catabolic pathways. In general, for every 100-calorie deficit, 0.2 to 0.3 g more nitrogen are required to maintain nitrogen balance.[12] Very-low-calorie diets, particularly if low in protein, may deplete lean body mass rapidly and have other untoward effects, such as hair loss.

Hypocaloric diets also increase the risk of deficits in other nutrients, especially those that tend to be low in American diets, such as iron, magnesium, calcium, phosphorus, zinc, and vitamin B6. When reducing diets consist of unusual types or amounts of food, intakes of many nutrients may not meet recommended levels. Biochemical and clinical deficiencies may become apparent when a person follows an inadequate diet for several weeks or more. When diets are less than 1,000 calories, it is difficult to meet Recommended Dietary Allowances (RDA) for several vitamins and minerals without the use of supplements.

A second reason for considering nutrition is to encourage the individual to make food choices that will facilitate a sensible transition from weight loss to maintenance. For example, the use of skim milk and low-calorie beverages can prove helpful throughout life. All diets must educate participants about both energy levels and nutritional properties of foods so decisions can be nutritionally informed.

Third, there is now evidence that inadequate nutrition during weight reduction can have serious and even fatal consequences. Low-calorie liquid protein formula diets that were inadequate not only in the quality of the protein they contained, but possibly in micronutrients such as potassium, magnesium, and trace elements, have been associated with increased risk of sudden death.[23,57] Later studies found an association between these diets and cardiac irregularities.[33] Negative nitrogen balance with possible losses in lean body mass on these and other very-low-calorie diets for several weeks have also been documented.[16,26]

Fourth, the nutrient composition of diets is critical during periods in the life cycle when nutrient needs are especially high. Inadequate nutrients and micronutrients can influence stature, growth, and lean body mass in children.[47,50] Weight reduction efforts should also be avoided during pregnancy because of possible adverse effects on maternal stores and fetal outcomes, particularly birth weights.[43,55] When energy is restricted to control pregnancy weight gain, the diet must account for the increased need for protein, iron, folic acid, and most other minerals and vitamins. During times of special nutrient requirements (infancy, childhood, puberty, pregnancy, lactation), it is best to stress weight control through small decreases in intake and increased energy expenditure. If overweight children eat properly, they can "grow into" the excess weight by keeping weight stable while height increases. This can limit accumulation of adipose tissue while permitting growth in lean body mass. There is less risk of nutrient compromise after growth has ceased, so weight loss is a viable goal.

Fifth, there is evidence that the composition of the diet can influence diuresis, appetite, and satiety, all important in weight reduction.[66] One example is the rapid diuresis that occurs in the initial stages of diets low in carbohydrate.[67] Although the rapid weight loss is welcome, true loss of fat is no different from that on other diets of the same calorie level. Protein-supplemented modified fasts that are very low in calories and carbohydrate also induce a diuresis, and the individual remains relatively dehydrated as long as the regimen continues.[32]

As another example, low-fat diets are often difficult for patients to adjust to because of their low satiety value, while diets high in fat and cholesterol can increase serum lipids.[34] During the first week on both high- and low-carbohydrate hypocaloric diets, appetite increases. After adjustments on both types of diets appetite remains constant in spite of greater ketosis when carbohydrate is low.[51]

The balance of micronutrients may also affect physiological variables such as insulin release, neurotransmitter release, sympathetic nervous system activity, and diet-induced thermogenesis. For example, very-low-carbohydrate diets have been shown to produce hypoinsulinemia leading to greater fat mobilization and ketosis.[16] Carbohydrate consumption affects and is affected by levels of serotonin, a neurotransmitter, and sympathetic nervous system activity has been shown to decrease with the consumption of pure protein diets.[74] It is possible that a subgroup of obese individuals who crave carbohydrate respond positively to treatment with drugs that release brain serotonin, thus suppressing carbohydrate craving.[73]

Experiments on diet-induced thermogenesis suggest that lean and obese mice and rats differ in their ability to burn off excess energy as heat.[63] It has been suggested that obesity represents a malfunction of mechanisms involving diet-induced thermogenesis, and that these differences are enhanced when diets consist largely of one nutrient and are minimized when diets are more balanced.[49] These effects have not been demonstrated in humans.

It remains to be seen whether these effects have clinical significance for weight reduction. Nevertheless, caution must be exercised when considering drastic modifications in dietary composition until the positive and negative effects are better understood.

The usual American diet provides approximately 20 percent of total calories from protein, 38 percent from fat, and 42 percent from carbohydrate. Drastic perturbations in macronutrients can affect both morale and adherence. Alteration of macronutrient composition has advantages and disadvantages. A diet that is radically different may promote short-term adherence because it sets dieters apart from their usual habits. However, drastic diets are difficult to follow in the long term because food choices are so different from what is usually available. The end result is to discourage rather than encourage adherence.

Popular Weight-Loss Diets

The number of diet books sold each year is evidence of the multimillion-dollar industry that caters to dieters. Many of these books give little attention to nutrition. Some offer nutritionally balanced weight loss plans including behavior modification and psychological tips. Others promote dangerous diets based on pseudoscientific theory and misinformation. An increasing number promise cures not only for obesity but cancer and a variety of other health problems.

Serious health problems and even deaths have resulted from several popular diets. The Food and Drug Administration has received reports of deaths associated with the liquid protein diet popularized by the *Last Chance Diet.*[35] Regulatory agencies cannot act in all cases where health risks arise from popular diets. Therefore, health care professionals have a responsibility to be familiar with these therapies and to object when necessary to protect the public's health.

In this section we analyze a number of popular diet books to illustrate their nutritional benefits and disadvantages. We also present a classification scheme that can be used more generally for analyzing new diets.

Six major bookstores in Boston were surveyed during December 1983 to determine what diet books were being sold. Books that appeared in the health, fitness, and diet sections in two or more of the bookstores during a two-month period from December 1983 to January 1984 were considered for analysis. In order to include any books that might not have been on the shelves during the survey period, we also reviewed the Sunday *New York Times* book review section during December 1983 and January 1984 for best-selling diet books. However, no diet books were listed during this time. From the books most frequently available we eliminated volumes that had been reviewed elsewhere.[15]

The books chosen for analysis were *Aerobic Nutrition,*[38] *The Diet Center Program,*[25] *The Delicious Quick-Trim Diet,*[4] *Nutraerobics,*[7] *Fasting: The Ultimate Diet,*[14] *Dr. Abravanel's Body Type Diet and Lifetime Nutrition Plan,*[1] *The Over-30 All-Natural Health and Beauty Plan,*[39] *California Diet and Exercise Program,*[72] and *The Diet That Lets You Cheat.*[45] The books were analyzed to identify specific methods used to motivate and promote adherence.[18] Representative three-day food intakes were chosen for each diet. If menus were not provided, typical menus were devised from the guidelines provided in the text.

The records were analyzed using the nutrient data base of the University of Massachusetts at Amherst. Mean intakes for the three representative days were determined and expressed as a percentage of the 1980 RDA for adult women aged 23 to 50 years.[13] This standard of comparison was chosen since this is the age and sex of adults most likely to use reducing diets.[22]

For descriptive purposes, the diets were divided into four groups according to their energy levels: moderately low—greater than 1,100 calories; low—1,100 calories or less; very low—800 calories or less; and extremely low—500 calories or less. Diets were classified as low in carbohydrate if they provided less than 100 g of this nutrient per day and high in carbohydrate if carbohydrate constituted more than 40 percent of total calories. Low-protein diets were defined as those from which less than 10 percent of calories (or less than the appropriate recommended allowance of 44 g) came from protein, and high-protein diets were those in which protein provided more than 40 percent of total calories. Low- and high-fat diets were defined as less than 10 or more than 40 percent of calories from this source.

The menus were also categorized as to how well they met the RDAs for women aged 23 to 50 for protein, vitamins A, D, E, and C, thiamin, riboflavin, niacin, folacin, vitamins B6 and B12, calcium, phosphorus, magnesium, iron, and zinc. Values for crude fiber, total fat, cholesterol, and the polyunsaturated to saturated fat (P:S) ratio were also calculated. Menus were defined as not meeting the standard if their means averaged less than 80 percent of the RDA or less than the lower limit of the range of safe and estimated allowances for the electrolytes sodium and potassium.[13]

Table 6.1 outlines the psychological techniques used in the books to capture the dieter's attention and promote adherence. Most of the books claimed a startling "new" development at science's "cutting edge," and guaranteed weight loss and better health.

Most of the books mentioned a famous name to give "authority" to the plan and used marketing techniques or gimmicks that attempted to distinguish the diet from others. They made untenable scientific assertions and claimed reduced risk of chronic degenerative diseases. The books did not provide evidence supporting these claims, and several were dangerous from the health standpoint.

Table 6.2 shows the calories, proportion of energy-yielding nutrients, type of fat as expressed by the P:S ratio, and cholesterol provided by the diets. Calorie levels ranged from zero to 1,800 with the majority falling in the range of 800 to 1,100 calories. Protein intake ranged from zero on the fast to 38 percent of total calories on Dr. Abravanel's "P-Type" basic weight-loss diet. None of the diets except the fast could be classified

TABLE 6.1
Psychological Techniques Used in Popular Reducing Diets

Function and Technique	Description and Comments	Utilized By
Motivates dieter to embark on regime by: Gimmick marketing techniques	Informs dieter of a "new" remedy to the old problem of weight loss. Promotes special food, service, or other substance as vital to the diet.	*Diet Center Program* *Over-30 All-Natural Health and Beauty Plan* *Diet That Lets You Cheat* *Dr. Abravanel's Body Type Diet and Lifetime Nutrition Plan* *Delicious Quick-Trim Diet* *Nutraerobics*
Use of a famous name	The name of a well-known person or institution is used to give credibility to the diet.	*Diet Center Program* *Over-30 All-Natural Health and Beauty Plan* *California Diet and Exercise Program* *Aerobic Nutrition* *Delicious Quick-Trim Diet* *Nutraerobics* *Fasting: The Ultimate Diet*
"Scientific" and biochemical claims	Diet makes "new" scientific claims. Biochemical claims may be valid or unproven and speculative. Weight loss is likely due to a placebo effect that increases motivation or adherence if claims are not valid.	*Diet Center Program* *Diet That Lets You Cheat* *California Diet and Exercise Program* *Dr. Abravanel's Body Type Diet and Lifetime Nutrition Plan* *Aerobic Nutrition* *Delicious Quick-Trim Diet* *Nutraerobics* *Fasting: The Ultimate Diet*
Prophylactic claims	Diet is claimed to have other health promotional properties, such as reducing risks of chronic degenerative diseases and so on.	*Diet Center Program* *Over-30 All-Natural Health and Beauty Plan* *Diet That Lets You Cheat* *California Diet and Exercise Program* *Aerobic Nutrition* *Delicious Quick-Trim Diet* *Nutraerobics* *Fasting: The Ultimate Diet*
Stimulate adherence by: Fixed menus	No fixed calorie intake is specified. Fixed menus for each day place constraints on the number, kinds, and portion size of foods permitted. Exchange system provides general patterns of types and amounts of food permitted. The dieter is freed from temptation and possible misjudgments by clear instructions.	*Diet Center Program* *Over-30 All-Natural Health and Beauty Plan* *Diet That Lets You Cheat* *Dr. Abravanel's Body Type Diet and Lifetime Nutrition Plan* *Aerobic Nutrition* *Delicious Quick-Trim Diet*

TABLE 6.1, continued

Function and Technique	Description and Comments	Utilized By
"Crash" phase	Very low calorie levels are used initially to cause rapid weight loss, reward efforts, and encourage adherence. Other techniques such as ketogenic diets and fluid restriction may be used as well to encourage diuresis.	*Dr. Abravanel's Body Type Diet and Lifetime Nutrition Plan* *Delicious Quick-Trim Diet* *Nutraerobics* *Fasting: The Ultimate Diet*
Special foods or supplements	Special foods such as "health" or "natural" foods may be provided with claims that they assist weight loss; they have only placebo effects. Dietetic foods are slightly lower in calories than usual items. Dietary fiber such as bran or bulk producers may contribute to satiety but do not alter energy output.	*Diet Center Program* *Over-30 All-Natural Health and Beauty Plan* *California Diet and Exercise Program* *Dr. Abravanel's Body Type Diet and Lifetime Nutrition Plan* *Nutraerobics*
Reward and incentive foods	Built-in rewards such as candy, sweets, alcohol, and days off are used as incentives to adhere to the diet. While food rewards may provide rest from the restrictions of the diet, they may also promote nonadherence at other times.	*Diet That Lets You Cheat* *California Diet and Exercise Program*
Unpalatable or monotonous foods	Altered taste, flavor, texture, temperature, color, or variety of foods may decrease palatability and thereby decrease food intake.	*Nutraerobics*
Eating rituals	Special order of eating foods, timing, cooking practices, or recipes may help satisfy dieter's sensory pleasure from food and need for routine.	*Delicious Quick-Trim Diet*
Special conditions on eating or availability of foods in the environment	Specifications on time, place, speed, or circumstances of eating and requirements for weighing, measuring, and recording foods eaten are employed. Social milieu or suitable emotional states for eating are outlined to assist dieters in overcoming problem eating behaviors.	*Fasting: The Ultimate Diet*

TABLE 6.1, continued

Function and Technique	Description and Comments	Utilized By
Monitoring by another person	Checks on adherence by another person may be helpful to some individuals.	
Groups	Provide social support and/or pressure for dieter.	*Diet Center Program* (if used in conjunction with commercial Diet Center group)
Cognitive techniques	Stress reduction techniques such as relaxation, meditation, yoga, and positive thinking may improve adherence by decreasing stress or emotion-related overeating.	*Diet Center Program* *Over-30 All-Natural Health and Beauty Plan* *California Diet and Exercise Program* *Dr. Abravanel's Body Type Diet and Lifetime Nutrition Plan* *Delicious Quick-Trim Diet* *Fasting: The Ultimate Diet*

as a low-protein diet. Over half of the diets were low in fat. Nearly two-thirds provided less than 50 percent of calories from carbohydrates. The P:S ratio was at or above the usual recommended level (1.0) in less than half of the twenty-seven separate diets that were analyzed. Cholesterol content ranged from zero on *Fasting: The Ultimate Diet* to 904 mg on *Dr. Abravanel's Body Type Diet,* but about half the diets achieved the recommended level of 300 mg or less.[2]

The diets were also analyzed by servings of food groups and how they conformed to the Basic Four *Guide to Good Eating,*[64] since this is a common way by which individuals judge dietary adequacy. As shown in table 6.3, only 15 percent of menus provided sufficient servings from food groups.

Diets that provide less than 100 g of carbohydrate or less than 800 calories stimulate ketosis, which induces diuresis and loss of fluid weight in the first few days on the diet. Sodium levels under 1,000 mg, low fluid intakes, or the use of weak diuretics such as coffee and tea can also stimulate diuresis or temporary shifts in fluid balance. One-third of the diets had one or more such characteristics, usually low levels of carbohydrate and sodium, which would induce diuresis. Table 6.4 shows these characteristics.

Table 6.5 shows that none of the diets met recommended levels for all vitamins and minerals. Nutrients most likely to be low were iron, zinc, folacin, and vitamin B6. The use of vitamin or mineral supplements did not guarantee nutrient adequacy; several diets that included supplements, such as the *Diet Center Program* and the *Over-30 All-Natural Health and Beauty Plan,* were still low in some micronutrients since only a vitamin or mineral supplement was provided. Some diets had serious shortcomings in many nutrients. The most limited was Baker's *Delicious Quick-Trim Diet;* four different diet plans were described and all provided less than 80 percent of recommended amounts of calcium, phosphorus, zinc, iron, and vitamins B6, B12, and C.

TABLE 6.2

Nutrient Composition of Popular Diets

	Calories	Protein[a]	Carbo-hydrate[a]	Fat[a]	P:S Ratio ≥ 1.0	Cholesterol ≤ 300 mg
Diet Center Program						
Conditioning	1,771	27	45	31	•[b]	
Reducing	983	32	41	30	•	
Stabilization	1,377	34	30	37		
Maintenance	1,396	28	47	29		
Over-30 All-Natural Health and Beauty Plan						
Basic	1,115	31	26	45	•	
Maintenance	1,524	27	40	37	•	
Diet That Lets You Cheat	1,319	21	53	30		•
California Diet and Exercise Program	1,312	25	48	31	•	•
Dr. Abravanel's Body Type Diet and Lifetime Nutrition Plan[c]						
G-Type:						
Basic weight loss	1,019	24	55	24		•
Last five pounds	1,029	19	54	33		•
Maintenance	1,217	25	59	19		•
A-Type:						
Basic weight loss	1,120	32	50	20	•	•
Last five pounds	986	28	62	15		•
Maintenance	1,248	26	48	29	•	•
T-Type:						
Basic weight loss	1,132	36	30	34		
Last five pounds	928	37	31	32		
Maintenance	1,431	29	45	28		
P-Type:						
Basic weight loss	1,046	38	45	19		
Last five pounds	1,163	32	32	39		
Maintenance	1,111	28	47	28	•	
Aerobic Nutrition	1,111	28	47	28		•
Delicious Quick-Trim Diet						
Basic	956	36	45	20		•
Variety	1,146	25	48	31	•	•
Vegetable	946	16	72	20	•	•
Liquid	915	28	64	9		•
Nutraerobics	607	18	59	24		•
Fasting: The Ultimate Diet	0	0	0	0	•	•

[a] Percent of calories.
[b] Bullets signify agreement with statements in column headings.
[c] Body types are assigned to the individual on the basis of a system devised by Dr. Abravanel that is neither widely accepted nor necessarily judged to be valid by physical anthropologists.

Diet Typologies

In the absence of controlled trials of effectiveness, content analysis can be helpful in analyzing the popular reducing diets. Four factors must be considered: calorie levels, composition (the mix of energy-yielding nutrients and other nutrients), psychological techniques used for motivation,

TABLE 6.3

Basic Four Food Groups in Popular Diets

	Basic Food Groups[a]			
	Milk and Milk Products	Meat and Meat Substitutes	Breads and Starches	Fruit and Vegetables
Diet Center Program				
Conditioning		•[b]		•
Reducing		•		•
Stabilization		•		•
Maintenance		•		•
Over-30 All-Natural Health and Beauty Plan				
Basic		•		•
Maintenance		•		•
Diet That Lets You Cheat	•	•	•	•
California Diet and Exercise Program	•	•	•	•
Dr. Abravanel's Body Type Diet and Lifetime Nutrition Plan[c]				
G-Type:				
Basic Weight Loss	•	•		•
Last five pounds	•			•
Maintenance	•	•	•	•
A-Type:				
Basic weight loss	•	•		•
Last five pounds		•		•
Maintenance	•	•		•
T-Type:				
Basic weight loss	•	•		•
Last five pounds		•		•
Maintenance	•	•	•	•
P-Type:				
Basic weight loss		•		•
Last five pounds		•		•
Maintenance		•		•
Aerobic Nutrition		•		•
Delicious Quick-Trim Diet				
Basic		•		•
Variety		•		•
Vegetable				•
Liquid	•			•
Nutraerobics				
Fasting: The Ultimate Diet				

[a] Based on *The Guide to Good Eating.*[64]
[b] Bullets signify recommended servings included.
[c] Body types are assigned to the individual on the basis of a system devised by Dr. Abravanel that is neither widely accepted nor necessarily judged to be valid by physical anthropologists.

and consumer-related marketing considerations. We used these factors to predict the likely physiological effects of the diets and their usefulness to consumers. Three categories emerged from the analysis: (1) reasonable regimens low in calories, adequate in nutrients, balanced in energy-yielding nutrients, scientifically objective in presentation, based on tested psychological techniques, and straightforward in marketing practices; (2) questionable regimens that do not meet one or more of the preceding

TABLE 6.4

Diuresis-promoting Characteristics of Popular Diets

	Energy intake ≤ 800 calories	Carbohydrate Intake ≤ 100 g	Sodium Intake ≤ 1000 mg	Composition Promotes Ketosis and Fluid Weight Loss
Diet Center Program				
Conditioning			•ᵃ 928	•
Reducing				
Stabilization				
Maintenance				
Over-30 All-Natural Health and Beauty Plan				
Basic		• 73	• 608	•
Maintenance				
Diet That Lets You Cheat				
California Diet and Exercise Program				
Dr. Abravanel's Body Type Diet and Lifetime Nutrition Plan[b]				
G-Type:				
Basic weight loss			• 925	•
Last five pounds				
Maintenance				
A-Type:				
Basic weight loss				
Last five pounds				
Maintenance				
T-Type:				
Basic weight loss		• 84		•
Last five pounds		• 75		•
Maintenance				
P-Type:				
Basic weight loss				
Last five pounds		• 93		•
Maintenance				
Aerobic Nutrition				
Delicious Quick-Trim Diet				
Basic				
Variety				
Vegetable				
Liquid			• 879	•
Nutraerobics	• 607		• 522	•
Fasting: The Ultimate Diet	• 0	• 0	• 0	•

ᵃ Bullets signify agreement with statements in column headings.
ᵇ Body types are assigned to the individual on the basis of a system devised by Dr. Abravanel that is neither widely accepted nor necessarily judged to be valid by physical anthropologists.

criteria; and (3) fad diets that present clear health hazards, that are not administered under a physician's direction, that advocate exaggerated or false theories, or that are marketed to put the consumer at unreasonable monetary risk.

TABLE 6.5
Vitamin and Mineral Content

	Vitamin A	Vitamin D	Vitamin C	Thiamin	Riboflavin	Niacin	Folacin	Vitamin B6	Vitamin D12	Calcium	Phosphorus	Absorbable Iron	Zinc	Nutrient Supplements Recommended
Diet Center Program														
Conditioning	A	I	M	A	A	A	A	I	A	A	A	A	I	yes
Reducing	A	I	M	I	A	A	I	I	I	A	A	I	I	yes
Stabilization	A	A	A	M	M	M	A	M	M	A	A	I	I	yes
Maintenance	A	A	A	A	A	A	A	I	A	A	A	I	I	yes
Over-30 All-Natural Health and Beauty Plan														
Basic	M	A	M	M	M	M	A	M	M	I	A	I	I	yes
Maintenance	A	A	M	M	M	M	A	M	M	I	A	I	I	yes
Diet That Lets You Cheat	A	A	A	A	A	A	I	I	A	A	A	I	I	
California Diet and Exercise Program	A	A	A	A	A	A	I	I	A	A	A	I	I	
Dr. Abravanel's Body Type Diet and Lifetime Nutrition Plan[a]														
G-Type:														
Basic weight loss	A	A	A	A	A	A	I	I	A	A	A	I	I	
Last five pounds	A	I	A	A	A	A	A	I	I	A	A	I	I	
Maintenance	A	A	A	A	A	A	A	I	A	A	A	I	I	
A-Type:														
Basic weight loss	A	A	A	A	A	A	A	I	A	A	A	I	I	
Last five pounds	A	I	A	A	A	A	I	I	I	A	A	I	A	
Maintenance	A	I	A	A	A	A	I	I	A	A	A	I	A	
T-Type:														
Basic weight loss	A	A	A	A	A	A	I	I	A	A	A	I	I	
Last five pounds	A	A	I	I	I	A	A	I	I	A	A	I	I	
Maintenance	A	A	A	A	A	A	A	I	A	A	A	I	I	
P-Type:														
Basic weight loss	A	A	A	A	A	A	I	I	A	I	A	A	I	
Last five pounds	A	I	A	A	A	A	A	I	I	I	A	I	I	
Maintenance	A	A	A	A	A	A	I	I	A	A	A	A	I	
Aerobic Nutrition	A	A	A	A	A	A	A	I	A	A	A	I	I	
Delicious Quick-Trim Diet														
Basic	A	I	A	A	A	A	I	I	I	A	A	I	I	
Variety	A	I	A	A	A	A	A	I	I	I	I	I	I	
Vegetable	A	A	A	A	A	A	A	I	I	I	A	A	I	
Liquid	A	A	A	A	A	A	A	A	A	A	A	A	I	
Nutraerobics	I	I	I	A	A	A	I	I	I	A	I	I	I	yes
Fasting: The Ultimate Diet	I	I	I	I	I	I	I	I	I	I	I	I	I	

[a] Body types are assigned to the individual on the basis of a system devised by Dr. Abravanel that is neither widely accepted nor necessarily judged to be valid by physical anthropologists.

A = Adequate (80 percent or more than RDAs). I = Less than 80 percent RDAs. M = Megadose (10–100 times RDAs).

EXAMPLES OF FAD DIETS

Three books we examined were clearly fad diets. They were questionable in all respects.

Cott's *Fasting: The Ultimate Diet*[14] recommends self-initiated total fasts from a day to a month in length. Fasting brings about rapid weight loss but is fraught with other problems.[5,10,70,75] These include hepatic dysfunction, infection, cardiovascular complications, potassium loss, ketosis, dehydration, hyperuricemia, and psychiatric disorders. The book also ignores the need for vitamin and electrolyte supplements during the fast and popularizes a number of dangerous myths about metabolism during fasting. For example, the author claims that the fasts are not starvation because they are short and end before "true starvation" begins. Inasmuch as fasts of as long as a month are suggested, starvation would occur. Another myth the author promotes is that side effects such as headaches, nausea, and dizziness are healthy signs that the body is "ridding itself of toxins." Cited as evidence are historical figures who believed that fasting could rid the body of disease and mentally ill persons who made remarkable recoveries while fasting. In fact, fasting for long periods of time is synonymous with starvation. Lean body mass is depleted and other undesirable side effects result from total fasting.[5,10,70] Total fasting can precipitate adverse emotional reactions and certainly does not cure psychotic breaks or other acute episodes in emotionally unstable individuals.[51,61]

The impressive initial weight loss of one to two pounds each day on a total fast is mostly fluid weight associated with the depletion of glycogen, protein, and fat stores. When eating resumes, a rapid gain of several pounds can be expected.[28] The fasting plan does not attempt to modify eating and exercise habits after the diet is over, so the chances of maintaining the weight loss are poor.

Bland's *Nutraerobics*[7] suggests a protein-sparing modified fast consisting of 600 to 800 calories. A protein supplement would replace two of three daily meals. General guidelines discuss what constitutes a high-quality protein supplement and what nutrients should be included in the diet.

Even a metabolically adept consumer would have difficulty in planning such a fast. The protein products available commercially in supermarkets and drug and health food stores are not necessarily as well supplemented with vitamins and minerals as the special products and diet plans that have been successfully utilized under medical supervision.[3,24,48] The proprietary protein supplement we chose for our analysis was similar to the protein product *Nutraerobics* recommends. However, the diet we developed following the book's instructions was inadequate in vitamins A, D, C, B6, B12, and folacin, as well as in calcium, phosphorus, iron, and zinc. Most consumers would not know the diet was inadequate and would not and could not supplement it.

Unless patients are screened and monitored by a physician experienced in clinical nutrition, medical contraindications to supplemented fasts cannot be ruled out. We do not recommend self-administration of these diets. Protein-supplemented modified fasts are recommended only for patients with severe obesity (greater than 30 to 40 percent above ideal weight) and only when ongoing medical supervision is provided so fat loss can occur without dangerous changes in lean body mass and other sequelae.[20] The patient should undergo a cardiac evaluation prior to commencing the diet and remain under close medical supervision for its duration. Moreover, most persons on these diets relapse, so a sound plan for maintenance is essential.[69] The *Nutraerobics* regimen[7] can be faulted on all these counts.

Dr. Abravanel's Body Type Diet and Lifetime Nutrition Plan[1] is another book in the fad category. Various plans are provided, each targeting different foods (e.g., meat, butter, eggs, starches, dairy foods, spices, fats, oils) as the causes of weight gain. The book is based on the untenable assumption that each individual has dominant glands (gonads, adrenals, thyroid, or pituitary) that determine the body's reaction to food, and if they are "overworked" weight gain results. Dieters are to identify their body type and the dominant gland, and are then to follow a diet for that combination that would purportedly stimulate the "weaker" glands and give the dominant gland a rest. Types of food allowed, spacing of meals, and meal patterns are rigidly specified for each diet. These unproven interpretations of endocrinology are excellent examples of the marketing of pseudoscience. Several of the menus in this diet are ketogenic, most of the diets are unbalanced, the entire rationale of the diet is unproven, and lifetime use of diets that are very low in several micronutrients is suggested. Long-term consumption of such a diet could produce clinically evident deficiencies.

EXAMPLES OF QUESTIONABLE DIETS

On *The Delicious Quick-Trim Diet*,[4] intake of over half of the nutrients is below 80 percent of recommended levels, the diet is very low in breads and cereals, and several unproven claims are made for the regimen. Written by Sam Sinclair Baker, the co-author of the Stillman and Scarsdale diets,[59,62] the diet capitalizes on the wish for quick weight loss, although the claims are not supported by evidence.

The Diet Center Program[25] is a book is based on the program offered at commercial Diet Center clinics. It is questionable because the diet plans are not adequate for some vulnerable groups even with the recommended supplements. Also, some statements are not supportable, such as that milk products cannot be used because lactose interferes with weight loss. The book's philosophy is that counting nutrients rather than calories and controlling the blood sugar level are the keys to loss and maintenance. The use of Diet Center food products is emphasized. While the program has positive aspects, it should not be used by children since the diet is inadequate in nutrients for this age group, especially calcium.

The Diet Center book illustrates our finding that diets that require supplements are not necessarily superior to those relying solely on food sources. The Diet Center program recommends calcium and vitamin C supplements. The calcium supplement is indicated because the diet excludes the use of milk, but vitamin C is widely available in the foods allowed on the diet, and with supplements it totals ten times recommended levels. Ascorbic acid intakes greater than 60 mg may decrease efficiency of absorption and increase rates of excretion of unmetabolized ascorbic acid,[13] so high doses may be self-defeating. Even though the diet has excess vitamin C, it is low in vitamins D, thiamin, folacin, B6, and B12, and in iron, and zinc.

An example of a high-fat, ketogenic diet is the *Over-30 All-Natural Health and Beauty Plan*'s Basic Weight Loss Diet,[39] which calls for consumption of 73 g of carbohydrate daily. The author, a former model, claims that there is increased inability after age 30 to handle starchy carbohydrate resulting in fluid retention and weight gain. A low-carbohydrate, ketogenic diet is recommended. There is no evidence for this theory. All hard liquor, instant and overprocessed foods, chemical preservatives, white-flour products, beef, pork, and processed meats are forbidden for unsupported reasons. Megadoses of vitamins such as B6 are recommended, which may cause toxicities, ataxia, and severe sensorinervous system dysfunction.[53]

The major problems with ketogenic diets are elevated serum uric acid levels, fatigue, postural hypotension, and ketosis.[66] The diet is very high (e.g., 45 percent of total calories) in fat. Inasmuch as current recommendations for a prudent diet suggest eating less rather than more fat, the diet is contrary to the elements of sound nutrition.

The *Over-30* plan relies heavily on megadoses of nutrients, including vitamin B6, yet is below recommended levels for calcium, iron, and zinc, so the consumer could suffer from too little of some nutrients and too much of others.

Another questionable diet is *Aerobic Nutrition*,[38] written by a former Director of Medical Services at the Pritikin Longevity Center. The extremely-low-fat, high-fiber plan aims at decreasing triglyceride levels and increasing oxygen delivery to tissues. The author claims that the combination of diet and aerobic exercises helps prevent chronic degenerative diseases. The problem is that there is no reason to suggest that this particular combination of diet and exercise is any more effective than other programs involving low-fat diets and vigorous physical activity. In addition, claims of effects are poorly documented.

Only two of the diets, the *Diet Center Program*[25] and the *Over-30* plan,[39] provide adequate iron. This deficiency is significant because women in child-bearing years are the most frequent dieters. Some of them may be mildly anemic due to menstrual losses and marginal iron intake. While absorption rates increase with reduced intake, iron uptake may still be insufficient to prevent anemia. None of the diet plans recommend iron supplements.

Many of the books claim to be lifetime nutrition plans. More than half of the diets provide some information for maintaining the desired body weight, but weight maintenance is usually given only cursory treatment. For example, *Aerobic Nutrition*[38] and *Over-30 All-Natural Health and Beauty Plan*[39] allow the addition of specific portions to adapt the diet to maintenance. However, the dieter is still restricted in food choices. Long-term adherence may suffer when the prescribed foods differ greatly from the normal diet. *The Delicious Quick-Trim Diet*[4] recommends that the dieter use the weight-loss diet when a five-pound weight gain occurs; no provisions are made for a maintenance diet.

EXAMPLES OF REASONABLE DIETS

Only two examples of nutritionally adequate and reasonable diets were found among the books reviewed. *The California Diet and Exercise Program*[71] is one of these. The plan emphasizes a progressive exercise or "play" program and a moderately hypocaloric diet designed for healthy adults who want to lose moderate amounts of weight. One strong feature is the careful consideration of exercise as an adjunct to weight reduction. This has a sound physiological basis. The body adapts to lowered intake by decreasing basal metabolic rate. Regular and vigorous physical activity increases basal metabolism as well as energy output from the work itself. Exercise can help to decrease hunger and appetite among obese individuals while preserving lean body mass.[17] In contrast to the weight loss achieved by diet alone (approximately 75 percent fat and 25 percent lean body mass), the combination of diet and exercise may increase fat loss and decrease loss of lean tissue.[8,66] Exercise programs have also decreased the percentage of body fat[6] and improved aerobic capacity.[31] The dietary aspects of the *California Diet* are also sensible. Diet plans ranging from 1,200 to 2,800 calories are provided. The eating plans become more liberal as the dieter increases physical activity.

A second reasonable diet is the *Diet That Lets You Cheat.*[45] The diet was adapted from the authors' experience with a community weight-loss program. It involves three phases, requiring increased participation by the dieter in menu planning while remaining within calorie restrictions. The dieter is rewarded by being allowed a 300-calorie "forbidden" food once each week. Although the book sometimes reads as a confusing mixture of a professional journal article (complete with literature review) and a popular diet book, the information provided is sound.

Providing Nutritional Advice to Obese Persons

No single regimen is appropriate for reduction of body fatness. However, there are general guidelines that are useful in the planning of the dietary aspects of treatment.[20,41,77]

The cornerstone to any obesity treatment program is a complete screening. The medical aspects of the workshop are detailed elsewhere.[11,20] They include, at a minimum, verification of the extent of the obesity, differential diagnosis to ascertain if the obesity is primary or secondary, and assessment of coexisting conditions such as high blood pressure, hyperlipidemias, glucose intolerance, cigarette smoking, excessive use of alcohol, sedentary life style, and other factors that may perpetuate the obesity or influence the treatment. Exercise evaluation and stress testing may also be in order if increased activity is recommended.

Often neglected are the motivational aspects of the screening. It is important to ascertain the patient's degree of commitment. Does the patient accept the inevitable long-term commitment to lose weight? Details of assessing motivation are provided elsewhere.[20] It is common to find motivation combined with fear of failure. It is important to work at the patient's level of motivation. Building confidence by setting attainable goals is preferable to seeking wholesale dietary reform immediately. Some patients find it easier to begin with physical activity and only moderate dietary changes, while others must lose weight before starting an exercise program. Guides for establishing a reasonable program are now available.[9,46]

Most patients are willing to attempt some dietary changes, so the next step in the screening involves diet and food habits. The dietary assessment is as important as the medical workup and requires equal care.[20] It involves assessing the nature and degree of the desire to lose weight, a personal history of weight status, a family history of obesity, diet and activity records, and an assessment of the personal, occupational, social, and environmental factors that are obstacles or incentives for weight control. In our experience this information is best obtained from food and activity records on which patients also note behavioral, situational, or emotional problems. These aid in later planning of behavioral programs.[27]

Patients should keep diet records prior to the first counseling session.[27,37] These can be mailed in and analyzed using microcomputer programs to assess energy and nutrient intakes and to determine patterns of food selection.[21] If records are to be useful, the patient must be instructed to keep exact accounts of type and amount of food.

The next step, usually at the second visit, is to set realistic weight goals with the patient. The recent revision of the Metropolitan Life Insurance Company reference weights has confused many patients and health personnel.[40,56] Actually, the midpoint weights for medium frames are slightly lower in most categories than the earlier tables. However, for females under 62 inches, midpoint weights are 5 to 7 pounds heavier than earlier recommendations, but in some instances somewhat lower targets may be appropriate. In general, however, individuals 20 percent over the midpoint of values in the new tables can be considered to be obese.[52] A medically realistic target weight for an individual will vary, depending on body build, cosmetic considerations, and the presence of coexisting medical conditions (i.e., high blood pressure, glucose intolerance, and hyperlipidemias) that may respond favorably to weight loss. While it is helpful to set a tentative, ultimate target, more attention should be paid to interim target weights. Specific weight targets are less important than the process of conjoint planning and decision making.

At this point, it is important to reassess the patient's motivation and understanding of the condition. Can the patient identify behaviors in the food records that contribute to obesity and analyze barriers to changing life style? Are the goals realistic, and is the individual able to put decisions to act into writing? If the answer to any of these questions is negative, the patient will need help on these issues before the weight-loss program begins in earnest.

The advisable treatment options vary depending on degree of overweight and health status. Moderate degrees of overweight (e.g., less than 30 percent overweight) and severe obesity carry different risks and suggest different treatments.[20] Since moderately obese patients are most commonly encountered in clinical practice, the options for them will be discussed. These include treatment by a physician or referral to a registered dietitian, commercial weight-loss group, voluntary self-help group, workplace prevention program, or some combination of these. Regardless of which is chosen, the person with medical responsibility should be involved in formulating the diet, exercise, and behavioral treatment plan.

Major aspects of nutritional care include an exchange plan or some other nutritionally adequate hypocaloric diet at a calorie level appropriate to the individual. Also included are therapeutic guidelines for special medical conditions, specific recommendations or referrals for exercise and behavior modification, targets, objectives and means of measuring them, and a schedule for follow-up.

Table 6.6 summarizes examples of basic principles of counseling sessions. The dieter should be instructed on choosing appropriate foods within a caloric restriction, changing eating behaviors, and increasing physical activity. Each area must be individualized to deal with the problems specific to the dieter and to the behavioral objectives specified in the treatment contract each session. Provisions for social and psychological support are also critical. The patient with a significant amount of weight to lose will require continued support and encouragement to make the needed life style changes.

TABLE 6.6
Guidelines for Weight Loss

Eat Within Calorie Restrictions

Use low-fat, low-calorie food preparation methods. Steaming, broiling, and baking provide fewer calories than frying.

Try skim and low-fat foods. Milk, yogurt, and cheese are available in a low-fat form. Poultry and fish are good examples of lean protein foods.

Choose a wide variety of foods from the "allowed" list. Limiting the variety eaten will limit the vitamin and mineral content of the diet as well as make it monotonous.

Avoid the "extras." Sauces, gravies, and breading as well as second helpings add unwanted calories.

Change Eating Behaviors

Keep a food diary. Having to write down the food eaten will call attention to problem foods and times.

Replace emotion-related eating with physical activity. Reach for a jumprope instead of the box of doughnuts when angry or depressed.

Limit the number of rooms eaten in. Excess calories are often consumed in bed or in front of the television.

Increase Physical Activity

Choose an activity program that can be followed. Interest, ability, and convenience will affect adherence.

Do it with a friend. Someone with similar abilities can offer support and encouragement.

Keep moving. Since calories are expended with activity, pace while talking on the phone, walk instead of driving whenever possible, and use the stairs instead of the elevator.

Conclusion

Obesity is among the most common health-related conditions afflicting Americans. Obesity varies according to socioeconomic circumstances, and it is common in all age groups, particularly middle-aged and older women.[54] Excessive weight is associated with increased mortality rates.[54] Many persons embark on reducing diets;[19] opinion polls estimate that at any one time approximately 16 percent of the population is dieting to lose weight and that only half regard their efforts as successful.[44] However, neither outpatient medical treatments nor longitudinal studies of populations provide much hope of long-term success.[30,60,65]

When diets were first advocated for the treatment of obesity, it was assumed that understanding caloric values of foods was sufficient to produce weight loss. When it became clear that knowledge alone was not enough, theories that both knowledge and motivation were necessary came into vogue. Later an emphasis on behavior modification, social support, and environmental influences became part of successful reducing formulas. Today, in addition to these factors, self-knowledge and learning of specific skills and behaviors to put motivation into action are also recognized as being important.[65]

We focused on popular diet books because these are among the worst offenders from the standpoint of nutritional and medical accuracy. Space permitted only a cursory review of the more common medically supervised interventions used in outpatient settings, but others have covered their strengths and weaknesses in greater depth.[36,58,65,76] They too may have nutritional shortcomings. Regardless of the modality utilized, it is important for professionals to assist laypersons in making nutritionally sound choices among treatments for obesity and to provide them with medical and psychological assistance when needed. At the same time, it is important to continue to extend our knowledge about the physiological effects of these regimens.[29,42,68]

REFERENCES

1. Abravanel, E. D., and King, E. A. 1983. *Dr. Abravanel's body type diet and lifetime nutrition plan.* New York: Bantam Books.
2. AMA Council on Foods and Nutrition and the Food and Nutrition Board of the National Academy of Sciences-National Research Council. 1972. Diet and coronary heart disease: A council statement. *Journal of the American Medical Association* 222:1647.
3. Amatruda, J. M., Biddle, T. L., Patton, M. L., and Lockwood, D. H. 1983. Vigorous supplementation of a hypocaloric diet prevents cardiac arrhythmias and mineral depletion. *American Journal of Medicine* 74:1016–1022.
4. Baker, S. S., and Schur, S. 1983. *The delicious quick-trim diet.* New York: Villard Books.
5. Ball, M. F., Canary, J. J., and Kyle, L. H. 1967. Comparative effects of calorie restitution and total starvation on body composition and obesity. *Annals of Internal Medicine* 67:60–67.
6. Björntorp, P. 1976. Exercise in the treatment of obesity. *Clinical Endocrinology and Metabolism* 5:431–451.
7. Bland, J. 1983. *Nutraerobics.* San Francisco: Harper & Row.
8. Brownell, K. D. 1984. The psychology and physiology of obesity: Implications for screening and treatment. *Journal of the American Dietetic Association* 84:406–413.
9. Brownell, K. D., and Stunkard, A. J. 1980. Physical activity in the development and control of obesity. In *Obesity*, ed. A. J. Stunkard, pp. 300–324. Philadelphia: W. B. Saunders.
10. Cahill, G. F., and Owen, O. E. 1970. Body fuels and starvation. *International Psychiatric Clinics* 7:25–40.
11. Calloway, C. W. 1985. Unproven but popular approaches in the treatment of obesity. In *Dietary treatment in the prevention of obesity: Proceedings of satellite conference on dietetics,* International monographs on obesity, ser. no. 2, ed. R. Frankle, J. Dwyer, L. Moragne, and A. Owen, pp. 11–20. London: John Libbey.
12. Calloway, D. H., and Spector, A. 1954. Nitrogen balance as related to caloric and protein intake in active young men. *American Journal of Clinical Nutrition* 2:405–411.
13. Committee on Dietary Allowances. 1980. *Recommended dietary allowances,* 9th rev. ed. Washington, D.C.: National Academy of Sciences.
14. Cott, A. 1981. *Fasting: The ultimate diet.* New York: Bantam Books.
15. Dazzi, A., and Dwyer, J. 1974. Nutritional analysis of popular reducing diets. *International Journal of Eating Disorders* 3:61.
16. Dehaven, J., Sherwin, R., Hendler, R., and Felig, P. 1980. Nitrogen and sodium balance and sympathetic nervous system activity in obese subjects treated with a low calorie protein or mixed diet. *New England Journal of Medicine* 302:477–482.
17. Durrant, M. L., Royston, J. P., and Wloch, R. T. 1982. Effect of exercise on energy intake and eating patterns in lean and obese humans. *Physiology and Behavior* 29:449–454.
18. Dwyer, J. 1980. Patient-oriented perspectives on management of obesity-related

problems of adolescents. In *Advances in human nutrition,* vol. 1, ed. R. Tobin and M. Mehlman, pp. 263–304. Park Forest, Ill.: Pathotox Publishers.

19. Dwyer, J. T., and Mayer, J. 1970. Potential dieters: Who are they? *Journal of the American Dietetic Association* 56:510–514.

20. ———. 1983. Obesity and coronary heart disease. In *Primary prevention of coronary heart disease: A practical guide for clinicians,* ed. R. N. Podell and M. M. Stewart, pp. 120–150. Menlo Park, N.J.: Addison-Wesley.

21. Dwyer, J., and Suitor, C. W. 1984. Caveat emptor: Assessing needs, evaluating computer options. *Journal of the American Dietetic Association* 84:302–312.

22. Dwyer, J. T., Feldman, J. J., and Mayer, J. 1970. The social psychology of dieting. *Journal of Health and Social Behavior* 11:269–287.

23. Felig, P. 1978. Four questions about protein diets (editorial). *New England Journal of Medicine* 298:1025–1026.

24. ———. 1984. Very low calorie protein diets (editorial). *New England Journal of Medicine* 310:589–591.

25. Ferguson, S. 1983. *The diet center program.* Boston: Little, Brown.

26. Fisler, J. S., Drenick, E. J., Blumfield, D. E., and Swenseid, M. E. 1982. Nitrogen economy during very low calorie reducing diets: Quality and quantity of dietary protein. *American Journal of Clinical Nutrition* 35:471–486.

27. Foreyt, J. P., and Gotto, A. M. 1979. Behavioral treatment of obesity. In *Atherosclerosis reviews,* ed. A. M. Gotto and R. Paoletti, pp. 179–201. New York: Raven Press.

28. Friedman, R. B., Kindy, P., and Reinke, J. A. 1982. What to tell patients about weight loss methods. *Postgraduate Medicine* 72:73–80.

29. Gariel, D. R., Todd, K. S., and Calloway, D. H. 1984. Effects of marginally negative energy balance on insulin binding to erythrocytes of normal men. *American Journal of Clinical Nutrition* 39:716–721.

30. Garn, S. M., and Cole, P. E. 1980. Do the obese remain obese and the lean remain lean? *American Journal of Public Health* 80:351–352.

31. Hadjiolova, I., et al. 1982. Physical working capacity in obese women after an exercise programme for body weight reduction. *International Journal of Obesity* 6:405–410.

32. Howard, A. N., and Baird, I. M. 1981. Physiopathology of protein metabolism in relation to very low calorie regimes. In *Recent advances in obesity research III,* ed. P. Björntorp, M. Cairella, and A. N. Howard, pp. 124–129. London: John Libbey.

33. Lantingua, R. A., et al. 1980. Cardiac arrhythmias associated with a liquid protein diet for the treatment of obesity. *New England Journal of Medicine* 303:735–738.

34. Lewis, S. B., Wallin, J. D., Kane, J. P., and Gerich, J. E. 1977. Effect of diet composition on metabolic adaptations to hypocaloric nutrition: Comparison of high carbohydrate and high fat isocaloric diets. *American Journal of Clinical Nutrition* 30:160–170.

35. Linn, R., and Stuart, S. L. 1976. *The last chance diet.* Secaucus, N.J.: Lyle Stuart.

36. McBean, C. 1984. Weight control. *Dairy Council Digest* 55:1–4.

37. Mahoney, M. J., and Mahoney, K. 1976. *Permanent weight control.* New York: W. W. Norton.

38. Mannerberg, D., and Roth, J. 1981. *Aerobic nutrition.* New York: Berkley Books.

39. Martin, E. 1982. *The over-30 all-natural health and beauty plan.* New York: Bantam Books.

40. Metropolitan Insurance Company. 1983. *Metropolitan height and weight tables.* New York: Metropolitan Insurance Company.

41. Munves, E. 1980. Managing the diet. In *Obesity,* ed. A. J. Stunkard, pp. 262–275. Philadelphia: W. B. Saunders.

42. Newmark, S. R., and Williamson, B. 1983. Survey of very low calorie weight reduction diets 1. Novelty diets II: Total fasting, protein sparing modified fasts, chemically defined diets. *Archives of Internal Medicine* 143:1195, 1198, 1423–1427.

43. Oldham, H., and Sheft, B. B. 1951. Effect of caloric intake on nitrogen utilization during pregnancy. *Journal of the American Dietetic Association* 27:847–854.

44. Pacific Mutual Life Insurance Company. 1978. *Health maintenance: Weight and obesity.* N.P.: Pacific Mutual Life Insurance Company.

45. Parr, R. B., Bachman, D. C., and Bates Noble, H. 1983. *The diet that lets you cheat.* New York: Crown.

46. Peab, C., and Tillotson, J. L. 1983. *Heart to heart: A manual on nutrition counseling for the reduction of cardiovascular disease risk factors.* NIH Publication no. 83-1528. Washington, D.C.: U.S. Department of Health and Human Services.

47. Phillips, L. S. 1981. Nutrition, metabolism and growth. In *Endocrine control of growth*, ed. W. H. Daughaday, pp. 121–173. New York: Elsevier.

48. Phinney, S. D., et al. 1983. Normal cardiac rhythm during hypocaloric diets of varying carbohydrate content. *Archives of Internal Medicine* 143:2258–2261.

49. Pothwell, N. J., Stock, M. J., and Tyzbir, R. S. 1982. Energy balance and mitochondrial function in liver and brown fat of rats fed cafeteria diets of varying protein content. *Journal of Nutrition* 112:1163–1172.

50. Pugliese, M. T., et al. 1983. Fear of obesity: A cause of short stature and delayed puberty. *New England Journal of Medicine* 309:513–518.

51. Rosen, J. C., Hunt, D. A., Sims, E. A. H., and Bogardus, C. 1982. Comparison of carbohydrate containing and carbohydrate restricted hypocaloric diets in the treatment of obesity: Effects on appetite and mood. *American Journal of Clinical Nutrition* 36:464–469.

52. Russell, R. M., McGandy, R. B., and Jellife, D. B. 1984. Reference weights: Practical considerations. Manuscript.

53. Schaumberg, H., et al. 1983. Sensory neuropathy from pyridoxine abuse. *New England Journal of Medicine* 309:445–448.

54. Simopoulos, A. P., and Van Itallie, T. B. 1984. Body weight, health and longevity. *Annals of Internal Medicine* 100:285–295.

55. Simpson, J. W., Lawless, R. W., and Mitchell, A. C. 1975. Responsibility of the obstetrician to the fetus. II. Influence of pregnancy weight and pregnancy weight gain on birthweight. *Obstetrics and Gynecology* 45:481–487.

56. Society of Actuaries and Associations of Life Insurance Medical Directors of America (New York). 1979. Blood pressure study.

57. Sours, H., et al. 1981. Sudden death associated with very low calorie weight reduction regimens. *American Journal of Clinical Nutrition* 34:453–461.

58. Stern, J. S., and Kane Nussen, B. 1979. Obesity: Its assessment, risks and treatments. In *Human nutrition: A comprehensive treatise*, ed. R. B. Alfin Slater and D. Kritchevsky, pp. 347–407. New York: Plenum Press.

59. Stillman, I. M., and Baker, S. 1977. *The doctor's quick weight loss diet*. New York: Dell.

60. Stunkard, A. J., and McLaren Hume, M. 1959. The results of treatment for obesity: A review of the literature and report of a series. *Archives of Internal Medicine* 103:29–85.

61. Stunkard, A. J., and Rush, J. 1974. Dieting and depression reexamined: A critical review of reports of untoward responses during weight reduction for obesity. *Annals of Internal Medicine* 81:526–533.

62. Tarnower, H., and Baker, S. S. 1978. *The complete Scarsdale medical diet*. New York: Bantam Books.

63. Tulp, O. B., Frink, R., and Danforth, E. 1982. Effect of cafeteria feeding on brown and white adipose tissue cellularity, thermogenesis, and body composition in rats. *Journal of Nutrition* 112:2250–2260.

64. U.S. Department of Agriculture, Food and Nutrition Service. 1979. *Building a better diet*, no. 1241. Washington, D.C.: U.S. Department of Agriculture.

65. Van Itallie, T. B. 1980. Dietary approaches to the treatment of obesity. In *Obesity*, ed. A. J. Stunkard, pp. 249–261. Philadelphia: W. B. Saunders.

66. ———. 1980. Diets for weight reduction: Mechanisms of action and physiological effects. In *Obesity: Comparative methods of weight control*, ed. G. Bray, pp. 15–24. London: John Libbey.

67. Van Itallie, T. B., and Yang, M. U. 1977. Current concepts in nutrition: Diet and weight loss. *New England Journal of Medicine* 297:1158–1160.

68. ———. 1984. Cardiac dysfunction in obese dieters: A potentially lethal complication of rapid massive weight loss. *American Journal of Clinical Nutrition* 39:695–702.

69. Wadden, T. A., Stunkard, A. J., and Brownell, K. D. 1983. Very low calorie diets: Their efficacy, safety, and future. *Annals of Internal Medicine* 99:675–684.

70. Weinsier, R. L. 1971. Fasting: A review with emphasis on electrolytes. *American Journal of Medicine* 50:233–239.

71. Wing, R. R., and Jeffery, R. W. 1979. Outpatient treatments of obesity: A comparison of methodology and clinical results. *International Journal of Obesity* 3:261–279.

72. Wood, P. 1983. *California diet and exercise program*. Mountain View, Calif.: Anderson World Books.

73. Wurtman, J. J., et al. 1981. Carbohydrate craving in obese people: Suppression by treatments affecting serotonergic transmission. *International Journal of Eating Disorders* 1:2–15.

74. Wurtman, R. S. 1983. Behavioral effects of nutrients. *Lancet,* 1145–1147.

75. Yang, M. U., and Van Itallie, T. B. 1976. Composition of weight lost during short term weight reduction. *Journal of Clinical Investigation* 58:722–728.

76. Yates, B. 1980. Improving the cost-effectiveness of obesity programs: Three basic strategies for reducing the cost per pound. In *Obesity: Comparative methods of weight control,* ed. G. Bray, pp. 151–168. London: John Libbey.

77. Zifferblatt, S. M., and Wilbur, C. S. 1977. Dietary counseling: Some realistic expectations and guidelines. *Journal of the American Dietetic Association* 70:591–595.

7

Obesity: The Role of Physical Activity

Judith S. Stern and Patricia Lowney

If there were a commandment for treating obesity it would be: "Thou shalt exercise." People who exercise regularly weigh less (see figure 7.1), have a lower percentage of body fat, and may eat more than sedentary individuals.[8,38] Yet, when surveying the scientific literature on the treatment of obesity, one cannot help but come away impressed with the dramatic effects of caloric restriction and underwhelmed by the minor contribution of exercise to most weight-loss programs. While this may be a democratic assessment of the literature, we think it is a shortsighted one. It ignores the possible contributions of exercise to the prevention of obesity (especially for those at high risk) and to the maintenance of a reduced weight. Exercise's contribution to weight loss and maintenance must be viewed over many months—even years. When evaluating the effectiveness of exercise in obesity treatment programs, there is the additional problem of adherence—50 percent of individuals who begin an exercise program drop out within the first six months.[16]

This chapter presents a brief overview of the contribution of physical activity to energy balance, and the role of exercise in obesity treatment programs and in the maintenance of a reduced body weight. Finally, suggestions are offered to improve adherence to exercise programs.

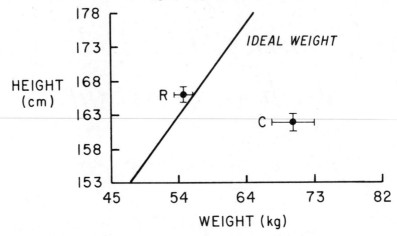

FIGURE 7.1

*Relative weights for twenty-seven long-distance female runners and forty-two controls
ranging in age from 35 to 59 years. Runners ran at least 24 km per week
(average = 55 km/wk). Average daily caloric intake was 2,386 kcal for runners
and 1,871 kcal for controls. "Ideal" weight is based on the 1959 Metropolitan Life
Height/Weight Table.*

SOURCE: S. N. Blair et al., 1981, Comparison of nutrient intake in middle-aged men and women runners
and controls, *Medicine and Science in Sports and Exercise* 13:310–315.

Energy Balance

Obesity is a disorder of energy balance that occurs when energy input
exceeds energy output. The components of energy expenditure include
resting metabolic rate, the thermic effect of food, the thermic effect of
activity, and thermogenesis produced in response to changes in environmental conditions.[54] Of these various components of energy expenditure,
activity or exercise is the "easiest" to increase. In a weight-stable 70-kg
man consuming 2,500 kcal per day, resting metabolism contributes approximately 60 percent, or 1,500 kcal, while physical activity is approximately 30 percent, or 750 kcal.[54] In a very active individual, the contribution of physical activity to energy expenditure can be several times
resting metabolism.

Some of the difficulty in evaluating the effectiveness of exercise in the
treatment of obesity is that its impact on energy intake or food intake is
variable. Exercise is reported to increase, decrease, or have no effect on
the amount of food consumed. Most studies of obesity in humans do not
include careful monitoring of food intake. Where monitoring occurs,
methods are usually inaccurate; in addition, the process of keeping records
or being observed can influence food intake.[43] In one study using self-
reports to assess food intake, obese subjects underreported their actual

food intake.[3] There are also a number of other methodological variables that make direct comparisons between studies difficult. The effects of exercise on food intake and body weight depend in part on the type, intensity, duration, and frequency of exercise as well as the individual's age, sex, and degree of obesity.

TYPE OF EXERCISE

In studies using rats, forced exercise programs include treadmill or wheel running or swimming. Running wheels are primarily used in spontaneous exercise protocols. Human exercise programs commonly studied include walking, cycling, and jogging.

Male rats forced to run on a treadmill typically decrease their twenty-four-hour food intake or decrease food intake while the lights are on, and decrease weight gain.[1,37,38] This is, in part, related to the intensity of the exercise. However, exercising rats increase their food intake on rest days.[47] Also, retirement from treadmill exercise is associated with a marked increase in food intake.[2,47,50]

In contrast, female rats do not decrease and may even increase food intake in response to an exercise program.[1,37,50] While weight gain is maintained in female rats, body fat is less in exercised than in sedentary rats.[1] This phenomena is age related. Older female rats (19 months) may initially lose weight or exhibit a decreased gain using a forced exercise protocol of intensity comparable to that of younger rats.*

How food intake is suppressed in male rats is unclear. Oscai has proposed that the "stress" of the forced exercise may cause a release of catecholamines which could then influence food intake.[38] In these experiments investigators often "motivate" the rats to run by shock grids. Since shock is commonly known to depress food intake in the rat, investigators who shock their rats frequently may be studying the effects of shock stress rather than the effects of exercise on food intake. A similar phenomenon may occur when rats are forced to swim. To ensure active participation by all rats, rats are often forced to swim with weights on their tails and in groups of four to five.

In our laboratory, a less stressful approach to treadmill exercise is used. Electric shock is used minimally or not at all, there is a long adaptation or training period, and rats are exercised in the dark—a time when they are normally active.[1,2] Under these conditions, a moderate exercise program (21 meters per minute, 1 hour daily) had no effect on total food intake in male rats. In another study, male rats that exercised voluntarily on running wheels actually increased their food intake.[48] The more the rats ran, the more they ate. The impact of exercise can be greater in obese rats. In a study of young genetically lean and obese male rats (*fafa*), running was associated with no change in food intake in lean rats but a

* R. McDonald, 1985. Personal communication.

TABLE 7.1

Approximate Energy Expenditure by a Healthy Adult Weighing About 150 Lb

Activity	Calories/Hour
Lying quietly	80–100
Sitting quietly	85–105
Standing quietly	100–120
Walking slowly, 2½ mph	210–230
Walking quickly, 4 mph	315–345
Light work (i.e., ballroom dancing, cleaning house, office work, shopping)	125–310
Moderate work (i.e., cycling, 9 mph; jogging, 6 mph; tennis; scrubbing floor; weeding garden)	315–480
Hard work (i.e., aerobic dancing; basketball; chopping wood; cross-country skiing; running, 7 mph; shoveling snow; spading garden; swimming, crawl stroke)	480–625

SOURCE: U.S. Department of Agriculture, U.S. Department of Health and Human Services, 1985, *Dietary Guidelines for Americans,* Home and Garden Bulletin no. 232, 2nd ed.

decrease in obese rats.[42] The percent of body fat is decreased in most studies using running wheels, but body weight can be decreased,[42] unchanged,[42] or even increased[39] in comparison to sedentary rats.

INTENSITY AND DURATION

Intensity refers to the energy cost per minute (kcal/min) of the activity. A healthy human adult weighing about 150 lb, for example, expends only 80 to 100 kcal per hour while sitting quietly and reading (see table 7.1).[49] In contrast, walking slowly doubles energy expenditure, and running may result in a four- to sixfold elevation. These figures do not take into account increases in metabolic rate that may occur for many hours following exercise* or the possible effects of exercise on the thermic effects of a meal.[14,24,] These would further increase the contribution of exercise to energy expenditure.

In male rats, exercise tends to depress food intake. Wilmore has postulated that this is related to the intensity of the exercise (for review, see Wilmore[53]). However, evaluation of the effects of intensity are complicated by the experimental designs of many studies. Total energy expenditure is often variable. When total energy expenditure of the exercise bout was held constant, exercise of moderate intensity (16 m/min, 10 percent grade, 50 min) resulted in a greater depression in twenty-four-hour food intake in male rats than did a very mild exercise program (5 m/min, 0 percent grade, 60 min).[31] The depression in food intake was greatest for the one hour following the exercise period.

In contrast, when total energy expenditure was variable, there was no correlation between intensity of exercise and food intake.[19] Rats were forced to run on a treadmill at a final speed of 20, 27, or 35 meters per

* See references 4, 21, 24, 32, and 41.

minute for one hour daily for seven weeks. In all three groups of exercised rats, despite equal reductions in food intake and unequal increases in energy expenditures, decreases in body weight gain and body fat were similar. These results are puzzling. In this study the differences in the intensity of exercise (20 m/min versus 27 versus 35) were not as great as in the first study (5 m/min, 0 percent grade versus 16 m/min, 10 percent grade), and seven weeks may not be a long enough time to detect small differences. A potential problem is that neither study[19,31] measured spontaneous activity in the home cage for the twenty-three hours when the rats were not exercising. It is possible that rats that ran 36 meters per minute were spontaneously less active than rats running 20 meters per minute. Nonetheless, in both studies, exercised rats ate less and gained less weight than did sedentary rats.

It is difficult to make direct comparisons between studies of rats and humans. In athletically untrained college-age females involved in an aerobic exercise program, caloric intake was inversely related to the mean running speed of a one- or two-mile run.[22] Those women who ran at the fastest rates (i.e., where intensity was the greatest) consumed more calories per day than did women who ran at a slower rate. However, caloric intake was not correlated with body weight.

In an often-quoted study by Mayer and coworkers, *duration* (the length of time of a bout of exercise) of a treadmill intermittent exercise/rest protocol was studied in adult female rats.[36] When rats exercised only twenty to sixty minutes daily, intake and body weight were actually less than sedentary values. With exercise bouts greater than one hour in duration, food intake increased and body weight was unchanged as the time spent exercising increased. This has been called the range of proportional response. With exercise duration greater than six hours, food intake and body weight decreased, probably due to exhaustion. Mayer and colleagues reported a similar relationship between duration and food intake in adults employed in a jute factory in West Bengal, India.[35] This, however, was a retrospective study.

These studies are often quoted to encourage sedentary obese individuals to exercise, in the hope that with a modest increase in physical activity food intake will actually decrease, but these results have not been replicated. An example is a carefully controlled study by Woo and colleagues, who studied six obese women at three activity levels (sedentary, mild, and moderate) for three nine day treatment periods (see table 7.2).[55] Subjects walked on a treadmill, and duration was varied. Food intake was unchanged with exercise, but energy expenditure increased as the duration of activity increased. Thus, caloric balance (caloric input minus caloric output) ranged from −41 kcal per day for sedentary and −423 kcal per day for moderate exercise. However, for moderately active people who are not obese, chronic exercise promotes increased caloric intake. For example, middle-aged men and women joggers consumed more calories than sedentary controls who were actually shorter and heavier (see figure 7.1 for women).[8]

TABLE 7.2

Effects of Exercise on Food Intake and
Energy Balance in Six Obese Women

Treatment	Caloric Balance (kcal / day)		
	Intake	*Output*	*Difference*
Sedentary	2180 ± 146	2221 ± 71	− 41
Mild Exercise	2267 ± 179	2419 ± 68	−152
Moderate Exercise	2291 ± 204	2714 ± 119	−423

SOURCE: R. Woo, J. S. Garrow, and Pi-Sunyer F. X., 1982, Effect of exercise on spontaneous calorie intake in obesity, *American Journal of Clinical Nutrition* 36: 470–477.

NOTE: Women were studied for three nine-day treatment periods: sedentary (no exercise), mild exercise (110 percent of sedentary expenditure), and moderate exercise (125 percent of sedentary expenditure). Subjects used a motorized treadmill (2.5 percent grade) and chose their own rate of walking (about 3 mph). Duration of exercise was based in individual rates of expenditure.

All of the aforementioned studies have looked at the chronic effects of exercise. In contrast, in adult rats, a single bout of exercise ranging in duration from two to six hours decreases food intake on the day of the experiment.[44] The decrease is greatest for the longest exercise period. Furthermore, the closer the next mealtime was to the termination of the exercise, the greater the anorexia. In humans, the acute effects of exercise also decrease food intake immediately after exercise. In a fourteen-day study of military cadets, food intake was carefully measured and energy expenditure was calculated from diaries.[20] Food intake was depressed on exercise days and increased on rest days. There was no correlation between food intake and energy expenditure in the same day; they were correlated two days later.

Exercise and Obesity Treatment

Although obese humans and laboratory animals are not always less active than those of normal weight, inactivity is often associated with obesity in individuals of all ages. Genetically obese rats and mice and rats made obese with electrolytic lesions are considerably less active than their lean littermates.[38] In obese humans, inactivity has been observed in infants,[40] children,[12] and adults.[13] For example, in one twenty-eight-day intensive study, obese housewives (N = 6) had normal to slightly elevated energy intake levels and sharply reduced activity levels.[13] Fifth-grade elementary schoolchildren who spent the greatest portion of their time (37.1 percent) in physical activities were the leanest and ate the most (1,976 kcal) (see table 7.3).[12] In contrast, the obese children spent only 22.7 percent of

TABLE 7.3

Comparison of Activity and Calories Consumed by Fifth-grade Elementary Schoolchildren Varying in Body Fat Levels

	Obese	Higher than Average Fat	Lower than Average Fat	Very Lean
N	12	15	12	11
Total activity (percent of time)	22.7%	30.2%	33.5%	37.1%
Average daily kcal	1814	1931	1908	1976
Age (years)	9.9%	9.7%	10%	10%
Weight (lb)	99.4%	78.5%	72.0%	67.4%
Percentage of body fat	28.0%	18.8%	11.9%	6.1%

SOURCE: C. B. Corbin and P. Pletcher, 1968, Diet and physical activity patterns of obese and nonobese elementary schoolchildren, *Research Quarterly* 39:922–931.

their time being physically active and had the lowest energy intake (1,814 kcal).

However, decreased spontaneous activity in obese persons does not necessarily mean decreased energy expenditure. Because of their higher body weight, obese individuals spend more energy for a given activity than do normal-weight individuals—a point that is often overlooked in most studies of obesity, food intake, and exercise. Waxman and Stunkard[51] studied caloric intake and expenditure of an obese boy and a nonobese brother in four families. In comparison to their lean brothers, the obese boys spent more energy outside the home and similar amounts inside the home.

While some obese individuals are clearly less active than those of normal body weight, the contribution of inactivity to the development of obesity remains unclear. In some cases, inactivity is a primary factor in the development of obesity. In one study of hospitalized patients with adult-onset obesity, onset in 68 percent of patients was linked with forced inactivity due to illness or injury.[26] In most cases of obesity, however, the link between onset and inactivity is not readily apparent. Such a link is more readily studied in experimental animals.

Forced inactivity can promote obesity in normally lean rats[30] and in genetically obese yellow (A^ya) mice.[10] In A^ya mice, moderate obesity develops when mice are housed normally in standard cages but is dramatically retarded when mice are allowed access to running wheels.[10] Exercise training also reduces excessive weight gain when normally lean rats are fed either a varied, palatable "cafeteria" diet[28] or a diet high in fat.[2] These effects were shortlived. When the exercise training program was terminated, rats gained weight more rapidly than did the sedentary controls.[2]

For the obese Zucker rat (*fafa*), the onset of inactivity is coincident with weaning, an age when body-weight differences are not readily apparent although carcass fat is elevated in the obese.[42] While both voluntary and involuntary exercise programs will slightly retard the development of obesity in these rats, the rats are still grossly obese.[42,50] Inactivity, while not a primary factor in the development of obesity in the Zucker rat, does contribute to fat accretion.

The effectiveness of exercise alone in the treatment of obesity is difficult to evaluate because of its variable effect on body weight and problems with adherence (which will be discussed later). Wilmore, in his excellent review of the effects of physical training on body composition, summarized the results of forty studies of men and nineteen of women that lasted from 6 to 104 weeks.[53] Initial percent of body fat ranged from 8.2 to 39.1 percent. Wilmore reported weight gain or slight losses (0.5 kg or less) in 37.5 percent of the studies of men and 52.6 percent of the studies of women. However, in 82.5 percent of the studies of men and 73.7 percent of the studies of women, percent of body fat decreased by at least 0.5 percent.

The amount of exercise needed to decrease body weight and body fat is a function of the duration and intensity of the exercise. Björntorp suggested that at least two months of training is necessary to significantly reduce body fat, provided the exercise is strenuous enough.[5] For example, in one such study, subjects exercised three times a week for six weeks.[7] Included in the exercise period were three 5-minute periods of cycling on an ergometer just below maximal working capacity. Body fat of nonobese and obese subjects decreased by approximately 1 kg. This approached significance in the nonobese ($p < .1$). In another study of patients who suffered a myocardial infarction, body fat decreased by approximately 7 kg over a nine-month period without restriction of energy intake.[6] Leon and colleagues[33] reported an average body-weight loss of 5.7 kg for six sedentary obese men who completed sixteen weeks of a vigorous walking program consisting of treadmill exercise for ninety minutes daily, five days per week, expending about 1,100 kcal per session. Food intake initially increased and progressively decreased so that by week sixteen it was actually below pretraining levels. Finally, Gwinup[27] reported that obese women who walked at least thirty minutes daily lost an average of 9.1 kg by the end of one year, while those who walked less than thirty minutes daily did not lose significant amounts of weight.

Adherence to Exercise Programs

Nearly 50 percent of American adults do not participate in vigorous physical activity. In addition, 50 percent of those who begin an exercise program typically discontinue their participation within six months.[23] Adherence is also a major problem in the treatment of obesity, where attrition ranges from 20 to 80 percent.[45]

TABLE 7.4

Five Strategies to Improve Adherence to an Exercise Program

1. Find a place to exercise that is conveniently located.
2. Make exercise enjoyable.
   a. Choose activities that you like to do.
   b. Vary the type of exercise and the setting.
   c. Make exercise more enjoyable by exercising alone, with another person, or in a group, as you prefer.
3. Don't expect too much too soon. Exercise doesn't have to hurt to be beneficial. Fitness takes time—think months rather than days.
4. Keep a daily exercise log. But avoid becoming excessively goal-oriented.
5. Finally, if you are having trouble staying with your exercise program, think of some activity that you really like to do or have to do. Don't do the preferred activity until you have exercised.

SOURCE: H. B. Falls, A. M. Baylor, and R. K. Dishman, 1980, *Essentials of fitness,* Philadelphia: Saunders College, p. 180.

Although it is not possible to predict with great accuracy who will drop out of an exercise program, several studies have attempted to characterize these individuals (for review see Dishman[17]). In comparison to the individual who completes an exercise program in a preventive medical exercise setting, dropouts tend to be overweight[15,18] and have low self-motivation.[18] No differences are observed with respect to attitudes toward physical activity, self-perceptions of physical abilities, and feelings of health responsibility.[17]

Adherence can usually be enhanced in a group setting,[17] although for some a personalized home-based program may be more practical.[52] Adherence also increases if the exerciser's spouse is supportive of the program and if the exercise is not excessively stressful in terms of discomfort or injury.[17] Accessibility of the exercise is critical. In one study of college professors, those who elected to participate in an exercise program and were still involved seven years later had offices significantly closer to the exercise facility than those who chose not to partake in the program.[23] Similarly, proximity to the exercise facility was a major determinant of exercise involvement for business executives. Table 7.4 offers some strategies to help the individual to improve adherence to an exercise program.

As suggested in a study by Brownell, Stunkard, and Albaum,[9] making people more aware of opportunities to be physically active and of some health benefits could alter exercise patterns. The authors made over 45,000 observations of individuals using stairs and an adjacent escalator at a shopping mall, a train station, and a bus station. In these settings only six percent of the people used the stairs (see figure 7.2). Obese subjects showed a significantly lower level of stair use than did nonobese subjects (1.5 percent versus 6.7 percent, respectively). When a simple sign pointing out the benefits of exercise was placed at the bottom of the stairs/escalator choice point, there was a dramatic increase in the use of the stairs (see figure 7.2). Once again, use was lower among obese subjects (7.8 percent) than among nonobese subjects (14.9 percent). In a second study, when

FIGURE 7.2

Lower panel represents percent of subjects using stairs where stairs and escalators were adjacent at a shopping mall, train station, and bus terminal. A total of 45,694 observations were made. Each baseline period represents two weekly measurements. Each "sign" period represents two weekly measurements during which a colorful sign (see upper panel) was positioned at the stair/escalator choice point.

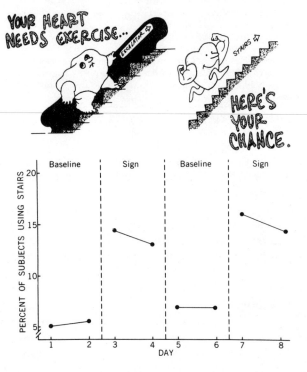

NOTE: K. D. Brownell, A. J. Stunkard, and J. M. Albaum, 1980, Evaluation and modification of exercise patterns in the natural environment, *American Journal of Psychiatry* 137:1540–1545.

the sign was present for fifteen consecutive days, stair use remained elevated.[9] Although stair use decreased during a one-month follow-up period, it took two more months to return to baseline.

Exercise and Weight Maintenance

In 1959, Stunkard and McLaren-Hume reviewed the results of thirty years of obesity treatment[46] and concluded that most obese persons will not stay in treatment for obesity. Of those who stay in treatment, most will not lose weight and, of those who do lose weight, most will regain it.

TABLE 7.5
Use of Exercise in Weight Loss and Maintenance[a]

Sex	Age (Yrs)	Weight Loss (Lb)	Method of Weight Loss			Important Factors in Weight Maintenance		
			Exercise Daily	Diet Only	Exercise and Diet	Increased Exercise	Vigorous Exercise	Nutritional Knowledge
Female (N = 41)	40.0	53.2	2%	93%	5%	78%	24%	66%
Male (N = 13)	45.5	76.2	8%	8%	85%	85%	85%	77%

SOURCE: R. H. Colven and S. B. Olson, 1983, A descriptive analysis of men and women who have lost significant weight and are highly successful at maintaining the loss, *Addictive Behaviors* 8:287–295.
[a] A descriptive analysis of male and female subjects who lost at least 20 percent of body weight and maintained loss for at least two years. Results represent averages.

Changes made in eating and exercise during a weight-loss program are often short-lived. However, when subjects continue to exercise after successfully losing weight, there is evidence that increased physical activity may help individuals maintain a reduced body weight.[11,25,29,34]

Colven and Olson[11] surveyed subjects who had lost at least 20 percent of their body weight and had maintained this loss for at least two years (see table 7.5). Very few subjects used exercise alone as a method to lose weight. Most women used diet only, while most men used a combination of diet and exercise. However, the overwhelming majority of women and men claimed that increased exercise was important to weight maintenance.

In another study, forty-seven individuals who had reached their goal weight within the preceding one to twelve months were followed for up to one year.[34] "Maintainers" were more likely to exercise several times weekly and less likely to eat for emotional reasons.

Conclusion

The restriction of caloric intake is perhaps the most important component of a weight-reduction program. The addition of exercise can increase the rate of fat loss, decrease the loss of lean body mass, and in some individuals could increase resting metabolic rate, improve glucose tolerance, improve mood, alleviate mild depression, and improve self-concept. There is increasing evidence that one very significant contribution of daily physical activity is increased success in weight maintenance. Finally, increased physical activity could be of special benefit to individuals with relatively low caloric requirements and to those who respond to a modest increase in activity by decreasing food intake.

REFERENCES

1. Applegate, E. A., Upton, D. E., and Stern, J. S. 1982. Food intake, body composition, and blood lipids following treadmill exercise in male and female rats. *Physiology and Behavior* 28:917–920.

2. ———. 1984. Exercise and detraining: Effect on food intake, adiposity and lipogenesis in Osborne-Mendel rats made obese on a high fat diet. *Journal of Nutrition* 114:447–459.

3. Beaudoin, R., and Mayer, J. 1953. Food intakes of obese and nonobese women. *Journal of the American Dietetic Association* 29:29–33.

4. Benedict, F. G., and Cathcart, E. P. 1913. *Muscular work: A metabolic study with special reference to the efficiency of the human body as a machine.* Washington, D.C.: Carnegie Institute Publication no. 187.

5. Björntorp, P. 1976. Exercise in the treatment of obesity. *Clinics Endocrinology and Metabolism* 5:431–453.

6. Björntorp, P., et al. 1972. Effects of physical training on glucose tolerance, plasma insulin and lipids and on body composition in men after myocardial infarction. *Acta Medica Scandinavica* 192:439–443.

7. Björntorp, P., et al. 1977. Physical training in human hyperplastic obesity. IV. Effects on hormonal status. *Metabolism* 26:319–328.

8. Blair, S. N., et al. 1981. Comparison of nutrient intake in middle-aged men and women runners and controls. *Medicine and Science in Sports and Exercise* 13:310–315.

9. Brownell, K. D., Stunkard, A. J., and Albaum, J. M. 1980. Evaluation and modification of exercise patterns in the natural environment. *American Journal of Psychiatry* 137:1540–1545.

10. Carpenter, K. J., and Mayer, J. 1958. Physiologic observations on yellow obesity in the mouse. *American Journal of Physiology* 193:499–504.

11. Colvin, R. H., and Olson, S. B. 1983. A descriptive analysis of men and women who have lost significant weight and are highly successful at maintaining the loss. *Addictive Behaviors* 8:287–295.

12. Corbin, C. B., and Pletcher, P. 1968. Diet and physical activity patterns of obese and nonobese elementary school children. *Research Quarterly* 39:922–931.

13. Curtis, D. E., and Bradfield, R. B. 1971. Long-term energy intake and expenditure of obese housewives. *American Journal of Clinical Nutrition* 24:1410–1417.

14. Davis, J. M., Sadri, S., Ward, D., and Rocchio, L. 1985. Effects of pre-prandial and post-prandial exercise on energy expenditure. *International Journal of Obesity* 9:A22.

15. Dishman, R. K. 1981. Biologic influences on exercise adherence. *Research Quarterly for Exercise and Sport* 52:143–159.

16. ———. 1982. Compliance/adherence in health-related exercise. *Health Psychology* 1:237–267.

17. ———. 1981. Contemporary sport psychology. *Exercise and Sport Sciences Reviews* 10:120–159.

18. Dishman, R. K., Ickes, W., and Morgan, W. P. 1980. Self-motivation and adherence to habitual physical activity. *Journal of Applied Social Psychology* 10:115–132.

19. Dohm, G. L., Beecher, G. R., Stephenson, T. P., and Womack, M. 1977. Adaptations to endurance training at three intensities of exercise. *Journal of Applied Physiology* 42:753–757.

20. Edholm, O. G., Fletcher, J. G., Widdowson, E. M., and McCance, R. A. 1955. The energy expenditure and food intake of individual men. *British Journal of Nutrition* 9:286–300.

21. Edwards, H. T., Thorndike, A., and Dill, D. B. 1935. The energy requirement in strenuous muscular exercise. *New England Journal of Medicine* 213:532–535.

22. Epstein, L. H., Wing, R. R., and Thompson, J. K. 1978. The relationship between exercise intensity, caloric intake, and weight. *Addictive Behaviors* 3:185–190.

23. Falls, H. B., Baylor, A. M., and Dishman, R. K. 1980. *Essentials of fitness.* Philadelphia: Saunders College.

24. Gleeson, M., Brown, J. F., Waring, J. J., and Stock, M. J. 1982. The effects of physical exercise on metabolic rate and dietary-induced thermogenesis. *British Journal of Nutrition* 47:173–181.

25. Gormally, J., Rardin, D., and Black, S. 1980. Correlates of successful response to a behavioral weight control clinic. *Journal of Counseling Psychology* 27:179–191.

26. Greene, J. A. 1939. Clinical study of the etiology of obesity. *Annals of Internal Medicine* 12:1797–1803.

27. Gwinup, G. 1975. Effect of exercise alone on the weight of obese women. *Archives of Internal Medicine* 135:676–680.

28. Hill, J. O., Davis, J. R., and Tagliaferro, A. R. 1983. Effects of diet and exercise training on thermogenesis in adult female rats. *Physiology and Behavior* 31:133–135.

29. Hoiberg, A., Berard, S., Watten, R. H., and Caine, C. 1984. Correlates of weight loss in treatment and at follow-up. *International Journal of Obesity* 8:457–465.

30. Ingle, D. J. 1949. A simple means of producing obesity in the rat. *Proceedings of the Society for Experimental Biology and Medicine* 72:604–605.

31. Katch, V. L., Martin, R., and Martin, J. 1979. Effects of exercise intensity on food consumption in the rat. *American Journal of Clinical Nutrition* 32:1401–1407.

32. Lennon, D., et al. 1985. Diet and exercise training effects on resting metabolic rate. *International Journal of Obesity* 9:39–47.

33. Leon, A. S., Conrad, J., Hunninghake, D. B., and Serfass, R. 1979. Effects of a vigorous walking program on body composition and carbohydrate and lipid metabolism of obese young men. *American Journal of Clinical Nutrition* 32:1776–1787.

34. Marston, A. R., and Criss, J. 1984. Maintenance of successful weight loss: Incidence and prediction. *International Journal of Obesity* 8:435–439.

35. Mayer, J., Roy, P., and Mitra, K. P. 1956. Relation between caloric intake, body weight and physical work: Studies in an industrial male population in West Bengal. *American Journal of Clinical Nutrition* 4:169–175.

36. Mayer, J., et al. 1954. Exercise, food intake and body weight in normal rats and genetically obese adult mice. *American Journal of Physiology* 177:544–548.

37. Nance, D. M., Bromley, B., Barnard, R. J., and Gorski, R. A. 1977. Sexually dimorphic effects of forced exercise on food intake and body weight in the rat. *Physiology and Behavior* 19:155–158.

38. Oscai, L. 1973. The role of exercise in weight control. *Exercise and Sport Sciences Reviews* 1:103–123.

39. Ring, G. C., Bosch, M., and Chu-Shek, L. 1970. Effects of exercise on growth, resting metabolism and body composition of Fischer rats. *Proceedings of the Society for Experimental Biology and Medicine* 133:1162–1165.

40. Rose, H. E., and Mayer, J. 1969. Activity, caloric intake, fat storage and the energy balance of infants. *Pediatrics* 41:18–29.

41. Schultz, C. L., et al. 1980. Effects of severe caloric restriction and moderate exercise on basal metabolic rate and hormonal status in adult humans. *Federation Proceedings* 39:783.

42. Stern, J. S., and Johnson, P. R. 1977. Spontaneous activity and adipose cellularity in the genetically obese Zucker rat (fafa). *Metabolism* 26:371–380.

43. Stern, J. S., Grivetti, L., and Castonguay, T. W. 1984. Energy intake: Uses and misuses. *International Journal of Obesity* 8:535–541.

44. Stevenson, J. A. F., Box, B. M., Feleki, V., and Beaton, J. R. 1966. Bouts of exercise and food intake in the rat. *Journal of Applied Physiology* 21:118–122.

45. Stunkard, A. J., and Brownell, K. D. 1979. Behavior therapy and self-help programs for obesity. In *The treatment of obesity,* ed. J. F. Munro, pp. 199–230. London: MTP Press.

46. Stunkard, A. J., and McLaren-Hume, M. 1959. The results of treatment for obesity. *Archives of Internal Medicine* 103:79–85.

47. Thomas, B. M., and Miller, A. T., Jr. 1958. Adaptation to forced exercise in the rat. *American Journal of Physiology* 193:350–354.

48. Tokuyama, K., Saito, M., and Okuda, H. 1982. Effects of wheel running on food intake and weight gain of male and female rats. *Physiology and Behavior* 28:899–903.

49. U.S. Department of Agriculture, U.S. Department of Health and Human Services. 1985. *Dietary Guidelines for Americans.* Home and Garden Bulletin no. 232, 2nd ed.

50. Walberg, J. L., Mole, P. A., and Stern, J. S. 1982. Effect of swim training on development of obesity in the genetically obese rat. *American Journal of Physiology* 242: R204–R211.

51. Waxman, M., and Stunkard, A. J. 1980. Caloric intake and expenditure of obese boys. *Journal of Pediatrics* 96:187–193.

52. Wilhelmsen, L., et al. 1975. A controlled trial of physical training after myocardial infarction. *Preventive Medicine* 4:491–508.

53. Wilmore, J. H. 1983. Body composition in sport and exercise: Directions for future research. *Medicine and Science in Sports and Exercise* 15:21–31.

54. Woo, R., Daniels-Kush, R., and Horton, E. S. 1985. Regulation of energy balance. *Annual Review of Nutrition* 5:411–433.

55. Woo, R., Garrow, J. S., and Pi-Sunyer, F. X. 1982. Effect of exercise on spontaneous calorie intake in obesity. *American Journal of Clinical Nutrition* 36:470–477.

8

Treatment of Childhood Obesity

Leonard H. Epstein

Obesity is prevalent in children and is associated with increased risk of adult obesity. The importance of treating childhood obesity and preventing these children from becoming obese adults is underscored by the poor treatment results with adults. Most programs produce small losses,[77] and maintenance is poor.[74] This chapter will provide information on the treatment of childhood obesity. The relative risks of childhood obesity at various ages will be considered, and the importance of family factors on the development of obesity will be reviewed. Behavioral risk factors associated with childhood obesity will be covered, and behavioral treatments of childhood obesity will be presented.

The Risks of an Obese Child Becoming an Obese Adult

At least four studies have evaluated the risk of obese children becoming obese adults (see table 8.1). Charney and associates[14] studied relationships between infant and adult weight, with infant obesity defined as weight greater than the ninetieth percentile at 6 months and adult obesity as greater than 20 percent over ideal weight. Fourteen percent of the over-

The preparation of this chapter and the research presented from our laboratory were supported in part by grants 12520 and 16411 from the National Institute of Child Health and Human Development. Special appreciation is expressed to Rena Wing, who has contributed much to my thinking about childhood obesity.

TABLE 8.1
The Relative Risk of an Obese Child Becoming an Obese Adult

Authors	N	Sex	Child Age in Months[a]	Child Definition[b]	Adult Age in Months[a]	Adult Definition[b]	Percent Obese[c]	Percent Nonobese[c]	Relative Risk[d]
Charney et al.[14]	366	M, F	6	>90%	20–30	>20%	14 (17/126)	6 (15/240)	2.33
Stark et al.[73]	7127	M, F	7	>20%	26	>20%	41 (84/203)	11 (740/6924)	3.73
Abraham, Collins, and Nordsieck[2]	100	M	10–13	>20%	31 (27–36)	>20%	74 (17/23)	31 (24/77)	2.39
	100	F	10–13	>20%	31 (26–35)	>20%	72 (26/36)	11 (7/64)	6.55
Abraham and Nordsieck[1]	717	M	10–13	>20%	33–38	>20%	63 (12/19)	10 (68/698)	6.30

[a] Age in childhood and adulthood when obesity was determined.
[b] Definition of obesity used >90 percent is greater than the ninetieth percentile for weight, while other definitions are greater than 20 percent over ideal weight for age, height, and sex.
[c] Percentage of obese and nonobese children who became obese adults.
[d] Determined by dividing the percentage of obese children who became obese by the percentage of nonobese children who became obese.

weight infants and 6 percent of the nonoverweight infants became obese adults, a relative risk of 2.33. Stark and coworkers[73] showed that 41 percent of obese 7-year-olds became obese adults, compared to 11 percent of thinner children, a relative risk of 3.73. Abraham, Collins, and Nord-sieck[2] showed that 74 percent of obese 10- to 13-year-old boys and 72 percent of obese girls became obese adults, compared to 31 and 11 percent of nonobese boys and girls, relative risks of 2.39 and 6.55. In another sample of 10- to 13-year-old boys, 63 percent of the obese boys became obese adults, compared to 10 percent of the nonobese boys, a relative risk of 6.30.[7]

The data in table 8.1 provide a clear picture of the developmental characteristics of childhood obesity. The percentage of obese children who become obese adults is 14 percent in infancy, 41 percent at age 7, and about 70 percent at 10 to 13 years of age. The percentage of nonobese children who become obese with advancing age increases only slightly. The relative risk at these three ages increases from 2.33 to 3.73 to 6.55. While normal-weight children can become obese adults, keeping a child thin throughout development will reduce the relative risk of the child becoming an obese adult.

Parental and Familial Effects on Childhood Obesity

Obesity runs in families. Garn and Clark[43] showed that children from two obese parents (defined by triceps skin folds) had skin folds that were two to three times as thick as children of two lean parents, depending on the child's age and sex. Skin-fold values increased with age for children of obese parents, with the values for girls being higher than those for boys.

Parental weight may add to the relative risk of an obese child becoming an obese adult. Overweight infants (greater than the seventy-fifth percentile for weight) are more likely to become obese adults if their parents are obese than if their parents are nonobese.[14] Fifty-one percent of the overweight infants with one or two obese parents became obese adults, compared to 20 percent of the obese infants with thin parents, a relative risk of 2.5. Thin infants, whether or not they had obese parents, were at lower risk for becoming obese adults, since less than 20 percent of non-overweight children became overweight adults.

Other studies have examined the relationship of a child's weight to weights of other family members. Garn and associates[44] assessed the probability of a family member in a four-member nuclear family being obese given the weight status of the other family members. If all other family members were lean, 3.2 percent of the boys and 5.4 percent of the girls were obese. If the remaining family members were obese, then 27.5 percent of the boys and 24.1 percent of the girls were obese. The relative risks for boys or girls were 8.6 and 4.7

Family size may also be important. Jacoby and others[51] showed that the prevalence of obesity is inversely related to family size. In their study 19.4 percent of only children were obese (determined by physician judgment) compared to 13.4 percent of children in two-child families, 8.2 percent in three- and four-child families, and 8.8 percent from families with five or more children. The relative risk of obesity in only children is 2.2 times that of children in families with four children and 1.52 times as great in two-child compared to four-child families. Ravelli and Belmont[69] also showed that only children were at greatest risk of becoming obese in a sample of male 19-year-olds.

Behavioral Risk Factors in Childhood Obesity

The discussion of behavioral factors will be organized according to social learning theory, which takes into account stimulus control, reinforcement control, and cognitive variables.[4] There are at least two types of stimulus control, or setting events, that may influence childhood eating. The first and least directive factor may be the availability or familiarity of the food in the environment. Birch[5,6] found that familiarity of the food is a major factor in child food preference, accounting for 25 to 30 percent of the variability in preference. The magnitude of this factor is equivalent to that shown for sweetness.[5,6] The best demonstration of familiarity was by Birch and Marlin,[8] who manipulated the exposure of children to novel cheeses and fruits. A linear relationship was shown between the amount of exposure and preference. This suggests that children will like what they see around the home. Likewise, children demonstrate aversions for foods their parents don't like.[62]

Parental prompting may also influence childhood eating. Klesges and colleagues[55,56] showed that child relative weight was related to parent prompts to eat in both 2- ($r = 0.81$) and 2½- ($r = 0.56$) year-old children. Parents of obese children prompted 2.3 times as much as parents of normal-weight children.

Research on prompting and physical activity shows similar results. Parental encouragement to be active is significantly correlated with child activity ($r = 0.53$; $r = 0.32$).[55,57] More active children have lower relative weights. Parental encouragements to be active correlate negatively with child relative weight ($r = -0.45$).

The importance of reinforcement on children's eating and activity has been shown in a number of studies. Masek, Marshall, and I[27] used stars and inexpensive tokens to regulate nutritionally balanced eating behavior in 5- and 6-year-old obese children. Stark, Collins, and Stokes[72] trained preschool children to make more nutritious snack choices at school by using colorful stickers and praise. The improved eating was maintained after the reinforcement ended. The new improved food choices did not generalize to the home until children were trained to cue their parents to praise improved food choices.

Eating may be a difficult behavior to change when parents use food as a reinforcer to manage behavior. Birch, Zimmerman, and Hind[9] showed that children will change their preferences for foods that are used as reinforcers or foods accompanied by parental attention, suggesting that children will prefer foods that parents use as reinforcers. While parents typically use sweets, children might learn to prefer other foods used as reinforcers. It would be interesting to study whether children would prefer raw vegetables if they were used as reinforcers.

Reinforcement can also influence physical activity. Our group found that activity in 5- to 8-year-old obese girls could be modified by reinforcing active movement.[39] The results of reinforcement compared to the control phases showed reinforcement increased activity by 24 percent and caloric expenditure by 40 percent.

Cognitive factors are also important in the study of eating by children. One such factor is cultural norms. The power of norms can be seen in the use of the chili pepper, a food that is widely accepted but that is initially aversive.[71] In fact, chili pepper is so aversive that animals cannot be trained to eat it.[71] Foods that are commonly eaten in one culture may be rejected in another (e.g., insects).

Parental beliefs are another determinant of what a child will eat. Parents often believe that children will not drink skim milk and that the temperature of the milk will influence consumption. In fact, children presented with different types of milk at different temperatures show no differences in consumption.[50] Parents who do not like skim milk may assume their children do not like it. Another example is that of baby food. The sugar and salt added to some baby foods may be for the parents who feel their preferences and their child's are the same.[41]

Parental expectations influence not only what but how much a child will eat. Waxman and Stunkard[76] reported that parents will feed obese children more than thin siblings, claiming that the obese child "needs" more to eat. Parents also expect the activity of their obese children to be less than that of their lean siblings.[76]

While cultural and parental factors may be strong, they can be changed. An interesting example of the modification of parental behavior was reported by Guthrie and associates[47] in their work in rural Philippine communities. When mothers did not change their feeding practices in response to traditional health education, the investigators showed that two reinforcement procedures for mothers could improve the growth of their infants.

A final cognitive variable that may be important in determining habit development in children is modeling. Peer modeling can influence food preference[7,21,63] and eating topography.[67] Peer modeling has its most durable effects on children without strong preferences for the foods studied. Adult models also affect food preferences. Harper and Sanders[48] compared adult prompts and modeling on two groups of 1- to 4-year-old children. In two studies, adult modeling was followed by child eating in 80 percent of the cases, while children ate in response to prompts to eat 48 and 47 percent of the time. Thus while prompts to eat do influence eating, an adult model is an even more powerful stimulus. Harper and Sanders[48] used unfamiliar adults as models, so studies must still be done on parental prompts and modeling.

The Treatment of Obesity in Children

The treatment of obesity in children is designed with two purposes. First, treatment should produce a significant reduction in weight, ideally until the child is not obese, or within 20 percent of the average weight for height. Second, treatment should teach appropriate eating and exercise habits so the child can maintain a lower relative weight while getting appropriate nutrition for growth and development. A program must be appropriate for the child's age, developmental capabilities, and parental influence. In addition, the program must incorporate a diet that lowers weight, a maintenance program that promotes growth, and an exercise program that the children will follow. Comprehensive programs must include a diet, an exercise program, and a behavior management program tailored to the child's age.

FOUR-STAGE TREATMENT MODEL

A multiple-stage model for the treatment of childhood obesity has been developed.[24] This model shifts the responsibility for habit change from the parent to the child based on the child's developmental capabilities. The first stage is for children ages 1 to 5. At this age a program must focus on parent management, as parents are the major influences on child eating and activity. While a child of this age responds to peers,[7] access to these models is limited compared to later ages when the child is in school. As children of this age cannot read or write, they cannot keep food or activity records and thus cannot self-regulate caloric intake or energy expenditure by use of feedback from self-monitoring. In addition, the average child of this age is probably not motivated to lose weight. There are neither the health and athletic nor social concerns to be thin that will be present as the child gets older.

From the ages 5 to 8, the child's sphere of social influence expands.

Children are at school and are exposed to new peer and adult models. There is increased access to food, yet children have limited reading, writing, and self-monitoring capabilities and still cannot play a major role in regulating their own caloric intake or expenditure. A program must focus on parent management, but the child must be trained to handle social situations in which food is offered. The child can learn to solicit parental cooperation so that reciprocal reinforcement occurs with the parent or significant adult.[45]

The third stage of treatment is designed for 8- to 12-year-old children, who are still responsive to parent management methods but can take greater responsibility for weight loss. Reading and writing skills are more advanced and children are capable of self-monitoring and goal setting. In addition, children this age are often motivated to lose weight to improve athletic performance, look better, and avoid criticism from peers.

The fourth stage is for adolescents 13 and older who possess the motivation and capability of managing their program with appropriate support from their parents. Programs for adolescents resemble those for adults, with planning for parent support. Behavior management programs for adolescents must be carefully planned, because conflict can arise when parents are involved as the adolescent is struggling for independence.

DIET

The diet for an obese child must be well balanced and have sufficient calories to promote growth, but must restrict intake enough to produce weight change. In addition, the diet must be structured to facilitate adherence. We use a traffic-light diet, developed at the Childhood Weight Control Program.[23] The diet divides foods into five groups (the basic four plus a group of other foods), with the foods in each group then divided into three colors that correspond to the colors in the traffic light, green (GO), yellow (CAUTION), and red (STOP). Green foods, which are only in the vegetable group, contain less than 20 calories per serving. Yellow foods have 20 calories per average serving for the average foods within that group and consist of foods from each group. Red foods are foods that exceed the caloric value of a yellow food, thereby lowering the nutrient density. Reduced-calorie foods designed to resemble red foods (e.g., low-calorie lasagna) are considered red foods because persons will not break the habit of eating lasagna if they often substitute low- for high-calorie lasagna. A food also becomes "red" when combined with other red foods (as in a casserole) or is over 300 calories per serving. This last rule is designed to teach parents and children to limit portion sizes.

The diet also emphasizes a balance of the major food groups while caloric intake is decreased. In a "habit book" the child (or parent) records food intake and the portions of foods that fall within the fruit and vegetable, grain, milk and dairy, and high-protein food groups. Parents are instructed to praise children for getting the appropriate portions of each food group for the dietary intake required for the child's age. We use three different programs—for children aged 1 to 5, 5 to 8, and 8 years and older—with different caloric intake requirements and different balance of the four food groups based on the recommended daily allowances for essential nutrients.[23]

EXERCISE PROGRAM

Exercise is a key component in the treatment of obesity. We have two types of exercise programs, structured (or programmed) aerobic exercise and life-style exercise.[12] Structured aerobic exercise is commonly prescribed, and it involves such activities as running, walking, cycling, or swimming, and is to be done several times per week at a specific duration and intensity. The goal is to both increase caloric expenditure and improve fitness, so exercise intensity is important. Life-style exercise involves a less structured exercise program that does not emphasize intensity. While this program can be made isocaloric to an aerobic program, the intensity of the exercise is likely to be lower and fitness effects may not be as pronounced. If the goal of the exercise is to produce weight loss, then the energy expenditure, and not the exercise intensity, is the important factor.

An important consideration is adherence to the exercise program. Many people who begin an exercise program will not sustain their participation.[66] One of the most important factors in predicting exercise nonadherence is exercise intensity.[22] Subjects will adhere less to higher-intensity programs. Thus exercise programs must be evaluated both in terms of weight change and adherence. Fitness may be measured to assess comparative effects of programs that vary in exercise intensity, but fitness improvements are not necessary endpoints. In addition, weight change will improve fitness when measured with a weight-dependent fitness test (treadmill or step test).

BEHAVIOR MODIFICATION

The behavior modification program must include specific skills to facilitate behavior change and also behavior management skills to encourage habit change. The behavioral skills most commonly used are self-monitoring, modeling, and stimulus control. The behavioral management techniques include structured parent training in social learning principles, with the emphasis on parental attention and reinforcement to support habit change. Parents are often taught to use reinforcement principles in the form of contingency management, such as a point economy or contract system,[53] in which specific behavior changes are operationalized and the contingencies used to reinforce behavior changes are detailed in advance.

TABLE 8.2
The Effects of Behavioral Treatment for Obese Children

Author	Age	Groups	N	Duration RX	FU[a]	Change in Percent Overweight[b] RX	FU[a]
Aragona, Cassidy, and Drabman[3]	5–10	1. Response cost and positive reinforcement	4	3	11	−14.4	−11.8
		2. Response cost	3			−13.3	−6.1
		3. No treatment control	5			+0.7	NA
Brownell, Kelman, and Stunkard[13]	12–16	1. Parent and child seen separately	12	4	16	−17.1	−20.5
		2. Parent and child seen together	12			−7.0	−5.5
		3. Child	12			−6.8	−6.0
Coates, Killen, and Slinkard[16]	13–17	1. Parent and child seen together	31	4.5	12	−8.6	−8.4
		2. Child				−5.1	−8.2
Coates et al.[17]	13–17	1. Daily contingency/ weekly contingency	8	4	10	−12.0	−8.0
		2. Weekly contingency/ weight loss	8			−5.2	+10.4
		3. Daily contingency/ calorie counting	11			−6.2	−2.4
		4. Weekly contingency/ calorie counting	11			−5.0	+5.8
Epstein et al.[36]	6–12	1. Behavior modification	6	2	5	−9.7	−17.5
		2. Health education	7			−5.7	−6.4
Epstein et al.[28,37]	6–12	1. Parent and child seen separately	24	8	60	−16.6	−13.6
		2. Child	21			−18.6	+3.3
		3. Nonspecific	22			−16.1	+7.0
Epstein et al.[38]	8–12	1. Diet and life-style exercise	10	5	17	−19.0	−13.8
		2. Life-style exercise	8			−13.8	−11.2
		3. Diet and programmed exercise	8			−10.3	+0.1
		4. Programmed exercise	11			−13.9	−9.7
Epstein et al.[31]	8–12	1. Diet	15	12	—	−20.1	−14.4
		2. Diet and life-style exercise	18			−14.9	−14.4
		3. No treatment control	14			+4.1	NA
Epstein et al.[35]	8–12	1. Diet and programmed exercise	10	6	12	−27.5	−25.4
		2. Diet	9			−18.8	−18.7

TABLE 8.2, continued

Author	Age	Groups	N	Duration RX	Duration FU[a]	Change in Percent Overweight[b] RX	Change in Percent Overweight[b] FU[a]
Epstein et al.[33]	8–12	1. Heavy parent/parent managed	10	12	36	−5.5	−5.8
		2. Heavy parent/child self-control	12			−9.6	+3.1
		3. Thin parent/parent managed	9			−15.6	−5.3
		4. Thin parent/child self-control	7			−17.3	−6.0
Epstein et al.[30]	8–12	1. Diet and programmed exercise	13	12	24	−16.4	−6.8
		2. Diet and life-style exercise	12			−16.1	−18.0
		3. Diet and calisthenics	10			−17.5	−7.2
Epstein et al.[40]	5–8	1. Behavior modification	8	12	—	−19.9	−26.3
		2. Health education	11			−13.4	−11.2
Epstein, Wing, and Valoski[29]	1–5	1. Behavior modification	21	12	—	−19.8	−18.1
Gross, Wheeler, and Hess[46]	13–17	1. Behavioral self-control	11	4	7	−4.7	−7.7
Harris, Kirschenbaum, and Tomarken[49]	9–12	1. Parent and child seen together	13	2.25	12	−6.3	−7.6
		2. Child	9			−7.7	−6.2
		3. No treatment control	8			+0.6	
Kingsley and Shapiro[54]	10–11	1. Parent and child seen together	8	2	5	+0.8	−4.1
		2. Child	10			−0.8	−2.2
		3. Parent	8			−5.3	−3.6
		4. No treatment control	10			−0.3	NA
Rivinus, Drummond, and Combrinck-Graham[70]	8–13	1. Behavior modification	10	2.5	30	−6.5	−29.1

[a] RX and FU refer to the change in percent overweight at the end of treatment and the furthest follow-up point, with the exception of the studies of Epstein et al.,[31,35,40] which involved a 12-month treatment. The 6-month treatment data are included under treatment for comparison to other studies.
[b] Refers to the change in relative weight from baseline to that measurement interval.

The emphasis on parent management may depend on the age of the child, with younger children requiring more structured programs that depend on immediate consequences.

Review of Obesity Treatment

The review of treatments for childhood obesity will focus on behavioral treatment methods. While previous reviews have compared behavioral and nonbehavioral methods,[11,15] this review will provide a more detailed examination of the effects of behavioral procedures. Following the review of traditional, clinic-based treatments a new form of treatment—school-based treatment—will be presented. Seventeen studies using behavioral treatments in clinic treatment were identified (see table 8.2).

TODDLER OBESITY PROGRAMS

There are no published studies on the behavioral treatment of obesity in young children. The one controlled study used a general health education approach, without specifying the particular behavior targeted or taught.[68] This study was designed to assess the effect of the "Prudent Diet" and a normal diet on weight in children who began the trial at 3 months of age. At 3 years of age, the prevalence of obesity in the treated group dropped from 25 percent to 1 percent, while the prevalence of obesity in the control group remained elevated, beginning at 34 percent and ending at 26 percent.

Our group[29] is completing a one-year trial with 1- to 5-year-old children. Twenty-one obese toddlers were provided a pilot family-based behavioral program to assess the feasibility of weight loss in young children with particular emphases placed on nutrient intake and growth. At the end of one year the average child lost 18.1 percent in percent overweight, with no significant decrease in height percentile. The magnitude of this weight loss is similar to that seen for older children.

OBESITY TREATMENT FOR THE 5- TO 8-YEAR OLD

Only one controlled study on the treatment of 5- to 8-year-old children has been done.[40] Nineteen obese girls were involved in the comparison of a parent-managed, family-based treatment program and a health education program. The children who participated in the behavioral program showed approximately double the changes (a loss of 27.3 percent) of the control children. This magnitude of change at the end of one year is the largest change at a comparable measurement time in our research program.

OBESITY TREATMENT FOR THE 8- TO 12-YEAR-OLD

The majority (ten of fifteen) of treatment studies on childhood obesity have focused on 8- to 12-year-old children. The studies can be divided into four groups based on the independent variable: (1) studies on the effectiveness of behavioral treatments; (2) studies on components of parent management; (3) studies on the role of the parents in treatment; and (4) research on the role of exercise.

One early group outcome study was designed to document the effectiveness of behavioral treatment.[70] This study reported impressive results. Ten obese children were treated with a behavioral treatment program that included self-monitoring, modeling, contracts, and reinforcement of appropriate habit change. Parents and children were seen in treatment, but it is not clear whether they were seen together or separately. In addition to the standard treatment meetings, children and parents ate an evening meal together at the end of each meeting. While the results at the end of the ten-week treatment are not large—a decrease of 6.5 percent overweight—the change obtained after thirty months—a decrease of 29.1 percent—is very impressive. These percent overweight changes are based on calculations using the height and weight data provided in the original report.

My associates and I[36] compared behavioral treatment to a group given similar education without the behavioral techniques. After five months the parents and the children in the behavior modification group had 2.7 times the change in percent overweight (−17.5 vs. −6.4 percent). As noted by Lavigne and Daruna[60] and Wing and I,[26] the effects of treatment were significantly different only for the adults, not for the children. However, the advantage for the behavioral treatment over education alone is similar (2.3 times the change) to that observed for younger children,[40] increasing confidence in the reliability of the effect.

If the behavioral approach is the treatment of choice, the specific technology of behavior change must be selected. One important dimension for parent management is the use of positive versus negative reinforcement (the presentation of reinforcers vs. the removal of an aversive event to increase the probability of a behavior). Aragona, Cassady, and Drabman[3] compared children of parents who were motivated by response cost to make the requested changes versus parents who were motivated by response cost plus a positive reinforcement system for appropriate child change, and a no-treatment control. Results of this small study ($N = 12$) suggested the superiority of response cost plus reinforcement to response cost alone. The magnitude of changes obtained for the response cost plus reinforcement group at both three and eleven months were good (−14.4 and −11.8 percent overweight).

Another treatment variable relevant to childhood obesity is child self-control. Self-control refers to the child's regulation of eating and exercise behavior by the manipulation of the important controlling variables, rather than parent management of the relevant variables. Self-control is conceptually related to success in weight control, and one study found self-control related to outcome.[18] For this reason one purpose of the study by coworkers and me[33] was to compare child self-management to parent management. The child self-control procedures were based on recommendations of O'Leary and Dubey.[65] Research in this area suggests that self-control in children is best accomplished when goal setting and rein-forcement are first developed under the control of an external change agent (parent) and then faded to the child. After three years of treatment no differences were found between these two treatment strategies.[33] The absence of weight differences suggests that there was no difference in the amount of behavior control produced by the child self-control or the parent control methods.

Four studies have assessed parental variables in the treatment of child-hood obesity. Three assessed the role of parental cooperation in child treatment. Kingsley and Shapiro[54] compared children in four groups: parent plus child seen together, child alone, parent alone, and a no-treatment control. There were very small weight changes at the end of two months of treatment, with the parent alone showing the best effect. At the end of five months, the groups did not differ. The effects were still very small, with an average change of only −3.3 percent overweight.

The next study compared families in which both the parent and child were targeted for weight loss, versus the child alone, versus a nonspecific target.[28,37] Targeting involved contingency management for habit and weight change. The contingencies for the parent and child group were arranged so that both parent and child had to lose weight. In all groups both the parent and child were seen, but separately. In addition, all the children had at least one obese parent, which is related to poorer prog-nosis.[33] No differences between groups were shown after eight months of treatment, with all groups showing good treatment effects (−16.1 to −18.6 percent overweight). At five years there was a significant treatment effect ($p < 0.01$); children in the parent-plus-child group maintained their treatment effect, while children in the other groups returned to baseline levels or higher. At the end of five years, 42 percent (10/24) of the children were not obese in the parent and child group, with 19 and 4 percent of the children in the other two groups not obese. This long-term treatment effect attests to the power of including the parent as an active participant in child treatment. There were no differential effects on parents.

Harris, Kirschenbaum, and Tomarken[49] compared groups in which the parent and child were seen together versus the child seen alone versus a no-treatment control. Three of these groups are identical to those stud-ied by Kingsley and Shapiro.[54] The results showed no differences as a function of treating both the parent and child together versus treating the child alone after nine weeks or one year. Changes in both groups were small, averaging −6.9 percent at the end of a year. An important distinction in studies in this area[37,49,54] is whether the parent and child are seen together or separately. As Brownell, Kelman, and Stunkard[13] have shown for adolescents, this is an important distinction, which can greatly influence treatment results.

The effects of parent weight (two thin parents vs. at least one obese one) on child weight loss success has also been studied.[33] The results showed that obese children with thin parents obtain significantly better weight change after one year than children with heavy parents. However, these effects did not persist over time. At three years, children with obese or thin parents did not differ in percent overweight.

Our group has completed four studies on the role of exercise in the treatment of childhood obesity. The first study[38] assessed the effects of isocaloric life style and programmed aerobic exercise crossed with diet/no diet. The results showed equal effects of life style and aerobic exercise during the initial two-month treatment, which was expected since the two exercise programs were isocaloric. The aerobic program showed greater fitness effects, also expected, since the aerobic exercise was of greater intensity. By six months, and continuing to seventeen months, the life-style exercise was superior to the aerobic exercise. The probable mechanism for the differences would be better adherence in the life-style than in the aerobic group. One interesting finding was the failure of diet to exert an independent effect on weight loss. This was probably due to voluntary dieting on the part of the subjects assigned to the exercise-alone group. Other studies have shown that exercise alone can produce equivalent effects to diet or diet plus exercise,[19] which must be due to dieting on the part of the exercise subjects. However, this voluntary dieting is problematic since it makes the comparison of diet versus exercise difficult.

The comparison of aerobic versus life-style exercise was replicated in a second study[30] with different methods. The study compared three groups that each dieted but differed in the type of exercise. Isocaloric aerobic and life-style exercises were compared to a plausible placebo exercise (calisthenics), which was similar in amount of exercise time, goal setting, and feedback, but which involved considerably less caloric expenditure. The inclusion of a control group provided a realistic, low-expenditure exercise program, which is important to control for nonspecific aspects of exercise that may influence weight but are not a function of exercise caloric expenditure.[25] There were no differences in weight change across the three groups at the end of one year. At the end of two years, the life-style group showed a further reduction in percent overweight, while the other two groups had significant increases in percent overweight. These results show differences in aerobic and life-style exercise are reliable over time.

We studied the effect of diet plus exercise on weight by randomizing obese parents and children to one of three groups: diet plus life-style exercise, diet, and no-treatment control.[31] The diet group was given a low-expenditure stretching exercise program. The expected superiority of diet plus exercise was observed for parents at six and twelve months, but there were no differences observed for the children. There are three possible explanations for this difference between adults and children. First, exercise may be less important for children than adults. Second, an exercise program for adults and children must be different. Third, children may adhere less to an exercise program than adults.

One way to test the effects of exercise would be to have children exercise as part of a standardized treatment. We tested this by comparing a standard diet treatment program to a diet program plus a six-week, three day per week, summer camp with an average of 300 calories-per-session expenditure.[35] After six and twelve months, the diet plus exercise group showed the expected superiority compared to the control group. These results suggest that beginning an exercise program by structuring the exercise behavior and controlling adherence may affect the long-term effects of exercise on weight loss, and also suggest that adherence played a role in the failure to show a difference between diet plus exercise versus diet alone.[31]

TREATMENT OF OBESE ADOLESCENTS

Four studies have been done with obese adolescents. The first study[46] used a behavioral self-control model with eleven children and found only small losses. One of the controlled studies assessed different types of contingency management, while the other two studies were on parental involvement. Coates and associates[17] compared the effects of reinforcing the children for weight or calorie change on a daily or weekly basis. Results favored the daily contingencies for weight loss, with only a moderate decrease in percent overweight of 8 percent after ten months.

Brownell, Kelman, and Stunkard[13] compared the effects of seeing the parent and child together, the parent and child separately, or seeing the child alone. The results at four and sixteen months show very powerful effects of seeing the parent and child separately, with a decrease in percent overweight of 20.5 percent after sixteen months. Seeing the parent and child together was not better than seeing the child alone. Coates, Killen, and Slinkard[16] compared the effects of seeing the parent and child together versus seeing the child alone, and as predicted from the previous study by Brownell, Kelman, and Stunkard[13] there were no significant differences over the year of observation.

GROWTH DURING WEIGHT REDUCTION

One goal of the diet is to achieve weight loss while adequate nutrients are provided for growth. Growth is sensitive to nutritional inadequacies and can be used to assess the adequacy of the caloric intake.[52] The results of height change over the five-year period in the weight-loss study previously reported[28] provide the most complete data set on height during weight reduction in children. For purposes of some analyses, the actual height for each subject was converted to height percentiles based on the age and sex of the child or parent.[20,64] There were no differences in growth as a function of treatment group (parent plus child, child alone, or nonspecific target), though these groups did show different weight losses, with the average child growing about 25.40 cm over the five years. When relative height is considered, the obese children are very tall compared to the average child, with a mean baseline height percentile of 74 percent. Since obese adults are not taller than average,[61] it is not likely that these obese children would be expected to maintain their average relative height percentile and become very tall adults. Rather it is likely that these obese children will resemble their parents in height, as would nonobese children.[61] Based on this hypothesis, the children were divided into three groups on the basis of their midparent height. Short parents were at the thirtieth percentile for adult height, average parents at the fifty-second percentile, and tall parents at the seventy-eighth percentile.[64] Children of short, average, and tall parents were at the fifty-eighth, seventy-eighth, and eighty-fifth percentile, respectively ($p < 0.01$). After five years of weight loss the children of short parents are now at the forty-fifth percentile, the children of average parents at the sixty-first percentile, and the children of tall parents at the seventy-eighth percentile. Thus the children of tall parents now resemble their parents in relative height, while children of average and short parents are still approximately 10 percent greater in relative height than their parents.

FAMILIAL EFFECTS ON CHILD WEIGHT LOSS

Family variables other than parental weight may influence child weight change. Family size is inversely related to obesity, with large families less likely to have obese children than smaller families.[51] The number of overweight siblings is associated with child weight; children with overweight siblings are more likely to be overweight. These two factors also relate to child weight loss. Family size and number of obese siblings predict weight loss. Children in families with more children and more obese children do not lose as much weight as children in small families with few obese siblings.[32]

SCHOOL-BASED TREATMENT PROGRAMS

The treatments presented in the previous sections are designed for clinic use and thus may be applied to only a small proportion of the population of obese children. It may be more effective to develop programs in the schools where there are large numbers of children. Four large-scale controlled studies have now been completed in the schools. Brownell and Kaye[10] compared a ten-week, behaviorally oriented program to a no-treatment control for 5- to 12-year-old children. Treatment children showed a mean decrease in percent overweight of 15.4 percent while the control group got heavier. The magnitude of the changes observed in this program were comparable to the changes seen in clinic programs. The school-based program was expanded to include peer counselors and was replicated in two new schools.[42] However, the results showed only a 5.3 percent decrease in relative weight, which was again superior to the control children who again became more obese. Lansky and Brownell[58] compared an eighteen-week behavioral program to a nutrition education/

exercise program for adolescents. Results showed small and comparable effects of the two treatments (−3 percent and −2.1 percent). Finally, Lansky and Vance[59] compared a behavioral treatment to no treatment in adolescents, and observed decreases in percent overweight of 5.7 percent while the control group gained 2.4 percent.

The results of these studies are generally consistent and may point to methods that can make treatment available to more children than is possible in clinics. Researchers in these studies report difficulty in getting cooperation of the parents in treatment, which may account for the lowered treatment effects in some studies.[42,58] Foster, Wadden, and Brownell[42] suggest that school-based programs may be best suited to the treatment of children who are moderately overweight but not appropriate for a clinic or for the prevention of obesity in children who are at high risk for becoming obese.

Summary and Discussion

This review shows several consistent findings about childhood obesity. First, obese children tend to become obese adults. There are developmental differences in relative risk: the risk goes from 2.3 for obese infants[14] to 6.3 to 6.6 for obese 10- to 13-year-olds.[1,2] Obese children of obese parents are at greater risk than obese children of thin parents, although this has been shown only for infants.[14] It is important to assess the interaction of parent and child weight across different developmental periods.

Parent variables are associated with childhood obesity. Parents may differentially prompt, model for, and reinforce obese and thin children for eating and exercise. This may be important in understanding both the etiology and treatment of childhood obesity. Most research has focused on differences between heavy and thin children, but a more interesting comparison, with clear implications for both the development and treatment of childhood obesity, might be to study differences in parent-child interactions, particularly in heavy and thin parents.

It appears that childhood obesity can be treated at a variety of ages. We have now shown that children receiving behavioral treatment were significantly less obese after five years than children given control treatments.[28] The variable that has most consistently influenced treatment outcome is parental participation, which is logical given the importance of parents in the etiology of childhood obesity. However, the manner in which parents are included is important.[13] The most effective way is to see the parents and children separately rather than together. In fact, results do not differ if the parent and child are seen together versus just the child is seen.[13] Though the effects of behavioral treatment are consistent across ages, additional research on matching treatments and treatment component to developmental capabilities is needed. The effects of exercise are not consistent across studies, but the results suggest the importance of exercise adherence.

In summary, significant developments in the treatment of childhood obesity have already been made. Future research directed at developing a better understanding of significant etiological and treatment variables will continue to increase the probability that childhood obesity can be prevented or treated.

REFERENCES

1. Abraham, S., and Nordsieck, M. 1960. Relationship of excess weight in children and adults. *Public Health Reports* 75:263–273.

2. Abraham, S., Collins, C., and Nordsieck, M. 1970. Relationship of child weight status to morbidity to adults. *Public Health Reports* 86:273–284.

3. Aragona, J., Cassady, J., and Drabman, R. S. 1975. Treating overweight children through parental training and contingency contracting. *Journal of Applied Behavior Analysis* 8:269–278.

4. Bandura, A. 1967. *Principles of behavior modification.* New York: Holt, Rinehart & Winston.

5. Birch, L. L. 1979. Dimensions of preschool children's food preferences. *Journal of Nutrition Education* 11:77–80.

6. ————. 1979. Preschool children's food preferences and consumption patterns. *Journal of Nutrition Education* 11:189–192.

7. ————. 1980. Effects of peer models' food choices and eating behaviors on preschoolers' food preferences. *Child Development* 51:489–496.

8. Birch, L. L., and Marlin, D. W. 1982. I don't like it; I never tried it: Effects of exposure on two-year-old children's food preferences. *Appetite: Journal of Intake Research* 3: 353–360.

9. Birch, L. L., Zimmerman, S. I., and Hind, H. 1980. The influence of social affective context on the formation of children's food preferences. *Child Development* 51:856–861.

10. Brownell, K. D., and Kaye, F. S. 1982. A school-based behavior modification, nutrition education, and physical activity program for obese children. *American Journal of Clinical Nutrition* 35:277–283.

11. Brownell, K. D., and Stunkard, A. J. 1978. Behavioral treatment of obesity in children. *American Journal of Diseases of Children* 132:403–412.

12. ————. 1980. Physical activity in the development and control of obesity. In *Obesity,* ed. A. J. Stunkard, pp. 300–324. Philadelphia: W. B. Saunders.

13. Brownell, K. D., Kelman, J. H., and Stunkard, A. J. 1983. Treatment of obese children with and without their mothers: Changes in weight and blood pressure. *Pediatrics* 71:515–523.

14. Charney, M., et al. 1976. Childhood antecedents of adult obesity: Do chubby infants become obese adults? *New England Journal of Medicine* 295:6–9.

15. Coates, T. J., and Thoresen, C. E. 1978. Treating obesity in children and adolescents: A review. *American Journal of Public Health* 68:143–151.

16. Coates, T. J., Killen, J. D., and Slinkard, L. A. 1982. Parent participation in a treatment program for overweight adolescents. *International Journal of Eating Disorders* 1: 37–48.

17. Coates, T. J., Jeffery, R. W., Killen, J. D., and Danaher, B. G. 1982. Frequency of contact and monetary reward in weight loss, lipid change, and blood pressure reduction with adolescents. *Behavior Therapy* 13:175–185.

18. Cohen, E. A., et al. 1980. Self-control practices associated with weight loss maintenance in children and adolescents. *Behavior Therapy* 11:26–37.

19. Dahlkoetter, J., Callahan, E. J., and Linton, J. 1979. Obesity and the unbalanced energy equation: Exercise versus eating habit change. *Journal of Consulting and Clinical Psychology* 47:898–905.

20. Department of Health, Education and Welfare. 1979. *Weight and height of adults 18–74 years of age: United States 1971–1974. Vital and Health Statistics,* series 11, no. 211. Washington, D.C.: DHEW publication (PHS).

21. Duncker, K. 1938. Experimental modification of children's food preferences through social suggestion. *Journal of Abnormal Psychology* 33:489–507.

22. Epstein, L. H. 1984. Adherence to exercise in obese children. *Journal of Cardiac Rehabilitation* 4:185–195.

23. ———. 1985. Behavioral treatment for childhood obesity. In *Pediatric clinics of North America,* ed. P. Penchanz. Philadelphia: W. B. Saunders.

24. ———. 1985. Family based treatment for childhood obesity. In *Advances in developmental and behavioral pediatrics,* ed. M. L. Wolraich and D. K. Routh. Greenwich, Conn.: JAI Press.

25. Epstein, L. H., and Wing, R. R. 1980. Aerobic exercise and weight. *Addictive Behaviors* 3:371–388.

26. ———. 1983. Reanalysis of weight changes in behavior modification and nutrition education for childhood obesity. *Journal of Pediatric Psychology* 8:97–100.

27. Epstein, L. H., Masek, B. J., and Marshall, W. R. 1978. A nutritionally based school program for control of eating in obese children. *Behavior Therapy* 9:766–788.

28. Epstein, L. H., Wing, R. R., and Koeske, R. In press. Long-term effects of family-based treatment of childhood obesity. *Journal of Consulting and Clinical Psychology.*

29. Epstein, L. H., Wing, R. R., and Valoski, A. In press. Family-based behavioral weight control in obese young children. *Journal of the American Dietetic Association.*

30. Epstein, L. H., Wing, R. R., Koeske, R., and Valoski, A. 1985. A comparison of lifestyle exercise, aerobic exercise, and calisthenics on weight loss of obese children. *Behavior Therapy* 16:345–356.

31. ———. 1984. The effects of diet plus exercise on weight change in parents and children. *Journal of Consulting and Clinical Psychology* 52:429–437.

32. ———. In press. The effects of family variables on child weight loss. *Health Psychology.*

33. ———. In press. The effects of parental weight on child weight loss. *Journal of Consulting and Clinical Psychology.*

34. ———. 1984. Parent height influences growth in obese children during weight reduction. Manuscript.

35. Epstein, L. H., Wing, R. R., Penner, B. C., and Kress, M. J. 1985. The effects of controlled exercise on weight change in obese preadolescent children. *Journal of Pediatrics* 107:358–361.

36. Epstein, L. H., et al. 1980. Comparison of family-based behavior modification and nutrition education for childhood obesity. *Journal of Pediatric Psychology* 5:25–36.

37. Epstein, L. H., et al. 1981. Child and parent weight loss in family-based behavior modification programs. *Journal of Consulting and Clinical Psychology* 49:674–685.

38. Epstein, L. H., et al. 1982. A comparison of lifestyle change and programmed aerobic exercise on weight and fitness changes in obese children. *Behavior Therapy* 13: 651–665.

39. Epstein, L. H., et al. 1984. The modification of activity patterns and energy expenditure in obese young girls. *Behavior Therapy* 15:101–108.

40. Epstein, L. H., et al. 1985. Effects of family-based treatment on obese 5–8 year old girls. *Behavior Therapy* 16:205–212.

41. Foman, S. J. 1974. *Infant nutrition.* Philadelphia: W. B. Saunders.

42. Foster, G. D., Wadden, T. A., and Brownell, K. D. 1985. Peer-led program for the treatment and prevention of obesity in the schools. *Journal of Consulting and Clinical Psychology* 53:538–540.

43. Garn, S. M., and Clark, D. C. 1976. Trends in fatness and the origins of obesity. *Pediatrics* 57:443–456.

44. Garn, S. M., Bailey, S. M., Solomon, M. A., and Hopkins, P. J. 1981. Effects of remaining family members on fatness prediction. *American Journal of Clinical Nutrition* 34: 148–153.

45. Graubard, P. S., Rosenberg, H., and Miller, M. B. 1974. Student applications of behavior modification to teachers and environments or ecological approaches to deviancy.

In *Control of human behavior,* vol. 3, ed. R. Ulrich, T. Stachnik, and J. Mabry, pp. 421–432. Glenview, Ill.: Scott, Foresman.

46. Gross, I., Wheeler, M., and Hess, K. 1976. The treatment of obesity in adolescents using behavioral self-control. *Clinical Pediatrics* 15:920–924.

47. Guthrie, G. M., Guthrie, H. A., Fernandez, T. L., and Estrera, N. O. 1982. Cultural influences and reinforcement strategies. *Behavior Therapy* 13:624–637.

48. Harper, L. V., and Sanders, K. M. 1975. The effect of adults eating on young children's acceptance of unfamiliar food. *Journal of Experimental Child Psychology* 20: 206–214.

49. Harris, E. S., Kirschenbaum, D. S., and Tomarken, A. J. In press. Effects of parental involvement in behavioral weight loss therapy for preadolescents. *Behavior Therapy.*

50. Herbert-Jackson, E., Cross, M. Z., and Risley, T. R. 1977. Milk types and temperature: What will young children drink. *Journal of Nutrition Education* 9:76–79.

51. Jacoby, A., Altman, D. G., Cook, J., and Holland, W. W. 1975. Influence of some social and environmental factors on the nutrient intake and the nutritional status of school children. *British Journal of Preventive and Social Medicine* 29:116–120.

52. Johnston, F. E. 1981. Anthropometry and nutritional status. In *Assessing changing food consumption patterns,* ed. National Research Council Assembly of Life Sciences-Food & Nutrition Board. Washington, D.C.: National Academy Press.

53. Kazdin, A. E. 1975. *Behavior modification in applied settings.* Homewood, Ill.: Dorsey.

54. Kingsley, R. G., and Shapiro, J. 1977. A comparison of three behavioral programs for the control of obesity in children. *Behavior Therapy* 8:30–36.

55. Klesges, R. C., Malott, J. M., Boschee, P. F., and Weber, J. M. In press. Parental influences on children's food intake, physical activity, and relative weight: An extension and replication. *International Journal of Eating Disorders.*

56. Klesges, R. C., et al. 1983. Parental influences on children's eating behavior and relative weight. *Journal of Applied Behavioral Analysis* 16:371–378.

57. Klesges, R. C., et al. 1984. An observational system for assessing physical activity in children and associated parent behavior. *Behavioral Assessment* 6:333–345.

58. Lansky, D., and Brownell, K. D. 1982. Comparison of school-based treatments for adolescent obesity. *Journal of School Health* 8:384–387.

59. Lansky, D., and Vance, M. A. 1983. School-based intervention for adolescent obesity: Analysis of treatment, randomly selected control, and self-selected subjects. *Journal of Consulting and Clinical Psychology* 51:147–148.

60. Lavigne, J. V., and Daruna, J. H. 1982. A comment on Epstein et al.'s "Comparison of family-based behavior modification and nutrition education for childhood obesity." *Journal of Pediatric Psychology* 7:95–98.

61. Lew, E. A., and Garfinkel, L. 1983. Variations in mortality by weight among 750,000 men and women. *Journal of Chronic Diseases* 32:563–576.

62. McCarthy, D. 1935. Children's feeding problems in relation to the food aversions of the family. *Child Development* 6:277–284.

63. Marinho, H. 1942. Social influence in the formation of enduring preferences. *Journal of Abnormal and Social Psychology* 37:448–468.

64. National Center for Health Statistics. 1977. *Growth curves for children birth–18 years of age, United States. Vital and Health Statistics,* series 11, no. 165. Washington, D.C.: DHEW publication (PHS).

65. O'Leary, S. G., and Dubey, D. R. 1979. Applications of self-control procedures by children: A review. *Journal of Applied Behavior Analysis* 12:449–466.

66. Oldridge, N. B. 1982. Compliance and exercise in primary and secondary prevention of coronary heart disease: A review. *Preventive Medicine* 11:56–70.

67. Perry, R. P., LeBow, M. D., and Buser, M. M. 1979. An exploration of observational learning in modifying selected eating responses of obese children. *International Journal of Obesity* 3:193–199.

68. Piscano, J. C., Lichter, H., Ritter, J., and Siegal, A. D. 1978. An attempt at prevention of obesity in infancy. *Pediatrics* 61:360–364.

69. Ravelli, G. P., and Belmont, L. 1979. Obesity in nineteen-year-old men: Family size and birth order associations. *American Journal of Epidemiology* 109:66–70.

70. Rivinus, T. M., Drummond, T., and Combrinck-Graham, L. 1976. A group behavior treatment program for overweight children: Results of a pilot study. *Pediatric and Adolescent Endocrinology* 1:55–61.

71. Rozin, P., and Fallon, A. E. 1981. The acquisition of likes and dislikes for foods. In *Criteria of food acceptance,* ed. J. Solms and R. L. Hall, pp. 35–48. Zurich: Foster Verlag AG.

72. Stark, L. J., Collins, F. L., and Stokes, T. F. 1984. Training preschool aged children to make nutritious snack choices. Manuscript.

73. Stark, D., Atkins, E., Wolff, D. H., and Douglas, J. W. B. 1981. Longitudinal study of obesity in the National Survey of Health and Development. *British Medical Journal* 283: 12–17.

74. Stunkard, A. J., and Penick, S. B. 1979. Behavior modification in the treatment of obesity: The problem of maintaining weight loss. *Archives of General Psychiatry* 36:801–806.

75. Tanner, J. M., Goldstein, H., and Whitehouse, R. H. 1970. Standards for children's height at ages 2–9 allowing for height of parents. *Archives of Diseases of Childhood* 45: 755–762.

76. Waxman, M., and Stunkard, A. J. 1980. Caloric intake and expenditure of obese boys. *Journal of Pediatrics* 96:187–193.

77. Wing, R. R., and Jeffery, R. J. 1979. Outpatient treatments of obesity: A comparison of methodology and results. *International Journal of Obesity* 3:261–279.

9

Behavior Therapy for Obesity: Modern Approaches and Better Results

Kelly D. Brownell and Thomas A. Wadden

How useful is behavior modification in treating obesity? At first glance, this would appear a question with an obvious answer. Behavioral approaches, known variously as behavior therapy, behavior modification, and behaviorism, are among the most widely used approaches for weight reduction. They have been incorporated into the Weight Watchers program, are mentioned frequently in popular magazines, and are part of the professional curriculum for many programs in nutrition, psychology, and even medicine. It is now the norm for programs, including profit-oriented commercial ones, to emphasize the three-pronged approach of nutrition, exercise, and behavior change. Does this not prove the effectiveness of behavior therapy?

What follows is our attempt to answer this basic question. However, the question must be framed to reflect a basic fact of the clinical management of obesity: every approach works for some people. A program must not be judged according to *whether* it is effective but as to how effective it is for specific individuals under specific circumstances. For example, approaches that have not been endorsed by the scientific community, such as hypnosis, ear stapling, and fad diets, have their success stories. The successes occur infrequently, but for the few persons who respond, the results are clear and powerful. Ear stapling could be a useful treatment if the small number of would-be responders could be identified.

Viewed in this light, it is difficult to embrace any single approach, because even the "winner" in such a contest cannot boast of meaningful results over the long term for a majority of individuals. It is useful, therefore, to examine behavioral approaches from a broad clinical perspective. The ultimate objective of such an examination would be to target behavioral approaches to the individuals who would most profit, but criteria for this matching do not yet exist. In their absence, we must draw inferences from group averages.

In this chapter, we begin with an examination of the changes in both the nature and results of behavioral programs over the fifteen years they have been popular. From this we offer our conclusions about the effectiveness of behavioral approaches and describe what we believe to be a comprehensive program for obesity, a program that includes more than just behavior therapy. We then move to clinical issues and focus specifically on the maintenance of weight loss and the utility of combining behavior therapy with other approaches.

Our work with obesity has included individual and group treatment, clinical studies, programs in work sites and schools, studies of fat cells and body composition, and research with animals. As we integrated this information and assembled material for this chapter, we came to several surprising conclusions, around which the chapter is organized:

1. Early behavioral approaches were more instructive for testing theory than for managing obesity.
2. Modern behavioral approaches have become increasingly comprehensive, with the key additions coming in the areas of exercise, attitudes, and social support.
3. The greater effectiveness of current approaches may come from longer treatment, not more potent treatment.
4. The modern approaches have intensified the emphasis on long-term weight loss. The average weight loss at follow-up is greater now than before, but the average loss during treatment is also greater. It is difficult to know the extent to which newer approaches are better at facilitating maintenance.
5. There is great promise in combining treatments for obesity, with behavior therapy providing the basic framework for life-style change. An example would be to produce large weight losses with very-low-calorie diets and to use behavior therapy to sustain the losses.

TABLE 9.1
*Summary of Data from Controlled Trials of Behavior
Therapy Completed Before and During 1974
and During 1978 and 1984*

	1974	1978	1984
Sample Size	53.1	54.0	71.3
Initial weight (lb)	163.0	194.0	197.0
Initial % overweight	49.4	48.6	48.1
Length of treatment (weeks)	8.4	10.5	13.2
Weight loss (lb)	8.5	9.4	15.4
Loss per week (lb)	1.2	0.9	1.2
Attrition (%)	11.4	12.9	10.6
Length of follow-up (weeks)	15.5	30.3	58.4
Loss at follow-up (lb)	8.9	9.1	9.8

NOTE: All values are means across studies.

A Comparison of Behavioral Approaches: Then and Now

When we began writing this chapter, we believed that behavioral approaches are more effective today than in the early 1970s. We also hypothesized a turning point around 1978 when programs began to increase in length and effectiveness.

To test our assumptions, we did summary statistics on studies published in three different periods. For the first period, before and during 1974, we included all studies in which subjects were randomly assigned to conditions. In studies where additions were made to the behavioral program, such as exercise or spouse training, only the behavioral groups were included. This was done to trace just the changes in the way behavior therapy is administered. The second and third periods involved all studies published during the years 1978 and 1984 in the journals *Behavior Therapy, Journal of Consulting and Clinical Psychology, Behaviour Research and Therapy,* and *Addictive Behaviors.* The summary data from these three periods are presented in table 9.1. We evaluated characteristics of the subjects, treatment duration, follow-up and outcome. From this, we can observe the progress of research in behavior therapy.

Behavior Modification: What It Used To Be

The origins of behavior modifications for obesity began with a paper by Ferster, Nurnberger, and Levitt[19] that appeared in the *Journal of Mathetics,* which published only one volume. Stuart[44] followed several years later with a series of case studies in which weight losses were unusually high. This history, and what followed, has been reported on many times and will be covered here only to show its effect on what occurs today.

Early studies on behavior therapy were done simply because obesity provided a convenient outcome measure (pounds lost) with which to evaluate self-management strategies.[51] An example is Mahoney's 1974[29] comparison of self-reinforcement and self-punishment approaches. This oft-cited study showed a statistical advantage for self-reinforcement, but the clinical advantage was negligible. Such studies taught us more about theory than practice.

Common to all programs were self-monitoring and stimulus control. Other techniques, including assertion training, relaxation, and token reward systems, were inserted and then removed with little effect on weight loss. Self-monitoring and stimulus control became mainstays and are still the backbone of many behavioral programs.

Programs remained remarkably similar in nature and outcome for many years. Jeffery, Wing, and Stunkard[24] reviewed studies from before 1976 and found average posttreatment losses of 11.5 lb. Wilson and Brownell[53] published a review in 1980 and found average losses of 10.4 lb. We found a mean loss of 8.5 lb in the studies from 1974 and before and of 9.4 lb in the studies from 1978. These are quite stable results considering differences among studies in characteristics of the subjects, cost, training of therapists, and other factors that might influence outcome.

Hidden within these averages is large variability among studies and among subjects within studies. The mean losses in the studies from 1974 and before ranged from 2.4 to 18.9 lb. The range in 1978 was 2.8 to 17.3 lb. This variability is easier to describe than explain. The large differences among studies cannot be attributed easily to therapist characteristics, length of treatment, components in the behavioral package, or other factors obtainable from published accounts of the studies. It is noteworthy that no satisfactory explanation has been proposed for these differences.

There were no substantial changes in the nature of the studies and the outcome from 1974 to 1978, except for the length of follow-up, which increased from 15.5 weeks to 30.3 weeks. This coincided with a call for longer follow-up,[51] which showed growing concern with obesity as a disorder rather than a proving ground for various treatments. There was an increase in the average weight of subjects, but not percentage overweight, which probably resulted from more men in the later studies. The average length of treatment increased from 8.5 to 9.4 weeks, a trend that continues in more recent studies.

To summarize the early studies, average weight losses were approximately one lb per week in programs of eight to nine weeks. The same average was present at follow-up, suggesting good maintenance. However, variability in most studies was greater at follow-up than after treatment, because some subjects went on to lose large amounts while others relapsed.[6] These results, while significant statistically, are relevant clinically only to those subjects who are mildly overweight. With these results in mind, the findings from recent studies are more impressive.

Behavior Therapy: What It Is Now

Current behavior therapy for obesity tends to be different from the self-monitoring and stimulus-control programs used earlier. Today most programs use a more comprehensive approach. Cognitive restructuring has been adopted in most programs, including our own. The emphasis on exercise has increased, and some programs are using social support interventions. Of these three newer approaches, only exercise can be supported by the literature.[10,46] (See chapter 7.) Cognitive restructuring and social support seem to be important clinically, but there is only preliminary evidence showing that their inclusion boosts program effectiveness.

Table 9.1 shows the results from this more comprehensive approach. There was a substantial increase in the average weight loss reported from the studies in 1984 (15.4 lb) compared to those from 1974 (8.5 lb) and 1978 (9.4 lb). The length of treatment increased, from 8.4 weeks in 1974 to 10.5 weeks in 1978, and finally to 13.2 weeks in 1984. One might ask, therefore, whether the greater weight loss in more recent studies results from better programs or simply from longer programs. The table provides a partial answer. The average weight loss per week has not increased from the 1974 and 1978 averages, suggesting that longer treatment is responsible for the better results.

This is a surprising finding, and stands in contrast to our strong clinical impression that today's program is better. Should we think otherwise? Perhaps not.

There is no guarantee that the earlier programs would have sustained the same weight loss per week if treatment duration were increased. The material added to the new programs may provide interesting and relevant information that enables the programs to be lengthened while sustaining the same weight loss per week. Also, the clinical issues faced by dieters are different early and late in the programs. The cognitive techniques, for example, may be helpful in the prevention of relapse[9] and so may be more relevant in later stages of treatment. There is also the possibility that the techniques added recently exert their strongest influence during the maintenance phase of a program.

The average weight loss at follow-up has improved in recent years. The mean weight loss at follow-up in 1984 (9.8 lb) is up from 9.1 lb in 1978 and 8.9 lb in 1974. This is not a large increase, but may be important considering that follow-ups are longer (58.4 weeks in 1984 versus 15.5

weeks and 30.3 weeks in 1974 and 1978). Therefore, the average follow-up loss has increased in the face of longer follow-up.

Conclusions about the maintenance of weight loss can be drawn from several perspectives. Observing only the final loss at follow-up, one sees a small increase in weight loss over a longer follow-up interval. However, the average loss during treatment is greater now, so the ability of subjects to maintain what they have lost has actually declined. In 1978, the average change from posttreatment to follow-up was from 9.4 lb to 9.1 lb, a regain of only 0.3 lb. In 1984, the change was from 15.4 lb to 9.9 lb, a regain of 5.6 lb. Even though the final weight loss at follow-up is slightly greater today, the course of weight change appears to be different. If this course, which is characterized by greater initial losses followed by some regain, has negative physiological or psychological effects, the higher weight loss at follow-up may have to be viewed in a different light. Little is known about the effects of different patterns of weight change, so we can only say that this issue deserves further attention.

The Clinical Utility of Behavioral Approaches

How effective is behavior therapy and what is its proper role in the treatment of obesity? It appears that the current version of the behavioral program produces weight losses of 1 or 1.5 lb per week for the duration of the program. Studies using programs of more than twelve weeks report substantial weight losses. The mean loss for a behavioral group in a fifteen-week program by Perri and associates[38] was 18.9 lb. Craighead, Stunkard, and O'Brien[15] reported a loss of 23.9 lb in a twenty-four-week program, and Brownell and Stunkard[11] found an 18.2-lb loss in sixteen weeks. Jeffery and colleagues reported losses of 21.9, 26.3, and 28.5 lb in studies of fifteen and sixteen weeks[25,26,27] using financial contracts in addition to the behavioral program. Wadden and Stunkard[47] reported a loss of 31 lb for a twenty-five-week program.

These large losses are quite impressive when viewed in terms of other approaches or of earlier behavioral programs. An average loss of 20 to 25 lb is good for persons who are mildly overweight, so behavior therapy may stand alone as a treatment for persons in this weight category.[6,45,53] Furthermore, the long-term maintenance is striking compared to the results from other approaches.[53] A possible strength of behavior therapy, therefore, may lie in its potential for long-term loss. This raises the possibility of combining behavior therapy with other approaches in hopes that more dramatic losses produced by other means, such as with a strict diet, can be maintained with the behavior change program. This issue is discussed in more detail later.

A Comprehensive Program for Managing Obesity

Research on behavioral programs has produced valuable information. It is generally agreed that behavioral approaches used alone miss several key issues in sensible, safe, and effective weight reduction. One such issue is nutrition and another is exercise. Programs vary in the emphasis placed on these factors and on the order in which they are introduced. The behavioral procedures generally take precedence in these programs, which is not surprising since this is the bias of their developers. For these reasons, we have developed a new program in an attempt to remedy these deficits.

FIVE FACTORS IN WEIGHT CONTROL

We now use a program with five components: behavior modification, exercise, cognitive change, social support, and nutrition. The program has been designed to incorporate behavior therapy into a broader program that differs in several fundamental ways from its predecessors. The behavioral techniques, such as self-monitoring, stimulus control, slowing eating, and others, that took precedence in earlier programs now form only one part of our program. Behavioral principles such as shaping and goal setting are used for changes in other areas (e.g., exercise).

This program is also designed to better fit the clinical realities of treating obesity. In working with individuals, we rarely follow the exact schedule cited in our books and manuals. Some dieters have difficulty shopping for food and others do not shop at all. Some are involved in social relationships that influence their eating and weight problems and others are not. This demands greater emphasis on certain parts of the program for some persons. Our program guides people to select the aspects most relevant to them. As an example that crosses the areas of social support and exercise, dieters are given guidelines to choose "social" or "solo" forms of physical activity, based on their personal needs to exercise alone or with others.

Most programs schedule topics sequentially, so that exercise may be covered in week 8, cognitive restructuring in week 10, and so forth. However, we feel that patients need some aspects of exercise early in the program and other aspects later. Therefore, in our program the five components are used throughout, so that in a given session, subjects are given the relevant information on each component.

Behavioral Techniques. Traditional behavioral techniques are used, including stimulus control, self-monitoring, slowing eating, preplanning, substituting alternative activities, and disruption of eating chains.

Exercise. The inclusion of exercise has been identified as one of the few predictors of success in weight-reduction programs.[8] Studies in which exercise has been manipulated have also shown favorable results, as described later. The challenge is to make exercise enjoyable enough for overweight persons so that long-term adherence is probable. This requires special consideration of the psychological and physical issues specific to obese persons. One way to incorporate exercise meaningfully is to begin it at a level that is reasonable, given a person's physical condition and attitudes about exercise. It is important that activity be monitored and reinforced throughout the program.

Cognitive Change. Our plan of cognitive change is an expanded version of the cognitive restructuring developed by Mahoney and Mahoney.[30] It includes goal setting, coping with mistakes, and motivation. There is a strong emphasis on attitudes in the later stages of the program, where relapse prevention becomes the major concern.[9,33] Attitude change is woven into the other parts of the program, so that positive attitudes facilitate adherence to the life style, exercise, relationship, and nutrition parts of the program.

Social Support. Social support is one determinant of health and recovery from illness.[13] It is a correlate of success in some weight studies[8] and can help with the long-term vigilance required for weight loss. We provide dieters with guidelines for evaluating their social environment and for determining whether any persons in this environment could aid their efforts. Specific approaches are described for eliciting and reinforcing supportive persons in their social network.

Nutrition. Nutrition receives little attention in most behavioral programs. Dieters may be taught to count calories but little more. We feel nutrition is important because improper dietary habits could lead to large losses of lean body tissue[48] and to other physical problems that could jeopardize health and the ability to exercise. Rules for proper nutrition are provided rather than specific meal plans, so that patients can choose an adequate diet within their own life-style.

THE USE OF A MANUAL

After the educational content of a program has been devised, the question remains about the best means for conveying the information to patients. While we discuss the material in group meetings, we also feel that written supplementation is necessary. We provide this in the form of a detailed manual, which in its 200 pages describes our entire program. This manual enables patients to review material between sessions, provides more detail than is possible within the time limits of meetings, and is a reference book once the program ends.*

* Information on receiving copies of this manual can be obtained from Dr. K. D. Brownell, Department of Psychiatry, University of Pennsylvania, 133 South 36th Street, Philadelphia, PA 19104.

Current Problems and Applications

Research on the behavioral treatment of obesity is currently directed at two problems—increasing weight losses in treatment and improving maintenance of these losses. The need for such research is readily apparent. A 15- to 25-lb weight loss, as produced by current behavioral programs, is beneficial to persons who are mildly overweight but is not sufficient for moderately obese persons needing to lose 50 to 100 lb. Similarly, although patients in current behavioral programs maintain roughly two-thirds of their weight loss at one-year follow-up, data suggest that patients may eventually gain back to their pretreatment weights. In the following sections we consider efforts to improve results in both of these areas.

Increasing Weight Losses

Methods to increase weight loss have included social support, pharmacotherapy, and, most recently, very-low-calorie diets. Social support has figured more prominently in the maintenance than in the induction of weight loss and, therefore, will be discussed in the section on improving maintenance.

PHARMACOTHERAPY

Anorexic agents were *the* treatment for obesity in the 1950s and 1960s. Their popularity was attributable to the large, yet effortless, weight losses they produced. Two factors, however, led to current restrictions in their use: the abuse potential of many of the drugs, particularly the amphetamines, and the regaining of weight that almost invariably followed termination of pharmacotherapy.

Craighead and her colleagues[14,15] conducted two studies exploring the combination of behavior therapy and pharmacotherapy. They reasoned that pharmacotherapy could produce the large weight losses often missing in behavioral treatment, while behavior therapy might maintain the large weight losses. In the first study, Craighead, Stunkard, and O'Brien[15] found that subjects treated for twenty-five weeks by either pharmacotherapy (fenfluramine hydrochloride) or pharmacotherapy plus behavior therapy lost significantly more weight than subjects treated by behavior therapy alone (losses of 32, 34, and 24 lb, respectively). At one-year follow-up, however, subjects in the first two conditions had regained 18 and 24 lb, respectively, while subjects in the behavior therapy–alone condition had regained only 4 lb. Behavior therapy clearly was not effective in maintaining the large weight losses produced by pharmacotherapy; however, it was an effective long-term treatment when used alone.

Pharmacotherapy and behavior therapy were administered simultaneously in the study just discussed. Craighead[14] then examined whether different sequences of the two therapies would improve results. The answer was a resounding no. Regardless of whether behavior therapy was administered before pharmacotherapy or vice versa, long-term results were no more effective than when the two treatments were administered simultaneously. Results of Craighead's two studies indicate that the long-term results of behavior therapy are not improved by the addition of pharmacotherapy; in fact, they are likely to be compromised. Pharmacotherapy is probably best reserved for cases of medical emergency in which patients need to lose large amounts of weight rapidly in order, for example, to undergo surgery.

VERY-LOW-CALORIE DIETS

The combination of behavior therapy and very-low-calorie diets holds the greatest promise of producing the weight losses needed by moderately and severely obese patients. Very-low-calorie diets are designed to produce the most rapid weight losses possible, while preventing the loss of lean body mass through the provision of 70 to 100 grams of protein a day in a total of 300 to 600 calories.[4,20,48] Protein may be consumed in two forms—as a liquid diet, composed of a milk- or egg-based protein formula, or as solid food including lean meat, fish, and fowl.[5] Both diets produce average weight losses of 45 lb in twelve weeks and appear to be safe when limited to this duration and conducted under careful medical supervision.[48] Current very-low-calorie diets should not be confused with the liquid protein diets of the 1970s, which were associated with at least fifty-eight fatalities.[42] (See chapter 10 for further information about physiological and medical aspects of very-low-calorie diets.)

The major problem with very-low-calorie diets has been weight regain following their termination. For example, 56 percent of Genuth, Vertes, and Hazelton's subjects[21] regained more than half of their 72-lb weight loss at twenty-two month follow-up, while Palgi and associates' patients[35] regained 30 lb of a 45-lb weight loss at a four-and-a-half year follow-up. Unfortunately, the full extent of this problem is not known because of the absence of follow-up data from most reports.[48]

Very-low-calorie Diet Plus Behavior Therapy. It is not surprising that weight losses produced by very-low-calorie diets have not been well maintained: most programs have included only minimal, if any, instruction in behavioral techniques. Our research team at the University of Pennsylvania has therefore been exploring the clinical viability and efficacy of a combined program in which a very-low-calorie diet is used to induce a large weight loss and behavioral methods are aimed at maintenance. Results of a pilot investigation were very encouraging.[49] Seventeen women, with an initial weight of 238 pounds, were treated weekly for six months. The first month they were prescribed a 1,000-calorie diet and instructed in behavioral methods of modifying eating and exercise habits. During months 2 and 3, they received a very-low-calorie diet (400 to 500 calories) and continued with their exercise program. During months 4, 5, and 6, they were returned to a 1,000-calorie diet and received instruction in cognitive-behavioral methods of weight control, which included training in relapse prevention (to be discussed later). Subjects lost 45 lb at the end of treatment and maintained a loss of 41 lb at one-year follow-up.

Controlled Clinical Trial. These very promising results led to a controlled clinical trial to assess the efficacy of this treatment combination.[47] Subjects were randomly assigned to one of three treatment conditions: (1) very-low-calorie diet alone, (2) behavior therapy alone, and (3) very-low-calorie diet plus behavior therapy (combined treatment). All subjects were treated weekly. Those in the diet-alone condition were treated for four months in a program that included two months of a very-low-calorie diet and two months of a 1,000-calorie diet. Subjects in this condition, which was designed to simulate treatment as delivered by most practitioners, received no formal training in behavioral methods of weight control. Behavior therapy–alone subjects were treated for six months using a modified version of our program (described earlier),[49] while combined-treatment subjects were treated for the same length of time following the protocol used in the pilot investigation.

At the end of treatment, subjects in the diet-alone, behavior therapy–alone, and combined-treatment conditions had lost 31.0, 31.5, and 42.5 lb, respectively. The results for combined treatment replicated those obtained in the pilot investigation by Wadden and associates[49] and thus demonstrate that we now have a therapy that will reliably produce clinically significant weight losses. Results for the behavior therapy–alone condition were also favorable and suggest that even larger weight losses might be obtained if standard behavioral treatment were extended beyond six months.

The end-of-treatment losses for the behavior therapy–alone and combined-treatment subjects were only partially maintained at one-year follow-up: both groups of subjects regained approximately one-third of their weight loss, resulting in net weight losses from pretreatment of 20.9 lb and 28.4 lb, respectively. These results appear more favorable, however, when compared with those for the diet-alone subjects, who regained two-thirds of their weight loss (net weight loss of 10.1 lb).

Two points about these findings should be emphasized. First, behavior therapy appeared to facilitate maintenance of weight lost by very-low-calorie diet; subjects who received a very-low-calorie diet plus behavior therapy regained only one-third of their weight loss, while those who received a very-low-calorie diet alone regained two-thirds. Second, a "slow but steady weight loss" produced by behavior therapy resulted in better long-term results than a "quick loss" produced by very-low-calorie diet. The very-low-calorie-diet-alone and behavior therapy–alone subjects lost identical amounts of weight during treatment (30 lb); however, at one-year follow-up, the behavior therapy–alone subjects regained only half as much weight as the diet-alone subjects (10.5 versus 20.9 lb).

Improving Maintenance of Weight Loss

There is a clear need for further research on weight-loss maintenance. Investigators have begun to respond to this need, and the three most promising interventions at this time are exercise, social support (including family and peers), and relapse prevention training.

EXERCISE

Patients who exercise while participating in a behavioral program tend to show better maintenance of weight loss than do patients who do not exercise. This finding, which has been reported by four research teams, was surprising because exercise was found to have little or no effect during treatment.[16,17,23,43] Only when patients were examined six months to one year after treatment did the positive effects appear. In all four studies, patients who received behavior therapy plus exercise continued to lose a small amount of weight (2 to 4 lb) during follow-up, while patients treated by behavior therapy gained a few pounds.

These positive results were achieved with modest levels of physical activity. In most cases, patients were encouraged to increase by 200 to 400 calories a day their energy expenditure by increasing their life-style activity (i.e., walking more, using stairs rather than elevators, etc.). A study of obese children by Epstein and coworkers,[18] in fact, showed that these less physically demanding changes in life-style produced better long-term weight losses than did programmed aerobic activity. Patients may be more likely to adhere to a program of life-style activity than to a rigorous program of aerobic exercise.[10]

Mechanisms of Action. Further research is needed to determine the mechanisms by which exercise acts to maintain body weight at a reduced level. There are several possibilities. The increased expenditure of calories resulting from physical activity may help patients to lose weight and to keep it off. Two miles of walking burns only about 200 calories, but would result in a year's weight loss of 10 lb if done daily. Alternatively, exercise may increase metabolic rate or decrease appetite, which in turn would affect body weight.[10] (See also chapter 7.) These events taken together might reflect or initiate the lowering of a body-weight set point.[3] A final possibility is that exercise positively affects mood and self-esteem; persons who engage in regular physical activity may be less prone to the dysphoric moods that can unleash eating.[46] All of these hypotheses need to be examined.

SOCIAL SUPPORT

Several investigators have examined the utility of including patients' spouses or friends in treatment. Family members may be important in the etiology or maintenance of obesity for some dieters and certainly may aid or hinder the patient's attempts to lose weight. One study found that including spouses in treatment improved weight losses slightly during treatment but improved the long-term results dramatically.[12] At a six-month follow-up, patients treated with their spouses (couples' group) had lost 30 lb while patients in two other standard behavioral conditions, in which spouses were not included, had lost only 19 and 15 lb. One-third of the total weight loss for patients in the couples' group occurred after treatment.

The positive results from this initial study were supported by findings from several other investigations conducted about the same time.[36,40,41] However, the effect of couples' training and social support has not been consistent across studies, as several investigators have failed to find an effect for this intervention.[11,34,50] Thus research efforts must examine the factors that mediate success or failure with family interventions. Issues such as the quality of the marital relationship and the dieter's ability to accept help from others are likely to be important.

Peer Support. Although it has never been systematically evaluated, peer support is likely to be an important factor in the success of behavioral treatment for obesity, just as it is in lay-led programs such as Take off Pounds Sensibly (TOPS) and Overeaters Anonymous (OA). Most behavioral treatment is conducted in groups. Friendships arise in these groups that serve to keep patients in treatment and provide participants, on occasion, with empathy and support of a different kind than that provided by professional therapists. Patients frequently make plans to continue to meet together once the formal program has ended.

Perri and associates[37] examined the effect on weight-loss maintenance of a follow-up program of peer support. At the end of treatment, patients in a "buddy group" continued to hold regular meetings in which they monitored each other's weight, praised those who were successful, and used problem-solving skills to assist persons having difficulty. These patients also had weekly contact with their therapist by telephone and mail. At twenty-one months' follow-up, patients in the buddy group maintained 10 lb of an original 13.5-lb loss. By contrast, patients, receiving standard behavior therapy and six biweekly booster sessions maintained only 0.8 pounds of an original 12.4-lb loss.

These findings, and those from several other studies, demonstrate

that booster sessions alone are not effective in maintaining weight loss.*
Also, as Perri and coworkers[37] pointed out, it was a shame that such
excellent follow-up results were coupled with such modest initial weight
losses (of 13.5 lb). The findings suggest, however, that this economical
follow-up procedure consisting of peer support and patient-therapist contact by mail and phone might be effective in maintaining the much larger
weight losses produced by treatments such as very-low-calorie diets.

RELAPSE PREVENTION TRAINING

The effort to improve the maintenance of weight loss will be aided
by increased understanding of the behavioral, cognitive, emotional, physiological, and social factors associated with regaining of lost weight. We
have little information about how these factors interact to cause weight
regain. The reason for our ignorance is clear: weight regain usually occurs
after patients have finished treatment and are no longer seen in our clinics.
Only after relapse do we see patients again, when they return for a second
round of treatment.

The study of relapse and relapse prevention initially focused on alcohol
use.[32] It soon became apparent, however, that there were striking similarities in relapse rates among programs for the treatments of alcoholism,
drug abuse, obesity, and smoking.[31] Moreover, there are similarities across
patients in the reports of the behavioral, cognitive, emotional, and social
factors associated with relapse.[9]

Marlatt and Gordon[32] describe the process of relapse as follows: (1)
individuals find themselves in a "high-risk situation" in which they are
exposed to the addictive stimulus (alcohol, food, etc.); (2) they do not
have a coping strategy with which to avoid the stimulus and simultaneously
anticipate pleasure from its use; (3) they use the stimulus and feel guilt
and loss of self-control (abstinence violation effect); and (4) as a result of
feeling that they have relapsed and have no self-control, they are more
likely to continue to use the addictive stimulus.

In relapse prevention training, patients are taught to identify high-
risk situations and learn skills needed to cope with such situations. In the
event that they *do* use the addictive stimulus or otherwise transgress their
desired behavior (i.e., gain weight rather than lose), they are taught to
view the episode as a temporary "lapse," from which they can recover,
rather than a "relapse," with its connotation of failure and hopelessness.[32]

Controlled Clinical Trial. Following a successful pilot investigation by
Rosenthal and Marx,[39] Perri and associates[38] conducted a large controlled
trial of relapse prevention training for obesity. Subjects who received a
fifteen-week program of behavior therapy, relapse prevention training,
and follow-up contact by telephone and mail (as described earlier) lost
21.2 lb at the end of treatment and maintained a loss of 22.8 lb at one-
year follow-up. In contrast, patients who received behavior therapy with

* See references 1, 2, 15, 22, and 52.

only relapse prevention training lost 18.8 lb at posttreatment but maintained only a 6.5-lb loss at the one-year follow-up. These latter results were inferior to those of subjects who received behavior therapy alone (losses of 16.5 and 13.8 lb at posttreatment and follow-up, respectively) or behavior therapy plus contact by phone and mail (losses of 19.2 and 12.7 lb at posttreatment and follow-up, respectively).

These findings are perplexing but have at least two implications. First, treatment programs with multiple maintenance components may be more effective than those with single components. If relapse is multiply determined, treatments providing multiple antidotes may be more effective. Second, in training patients in relapse prevention methods, therapists must be careful not to give patients implicit expectations that they will fail to maintain their weight loss (and thus legitimate such failure). This is a difficult task; therapists must help patients to adopt a realistic but optimistic view of what is a difficult task—maintaining weight loss in the face of multiple pressures. Different methods of approaching this problem need to be explored.

Recommendations for Practice and Research

1. Increase the length of treatment. Since programs appear to produce average losses of 1 to 1.5 lb a week for at least sixteen to twenty weeks, the traditional program of ten to twelve weeks should give way to longer initial treatment. Programs of one year may produce losses of 50 lb and give patients greater time to learn maintenance skills. Ultimately, longer treatment may be more cost effective than having patients repeat brief programs that provide brief success. It is unrealistic to expect that nine hours of training in relapse prevention, as provided in the Perri and associates study,[38] is going to reverse what is often a lifelong problem.

2. Increase the use of *in vivo* techniques in clinical settings. Therapists and researchers appear to work almost exclusively with patients' "reports" of their eating behavior rather than the behavior itself. In addition to assessing patients' eating behavior (amount and type of food eaten, rate of eating, etc.) in the clinic, practitioners could teach and observe stimulus-control techniques (leaving food on the plate, slowing eating, etc.). Similarly, the accuracy of patients' self-monitoring and calorie counts could be checked,[28] and nutrition education could be taught with cooking demonstrations. Such *in vivo* practice might help to bridge the gap between what patients report they know and what they actually do.

3. Examine cognitive and emotional factors that appear to disrupt efforts at weight control. Techniques used with bulimic patients of allowing them to overeat and then discussing maladaptive cognitions could be used with

obese patients who are prone to binging after initially overeating by only a small amount. Appropriate self-statements could be modeled for patients while they were actually experiencing emotional distress.

4. Further identify the factors that differentiate weight loss from maintenance. The goal of weight loss is change; the goal of maintenance is no change. Weight loss produces internal and external reinforcement that is often not present during maintenance. The goal of weight loss is to lose large amounts of weight; maintenance involves the quick reversal of small gains. Patients rarely get supervised practice in the latter task because weight regain usually occurs only once treatment has ended.

5. Examine relationship patterns between obese persons and their spouses, friends, coworkers, and others. This may explain why social support interventions are powerful in some cases and ineffective in others. The ultimate aim is to identify persons whose relationships would allow a support program to facilitate weight loss or to tailor programs to an individual's social environment.

6. Evaluate exercise patterns in obese persons asked to increase physical activity. This information would be used to design exercise activities that are enjoyable and beneficial, given the special limitations imposed by patients' excess weight and negative feelings about exercise.

7. Identify methods of combining behavioral techniques with other approaches (e.g., very-low-calorie diet) to produce large losses that are sustained. While this combination of techniques offers promise, precise methods must be developed in response to studies on the timing of various components and the nature and process of relapse.

REFERENCES

1. Ashby, W. A., and Wilson, G. T. 1977. Behavior therapy for obesity: Booster sessions and long-term maintenance of weight loss. *Behaviour Research and Therapy* 15:451–464.

2. Beneke, W. B., et al. 1978. Long-term results of two behavior modification weight loss programs using nutritionists as therapists. *Behavior Therapy* 9:501–507.

3. Bennett, W., and Gurin, J. 1982. *The dieter's dilemma: Eating less and weighing more.* New York: Basic Books.

4. Bistrian, B. R. 1978. Clinical use of a protein-sparing modified fast. *Journal of the American Medical Association* 240:2299–2302.

5. Blackburn, G. L., Bistrian, B. R., and Flatt, J. P. 1975. Role of protein-sparing modified fast in a comprehensive weight reduction program. In *Recent advances in obesity research,* ed. A. N. Howard, pp. 279–281. London: Newman.

6. Brownell, K. D. 1982. Obesity: Understanding and treating a serious, prevalent, and refractory disorder. *Journal of Consulting and Clinical Psychology* 50:820–840.

7. ———. 1985. *The LEARN program for weight control.* Philadelphia: University of Pennsylvania Press.

8. Brownell, K. D. 1984. Behavioral, psychological, and environmental predictors of obesity and success at weight reduction. *International Journal of Obesity* 8:543–550.

9. Brownell, K. D., Marlatt, G. A., Lichtenstein, E., and Wilson, G. T. In press. Understanding and preventing relapse. *American Psychologist.*

10. Brownell, K. D., and Stunkard, A. J. 1980. Exercise in the development and control of obesity. In *Obesity*, ed. A. J. Stunkard, pp. 300–324. Philadelphia: W. B. Saunders.

11. Brownell, K. D., and Stunkard, A. J. 1981. Couples training, pharmacotherapy, and behavior therapy in treatment of obesity. *Archives of General Psychiatry* 38:1223–1229.

12. Brownell, K. D., et al. 1978. The effect of couples training and partner cooperativeness in the behavioral treatment of obesity. *Behaviour Research and Therapy* 16:323–333.

13. Cohen, S., and Syme, S. L. 1985. *Social support and health*. New York: Academic Press.

14. Craighead, L. W. 1984. Sequencing of behavior therapy and pharmacotherapy for obesity. *Journal of Consulting and Clinical Psychology* 52:190–199.

15. Craighead, L. W., Stunkard, A. J., and O'Brien, R. 1981. Behavior therapy and pharmacotherapy for obesity. *Archives of General Psychiatry* 38:763–768.

16. Dahlkoetter, J., Callahan, E. J., and Linton, J. 1979. Obesity and the unbalanced energy equation. *Journal of Consulting and Clinical Psychology* 47:898–905.

17. Epstein, L. H., Wing, R. R., Koeske, R., and Valoski, A. 1984. Effects of diet plus exercise on weight change in parents and children. *Journal of Consulting and Clinical Psychology* 52:429–437.

18. Epstein, L. H., et al. 1982. A comparison of lifestyle change and programmed aerobic exercise on weight and fitness changes in obese children. *Behavior Therapy* 13:651–665.

19. Ferster, C. B., Nurnberger, J. I., and Levitt, E. B. 1962. The control of eating. *Journal of Mathetics* 1:87–109.

20. Genuth, S. 1979. Supplemented fasting in the treatment of obesity and diabetes. *American Journal of Clinical Nutrition* 32:2579–2586.

21. Genuth, S. M., Vertes, V., and Hazelton, J. 1978. Supplemented fasting in the treatment of obesity. In *Recent advances in obesity research*, ed. G. Bray, pp. 370–378. London: Newman.

22. Hall, S. M., Hall, R. G., Borden, B. L., and Hanson, R. W. 1975. Follow-up strategies in the behavioral treatment of overweight. *Behaviour Research and Therapy* 13:167–172.

23. Harris, M. B., and Hallbauer, E. S. 1973. Self-directed weight control through eating and exercise. *Behaviour Research and Therapy* 11:523–529.

24. Jeffery, R. W., Wing, R. R., and Stunkard, A. J. 1978. Behavioral treatment of obesity: State of the art in 1976. *Behavior Therapy* 6:189–199.

25. Jeffery, R. W., et al. 1984. Behavioral treatment of obesity with monetary contracting: Two-year follow-up. *Addictive Behaviors* 9:311–313.

26. Jeffery, R. W., et al. 1984. Calorie requirements in weight loss: An estimate based on self-reported food intake in middle-aged men. *Addictive Behaviors* 9:231–233.

27. Jeffery, R. W., et al. 1984. Effectiveness of monetary contracts with two repayment schedules on weight reduction in men and women from self-referred and population samples. *Behavior Therapy* 15:273–279.

28. Lansky, D., and Brownell, K. D. 1982. Estimates of food quantity and calories: Errors in self-reports among obese patients. *American Journal of Clinical Nutrition* 35:727–732.

29. Mahoney, M. J. 1974. Self-reward and self-monitoring techniques for weight control. *Behavior Therapy* 5:48–57.

30. Mahoney, M. J., and Mahoney, B. K. 1976. *Permanent weight control: A total solution to the dieter's dilemma*. New York: W. W. Norton.

31. Marlatt, G. A. 1985. Relapse prevention: General overview. In *Relapse prevention*, ed. G. A. Marlatt and J. R. Gordon, pp. 3–70. New York: Guilford Press.

32. Marlatt, G. A., and Gordon, J. R. 1980. Determinants of relapse: Implications for the maintenance of behavior change. In *Behavioral medicine: Changing health lifestyles*, ed. P. O. Davidson and S. M. Davidson, pp. 410–452. New York: Brunner/Mazel.

33. Marlatt, G. A., and Gordon, J. 1985. *Relapse prevention*. New York: Guilford Press.

34. O'Neil, P. M., et al. 1979. Effects of sex of subject and spouse involvement on weight loss in a behavioral treatment program: A retrospective investigation. *Addictive Behaviors* 4:167–177.

35. Palgi, A., et al. 1985. Multidisciplinary treatment of obesity with a protein-sparing modified fast: Results in 668 outpatients. *American Journal of Public Health* 75:1190–1194.

36. Pearce, J. W., LeBow, M. D., and Orchard, J. 1981. The role of spouse involvement in the behavioral treatment of obese women. *Journal of Consulting and Clinical Psychology* 49:236–244.

37. Perri, M. G., McAdoo, W. G., Spevak, P. A., and Newlin, D. B. 1984. Effects of a

multicomponent maintenance program on long-term weight loss. *Journal of Consulting and Clinical Psychology* 52:480–481.

38. Perri, M. G., et al. 1984. Maintenance strategies for the treatment of obesity: An evaluation of relapse prevention training and posttreatment contact by mail and telephone. *Journal of Consulting and Clinical Psychology* 52:404–413.

39. Rosenthal, B. S., and Marx, R. D. 1979. A comparison of standard behavioral and relapse prevention weight control program. Paper presented at the meeting of the Association for Advancement of Behavior Therapy, Chicago, December.

40. Rosenthal, B. S., Allen, G. J., and Winter, C. 1980. Husband involvement in the behavioral treatment of overweight women: Initial effects and long-term follow-up. *International Journal of Obesity* 4:165–173.

41. Saccone, A. J., and Israel, A. C. 1978. Effects of experimenter versus significant other–controlled reinforcement and choice of target behavior on weight loss. *Behavior Therapy* 9:271–278.

42. Sours, H. E., et al. 1981. Sudden death associated with very low calorie weight reduction regimens. *American Journal of Clinical Nutrition* 34:453–461.

43. Stalonas, P. M., Johnson, W. G., and Christ, M. 1978. Behavior modification for obesity: The evaluation of exercise, contingency management, and program adherence. *Journal of Consulting and Clinical Psychology* 46:463–469.

44. Stuart, R. B. 1967. Behavioral control of overeating. *Behaviour Research and Therapy* 5:357–365.

45. Stunkard, A. J. 1984. The current status of treatment for obesity in adults. In *Eating and its disorders,* ed. A. J. Stunkard and E. Stellar, pp. 157–174. New York: Raven Press.

46. Thompson, J. K., Jarvie, G. J., Lahey, B. B., and Cureton, K. J. 1982. Exercise and obesity: Etiology, physiology, and intervention. *Psychological Bulletin* 91:55–79.

47. Wadden, T. A., and Stunkard, A. J. In press. A controlled trial of very-low-calorie diet in the treatment of obesity. *Journal of Consulting and Clinical Psychology.*

48. Wadden, T. A., Stunkard, A. J., and Brownell, K. D. 1983. Very low calorie diets: Their efficacy, safety, and future. *Annals of Internal Medicine* 99:675–684.

49. Wadden, T. A., Stunkard, A. J., Brownell, K. D., and Day, S. C. 1984. Treatment of obesity by very-low-calorie diet and behavior therapy: A pilot investigation. *Journal of Consulting and Clinical Psychology* 52:692–694.

50. Weisz, G., and Butcher, B. 1980. Involving husbands in the treatment of obesity: Effects on weight loss, depression, and marital satisfaction. *Behavior Therapy* 11:643–650.

51. Wilson, G. T. 1978. Methodological considerations in treatment outcome research on obesity. *Journal of Consulting and Clinical Psychology* 46:687–702.

52. Wilson, G. T., and Brownell, K. D. 1978. Behavior therapy for obesity: Including family members in the treatment process. *Behavior Therapy* 9:943–945.

53. Wilson, G. T., and Brownell, K. D. 1980. Behavior therapy for obesity: An evaluation of treatment outcome. *Advances in Behavior Research and Therapy* 3:49–86.

10

The Very-Low-Calorie Diet: A Weight-Reduction Technique

George L. Blackburn, Margaret E. Lynch, and Stacie L. Wong

Increased mortality and morbidity are associated with body weight greater than 30 percent of ideal. Only a small minority of obese patients seeking professional help achieve and sustain weight loss by conventional dieting. Correlates of obesity such as hyperglycemia, hypertension, orthopedic disability, increased risk from surgery, and psychological distress accentuate the medical significance of obesity and sensitize physicians to the difficulties of treatment. Within the past decade new approaches have been recognized, including gastric bypass surgery for the treatment of morbid refractory obesity, behavior modification, and special diets. This chapter discusses the very-low-calorie diet (VLCD), a weight-reduction diet that has been administered and studied in clinics of North America and Europe over the past two decades. Essentially, it is a modification of the fasting approach to weight loss.

Supplemented Fast

Total fasting has been accepted by some researchers as a valid approach to in-hospital weight reduction in cases of refractory obesity. A total fast results in rapid, significant weight loss. If much of this weight loss consists of lean body tissue, no good end is served. Loss of body fat—not protein—is the goal of dieting. Total fasting is associated with significant losses of body protein. This protein malnutrition may have serious consequences on hepatic, renal, and pulmonary function.[16,21,23] The state of malnutrition created by total fasting may be self-defeating. Restoration of lean tissue loss following a fast requires ample dietary intake and is accompanied by some fat reaccumulation.[22] Long-term therapeutic results with total fasting are very poor.[12] Weight regain is obligatory and the internal signals to overeat may be exacerbated.

VLCDs are supplemented fasts that physiologically modify the protein catabolism associated with total fasting. They are designed to spare body protein while maximizing fat loss. The VLCD is a modification of a total fast, not of a balanced diet of moderate caloric intake. Patients remain in a physiologically fasting state. Protein intake minimizes protein catabolism. VLCDs provide 200 to 800 kcal per day, primarily of protein of high biologic value (with or without carbohydrates) and proper mineral, vitamin, and electrolyte supplementation. Some VLCDs currently in use include the Cambridge Diet,[19] Optifast,[17] Modifast, and the Protein-Sparing Modified Fast (PSMF).[9]

VLCDs may be administered as formulas, powders, or conventional foodstuffs. The Cambridge Diet, Optifast, and Modifast are chemically defined formulas or powders. Protein, carbohydrate, minerals, electrolytes, and essential fatty acids are included. Caloric and nutrient levels remain constant, obviating calorie counts by the physician. The PSMF consists of conventional food items. These are animal protein foods of high biological value, (meat, fish, or fowl), very limited use of low-carbohydrate vegetables, high fluid intake (noncaloric beverages), and vitamin, mineral, and electrolyte supplementation.

The rapid weight loss experienced during supplemented fasting encourages diet adherence. Paradoxically, VLCDs are easier to follow than conventional weight-reducing balanced diets if patient motivation is high. VLCDs are simple, restrictive, and clearly defined. Most patients report loss of hunger—an incompletely explained phenomenon possibly related to the mild ketoacidosis brought about by the diets. Short-term results with the diets are excellent.

VLCDs are not new. The earliest scientific studies are Mason's in 1924.[29] More extensive experience was reported by Allen, Stillman, and Fritz in 1919 in their study of diabetic patients in the preinsulin era[1] and by Evans and Strang in 1931.[13] In 1966 Bolinger and coworkers were the first researchers to formulate the concept of a "protein-sparing fast."[10]

Nitrogen Balance

The role of protein in VLCDs cannot be overemphasized. Amino acid supplementation suppresses insulin secretion, thereby modifying the inhibition of fat mobilization, and replenishes the amino acid pool, thereby facilitating protein anabolism. Limited amounts of exogenous amino acids do not markedly affect weight loss and prevent nitrogen imbalance. It is assumed that the measurement of nitrogen balance (N bal), the amount of nitrogen entering the body versus the amount excreted in the urine and feces, reflects the status of body protein metabolism. N bal is assessed by the formula:

N bal = N intake − (urinary N + fecal N

+ estimated integumental and miscellaneous N losses).

The latter variable is estimated to be 5 mg N per kg body weight. Negative N bal—nitrogen loss greater than nitrogen intake—reflects excessive protein catabolism associated with total fasting. A near equilibrium or positive N bal is the goal of VLC dieting. This balance reflects the preservation of body protein stores. Measures of N bal obtained during periods of modified fasting have shown that body protein can be maintained as long as adequate protein is provided by the diet.[5] Again, this finding is based on the premise that N bal equals body protein preservation.

The optimal composition of a VLCD is estimated to be 1.5 g protein per kg ideal body weight (IBW) per day. Nitrogen equilibrium is attained after fourteen to twenty-one days of supplemented fasting.[8] Protein intake (of hydrolyzed collagen fortified with tryptophan, egg albumin, or lean meat) must be supplemented with potassium, magnesium, phosphate, sodium, and calcium. Positive N bal in patients receiving less than 1.5 g protein per kg IBW have been reported. Such findings could reflect failure to account for fecal and cutaneous nitrogen losses.

Total urinary nitrogen (TUN) is the classic method of assessing N bal. This technique requires nitrogen analysis after micro-Kjeldhal digestion. It is expensive and difficult to perform. Based on their findings that urinary urea nitrogen (UUN) correlates linearly with TUN, Makenzie and associates have proposed that TUN can be inferred by adding a constant of 2 to the UUN value.[28] In order to conservatively estimate nitrogen loss, these researchers recommend adding a constant of 4 to the UUN. This equation is a cost-effective and accurate technique for assessing N bal.

When comparing N bal studies in obese individuals, initial body weight is a consideration. Morbidly obese individuals may have increased lean body mass. At a given protein intake, they may be in more negative N bal than moderately obese patients because of increased lean body mass. Dietary factors influencing N bal include total caloric value of the diet,

FIGURE 10.1

Nitrogen balance (N bal) at different weeks for two VLCD. Open bars indicate N bal for the higher protein diet (1.5 g/kg ideal body weight/day [IBW/d]); shaded bars indicate N bal for the lower protein diet (0.8 g/kg IBW/d).

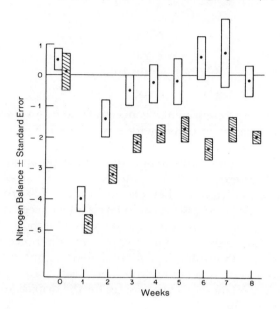

NOTE: Reprinted, by permission of the publisher, from L. J. Hoffer et al., 1984, Metabolic effects of very low calorie weight reduction diets, *Journal of Clinical Investigation* 73:754.

amount and type of protein, and characteristics of the patient's diet prior to the modified fast. There exists individual variation in the response to VLC dieting. Variables affecting N bal include age, sex, hormonal status, and levels of specific micronutrients.[32,35]

Discrepancy surrounds the optimal amount of protein required for N bal. Variable results may be explained by difficulties with the N bal technique and its interpretations. Investigators are familiar with the limitations of the N bal technique. It illustrates nitrogen input and output but not the adaptations, perhaps undesirable, that the body must undergo to accommodate inadequate nutrition. Research comparing varying protein levels of VLCDs shows that the proportion of body protein that undergoes continuous synthesis and breakdown diminishes during protein deficient VLCDs as a mechanism to conserve body protein stores.[4] Measurements of body protein turnover rates may be important. Although a VLCD shows favorable N bal, this may occur via major decrease in body protein turnover rates. VLCDs with a high protein content are associated with better N bal and, thus, better protein retention than lower protein diets as illustrated in figure 10.1. This finding can be explained as a more favorable balance between protein intake and oxidation. Perhaps no reduction in amino acid oxidation is necessary to establish N bal with the higher-protein diet. The generous protein allotments permit nitrogen equilibrium despite inefficient amino acid utilization caused by energy deficit.

Carbohydrate Intake

It is clear that a high protein intake is necessary to ensure protein equilibrium. The importance of carbohydrate is debated. Some researchers favor the addition of carbohydrate as an electrolyte-retaining adjunct that minimizes the diuresis and subsequent orthostatic hypotension associated with VLCDs. Other researchers favor the exclusion of carbohydrate. By omitting carbohydrate from the diet, plasma insulin levels are suppressed and ketosis is induced. Depressed insulin levels effect accelerated release of free fatty acids from adipose tissue and increased fat mobilization. The ketonuria that results aids in monitoring patient adherence to the diet. Except for patients with insulin-dependent diabetes, gout, or sodium depletion, the ketotic state is generally considered safe. More generous sodium chloride supplementation compensates for the urinary sodium losses that accompany ketonuria.

During the keto-adaptive phase encompassing the first few weeks of the diet, protein metabolism may be more sensitive than fat metabolism to reduced insulin levels. With the progressive increase in ketone production and reduction in nitrogen excretion, it is believed that reduced insulin levels stimulate both protein anabolism and fat utilization. Ketone bodies serve as a substitute fuel source for the brain. By replacing glucose as an energy source, ketone bodies reduce gluconeogenesis. Ketone bodies also reduce glucose requirements by the brain and bone marrow. Physiological increases in betahydroxybutyrate inhibit oxidation of branched-chain amino acids in muscle. The overall effect is reduced catabolism in muscle. The interrelationship of these metabolic fuels is illustrated in figure 10.2.

Vitamin and Mineral Intake

It is crucial to supplement VLCDs in order to meet the Recommended Daily Allowances of vitamins and minerals. Adequate potassium is necessary in order to achieve optimal protein-sparing. The protein-sparing characteristics of VLCDs increase potassium requirements beyond those

FIGURE 10.2

Metabolic fuel regulatory system showing the relationships between the concentration of metabolic fuels and insulin. Arrows describe how concentrations in the blood are influenced. Metabolic pathways for the oxidative degradation of the various fuels lead to common terminal reactions and have the effect of a metabolic funnel.
In this manner the oxidation of all the metabolic fuels is integrated so that the total energy generated equals energy expenditure.

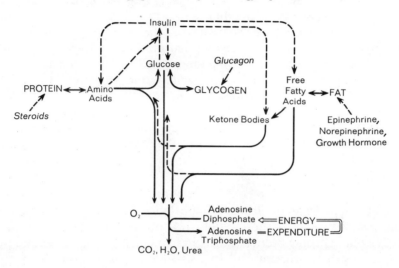

NOTE: Reprinted, by permission of the publisher, from J. P. Flatt and G. L. Blackburn, 1974, Implications for therapies during caloric deprivation and disease, *American Journal of Nutrition* 27:176.

for a total fast. The recommended daily allowance of potassium is 2 g. A liquid form of potassium taken via a sugar-free vehicle is permissible. Any metabolizable anion (i.e., glucenate or citrate) or bicarbonate must be excluded, for these counteract ketosis. Slow-release potassium chloride tablets should be avoided because of reduced gut mobility in semistarved patients. Salt is not restricted. In fact, sodium intake should be at least 5 g per day in order to counteract sodium loss through diuresis. Eight hundred mg of daily calcium supplementation is required.

Patient Population

Because of the manageable yet unavoidable risks of VLC dieting, mildly overweight patients who weigh less than or equal to 30 percent more than ideal body weight should be administered an 800 to 1,500 kcal balanced diet. For this population, excess weight is a cosmetic and psychological problem rather than a medical one and does not justify a more calorically restricted weight-loss program. Moderate obesity, or body weight greater than 30 percent and less than 100 percent more than ideal body weight, is clinically significant and is correlated with increased morbidity and mortality. Successful weight loss by conventional dietary therapy is marginal in this population. VLC dieting coupled with behavior modification and careful physician-supervised follow-up care is the preferred approach to weight reduction.

In morbidly obese patients—those weighing more than twice ideal body weight—recidivism of weight lost by VLC dieting is nearly universal. Surgical bypass is considered the treatment of choice. Preoperative weight loss of 20 to 50 pounds by VLC dieting is surgically advantageous especially for those patients with restrictive pulmonary disease, mild heart failure, and/or obesity-hypoventilation syndrome. In many patients, a fatty liver accompanies diabetes, hyperlipidemia, or simply extreme obesity. VLC dieting produces a rapid mobilization of hepatic fat. The liver returns to a more normal size and surgery can be performed with greater safety and ease.

PEDIATRIC PATIENTS

Protein-sparing is of primary importance in pediatric patients for whom net anabolism is the physiological norm. VLCDs may be more effective than chronic reducing diets in maximizing weight loss and preventing growth retardation.[11,31] In a six-month follow-up study of eight pediatric patients who had dieted for one to eight months, there was no change in height for age.[30] Rapid, protracted, safe weight reduction is essential in markedly obese adolescents, especially those in whom obesity is accompanied by other morbidity such as hypertension, abnormal carbohydrate metabolism, or respiratory difficulties.

DIABETIC PATIENTS

VLCDs best maintain lean body mass in obese diabetic patients having some endogenous insulin and allow the early withdrawal of exogenous insulin. VLCDs should be administered only to inpatient obese diabetic individuals until further experience is gained.[6] Although the optimal schedule is unknown, discontinuation of insulin can be performed over one to two weeks at one-half of the customary dose. Insulin can be withdrawn immediately from obese diabetic patients who require only thirty to thirty-five units of insulin per day.

Contraindications

VLCDs may be administered to patients with chronic cardiovascular disease since weight loss improves their cardiovascular function. VLCDs are contraindicated in patients with cerebrovascular insufficiency because of the risk of postural hypotension. These diets are also not recommended for patients with recent myocardial infarction. Free fatty acid elevation may affect cardiac arrhythmias in these patients. Because of the protein content of VLCDs, they should not be administered to patients with severe liver or kidney complications. Nor should patients with juvenile-onset diabetes be administered VLCDs since their disease precludes discontinuation of insulin. Pregnancy, lithium therapy, and psychological instability contraindicate VLC dieting. VLCDs are not administered to geriatric patients because of limited information and the potential for harm.

Side Effects

Adaptive changes that occur during the first seven to ten days of the dieting may lead to mild postural hypotension. As discussed later, this can be minimized by prescribing a balanced diet several weeks prior to initiation of the VLCD. Salt and water should be provided in the VLCD. Constipation may occur and can be alleviated by a mild laxative or fiber such as low-carbohydrate vegetables. In cases of temporary amenorrhea, a pregnancy test should be performed since pregnancy contraindicates the VLCD. Possible changes in blood chemistry involve increased uric acid and decreased triglycerides and cholesterol. Patients may experience dry skin, mild fatigue, hair loss, and cold intolerance.

Weight Loss

Weight loss produced by the diets is proportional to the duration of treatment. There is a significant difference in body mass index (BMI) and percent of body fat at the end of the weight-loss period. The mean rate of weight loss for men is 1.5 to 2.5 kg per week; for women it is 1.0 to 2.0 kg per week. The weight loss is primarily fat. Weight loss produced by VLCDs is much greater than that produced by other nonsurgical treatments. Most conventional treatments result in mean weight losses of less than 7 kg. Losses on VLCDs are 7 to 10 kg for four weeks, 20 kg for twelve weeks, and 31 to 41 kg for twenty-four weeks. Table 10.1 provides a more descriptive summary of weight lost on VLCDs.

Refeeding

Refeeding is accomplished over at least four weeks. Milk and milk products, vegetables, cereals, and fruits are slowly introduced in that order. Simple sugars are avoided. In the case of carbohydrate-free diets, potassium supplementation ceases once ketonuria disappears. This approach avoids the abrupt fluid gain that would occur if carbohydrates were immediately introduced.

Comprehensive Weight Control Program

VLCDs are not used as sole therapy for weight control. The VLCD is a therapeutic measure used to achieve substantial weight loss within a program oriented toward permanent weight control. This program can be divided into three phases, as shown in figure 10.3. The first phase involves a clinical evaluation of the patient and his or her dietary intake. As discussed earlier, only those individuals who can tolerate the physical and emotional demands of the program are included.

Clinical evaluation includes physical examination, medical history, personality inventory, dietary questionnaire, personal interview, and anthropometrics. Body density may also be included. A complete blood chemistry including serum electrolytes, urea nitrogen (BUN), bilirubin, protein albumin, uric acid, triglycerides, cholesterol, glutamic oxaloacetic and/or peptide transaminase, lactic dehydrogenase, alkaline phosphatase, calcium, phosphorus, hemogram, and thyroid (T_4) is obtained. A complete urinalysis is performed in addition to a chest x-ray and electrocardiogram. Patients are given a food diary at the initial clinic visit, which is to be returned at the following visit. At that visit, patients may be administered a balanced diet of 800 to 1,200 kcal. By beginning the program with balanced dieting, the patient receives a gradual introduction to caloric deprivation. Gradual diuresis occurs, preventing the rapid sodium loss associated with the abrupt institution of the VLCD. In addition, adherence to a balanced diet is an index of potential adherence to the VLCD.

The next phase of the program is the rapid weight loss program.

TABLE 10.1

Summary Analysis of Eight Major Studies Using VLCD

Study	Subjects[a] N	Sex	Mean Pretreatment Weight (kg)	Mean Age (Years)	Diet Regimen	Mean Treatment Duration (Weeks)	Mean Weight Loss (kg)	Mean Weight Loss at Follow-up[b] (kg)
Howard et al.[20]	22	19 F, 3 M	107.8	—	Formula (protein, 31 g; carbohydrate, 44 g)	4	9.6	13.2 (7 subjects stayed on diet 6 wks)
	28 (22)	25 F, 3 M	96.3	—	Formula (same as above)	6	9.0	15.7 (6 subjects stayed on diet 12 wks)
McLean Baird and Howard[27]	38 (25)	30 F, 8 M	104.4	17–62 (range)	Formula (protein, 25 g; carbohydrate, 40 g)	8	13.8	12.2 kg (1 mo)
Atkinson and Kaiser[2]	234	200 F, 34 M	104.5	37.9	Formula (protein, 1 g/kg ideal body weight; sucrose, 0.5 g/kg ideal body weight)	Maximum of 12	18.7 (at 12 wks)	—
Tuck et al.[37]	25	14 F, 11 M	103.9	40.7	Formula (Optifast)	12	20.2	18.4 kg (12 mos); 14.5 (18–24 mos)
Linder and Blackburn[25]	67	57 F, 10 M	93.6	48	Formula (Hentex P-20; training in nutrition and behavior modification)	16.7	20.8	
Palgi et al.[33]	668	564 F, 104 M	98	38.5	Animal protein (protein, 1.5 g/kg ideal body weight; training in nutrition and behavior modification)	17	21	6.6 (216 subjects sampled at 4.5 yrs)
Vertes, Genuth, and Hazelton[39,c]	411	F	109.6	40	Formula (protein, 45 g; glucose, 30 g)	23.8	31.2	—
Genuth, Castro, and Vertes[17]	119	M	136.6	40	Same as above	19.9	37.6	56% of total regained 50% of weight lost (22 mos)
	45 (28)	F	112.5	42	Formula (protein, 45 g; glucose, 30 g)	23	32.5	
	30 (19)	M	137.8	44	Same as above	19	41.1	—

NOTE: Reprinted, by permission of the publisher, from T. A. Wadden, A. J. Stunkard, and K. D. Brownell, 1983, Very low caloric diets: their efficacy, safety and future, *Annals of Internal Medicine* 99: 679.

[a] All subjects seen as outpatients except for 22 subjects in Howard and associates.[20] Subjects in Genuth, Castro, and Vertes's study[17] were seen as inpatients for first week, but as outpatients thereafter. Number in parentheses is number of subjects after attrition.

[b] All follow-up weights calculated from pretreatment values.

[c] Data show mean weight loss for all patients, rather than percentage of patients meeting weight loss criteria as in original study.

FIGURE 10.3

*Example of a comprehensive weight control program illustrating priority levels and
interactions of various components across phases of the program.*

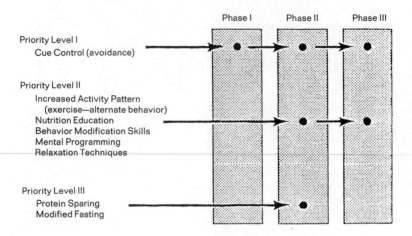

NOTE: Reprinted, by permission of the publisher, from G. L. Blackburn and I. Greenberg, 1978,
Multidisciplinary approach to adult obesity therapy, *International Journal of Obesity* 2:136.

During the VLCD patients should be seen weekly by personnel knowledgeable in the metabolism of fasting. Each weekly follow-up includes a
check for medical symptoms and measurements of blood pressure, weight,
and urine or breath ketones, if applicable. Serum electrolytes, BUN, glucose, and hemoglobin are checked periodically.

Weight maintenance is the goal of the program. The weight-loss and
maintenance components are separate entities. Techniques suitable for
the weight-loss phase are inappropriate for weight maintenance. Successful
weight maintenance is defined as the adoption of normal eating patterns,
recovery from dysphoria encountered at the completion of VLC dieting,
and voluntary restriction of eating during periods of emotional stress.
Maintenance techniques such as nutrition education, mental recondition-
ing, behavior modification, relaxation, and exercise can be introduced
during the fasting period. An exercise regimen is crucial to successful
weight control. It is not only the increased caloric expenditure but also
the life-style changes introduced by regular exercise that will prevent
patients from regaining weight.

There have been few studies of weight-loss maintenance following
VLC dieting. What studies exist show the necessity of research in this
area. Moderately obese patients who underwent a multidisciplinary weight-
control program were contacted at two-year follow-up. They had regained
only 6.3 kg of their 20.8 kg weight loss.[25] At five-year follow-up Palgi
and associates[33] found that patients had regained 16.1 kg of a 22.7 kg
loss. These results illustrate the necessity of research on VLCDs regarding
maintenance of weight loss.

Liquid Protein Diet

The VLCD should not be mistakenly identified with the liquid protein diet (LPD) popularized by Linn and Stuart.[26] Dubbed "The Last Chance Diet," the LPD consisted of liquid collagen of poor biological quality. VLCDs use high biological quality protein and are administered under the supervision of a physician. Any discussion of diet regimens should clarify the distinction between these two diets. The Food and Drug Administration and the Centers for Disease Control investigated forty-six deaths associated with LPDs. In retrospective studies of this "liquid protein mayhem," no single factor seemed responsible, although ventricular tachycardia and fibrillation were frequently the principal events immediately preceding death.[15,36] Morbidly obese patients are at a naturally higher risk for cardiac-related mortality. The death rate of LPD patients greatly exceeded the death rate of other VLCD patients. Four deaths out of 1,300 VLCD patients, as reported by Vertes, Genuth, and Hazelton, is an expected number for this patient population.[38]

Determining the cause of the high death rate associated with the LPD is difficult. Events often ignored but important are the fasting and refeeding procedures themselves. Compliance with protein and nutritional supplements is questionable when patients are not under the care of a competent physician. The vulnerability of patients to cardiac complications during the refeeding state is exacerbated by the discontinuation of supplements (potassium), the reintroduction of diuretics, and binge eating (especially of high-carbohydrate foods), which combine to set up rapid cellular shifts of potassium, sodium, and water. It is possible that a potassium deficiency may develop with LPDs despite normal serum potassium values and potassium supplementation. This may lead to damage of the myocardium. The mechanism of sudden death on LPDs is unknown. It is uncertain whether the deaths resulted from dietary deficiencies (of protein, potassium, or trace elements), the presence of a toxic agent, or an unidentified cause. The deaths associated with use of the LPD illustrate the importance of understanding the potential dangers of any semistarvation regimen and, more important, emphasize the necessity of close physician supervision.

Safety of VLCDs

In contrast to adverse effects of the LPDs, VLCDs are safe. In the course of seven years during which 1,200 patients were on a VLCD for a mean of four months, no deaths occurred.[3] While deterioration in cardiac performance has been documented with the LPD, electrocardiograms and twenty-four-hour Holter monitoring have indicated actual improvement with VLCDs. Twenty-four-hour Holter monitoring has been used as a sensitive detector of cardiac arrhythmias.[24] Patton and colleagues[34] found no alterations in pre- and postdiet monitoring readings in patients on a VLCD providing high biological value protein.

The course of patients on hypocaloric protein- and mineral-supplemented diets for a maximum of twelve weeks has generally been devoid of major medical complications. Because of the lack of evidence regarding the safety and efficacy of these diets beyond twelve weeks, physicians and patients should be aware of potential dangers especially if adherence to the diet continues for more than three consecutive months.

Conclusion

The virtue of VLCDs lies in their large and rapid weight losses. These regimens should *not* be used independently. The VLCD is one component of a comprehensive weight-control program involving education, behavior modification, exercise, and cognitive training. The weight control program lasts for a minimum of twenty, a mean of thirty, and a maximum of fifty weeks. It should be considered a preparatory stage allowing the patient to develop a set point to which he or she can adapt.

Maintenance of this set-point weight cannot be overemphasized. There is no benefit from weight that is lost only to be regained in a "yo-yo" process. In addition to the psychological trauma that accompanies such weight fluctuation, there may be physiological trauma. A second attempt at weight loss is made more difficult by the possibility that the body has adapted to the lower caloric intake responsible for the initial weight loss. The dangers of such weight fluctuation reinforce the importance of including the VLCD in a comprehensive weight-loss program whose ultimate goal is life-style change and weight maintenance.

VLCDs are especially suited for patients with medically significant obesity who are at increased risk for morbidity and mortality. Obesity should be considered a contributing factor in the etiology and development of disease, and a comprehensive weight-loss program should be considered a primary intervention in the treatment of these pathological states. A second group of patients who benefit from VLCDs are those with surgically significant obesity. Preoperative weight loss decreases the risks not only for cardiovascular and respiratory surgical complications but also for wound infection and dehiscence.

REFERENCES

1. Allen, F. M., Stillman, E., and Fritz, R. 1919. *Total dietary regulation in the treatment of diabetes.* Monograph 11. New York: Rockefeller Institute of Medical Research.

2. Atkinson, R. L., and Kaiser, D. L. 1981. Nonphysician supervision of a very-low-calorie diet: Results in over 200 cases. *International Journal of Obesity* 5:237–241.

3. Bistrian, B. R., and Hoffer, J. 1982. The treatment of obesity. In *Current therapy,* ed. H. F. Conn, pp. 444–447. Philadelphia: W. B. Saunders.

4. Bistrian, B. R., Sherman, M., and Young, V. 1981. The mechanism of nitrogen sparing in fasting supplement by protein and carbohydrate. *Journal of Clinical Endocrinology and Metabolism* 53:874–878.

5. Bistrian, B. R., et al. 1975. Protein requirements for net anabolism with a hypocaloric diet. *Clinical Research* 23:315A.

6. Bistrian, B. R., et al. 1976. Nitrogen metabolism and insulin requirements in obese diabetic adults on a protein-sparing modified fast. *Diabetes* 25:494–504.

7. Blackburn, G. L., and Greenberg, I. 1978. Multidisciplinary approach to adult obesity therapy. *International Journal of Obesity* 2:133–142.

8. Blackburn, G. L., Bistrian, B. R., and Flatt, J. P. 1974. Preservation of the physiological responses in a protein-sparing modified fast. *Clinical Research* 22:461A.

9. ————. 1974. Role of a protein sparing fast in a comprehensive weight reduction programme. In *Recent advances in obesity research: 1. Proceedings of the first International Congress on obesity,* ed. A. Howard, pp. 279–281. London: Newman Publishing.

10. Bolinger, R. E., et al. 1966. Metabolic balance of obese subjects during fasting. *Archives of Internal Medicine* 118:3–8.

11. Dietz, W. H., and Schoeller, D. A. 1982. Optimal dietary therapy for obese adolescents: Comparison of protein plus glucose and protein plus fat. *Journal of Pediatrics* 100: 638–644.

12. Drenick, E. J., and Johnson, D. 1980. Weight reduction by fasting and semi-starvation in morbid obesity: Long-term followup. In *Obesity: Comparative methods of weight control,* ed. G. A. Bray, pp. 25–34. Westport, Conn.: Technomic Publishing.

13. Evans, F. A., and Strang, J. M. 1931. The treatment of obesity with very low calorie diets. *Journal of the American Medical Association* 97:1063–1069.

14. Flatt, J. P., and Blackburn, G. L. 1974. Implications for protein-sparing therapies during caloric deprivation and disease. *American Journal of Clinical Nutrition* 27:175–187.

15. Frank, A., Graham, C., and Frank, S. 1981. Fatalities on the liquid protein diet. An analysis of possible causes. *International Journal of Obesity* 5:243–248.

16. Garnett, E. S., et al. 1969. Gross fragmentation of cardiac myofibrils after therapeutic starvation for obesity. *Lancet* 1:914–916.

17. Genuth, S. M., Castro, J., and Vertes, V. 1974. Weight reduction in obesity by outpatient semi-starvation. *Journal of the American Medical Association* 230:987–991.

18. Hoffer, L. J., et al. 1984. Metabolic effects of very low calorie weight reduction diets. *Journal of Clinical Investigation* 73:750–758.

19. Howard, A. N., and McLean Baird, I. 1977. Very low calorie semi-synthetic diets in the treatment of obesity: An inpatient/outpatient study. *Nutrition and Metabolism* 21 (Suppl. 1):59–61.

20. Howard, A. N., et al. 1978. The treatment of obesity with a very-low-calorie liquid-formula diet: An inpatient/outpatient comparison using skimmed milk as the chief protein source. *International Journal of Obesity* 2:321–332.

21. Isner, J. M., et al. 1979. Sudden unexpected death in avid dieters using the liquid protein modified fast diet. *Circulation* 60:1401–1412.

22. Jackson, A. A., Chir, B., Picou, D., and Reeds, P. J. 1977. The energy cost of repleting tissue deficits during recovery from protein-energy malnutrition. *American Journal of Clinical Nutrition* 30:1514–1519.

23. Keys, A., et al. 1950. *The biology of human starvation.* Minneapolis: University of Minnesota Press.

24. Lantigua, R. A., et al. 1980. Cardiac arrhythmia associated with a liquid protein diet for the treatment of obesity. *New England Journal of Medicine* 303:735–738.

25. Lindner, P. G., and Blackburn, G. L. 1976. Multidisciplinary approach to obesity utilizing fasting modified by protein-sparing therapy. *Obesity/Bariatric Medicine* 5:198–216.

26. Linn, R., and Stuart, S. L. 1976. *The last chance diet.* Secaucus, N.J.: Lyle Stuart.

27. McLean Baird, I., and Howard, A. N. 1977. A double-blind trial of mazindal using a very low calorie formula diet. *International Journal of Obesity* 1:271–278.

28. Makenzie, T. A., et al. 1984. A simple method for estimating nitrogen balance in hospitalized patients. Manuscript.

29. Mason, E. H. 1924. The treatment of obesity. *Canadian Medical Association Journal* 14:1052–1056.

30. Merritt, R. J. 1978. Treatment of pediatric and adolescent obesity. *International Journal of Obesity* 2:207–214.

31. Merritt, R. J., Bistrian, B. R., Blackburn, G. L., and Suskind, R. M. 1980. Consequences of modified fasting in obese pediatric and adolescent patients. I. Protein-sparing modified fast. *Journal of Pediatrics* 96:13–19.

32. Munro, H. N., and Crim, N. C. 1980. The proteins and amino acids. In *Modern nutrition in health and disease,* ed. R. S. Goodhart and M. E. Shils, pp. 51–98. Philadelphia: Lea & Febiger.

33. Palgi, A., et al. 1985. Multidisciplinary treatment of obesity with a protein-sparing modified fast: Results in 668 outpatients. *American Journal of Public Health* 75:1190–1194.

34. Patton, M. L., et al. 1981. Prevention of life-threatening cardiac arrhythmias associated with a modified fast by dietary supplementation with trace metals and fatty acids. *Clinical Research* 29:663A.

35. Rudman, D., et al. 1975. Elemental balances during intravenous hyperalimentation of underweight adult subjects. *Journal of Clinical Investigation* 55:94–104.

36. Sours, H. E., et al. 1981. Sudden death associated with very low caloric weight reduction regimens. *American Journal of Clinical Nutrition* 34:453–461.

37. Tuck, M. L., et al. 1981. The effect of weight reduction on blood pressure, plasma renin activity, and plasma aldosterone levels in obese patients. *New England Journal of Medicine* 304:930–933.

38. Vertes, V., Genuth, S. M., and Hazelton, I. M. 1977. Precautions with supplemented fasting (letter). *Journal of the American Medical Association* 238:2142.

39. ———. 1977. Supplemented fasting as a large scale outpatient program. *Journal of the American Medical Association* 238:2151–2153.

40. Wadden, T. A., Stunkard, A. J., and Brownell, K. D. 1983. Very low caloric diets: Their efficacy, safety and future. *Annals of Internal Medicine* 99:675–684.

11

The Control of Obesity: Social and Community Perspectives

Albert J. Stunkard

Social and community perspectives are of value in understanding any disorder. But when clinical measures are limited, as with obesity, such perspectives can be particularly useful. The precedents are many and of long-standing. In 1854, for example, when cholera was overwhelming the clinical efforts of London's physicians, John Snow traced its origins to the social group at risk—users of the Broad Street pump. When he removed the pump handle, he did more than stop an epidemic, he established a model of public health practice.[23] Since then the details have changed but not the principles.

Changes in public health practice since the days of John Snow reflect the changes in the burden of illness. The conquest of cholera and the other infectious diseases has left as our greatest burden the chronic and degenerative diseases, with their very different demands. In the era of infectious disease, the major public health efforts were exerted by the experts and little was demanded of the population other than its passive participation—in allowing swamps to be drained and sewers to be built. At most, it required visiting the doctor's office for immunizations. By contrast, public health measures for the control of obesity may require an extraordinary degree of participation on the part of the citizenry.

Such active participation is needed because obesity is so largely a result of the way we live, of our life styles and personal habits. Controlling obesity may well require major changes in those life styles and personal habits. Such an undertaking is clearly an ambitious endeavor. It would

FIGURE 11.1

Decreasing prevalence of obesity with increase in socioeconomic status (SES) among women. Note that the relationship between SES of origin and obesity is almost as strong as that between current SES and obesity.

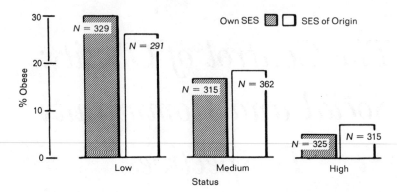

NOTE: Reprinted, by permission of the publisher, from P. B. Goldblatt, M. E. Moore, and A. J. Stunkard, 1965, Social factors in obesity, *Journal of the American Medical Association* 192:1040.

be much easier if we understood better the social and economic forces that help to determine the life styles that promote and control obesity.

One way of increasing this understanding is to learn more about the population at risk. Who, today, corresponds to the users of the Broad Street pump? Are there groups at high risk of obesity? Are there those at low risk? If so, what distinguishes the two?

Fortunately, recent research has provided preliminary answers. It has uncovered differences in the prevalence of obesity that suggest special vulnerabilities of some populations and special resistances of others. These differences help to identify points of therapeutic leverage in community efforts to control obesity.

Social Factors and Obesity

The first evidence of the special patterning of obesity within the population was obtained by the Midtown study of a population of 110,000 adults in an area of Manhattan selected so that it represented extremes in socioeconomic status (SES), from extremely high to extremely low.[25] The results were based on intensive interviews with 1,660 persons selected as representative of the population by systematic probability sampling.

The Midtown study showed a striking association between SES and the prevalence of obesity, particularly among women.[14] Figure 11.1 shows the strong inverse correlation between these variables. Fully 30 percent of women of lower SES were obese, compared to 16 percent of those of middle status and no more than 5 percent in the upper-status group. Among men the differences between social classes were similar but of considerably lesser degree. Men of lower SES, for example, showed a prevalence of obesity of 32 percent, compared to that of 16 percent among upper-class men.

A notable feature of this study was that it permitted causal inferences about the influence of SES. This was achieved by ascertaining not only the SES of the respondents at the time of the study but also that of their parents when the respondents were 8 years old. Although a person's obesity might influence his or her own social class, it is unlikely that the person's obesity in adult life could have influenced his or her parents' social class. Therefore, associations between parental social class and obesity can be viewed as causal. Figure 11.1 shows that these associations were almost as powerful as those between the respondents' own social class and obesity. For example, 7 percent of the female offspring of upper-class parents were obese, compared to 5 percent of the members of the upper class; 26 percent of the female offspring of lower-class parents were obese, compared to 30 percent of members of the lower class.

The relationship between social factors and obesity is a two-way street. Just as SES influences obesity (strongly), so does obesity influence SES (less strongly). Thus obesity was more prevalent among downwardly socially mobile persons (22 percent) than among those who remained in the social class of their parents (18 percent), and far more prevalent than among those who were upwardly socially mobile (12 percent).[27] Generation in the United States was also strongly linked to obesity. Persons were divided into four groups on the basis of the number of generations that their families had been in the United States. Of first-generation women, 24 percent were overweight, and the prevalence fell to 22 percent, 6 percent, and 4 percent with succeeding generations.[27] Even ethnicity and religion were found to influence the prevalence of obesity among women.[27]

The influence of social factors on the prevalence of obesity begins early in life. On entry into school, 8 percent of girls of lower SES are already obese, at a time when there are no obese girls of upper SES.[29] Even when obesity finally appears among girls of upper SES, it is infrequent. Obesity is thus not only more prevalent among lower-class girls, but its greater prevalence begins earlier and increases at a more rapid rate than among upper-class girls.

The relationship between social factors and obesity has been confirmed many times since it was discovered in New York in the early 1960s.[22] It is now well established in Western societies that, as SES rises, the prevalence of obesity among women falls. (The relationship is more variable among men.) Social factors must be considered as one of the most important influences on the prevalence of obesity in Western society.

The most recent indication of the generality of these findings comes from a study twenty years after Midtown, in another region (Texas), using

FIGURE 11.2

Relationship of social class, ethnicity, gender, and overweight. The Quetelet Index, also known as the body mass index (BMI), is calculated as weight / height² (kg / m²). With increasing social class, overweight decreases for women but increases very slightly for men. Mexican women are heavier than Anglo women, while Anglo men are slightly heavier than Mexican men. The relationship of social class and overweight is the same in both cultures.

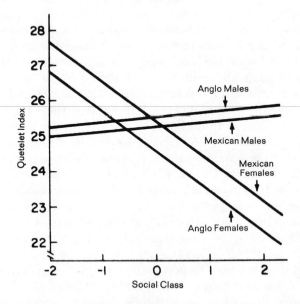

NOTE: Reprinted, by permission of the publisher, from C. E. Ross and J. Mirowsky, 1983, Social epidemiology of overweight: A substantive and methodological investigation, *Journal of Health and Social Behavior* 24:293.

a different measure of obesity and different ethnic groups. Ross and Mirowsky[21] once again found an inverse relationship among women, this time between SES and the mean body mass index (BMI) (rather than the prevalence of obesity). Furthermore, as figure 11.2 shows, this relationship was precisely the same for Mexican and for Anglo (Americans of non-Hispanic origin) women, despite the greater mean BMI of the former group. In contrast to the strong inverse relationship among women, there was essentially no difference in degree of overweight among men in any social class. To a greater extent than in the Midtown study, Ross and Mirowsky established the independent effect of ethnicity, among both women and men, thus confirming the importance of still another social factor in our understanding of obesity.

The full implications of these findings for the understanding and control of obesity have yet to be realized. They mean that whatever its genetic determinants and biochemical pathways, obesity is under the control of the social environment to an unusual degree. These findings suggest that a broad-scale assault on obesity need not await definitive understanding of biochemical determinants; understanding of its social determinants may be enough.

The most instructive of these results is the extent to which obesity has been controlled by upper-class women. Subjected to the same environment of media pressure, palatable and high-calorie foods, and labor-saving devices that has so strongly influenced lower-class women, upper-class women have somehow managed to avoid obesity. Their example can teach us much about the control of obesity. There is, for example, no evidence that their success is due to more information—women's magazines with their advice on dieting are widely available. Their diets are as high in obesity-promoting fat content as are those of lower-class women. Upper-class women are not thinner because they have had access to more effective treatment; treatment is simply not that effective. Their resistance to obesity seems to lie rather in the demands of their social station, in the rewards and punishments with which upper-class women are raised and in the communities that enforce these standards. Ultimately their resistance to obesity lies in their motivation to remain slim.

How can the findings of this experiment of nature be refined and applied? How can the effective ingredients of upper-class life be brought to bear upon women in other social classes, and upon men? The effective ingredient could well be the same as that through which upper-class values are transmitted—the community.

The idea of community brings to mind the place we live, our neighborhood, our city, our nation. But we are all part of a large number of different, and overlapping, communities. For "community" simply means people with common interests or characteristics.[8] Different communities involve us in different ways. Some have a profound effect upon the way we live, upon our life styles. Some are far better able to influence behavior than are physicians and psychologists, seeing patients one by one in their offices. And some communities are beginning to exert that influence in order to improve the health behavior of their members.

Three kinds of communities might be termed the Community of the Afflicted, the Community at the Work Site, and the Geographical Community. The control exercised within each of these three types of communities is based on different premises, is concerned with different groups, and utilizes different measures. In the Community of the Afflicted, for example, the control of obesity has its origins in the self-help movement and, more recently, in commercial enterprises. In the Community at the Work Site, attempts to control obesity have arisen largely from efforts of enterprising young behavior therapists. In the Geographical Community, the leaders have been epidemiologists and communication experts.

The Community of the Afflicted

In the early days of our nation, de Tocqueville described the proclivity of Americans to organize in informal groups to achieve ends that are the responsibility of government in other societies.[31] Nowhere is this proclivity expressed more impressively than in the organization of patients to cope with their illnesses. Although the origins of the self-help movement can be traced to nineteenth-century England and beyond, the pioneering American institution was Alcoholics Anonymous, and many of the current self-help groups have been modeled after it. The largest of these is TOPS (Take Off Pounds Sensibly), a thirty-eight-year-old organization that enrolls more than 300,000 members in 12,000 chapters in all parts of the country.[13]

The membership of TOPS is almost exclusively female, white, and middle class. The average member is a 42-year-old woman whose ideal weight is 119 lb and who entered TOPS weighing 180 lb, or 58 percent overweight. The key elements of TOPS are weekly meetings to provide group support, weekly weigh-ins that are high points of the meetings, and policy supervision from national headquarters. The effectiveness of self-help groups is difficult to assess because of their single most serious problem—very high attrition rates. In one study 67 percent of members dropped out during their first year; and these were persons who had lost the least amount of weight. TOPS membership at any one time appears to consist of a relatively small pool of longer-term members and a much larger pool of members who have been in the organization for only a short time. The short-term members lose only small amounts of weight. The longer-term members lose larger amounts of weight (20 lb in one study) and then slowly regain it, even while remaining in TOPS.

The results of TOPS can be improved by the introduction of behavior modification. An experimental program involving 298 members of sixteen TOPS chapters was able to significantly reduce the dropout rate—from 67 percent in the control chapters to 40 percent—and to increase the amount of weight lost.[17] TOPS did not capitalize upon this demonstration of the value of behavior modification and has continued its traditional approach. Commercial weight-reduction organizations, however, have incorporated behavioral components into their programs.

Commercial weight-loss organizations appeal to much the same clientele as do the nonprofit ones, and with somewhat greater success—500,000 persons a week attend just one such organization, Weight Watchers.[26] The commercial organizations have added three important elements to the programs pioneered by the nonprofit groups—behavior modification, inspirational lecturers drawn from successful members, and a carefully designed nutritional program. They are readily available to persons with even a casual interest in weight reduction.

The commercial organizations also suffer from the problem of attri-

FIGURE 11.3

Life table of participants in six treatment programs showing dropout rates during the first year of membership, recalculated assuming the subjects not responding to the questionnaire had dropped out of treatment.

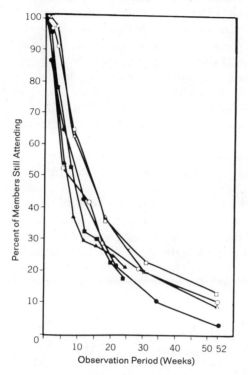

NOTE: Reprinted, by permission of the publisher, from F. R. Volkmar, A. J. Stunkard, J. Woolston, and B. A. Bailey, 1981, High attrition rates in commercial weight reduction programs, *Archives of Internal Medicine* 141:427.

tion, perhaps even more severely than do the self-help groups. Although these organizations release no information about their results, two prospective studies have recorded the attrition rates in a representative sample of the membership of a large commercial organization. Figure 11.3 shows the attrition rate in one study in which 50 percent of members dropped out in six weeks, 70 percent in twelve weeks and 80 percent in twenty-four weeks.[32] The other prospective study found attrition rates remarkably similar to these and, in addition, that persons joining this group had previously joined and dropped out an average of three times.[19]

The results of four retrospective studies[32] are also shown in figure 11.3. They represent data from programs conducted by Weight Watchers, Silhouette Slimming Clubs, and *Slimming Magazine* Slimming Clubs. The most notable aspects of all these reports is the striking similarity in the attrition rates of programs conducted on three continents with different procedures and different clientele. Dropout rates of this magnitude make it difficult to assess reports of weight loss by the survivors and warrant skepticism in evaluating the results of any commercial weight-loss program.

Despite these serious problems, the low cost and ready availability of lay-led groups make them an important resource for the control of mild obesity. Very large numbers of persons can be reached by these measures. Even the high dropout rates are not necessarily a weakness. The ease of withdrawal from treatment plus the parallel ease of reentry permits members to avail themselves of service when needed.[26] Finally, despite the limited effectiveness of these programs, their very low costs result in favorable cost-effectiveness ratios. For example, it costs far more to lose comparable amounts of weight in an exemplary university clinic than in a neighboring commercial program, even with its high dropout rate.[33] For the well-motivated person with mild obesity, commercial weight-loss programs are probably the treatment of choice.

The full potential of lay-led weight control groups may not have been realized in the English-speaking world. In Norway, for example, a program that has enrolled 80,000 persons (of a population of 4 million) has achieved surprising success.[15] Dropout rates are less than 10 percent, weight losses average 14 lb, and, with the aid of follow-up sessions, they are relatively well maintained. These results suggest that efforts to improve the performance of lay-led groups in the United States may pay large dividends.

The Community at the Work Site

The second community is the Community at the Work Site, which may well be the most promising site for health behavior change. Many people spend more of their time at work than at any other activity, and their relationships with their fellow workers are often among the most important of their lives. Health promotion programs conducted at the work site keep to a minimum time lost from work. Furthermore, the work site provides access to large numbers of persons who can be reached at relatively low cost, and many of them want health promotion programs.

The work site can provide two elements to which social learning theory ascribes primary importance in the control of behavior—its cues and its consequences.[3] These elements have already been used successfully in health behavior change. Cues were used with great effect in the United Store Workers Program for hypertension control. Very high participation rates were obtained by a union secretary calling members to remind them of their appointments at a nearby work site.[2] Consequences have been used with increasing frequency, particularly in the form of rewards for stopping smoking. A striking example occurred in Speedcall, a small electronics firm, whose president found that a seven-dollar-a-week bonus for not smoking at work was sufficient to decrease the number of on-the-job

TABLE 11.1

Weight Reduction at the Work Site: "Clinical" Programs

Study	N	Duration (Weeks)	Percent of Attrition	Weight Loss (lb)
Abrams and Follick[1]	133	10	48	7.0
Brownell, Stunkard, and McKeon[5]	172	16	42	7.9
Fisher et al.[11]	40	10	44	9.9
Follick, Fowler, and Brown[12]	48	14	40	9.7

smokers from twenty-four to four.[22] A recent survey revealed that 90 percent of California employers sponsor health promotion programs at the work site.[10]

In spite of the demonstrated effectiveness of work-site programs in many areas of health promotion, the control of obesity at the work site has lagged. There have been four reports of programs of weight reduction at the work site, and the results have been remarkably similar and remarkably poor.[1,5,11,12] Table 11.1 shows that these work-site programs have been afflicted with the same problems that afflict lay-led groups—high dropout rates and modest weight losses among the survivors.

There is a striking consistency in the very high dropout rates over short periods of time in programs that vary widely in setting and in the nature of the populations under treatment. This consistency suggests that some factor inherent in this type of program is responsible for these problems, which are so much more severe than those occurring in the clinical programs from which they were derived.

The problems may lie in the origins of these programs, which were basically clinical ones, devised for office use in the treatment of highly motivated, paying clients. Transferring them to a work setting may have lessened their special strengths without, at the same time, taking advantage of the special characteristics of the work site. Differential utilization of the work-site environment may explain the striking difference in effectiveness of two programs that contained the same substantive program but that differed in the method of delivery.

The first program was carried out under the auspices of the United Store Workers Union, the aforementioned pioneer in work site control of hypertension. Three consecutive cohorts totaling 172 women were treated in this program over a period of four years with a standard behavioral program that had proven effective in a clinical setting.[4] Despite the enlightened support of the union and the prior effectiveness of the program in a clinical setting, the results were disappointing. Figure 11.4 shows the high dropout rate in the first cohort, which received four variations of the basic program. Note the similarity of the dropout rate to that of self-help and commercial groups.

Information obtained from the treatment of each cohort was used to improve the program for the next cohort, and some improvement in

FIGURE 11.4

Life table of participants in first cohort of weight-loss program conducted by the United Store Workers Union. Three programs were carried out at the work site and one, for contrast, at a medical site. Two programs were conducted by union leaders (lay) while two were conducted by a psychologist (professional). One program met four times a week (frequent) while three met once a week (standard). Note the high dropout rate in each of these four variants of the basic behavioral program during the sixteen-week treatment period.

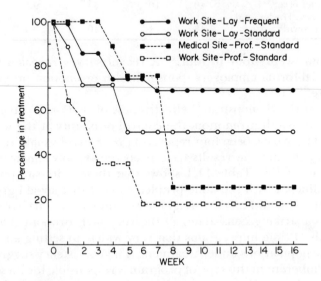

SOURCE: K. D. Brownell, A. J. Stunkard, and P. E. McKeon, Weight reduction at the work site: A promise partially fulfilled (manuscript).

performance occurred.[5] The dropout rate was reduced from 57.5 percent in the first cohort to 42.6 percent in the second cohort and then to 33.8 percent in the third. There was, however, no significant change in weight loss and maintenance of weight losses was poor. Although the program was judged a success by the union, which assumed its financial support, its clinical effectiveness must be viewed as marginal at best.

Quite different results were obtained when the same basic program was delivered in a way that took advantage of the special characteristics of the work site. One of these characteristics is the opportunity for competition that the work site provides. Competition is a powerful human motive that has driven persons as varied as athletes, businesspeople, and politicians to surpass their own expectations. It can also be used to motivate health behavior change.

The first description of a weight-loss competition was reported by the vice president of the Colonial Bank of Chicago in 1980 at a meeting on health promotion.[16] The competition was initiated by a challenge from the Colonial Bank to two other banks; the weight-loss program itself was implemented in conjunction with a commercial weight-reduction organization. Although it was noted that members of the Colonial Bank lost

TABLE 11.2
Competition Versus "Clinical" Programs

Group	N	Duration (Weeks)	Percent of Attrition	Weight Loss (lb)
United Store Workers Union[5]	172	16	42	7.9
Banks[6]	175	12	0.5	13

half a ton of fat and that it nevertheless lost the competition, few details of the program were described.

It was not until the report of Brownell and his colleagues in 1984 that the full effectiveness of a weight-loss competition became apparent.[6] In this competition, too, a bank challenged two other banks to a competition and the challenger lost the competition. This first competition and several subsequent ones were conducted under the auspices of the Pennsylvania County Health Improvement Program (CHIP). CHIP is a community-based multiple-risk-factor reduction program designed to reduce mortality and morbidity from cardiovascular disease in a county of 118,000 persons in north-central Pennsylvania.[28] Obesity is one of the risk factors targeted by the CHIP program, but until the competitions, little progress had been made in this area.

The first work-site competition was *between* institutions—the three banks. All employees were invited to participate and almost all did. Weight-loss goals were kept modest in order to discourage crash dieting. Each participant paid five dollars to enter the program and the pool was awarded to the winning bank. A large bulletin board, similar to a United Way thermometer, was placed in a prominent location in each bank to show the weekly progress of each team.

Weigh-ins occurred weekly in a central location in each bank, accompanied by considerable local publicity and a high level of employee interest. At each weigh-in, employees were given an installment of the same weight-loss manual[4] that had been used with such indifferent success in the program sponsored by the United Store Workers Union. Professional time devoted to this first program was minimal, confined to planning, preparation, and initial implementation. Since then, competitions have required even less assistance and only from nonprofessional personnel.

The results of the weight-loss competition at the banks were striking and without precedent among weight-loss programs at the work site. They are summarized in table 11.2, which contrasts the results of this competition with those of the United Store Workers Union program. Note the remarkably low dropout rate of 0.5 percent, unusual even in the best clinical programs. Furthermore, the bank program, in which participants averaged a loss of 13 lb, lasted for only twelve weeks, in contrast to the sixteen-week program in the United Store Workers Union, which produced only a 7.9-lb weight loss. These large weight losses were paralleled by a marked improvement in a number of psychological parameters, such as employee morale and energy level.

A number of subsequent competitions have been held under CHIP auspices *within* industries.[7,28] Competitions have been carried out among different divisions of a single industry and among employees of a single industry who were randomly assigned to different teams. The results of these programs suggest that competition *between* industries is more effective than is competition *within* industries. This result suggested that it was not competition alone but rather competition on behalf of an in-group that was the critical element. To test this hypothesis, a program was carried out in which individuals competed against each other.[7] The results fully confirmed the hypothesis: Dropouts were even higher and weight losses even lower than in traditional programs of weight loss at the work site. *Cooperation* within the competitive unit is the key to the effectiveness of competition.

Another competition assessed the effects upon women as compared to men.[7] Men not only lost more weight, as might be expected from their greater weight, but also lost a greater percentage of overweight. This suggestion that competitions are effective with men is of great importance in view of the limited appeal of traditional weight-loss programs to men. Men usually constitute less than 10 percent of the participants in weight-loss programs.

Weight-loss competitions also seem to be useful for involving a group that is particularly resistant to health promotion programs—blue-collar workers. If competition can be utilized as a means of involving them, it may have important, unexpected benefits. An indirect method of involving blue-collar workers at one CHIP work site through a competition between their wives showed considerable promise.

The very low costs of weight-loss competitions suggested that a cost-effectiveness analysis might highlight their attractions. The costs for each competition included personnel time for management and for the staff to organize and oversee the program, along with small costs for materials. The cost per pound of weight lost was $2.21.[6] This analysis overestimates even this low cost because the greatest expense was incurred in the first competition. In the second and third competitions, the costs per pound lost were $1.16 and $0.85 respectively. With further experience and with the development of a manual specially devised for weight-loss competitions,[30] costs have continued to fall and effectiveness has continued to rise.

A comparison of the cost-effectiveness of the work-site competitions relative to other programs for the control of obesity is possible through Yates's report of the cost of losing a somewhat different measure—decrease in percentage overweight.[33] Figure 11.5 shows the cost for a 1-percent decrease in percentage overweight in a university clinic ($44.60), the United Store Workers work-site program conducted by either professional leaders ($25.14) or lay leaders ($8.26), a leading commercial program ($3.00), and the first work-site competition described here ($2.93).

FIGURE 11.5

The cost per 1-percent reduction in percentage overweight.

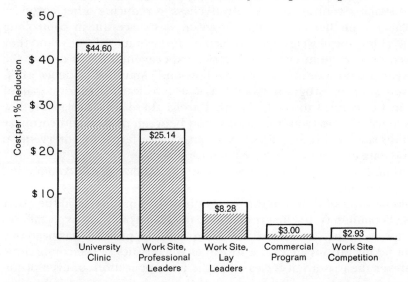

NOTE: Reprinted, by permission of the publisher, from K. D. Brownell et al., 1984, Weight loss competitions at the work site: Impact on weight, morale and cost-effectiveness, *American Journal of Public Health* 74: 1284.

Geographical Community

When we think of community, most of us think first of our geographical community, where we live and what we call home. It is in our geographical community where impersonal social forces and intimate personal forces combine to affect us. The sixfold lesser prevalence of obesity among upper-class women is a striking example. Here would seem to be the place, *par excellence,* where favorable changes in health behavior can be taught and learned. A new type of research enterprise, focusing on geographical communities, has begun to explore this possibility. Two such efforts have produced promising results.

The Stanford Three-Community Study attempted to reduce coronary risk factors in two small towns through a health promotion program that relied in great measure upon an intensive media campaign.[9] This program produced a marked reduction in coronary risk factors in the two experimental towns as compared with a control town, but the sample size was too small to demonstrate reduction in mortality and morbidity.

The North Karelia Project, a multiple-risk-factor intervention trial in a province in Finland, also reduced coronary risk factors.[20] In addition, because of the far larger size of the community (180,000 persons), this reduction in risk factors was translated into reductions in mortality and morbidity as compared with a control province.

In striking contrast to this effectiveness in reducing other coronary risk factors, neither community program was successful in controlling obesity. Only mean weights are available for the Stanford study, and they showed no change in either of the two experimental towns during the two-year program or at a one-year follow-up.[18] Marginal evidence of effectiveness of the program depended on a statistically significant gain of 1 lb in the control town. In North Karelia there was a relatively low prevalence of obesity and no association between obesity and coronary heart disease. As a result, obesity was not a major target for intervention and no data on weight loss have been reported.

In the geographical community, as in the other types of community, there are strong theoretical reasons to expect that weight-loss programs should be successful. But in the geographical community, as in the other types of community, the first results have not borne out these expectations. Perhaps, as in the case of work site programs, the problem has been one of not taking advantage of the special characteristics of the community. Whatever the reasons, it is clear that the first applications of even promising interventions may fall far short of the mark.

Summary and Conclusions

Social and commercial approaches may be particularly useful in a disorder such as obesity, for which clinical measures are of limited effectiveness. This view is supported by epidemiological studies that reveal striking vulnerabilities and resistances specific to different populations: Obesity is common among lower-class women and rare among upper-class women. Attempts to mobilize social pressures to control obesity through lay-led groups have a strong theoretical rationale and have been widely applied. Their impact, however, has been blunted by high dropout rates among the participants. Work site programs, likewise, have a strong theoretical rationale and have had problems of implementation. The recent introduction of weight-loss competitions at the work site has markedly improved the results. Programs in the geographical community have as yet had little impact upon obesity despite their effectiveness in controlling other coronary risk factors.

The first results of social and commercial approaches to the control of obesity are sufficiently encouraging to warrant further vigorous effort.

REFERENCES

1. Abrams, D. B., and Follick, M. J. 1983. Behavioral weight loss intervention at the work site: Feasibility and maintenance. *Journal of Consulting and Clinical Psychology* 51: 226–233.
2. Alderman, M. H., and Schoenbaum, E. E. 1975. Detection and treatment of hypertension at the worksite. *New England Journal of Medicine* 293:65–68.
3. Bandura, A. 1977. *Social learning theory.* Englewood Cliffs, N.J.: Prentice-Hall.
4. Brownell, K. D. 1979. *Behavior therapy for obesity: A treatment manual.* Philadelphia: University of Pennsylvania Press.
5. Brownell, K. D., Stunkard, A. J., and McKeon, P. E. 1985. Weight reduction at the work site: A promise partially fulfilled. *American Journal of Psychiatry* 141:47–51.
6. Brownell, K. D., et al. 1984. Weight loss competitions at the work site: Impact on weight, morale and cost-effectiveness. *American Journal of Public Health* 74:1283–1285.
7. Cohen, R. Y., Stunkard, A. J., and Felix, M. R. J. A comparison of three worksite weight loss competitions. Manuscript.
8. Durkheim, E. 1966. *The division of labor in society.* New York: Free Press.
9. Farquhar, J. W., et al. 1977. Community education for cardiovascular disease. *Lancet* 1:1192–1195.
10. Fielding, J. E., and Breslow, L. 1983. Health promotion programs sponsored by California employers. *American Journal of Public Health* 73:538–542.
11. Fisher, E. B., Jr., Lowe, M. R., Levenkron, J. C., and Newman, A. 1982. Reinforcement and structural support of maintained risk reduction. In *Adherence, compliance and generalization in behavioral medicine,* ed. R. B. Stuart, pp. 145–168. New York: Brunner/ Mazel.
12. Follick, M. J., Fowler, J. L., and Brown, R. 1984. Attrition in work site interventions: The effects of an incentive procedure. *Journal of Consulting and Clinical Psychology* 52: 139–140.
13. Garb, J. R., and Stunkard, A. J. 1972. Effectiveness of a self-help group in obesity control: A further assessment. *Archives of Internal Medicine* 134:716–720.
14. Goldblatt, P. B., Moore, M. E., and Stunkard, A. J. 1965. Social factors in obesity. *Journal of the American Medical Association* 192:1039–1044.
15. Grimsmø, A., Helgesen, G., and Borchgrevink, C. F. 1981. Short-term and long-term effects of lay groups on weight reduction. *British Medical Journal* 283:1093–1095.
16. Hynes, O. 1980. Presentation on the Colonial Bank of Chicago Weight Loss Program at the Healthy America conference on the Corporate Commitment to Health, Washington, D.C., June 9–10.
17. Levitz, L. S., and Stunkard, A. J. 1974. A therapeutic coalition for obesity: Behavior modification and patient self-help. *American Journal of Psychiatry* 131:423–427.
18. Maccoby, N. 1984. Personal communication, June 29.
19. Nash, J. D. 1977. Curbing drop-out from treatment for obesity. Doctoral Diss., Stanford University.
20. Puska, P., et al. 1983. Ten years of the North Karelia project: Results with community-based prevention of coronary heart disease. *Scandinavian Journal of Social Medicine* 11:65–68.
21. Ross, C. E., and Mirowsky, J. 1983. Social epidemiology of overweight: A substantive and methodological investigation. *Journal of Health and Social Behavior* 24.288–298.
22. Shepard, D. S. 1980. Presentation on the Speedcall Corporation Smoking Control Program at the Healthy American conference on the Corporate Commitment to Health, Washington, D.C., June 9–10.
23. Snow, J. 1936. *The mode of transmission of cholera.* New York: The Commonwealth Fund. (Orig. published 1855.)
24. Sobal, J., and Stunkard, A. J. Socioeconomic status and obesity: A review of the literature. Manuscript.
25. Srole, L., et al. 1962. *Mental health in the metropolis: The midtown Manhattan study.* New York: McGraw-Hill.
26. Stuart, R. B. 1977. Self-help group approach to self-management. In *Behavioral self-management,* ed. R. B. Stuart, pp. 278–305. New York: Brunner/Mazel.

27. Stunkard, A. J. 1975. From explanation to action in psychosomatic medicine: The case of obesity. *Psychosomatic Medicine* 37:195–236.

28. Stunkard, A. J., Cohen, R. Y., and Felix, M. R. J. 1985. Mobilizing a community to promote health: The Pennsylvania County Health Improvement Program (CHIP) In *Prevention in health psychology*, ed. J. C. Rosen and L. J. Solomon, pp. 143–190. Hanover, N.H.: University Press of New England.

29. Stunkard, A. J., D'Aquili, E., Fox, S., and Filion, R. D. L. 1972. The influence of social class on obesity and thinness in children. *Journal of the American Medical Association* 22: 579–584.

30. Stunkard, A. J., et al. 1984. *Worksite weight loss competitions: A "how-to" manual.* Williamsport, Pa.: Lycoming College.

31. Tocqueville, A. C. H. M. C. de. 1966. *Democracy in America,* trans. George Lawrence. New York: Harper & Row.

32. Volkmar, F. R., Stunkard, A. J., Woolston, J., and Bailey, B. A. 1981. High attrition rates in commercial weight reduction programs. *Archives of Internal Medicine* 141:426–428.

33. Yates, B. T. 1978. Improving the cost-effectiveness of obesity programs. Three basic strategies for reducing the cost per pound. *International Journal of Obesity* 2:249–266.

PART II

ANOREXIA NERVOSA

12

Anorexia Nervosa: History and Psychological Concepts

Michael Strober

Although the condition has been known to medicine for centuries, scientific interest in anorexia nervosa has increased with dramatic suddenness in recent years.[14] This chapter reviews the historical underpinnings of the modern-day concept of anorexia nervosa and discusses its descriptive and psychopathological features, epidemiology, and etiology.

Historical Antecedents

Literary accounts of self-inflicted starvation and weight loss can be traced back to the Middle Ages. A detailed review of this literature may be found in William Hammond's monograph, *Fasting Girls: Their Physiology and Pathology,* published in 1879.[24] Several cases are intriguing. A Leichester nun (circa 1225) claimed to have ingested nothing but the eucharist for seven years. Learning of this report, the Bishop of Lincoln dispatched fifteen clerks to her bedside to observe without interruption for fifteen days, whereupon the fast was indeed confirmed. Liduine of Schiedam, a female saint living in the fourteenth century, is said to have existed for years on nothing but "a little piece of apple the size of a holy wafer." The physician Bucoldianus, writing in 1542, described the case of Margaret

Weiss, ten years of age, who abstained from food for three years, while "walking about, laughing, and talking like other children." The following account by the physician Fabricius, published in 1611, concerns a thirteen-year-old girl said to have lived without food or drink for three years.

> She was of a sad and melancholy countenancy; her body was sufficiently fleshy except only her belly, which was compressed so as that it seemed to cleave to her back-bone. . . . As for excrements she voided none; and did so abhor all kinds of food. That when one, who came to see her privately, put a little sugar in her mouth she immediately swooned away. But what was most wonderful was, that this maid walked up and down, played with other girls, danced and did all other things that were done by girls of her age; neither had she any difficulty of breathing, speaking or crying out. (Quoted in Hammond,[24] p. 10)

One of Hammond's principal sources, the nineteenth-century writer Gorres, offered the following spiritually conceived explanation of these phenomena:

> In ordinary nourishment he who eats being superior to that which is eaten, assimilates the aliments which he takes, and communicates then his own nature. . . . It is no longer therefore the nourishment which is assimilated, but on the contrary, it assimilates the man, and introduces him to a superior sphere. . . . The supernatural life in some way or other absorbs the natural life, and the man instead of living on earth lives henceforth by grace and by heaven. (Quoted in Hammond,[24] p. 3)

Interestingly, Hammond denounced these accounts for their lack of scientific credibility, citing deception, fraud, or organic disease as more parsimonious explanations. Although other possibilities necessitate consideration as well (e.g., religiously inspired ascetic practices or primary psychiatric illness), the clinical resemblance to true anorexia nervosa is self-evident.

The earliest comprehensive description of anorexia nervosa is credited to Richard Morton, whose 1694 treatise on tubercular disease[36] described a state of nervous atrophy (phthisis nervosa) characterized by decreased appetite, amenorrhea, food aversion, emaciation, and hyperactivity. Although Morton proclaimed the etiology of these phenomena to be neurogenic in origin—a malfunction of the brain and nerves—his comments on the mutual influences between mental and bodily processes operating in these patients and the pathogenic role of the emotions heralded contemporary psychosomatic thought. He described the condition in this manner:

> A Nervous Atrophy or Consumption is a wasting of Body without any remarkable Fever, Cough, or Shortness of Breath; but it is attended with a want of Appetite, and a bad Digestion, upon which there follows a Languishing Weakness of Nature, and a falling away of the Flesh every day more and more. . . .

The immediate cause of the Distemper I apprehend to be in the System of the Nerves proceeding from a Preternatural state of the Animal Spirits, and the destruction of the Tone of the Nerves; whereupon I have used to call this a Consumption in the Habit of the Body. For as the Appetite and Concoction are overthrown by the weak and infirm Tone of the Stomach, so also the Assimilation, the Fermentation, and Volatilization of the Nutritious Juice are hindered in the whole Habit of the Body from the distemper'd state of the Brain and Nerves.

The Causes which dispose the Patient to this Disease, I have for the most part observed to be violent Passions of the Mind, the intemperate drinking of Spirituous Liquors, and an unwholsom Air, by which it is no wonder if the Tone of the Nerves, and the Temper of the Spirits are destroy'd. (Quoted in Bliss and Branch,[4] pp. 9–10)

As is amply illustrated in the following excerpt from one of his case reports, Morton was intrigued by his patient's indifference to her malnourished state and the apparent preservation of basic mental faculties:

Mr. Duke's Daughter in St. Mary Axe, in the Year 1684 and the eighteenth Year of her Age, in the month of July fell into a total suppression of her Monthly Courses from a multitude of Cares and Passions of her Mind, but without any Symptom of the Green-Sickness following upon it. From which time her Appetite began to abate, and her Digestion to be bad; her flesh also began to be flaccid and loose, and her looks pale. . . . the Winter following, this Consumption did seem to be not a little improved; for that she was wont by her studying at Night, and continual poring upon Books, to expose herself both Day and Night to the injuries of the Air, which was at that time extreamly cold. . . . So from that time loathing all sorts of Medicaments, she wholly neglected the care of her self for two full Years, till at last being brought to the last degree of a Marasmus, or Consumption, and thereupon subject to Frequent Fainting Fits, she apply'd her self to me for advice.

I do not remember that I did ever in all my Practice see one, that was conversant with the Living so much wasted with the greatest degree of a Consumption (like a Skeleton only clad with skin) yet there was no Fever, but on the contrary a coldness of the whole Body. . . . (Quoted in Bliss and Branch,[4] pp. 10–11)

In keeping with the structural traditions of eighteenth-century medicine, and no doubt influenced by new advances in anatomy and reflex neurophysiology, the English scientist Richard Whytt speculated in 1767[56] that the cause of unusual food aversion and states of compulsivelike food cravings could be localized in the gastric nerves. Further reference in eighteenth-century medical literature to nervous conditions associated with repugnance for food and extreme malnutrition appeared in the writings of Mesmer and the French physician Naudeau,[4] although it is not clear whether the cases cited would fulfill current criteria for anorexia nervosa.

It is generally agreed that anorexia nervosa emerges as a distinctive syndrome with the near-simultaneous reports by Sir William Gull[22] and

Charles Lasegue[31] in the latter part of the nineteenth century. Gull's first reference to the condition came in a brief, passing remark during an address to the British Medical Association meeting in Oxford in 1868. A more complete description appeared subsequently in 1874,[22] at which time Gull coined the term anorexia nervosa. The following is one of the two cases reported.

> Miss A., age 17 . . . was brought to me on Jan. 17, 1866. Her emaciation was very great. It was stated that she had lost 33 lbs. in weight. She was then 5 st. 12 lbs. Height 5 ft. 5 in. Ammorrhoea for nearly a year. . . . Complete anorexia for animal food, and almost complete anorexia for everything else. Abdomen shrunk and flat, collapsed. . . . The condition was one of simple starvation. There was but slight variation in her condition, though observed at intervals of three or four months. . . . The case was regarded as one of simple anorexia.
>
> Various remedies were prescribed . . . but no perceptible effect followed their administration. The diet also varied, but without any effect upon the appetite. Occasionally for a day or two the appetite was voracious, but this was very rare and exceptional. The patient complained of no pain, but was restless and active. This was in fact a striking expression of the nervous state, for it seemed hardly possible that a body so wasted could undergo the exercise which seemed agreeable. There was some peevishness of temper, and a feeling of jealousy. No account could be given of the exciting cause.
>
> Miss A. remained under my observation from Jan. 1866 to March 1868, when she had much improved, and gained in weight from 82 to 128 lbs. . . . It will be noticeable that as she recovered she had a much younger look, corresponding indeed to her age, 21. . . .
>
> It will be observed that all the conditions in this case were negative, and may be explained by the anorexia which led to starvation, and a depression of all the vital functions; viz., amenorrhoea, slow pulse, slow breathing. In the stage of greatest emaciation one might have been pardoned for assuming that there was some organic lesion, but from the point of view indicated such an assumption would have been unnecessary.
>
> This view is supported by the satisfactory course of the case to entire recovery, and by the continuance of good health. (Pp. 22–23)[22]

Gull's discussion of the condition took note of its characteristic onset during adolescence, preponderance in females, and significant psychological component; the influence of prolonged starvation and calorie depletion on general metabolic functioning; and the importance of timely intervention under strict professional supervision. He writes:

> The want of appetite is, I believe, due to a morbid mental state. I have not observed in these cases any gastric disorder to which the want of appetite could be referred. I believe, therefore, that its origin is central and not peripheral. That mental states may destroy appetite is notorious, and it will be admitted that young women at the ages named are specially obnoxious to mental perversity. . . . The importance of discriminating such cases in practice is obvious; otherwise prognosis will be erroneous, and treatment misdirected.
>
> In one of the cases I have named the patient had been sent abroad for one or two winters, under the idea that there was a tubercular tendency. I

have remarked above that these wilful patients are often allowed to drift their own way into a state of extreme exhaustion, when it might have been prevented by placing them under different moral conditions.

The treatment required is obviously that which is fitted for persons of unsound mind. The patients should be fed at regular intervals, and surrounded by persons who would have moral control over them; relations and friends being generally the worst attendants. (Pp. 25–26)[22]

Lasegue's 1873 report[31] on "anorexia hysterique" was impressive in several respects. He clearly viewed its distinctive phenomenology to be the morbid belief that food is injurious and must be avoided. He also perceptively noted the now widely recognized psychopathological features of self-doubt and drive for approval, along with the family's contribution to the maintenance of symptoms once developed. He described the condition and its development in these terms:

A young girl, between fifteen and twenty years of age, suffers from some emotion which she avows or conceals. Generally it relates to some real or imaginary marriage project, to a violence done to some sympathy, or to some more or less conscient desire. At other times, only conjectures can be offered concerning the occasional cause, whether that the girl has an interest in adopting the mutism so common in the hysterical, or that the primary cause really escapes her. . . .

At first she feels uneasiness after food. . . . At the end of some weeks there is no longer a supposed temporary repugnance, but a refusal of food that may be indefinitely prolonged. The disease is now declared, and so surely will it pursue its course that it becomes easy to prognosticate the future. . . . Ever on the watch for the judgments concerning themselves, especially such as are approved by the family, they never pardon; and considering that hostilities have been commenced against them they attribute to themselves the right of employing these with implacable tenacity.

The repugnance for food continues slowly progressive meal after meal is discontinued. . . . Things may be thus prolonged during weeks or months without the general health seeming to be unfavourably influenced, the tongue being clean and moist and thirst entirely absent. . . . Another ascertained fact is, that so far from muscular power being diminished, this abstinence tends to increase the aptitude for movement. The patient feels more light and active, rides on horseback, receives and pays visits, and is able to pursue a fatiguing life in the world without perceiving the lassitude she would at other times have complained of.

If the situation has undergone no change as regards the anorexia and refusal of food, the mental condition of the patient is brought out more prominently, while the dispositions of those surrounding her undergo modification as the disease becomes prolonged. If the physician had promised rapid amendment, or if he has suspected a bad disposition on the part of his patient, he has long since lost all moral authority.

The family has but two methods at its service which it always exhausts— entreaties and menaces, and which both serve as a touchstone. The delicacies of the table are multiplied in the hope of stimulating the appetite; but the more the solicitude increases, the more the appetite diminishes. The patient

disdainfully tastes the new viands, and after having thus shown her willingness,
holds herself absolved from any obligation to do more. She is besought, as a
favour and as a sovereign proof of affection, to consent to add even an additional mouthful to what she has taken; but this excess of insistence begets
an excess of resistance. (Pp. 265–266)

Interestingly enough, the Gull and Lasegue reports spurred widely
polarized viewpoints on what constituted the appropriate and most effective treatment of this condition. Thus, while Playfair[41] boldly asserted
that successful treatment always required the removal of the patient from
her "unwholesome usual domestic surroundings," Myrtle[38] countered
that the isolation of patient from her family was, in the end, therapeutically
unnecessary, too costly, and a cruel punishment.

With the importance and clinical diagnosis of anorexia nervosa now
widely accepted, questions arose pertaining to its precise nosology and
relation to other forms of mental and psychosomatic disturbance. A major
revision in thinking about the primacy of psychological factors was spurred
in 1914 by Simmond's report[44] of a case of cachexia associated with pituitary atrophy. There rapidly followed a medicalization of the diagnosis,
conceptualization, and treatment of anorexia nervosa that held for some
two to three decades, until reanalysis of Simmond's original cases refuted
the link between hypophyseal insufficiency and weight loss and clarified
several important descriptive and physiological distinctions between Simmonds' disease and anorexia nervosa.[43]

Theories of psychological causality flourished anew during the 1940s
and 1950s, greatly influenced by the assimilation of psychoanalytic concepts into the mainstream of psychiatric theory and practice. In keeping
with the basic tenets of psychoanalytic understanding, various writers[2,37,55]
espoused the view that anorexia nervosa was symbolic of fixated unconscious conflicts relating to oral-sadistic fears, oral impregnation, and other
regressive wishes and primitive fantasies. However, the most influential
and lasting contribution to the modern conceptualization of anorexia
nervosa emerged in the writings of Hilde Bruch,[5] whose clinical studies
spanned nearly three decades and inspired a more formal approach to
the investigation of developmental factors in etiology and pathogenesis
previously neglected by psychoanalytically oriented theorists. As a result
of extensive experience in the long-term treatment of patients, Bruch
came to doubt that drive dynamics and intrapsychic conflict were as specific
or theoretically relevant to the disorder as previously postulated. Rather,
what she eventually conceived to be of primary importance was the fal-
sification of early developmental learning experiences—the failure of early
parent-child interactions to effectively discriminate or reinforce the child's
incipient psychological identity. The core psychopathology, she asserted,
was invariably present in a specific constellation of ego and personality
deficits, consisting of inaccurate perception and cognitive labeling of visceral and affective states, faulty perception of body boundaries, and a
deeply rooted sense of ineffectiveness and lack of autonomy. In her clinical

view, the driven and remorseless self-starvation of the anorexic patient was best understood in regard to its ultimate functional and adaptational effects; specifically, the undoing of feelings of passivity, ineffectiveness, and control by outside forces.

Current Perspectives

DESCRIPTIVE AND PSYCHOPATHOLOGICAL FEATURES

The descriptions of Morton, Gull, and Lasegue point up the remarkable secular stability of anorexia nervosa as a descriptive syndrome entity over the course of three centuries. In recent years different sets of more formalized diagnostic criteria have been proposed by various investigators,[15] yet several discriminating features continue to be unanimously emphasized:

1. Self-inflicted weight loss accompanied thereafter by a sustained avoidance of mature body shape, which cannot be directly ascribed to other identifiable psychiatric causes, cachexia-inducing diseases, or externally imposed demands for reduced food intake.
2. A morbid and persistent dread of fat.
3. The manipulation of body weight through dietary restraint, self-induced vomiting, abuse of purgatives, or excessive exercise.
4. Disturbances in body image, manifest in the misrepresentation of actual body dimensions or extreme loathing of bodily functions.
5. Amenorrhea and the development of other behavioral-physiological sequelae of starvation.

As noted, psychological factors have historically received primary emphasis in etiological theories of anorexia nervosa, although the existence of a distinct predisposing personality has yet to be demonstrated. Still, a number of reports* are consistent in describing such traits as extreme compliancy, emotional reserve, compulsivity, and lack of independence as unusually common among anorexic patients. Psychometric studies[1,40,45,46] have likewise reported the presence of neuroticism, introversion, obsessionality, and self-doubt as well as increases in interpersonal anxiety coinciding with return to normal body weight. However, the interpretation of these data is confounded by the chronicity of the patient samples and the absence of suitable control groups for assessing the relative specificity of these symptom and personality variables.

In this regard, two recent psychometric studies[47,48] comparing younger, nonchronic anorexic patients to age-matched depressive and

* See references 5, 23, 28, 30, and 35.

personality-disorder controls are worthy of note. In both cases, anorexic patients were found to differ significantly from controls on a range of personality trait variables. To summarize, the prototypical pattern found was that of a young woman somewhat obsessional in character; introverted, emotionally reserved, and socially insecure; self-denying, deferential to others, and given to overcompliance; prone to self-abasement and limited autonomy; and overly rigid and stereotyped in thinking. Follow-up testing conducted when patients were weight-recovered revealed little change in these characteristics, suggesting they represent more stable and robust features of personality rather than consequences of malnutrition and chronic social morbidity.

CLASSIFICATION

With the recognition that anorexia nervosa is probably multifactorial in causation, there has been increasing interest in the subclassification of patients into more clinically and psychobiologically homogenous groups. What has emerged from these efforts is a growing consensus that different patterns of dietary control and consummatory behavior among patients may be one distinction having particular heuristic and clinical importance. Within this classificatory system, anorexic patients have been divided into two broad groups—restricters, who maintain a relatively uninterrupted pattern of dietary restriction, and bulimics, who exhibit periodic episodes of binge eating and self-induced purgation. By and large, comparative studies employing this distinction[7,16,30,50] have attested to its external validity in showing that differences between these groups extend beyond the topography of their eating behavior. Specifically, it is reported that bulimic patients have a greater incidence of personal and familial obesity; are more likely to show evidence of childhood maladjustment; are more prone to depressive mood swings and impulse-related problems; have increased familial loadings of affective illness and alcoholism; and experience greater conflict and negativity in family relationships. Judging from these findings, it would seem that increased risk for bulimia in anorexic patients is determined by, or at least correlated with, any of several mechanisms involved in the overall regulation of affect and tension states and the body's natural compensatory physiological response to deprivational conditions and weight loss.

However valid, the bulimia-restricter distinction is probably an oversimplification of the heterogeneity intrinsic to anorexic patients. For instance, multiple-regression techniques applied to measures of personality and body image obtained on young anorexic patients suggest that certain personality traits are uniquely associated with specific and empirically distinct components of body-image disturbance.[49] Similarly, a recent typology of patients derived through cluster analysis[51] suggests three prototype patterns, varying along the dimensions of self-esteem, affective stability, general ego strength, and regulatory control over impulses. That the three groups were shown to differ in terms of premorbid adjustment, family history, and short-term treatment response adds to the validity of a multidimensional conceptualization that views anorexia nervosa as a final common pathway for diverse causal factors and personality dynamics.

Parental and Familial Correlates

Research in the area of parental and familial correlates is disappointingly sparse and plagued by problems of poor methodology. Chief among the criticisms are the infrequent use of validated measures of personality or systematic observations of family interaction, lack of appropriate controls, and the assumption of causality in the absence of direct empirical support. Bearing this caveat in mind, maladaptive tendencies that have been attributed to parents include neurotic constitution, obsessionality, phobic avoidance, emotional rigidity, and passivity[4,13,27]; however, the reported incidence of these behaviors in parents is extremely variable, ranging from 10 to 40 percent. The few psychometric studies of parents[10,53] have likewise indicated the presence of emotional disturbance, expressed mainly in overcontrolled hostility, social maladjustment, impulsivity, and rigid expectations, particularly in fathers of young bulimic-anorexic patients.

Equally difficult to interpret are largely anecdotal and impressionistic accounts of interactional problems in anorexic families. Morgan and Russell[35] found demonstrable family disturbance preceding onset of illness in some 50 percent of cases, while other reports[3,27,28] have commented on contrasting patterns of maternal intrusiveness and paternal underinvolvement in some 30 to 40 percent of cases. A recent case-controlled study by Garfinkel and colleagues[17] found that while parents of young anorexic patients differed little from normal control parents on measures of depressive symptomatology, personality function, or attitudes toward weight control and dieting, anorexic families as a group acknowledged significantly greater difficulty in accommodating to change, in their role performance, in the clarity of their expressed communication, and in affective expression.

Recent interest has also begun to focus on specific patterns of psychiatric morbidity and weight pathology in anorexic families and their bearing on social, and possibly genetic, transmission of vulnerability. In a preliminary study, Gershon and associates[21] found that eating disorders occurred in 6.4 percent of first-degree relatives of anorexia nervosa patients, as compared to 1.3 percent of control relatives. Similarly, this author[52] observed diagnoses of eating disorder to aggregate more in the first- and second-degree relatives of anorexic probands than in the relatives of well-matched probands with affective illness. A generation effect was also present, with sisters more likely to be affected than mothers, aunts, or grandparents. Kalucy, Crisp, and Harding[27] reported an explicit history of significantly low adolescent weight, anorexia nervosa, or weight phobia in 27 percent of mothers and 16 percent of fathers in fifty-six cases. Crisp and coworkers[12] also reported a history of probable anorexia nervosa in a first-degree relative in 29 percent of 102 consecutive cases. The estimated prevalence of anorexia nervosa among female first-degree relatives of anorexic patients reported in other studies ranges between 3 and 10 percent.[3,16,35,54] With respect to twins, both members of a monozygotic pair are afflicted in 50 percent of cases, while concordance in dizygotic pairs has been estimated at 7 percent.[15] Also noteworthy are studies that have examined lifetime prevalence rates of other psychiatric disorders in relatives, over and above the frequency of problems in the family's general adaptive functioning. By and large, these studies indicate substantially greater rates of major affective illness among first- and second-degree relatives of anorexic patients compared to the expected prevalence in the general population.[21,25,52,58] However, data this author reported[52] also suggest a differential pattern of family transmission, with greater aggregation of affective illness in relatives of depressed anorexic patients compared to relatives of nondepressed anorexic patients. At the same time, rates of anorexia nervosa and weight phobia were found to be negligible in relatives of affective-disorder probands, thus arguing against a straightforward genetic hypothesis that anorexia nervosa and affective illnesses share a single common predisposition.

Taken together, then, studies of abnormalities in parenting and family life experiences are currently too preliminary to be clearly interpretable. Yet there is a consensus that prevalences of anorexia nervosa and affective illness are significantly elevated in relatives of anorexic patients, thus suggesting the operation of specific transmissible factors, or heritability. However, the precise nature of this transmitted vulnerability—its psychosocial, developmental, or biological substrate—remains poorly understood.

Epidemiological Patterns

Several aspects of the epidemiology of anorexia nervosa are reasonably well established and will be summarized briefly. They are modal age of onset during adolescence, greatly increased prevalence among females, and overrepresentation in the middle and upper social classes.[15] Existing studies have put the lifetime prevalence of the disorder in representative populations between 0.5 and 2.1 percent.[11,42] Etiologically, the conclusions most often drawn from these data are that the disorder is intimately related to maturational problems brought on by pubertal stresses[8] and that various social class or culturally mediated factors are conducive to its expression in psychologically vulnerable young women. Social class phenomena that have been speculated to heighten vulnerability include high and competitive achievement standards, feminine role definitions and attitudes toward sexuality, and the social reinforcement of affiliation and dependency behaviors.[19]

Not surprisingly, converging evidence from large-scale epidemiological surveys points to a rising incidence of the disorder in the United States and Europe. Based on a survey of first admissions to two university hospitals in southern Sweden between 1931 and 1960, Theander[54] reported an overall figure of 0.24 cases per 100,000 population, with the number of new cases per year increasing steadily over time from 1.1 in 1931 to 5.8 (0.45 per 100,000 annual incidence) during the period 1951 through 1960. Kendell and associates[29] reviewed psychiatric case registry data from northeast Scotland, upstate New York, and the London district of Camberwell and found annual incidence rates ranging from 0.37 per 100,000 to 1.6 per 100,000, with a near doubling of new cases reported in each geographic area over the five- to ten-year period of study. Jones and coworkers[26] used the Monroe County, New York, psychiatric case registry and general medical records from the region's major university teaching and research hospital to examine changes in annual incidence between 1960 and 1976, as well as age, sex, and social class specific rates. A total of fifty-four first-admission cases were identified during the seventeen-year period; of these, thirty-two were diagnosed during the period 1970 to 1976, giving an annual incidence of 0.64 per 100,000 compared to 0.35 per 100,000 for the period 1960 to 1969. The increased incidence between 1970 and 1976 was seen most dramatically in adolescent and young-adult females from the upper social classes; rates of illness in males declined slightly during this period, while the rate in middle-class females remained constant. Willi and Grossman[57] calculated incidence rates of anorexia nervosa in Zurich for three randomly selected sampling periods between 1956 and 1975 using nearly all case records from regional psychiatric and medical facilities. They similarly found a steady rise in incidence, from 0.38 per 100,000 for 1956 to 1958 to 1.12 per 100,000 for 1973 to 1975.

What is less clear at present is whether anorexia nervosa occurs on a continuum of severity and if the intensifying preoccupation with body shape and dieting behavior so common in nonclinical adolescent populations might, in some cases, be indicative of a symptomatically milder or partial expression of the illness. Although work in this area is still quite preliminary, the consensus from several large screening studies of abnormal eating attitudes in female adolescents is that milder, subsyndromal variants of anorexia nervosa may be present in some 5 to 10 percent of this age group.[6,33] In all likelihood, however, women with significant weight preoccupation comprise a heterogenous population. While extreme dieting and body-image dissatisfaction in some teenage and young-adult women may indeed by psychopathological precursors of later anorexia nervosa, the majority of young women who are preoccupied with weight differ in fundamental psychological ways from those who go on to develop the classical syndrome.[20]

Theoretical Paradigms

As befitting the complex nature of its characteristics, current theoretical models of anorexia nervosa take as their point of departure the interplay and centrality of multiple predisposing and pathogenic factors.[15] Each is more or less a heuristic framework for developing and testing specific hypotheses concerning these individual factors. Because a detailed consideration of these models is well beyond the scope of this chapter, they are outlined only briefly.

Biological models postulate that since endogenously influenced changes in hormone output and regulation occurring at the time of puberty have far-reaching biochemical influences, including effects on eating behavior, there are, at least in certain individuals, specific links between abnormalities in these mechanisms and concomitant changes in eating behavior and weight control. Most attention in this regard has focused on possible dysfunction within hypothalamic catecholamine and opioid receptor systems normally involved in the regulation of natural eating behavior.[32] Thus a variety of biogenic amines and neuroregulatory agents and their metabolites have been measured in the urine, blood, and spinal fluid of anorexic patients[15] to determine if, under certain conditions, changes in the level, biosynthesis, or utilization of these neuroregulators might be correlated with abnormal eating patterns. Although this research has the promise of identifying crucial points of vulnerability in these biological systems, a direct relation to anorexia nervosa has yet to be established.

Theories emphasizing the contributory role of sociocultural factors to the expression of anorexia nervosa have gained increasing prominence in recent years. For instance, Garner, Garfinkel, and Olmsted[19] note that the recent trend toward greater average body weight among young-adult females in the general population is in direct conflict with aesthetic and socially reinforced preferences for a thinner body shape, and speculate that such a tension between prevailing cultural norms and biological realities is augmenting risk for anorexia nervosa in psychologically vulnerable women. Evidence that severe cases and milder variants of the disorder are overrepresented among individuals who experience occupational pressures to maintain a thin body frame[18] offers direct support for this hypothesis. Other cultural shifts believed to heighten expression of the disorder in recent years include contradictory role expectations and escalating achievement standards affecting young women in contemporary society.[19]

Family systems models of anorexia nervosa have also enjoyed much popularity recently with renewed interest in the role of familial factors in the psychopathogenesis of deviant behavior.[34] This approach criticizes as reductionistic all models of anorexia nervosa giving primacy to individual psychopathology or biological deficit. Rather the condition is viewed in broader context as a link in a chain of nonlinear, circular, and self-regulatory interactions among all family members. Chief among the dysfunctional patterns of family interaction hypothesized to increase risk for anorexia nervosa and to sustain its symptoms once developed include the avoidance or minimization of conflict; involvement of the child in marital tensions; extreme proximity, overintrusive concern, and poorly demarcated generational boundaries among members; and intolerance of change. Although the relevance of these characteristics to the problem of anorexia nervosa is certainly known to the practicing clinician, the exact manner in which they contribute to the illness has not been made clear, and empirical validation of the presence or specificity of these so-called psychosomatic family patterns is still lacking.

Last, anorexia nervosa has been viewed conceptually as a psychobiologically regressive state in which starvation-induced changes in metabolic activity, reproductive drive, and physical appearance help sustain an avoidance of deeply rooted maturational problems (e.g., incomplete individuation from family, unstable self-esteem, deficits in autonomy) that the teenager has come to experience as insurmountable and that she now construes in terms of body shape.[9] A somewhat related view, offered by psychoanalytic theorists,[39] is that suppression of the body's growth and further pubertal development is aimed, at least in part, at preventing fusion with parental objects by repudiating physical likeness to that object. While intriguing, this latter speculation is without empirical support.

In summary, anorexia nervosa is today no less perplexing or therapeutically challenging a disorder than when it was first described some three centuries ago. It is hardly surprising that investigative approaches to this problem have become more technical and specialized in recent years and that simplistic, unicausal models of etiology no longer receive serious consideration. As new hypotheses have been developed, the need for a cohesive biopsychosocial framework that unites data and research methods from a broad range of scientific disciplines has become more widely accepted.

REFERENCES

1. Ben-Tovim, D., Marilov, V., and Crisp, A. H. 1979. Personality and mental state (P.S.E.) within anorexia nervosa. *Journal of Psychosomatic Research* 23:321–325.

2. Benedek, T. 1936. Dominant ideas and their relation to morbid cravings. *International Journal of Psychoanalysis* 17:40–56.

3. Beumont, P. J. V., et al. The onset of anorexia nervosa. *Australia and New Zealand Journal of Psychiatry* 12:145–149.

4. Bliss, E. L., and Branch, H. C. H. 1960. *Anorexia nervosa: Its history, psychology, and biology.* New York: Paul B. Hoeber.

5. Bruch, H. 1973. *Eating disorders: Obesity, anorexia nervosa, and the person within.* New York: Basic Books.

6. Button, E. J., and Whitehouse, A. 1981. Subclinical anorexia nervosa. *Psychological Medicine* 11:509–516.

7. Casper, R. C., et al. 1980. Bulimia: Its incidence and clinical importance in patients with anorexia nervosa. *Archives of General Psychiatry* 37:1030–1034.

8. Crisp, A. H. 1980. *Anorexia nervosa: Let me be.* New York: Grune & Stratton.

9. ———. Anorexia nervosa: Getting the heat out of the system. *Psychiatric Annals* 13: 939–950.

10. Crisp, A. H., Harding, B., and McGuinness, B. 1974. Anorexia nervosa: Psychosomatic characteristics in parents: Relationship to prognosis. A quantitative study. *Journal of Psychosomatic Research* 18:167–173.

11. Crisp, A. H., Palmer, R. L., and Kalucy, R. S. 1976. How common is anorexia nervosa: A prevalence study. *British Journal of Psychiatry* 142:133–138.

12. Crisp, A. H., Hsu, L. K. G., Harding, B., and Hartshorn, J. 1980. Clinical features of anorexia nervosa: A study of a consecutive series of 102 female patients. *Journal of Psychosomatic Research* 24:179–191.

13. Dally, P. J. 1969. *Anorexia nervosa.* New York: Grune & Stratton.

14. Darby, P. L., Garfinkel, P. E., Garner, D. M., and Coscina, D. C., eds. 1983. *Anorexia nervosa: Recent developments in research.* New York: Alan R. Liss.

15. Garfinkel, P. E., and Garner, D. M. 1982. *Anorexia nervosa: A multidimensional perspective.* New York: Brunner/Mazel.

16. Garfinkel, P. E., Moldofsky, H., and Garner, D. M. 1980. Heterogeneity of anorexia nervosa: Bulimia as a distinct syndrome. *Archives of General Psychiatry* 37:1036–1040.

17. Garfinkel, P. E., et al. 1983. A comparison of characteristics in the families of patients with anorexia nervosa and normal controls. *Psychological Medicine* 13:821–828.

18. Garner, D. M., and Garfinkel, P. E. 1980. Socio-cultural factors in the development of anorexia nervosa. *Psychological Medicine* 10:647–656.

19. Garner, D. M., Garfinkel, P. E., and Olmsted, M. 1983. An overview of sociocultural factors in the development of anorexia nervosa. In *Anorexia nervosa: Recent developments in research,* ed. P. L. Darby, P. E. Garfinkel, D. M. Garner, and D. V. Coscina, pp. 65–82. New York: Alan R. Liss.

20. Garner, D. M., Olmsted, M. P., Polivy, J., and Garfinkel, P. E. 1984. Comparison between weight-preoccupied women and anorexia nervosa. *Psychosomatic Medicine* 46: 255–266.

21. Gershon, E. S., et al. 1983. Anorexia nervosa and major affective disorders associated in families: A preliminary report. In *Childhood psychopathology and development,* ed. S. B. Guze, F. J. Earls, and J. E. Barrett, pp. 279–284. New York: Raven Press.

22. Gull, W. W. 1874. Anorexia nervosa (apepsia hysterica, anorexia hysterica). *Transactions of the Clinical Society of London* 7:22–28.

23. Halmi, K. A. 1974. Anorexia nervosa: Demographic and clinical features in 94 cases. *Psychosomatic Medicine* 36:18–25.

24. Hammond, W. A. 1879. *Fasting girls: Their physiology and pathology.* New York: Putnam.

25. Hudson, J. I., Pope, H. G., Jonas, J. M., and Yorgelun-Todd, D. 1983. A family study of anorexia nervosa and bulimia. *British Journal of Psychiatry* 142:133–138.

26. Jones, D. J., Fox, M. M., Babigian, H. M., and Hutton, H. E. 1980. The epidemiology of anorexia nervosa in Monroe County, New York: 1960–1976. *Psychosomatic Medicine* 42: 551–558.

27. Kalucy, R. S., Crisp, A. H., and Harding, B. 1977. A study of 56 families with anorexia nervosa. *British Journal of Medical Psychology* 50:381–395.

28. Kay, D. W. K., and Leigh, D. 1954. The natural history, treatment, and prognosis of anorexia nervosa, based on a study of 38 patients. *Journal of Mental Science* 100:411–439.

29. Kendell, R. E., Hall, D. J., Hailey, A., and Babigian, H. M. 1973. The epidemiology of anorexia nervosa. *Psychological Medicine* 3:200–203.

30. King, A. 1963. Primary and secondary anorexia nervosa syndromes. *British Journal of Psychiatry* 109:470–479.

31. Lasegue, C. 1873. On hysterical anorexia. *Medical Times Gazette* 2:265–266.

32. Leibowitz, S. F. 1983. Hypothalamic catecholamine systems controlling eating behavior: A potential model for anorexia nervosa. In *Anorexia nervosa: Recent developments in research*, ed. P. L. Darby, P. E. Garfinkel, D. M. Garner, and D. V. Coscina, pp. 221–229. New York: Alan R. Liss.

33. Mann, A. H., et al. 1983. Screening for abnormal eating attitudes and psychiatric morbidity in an unselected population of 15-year-old school girls. *Psychological Medicine* 13: 573–580.

34. Minuchin, S., Rosman, B. L., and Baker, L. 1978. *Psychosomatic families: Anorexia nervosa in context.* Cambridge, Mass.: Harvard University Press.

35. Morgan, H. G., and Russell, G. F. M. 1975. Value of family background and clinical features as predictors of long-term outcome in anorexia nervosa: Four year follow-up study of 42 patients. *Psychological Medicine* 5:355–371.

36. Morton, R. 1694. *Phthisiologica: Or a treatise of consumptions.* London: S. Smith & B. Walford.

37. Moulton, R. 1942. A psychosomatic study of anorexia including the use of vaginal smears. *Psychosomatic Medicine* 4:62–74.

38. Myrtle, A. S. 1888. Letters to the editor. *Lancet* 1:899.

39. Palazzoli, M. S. 1978. *Self-starvation.* New York: Jason Aronson.

40. Pillay, M., and Crisp, A. H. 1977. Some psychological characteristics of patients with anorexia nervosa whose weight has been newly restored. *British Journal of Medical Psychology* 50:375–380.

41. Playfair, W. S. 1888. Note on the so-called anorexia nervosa. *Lancet* 1:817.

42. Pope, H. G., Hudson, J. I., Yorgelun-Todd, D., and Hudson, M. 1984. Prevalence of anorexia nervosa and bulimia in three student populations. *International Journal of Eating Disorders* 3:53–62.

43. Sheehan, H. L., and Summers, V. K. 1949. The syndrome of hypopituitarism. *Quarterly Journal of Medicine* 18:319–378.

44. Simmonds, M. 1914. Uber embolische prozesse in der hypophysis. *Archives of Pathology and Anatomy* 217:226–239.

45. Smart, D. E., Beumont, P. J. V., and George, G. C. W. 1976. Some personality characteristics of patients with anorexia nervosa. *British Journal of Psychiatry* 128:57–60.

46. Stonehill, E., and Crisp, A. H. 1977. Psychoneurotic characteristics of patients with anorexia nervosa before and after treatment and at follow-up 4–7 years later. *Journal of Psychosomatic Research* 21:187–193.

47. Strober, M. 1980. Personality and symptomatological features in young, nonchronic anorexia nervosa patients. *Journal of Psychosomatic Research* 24:353–359.

48. ———. 1981. A comparative analysis of personality organization in juvenile anorexia nervosa. *Journal of Youth and Adolescence* 10:285–295.

49. ———. 1981. The relation of personality characteristics to body image disturbances in juvenile anorexia nervosa. *Psychosomatic Medicine* 43:323–330.

50. ———. 1981. The significance of bulimia in juvenile anorexia nervosa: An exploration of possible etiologic factors. *International Journal of Eating Disorders* 1:28–43.

51. ———. 1983. An empirically derived typology of anorexia nervosa. In *Anorexia nervosa: Recent developments in research*, ed. P. L. Darby, P. E. Garfinkel, D. M. Garner, and D. V. Coscina, pp. 185–196. New York: Alan R. Liss.

52. ———. 1983. Family associations between anorexia nervosa and affective illness. Paper presented at the annual meeting of the American Psychiatric Association, New York, May 7.

53. Strober, M., Salkin, B., Burroughs, J., and Morrell, W. 1982. Validity of the bulimia-restricter distinction in anorexia nervosa: Parental personality characteristics and family psychiatric morbidity. *Journal of Nervous and Mental Disease* 170:345–351.

54. Theander, S. 1970. Anorexia nervosa: A psychiatric investigation of 94 female cases. *Acta Psychiatrica Scandinavica* 214 (Suppl.):1–94.

55. Waller, J. V., Kaufman, M. R., and Deutsch, F. 1940. Anorexia nervosa: Psychosomatic entity. *Psychosomatic Medicine* 2:3–16.

56. Whytt, R. 1767. *Observations on the nature, causes and cure of those disorders which have been commonly called nervous hyponchrondriac or hysteric: To which are prefixed some remarks on the sympathy of the nerves,* 3rd ed. London: T. Beckett, P. A. DeHondt, and J. Balfour.

57. Willi, J., and Grossman, S. 1983. Epidemiology of anorexia nervosa in a defined region of Switzerland. *American Journal of Psychiatry* 140:564–567.

58. Winokur, A., March, V., and Mendels, J. 1980. Primary affective disorder in relatives of patients with anorexia nervosa. *American Journal of Psychiatry* 137:695–698.

13

Anorexia Nervosa: Medical and Physiological Aspects

James E. Mitchell

Several important areas must be considered when examining the relationship between anorexia nervosa and physical status. The first is the well-recognized problem that certain medical illnesses can mimic primary anorexia nervosa. Space-occupying lesions of the central nervous system (CNS) represent one serious example. The second area concerns the medical complications of anorexia nervosa, some of which are serious. The third area concerns the pathophysiology of the disorder itself and centers on the question of whether the hypothalamic dysfunction seen in patients with anorexia nervosa is a cause or a consequence of the disorder. Is anorexia nervosa best considered a medical illness resulting from hypothalamic dysfunction that manifests itself in physical, psychological, and behavioral changes? Or does hypothalamic dysfunction result from the weight loss engendered by the psychopathology?

The first two considerations, medical causes and medical consequences, can be approached directly. The question of hypothalamic dysfunction remains a matter of considerable debate. This chapter reviews the physical causes and consequences of anorexia nervosa or anorexia-like illnesses and relates these findings to the question of causality.

Most of the physical abnormalities that have been demonstrated in anorexia nervosa patients have also been described in starved individuals who do not have anorexia nervosa. For example, the endocrine abnormalities of anorexia nervosa are similar to those of individuals undergoing starvation.* Experimental starvation research shows that many behavioral sequelae of anorexia nervosa, including irritability, difficulty with concentration, depression, mood lability, indecisiveness, and obsessive think-

---

* See references 11, 87, 126, 145, 146, and 154.

TABLE 13.1

Symptoms and Signs of Anorexia Nervosa

Symptoms	Prevalence of Symptoms (%)	Signs	Prevalence of Signs (%)
Amenorrhea	100	Hypotension	20–85
Constipation	20	Hypothermia	15–85
Bloating	30	Dry skin	25–85
Abdominal pain	20	Bradycardia	25–90
Cold intolerance	20	Lanugo	20–80
Lethargy	20	Edema	20–25
Excess energy	35	Petechiae	10

ing, can also be seen in starved normal subjects. However, such subjects do not develop the intense fear of food, the body-image distortion, or the ability to suppress hunger that is commonly seen in patients with anorexia nervosa. Therefore, experimental starvation explains only part of the problem.

Signs and Symptoms

The prevalence of signs and symptoms encountered in patients with anorexia nervosa are shown in table 13.1. These are based on several series of patients reported in the literature.* Amenorrhea is present invariably and is used by some researchers as a criterion for diagnosis. Constipation is also commonly reported. Common signs of the disorder noted on physical examination include hypotension, hypothermia, skin changes including dryness of the skin and the presence of lanugo, bradycardia, and, in a small percentage of patients, pitting edema. Some of these physical signs, such as hypothermia, bradycardia, and petechiae, may indicate serious underlying medical complications. These will be discussed in more detail under the various organ systems.

Medical Complications by Organ Systems

METABOLIC ABNORMALITIES

Patients with anorexia nervosa frequently fast for prolonged periods. Hypoglycemia can be seen and is sometimes profound.[78,108] Another problem in glucose homeostasis is abnormalities on glucose tolerance test-

* See references 66, 89, 136, 141, and 165.

TABLE 13.2

Common Laboratory Abnormalities Seen in Patients with Anorexia Nervosa

Metabolic Abnormalities
Hypercholesterolemia
Hypercarotenemia
Hypozincemia
Abnormal liver functions
Abnormal glucose tolerance
Fasting hypoglycemia
Hypocalcemia

Gastrointestinal Abnormalities
Elevated amylase

Cardiovascular Abnormalities
Electrocardiogram abnormalities

Renal Abnormalities
Elevated blood urea nitrogen
Decreased glomerular filtration rate
Urinary concentrating defect

Central Nervous System Abnormalities
Electroencephalogram abnormality
Computerized-axial-tomography scan
abnormality

Fluid and Electrolyte Abnormalities
Hypochloremia
Hypokalemia
Metabolic alkalosis
Metabolic acidosis

Hematological Abnormalities
Pancytopenia
Relative lymphocytosis
Bone marrow hypocellularity
Thrombocytopenia

Endocrine Abnormalities
Low luteinizing hormone, follicle-
stimulating hormone
Low urinary gonadotropins
Low urinary estrogen
Low triiodothyronine
Elevated growth hormone
Elevated cortisol
Dexamethasone suppression test
nonsuppression

ing. Both diabetic glucose tolerance curves and flat curves have been reported.[165] The available research indicates that glucose tolerance improves with weight gain.[30] Anorexic patients have also shown relative insulin resistance, which appears to correlate with degree of weight loss. These changes are summarized in tables 13.2 and 13.3.

TABLE 13.3

Medical Complications of Anorexia Nervosa

Metabolic Complications
Yellowing of skin
Impaired taste
Hypoglycemia

Gastrointestinal Complications
Altered gastric emptying
Salivary gland swelling
Superior mesenteric artery syndrome
Gastric dilatation
Constipation

Cardiovascular Complications
Bradycardia
Arrhythmias
Pericardial effusion
Edema
Heart failure

Renal Complications
Water concentration defect
Kaliopenic nephropathy

Fluid and Electrolyte Complications
Dehydration
Weakness
Tetany

Hematological Complications
Bleeding diathesis
Anemia

Dental Problems
Decalcification
Caries

Endocrine Complications
Amenorrhea
Lack of sexual interest
Impotence

General Complications
Weakness
Hypothermia

Wachslicht-Rodbard and associates[156] reported increased insulin binding to erythrocytes in patients with anorexia nervosa, which normalized following refeeding. Their interpretation of the Scatchard analysis—which allows for differentiation between changes in receptor numbers and receptor affinities—indicated a change in binding characteristics reflecting an actual increase in the number of receptors rather than a change in receptor affinity. However, these conclusions have been debated.[81,143]

An interesting association between anorexia nervosa and diabetes mellitus has been reported. Powers and associates[128] reported four such cases and illustrated that these patients employed a variety of techniques to lose weight, including self-induced vomiting, the use of excess insulin while not eating, and purposefully spilling large amounts of glucose in the urine by staying hyperglycemic.

Liver function abnormalities have been described in patients with anorexia nervosa. These may be present during weight loss and may increase during weight gain in treatment, suggesting mild fatty degeneration secondary to refeeding.[68,85] Elevated serum cholesterol levels have been reported frequently in patients with anorexia nervosa.[69,91,116] Halmi and Fry[69] reported considerable variability in cholesterol values in anorexic patients and stressed that frank hypercholesterolemia was rare. The etiology of the cholesterol elevation is not known. Nestle[116] suggested that the elevated cholesterol reflected diminished bile and cholesterol acid turnover and demonstrated that bile acid excretion was decreased in some patients with anorexia. Mordasini and associates[111] suggested that diminished cholesterol turnover might explain the elevation. Serum triglyceride levels are normal in most patients.[78]

Zinc levels relate to taste perception, and impaired taste perception has been reported in patients with anorexia nervosa.[9,31,77] Casper and associates[31] measured trace minerals in patients with anorexia nervosa and correlated these levels with abnormalities in taste function. Although low zinc levels were present, plasma zinc levels did not correlate with the taste recognition scores. Currently, the role of zinc deficiency in anorexia nervosa is unclear.

Elevated serum carotene levels have also been described in patients with anorexia nervosa.[17,95,131] Various explanations have been offered for this elevation, including increased intake of foods high in carotene or some defect in the utilization or metabolism of vitamin A.

GASTROINTESTINAL COMPLICATIONS

Complaints of abdominal pain, bloating, and postprandial distress are very common in patients with anorexia nervosa. These complaints are particularly troublesome early in treatment when patients are expected to eat more to gain weight.

Investigations of gastrointestinal physiology in these patients have clarified the pathophysiology of these problems. Initial work was reported by Silverstone and Russell[143] in 1967 using a pressure transducer system to measure gastric contractions. No difference was found in gastric motility between patients with anorexia nervosa and controls. However, the patients with anorexia nervosa demonstrated increased motility after treatment. More recently, Dubois and associates† used a dye dilution technique to measure intragastric volume, fractional emptying rate, gastric hydrogen output, and gastric fluid output in a series of fifteen patients and eleven controls. They found decreased fractional emptying rate and decreased hydrogen ion output in the anorexia nervosa patients. When retested after weight gain, the patients had improved fractional gastric emptying but were still significantly different from the controls. Gastric hydrogen output had not improved significantly. Saleh and Lebwohl[133] used a gamma camera technique to study gastric retention of Technetium-labeled meals in patients with anorexia nervosa and demonstrated delayed gastric emptying compared to controls. Patients were then treated with metoclopramide hydrochloride, a dopamine (DA)-blocking agent that stimulates gastric peristalsis. Five patients showed improved gastric emptying. The authors suggested that this drug might be a useful adjunct in the treatment of anorexia nervosa. Changes in gastric secretion or gastric emptying in anorexia nervosa have also been demonstrated by others.[76,90] Taken together, these studies suggest impaired gastric functioning in anorexia nervosa patients when they are low in weight and a probable decrease in gastric fluid and hydrogen output. Available studies suggest improvement with weight gain.

The superior mesenteric artery syndrome is a condition important to this review for two reasons: this condition can be confused with anorexia nervosa, and patients with anorexia nervosa may be at risk for developing this complication.[2,124,147,168] This syndrome involves compression of the third portion of the duodenum by the superior mesenteric neurovascular bundle as it crosses the duodenum. The problem also has been described in patients following severe weight loss not associated with anorexia nervosa.[168] It can be acute or chronic and may at times be intermittent and positional. Patients usually present with vomiting, abdominal pain, and, if the problem has been chronic, weight loss.[2] The condition can sometimes be managed supportively but may require surgical intervention. Patients with anorexia nervosa, particularly if placed at bed rest, may be at risk for this complication because of the lack of a fat cushion surrounding the neurovascular bundle.[147]

Another potentially serious complication of anorexia nervosa is acute gastric dilatation where the stomach expands and may rupture.* This complication has been reviewed by Saul,[134] who compiled a series of sixty-six cases of spontaneous rupture of the stomach. In about half of the cases, Saul concluded that the situation had resulted from the ingestion of large amounts of food and/or gastric dilatation. Eleven of these cases

---

* See references 18, 24, 34, 36, 49, 83, 96, 105, 107, 132, 134, and 137.
† Dubois, A., Gross, H. A., Ebert, M. H., and Castle, D. O. 1979. Altered gastric emptying and secretion in primary anorexia nervosa. *Gastroenterology* 77:319–323.

had been diagnosed as having anorexia nervosa, most of them undergoing refeeding. Gastric dilatation has also been documented in prisoners of war undergoing refeeding.[105] The mechanism appears to be obstruction of the gastroesophageal junction associated with the intake of a large amount of food.

Swelling of the salivary glands, particularly the parotid gland, has also been described.* This complication is also common in patients with bulimia and is discussed in detail in Chapter 21.

Recent reports suggest the possibility of pancreatic dysfunction in patients with anorexia nervosa. Pancreatitis associated with anorexia nervosa has been reported, as has reduced echogenicity on ultrasound evaluation, suggesting pathological changes in the organ.[37,135]

RENAL COMPLICATIONS

Dehydration is a common complication of anorexia nervosa.[128] An elevated blood urea nitrogen level is frequently discovered on screening, but serum creatinine is usually normal. More sophisticated renal testing has also been done. Aperia and associates[7] studied urine concentrating capacity following water deprivation and vasopressin augmentation, glomerular filtration rate (GFR) using insulin clearance, and renal blood flow. Urinary concentrating capacity was moderately depressed both before and during vasopressin augmentation, but the differences were not significant compared to controls. GFR was generally reduced in the anorexia nervosa patients.

The effects of chronic dehydration and low serum potassium on renal function is of considerable concern. Wigley[174] revealed seventeen cases of patients with anorexia nervosa who developed hypokalemic alkalosis and found a history of some renal problem in eight cases. He added three additional cases and felt that the renal problems were secondary to the potassium depletion. Riemenschneider and Bohle[130] studied renal biopsy results in patients with hypokalemia and hyponatremia from a variety of causes including laxative abuse, diuretic abuse, anorexia nervosa, and chronic vomiting, and found evidence of interstitial fibrosis. This pattern, described as kaliopenic nephropathy, can result in renal impairment. Further studies of renal functions should be done in patients with anorexia nervosa, and the possibility of renal damage should be considered in each case.

There has also been interest in the regulation of urinary concentrating capacity in patients with anorexia nervosa. Several studies found increases in urine osmolality following vasopressin administration, suggesting partial diabetes insipidus.[108,155] Gold and associates[60] studied cerebrospinal fluid (CSF) and plasma arginine vasopressin in patients with anorexia nervosa and demonstrated abnormalities in regulation following challenge with

* See references 5, 12, 43, 98, 144, and 162.

intravenous hypertonic saline. Most subjects had increased urinary output and increased CSF levels of arginine vasopressin. The pathophysiology of these abnormalities is unclear.

CARDIOPULMONARY COMPLICATIONS

Bradycardia is common in patients with anorexia nervosa and reflects the adaptive metabolic effects of starvation. A growing number of reports suggest additional cardiovascular problems. Electrocardiograms frequently reveal abnormalities, including T-wave morphology changes and ST segment depression.[122,151] Several cases involving the development of arrhythmias have been reported. Those described include sinus arrest with ectopic atrial rhythm,[51] nodal escape beats,[151] and junctional rhythm with retrograde atrial conduction.[109] Electrolyte abnormalities may account for many such problems, yet the arrhythmias have developed despite normal electrolytes.[109] There are no studies that would allow an estimate of the incidence of such problems.

Circulatory dynamics have also been evaluated in patients with anorexia nervosa. Gottdiener and associates[64] studied a series of patients using echocardiography and found a decrease in cardiac chamber dimensions greater than expected on the basis of the decreased body surface areas. Kalager and associates[84] found evidence of left ventricular functional impairment with probable reduced cardiac contractility using systolic ejection time measures. Powers[127] reported cardiac failure in anorexia nervosa patients undergoing refeeding and stressed the role of refeeding as a predisposing complication. Pericardial effusions have also been described in patients with anorexia nervosa.[142]

Pneumomediastinum, or the presence of air in the mediastinum, has been reported in both anorexia nervosa and hyperemesis graviderum, a condition associated with protracted vomiting.[33,46] The pathophysiology of this completion is not well understood but may relate to vomiting behavior.

HEMATOLOGICAL AND IMMUNOLOGICAL COMPLICATIONS

Several hematological abnormalities have been described in patients with anorexia nervosa. The most common is leukopenia, with a white blood cell count of less than 5,000.* Bowers and Eckert[19] compared hematological indices in patients with anorexia nervosa and in matched controls with psychiatric problems. The anorexia nervosa patients had significantly decreased leukocyte counts and absolute neutrophil, lymphocyte, and monocyte counts, a pattern best characterized as panleukopenia. Thrombocytopenia has also been reported in these patients.[19,93] The hematological abnormalities seen in patients with

* See references 19, 28, 92, 115, 123, 129, and 165.

anorexia nervosa can improve with weight gain and are secondary to malnutrition.[68,92]

Bone marrow findings have been reported in several series.* The pattern found is usually one of marked hypocellularity of the marrow and deposition of gelatinous acid mucopolysaccharide, a pattern secondary to starvation. These changes are reversible with weight gain.[92]

Studies of immune function in anorexia suggest a mixed picture. Pertschuk and associates[125] found that cellular immunity endured until the patients became severely emaciated. Golla and associates[62] studied lymphocyte functioning and found intact cell-mediated immunity and normal T lymphocyte populations with unimpaired proliferative lymphocyte responsiveness to mitogenic stimulation. However, granulocytes obtained from patients with anorexia nervosa have reduced killing rate for *Staphylococcus aureus* and *Escherichia coli in vitro*.[63,121] Such findings add to speculation that patients with anorexia nervosa might be at increased risk for infections. However, Bowers and Eckert[19] examined the frequency of infections in a group of patients with anorexia and a group of matched controls. While the patients with anorexia nervosa did have lower leukocyte counts, there was no significant difference in the rate of infections between the two groups. Clinically, patients with anorexia nervosa often become ill during the period of weight gain rather than when they are low in weight. This is intriguing and suggests a protective mechanism against infection at low weight.

Clotting mechanisms have also been evaluated in patients with anorexia nervosa. Reduced serum levels of certain complement factors have been demonstrated,[88,120] as have low levels of fibrinogen.[176] These data, coupled with the low platelet counts that are seen, suggest the possibility of bleeding tendencies.

DENTAL PROBLEMS

Dental problems are common in patients with anorexia nervosa and appear to be attributable to certain problem behaviors, particularly the self-induced vomiting seen in the subgroup of patients who are characterized as bulimic anorexics. Several authors have described these complications in detail.[75,79,148] Since they relate to the bulimic symptoms of the disorder, they are discussed in more detail in chapter 21.

FLUID AND ELECTROLYTE COMPLICATIONS

Considering the fluid restriction, vomiting, and laxative abuse that can accompany anorexia nervosa, it is not surprising that electrolyte abnormalities have been described in these patients. Metabolic alkalosis has been most frequently described†; also seen are hypochloremia and hy-

* See references 4, 35, 92, 93, 104, and 115.
† See references 47, 148, 150, 160, 164, 165, and 175.

pokalemia. The fluid and electrolyte abnormalities appear to result from the associated bulimic behaviors, such as vomiting, although prolonged fasting may contribute. These abnormalities are covered in greater detail in chapter 21.

CENTRAL NERVOUS SYSTEM COMPLICATIONS

In considering the role of CNS dysfunction in anorexia nervosa, we must first consider reports of primary neurological problems presenting with disordered eating. For example, patients with space-occupying lesions such as hypothalamic tumors may present with the symptoms of anorexia nervosa.[99,170] The possibility of a primary CNS lesion must be considered in each patient.

Electroencephalogram abnormalities have been described by Crisp and associates[38] in some patients with anorexia nervosa. The authors stressed that such abnormalities could be attributable to the profound metabolic disturbance seen in these patients. Computerized-axial-tomography studies have been used to evaluate CNS structure, and several case reports or small series[48,74,119,138] have demonstrated abnormalities suggesting cortical atrophy and ventricular dilatation. In one series, the changes were reversible with weight gain, suggesting that they related directly to the emaciation rather than being evidence of any stable ongoing neurological deficit.[138] A case of Wernicke's encephalopathy has been reported in a patient with anorexia nervosa; the authors of this report suggested that this might be a frequently overlooked problem, a suggestion that should be evaluated further, considering the cognitive impairment anorexic patients may manifest.[73]

ENDOCRINE COMPLICATIONS

The endocrine system has been intensively investigated in patients with anorexia nervosa.* This attention reflects both the variety of endocrine abnormalities seen in these patients as well as the research potential of using neuroendocrine measures to evaluate hypothalamic dysfunction. A large literature exists in this area and can only be briefly reviewed here. While it has been noted that most of the endocrine abnormalities that have been described appear to remit with weight gain, some abnormalities seem to persist, although long-term follow-up studies employing neuroendocrine measures are lacking.

Gonadotropins, Gonadal Steroids, and Menstrual Functioning. Amenorrhea is invariably present in anorexia nervosa, and the pituitary-gonadal axis has been carefully studied. Studies have demonstrated hypofunctioning of the hypothalamo-pituitary-ovarian axis in anorexic patients. Reduced levels of luteinizing hormone (LH) and follicle-stimulating hormone (FSH)

* See references 16, 55, 106, 117, and 161.

have usually been reported.* LH responsiveness to LH releasing hormone (RH) has also been shown to be impaired when patients are low in weight, although results are inconsistent.† LHRH priming[177] or weight gain‡ improves responsiveness to LHRH, suggesting a possible underlying lack of endogenous LHRH stimulation. Using serial monitoring techniques, LH secretory patterns have been found to be "immature," that is, to resemble the patterns of premenarchal girls.[20,21,152] This pattern "matures" with weight gain when the gain is accompanied by symptomatic improvement in such areas as attitudes toward food.[80] This would indicate that simple weight gain is not sufficient to correct the abnormality.[21]

Abnormalities of estrogen metabolism have also been found. This area has been investigated by Weiner and his colleagues and has been recently reviewed.[169] Estrogen metabolism generates less estradiol and more 2-hydroxyestrone than is seen in normal subjects. This pattern is opposite of that seen in obese women.[50] There is also an abnormality in hypothalamic responsiveness to the negative feedback effects of estrogen.[158,159] Plasma and urinary estrogen levels are low§ but return toward normal with weight gain. Low testosterone levels have also been demonstrated in both male and female patients with anorexia nervosa¶; testosterone levels appear to improve with weight gain. An impairment in LH responsiveness to LHRH has also been demonstrated in male anorexic patients.[6,39]

As stated previously, amenorrhea is invariably present in anorexia nervosa. The most common pattern is one of secondary amenorrhea, although primary amenorrhea is also seen. In a significant minority of cases, amenorrhea may actually precede weight loss by several months.[140]

Thyroid Function. Abnormalities on thyroid function tests are common in patients with anorexia nervosa; the changes may be adaptational to starvation. Low serum triiodothyronine (T_3) levels are consistently found,** with thyroxine (T_4) values usually normal or low.[110,114] The low T_3 values may represent a low T_3 syndrome secondary to the decreased peripheral conversion of T_4 to T_3, a pattern that is adaptational to starvation.[54,110,149,153] Reverse T_3, which is the less active form of the hormone, has been found to be elevated.[29] The bradycardia and cold intolerance seen in these patients may in part reflect this hypometabolic state.

Low thyroid-stimulating hormone (TSH) values have been described in some, but not all, patients with anorexia nervosa.[78,110,114] Of particular interest has been the demonstration of abnormalities in TSH response to thyroid-releasing hormone (TRH),[29,97,110] including a delay in the fall of TSH[40] and a blunted TSH response to TRH.[101] Weight recovery is accompanied by improvement in this pattern, but some patients continue

---

* See references 10, 15, 21, 25, 42, 56, 70, 82, 118, and 140.
† See references 41, 112, 139, 164, 166, and 173.
‡ See references 70, 80, 164, 166, and 173.
§ See references 15, 70, 78, 108, 118, and 140.
¶ See references 39, 97, 102, 171, and 172.
** See references 26, 27, 40, 82, 110, 113, 114, and 165.

to show a delay in peak response despite weight gain,[29] suggesting a persistence of neuroendocrine regulatory dysfunction.

Growth Hormone. Fasting growth hormone (GH) levels are elevated in many patients with anorexia nervosa at low weight.* Some reports have shown pathological GH increases in response to glucose administration and TRH stimulation,[3,61,101,103] but some have not.[52,106] Attenuated GH responsiveness to levodopa,[139] apomorphine,[30] and insulin-induced hypoglycemia[23] have also been reported. The clinical implications of these GH regulatory abnormalities are unknown.

Prolactin. Fasting prolactin levels have generally been reported to be normal.† Paradoxical increase in prolactin has been reported in response to gonadotropin releasing hormone.[14] Responsiveness to TSH and sulperidine appear to be normal,[16,59,101] but has been reported to be exaggerated in at least two patients.[152]

Halmi and associates suggested that a dopaminergic abnormality as reflected by prolactin regulatory disturbance might be masked by the elevation in cortisol.[71] These authors assessed prolactin responsiveness to chlorpromazine while controlling for cortisol levels. Two of six patients had clearly impaired responsiveness, and responsiveness was less than optimal in three others. These authors suggested that this finding indicated possible impairment at postsynaptic DA receptor sites.

Adrenal Function. Regulation of adrenal cortisol secretion has also been studied intensively in patients with anorexia nervosa. Elevated basal cortisol levels,‡ inadequate cortisol suppression following dexamethasone,[8,42,163] and disturbed secretory patterns of cortisol[20,32,97] have all been described. These patients have increased secretion and decreased clearance of cortisol with a prolonged half-life for cortisol.[22,162] The low weight may be responsible for the nonsuppression on the dexamethasone suppression test in that a weight gain of only 10 percent will normalize dexamethasone suppression in most patients.[45]

CHANGES IN HYPOTHALAMIC REGULATION

The foregoing discussion documents that neuroendocrine abnormalities are frequent in anorexia nervosa patients. What these reports have not done is separate cause from effect. We know that many of the neuroendocrine abnormalities can be attributed to the weight loss. However, not all of these abnormalities normalize promptly with restoration of a normal weight. Also, some anorexia nervosa patients will experience amenorrhea prior to weight loss. Whether the persistence of neuroendocrine dysfunction or onset of amenorrhea prior to weight loss indicates primary hypothalamic dysfunction in a subgroup of these patients is unclear.

* See references 44, 61, 78, 94, and 101.
† See references 16, 32, 59, 101, and 108.
‡ See references 20, 25, 56, 78, and 163.

Several other functions that are under hypothalamic control also are disordered in anorexia nervosa. One is temperature regulation. Anorexia nervosa patients show exaggerated fluctuations in core body temperature when exposed to temperature extremes, have a lowered threshold for thermal regulatory sweating and vasodilatation, and demonstrate reduced and irregular vasodilatation on exposure to indirect heating.[53,100,157]

Another area of possible disordered hypothalamic functioning is appetite regulation. Researchers have studied the neurotransmitters in the hypothalamus that are known to be associated with appetite control. Of the neurotransmitters involved, DA, norepinephrine (NE), epinephrine, and serotonin (5HT) all appear to be involved in appetite and weight regulation. Halmi and associates measured 3-methoxy, 4-hydroxy-phenolglycol (MHPG), a metabolite of NE, and other biogenic amine metabolites in the urine of patients with anorexia nervosa.[72] MHPG levels were quite low when weight was low but increased with weight gain. Increasing MHPG correlated with decreasing depression scores, suggesting a relationship between these factors.[72] Other groups have also found decreased MHPG in the urine of patients with anorexia nervosa with low weight.[1,57,65,67] CSF levels of homovanillic acid and 5-hydroxyindoleacetic acid (metabolites of DA and 5HT) have also been shown to be low in anorexia nervosa patients.[58,86] Various other transmitters are now being evaluated (DA, endorphin, and dynorphin) in an attempt to correlate changes with the dysfunction seen in these patients. Research into the control of appetite has grown immensely in the last few years, and many new transmitter substances, particularly peptides such as corticotrophin-releasing factor (CRF), cholecystokinin (CCK), and neurotensin, have been shown to have a role in appetite regulation. Most of these substances have yet to be examined in patients with anorexia nervosa.

Conclusions

From the information reviewed, one can only conclude that anorexia nervosa is not a medically benign condition and that these patients must be carefully evaluated and monitored to prevent serious complications or death.

Certain general guidelines can be suggested concerning the evaluation of these patients. A careful history and physical examination should be part of the evaluation process. On physical examination, careful attention should be given to the state of hydration, oral hygiene, cardiac functioning, and vital signs. Careful neurological assessment is also indicated to rule out primary neurological dysfunction. Nonmedical therapists who work with these patients should work closely with physicians to ensure that medical stability can be monitored. Routine laboratory screening is also indicated and should include a complete blood count with platelet count, screening renal function tests, screening liver function tests, glucose and electrolyte determination, thyroid functions, and an electrocardiogram as a minimum battery. Some experts in this area also favor in-depth routine neurological evaluation including skull films with sella views, visual field examination, computerized-axial-tomography scan, fasting prolactin, and LH and FSH tests. Regardless of the tests used, a careful history and physical examination remain the most important parts of the diagnostic evaluation.

REFERENCES

1. Abraham, S. F., Beumont, P. J. V., and Cobbin, D. M. 1981. Catecholamine metabolism and body weight in anorexia nervosa. *British Journal of Psychiatry* 138:244–247.
2. Akin, J. T., Jr., Gray, S. W., and Skandelakis, J. E. 1976. Vascular compression of the duodenum: Presentation of ten cases and review of the literature. *Surgery* 79:515–522.
3. Alvarez, L. C., et al. 1972. Growth hormone in malnutrition. *Journal of Clinical Endocrinology and Metabolism* 34:400–409.
4. Amrein, P. C., Friedman, R., Kosinski, K., and Ellman, L. 1979. Hematologic changes in anorexia nervosa. *Journal of the American Medical Association* 241:2190–2191.
5. Anders, D., Harms, D., Kriens, O., and Schmidt, H. 1975. Zur frage der sialadenose als sekundärer organmanifestation der anorexia nervosa—beobachtungen en einem 13 jahrigen knaben. *Klinische Pädiatric* 187:156–162.
6. Andersen, A. E., Wirth, J. B., and Strahlman, E. R. 1982. Reversible weight-related increase in plasma testosterone during treatment of male and female patients with anorexia nervosa. *International Journal of Eating Disorders* 2:74–84.
7. Aperia, A., Broberger, O., and Fohlin, L. 1978. Renal function in anorexia nervosa. *Acta Paediatrica Scandinavica* 67:219–224.
8. Auerbach, M. 1977. Anorexia nervosa: Circadian rhythm of plasma hormones. *New England Journal of Medicine* 296:1069.
9. Bakan, R. 1979. The role of zinc in anorexia nervosa: Etiology and treatment. *Medical Hypotheses* 5:731–736.
10. Baranowska, B., and Zgliczynski, S. 1979. Enhanced testosterone in female patients with anorexia nervosa: Its normalization after weight gain. *Acta Endocrinologica* (Copenhagen) 90:328–335.
11. Barbosa-Saldivar, J. L., and Van Itallie, T. B. 1979. Semistarvation: An overview of an old problem. *Bulletin of the New York Academy of Medicine* 55:744–797.
12. Bernard, J. D., and Shern, M. A. 1974. Psychogenic pseudo-Sjögren's syndrome. *Western Journal of Medicine* 120:247–248.
13. Beumont, P. J. V. 1979. The endocrinology of anorexia nervosa. *Medical Journal of Australia* 1:611–613.
14. Beumont, P. J. V., Abraham, S. F., and Turtle, J. 1980. Paradoxical prolactin response to gonadotropin-releasing hormone during weight gain in patients with anorexia nervosa. *Journal of Clinical Endocrinology and Metabolism* 51:1283–1285.
15. Beumont, P. J. F., Carr, J. P., and Gelder, M. G. 1973. Plasma levels of luteinizing hormone and of immunoreactive oestrogens (oestradiol) in anorexia nervosa: Response to clomiphene citrate. *Psychological Medicine* 3:495–501.
16. Beumont, P. J. V., George, G. C. W., Pimstone, B. L., and Vinik, A. I. 1976. Body weight and the pituitary response to hypothalamic releasing hormones in patients with anorexia nervosa. *Journal of Clinical Endocrinology and Metabolism* 43:487–496.
17. Bjanji, S., and Mattingly, D. 1981. Anorexia nervosa: Some observations on "dieters"

and "vomiters," cholesterol and carotene. *British Journal of Psychiatry* 139:238–241.

18. Bossingham, D. 1977. Acute gastric dilatation in anorexia nervosa. *British Medical Journal* 2:959.

19. Bowers, T. K., and Eckert, E. 1978. Leukopenia in anorexia nervosa. *Archives of Internal Medicine* 138:1520–1523.

20. Boyar, R. M., and Katz, J. 1977. Twenty-four hour gonadotropin secretory patterns in anorexia nervosa. In *Anorexia nervosa*, ed. R. A. Vigersky, pp. 177–187. New York: Raven Press.

21. Boyar, R. M., et al. 1974. Anorexia nervosa—immaturity of the 24-hour luteinizing hormone secretory pattern. *New England Journal of Medicine* 291:861–865.

22. Boyar, R. M., et al. 1977. Cortisol secretion and metabolism in anorexia nervosa. *New England Journal of Medicine* 296:190–193.

23. Brauman, H., and Gregoire, F. 1975. The growth hormone response to insulin induced hypoglycaemia in anorexia nervosa and control underweight or normal subjects. *European Journal of Clinical Investigation* 5:289–295.

24. Brook, G. K. 1977. Acute gastric dilatation in anorexia nervosa. *British Medical Journal* 2:499–500.

25. Brown, G. M., et al. 1977. Endocrine profiles in anorexia nervosa. In *Anorexia nervosa*, ed. R. A. Vigersky, pp. 123–135. New York: Raven Press.

26. Burman, K. D., et al. 1977. Investigations concerning thyroxine deiodinative pathways in patients with anorexia nervosa. In *Anorexia nervosa*, ed. R. A. Vigersky, pp. 255–262. New York: Raven Press.

27. Buvat, J., et al. 1983. Psychoneuroendocrine investigations in 115 cases of female anorexia nervosa at the time of their maximum emaciation. *International Journal of Eating Disorders* 2:117–128.

28. Carryer, H. M., Berkman, J. M., and Mason, H. L. 1959. Relative lymphocytosis in anorexia nervosa. *Staff Meetings of the Mayo Clinic* 34:426–432.

29. Casper, R. C., and Frohman, L. A. 1982. Delayed TSH release in anorexia nervosa following injection of thyrotropin-releasing hormone (TRH). *Psychoneuroendocrinology* 7:59–68.

30. Casper, R. C., Davis, J. M., and Pandey, G. N. 1977. The effect of the nutritional status and weight changes on hypothalamic function tests in anorexia nervosa. In *Anorexia nervosa*, ed. R. A. Vigersky, pp. 137–147. New York: Raven Press.

31. Casper, R. C., et al. 1980. An evaluation of trace metals, vitamins, and taste function in anorexia nervosa. *American Journal of Clinical Nutrition* 33:1801–1808.

32. Caufriez, A., Wolter, R., Robyn, C., and L'Hermite, M. 1980. Prolactin secretion in anorexia nervosa. *Acta Psychiatrica Belgica* 80:546–550.

33. Chatfield, W. R., Bowditch, J. D. P., and Forrest, C. A. 1979. Spontaneous pneumomediastinum complicating anorexia nervosa. *British Medical Journal* 1:200–201.

34. Conrad, C., and Anderson, M. T. 1976. Akut ventrikelatoni efter umodeholden fodeindtagelse. *Ugeskrift for Laeger.* 138:2007–2008.

35. Cornbleet, P. J., Moir, R. C., and Wolf, P. L. 1977. A histochemical study of bone marrow hypoplasia in anorexia nervosa. *Virchows Archives* 374:239–247.

36. Costanzo, J., et al. 1975. Dilatation aigue gastrique et anorexie mental. *Nouvelle Presse Médicale* 4:509.

37. Cox, K. L., et al. 1983. Biochemical and ultrasound abnormalities of the pancreas in anorexia nervosa. *Digestive Diseases and Sciences* 28:225–229.

38. Crisp, A. H., Fenton, G. W., and Scotton, L. 1968. A controlled study of the EEG in anorexia nervosa. *British Journal of Psychiatry* 114:1149–1160.

39. Crisp, A. H., Hsu, L. S., Chen, C. N., and Wheeler, M. 1982. Reproductive hormone profiles in male anorexia nervosa before, during and after restoration of body weight to normal. *International Journal of Eating Disorders*, 1:3–9.

40. Croxson, M. S., and Ibbertson, H. K. 1977. Low serum triiodonthyronine (T₃) and hypothyroidism in anorexia nervosa. *Journal of Clinical Endocrinology and Metabolism* 44:167–174.

41. Cutler, W. B., and Garcia, C. R. 1980. The psychoneuroendocrinology of the ovulatory cycle of woman: A review. *Psychoneuroendocrinology* 5:89–111.

42. Danowski, T. S., et al. 1972. Fractional and partial hypopituitarism in anorexia nervosa. *Hormones* 3:105–118.

43. Dawson, J., and Jones, C. 1977. Vomiting-induced hypokalemic alkalosis and parotid swelling. *Practitioner* 218:267–268.

44. De la Fuente, J., and Wells, L. 1981. Human growth hormone in psychiatric disorders. *Journal of Clinical Psychiatry* 42:270–274.

45. Doerr, P., Fichter, M., Pirke, K. M., and Lund, R. 1980. Relationship between weight gain and hypothalamic pituitary adrenal function in patients with anorexia nervosa. *Journal of Steroid Biochemistry* 13:529–537.

46. Donley, A. J., and Kemple, T. J. 1978. Spontaneous pneumomediastinum complicating anorexia nervosa. *British Medical Journal* 2:1604–1605.

47. Elkinton, J. R., and Huth, E. J. 1958. Body fluid abnormalities in anorexia nervosa and undernutrition. *Metabolism* 5:376–403.

48. Enzmann, D. R., and Lane, B. 1977. Cranial computer tomography findings in anorexia nervosa. *Journal of Computer Assisted Tomography* 1:410–414.

49. Evans, D. S. 1968. Acute dilatation and spontaneous rupture of the stomach. *British Journal of Surgery* 55:940–942.

50. Fishman, J., Boyar, R. M., and Hellman, L. 1975. Influence of body weight on estradiol metabolism in young women. *Journal of Clinical Endocrinology and Metabolism* 41:989–991.

51. Fohlin, L. 1977. Body composition, cardiovascular and renal functions in adolescent patients with anorexia nervosa. *Acta Paediatrica Scandinavica* 268 (Suppl.):7–19.

52. Frankel, R. J., and Jenkins, J. S. 1975. Hypothalamic-pituitary function in anorexia nervosa. *Acta Endocrinologica* (Copenhagen) 78:209–221.

53. Freyschuss, U., Fohlin, L., and Thoren, C. 1978. Limb circulation in anorexia nervosa. *Acta Paediatrica Scandinavica* 67:225–228.

54. Gardner, D. F., Kaplan, M. M., Stanley, C. A., and Utiger, R. D. 1979. Effect of triiodothyronine replacement on the metabolic and pituitary responses to starvation. *New England Journal of Medicine* 300:579–584.

55. Garfinkel, P. E., Brown, G. M., and Darby, P. L. 1981. The psychoendocrinology of anorexia nervosa. *International Journal of Mental Health* 9:162–193.

56. Garfinkel, P. E., Brown, G. M., Stancer, H. C., and Moldofsky, H. 1975. Hypothalamic-pituitary function in anorexia nervosa. *Archives of General Psychiatry* 32:739–744.

57. Gerner, R. H., and Gwirtsman, H. E. 1981. Abnormalities of dexamethasone suppression test and urinary MHPG in anorexia nervosa. *American Journal of Psychiatry* 138:650–653.

58. Gillberg, C. 1983. Low dopamine and serotonin levels in anorexia nervosa. *American Journal of Psychiatry* 140:948–949.

59. Giusti, M., et al. 1981. Prolactin secretion in anorexia nervosa. *Hormone and Metabolic Research* 13:585–586.

60. Gold, P. W., Kaye, W., Robertson, G. L., and Ebert, M. 1983. Abnormalities in plasma and cerebrospinal-fluid arginine vasopressin in patients with anorexia nervosa. *New England Journal of Medicine* 308:1117–1123.

61. Gold, M. S., et al. 1980. Further evidence of hypothalamic-pituitary dysfunction in anorexia nervosa. *American Journal of Psychiatry* 137:101–102.

62. Golla, J. A., et al. 1981. An immunological assessment of patients with anorexia nervosa. *American Journal of Clinical Nutrition* 34:2756–2762.

63. Gotch, F. M., et al. 1975. Reversible granulocyte killing defect in anorexia nervosa. *Clinical and Experimental Immunology* 21:244–249.

64. Gottdiener, J. S., et al. 1978. Effects of self-induced starvation on cardiac size and function in anorexia nervosa. *Circulation* 58:425–433.

65. Gross, H. A., et al. 1979. Catecholamine metabolism in primary anorexia nervosa. *Journal of Clinical Endocrinology and Metabolism* 49:805–809.

66. Halmi, K. A. 1974. Anorexia nervosa: Demographic and clinical features in 94 cases. *Psychosomatic Medicine* 36:18–26.

67. ———. 1981–82. Catecholamine metabolism in anorexia nervosa. *International Journal of Psychiatry in Medicine* 11:251–254.

68. Halmi, K. A., and Falk, J. R. 1981. Common physiological changes in anorexia nervosa. *International Journal of Eating Disorders* 1:16–27.

69. Halmi, K., and Fry, M. 1974. Serum lipids in anorexia nervosa. *Biological Psychiatry* 8:159–167.

70. Halmi, K. A., and Sherman, B. M. 1975. Gonadotropin response to LH-RH in anorexia nervosa. *Archives of General Psychiatry* 32:875–878.

71. Halmi, K. A., Owen, W. P., Lasley, E., and Stokes, P. 1983. Dopaminergic regulation in anorexia nervosa. *International Journal of Eating Disorders* 2:129–133.

72. Halmi, K. A., et al. 1978. Catecholamine metabolism in anorexia nervosa. *Archives of General Psychiatry* 35:458–460.

73. Handler, C. E., and Perkin, G. D. 1982. Anorexia nervosa and Wernicke's encephalopathy: An underdiagnosed association. *Lancet* 2:771–772.

74. Heinz, E. R., Martinez, J., and Haenggeli, A. 1977. Reversibility of cerebral atrophy in anorexia nervosa and Cushing's syndrome. *Journal of Computer Assisted Tomography* 1: 415–418.

75. Hellstrom, I. 1977. Oral complications in anorexia nervosa. *Scandinavian Journal of Dental Research* 85:71–86.

76. Holt, S., Ford, M. J., Grant, S., and Heading, R. C. 1981. Abnormal gastric emptying in primary anorexia nervosa. *British Journal of Psychiatry* 139:550–552.

77. Horrobin, D. F., and Cunnane, S. C. 1980. Interactions between zinc, essential fatty acids and prostaglandins: Relevance to acrodermatitis enteropathica, total parenteral nutrition, the glucagonoma syndrome, diabetes, anorexia nervosa and sickle cell anemia. *Medical Hypotheses* 6:277–296.

78. Hurd, H. P., Palumbo, P. J., Gharib, H. 1977. Hypothalamic-endocrine dysfunction in anorexia nervosa. *Mayo Clinic Proceedings* 52:711–716.

79. Hurst, P. S., Crisp, A. H., and Lacey, J. H. 1977. Teeth, vomiting and diet: A study of the dental characteristics of seventeen anorexia nervosa patients. *Postgraduate Medical Journal* 53:298–305.

80. Isaacs, A. J., Leslie, R. D. G., Gomez, J., and Bayliss, R. 1980. The effect of weight gain on gonadotrophins and prolactin in anorexia nervosa. *Acta Endocrinologica* (Copenhagen) 81:252–262.

81. Jameson, L. 1979. Insulin binding in anorexia nervosa. *New England Journal of Medicine* 301:386–387.

82. Jarrell, J., Meltzer, S., and Tolis, G. 1979. A review of the endocrine abnormalities in the hypothalamus-pituitary axis. In *Clinical pharmacology: A pathophysiological approach,* ed. G. Tolis et al., pp. 355–365. New York: Raven Press.

83. Jennings, K. P., and Klidjian, A. M. 1974. Acute gastric dilatation in anorexia nervosa. *British Medical Journal* 1:477–478.

84. Kalager, T., Brubakk, O., and Basse, H. H. 1978. Cardiac performance in patients with anorexia nervosa. *Cardiology* 63:1–4.

85. Kanis, J. A., et al. 1974. Anorexia nervosa: A clinical, psychiatric, and laboratory study. *Quarterly Journal of Medicine* 43:321–338.

86. Kaye, W. H., Ebert, M. H., Raleigh, M., and Lake, C. R. 1984. Abnormalities in CNS monoamine metabolism in anorexia nervosa. *Archives of General Psychiatry* 41:350–355.

87. Keys, A., Henschel, A., and Taylor, H. L. 1947. The size and function of the human heart at rest in semi-starvation and in subsequent rehabilitation. *American Journal of Physiology* 150:153–169.

88. Kim, Y., and Michael, A. F. 1975. Hypocomplementemia in anorexia nervosa. *Journal of Pediatrics* 87:582–585.

89. King, A. 1963. Primary and secondary anorexia nervosa syndromes. *British Journal of Psychiatry* 109:470–479.

90. Kishi, S. 1980. Gastric secretory capacity in anorexia nervosa. *Tokushima Journal of Experimental Medicine* 27:29–35.

91. Klinefelter, H. F. 1965. Hypercholesterolemia in anorexia nervosa. *Journal of Clinical Endocrinology and Metabolism* 25:1520–1521.

92. Kubanek, B., Heimpel, H., Paar, G., and Schoengen, A. 1977. Hämatologische Veranderungen bei anorexia nervosa. *Blut* 35:115–124.

93. Lampert, F., and Lau, B. 1976. Bone marrow hypoplasia in anorexia nervosa. *European Journal of Pediatrics* 124:65–71.

94. Landon, J., Greenwood, F. C., Stamp, T. C. B., and Wynn, V. 1966. The plasma sugar, free fatty acid, cortisol, and growth hormone response to insulin, and the comparison of this procedure with other tests of pituitary and adrenal function. II. In patients with hypothalamic or pituitary dysfunction of anorexia nervosa. *Journal of Clinical Investigation* 45:437–449.

95. Laszlo, J. E. 1981. Vitamin A (carotene) and anorexia. *Medical Journal of Australia* 1:146.

96. Lebriquir, M., et al. 1978. Dilatation aigue gastrique et anorexie mental. *Semaine Hôpitaux de Paris* 54:1175–1176.

97. Lemaire, A., et al. 1983. Gonadal hormones in male anorexia nervosa. *International Journal of Eating Disorders* 2:135–144.

98. Levin, P. A. et al. 1980. Benign parotid enlargement in bulimia. *Annals of Internal Medicine* 93:827–829.

99. Lewin, K., Mattingly, D., and Millis, R. R. 1972. Anorexia nervosa associated with hypothalmic tumor. *British Medical Journal* 2:629–630.

100. Luck, P., and Wakeling, A. 1980. Altered thresholds for thermoregulatory sweating and vasodilatation in anorexia nervosa. *British Medical Journal* 281:906–908.

101. Macaron, C., Wilber, J. F., Green, O., and Freinkel, N. 1978. Studies of growth hormone (GH), thyrotropin (TSH) and prolactin (PRL) secretion in anorexia nervosa. *Psychoneuroendocrinology* 3:181–185.

102. McNab, D., and Hawton, K. 1981. Disturbances of sex hormones in anorexia nervosa in the male. *Postgraduate Medical Journal* 57:254–256.

103. Maeda, K. 1976. Effects of thyrotropin-releasing hormone on growth hormone release in normal subjects and in patients with depression, anorexia nervosa and acromegaly. *Journal of Medical Science* 22:263–272.

104. Mant, M. J., and Faragher, B. S. 1972. The haematology of anorexia nervosa. *British Journal of Haematology* 23:737–749.

105. Markowski, B. 1947. Acute dilatation of the stomach. *British Medical Journal* 2: 128–130.

106. Marks, V., and Bannister, R. G. 1963. Pituitary and adrenal function in under-nutrition with mental illness. *British Journal of Psychiatry* 109:480–484.

107. Matikainen, M. 1979. Spontaneous rupture of the stomach. *American Journal of Surgery* 138:451–452.

108. Mecklenburg, R. S., et al. 1974. Hypothalamic dysfunction in patients with anorexia nervosa. *Medicine* 53:147–159.

109. Mitchell, J. E., and Gillum, R. 1980. Weight-dependent arrhythmia in a patient with anorexia nervosa. *American Journal of Psychiatry* 137:377–378.

110. Miyai, K., et al. 1975. Serum thyroid hormones and thyrotropin in anorexia nervosa. *Journal of Clinical Endocrinology and Metabolism* 40:334–338.

111. Mordasini, R., Klose, G., and Greten, H. 1978. Secondary type II hyperlipoproteinemia in patients with anorexia nervosa. *Metabolism* 27:71–79.

112. Morimoto, Y., et al. 1980. Interrelations among amenorrhea, serum gonadotropins and body weight in anorexia nervosa. *Endocrinologica Japonica* 27:191–200.

113. Moshang, T., and Utiger, R. D. 1977. Low triiodothyronine euthyroidism in anorexia nervosa. In *Anorexia nervosa,* ed. R. A. Vigersky, pp. 263–270. New York: Raven Press.

114. Moshang, T., et al. 1975. Low serum triiodothyronine in patients with anorexia nervosa. *Journal of Clinical Endocrinology and Metabolism* 40:470–473.

115. Myers, T. J., Perkerson, M. D., Witter, B. A., Granville, N. B. 1981. Hematologic findings in anorexia nervosa. *Connecticut Medicine* 45:14–17.

116. Nestel, P. J. 1973. Cholesterol metabolism in anorexia nervosa and hypercholesterolemia. *Journal of Clinical Endocrinology and Metabolism* 38:325–328.

117. Neufield, N. D. 1979. Endocrine abnormalities associated with deprivation dwarfism and anorexia nervosa. *Pediatric Clinics of North America* 26:199–208.

118. Nillius, S. J., and Wide, L. 1977. The pituitary responsiveness to acute and chronic administration of gonadotropin-releasing hormone in acute and recovery stages of anorexia nervosa. In *Anorexia nervosa,* ed. R. A. Vigersky, pp. 225–242. New York: Raven Press.

119. Nussbaum, M., Shenker, I. R., March, J., and Klein, M. 1980. Cerebral atrophy in anorexia nervosa. *Journal of Pediatrics* 96:867–869.

120. Ogston, D., and Ogston, W. B. 1976. The fibrinolytic enzyme system in anorexia nervosa. *Acta Haematologica* 55:230–233.

121. Palmblad, J., Fohlin, L., and Lundstrum, M. 1977. Anorexia nervosa and polymorphonuclear (PMN) granulocyte reactions. *Scandinavian Journal of Haematology* 19: 334–342.

122. Palossy, B., and Oo, M. 1977. ECG alterations in anorexia nervosa. *Advances in Cardiology* 19:280–282.

123. Pearson, H. A. 1967. Marrow hypoplasia in anorexia nervosa. *Journal of Pediatrics* 71:211–215.

124. Pentlow, B. D., and Dent, R. G. 1981. Acute vascular compression of the duodenum in anorexia nervosa. *British Journal of Surgery* 68:665–666.

125. Pertschuk, M. J., Crosby, L. O., Barot, L., and Mullen, J. L. 1982. Immunocompetency in anorexia nervosa. *American Journal of Clinical Nutrition* 35:968–972.

126. Pimstone, B. L., Barbezat, G., Hansen, J. D. L., and Murray, P. 1968. Studies on

growth hormone secretion in protein-calorie malnutrition. *American Journal of Clinical Nutrition* 21:482–487.

127. Powers, P. S. 1982. Heart failure during treatment of anorexia nervosa. *American Journal of Psychiatry* 139:1167–1170.

128. Powers, P. S., Malone, J. I., and Duncan, J. A. 1983. Anorexia nervosa and diabetes mellitus. *Journal of Clinical Psychiatry* 44:133–135.

129. Rieger, W., Brady, J. P., and Weisberg, E. 1978. Hematologic changes in anorexia nervosa. *American Journal of Psychiatry* 135:984–985.

130. Riemenschneider, T. H., and Bohle, A. 1983. Morphologic aspects of low-potassium and low-sodium nephropathy. *Clinical Nephrology* 19:271–279.

131. Robboy, M. S., Sato, A. S., and Schwabe, A. D. 1974. The hypercarotenemia in anorexia nervosa: A comparison of vitamin A and carotene levels in various forms of menstrual dysfunction and cachexia. *American Journal of Clinical Nutrition* 27:362–367.

132. Russell, G. F. M. 1966. Acute dilatation of the stomach in a patient with anorexia nervosa. *British Journal of Psychiatry* 112:203–207.

133. Saleh, J. W., and Lebwohl, P. 1980. Metoclopramide-induced gastric emptying in patients with anorexia nervosa. *American Journal of Gastroenterology* 74:127–132.

134. Saul, S. H., Dekker, A., and Watson, C. G. 1981. Acute gastric dilatation with infarction and perforation. *Gut* 22:978–983.

135. Schoettle, U. C. 1979. Pancreatitis: A complication, a concomitant, or a cause of an anorexia nervosa-like syndrome. *Journal of the Academy of Child Psychiatry* 18:384–390.

136. Schwabe, A. D., et al. 1981. Anorexia nervosa. *Annals of Internal Medicine* 94: 371–381.

137. Scobie, B. A. 1973. Acute gastric dilatation and duodenal ileus in anorexia nervosa. *Medical Journal of Australia* 2:932–934.

138. Sein, P., Searson, S., and Nicol, A. R. 1981. Anorexia nervosa and pseudo-atrophy of the brain. *British Journal of Psychiatry* 139:257–258.

139. Sherman, B. M., and Halmi, K. A. 1977. Effect of nutritional rehabilitation on hypothalamic-pituitary function in anorexia nervosa. In *Anorexia nervosa*, ed. R. A. Vigersky, pp. 211–223. New York: Raven Press.

140. Sherman, B. M., Halmi, K. A., and Zamudio, R. 1975. LH and FSH response to gonadotropin-releasing hormone in anorexia nervosa: Effect of nutritional rehabilitation. *Journal of Clinical Endocrinology and Metabolism* 41:135–142.

141. Silverman, J. A. 1983. Anorexia nervosa: Clinical and metabolic observations. *International Journal of Eating Disorders* 2:159–166.

142. Silverman, J. A., and Krongrad, E. 1983. Anorexia nervosa: A cause of pericardial effusion? *Pediatric Cardiology* 4:125–127.

143. Silverstone, J. T., and Russell, G. F. M. 1967. Gastric "hunger" contractions in anorexia nervosa. *British Journal of Psychiatry* 113:257–263.

144. Simon, D., Laudenbach, P., Lebovici, M., and Mauvais-Jarvis, P. 1979. Parotid-omegalie au cours des dysorexies mentales. *Nouvelle Presse Médicale* 9:2399–2402.

145. Smith, S. R., Bledsoe, T., and Chhetri, M. K. 1975. Cortisol metabolism and the pituitary-adrenal axis in adults with protein-calorie malnutrition. *Journal of Clinical Endocrinology and Metabolism* 40:43–52.

146. Smith, S. R., et al. 1974. Growth hormone in adults with protein-calorie malnutrition. *Journal of Clinical Endocrinology and Metabolism* 39:53–62.

147. Sours, J. A., and Vorhaus, L. J. 1981. Superior vascular compression of the duodenum in anorexia nervosa. *British Journal of Surgery* 68:665–666.

148. Stege, P., Visco-Dangler, L., and Rye, L. 1982. Anorexia nervosa: Review including oral and dental manifestations. *Journal of the American Dental Association* 104:648–652.

149. Suda, A. K., Pittman, C. S., Shimizu, T., and Chambers, J. B. 1978. The production and metabolism of 3,5,3'-triiodothyronine and 3,3',5'-triiodothyronine in normal and fasting subjects. *Journal of Clinical Endocrinology and Metabolism* 47:1311–1319.

150. Sunderman, F. W., and Rose, E. 1948. Studies in serum electrolytes. XVI. Changes in the serum and body fluids in anorexia nervosa. *Journal of Clinical Endocrinology and Metabolism* 8:209–220.

151. Thurston, J., and Marks, P. 1974. Electrocardiographic abnormalities in patients with anorexia nervosa. *British Heart Journal* 36:719–723.

152. Travaglini, P., et al. 1976. Some aspects of hypothalamic-pituitary function in patients with anorexia nervosa. *Acta Endocrinologica* (Copenhagen) 81:252–262.

153. Vagenakis, A. G. 1977. Thyroid hormone metabolism in prolonged experimental

starvation in man. In *Anorexia nervosa,* ed. R. A. Vigersky, pp. 243–254. New York: Raven Press.

154. Vigersky, R. A., Andersen, A. E., Thompson, R. H., and Loriaux, D. L. 1977. Hypothalamic dysfunction in secondary amenorrhea associated with simple weight loss. *New England Journal of Medicine* 297:1141–1145.

155. Vigersky, R. A., Loriaux, D. L., Andersen, A. E., and Lipsett, M. 1975. Anorexia nervosa: Behavioral and hypothalamic aspects. *Clinical Endocrinology* 5:517–535.

156. Wachslicht-Robard, H., et al. 1979. Increased insulin binding to erythrocytes in anorexia nervosa. *New England Journal of Medicine* 300:882–887.

157. Wakeling, A., and Russell, G. F. M. 1970. Disturbances in the regulation of body temperature in anorexia nervosa. *Psychological Medicine* 1:30–39.

158. Wakeling, A., DeSouza, V. A., and Beardwood, C. J. 1977. Assessment of the negative and positive feedback effects of administered oestrogen on gonadotrophin release in patients with anorexia nervosa. *Psychological Medicine* 7:397–405.

159. ———. 1977. Effects of administered estrogen on luteinizing hormone release in subjects with anorexia nervosa in acute and recovery stages. In *Anorexia nervosa,* ed. R. A. Vigersky, pp. 199–210. New York: Raven Press.

160. Wallace, M., Richards, P., Chesser, E., and Wrong, O. 1968. Persistent alkalosis and hypokalaemia caused by surreptitious vomiting. *Quarterly Journal of Medicine* 37: 577–588.

161. Walsh, B. T. 1980. The endocrinology of anorexia nervosa. *Psychiatric Clinics of North America* 3:299–312.

162. Walsh, B. T., Croft, C. B., and Katz, J. A. 1981–82. Anorexia nervosa and salivary gland enlargement. *International Journal of Psychiatry in Medicine* 11:255–261.

163. Walsh, B. T., et al. 1978. Adrenal activity in anorexia nervosa. *Psychosomatic Medicine* 40:499–506.

164. Warren, M. P. 1977. Weight loss and responsiveness to LH-RH. In *Anorexia nervosa,* ed. R. A. Vigersky, pp. 189–198. New York: Raven Press.

165. Warren, M. P., and Van de Wiele, R. L. 1973. Clinical and metabolic features of anorexia nervosa. *American Journal of Obstetrics and Gynecology* 117:435–499.

166. Warren, M. P., et al. 1975. The significance of weight loss in the evaluation of pituitary response to LH-RH in women with secondary amenorrhea. *Journal of Clinical Endocrinology and Metabolism* 40:601–611.

167. Warren, S. E., and Steinberg, S. M. 1979. Acid-base and electrolyte disturbances in anorexia nervosa. *American Journal of Psychiatry* 136:415–418.

168. Wayne, E., Miller, R. E., and Eiseman, B. 1971. Duodenal obstruction by the superior mesenteric artery in bedridden combat casualties. *Annals of Surgery* 174:339–345.

169. Weiner, H. 1983. The hypothalamic-pituitary-ovarian axis in anorexia and bulimia nervosa. *International Journal of Eating Disorders* 2:109–116.

170. Weller, R. A., and Weller, E. B. 1982. Anorexia nervosa in a patient with an infiltrating tumor of the hypothalamus. *American Journal of Psychiatry* 139:824–826.

171. Wesselius, C. L., and Anderson, G. 1982. A case study of a male with anorexia nervosa and low testosterone levels. *Journal of Clinical Psychiatry* 43:428–429.

172. Wheeler, M. J., Crisp, A. H., Hsu, L. K. G., and Chen, C. N. 1983. Reproductive hormone changes during weight gain in male anorectics. *Clinical Endocrinology* 18:423–429.

173. Wiegelmann, W., and Solbach, H. G. 1972. Effects of LH-RH on plasma levels of LH and FSH in anorexia nervosa. *Hormone and Metabolic Research* 4:404.

174. Wigley, R. D. 1960. Potassium deficiency in anorexia nervosa, with reference to renal tubular vacuolation. *British Medical Journal* 2:110–113.

175. Wolff, H. P., et al. 1968. Psychiatric disturbance leading to potassium depletion, sodium depletion, raised plasma-renin concentration, and secondary hyperaldosteronism. *Lancet* 1:257–261.

176. Wyatt, R. J., et al. 1982. Reduced alternative complement pathway control protein levels in anorexia nervosa: Response to parenteral alimentation. *American Journal of Clinical Nutrition* 34:973–980.

177. Yoshimoto, Y., Moridera, K., and Imura, H. 1975. Restoration of normal pituitary gonadotropin reserve by administration of luteinizing-hormone-releasing hormone in patients with hypogonadotropic hypogonadism. *New England Journal of Medicine* 292:242–245.

14

Anorexia Nervosa: Diagnostic Conceptualizations

Paul E. Garfinkel and Allan S. Kaplan

Introduction

Anorexia nervosa is an increasingly common and complex disorder; it is characterized by an all-consuming pursuit of thinness[8] that overrides the patient's physical and psychological well-being. The person begins to diet ostensibly to alter her weight, but this desire is often a screen that masks a pervasive sense of helplessness.[8] Pursuing a thin body becomes an isolated area of control in a world in which the individual feels ineffective; the dieting provides an artificially dangerous sense of mastery and control. As the weight loss progresses, a starvation state ensues, which eventually develops a life of its own, leading to the features of anorexia nervosa.

Diagnostic thinking about the illness has passed through several phases (see chapter 12). It has been considered entirely somatic and entirely psychological. It was first described by Gull[36] and Lasegue[48] as a psychological disorder with physical manifestations. For the first quarter of this century, conceptualization of anorexia nervosa was greatly influenced by Simmonds'[67] description of pituitary insufficiency. More recently there has been a clearer distinction made between the biological and psychological nature of the illness. This chapter will review changes in the diagnostic understanding of anorexia nervosa.

The authors are grateful to Velma Varey for her valuable assistance in the preparation of the manuscript. Our work was supported by grants from the Ontario Mental Health Foundation and the Medical Research Council of Canada.

Advances in Diagnostic Conceptualizations

Recent diagnostic advances can be categorized as follows:

1. Further distinction between primary pituitary disease and anorexia nervosa.
2. The contribution of the starvation syndrome to anorexia nervosa.
3. The heterogeneity of anorexia nervosa with bulimic and restricting subtypes.
4. The differentiation of anorexia nervosa patients from a continuum of women with weight preoccupation.
5. The recognition of other emotional states that present with weight loss but that are clinically distinct from anorexia nervosa.

PRIMARY PITUITARY DISEASE AND ANOREXIA NERVOSA

In 1914 pathologist Morris Simmonds[67] described a patient in whom cachexia was associated with destruction of the adenohypophysis. For the next quarter of a century this condition (Simmonds' disease) was thought to be responsible for many cases of weight loss with undetermined etiology. Hundreds of cases were reported in the literature during this time, of which many were not related to anatomic destruction of the pituitary gland; some could be cases of anorexia nervosa. The distinction between anorexia nervosa and primary pituitary pathology was not elucidated until the late 1930s. This distinction became clearer over the next fifteen years. Sheehan and Summers[66] noted only two features exhibited by these two conditions: amenorrhea and low basal metabolic rate. They correctly emphasized that patients with anorexia nervosa show hyperactivity and extreme weight loss, unlike those with pituitary insufficiency, who often have lassitude and limited weight loss. With the recent clarification of psychopathology in patients with anorexia nervosa, a drive for thinness, denial of illness, body-image disturbance, and vigorous efforts at weight loss, including purging behavior, are all recognized as hallmarks of the disorder and are absent in cases of primary pituitary disorders.

The hypothalamic-pituitary abnormalities present in anorexia nervosa are largely due to either the degree of weight loss or caloric deprivation.[6] Weight loss seems responsible for alterations in thermoregulation, water conservation, the thyroid-stimulating hormone (TSH) response to thyroid-releasing hormone (TRH), resting gonadotropin levels, and luteinizing hormone (LH) responses to provocative tests. These abnormalities correct with weight gain. Caloric deprivation, on the other hand, seems responsible for alterations in resting plasma growth hormone (GH), plasma triiodothyronine (T_3) and reverse T_3. These abnormalities correct when adequate caloric intake is resumed. Amenorrhea may precede weight loss and may not change with weight gain. The mechanisms underlying these findings are unclear.

THE STARVATION SYNDROME

The extent to which starvation influences behavior and cognition has been appreciated only recently, although information about the clinical effects of starvation has been available for more than three decades. This information comes from studies of starving people such as those done by Keys and associates[59] in Minnesota, published in 1950. Normal young men were put on semistarvation diets for several months. They developed many of the symptoms thought to typify anorexia nervosa. These symptoms were food related, related to cognitive disturbances, and related to affective and personality changes.

Subjects in the Keys and associates studies developed a preoccupation with food, food-related thoughts, and dreams about food. They experienced intense hunger and, on occasion, felt hungrier after eating than before. A few men had bulimic episodes. Eating generally slowed down, and bizarre food fads were common, including increased coffee and tea consumption, cigarette smoking, nail biting, and gum chewing. Some men collected recipes and decided to become chefs.

Cognitively, these men experienced indecisiveness, poor concentration, and reduced self-discipline, alertness, and ambition. Affectively, many subjects became irritable, anxious, and had labile moods. Previous personality traits became exaggerated; some subjects withdrew socially and had elevated Minnesota Multiphasic Personality Inventory scores on the depression, hypochondriasis, and hysteria scales compared to prestarvation scores.

All of these symptoms are prominent in anorexia nervosa. That they result from starvation per se and not from a pathophysiological process unique to anorexia nervosa has allowed greater diagnostic specificity and more emphasis on weight gain as a critical aspect of treatment. Understanding the nature of these starvation-related symptoms has clarified their contribution to the factors that fuel the illness and contribute to its resistance to treatment before weight gain.[26]

HETEROGENEITY OF ANOREXIA NERVOSA

Subtypes of anorexia nervosa have been recognized since Janet[40] described obsessional and hysterical forms. He differentiated these on the presence or absence of hunger; obsessional anorexic patients were thought to maintain their hunger while hysterical patients lost it. This distinction was reintroduced by Dally,[17] who described three groups of patients with anorexia nervosa: an obsessional group, a hysterical group, and a group having mixed features. The distinction among these groups was based largely on the presence or absence of hunger, but this has not been supported by research, which has shown that true anorexia is rare until late in the starvation process and that most patients with anorexia nervosa maintain their feelings of hunger.[25] However, Janet's and Dally's observation that certain symptoms such as vomiting, bulimia, and mood lability clustered together in one group of patients was an important insight.

Meyer[52] noted clinical differences between patients who lose weight because they abstain from eating and those in whom vomiting was a major symptom. Beumont and his group[3] were the first to consider this in a systematic way. In a retrospective study of thirty-one hospitalized patients with anorexia nervosa, they described seventeen as pure restricters and fourteen as "vomiters" and "purgers." Clinical differences were found on many variables, including personality traits, social history, eating behavior, and the course of the illness. The vomiters and purgers were more likely to have been premorbidly obese, sexually active, and to have histrionic personalities. They had a chronic course with poor prognosis. The restricter group exhibited marked obsessionality manifested clinically as extreme self-denial; they also demonstrated social withdrawal and few sexual experiences. They were not premorbidly obese and tended to recover. Beumont[3] later found that the restricters were more introverted, anxious, and independent than both controls and the vomiter-purger group.

Bulimia as a symptom of other illnesses has been recognized dating back to the Babylonian Talmud,[43] which was written around the year A.D. 400. It was associated with anorexia nervosa in several descriptions in the nineteenth century. For example, Gull[35] mentioned overeating in a patient with anorexia nervosa. He noted: "Occasionally for a day or two the appetite was voracious" (p. 133), but this was rare and exceptional.[36] A vivid case of bulimia is in Binswanger's classic description of Ellen West[4]; she stated: "Fate wanted me to be heavy and strong but I wanted to be thin and delicate."

Russell[62] recently described thirty patients with "bulimia nervosa." His criteria for this diagnosis included: (1) an irresistible urge to overeat, (2) self-induced vomiting or purging, and (3) a morbid fear of becoming fat. Russell[63] recently stated that a fourth criterion—a history of anorexia nervosa—should be added to make this group homogeneous.

Two recent studies[12,28] have more fully described the significance of bulimia in anorexia nervosa. In both studies the presence of bulimia characterized a group of anorexic patients with special features. Garfinkel, Moldofsky, and Garner[28] found that bulimic anorexics were more likely than restricters to have been premorbidly obese, to have mothers who were obese, to vomit, and to abuse laxatives. The bulimic subjects were more impulsive than the restricting group. They were more likely to use alcohol or street drugs, to steal, to mutilate themselves, to be more sexually active, and to have labile moods. This group was more difficult to treat and had a poorer prognosis.

Casper and associates[12] reported many similar findings. Bulimic patients had a stronger sense of hunger. This was perceived as an uncomfortable experience, in contrast to the abstainers' experience, where this sensation was cherished as a sense of mastery over their bodies. Alcoholism and stealing were more common in the bulimic-anorexic group. Kleptomania in this group has been reported by others.[16] The Casper and associates study[12] found that the bulimic patients had poorer relationships with their fathers and a greater degree of distress. This included feelings of depression, guilt, and frequent somatization. The bulimic subgroup, unlike the abstainers, were not characterized by low body weight, body-image disturbance, or marked denial of illness.

A number of studies have confirmed the validity of these subtypes with psychometric instruments. Strober[70] assessed the need for approval, personality organization, general psychopathology, and obsessional symptoms. The bulimic subgroup was more flexible in their general thinking pattern and behavior. This flexibility was also demonstrated in their greater psychological-mindedness. The bulimic patients were more socially outgoing but had less self-control. Hood, Moore, and Garner[39] found that an external locus of control was characteristic of the bulimic subgroup and was correlated with greater distress. Garner, Garfinkel, and O'Shaughnessy[32] found that when bulimic patients who never met weight-loss criteria for anorexia nervosa ("normal-weight" bulimic patients), anorexic-bulimic patients, and anorexic-restricter groups were compared on demographic, clinical, and psychometric variables, the normal-weight bulimic group closely resembled the anorexic-bulimic group. They argued that the presence or absence of bulimia could be of greater diagnostic and etiologic significance than a history of weight loss.

Bulimic patients may also differ from restricters by their family history and their course. Alcoholism and depression are more common in families of anorexic patients, and this may be due to a particularly high frequency in the first-degree relatives of bulimic individuals. Piran and coworkers[59] found a family history of affective disorder in 61 percent of bulimic patients and in 23 percent of restricters.

Bulimia has been shown to be a sign of poor prognosis in anorexia nervosa.[27] This is related to the frequent metabolic complications and increased incidence of other disorders, including alcoholism and possibly depression. It is not clear whether bulimic patients respond more favorably to antidepressants (see chapter 24).

Bulimia is thus an important diagnostic feature. It identifies a group of patients with anorexia nervosa who have common personality traits, are at risk for serious metabolic complications, and who generally experience more serious psychopathology.

ANOREXIA NERVOSA AND THE CONTINUUM OF WEIGHT-PREOCCUPIED WOMEN

The epidemiology of anorexia nervosa has changed. Traditionally, it has been considered an uncommon disorder of young adolescents from upper socioeconomic classes. However, several recent reports* find increased incidence of the illness (in females only), more equal occurrence

* See references 21, 26, 41, 45, and 71.

in all socioeconomic classes, and more frequent occurrence in women in their twenties.

There are several possible explanations for these changing epidemiological figures. These include greater public and medical awareness of the disorder, but a strong argument can be made for the effects of sociocultural influences. Garner, Garfinkel, and Olmsted[31] argued that the pressures on women to meet the current thinner standard for physical attractiveness are responsible for preoccupation with dieting. The fashion industry and media have encouraged the association between thinness and success, beauty, wealth, and happiness. Selvini-Palazzoli[65] also notes that culture places powerful and often contradictory pressures on women to be successful, fashionable, and slim. Bruch[8] proposed that pressure to be successful may play a role in the genesis of anorexia nervosa when the success is seen as achievement for someone else and not for oneself.

Most adolescents and young adult women are exposed to these sociocultural pressures, yet few develop a psychiatric illness with eating pathology. Many women actively diet in the pursuit of thinness but never present to physicians with an illness. Does anorexia nervosa represent the extreme of this continuum, or is anorexia nervosa a distinct syndrome?

Some investigators regard anorexia nervosa as qualitatively distinct while others support its existence along a continuum. Crisp[14,15] argued that the disorder represents a psychobiological regression to a prepubertal state that is distinct and different from other forms of dieting behavior. Diagnostically, Crisp emphasized the need for a specific degree of weight loss below a critical menstrual weight threshold. Bruch[8] has considered the psychopathology that she feels is responsible for the development of the disorder, to distinguish it from other forms of dieting. She has described ego deficits that are manifest as an overwhelming sense of ineffectiveness and disturbances in body image and affective and visceral perceptions.

A recent study by Garner, Olmsted, and Garfinkel[33] supports this view. Using psychometric instruments, they compared patients with anorexia nervosa with extremely weight-preoccupied women selected from college and ballet students. They found a continuum of weight concerns that did not parallel the continua of psychopathology that were observed in patients with anorexia nervosa. The weight-preoccupied, nonclinical sample had disturbances in dieting, perfectionism, and attitudes about shape that were similar to the anorexic group. Other disturbances in psychological functioning, such as feeling ineffective, lack of interoceptive awareness, and interpersonal distrust, were much less common in the nonclinical group. These findings support Bruch's contention that patients with anorexia nervosa are unique not only in dieting behavior and weight loss but, more importantly, in the underlying psychopathology responsible for it.

There is also support for viewing anorexia nervosa on a continuum. Berkman[2] first suggested this:

... in which the symptoms are so mild that the individual merely appears thin, to instances in which the symptoms are so severe that the starvation results in emaciation and cachexia. In other words, no sharp diagnostic line separates simple malnutrition from anorexia nervosa and the minimum requirements for the making of the diagnosis of the latter are, to a certain extent, only a matter of personal opinion. (P. 237)

Loeb,[50] Fries,[24] and Russell[64] have all implied that such a continuum exists. Nylander[57] was the first to study this systematically. He studied Swedish adolescents and found that 10 percent had at least three "anorexic" symptoms associated with weight loss, while 0.06 percent presented with actual anorexia nervosa. He stated that the difference between these "mild" and "serious" cases was of degree only, related to the intensity of the starvation symptoms. Button and Whitehouse[9] have recently described a group of patients with "subclinical anorexia nervosa." These women were thought to be abnormally preoccupied with weight and to have many of the behavioral symptoms of anorexia nervosa. They imply that these patients have a milder form of the illness. In a similar way, Lowenkopf[51] has proposed a diagnostic category of "pursuit of thinness" where these "minor disorders" would lie.

We feel that anorexia nervosa does exist as a distinct clinical entity separate from other psychiatric disorders and from other dieting behavior. Although aspects of the psychopathology that predispose to anorexia nervosa are found in other psychiatric illnesses and in the population, and although the starvation effects that account for the dramatic presentation of the illness occur on a continuum, the combination of these two with the distorted drive for thinness distinguish the true syndrome of anorexia nervosa.

ANOREXIA NERVOSA AND OTHER EMOTIONAL STATES ASSOCIATED WITH WEIGHT LOSS

There has been uncertainty about whether anorexia nervosa is a discrete entity or is a variant of other psychiatric illnesses. A third viewpoint is that it represents a non-specific symptom that can occur in many emotional disorders in which weight loss is a feature. We feel that it does represent a distinct illness.

Anorexia as a Variant of Other Illnesses. While the earliest writers, such as Gull,[36] Gilles de la Tourette,[49] and Dejerine and Gauckler[44] considered anorexia nervosa a distinct disorder, others have considered it a variant of affective disorder, schizophrenia, obsessional disorder, and hysteria. In table 14.1 we present the clinical features of anorexia nervosa and these other disorders.

AFFECTIVE DISORDER. It is understandable that anorexia nervosa might be considered a variant of depression. Many features are common to both, including the clinical presentation, family history, response to treatment, and outcome. Depressed mood is very common in anorexic pa-

TABLE 14.1

Clinical Features of Anorexia Nervosa, Conversion Disorder, Schizophrenia, and Depression

Feature	Anorexia Nervosa	Conversion Disorder	Schizophrenia	Depression
Intense drive for thinness	Marked	None	None	None
Self-imposed starvation	Marked (due to fear of body size)	None	Marked (due to delusions about food)	None
Disturbance in body image	Present (lack of awareness of change in body size and lack of satisfaction or pleasure in the body)	None	None	None
Appetite	Maintained (but with fear of giving in to impulse)	Variable	Maintained	True anorexia
Satiety	Usually bloating, nausea, early satiety	Variable	Variable	Variable
Avoidance of specific foods	Present (for carbohydrates or foods presumed to be high in "calories")	None	Present (of foods that are thought to be poisoned)	Loss of interest in all food
Bulimia	Present in 30 to 50%	May occur	Rare	Rare
Vomiting	Present (to prevent weight gain)	Present (expresses some symbolic meaning)	Rare (to prevent undesirable effects on the body)	None
Laxative abuse	Present (to prevent weight gain)	Infrequently present (expresses some symbolic meaning)	None	None
Activity level	Increased	Reduced or no change	No change	Reduced
Amenorrhea	Present	Present	Present	Present

NOTE: Reprinted, by permission of the publisher, from P. E. Garfinkel et al., 1983, Differential diagnosis of emotional disorders that cause weight loss, *Canadian Medical Association Journal* 129:940.

tients.[44] However, Carlson and Cantwell[11] found that although anorexic adolescents described dysphoric mood, low self-esteem, hopelessness, and suicidal ideation, their global ratings of depression were significantly less than those of adolescents with primary affective disorder. Clinical features such as the neurovegetative symptoms of sleep disturbance, weight loss, reduced libido, and amenorrhea are symptoms of both anorexia nervosa and depression. Cognitive disturbances and a reduced sense of self-esteem occur in both states; however, the quality of the latter is different in anorexia nervosa, as it is specifically tied to body weight and appearance. In people with anorexia nervosa, many of these signs and symptoms result from starvation.

Another reason tying anorexia nervosa to depressive illness is the prevalence of depression in anorexic patients and their parents. Cantwell and associates[10] found a high prevalence of depression in anorexic subjects and their mothers. Others have confirmed this familial association.[42,59,73]

Some have used the clinical responsiveness of anorexic patients to tricyclic drugs as evidence of a link with depression,[54] but their efficacy has not been established, and even if found to be effective, it is a weak argument to link two illnesses based on a common response to medications.

SCHIZOPHRENIA. In 1913 Dubois[20] first described anorexia nervosa as occurring in an adolescent girl with signs of schizophrenia. Since that time several writers[4,55] have felt that anorexia nervosa is a variant of schizophrenia. Some features of schizophrenia can appear to be present in patients with anorexia nervosa. Volitional defects seen in schizophrenia may seem present in patients with anorexia nervosa because of their general negativism, indecisiveness, and social withdrawal. The body-image distortion may reach delusional proportions and resemble psychotic perceptions and delusions. However, the fundamental schizophrenic disturbances in affect, thought processes, and volition are not found in anorexia nervosa. Several studies[17,71] have shown no increased risk for schizophrenia in anorexic patients or in their families.

OBSESSIONAL DISORDER. Many patients with anorexia nervosa display obsessional symptomatology, leading some[19,58] to conclude that it is a form of obsessive compulsive neurosis. Smart, Beumont, and George[68] and Solyom[69] have confirmed the obsessive nature of a group of patients with anorexia nervosa with psychometric testing. It is our belief that the obsessional symptomatology in some patients is magnified by the severe starvation state. Although some patients have obsessional character traits, this does not signify an obsessive-compulsive disorder. Many of the anorexic patient's obsessional-like symptoms are not viewed by her as ego-alien, as are true symptoms of an obsessive-compulsive disorder. Only the anorexic patient's preoccupation with food is seen as ego-alien, while her preoccupation with weight, body shape, and drive for thinness are not.

HYSTERIA (CONVERSION DISORDER). At several points in the last one hundred years, investigators have felt that anorexia nervosa was a hysterical symptom. Lasegue[48] termed this disorder "anorexie hysterique" after observing hysterical symptoms in a patient with anorexia nervosa.

Gilles de la Tourette[49] considered anorexia nervosa to be a manifestation of hysteria and different from what he termed "anorexie gastrique," which was due to gastrointestinal symptoms. Both Janet[40] and Dally[17] felt there was a subgroup of patients with anorexia nervosa who also had hysteria. Because of the confusion regarding hysteria itself, its relationship to anorexia nervosa is not clear. Hysterical personality disorder, somatization disorder, and conversion disorder have all been linked to hysterical phenomena, but anorexia nervosa does not clearly resemble any of these. Garfinkel and associates[29] have reported significant differences between patients who they feel have a conversion disorder and those who have anorexia nervosa.

ANOREXIA NERVOSA AS A NONSPECIFIC SYMPTOM. Bliss and Branch[5] introduced the concept that anorexia nervosa was a nonspecific symptom that occurred in many emotional disorders that presented with significant weight loss and that it was virtually impossible to distinguish it from other forms of emaciation. Anorexia nervosa then became an umbrella diagnosis that encompassed illnesses such as schizophrenia, depression, conversion disorder, and other emotional states in which there was significant weight loss. They stated: "Anorexia nervosa is a symptom found at times in almost all psychiatric categories" (p. 18). This view is not accepted today. Many investigators* view anorexia nervosa as distinct from other causes of weight loss. The distinguishing features center around the fundamental drive for thinness that overrides the patient's physical and psychological well-being. In the past, this form of the disorder was referred to as primary anorexia nervosa, with the secondary forms occurring not because of a pursuit of thinness but rather related to other reasons for food refusal. Bruch[8] has added a group of "atypical anorexics" in whom weight loss occurs because of symbolic misinterpretation of eating rather than fear of weight gain. We feel that these so-called secondary forms of the illness should be described according to the primary diagnosis that leads to weight loss—that is, depression, conversion disorder, or schizophrenia.

Garfinkel and associates[30] described differences in the clinical presentation of the emotional disorders that cause weight loss (see table 14.1). Clinical features often allow the differentiation of patients with major depression from patients with anorexia nervosa. Patients with major depressive illness lack the drive for thinness that is present in anorexia nervosa. Depressed patients have true anorexia, whereas patients with anorexia nervosa maintain their appetite until they are very emaciated. The depressed patient feels a general sense of worthlessness, while the loss of self-esteem in the anorexic patient is linked to weight.

There is a group of patients with a conversion disorder who present with weight loss and vomiting and who superficially resemble patients with anorexia nervosa. In a recent study 20 patients out of 360 referred over ten years with a provisional diagnosis of anorexia nervosa lacked the core features of anorexia nervosa and were described as having a con-

* See references 8, 13, 23, 28, 47, 61, and 72.

version disorder.[29] These patients, referred to earlier by Bruch[8] as "atypical anorexics," can be readily differentiated from patients with anorexia nervosa on clinical grounds. Their vomiting and weight loss result from the symbolic meaning that food or eating has assumed. Vomiting, for example, may signify revulsion or disgust. Weight loss may not result from a drive for thinness or a fear of fat. Their symptoms may serve to control others or to allow the person to avoid unconscious conflicts, but are less related to problems with identity and self-control than is the case with anorexia nervosa. Often a traumatic event precipitates symptoms and causes food to assume symbolic significance in conversion-disorder patients. Their psychological disturbances are more circumscribed with less pervasive psychosocial deficits. In contrast to patients with anorexia nervosa, patients with a conversion disorder have a stronger sense of self-control, less obsessive/compulsive behavior, more consistent social relationships, and less evidence of body-image disturbance.[29]

Finally, schizophrenia can present with weight loss secondary to vomiting or to a refusal to eat. However, the reason for this food refusal is very different from that in anorexia nervosa. In the schizophrenic patient, there may be delusions about food (the food may have been poisoned) or about the effects food will have on the body (e.g., that food will cause the stomach to rot). Food refusal may be a rare manifestation of negativistic behavior found in catatonia. The premorbid personality, family history, and response to antipsychotic medication all differentiate these patients from patients who have anorexia nervosa.

Diagnostic Criteria

Diagnostic conceptualization of anorexia nervosa has been influenced by the fact that its features result from several etiological factors. These factors are:

1. The drive for thinness and resulting behavior (starvation, purging).
2. The effects of starvation.
3. Psychopathology.
4. Complications or sequelae of the illness.

Investigations have generally focused on only one or two of these factors in establishing criteria for diagnosis.

There is general agreement that a drive for thinness is necessary for the diagnosis. Different investigators describe this in different ways. Bruch[7] wrote of the "relentless pursuit of thinness." Theander[71] emphasized the changed attitude toward food and eating that results from "the pursuit of thinness." Selvini-Palazzoli[65] referred to this as the "deliberate wish to be slim." Ziegler and Sours[74] stated that "the pursuit of thinness as a pleasure in itself" is required for diagnosis. Crisp[15] wrote of a "weight phobia" in which there is the preoccupation to maintain subpubertal body weight and to avoid weight gain. More recently, the authors of the *Diagnostic and Statistical Manual* (DSM-III)[1] included "a refusal to maintain body weight over a minimal normal weight for age and height" as one of the specific criteria for the diagnosis (p. 64). Despite different terminology, all these investigators address the importance that this feature plays in the illness.

Some have concentrated on psychopathology for the diagnostic criteria. These are often difficult to determine objectively and may not be present in all patients. For example, in addition to the basic drive for thinness, Bruch[8] bases the diagnosis on three psychopathological features: a disturbance in body image, a disturbance in interpreting internal affective and visceral perceptions, and an overall sense of personal ineffectiveness.

Others have focused on related psychopathology. Rollins and Piazza[60] described a sense of inadequacy that pervades the lives of anorexic patients. However, they note that this feature is not pathognomonic of or distinct to anorexia nervosa patients.

Since 1969, a variety of operational criteria have been proposed for the diagnosis of anorexia nervosa (see table 14.2). These criteria have been developed for both clinical and research use, and usually require evidence of both a psychobiological as well as a psychopathological disturbance.

As is evident from the table, there are significant differences in the various criteria. Some rely on implied psychopathology (e.g., Norris[56]), but most emphasize signs and symptoms. Of the latter, prominent differences relate to: (1) the degree of weight loss required; (2) a particular age of onset; (3) the presence of an endocrine disturbance manifested as amenorrhea.

Degree of weight loss can be measured from premorbid weight or from a normal ideal weight for a given age and height. Russell[61] proposed that a 25-lb weight loss was required for a diagnosis of anorexia nervosa. Current controversy relates to the percentage of weight loss required. Feighner and associates[22] and the authors of *DSM-III*[1] require 25 percent weight loss from one's original body weight. However, if an individual lost only 20 percent of her original body weight and if relatively thin or still growing at the onset, she would still qualify. Rollins and Piazza[60] recommended either weight loss that is 20 percent or more of original body weight or weight loss that brings weight 20 percent or more below average for height and age. Halmi and coworkers[38] employed a criterion of 25 percent weight loss of original body weight or 15 percent weight loss below normal weight and height. Thus, although the concept of weight loss is central to the diagnosis, not all investigators agree on the degree of weight loss required or on the method of calculating this weight loss.

Age of onset has also varied as a criterion for diagnosis. Dally[17] re-

TABLE 14.2
Diagnostic Criteria for Anorexia Nervosa

Dally (1969)[17]

---

1. Refusal to eat.
2. Weight loss of at least 10 percent of previous body weight.
3. Amenorrhea of at least three months' duration if menses were previously regular.
4. Age of onset between 11 and 35 years.
5. No evidence of preexisting schizophrenia, depression, or organic disease.

Russell (1970)[61] *and Morgan and Russell (1975)*[53]

---

1. Patient resorts to a variety of devices aimed at achieving weight loss (starvation, vomiting, laxatives, etc.)
2. Evidence of an endocrine disorder, amenorrhea in the female, and loss of sexual potency and interest in the male.
3. Patient manifests the characteristic psychopathology of a morbid fear of becoming fat. This is accompanied by a distorted judgment by the patient of her body size.

Feighner and associates (1972)[22]

---

1. Onset prior to age 25.
2. Anorexia with accompanying weight loss of at least 25 percent of original body weight.
3. A distorted implacable attitude toward eating food or weight that overrides hunger, admonitions, reassurances, and threats.
4. No known medical illness accounts for the anorexia and weight loss.
5. No other known psychiatric disorder, with particular reference to primary affective disorders, schizophrenia, obsessive, and compulsive and phobic neurosis.
6. At least two of the following manifestations: amenorrhea, lanugo, bradycardia, periods of overactivity, episodes of bulimia, vomiting.

The Pathology of Eating Group (Garrow et al. 1975)[34]

---

1. Self-inflicted severe loss of weight using one or more of the following devices: avoidance of food considered to be fattening, self-induced vomiting, use of purgatives, excessive exercise.
2. A secondary endocrine disorder of the hypothalamic and anterior pituitary gonadal axis manifest in the female as amenorrhea and in the male by a diminution of sexual interest and activity.
3. A psychological disorder that has as its central theme a morbid fear of being unable to control eating and hence becoming too fat.

Rollins and Piazza (1978)[60]

---

1. Psychopathologic disturbance as follows:
   a. Evidence of weight phobia and/or distorted body image.
   b. Pervasive sense of inadequacy.
2. Biological disturbance as follows:
   a. Weight loss of 20 percent or more of body weight or weight loss to less than 80 percent of average for age and height.
   b. Amenorrhea.

Norris (1979)[56]

---

1. "Positive" perception of family.
2. Psychosexual unawareness of guilt.

TABLE 14.2, continued

Norris (1979)[56]

3. Onset of illness between 13 and 15 years.
4. Any two of the following psychological features: shy, obsessional and compulsive, compliant or dependent.
5. Enmeshment with a parent.
6. Close intact family denying conflict.
7. Above-average intelligence.
8. More female children than males.
9. Change of personality at or before onset.
10. Dominant mothers.
11. Mothers anxious and overprotective or indulgent and self-martyring.

DSM-III (1980)[1]

1. Intense fear of becoming obese that does not diminish as weight loss progresses.
2. Disturbance of body image (e.g., claiming to "feel fat" even when emaciated).
3. Weight loss of at least 25 percent of original body weight or, if under 18 years of age, weight loss from original body weight plus projected weight gain expected from growth charts may be combined to make the 25 percent.
4. Refusal to maintain body weight over a minimal normal weight for age and height.
5. No known physical illness that would account for the weight loss.

quired an onset between the ages of 11 and 35 years. Feighner and others[22] specified an age of onset prior to 25. However, many recent investigators* have omitted an age of onset criterion. This is valuable, especially since more women are developing anorexia nervosa at a later age. Most investigators do require the evidence of an endocrine disturbance that manifests as amenorrhea in the female. Thus Halmi,[37] Bruch,[8] and Rollins and Piazza[60] consider amenorrhea as a central symptom, whereas Feighner and associates[22] and Russell[61] consider it as one of several possible biological disturbances that may be present. Surprisingly, there is no mention of amenorrhea or other endocrine disturbance in *DSM-III.*[1]

Some of the listed criteria were developed for research purposes and have limited clinical application. Most notably, Feighner and associates' criteria are too restrictive and exclude many individuals who present with essential features of the disorder but lack some accompanying symptoms. Their requirement for anorexia is misleading, as it has been shown that most patients with anorexia nervosa do not develop true anorexia. Their requirement for an onset prior to age 25 is too restrictive. Norris's criteria are much too vague and overemphasize individual and familial psycho pathology to the exclusion of signs and symptoms of the illness. The criteria of the Pathology of Eating Group[34] and of *DSM-III*[1] provide valid and reliable features that are useful clinically in making a diagnosis of the illness. However, we feel that there should be two additional criteria to *DSM-III:* one addressing the endocrine disturbance that is present in anorexia nervosa and another recognizing bulimic and restricter subtypes of the illness.

* See references 1, 34, 37, 38, 60, and 61.

Summary

In this chapter we have discussed diagnostic conceptualizations of anorexia nervosa. We have elaborated on the recent clinical advances in understanding this illness that have influenced diagnostic thinking. We have emphasized various diagnostic criteria that have been proposed for establishing the diagnosis and have also critically reviewed the controversies present in these criteria and have proposed additional criteria to the current edition of the *Diagnostic and Statistical Manual* of the American Psychiatric Association.

REFERENCES

1. American Psychiatric Association. 1980. *Diagnostic and statistical manual of mental disorders*, 3rd ed. Washington, D.C.: American Psychiatric Association.

2. Berkman, J. M. 1948. Anorexia nervosa, anterior-pituitary insufficiency, Simmonds' cachexia, and Sheehan's disease, including some observations on disturbances in water metabolism associated with starvation. *Postgraduate Medicine* 3:237–246.

3. Beumont, P. J. V. 1977. Further categorization of patients with anorexia nervosa. *Australia and New Zealand Journal of Psychiatry* 11:223–226.

4. Binswanger, L. 1944. Der fall Ellen West. *Schweiz Archives of Neurological Psychiatry* 54:69–117.

5. Bliss, E. L., and Branch, C. H. H. 1960. *Anorexia nervosa: Its history, psychology and biology.* New York: Paul B. Hoeber.

6. Brown, G. M., et al. 1983. A critical appraisal of neuroendocrine approaches to psychiatric disorder. In *Neuroendocrine perspectives*, vol. 2, ed. E. E. Mueller and R. M. MacLeod, pp. 329–364. New York: Elsevier.

7. Bruch, H. 1970. Instinct and interpersonal experience. *Comparative Psychiatry* 11:495–506.

8. ————. 1973. *Eating disorders.* New York: Basic Books.

9. Button, E. J., and Whitehouse, A. 1981. Subclinical anorexia nervosa. *Psychological Medicine* 11:509–516.

10. Cantwell, D. P., et al. 1977. Anorexia nervosa: An affective disorder? *Archives of General Psychiatry* 34:1087–1093.

11. Carlson, G. A., and Cantwell, P. P. 1980. Unmasking masked depression in children and adolescents. *American Journal of Psychiatry* 37:445–449.

12. Casper, R. C., et al. 1980. Bulimia: Its incidence and clinical importance in patients with anorexia nervosa. *Archives of General Psychiatry* 37:1030–1034.

13. Crisp, A. H. 1965. Clinical and therapeutic aspects of anorexia nervosa: Study of 30 cases. *Journal of Psychosomatic Research* 9:67–78.

14. ————. 1970. Premorbid factors in adult disorders of weight with particular reference to primary anorexia nervosa (weight phobia): A literature review. *Journal of Psychosomatic Research* 14:1–22.

15. ————. 1977. Diagnosis and outcome of anorexia nervosa: The St. George's view. *Proceedings of the Royal Society of Medicine* 70:464–470.

16. Crisp, A. H., Harding, B., and McGuinness, B. 1980. The starving hoarder and voracious spender: Stealing in anorexia nervosa. *Journal of Psychosomatic Research* 24:225–231.

17. Dally, P. J. 1969. *Anorexia nervosa.* New York: Grune & Stratton.

18. Dejerine, J., and Gauckler, E. 1911. *Les manifestations fonctionelles des psychonevroses, leur traitement par la psychotherapie.* Paris: Masson.

19. Du Bois, F. S. 1949. Compulsion neurosis with cachexia (anorexia nervosa). *American Journal of Psychiatry* 106:107–115.

20. Dubois, R. 1913. De l'anorexie mentale comme prodrome de la démence précoce. *Annals of Medical Psychology* 10:431–438.

21. Duccle, M. 1973. An increase of anorexia nervosa in a university population. *British Journal of Psychiatry* 123:711–712.

22. Feighner, J. P., et al. 1972. Diagnostic criteria for use in psychiatric research. *Archives of General Psychiatry* 26:57–63.

23. Frazier, S. A. 1965. Anorexia nervosa. *Diseases of the Nervous System* 26:155–159.

24. Fries, H. 1977. Studies on secondary amenorrhea, anorectic behavior and body image perception: Importance for the early recognition of anorexia nervosa. In *Anorexia nervosa,* ed. R. Vigersky, pp. 163–176. New York: Raven Press.

25. Garfinkel, P. E. 1974. Perception of hunger and satiety in anorexia nervosa. *Psychological Medicine* 4:309–315.

26. Garfinkel, P. E., and Garner, D. M. 1982. *Anorexia nervosa: A multidimensional perspective.* New York: Brunner/Mazel.

27. Garfinkel, P. E., Moldofsky, H., and Garner, D. M. 1977. The outcome of anorexia nervosa: Significance of clinical features, body image and behavior modification. In *Anorexia nervosa,* ed. R. Vigersky, pp. 315–329. New York: Raven Press.

28. ———. 1980. The heterogeneity of anorexia nervosa: Bulimia as a distinct subgroup. *Archives of General Psychiatry* 37:1036–1040.

29. Garfinkel, P. E., Kaplan, A. S., Garner, D. M., and Darby, P. L. 1983. The differentiation of vomiting and weight loss as a conversion disorder from anorexia nervosa. *American Journal of Psychiatry* 140:1019–1022.

30. Garfinkel, P. E., et al. 1983. Differential diagnosis of emotional disorders that cause weight loss. *Canadian Medical Association Journal* 129:939–945.

31. Garner, D. M., Garfinkel, P. E., and Olmsted, M. P. 1983. An overview of sociocultural factors in the development of anorexia nervosa. In *Anorexia nervosa: Recent developments in research,* ed. P. L. Darby, P. E. Garfinkel, D. M. Garner, and D. V. Coscina, pp. 65–82. New York: Alan R. Liss.

32. Garner, D. M., Garfinkel, P. E., and O'Shaughnessy, M. 1983. Clinical and psychometric comparison between bulimia in anorexia nervosa and bulimia in normal weight women, In *Understanding anorexia nervosa and bulimia: Report of Fourth Ross Conference on medical research,* pp. 6–14. Columbus, Oh.: Ross Laboratories.

33. Garner, D. M., Olmsted, M. P., and Garfinkel, P. E. 1983. Does anorexia nervosa occur on a continuum? *International Journal of Eating Disorders* 2:11–20.

34. Garrow, J. S., et al. 1975. Pathology of eating, group report. In *Dahlem Konferezen Life Sciences Research Report,* ed. T. Silverstone. Berlin: N.p.

35. Gull, W. W. 1868. The address in medicine delivered before the annual meeting of the BMA at Oxford. *Lancet* 2:171.

36. ———. 1964. Anorexia nervosa. In *Evolution of psychosomatic concepts. Anorexia nervosa: A paradigm,* ed. R. M. Kaufman and M. Heiman, pp. 132–139. New York: International Universities Press. (Originally published 1874.)

37. Halmi, K. 1978. Anorexia nervosa: Recent investigations. *Annual Review of Medicine* 29:137–148.

38. Halmi, K., et al. 1977. Pretreatment evaluation in anorexia nervosa. In *Anorexia nervosa,* ed. R. Vigersky, pp. 43–54. New York: Raven Press.

39. Hood, J., Moore, T. E., and Garner, D. M. 1982. Locus of control as a measure of ineffectiveness in anorexia nervosa. *Journal of Consulting and Clinical Psychology* 50:3–13.

40. Janet, P. 1919. *Les obsessions et la psychasthenie.* Paris: Felix Alcan.

41. Jones, D. J., Fox, M. M., Babigan, H. M., and Hutton, H. E. 1980. Epidemiology of anorexia nervosa in Monroe County, New York, 1960–1976. *Psychosomatic Medicine* 42:551–558.

42. Kalucy, R. S., Crisp, A. H., and Harding, B. 1977. A study of 56 families with anorexia nervosa. *British Journal of Medical Psychology* 50:381–395.

43. Kaplan, A. S., and Garfinkel, P. E. 1984. Bulimia in the Talmud. *American Journal of Psychiatry* 141:721.

44. Kay, D. W. K. 1953. Anorexia nervosa: Study in prognosis. *Proceedings of the Royal Society of Medicine* 46:669–674.

45. Kendell, R. E., Hall, D. J., Hailey, A., and Babigan, H. M. 1973. The epidemiology of anorexia nervosa. *Psychological Medicine* 3:200–203.

46. Keys, A., et al. 1950. *The biology of human starvation.* Minneapolis: University of Minnesota Press.

47. King, A. 1963. Primary and secondary anorexia nervosa syndromes. *British Journal of Psychiatry* 109:470–479.

48. Lasegue, G. 1964. De l'anorexie hysterique. In *Evolution of psychosomatic concepts. Anorexia nervosa: A paradigm,* ed. R. M. Kaufman and M. Heiman, pp. 141–155. New York: International Universities Press. (Originally published 1873.)

49. La Tourette, Gilles de. 1895. *G.A.E.B.: Traite clinique et therapeutique de l'hysteric.* Paris: Plou, Nourit et Co.

50. Loeb, L. 1964. The clinical course of anorexia nervosa. *Psychosomatics* 5:345–347.

51. Lowenkopf, E. L. 1982. Anorexia nervosa: Some nosological considerations. *Comparative Psychiatry* 23:233–240.

52. Meyer, J. E. 1961. The anorexia nervosa syndrome: Catemnestic research. *Archives fuer Psychiatrie und Nervenkrankheiten* 202:31–59.

53. Morgan, H. G., and Russell, G. F. M. 1975. Value of family background and clinical features as predictors of long-term outcome in anorexia nervosa: Four-year follow-up study of 41 patients. *Psychological Medicine* 5:355–371.

54. Needleman, H. L., and Waber, D. 1976. Amitriptyline therapy in patients with anorexia nervosa. *Lancet* 2:580.

55. Nicolle, G. 1939. Prepsychotic anorexia. *Proceedings of the Royal Society of Medicine* 32:153–162.

56. Norris, D. 1979. Clinical diagnostic criteria for primary anorexia nervosa. *AUX* (South African medical journal) 56:987–992.

57. Nylander, I. 1971. The feeling of being fat and dieting in a school population: An epidemiologic interview investigation. *Acta Sociomedica Scandinavica* 3:17–26.

58. Palmer, H. D., and Jones, M. S. 1939. Anorexia nervosa as a manifestation of compulsive neurosis. *Archives of Neurology and Psychiatry* 41:856–860.

59. Piran, N., Kennedy, S., Owens, M., Garfinkel, P. E. N.D. Anorexia nervosa, bulimia and affective disorder. Manuscript.

60. Rollins, N., and Piazza, E. 1978. Diagnosis of anorexia nervosa: A critical appraisal. *Journal of the American Academy of Child Psychiatry* 17:126–137.

61. Russell, G. F. M. 1970. Anorexia nervosa: Its identity as an illness and its treatment. In *Modern trends in psychological medicine,* ed. J. H. Price, pp. 131–164. London: Buttersworth.

62. ———. Bulimia nervosa: An ominous variant of anorexia nervosa. *Psychological medicine* 9:429–448.

63. ———. 1984. Proceedings of the first international conference on eating disorders, New York. Unpublished comments.

64. ———. 1972. Psychosocial aspects of weight loss and amenorrhea in adolescent girls. Proceedings from *III International Congress of Psychosomatic Medicine in Obstetrics and Gynecology* (London):593–595.

65. Selvini-Palazzoli, M. P. 1974. *Self starvation.* London: Chaucer Publishing.

66. Sheehan, H. L., and Summers, V. K. 1949. The syndrome of hypopituitarism. *Quarterly Journal of Medicine* 18:319–378.

67. Simmonds, M. 1914. Ueber embolische prozesse in des hypophysis. *Archives of Pathology and Anatomy* 217:226–239.

68. Smart, D. E., Beumont, P. J. V., and George, G. C. W. 1976. Some personality characteristics of patients with anorexia nervosa. *British Journal of Psychiatry* 128:57–60.

69. Solyom, L., Miles, J. E., and O'Kane, J. 1982. A comparative psychometric study of anorexia nervosa and obsessive neurosis. *Canadian Journal of Psychiatry* 27:282–286.

70. Strober, M. 1980. A cross-sectional and longitudinal analysis of personality and symptomological features in young non-chronic anorexia nervosa patients. *Journal of Psychosomatic Research* 24:353–359.

71. Theander, S. 1970. Anorexia nervosa: A psychiatric investigation of 94 female patients. *Acta Psychiatrica Scandinavica* 214 (Supplement):1–194.

72. Thoma, H. 1967. *Anorexa nervosa,* trans. G. Brydone. New York: International Universities Press.

73. Winokur, A., March, V., and Mendels, J. 1980. Primary affective disorder in relatives of patients with anorexia nervosa. *American Journal of Psychiatry* 137:695–698.

74. Ziegler, R., and Sours, J. A. 1968. A naturalistic study of patients with anorexia nervosa admitted to a university medical center. *Comparative Psychiatry* 9:644–651.

15

Outcome and Prognosis of Anorexia Nervosa

George I. Szmukler and Gerald F. M. Russell

For the clinician, a knowledge of the likely outcome for a patient with a disorder is of great value. It helps in the formulation of management, particularly if it is likely to be long term, and in advising the patient and relatives as to what they may expect for the future.

Most disorders seen by psychiatrists are characterized by considerable variability in outcome, and anorexia nervosa is no exception. A number of comprehensive reviews in this area[6,8,15] reveal that outcome varies from full recovery to a chronic severe illness. As the majority of patients are female, the feminine gender will be used in the text when referring to an individual patient. There will be a section on male patients at the end of this chapter.

What Is a Good Outcome?

The question of what represents a good outcome in anorexia nervosa is not a straightforward one. The answer varies from one authority to the next and depends to a large degree on assumptions about the etiology of the disorder and the nature of the illness "process."

At least three possibilities can be considered: First, the illness comprises the basic syndrome of deliberate weight loss, amenorrhea, and a psychopathology concerning a morbid fear of "fatness." There are perhaps important predisposing factors but these are distinct from the illness process itself. A "cure" is represented by a sustained recovery to a healthy weight, resumption of menses, and a loss of the characteristic psychopathology. A requirement that the predisposing factors, for example a particular personality structure, should also be changed is unreasonable in the same way that recovery from tuberculosis can occur when active infection has ceased without a change in predisposing causes such as an unhygienic environment. Thus if a patient suffered from particular personality vulnerabilities prior to the illness, even if these contributed to its onset, recovery would not demand that they should have changed.

Secondly, the syndrome of anorexia nervosa is a manifestation of a deeper psychological disturbance, and for "true" recovery this must also be ameliorated. There must be improvement in psychological functioning in the relevant areas. It might be predicted that if the underlying disturbance was not improved but recovery from the features of the syndrome did occur, then other symptoms would arise.

Thirdly, even if no assumptions were made about etiology, a broader view of outcome than a simple remission of the features of the syndrome could still be justified. Anorexia nervosa is associated with serious effects on the patient's psychological and social functioning quite apart from the eating-related disturbances. It is reasonable to examine whether these impairments persist after recovery from the basic syndrome. The significance of a broader assessment of outcome differs here from that in the second case just discussed. The examination is for impairments that were not present before the illness developed. Such an assessment needs to be made against a baseline of the patient's previous functioning. For example, if a patient's obsessionality, though marked, is not any more severe than before she developed her illness, then it might be said that she had recovered in this respect.

Each standpoint just described is oversimplified, yet the possibilities are worth bearing in mind when looking at outcome studies since they clarify the assumptions underlying the selection of the measures employed.

In our current state of knowledge about anorexia nervosa, the second point seems the most difficult to support. Theories about etiology are essentially untested and the specification of what should improve will vary from one authority to the next. There is also a difficulty, when complex chains of causes including circular ones are operating, in distinguishing what is an integral part of the disorder.

The first option seems too narrow if we are interested in a full description of outcome, although at present this is all that may be justified. The third option presents the difficulty of assessing premorbid functioning. This generally must be done retrospectively, and for young, still maturing patients, the premorbid state is only temporary. Despite these difficulties, an attempt to measure changes against a personal baseline is useful.

In theory, the results of outcome studies should help us in deciding which of the three options just described is most appropriate. Clues about etiology might be uncovered. If symptom substitution did occur, it might be asked how recovered patients with new symptoms differ from those without new symptoms. Such an examination might point to specific underlying pathogenic mechanisms.

Problems Associated with the Evaluation of Outcome Studies

There are a number of problems in reaching general conclusions from a review of outcome studies. While some have been discussed previously,[6,8,15] we should like to make some comments about methodological issues.

SAMPLING BIASES

Different treatment centers see different populations of patients even though they all share a diagnosis of anorexia nervosa. Some of these biases, such as age, are obvious, but others are subtle and reflect selection factors that depend on the type of treatment unit involved and local practice. Large samples tend to be reported from specialty treatment units that attract referrals from far and wide, many resulting from failed attempts at treatment by local services. The hospital patient population is therefore biased toward the already chronic.

Patients with anorexia nervosa are often reluctant to accept treatment, and this allows for selection by patient motivation. A unit may be prepared to accept for treatment only patients who agree to comply. The outcome for such a group is likely to differ substantially from that for patients who have been coerced into treatment, on occasions on a compulsory treatment order.

Patients may find their way to different hospital specialists including general physicians, endocrinologists, gynecologists, gastroenterologists, and psychiatrists. With the last the treatment may be conducted in a general hospital or a mental hospital. The populations of patients in these settings may differ substantially. It is difficult, when assessing reports from diverse units, to separate out selection factors from the influence of the treatment setting.

A description of the patient population is thus important, but some characteristics are difficult to define. One often learns much of importance about the practices of other units through informal discussion with staff members.

A less obvious bias may be introduced when patients from different epochs are included in different series. The number of cases of anorexia nervosa presenting for treatment has increased markedly over the past few decades, and patients presenting today may differ in several respects from patients who presented a decade ago. It is possible that patients presenting today have less vulnerability to the disorder and that they have acquired it in response to increased exposure to adverse influences in contemporary society. Less vulnerability might be associated with a better outcome.

TRACING ALL PATIENTS

Patients who fail to respond to invitations for follow-up interviews may have a different outcome from those who do participate in such interviews. Vandereycken and Pierloot[21] were unable to trace over 30 percent of their series for follow-up. On studying the data collected previously, they found that the nonresponders differed by being older, having longer illnesses, having been more emaciated, and having dropped out of treatment more often. It thus appears that those who cannot be followed up are more likely to have done badly.

Ensuring the cooperation of all patients in a follow-up study is something of an art. It is more readily achieved when the investigator has a good relationship with the patient and when the follow-up is prospective, with special attention to ensuring the patient's goodwill. As a consequence of a long-term follow-up study that we are undertaking, we have discovered the value of anticipating difficulties, of maintaining occasional contact after discharge, and of sending a personal invitation to the patient written in a manner that takes account of her particular likes and dislikes. The thought behind such a letter is not dissimilar to that which goes into the formulation of a therapeutic intervention.

DEFINITION OF THE DISORDER

If the disorder is variously defined, the value of comparison is seriously undermined. The categorization of atypical cases is particularly troublesome, and this has been well discussed, with examples, by Theander.[19] Diagnostic criteria that are very strict may lead to the exclusion of patients who would confidently be diagnosed as suffering from the disorder. This will limit the generalizability of the results.

OUTCOME MEASURES AND THE QUALITY OF INFORMATION

The outcome measures employed will be influenced by the assumptions described previously concerning the meaning of a "good" outcome. Apart from information about weight, menstruation, and attitudes to body shape, there has been considerable variation in the measures that have been adopted. Comparison between studies thus becomes a dubious exercise.

The quality of information depends on its source. Personal interviews seem the most reliable, particularly when they are semistructured. Standardized self-report inventories are popular, but have questionable validity for patients who deny many aspects of their experiences. An interview has the advantage of permitting an assessment of the reliability of the patient's responses and also allows for clarification of terms such as "eating binges" with further probing. The nature of the relationship between the interviewer and the patient may have an important bearing on what is revealed, and this needs to be considered.

Some comment on the manner in which the patient's weight is reported is in order. Although ostensibly a straightforward measure, its interpretation can pose some difficulties. The problem concerns what should be regarded as a "normal" weight for a particular patient. A percentage of the matched population mean weight (MPMW) can sometimes be misleading. For example, a girl or young woman might have been perfectly healthy at a weight far below the population average before her illness. Should she recover to this level, she might appear quite underweight by table averages. Conversely, a previously overweight young woman might at 85 percent MPMW be considerably underweight by her own premorbid standard. Because of this difficulty, it would be reasonable for the patient's weight to be reported both as a percent of MPMW and as a percent of her premorbid weight. A special problem is posed by patients whose onset of illness antedated the completion of the pubertal growth spurt and who never achieved a stable premorbid weight.

THE DURATION OF FOLLOW-UP

There is good evidence that outcome varies with the duration of follow-up.[5,19,21] In the study of Vandereycken and Pierloot,[21] the proportion of patients reported to have recovered was only 13 percent at two years or less, rising to 56 percent at five years or more. Continued improvement with time was noted also for the resumption of menses and the achievement of satisfying sexual experiences. Therefore, a study that reports on an outcome ranging from one to nine years is virtually impossible to interpret. A minimum period of four years has been recommended by Morgan and Russell.[11] This appears reasonable, but even longer is necessary for a full picture of outcome as some patients may recover even after ten years while others, apparently recovered, may still relapse.[19]

Given the difficulties just described, we believe that a comparison of different studies based on varying populations, variously defined and assessed in different ways, is of limited usefulness. Previous reviewers[6,8,15] have taken this kind of analysis as far as it can be taken. The conclusion to be drawn from their work is that the outcome of anorexia nervosa varies considerably both across and within studies. For this reason this chapter will be more restricted in its scope and will examine studies where comparisons can be made with reasonable confidence. Two types of study will be discussed. The first deals with the long-term course of the illness and the second deals with a cross-sectional view of groups of patients followed four or more years after the onset of the illness.

The Long-term Course of the Illness

Two studies, those of Theander[19] and of Dally and Gomez,[5] provide useful data on the long-term course of anorexia nervosa. The ninety-four patients described by Theander were drawn from a defined area in Sweden and were treated in a variety of hospital-based settings between 1930 and 1960. The 140 patients described by Dally and Gomez were referred to one psychiatrist, 78 percent being admitted to a hospital. Both studies involved follow-ups of eight years or longer. Diagnostic criteria were clearly defined.

Theander found a wide variation in the duration of the illness. Only 15 percent of the patients recovered in less than two years, and by three years about 33 percent had recovered. The illness persisted in about 25 percent for more than six years and in about half of these for more than ten years. Although "recovery" was clearly defined by the author, he noted that "hardly any of the probands seemed to have been completely free from neurotic fixations on body and diet at the time of the review" (p. 94), even when their weight was normal and menstruation had returned. A further relapse following a period of apparent recovery was unusual and occurred in about 12 percent of the patients.

The results reported by Dally and Gomez are similar. The assessment of a good outcome was made when the patient achieved more than 90 percent of standard weight or premorbid weight (whichever was the lower) and maintained it for at least a year. By the end of the second year 38 percent of the patients had achieved this goal; by the end of four years, 67 percent; and by ten years, 70 percent. Patients with an onset of the disorder before 14 years, when compared with those with an onset between 15 and 18, were more likely to recover within two years, but after four years a similar proportion had reestablished a healthy weight (72 percent and 65 percent respectively). These authors reported that the resumption of menstruation occurred an average of nine months after weight had been restored to normal. Eighty percent of patients who regained an adequate and stable weight menstruated spontaneously within two years of this.

Both studies therefore show a similar pattern in the rate of recovery, with a steady upward trend up to the end of about four years and tapering off thereafter. The mortality rate in Theander's study was 13 percent. The mortality rate in the study by Dally and Gomez is not clearly stated. Both studies found that about one-third of the patients who recovered developed bulimia as a temporary feature. Obesity was a rare development.

Theander[20] has continued to follow-up this cohort of patients and has reported briefly on the further course of their illnesses sixteen years after his first assessment, the period of follow-up now being twenty-two to fifty years. A further five patients had died from malnutrition or suicide, bringing the mortality rate up to 18 percent. The mortality rate was noted to double as the observation time extended from five to ten years and to treble if extended to twenty-five to thirty years. Of the seven probands still seriously ill with anorexia nervosa at the time of the first follow-up, four had died by the date of the second follow-up. These patients had been ill for twenty years or more. Theander commented that, compared with the initial assessment, more patients had recovered and there was a decline in psychiatric symptoms and adjustment problems. Only one patient in the cohort developed a schizophrenic illness.

Patients' Status After Four or More Years Follow-Up

THREE STUDIES FROM SPECIALIZED PSYCHIATRIC CENTERS

Three studies have produced findings that are directly comparable in terms of the outcome measures employed.[9,11,12] Two emanated from specialized treatment centers[9,11] while the third[12] provides a valuable comparison since it came from a unit providing a more local service. Each study was carefully planned and a wide range of outcome variables was considered.

Some of the details of the patients studied are presented in table 15.1. The data provided do not permit a ready comparison on some of the items, but important differences are evident, particularly when the Maudsley series[11] is compared with the Bristol series.[12] These differences are most marked in the duration of illness, previous attempts at psychiatric treatment, the social class distribution, and the proportion of married patients. The Bristol patients had shorter histories of illness, had been treated elsewhere less often, and were less likely to come from upper-class families. It is not known to what extent these differences are related to the patient referral pattern to each unit or to changes in the patient population that might have occurred with the passage of time, although the former is probably the more influential factor.

Another point of difference between the three series is that in the Bristol study most of the patients were managed as outpatients, while the majority in the St. George's series[9] and all of the Maudsley series were admitted at some stage. At least two interpretations can be made of this fact. The first is that the Bristol patients were less severely ill and the second that there was a bias there against admitting patients to a hospital. Both factors probably played a part. The Maudsley and St. George's series contained a higher proportion of patients who had failed to respond to earlier psychiatric treatment and hence had more severe problems. On the other hand, the authors stated that there was a shortage of admission beds in Bristol, and this must clearly have influenced treatment practice.

TABLE 15.1

Comparison of Patients in Three Studies Using Similar Methods

	Maudsley Series (Morgan and Russell[11]) N = 41	St. George's Series (Hsu, Crisp, and Harding[9]) N = 102	Bristol Series (Morgan, Purgold, and Wellbourne[12]) N = 78
Age at presentation (years)	<18 51% 18–30 32% 30+ 17%	Mean 20.8 (s.d. 6.2)	<18 35% 18–30 62% 30+ 4%
Age at onset (years)	Mean 15.5 (s.d. 3.1)	Not known	Mean 17.2 (s.d. 3.3)
Duration of illness (years)	<1 14% 1–2 37% 2–3 14% 3–7 13% >7 22% Median 2.0	Mean 3.5	<1 38% 1–2 17% 2–3 15% 3–7 15% >7 15% Median 1.6
Social class	I. 44% II. 22% III. 32% IV. 2% V. 0%	I. 31% II. 39% III. 19% IV. 5% V. 6%	I. 6% II. 49% III. 33% IV. 8% V. 0%
Ever married	5%	15%	13%
Lowest mean body weight (% matched normal population)	63.3 (s.d. 9.1)	68.1 (s.d. 8.2)	67.8 (s.d. 8.2)
Previous psychiatric treatment for anorexia nervosa	49%	47%	12%

Tables 15.2, 15.3, and 15.4 show the main results of the follow-up assessments. The "General Outcome Category" is derived purely from the patient's weight and menstrual status. A "good" outcome means that body weight has been maintained within 15 percent of average for height, sex, and age, and is accompanied by regular cyclical menstruation. "Intermediate" outcome includes those patients whose weight has only in-

TABLE 15.2

*Comparison of Outcome in Three Studies
Using Similar Methods*

"General Outcome Categories"	Maudsley[11] (%)	St. George's[9] (%)	Bristol[12] (%)
Good	39	48	58
Intermediate	27	30	19
Poor	29	20	19
Died	5	2	1

TABLE 15.3

Comparison of "General Outcome Categories" with Scores on Three Rating Scales in the Maudsley[11] and St. George's[9] Series

"General Outcome Categories"	Rating Scales					
	Mental State		Psychosexual		Socioeconomic	
	Maudsley	St. George's	Maudsley	St. George's	Maudsley	St. George's
Good	10.2	10.2	10.9	10.8	10.2	9.6
Intermediate	9.0	9.1	8.0	9.4	7.1	8.2
Poor	5.4	7.2	6.2	5.7	5.7	5.9

NOTE: A higher score on each rating scale represents a better outcome and is scored on a 12-point scale.

termittently risen to within 15 percent of standard weight or who have continuing menstrual disturbance. In the "poor" outcome category, body weight has never approached 85 percent of the standard and menstruation has been absent or sporadic. The other outcome score shown in tables 15.3 and 15.4 is the "Average Outcome Score," which comprises a composite rating on a twelve-point scale derived from five independent measures of the patient's state over the previous six months. These concerned (1) nutritional status, (2) menstrual function, (3) mental status, (4) psychosexual adjustment, and (5) social and economic functioning. The higher the score, the better the outcome.

It will be seen in table 15.2 that the results from the Maudsley study on "General Outcome" differ considerably from those of the Bristol study, with those of the St. George's study falling in between, but closer to the Maudsley results. Table 15.3 shows that in both the Maudsley and St. George's studies, the scores on three of the rating scales (mental state, psychosexual, socioeconomic) are very similar for each of the "General Outcome" categories, and these decline in parallel with a progressively poorer weight and menstrual outcome. These data are not available for the Bristol series. Table 15.4 shows that in the Bristol series the "Average Outcome" scores are significantly higher than in the Maudsley series. These data are not available for the St. George's series.

TABLE 15.4

Comparison of "Average Outcome Scores" in the Maudsley[11] and Bristol[12] Series

"Average Outcome Scores"	Maudsley (%)	Bristol (%)
0–2.9	15	0
3–5.9	20	5
6–8.9	25	35
9–12	40	60

NOTE: A higher score represents a better outcome on a 12-point scale.

TABLE 15.5

Outcome for Specific Disturbances in Three Studies Using Similar Methods

	Maudsley Series[11] (%)	St. George's Series[9] (%)	Bristol Series[a][12] (%)
Anorexic Symptoms			
Weight 85 percent standard weight	55	62	72
15 percent overweight	2	2	
Normal eating	33	35	
Vomiting	25	21	23
Purgative abuse	33	34	21
Anxiety eating with others	51	31	
Concern about body shape	65		
Menstrual Function			
Regular periods	50	51	54
Amenorrhea	42	28	15
Other Psychiatric Symptoms			
Free from psychiatric disturbance	40	45	
Depression	45	38	
Obsessions	23	21	
Social phobia	45	24	
Psychosexual Symptoms			
Normal attitudes and behavior	60	57	
Clearly abnormal	23	20	
Socioeconomic Symptoms			
Significant difficulties with family	55	37	33
Full-time employment/ housewife/student	73	78	80

[a] Information provided by Professor H. G. Morgan and Ms. J. Purgold.

Table 15.5 shows some of the results concerning more specific areas of functioning. The similarities between the Maudsley and St. George's series are very striking on nearly all of these. Some of the data from the Bristol series have kindly been provided by Professor H. G. Morgan and Ms. J. Purgold, and these show a better outcome for weight and menstruation (fewer patients with amenorrhea) but not for self-induced vomiting. Vomiting, however, was infrequently carried out by half of these patients.

The results from the Maudsley and St. George's studies indicate that a recovery of weight and menses is associated with fewer related psychological disturbances. It is not possible to tell from the information provided exactly to what degree these improvements run in parallel. More details are provided by Morgan[10] for the Maudsley series, where it is possible to calculate correlation coefficients between the Nutrition Scale ("dietary restriction, concern about body weight"), weight maintenance, and the other scales contributing to the "Average Outcome Score" ("mental state, psychosexual adjustment, and socioeconomic functioning"). The correlations are 0.72, 0.54, and 0.72 respectively and all are statistically significant at the 0.001 level. A finding common to these studies as well as most others is that many patients, despite returning to normal weight and resuming menstruation, continue to be preoccupied with their weight. However, many young women in a normal population have similar concerns, and it would be unrealistic to expect recovered patients not to share these. Whether their fears are in some way different is difficult to evaluate.

Table 15.5 shows that symptoms of depression and obsessionality were common on follow-up. Despite this, the authors were impressed with the consistency of the basic clinical picture of anorexia nervosa in 80 percent or so of the patients.

One result reported from the St. George's study that probably demonstrates the operation of selection factors in influencing the final outcome concerns a comparison between patients admitted and those treated only on an outpatient basis. Seventy-one percent of the outpatients fell into the "Good Outcome" category compared with 45 percent of those in the inpatient group. Only 6 percent of the outpatient group fell into the "Intermediate" category compared with 37 percent of the inpatient group, while both groups had about 20 percent in the "Poor Outcome" category. This finding is unexplained but might be due to the fact that patients likely to have a good outcome are considered not to require admission while some of those likely to have a poor outcome reject admission even when it is offered.

These three studies, when considered side by side, are extremely valuable in providing information on the outcome of patients referred to specialized centers and to a psychiatric service with a more local commitment. The pattern of the results from these studies speaks strongly for their reliability and validity.

TWO RECENT STUDIES FROM GENERAL MEDICAL TREATMENT CENTERS

Two recent studies from Scandinavia provide useful information about the outcomes of patients treated in a general medical setting rather than a psychiatric service. Definitions of the outcome measures are not as clearly specified as in the studies just considered, but the results reported are of interest when compared with these studies. Both provide data on follow-up periods of at least four years.

Askevold[1] found that 60 percent of his series of fifty-three patients had recovered "socially, sexually, and in their eating habits and weight, and had good interpersonal relationships" (p. 195). A further 25 percent were partially improved, that is, they "were functioning well in social situations, but occasionally had food peculiarities or still had amenorrhoea" (p. 195). Thirteen percent were considered to be only slightly improved and 4 percent had died. Overall, 82 percent were said to be physically cured. Within the series there was a tendency for patients who had received long-term psychotherapy to fare worse. This is probably an artifact reflecting the tendency for more difficult patients to be referred for psychiatric treatment.

The other study, by Bassoe and Eskeland,[2] reported the outcome for seventy-seven patients treated by an endocrinologist and followed-up for four or more years. Some patients were also referred to a psychiatrist. The doctor "played the role of an instructor in the pathophysiology of hunger without discussing social or psychological problems" (p. 127). Fifty-eight percent of the patients had a "good" outcome (i.e., "the patients were healthy and symptom-free and all the women had regular menstrual cycles" [p. 129]), 28 percent were "intermediate" (i.e., they had "recovered or nearly recovered normal body weight and felt healthy, in 50% of them the menstrual cycle had become normal, some of the patients had vague gastrointestinal symptoms and anxiety concerning further gains in body weight" [p. 129]); and 14 percent were "poor or unchanged." Again there was a tendency for patients referred to a psychiatric clinic to have a poorer outcome.

The evidence from those studies suggests that patients treated in a medical setting tend to have a better outcome than those treated by psychiatrists and that those treated in an outpatient clinic tend to do better than those admitted. It is of course difficult to assess the influence of the treatments themselves, but the most likely explanation for the differences in outcome is the operation of selection biases; different populations of patients find their way to different treatment settings. It is likely, for example, that patients who are more psychologically disturbed find their way to psychiatric clinics and that this disturbance also affects their prognosis for recovery.

In all of these studies there appears to be a core of about 15 to 20 percent of patients who show little improvement. The mortality rates were 5 percent or less.

Factors Predicting Eventual Outcome

The studies of Morgan and Russell,[11] Hsu, Crisp, and Harding,[9] and Morgan, Purgold, and Wellbourne[12] examined a similar set of factors for their prognostic significance. The first two studies produced similar results; the third identified only a few factors that were associated with a differential outcome.

The following were of prognostic significance in both the Maudsley and the St. George's studies and predicted a poorer outcome:

1. An older age of onset.
2. A longer duration of illness.
3. A lower body weight at presentation.
4. A poorer adjustment in childhood.
5. Disturbed family relationships (a poor relationship between the patient and other family members in the Maudsley study, or a disturbed relationship between the parents in the St. George's study).
6. A history of previous psychiatric treatment.

In general, the correlations between the features just described and outcome were fairly modest in the Maudsley study, being significant at around the 0.05 level. Poor childhood adjustment and family disturbance were significant at the 0.01 level. The St. George's study showed stronger correlations overall and also found other factors associated with a differential outcome. A poorer outcome was associated with lower social class status, married status, and bulimia. The last two were associated with a longer duration of illness, which is thus a confounding variable. In the Maudsley study, the short-term response to treatment and even the need for readmission did not predict eventual outcome. In the St. George's study, the patient's outcome at one year was significantly correlated with the outcome at four or more years.

Only two factors were associated with "General Outcome" in the Bristol study: the duration of illness and a disturbed relationship between the patient and other members of the family were related to a poorer outcome. Family hostility and personality difficulties were associated with a poorer outcome on the "Average Outcome Score."

The identification of prognostic factors in a particular series will depend on the population of patients included and the extent of within-group variation. For example, if the age of onset of the disorder is limited in the group of patients to 15 to 18 years, then it is unlikely that this factor will have much value in predicting eventual outcome. In the end, all that might be reasonably concluded is that in a population of patients seen in a particular clinic, certain factors are associated with a certain outcome. This might help explain the major differences among many studies in the identification of prognostic factors.[15] Varying populations may also be the explanation for the differences among the three studies just scrutinized.

Although bulimia and self-induced vomiting are often said to be associated with a poor outcome,[3,7,19] the three studies cited provide little support for this view. It should be borne in mind, however, that the special interest in these features is fairly recent and that earlier studies may not have attended closely to them. It is also possible that self-induced vomiting may be a bad prognostic sign when part of the bulimic syndrome and not when associated with classical anorexia nervosa.

Morgan, Purgold, and Wellbourne[12] have commented on the finding that a longer duration of illness is associated with a lesser chance of recovery. It may be that earlier intervention in those who develop the disorder could improve the likelihood of a good outcome (that is, through better "secondary prevention"). However, it is also possible that there are factors, such as personality variables, important in facilitating recovery that also lead the patient to present for treatment at an earlier stage in the illness.

The prediction of outcome in an individual case is generally believed to remain something of a guess. Single factors of the type discussed earlier are of limited usefulness, and it has been suggested that multivariate statistical techniques might improve matters considerably. However, the application of such procedures requires the study of very large groups of patients and these are, in practice, difficult to assemble. In addition, "stronger" data than those generally collected are probably required. Another approach might be to study more complex measures such as the nature of the relationships within the family or the patient's premorbid level of functioning. These assessments cannot be realistically performed retrospectively, and the results from prospective studies are slow to emerge. In fact, no outcome study to date has been a truly prospective one in which hypotheses concerning the prediction of outcome have been drawn up and then tested.

In most outcome studies the effects of treatment are ignored. Although at this stage there is little evidence to suggest that any particular treatment is superior to any other in influencing the eventual outcome, this may not in fact be the case. Morgan, Purgold, and Wellbourne[12] raise the possibility that the improvement seen in their outcomes over those in the Maudsley and St. George's series might be in part due to the fact that hospital admission was employed less often. A good case for testing such a hypothesis can be made in a study where patients are randomly allocated to inpatient or outpatient care, but it would prove difficult to avoid admission for those whose state of emaciation is dangerous.

ANOREXIA NERVOSA IN YOUNGER PATIENTS

Swift[17] has reviewed the literature in an attempt to determine whether the outcome for younger patients in the age range 11 to 15 differs from that in patients presenting in late adolescence. Studies that have examined groups of patients of all ages provide little useful information on this subject. Swift[17] examined seven studies that dealt specifically with young patients, but most of these suffered from such drawbacks that conclusions could not be drawn. Two sounder studies[16,23] reached opposite conclusions; Warren's study[23] provided evidence for a better outcome in younger patients, while Sturzenberger and associates' study[16] did not. The evidence remains inconclusive.

An important observation has been made with regard to a sinister consequence that may arise in patients who develop the illness before the completion of puberty.[13] A series of twenty patients was presented in whom the pubertal sequence was arrested with the onset of the illness and the possibility raised that this might prove eventually irreversible. The developmental failures described were a diminished stature, an impaired growth of the breasts, and a persistent primary amenorrhea. Those patients with the longest histories of emaciation showed the least breast development after weight gain and they remained stunted in their growth. Menstruation had begun in eleven of the patients, in one case being delayed until the age of 25 years. How long the menarche can be delayed through the development of the illness is not known.

ANOREXIA NERVOSA IN MALES

Burns[4] has provided information on the outcome of the disorder in males based on the largest series of such patients yet reported. Thirty-six patients seen at St. George's Hospital over a twenty-year period were described. The clinical picture was remarkably similar to that seen in females apart, of course, from the menstrual disturbance.

Twenty-seven patients were followed up from two to twenty years in a manner similar to that of Morgan and Russell,[11] Hsu, Crisp, and Harding,[9] and Morgan, Purgold, and Wellbourne.[12] The patients were classified at follow-up in terms of "General Outcome" categories that paralleled those used for female patients.

A "good" outcome was defined as a weight greater than 85 percent MPMW and regular sexual activity (intercourse or masturbation taken as an indicator of sexual potency). An "intermediate" outcome was defined as a weight greater than 85 percent MPMW with intermittent or no sexual activity or as a weight between 75 and 85 percent MPMW with regular sexual activity. A "poor" outcome consisted of a weight less than 75 percent MPMW with intermittent or absent sexual activity. Using these criteria, the outcome was good in 44 percent of the patients, intermediate in 26 percent, and poor in 30 percent. Using the criterion of weight alone, 59 percent were heavier than 85 percent MPMW at follow-up. Sixty-three percent of the patients were rated as psychiatrically "normal" at follow-up, and the general absence of depressive episodes compared with females was noted. Eight patients were married (only two had been at the time of presentation), but 37 percent were noted to avoid sexual contacts. The disorder "bred true" over time as for female patients.

A number of factors associated with a poor "General Outcome" were detected. These were a lower weight during the illness, a poor relationship with the mother during the illness, poor school performance during the illness, a poor relationship with the parents during childhood, and, most significant statistically, the absence of premorbid sexual fantasies and masturbation.

From these findings, one may conclude that for patients seen in a specialized clinic, the overall outcome for males does not differ substantially from that for females.

Conclusions

Some of the major difficulties in reviewing a series of outcome studies performed in different centers have been discussed, as have differing conceptualizations of what may constitute a "good" outcome for anorexia nervosa.

Studies in hospital clinic patients do not help us to reach a general conclusion concerning the outcome of anorexia nervosa since the course of the disturbance may be quite different in cases arising in the general population and who never arrive at a clinic. A study on a representative sample of the population has not, so far, been conducted.

A striking observation when outcome studies from different centers are compared is the variability in outcome even within these centers. Some patients recover completely, others remain chronically ill, and an appreciable proportion die.

Long-term studies show that the proportion of patients recovering increases almost linearly for the first four years and then tapers off. However, all hope is not lost as a small proportion of cases may recover even after six or ten years of illness. In patients with a chronic illness, the clinical picture remains primarily that of anorexia nervosa although other psychiatric symptoms, particularly depressive and obsessional, may be prominent.

To gain a reliable view of the outcome of a group of patients, a follow-up period of four years or more is necessary. The results of a "cross-sectional" study of the patients' status after such an interval depends to a significant degree on the clinical population studied. In a specialized center, 40 to 50 percent have achieved a good outcome in terms of weight and resumption of normal menses. In a psychiatric service with a more local commitment, this proportion may be 60 percent or more. In non-psychiatric clinics the proportion may be higher still. Patients who recover in terms of their weight and menses tend also to show the least psychiatric disturbance. Without knowing the patients' level of psychological and social functioning before the commencement of the illness, it is not possible to know whether these other disturbances had to be ameliorated to permit recovery from the anorexic symptoms or whether the fact that patients were functioning better premorbidly facilitated their eventual recovery. The finding by Morgan and Russell[11] and Hsu, Crisp, and Harding[9] that a poor childhood adjustment was associated with a poorer outcome provides some support for the latter possibility.

The delineation of important prognostic factors has been disappointing. Inconsistencies in the results, even in the three studies given special attention in this review, can to some extent be accounted for by varying clinic populations, but they also suggest that the variables examined so far are of limited usefulness. A more fruitful approach requires the prospective evaluation of more complex variables, such as those pertaining to premorbid personality and family relationships. The quality of the latter, even when quite crudely assessed, has been implicated in influencing the outcome in each of the studies reviewed herein. An example of a more complex variable that might prove valuable is the "Expressed Emotion" measure, which has been shown to be strongly associated with relapse in schizophrenia.[22] This measure assesses, on the basis of an audiotaped semistructured interview with the parents, a number of attitudes toward the patient. Ratings are standardized and achieve high levels of reliability. We have used this measure at the time of intake and found it the only one that has predicted, to a highly significant extent, early dropouts from treatment.[18] The application of measures such as this may improve our ability to predict which patients are at greatest risk for a poor eventual outcome and may suggest appropriate treatment measures.

The effects of different treatment approaches on long-term outcome have not been studied. The finding that a longer duration of illness is associated with a lesser chance of recovery raises the possibility that earlier intervention may boost the chances of a better outcome. This hypothesis is difficult to test in practice as it is extremely difficult to influence patients to present for treatment earlier.

The outcome for patients suffering from bulimia nervosa[14] or bulimia is at present unknown. The occurrence of bulimic symptoms or self-induced vomiting in patients with anorexia nervosa has not yet been shown conclusively to affect adversely the eventual outcome.

REFERENCES

1. Askevold, F. 1983. What are the helpful factors in psychotherapy for anorexia nervosa? *International Journal of Eating Disorders* 2:193–197.

2. Bassoe, H. H., and Eskeland, I. 1982. A prospective study of 133 patients with anorexia nervosa: Treatment and outcome. *Acta Psychiatrica Scandinavica* 65:127–133.

3. Beumont, P. J. V., George, G. C. W., and Smart, D. E. 1976. "Dieters" and "vomiters and purgers" in anorexia nervosa. *Psychological Medicine* 6:617–622.

4. Burns, T. P. 1984. Anorexia nervosa in the male: A prognostic study. M.D. thesis, Cambridge University.

5. Dally A., and Gomez, J. 1979. *Anorexia nervosa.* London: Heinemann.

6. Garfinkel, P. E., and Garner, D. M. 1982. *Anorexia nervosa: A multidimensional perspective.* New York: Brunner/Mazel.

7. Garfinkel, P. E., Moldofsky, H., and Garner, D. M. 1977. The outcome of anorexia nervosa: Significance of clinical features, body image and behavioural modification. In *Anorexia nervosa,* ed. R. A. Vigersky, pp. 315–329. New York: Raven Press.

8. Hsu, L. K. 1980. Outcome of anorexia nervosa: A review of the literature. *Archives of General Psychiatry* 37:1041–1046.

9. Hsu, L. K., Crisp, A. H., and Harding, B. 1979. Outcome of anorexia nervosa. *Lancet* 1:61–65.

10. Morgan, H. G. 1972. Anorexia nervosa: A prognostic study. M.D. thesis, Oxford University.

11. Morgan, H. G., and Russell, G. F. M. 1975. Value of family background and clinical

features as predictors of long-term outcome in anorexia nervosa: Four-year follow-up study of 41 patients. *Psychological Medicine* 5:355–371.

12. Morgan, H. G., Purgold, J., and Wellbourne, J. 1983. Management and outcome in anorexia nervosa: A standardized prognostic study. *British Journal of Psychiatry* 143: 282–287.

13. Russell, G. F. M. 1985. Premenarchal anorexia nervosa and its sequelae. *Journal of Psychiatric Research* 19:363–369.

14. ———. 1983. Anorexia nervosa and bulimia nervosa. In *Handbook of psychiatry*, vol. 4, *The neuroses and personality disorders*, ed. G. F. M. Russell and L. A. Hersov, pp. 285–298. Cambridge: Cambridge University Press.

15. Steinhausen, H. C., and Glanville, K. 1982. Follow-up studies of anorexia nervosa: A review of research findings. *Psychological Medicine* 13:239–249.

16. Sturzenberger, S., et al. 1977. A follow-up study of adolescent psychiatric inpatients with anorexia nervosa. *Journal of the American Academy of Child Psychiatry* 16:703–715.

17. Swift, W. J. 1982. The long-term outcome of early onset anorexia nervosa: A critical review. *Journal of the American Academy of Child Psychiatry* 21:38–46.

18. Szmukler, G. I., Eisler, I., Russell, G. F. M., and Dare, C. 1984. Anorexia nervosa: Parental "expressed emotion" and dropping out of treatment. *British Journal of Psychiatry* 147:265–271.

19. Theander, S. 1970. Anorexia nervosa: A psychiatric investigation of 94 female patients. *Acta Psychiatrica Scandinavica* 214(Suppl.):1–194.

20. ———. 1983. Research on outcome and prognosis of anorexia nervosa and some results from a Swedish long-term study. *International Journal of Eating Disorders* 2:167–174.

21. Vandereycken, W., and Pierloot, R. 1983. Long-term outcome research in anorexia nervosa. *International Journal of Eating Disorders* 2:237–242.

22. Vaughn, C. E., and Leff, J. P. 1976. The measurement of expressed emotion in the families of psychiatric patients. *British Journal of Social and Clinical Psychology* 15: 157–165.

23. Warren, W. 1968. A study of anorexia nervosa in young girls. *Journal of Child Psychology and Psychiatry* 9:27–40.

16

Cognitive Therapy for Anorexia Nervosa

David M. Garner

Distorted attitudes about food, weight, and the body have been consistently recognized as characteristic of anorexia nervosa. Moreover, it has frequently been observed that maladaptive thinking in anorexia nervosa extends beyond food and weight to other areas of experience.[16,17] These observations as well as the clinical experience of our group in treating the disorder have led to cognitive-behavioral management principles aimed at the broad range of misconceptions that appear to maintain the syndrome.[43,44,50] These principles are derived from models described by Beck and his colleagues and by other cognitive theorists.* However, the form and content of cognitive therapy for anorexia nervosa have been adapted to meet the special needs of these patients. This chapter will present an overview of techniques that have been described in detail elsewhere.[43,44,50] The cognitive strategies proposed for anorexia nervosa are also applicable for nonemaciated patients with bulimia. Similar cognitive and behavioral methods have been recommended for both disorders.†

I am indebted to Kelly Bemis and Victoria Mitchell for their contributions to this chapter. I also would like to acknowledge continued support from Health and Welfare Canada, the Ontario Mental Health Foundation, and the Medical Research Council of Canada.

* See references 5, 6, 7, 30, 59, 81, and 86.

† See references 31, 34, 43, 44, 78, and 94.

The Cognitive Model

Anorexia nervosa has been conceptualized from a range of theoretical perspectives. Explanations have been offered that emphasize early development, faulty interactional patterns, fears of psychosexual maturity, specific personality traits, behavioral contingencies, biological determinants, and the social context.[42,47] Each may be relevant to a subset of patients. Thus anorexia nervosa is probably best understood as a final common pathway that may be entered through the interaction of various psychological, familial, and social predisposing factors.[42]

The cognitive approach to understanding anorexia nervosa emphasizes how the symptom pattern logically derives from the patient's faulty assumptions. The apparently bizarre eating patterns and the resolute refusal of adequate nourishment become plausible given the anorexic patient's conviction that thinness is essential for her* happiness or well-being. The surplus meaning that has become attached to thinness also provides a window into the patient's broader system of self-evaluation. One advantage of a cognitive approach to anorexia nervosa is that it is not incompatible with other models. Some of these formulations emphasize events that are remote in time from the expression of symptoms, while others concentrate on more proximal events. Recently a number of authors have accounted for the development and maintenance of anorexia nervosa by an analysis of functional relationships among antecedent events, positive reinforcers, and negative reinforcers.†

Speculation regarding pathogenesis presumes that behavior is maintained by its ability to reduce aversive consequences (i.e., a conditioned avoidance model). A number of theories explain the anorexic patient's behavior as an adaptive avoidance of real or perceived fears associated with separation, sexuality, and performance expectations. Crisp[26,27] has most fully developed this viewpoint of anorexia nervosa as a "weight phobia" whereby dieting becomes the mechanism by which threatening aspects of psychosexual maturity may be avoided or reversed. Avoidance behavior is resistant to extinction because it prevents the individual from recognizing when the aversive contingencies are no longer operating. However, the anorexic patient's behavior is motivated not simply by a fear of body weight and all that it might imply, but also by a "drive to be thinner."[15,17] The relentless dietary restraint is fueled by the gratification and sense of mastery it provides. The tangible success at weight loss or the hope of anticipated rewards provides pleasure and a sense of supreme accomplishment. This explains the patient's reluctance to part with certain symptoms. As Slade[104] indicated, these feelings are particularly potent when the individual experiences extreme dissatisfaction in other areas of

* The feminine pronoun is used throughout this chapter because most patients with anorexia nervosa are female.
† See references 9, 43, 44, 50, and 104.

her life. Noting that perfectionistic tendencies have also been associated with anorexia nervosa, Slade[104] postulates that the combination of perfectionism and general dissatisfaction are setting conditions for the disorder. They optimize the likelihood that the potential anorexic individual will turn to self-control in general and control over her body in particular as means of consolation. My associates and I also have emphasized how the anorexic patient's relentless dieting is maintained by *cognitive self-reinforcement* from the sense of mastery, virtue, and self-control that it provides.[43,44,50] An adolescent who is struggling with extreme feelings of ineffectiveness might embrace the idea that a thinner shape leads to a greater sense of adequacy. The message that thinness is an assured pathway to beauty, success, and social competence is a consistent theme transmitted through the fashion and dieting industries.[53,58,113,114]

Thus simultaneous positive and negative reinforcement may distinguish anorexia nervosa from the phobic or depressive disorders and may also account for its recalcitrance. What is important for the discussion here is that these contingencies may be covert or cognitive events that are often maintained by distorted beliefs and faulty reasoning.

While there are differences in theory, there are remarkable similarities in the clinical approaches based on experience. Cognitive therapy offers powerful strategies for modifying distorted beliefs associated with eating and body shape as well as a range of developmental, interpersonal, and self-attributional themes. On some level, most psychological theories focus on beliefs, meaning, misperceptions, and misattributions. As long as interventions are relevant to the patient's belief structure, the cognitive model may retain its conceptual integrity while borrowing from traditional formulations. The distinctions between cognitive therapy and other approaches are more philosophical and methodological than procedural. Drawing from other writers, Bemis and I[44] have delineated the five main features of cognitive therapy. These include:

1. Reliance on conscious and preconscious experience rather than unconscious motivation.
2. *Explicit* emphasis on meaning and cognitions as mediating variables accounting for maladaptive feelings or emotions.
3. Use of questioning as a major therapeutic device.
4. Active and directive involvement on the part of the therapist.
5. Methodological allegiance to behavioral and scientific psychology in which theory is shaped by empirical findings; this involves a commitment to specification of treatment methods and objective assessment of target behaviors.

Conventional cognitive therapy must be adapted to the specific needs of the anorexia nervosa patient; including (1) idiosyncratic beliefs related to food and weight, (2) the interaction between physical and psychological components of the disorder, (3) the patient's desire to retain certain focal symptoms, (4) the development of motivation for treatment with emphasis on the gradual evolution of a trusting therapeutic relationship, (5) the prominence of fundamental self-concept deficits related to self-esteem and trust in internal state, and (6) a longer duration of therapy than is typical for depression or anxiety disorders because of the time required to reverse the patient's deteriorated physical state and because of the nature of her focal symptoms.

Two-track Approach to Treatment

Throughout the course of therapy, my associates and I recommend that the therapist adhere to a conscious "two-track" approach to treatment.[48] The first track pertains to eating behavior and physical condition. The therapist must be aware of these at all times and plan specific cognitive and behavioral interventions aimed at their normalization. The second track involves the more complex task of assessing and modifying misconceptions reflected in self-concept deficiencies, perfectionism, separation or autonomy fears, and disturbed relationships. Often these issues are directly tied to beliefs about weight, but at other times they appear to be relatively independent. Since both tracks are characterized by reasoning errors, faulty beliefs, and distorted underlying assumptions, they may be addressed using cognitive therapy principles. An emphasis on the first track is required early in therapy since other contributing factors cannot be assessed until starvation symptoms and chaotic eating patterns are ameliorated. It is essential for the therapist to begin with a thorough understanding of methods for normalizing eating and weight. Starvation, severe dieting, or electrolyte disturbances resulting from vomiting and purgative abuse all may have a dramatic effect on mood, thinking, and personality.[42] The first step is to motivate the patient to gain weight and to discontinue dangerous weight-control practices.

Developing Motivation for Treatment

The circumstances surrounding the initiation of treatment and the manner in which the therapist deals with them are particularly important in anorexia nervosa. It is not uncommon for the patient to arrive for an initial consultation opposed or at least ambivalent to treatment. Agreeing to a consultation may have been a reluctant compromise under pressure from family or friends. The patient is poised to resist an assault on her "ego-syntonic" symptoms. Standard cognitive therapy has been developed for less reluctant depressed and anxious patients who voluntarily seek help. With anorexia nervosa, formal cognitive therapy methods must be introduced more gradually once the patient has begun to express a desire to change.

During the initial phase of therapy there must be a gradual evolution of trust and openness. Rather than focusing exclusively on weight, the goal is to understand the emotional distress that has led to weight loss. If distress is denied, the point should not be pressed and greater attention should be focused on describing the effects of starvation and conveying information about anorexia nervosa or bulimia. The format of the initial interview and other recommendations for eliciting motivation for therapy have been presented in detail elsewhere.[43,44,50]

The patient must be helped to recognize that her symptoms have disastrous long-term consequences even though they provide short-term gratification. For most patients anorexia nervosa is a misdirected attempt to achieve mastery and well-being. Patients become genuinely motivated for recovery once they recognize that the effort required to maintain the disorder and its emotional consequences virtually preclude sustaining interpersonal and vocational goals.

The sequence of events in psychotherapy is crucial. Most patients share the orthodox view that eating and weight-related symptoms will disappear naturally once the underlying unhappiness has been resolved. For reasons that will be explained later, this sequence of events rarely applies in anorexia nervosa because of the self-perpetuating nature of the syndrome.

Weight gain and "normal" eating elicit intense anxiety for the patient. Since therapy requires the patient to gradually discard her symptoms and actually feel worse as a result, motivation must be elicited repeatedly during the course of treatment. Stringent dieting, retaining a suboptimal weight, avoiding fattening foods, and vomiting must be repeatedly redefined as inconsistent with the ultimate goal of recovery. The therapist may help the patient redefine the short-term goal of therapy as amelioration of her starvation symptoms rather than simply weight gain. She must be encouraged to examine the long-term consequences of her behavior on a daily basis. A trusting therapeutic relationship is the key ingredient in the patient's willingness to exchange control over eating and weight for the promise of ultimate improvement.

THE THERAPEUTIC RELATIONSHIP

Various systems of psychotherapy have acknowledged the role of the therapeutic relationship in promoting change,[38,85] and cognitive therapy is no exception.[7,63,81] In adapting the cognitive approach to anorexia nervosa, several authors have maintained that a strong therapeutic alliance is a prerequisite for treatment.[43,44,50,63] As mentioned earlier, the quality of the relationship plays a vital role in motivation for recovery. Bemis and I[44] have emphasized that a trusting relationship is crucial in cognitive therapy since this approach places a premium on assessment of cognition, affect, and behavior through self-reported, introspective data. Moreover, the relationship provides a conduit for examining distortions and misperceptions that the patient applies to her interpersonal world. When the patient's reactions to the therapist are viewed within the context of other relationships, data are provided that may illuminate salient beliefs, assumptions, and attitudes.[44]

Normalization of Eating and Weight

The process of psychotherapy is influenced by weight because starvation exerts a profound effect on cognitive and emotional functioning. Although cognitive interventions will be described later, a number of practical concerns may be outlined here.

EDUCATIONAL MATERIAL

Educational material related to starvation, physical complications, the biology of weight regulation, consequences of dieting, nutrition, obesity, self-monitoring, and the social context of eating disorders has become an integral component of many programs.* Didactic instruction in therapy meetings may be supplemented by written material.[58] The material is helpful in enlisting motivation and complements the attitude change emphasized in cognitive therapy.

EFFECTS OF STARVATION

One important recent contribution to the understanding of anorexia nervosa has been the differentiation of the primary psychopathology of the disorder from the effects of starvation.† It is useful to provide some patients with selected chapters from the classic study of experimental semistarvation by Keys and associates[74] or a synopsis of this and other studies.[58] A summary of starvation symptoms is presented in Table 16.1. Patients usually do not attribute these symptoms to a common cause, and the description of the starvation state helps them to integrate their experiences.

---

* See references 34, 43, 44, 71, 77, 88, and 115.
† See references 4, 8, 17, 21, 22, 28, 42, 45, 80, 84, and 103.

TABLE 16.1

Effects of Starvation

Attitudes and Behavior Toward Food
Food preoccupations
Collection of recipes, cookbooks, and menus
Unusual eating habits
Increased consumption of coffee, tea, and spices
Binge eating

Emotional and Social Changes
Depression
Anxiety
Irritability, anger
Lability
"Psychotic" episodes
Personality changes on psychological tests
Social withdrawal

Cognitive Changes
Decreased concentration
Poor judgment
Apathy

Physical Changes
Sleep disturbances
Weakness
Gastrointestinal disturbances
Hyperacuity to noise and light
Edema
Hypothermia
Paresthesia
Decreased basal metabolic rate
Decreased sexual interest

SOURCE: A. Keys et al., *The biology of human starvation* (Minneapolis: University of Minnesota Press, 1950).

MINIMUM WEIGHT

Outpatient psychotherapy may proceed only if weight does not fall below a certain level[18,102] and if the patient is not in imminent danger due to other complications (e.g., hypokalemia, cardiac irregularities). There are no absolute rules regarding minimum weight since it depends on the patient's overall health. In general, the patient's weight should be monitored regularly by a physician if it drops precipitously or if it approaches 75 percent of premorbid weight.[50]

TARGET WEIGHT

The vast number of studies that illuminate the biological consequences of under- and overfeeding[58] may be used to convey to the patient the concept that body weight appears to be homeostatically regulated around a "set point."[91] Significant deviations from this weight result in physiological compensations designed to return the organism to a state of equilibrium. Although there is considerable controversy surrounding the set point construct, there is convincing evidence that it is a useful concept with sound empirical support.[73,90] (See also chapter 3.) Studies of body-weight regulation have clinical implications when determining an appropriate target weight for treatment. Although there has been a convention of setting a target weight of 90 to 100 percent of expected weight based on population norms, this practice does not take into account the likelihood that "healthy" body weights,[100] like other physical attributes, are distributed normally in the population.[58] (See also chapter 1.) Therefore, a realistic body weight must be consistent with the patient's weight history in order to reduce the biological pressure to gain weight. Based on clinical experience, my associates and I recommend a goal weight range of 3 to 5 pounds above the patient's menstrual weight threshold and as close as can be tolerated to about 10 percent below her highest weight prior to the onset of the disorder.[58] However, this is simply a guideline and may have to be accomplished very gradually or in stages; it may have to be modified based on the patient's capacity for change.

MONITORING WEIGHT

If the patient's weight is low or unstable, it should be monitored regularly. Presuming a trusting relationship, it is ideal for this to occur within the context of therapy. Just as it is inappropriate to ignore other acts of self-harm, it is not advisable to disregard weight loss. Weighings are not a punitive action and should convey a realistic concern about the patient's physical and psychological status.[43,44] Some patients prefer to be informed of their weight so that potential distress may be addressed in therapy; others who tend to become preoccupied with minute shifts in weight prefer to be "blind" to the weighings and informed only if there is a consistent trend up or down over several weeks.

MEAL PLANNING

Anorexic patients are invariably confused about what constitutes appropriate eating. Establishing precise guidelines for the quality, quantity, and spacing of meals is useful in helping patients tolerate guilt experienced when they deviate from symptomatic eating patterns.[58] Patients should be encouraged to eat "mechanically" according to predetermined plans.[44] Minimizing choice at mealtimes will assist the patient in resisting the urge to "choose" dietetic foods at every opportunity. In cases in which the patient is having difficulty maintaining an appropriate body weight, the therapist must focus on the details of daily food intake. Once cooperation and trust have been established, most patients are relieved to have assistance in planning their meals. Structured eating and monitoring of food intake through detailed records may be gradually replaced by more natural eating behavior.

INTRODUCTION OF AVOIDED FOODS

Small, predetermined amounts of "nonanorexic" foods (those foods that are currently avoided but were consumed prior to the onset of the eating disorder) should be gradually incorporated into the meal plan. This is the practice of most inpatient programs that emphasize the consumption of previously avoided foods in reasonable quantities.[27,100] This strategy should be complemented with cognitive methods (to be outlined later) that challenge the practice of dividing food into good (i.e., diet) and bad (i.e., nondiet) categories. Bulimic patients should be presented with the evidence that dieting or rigid avoidance of desired foods may create the cognitive and physiological conditions that increase the probability of binge eating.[58]

In summary, while dealing with eating and weight in therapy may seem like a mundane, "nonpsychological" task, it is vital for reasons beyond the obvious physical implications. The therapist's concern in these areas emphasizes the interdependence between mental and physical issues. Moreover, even the most resistant patients are willing to discuss the topic of food as part of an evaluation of their condition. The understanding shown by the therapist in this area often leads to trust with more sensitive topics. Weight gain and modifications in eating patterns should be presented as experiments that will provide the patient with data to evaluate various assumptions which determine her behavior. Resistance and fear of deviating from symptomatic behavior provide valuable opportunities to examine dysfunctional attitudes. Normalizing eating and weight through behavioral interventions is one of the primary vehicles for eliciting dysfunctional attitudes, which may then be exposed to cognitive interventions.

Medical Consultation and Hospitalization

Anorexia nervosa is a serious disorder with significant risks of mortality or morbidity. Awareness of the complications is a prerequisite for outpatient psychotherapy.[4,42,87] Patients who are at a low weight, lose weight precipitously, induce vomiting, or abuse purgatives or other medications should be monitored frequently by a physician.

Hospitalization may be required for renourishment, to control binging and vomiting, to assess or treat various physical complications, or to disengage the patient from an interpersonal system that is maintaining the disorder.[42] When hospitalization is required for renourishment, care must be taken to enlist the patient's cooperation, otherwise the process of weight gain may inflict psychological damage.[19] The patient's collaboration in the treatment process may be enhanced by explaining the details of the inpatient protocol and giving her the opportunity to meet with the ward staff.[27,42]

Assessment of Beliefs

Functional analysis has been recommended for exploring the thinking patterns in anorexia nervosa[67,104] and in bulimia.[41,94] This methodology not only offers explanations of symptom development or maintenance in individual cases but also provides meaningful data for theory development. Studies with the repertory technique have documented the anorexic patient's tendency to construe herself in terms of body weight.[10,20,39,40] Button[20] reported marked individual differences between anorexic patients' assessment of the meaningfulness of "self" in terms of the "thin-fat" construct. Moreover, patients whose evaluation of self went beyond the concept of weight had a positive treatment outcome.

Various standardized self-report measures have been proposed to assess eating patterns or symptoms of anorexia nervosa and bulimia.[56,66] Although these instruments are useful for measuring thoughts or behaviors related to food, eating, and the body, they are limited by the narrow range of cognitive material that they assess. The Eating Disorder Inventory (EDI) is a somewhat broader, standardized, self-report instrument that measures eight cognitive-behavioral dimensions relevant to anorexia nervosa and bulimia.[49,54,55] Table 16.2 presents the EDI subscales and illustrates sample items. Recent studies with the EDI indicate that distorted attitudes related to self-concept may best distinguish the clinical syndrome of anorexia nervosa and subgroups of weight-preoccupied women.[57,93]

Reasoning Errors

Based on Beck's[6] taxonomy of logical errors in the thinking of depressed and phobic patients, my associates and I have described faulty thinking patterns that occur in anorexia nervosa.[43,50] The more common reasoning errors to be discussed include dichotomous reasoning, personalization and self-reference, superstitious thinking, magnification, selective ab-

TABLE 16.2

Eating Disorder Inventory Subscales and Sample Items

Drive for Thinness
   "I am preoccupied with the desire to be thinner."
   "I am terrified of gaining weight."

Bulimia
   "I stuff myself with food."
   "I have gone on eating binges where I have felt that I could not stop."

Body Dissatisfaction
   "I think that my stomach is too big."
   "I think that my thighs are too large."

Ineffectiveness
   "I feel ineffective as a person."
   "I have a low opinion of myself."

Perfectionism
   "I hate being less than best at things."
   "I have extremely high goals."

Interpersonal Distrust
   "I am open about my feelings."[a]
   "I have close relationships."[a]

Interoceptive Awareness
   "I get confused about what emotion I am feeling."
   "I have feelings I can't quite identify."

Maturity Fears
   "I wish that I could be younger."
   "I wish that I could return to the security of childhood."

---

[a] Indicates negatively keyed item.

straction, overgeneralization, faulty underlying assumptions, and self-concept deficits. The order of presentation does not reflect their relative prominence or sequence of appearance in psychotherapy.

DICHOTOMOUS REASONING

Dichotomous reasoning involves thinking in extreme, absolute, or all-or-none terms and is typically applied to food, eating, and weight. The patient divides foods into good ("calorie sparing") and bad ("fattening") categories. A one-pound weight gain may be equated with incipient obesity. Breaking a rigid eating routine produces panic because it means a *complete* loss of control. Rigid attitudes and behaviors are not restricted to food and weight but extend to the pursuit of sports, careers, and school. It is most evident in the area of self-evaluation. Patients evaluate themselves harshly and in extreme terms but view others realistically. The anorexic individual often believes that such personal attributes as self-control, independence, self-confidence, and social ability must be completely and continually maintained. This leads to idealized and unattainable notions of happiness, contentment, and success.[50]

PERSONALIZATION AND SELF-REFERENCE

Personalization and self-reference involve the egocentric interpretations of impersonal events or the overinterpretation of events relating to the self. The anorexic patient frequently seems convinced that strangers or casual friends would notice if she gained a pound or ate a forbidden food. This style of thinking extends to other interpersonal situations in which the patient is unusually sensitive to disapproval from others. Given the enmeshed and overprotective family environment of many patients, it is understandable how this thinking style could develop.

SUPERSTITIOUS THINKING

The error of superstitious reasoning reflects belief in cause-effect relationships of noncontingent events. It often involves magical thinking, which is applied in the maintenance of eating or exercise rituals. Eating a small amount of a "forbidden food" may precipitate taking laxatives despite the knowledge that they do not result in malabsorption. Extreme anxiety is often experienced following a minute deviation from exercise rituals because of the belief that some vague punishment will accrue. This is often unrelated to the calorie-burning effect of exercise since patients will display great reluctance to perform even one less of a particular calisthenic after a standard has been set.[50]

MAGNIFICATION

Magnification involves overestimation of the significance of undesirable consequent events. For the anorexic patient, the significance of small increases in weight are reliably overinterpreted. Moreover, momentary lapses in willpower are viewed as a precedent for consistent poor self-discipline. In a manner similar to that observed in depressed patients, anorexic patients magnify poor performances and minimize accomplishments in their self-evaluation.

SELECTIVE ABSTRACTION

The error of selective abstraction in thinking is characterized by focusing on isolated details while ignoring contradictory or more salient evidence. This style of thinking is illustrated by the belief that thinness is the sole frame of reference for inferring self-worth. It is also represented by the reciprocal belief that fatness is a clear indication of incompetence. These beliefs persist in defiance of examples to the contrary.

OVERGENERALIZATION

Overgeneralization involves extracting a rule on the basis of one event and applying it to dissimilar situations. Overgeneralization is evident in the inferences drawn about thinness. For example, a patient may conclude that weight loss would be the secret to competence because someone she knows who is competent is also thin. She may assume that because she was unhappy at a normal weight, weight gain will produce unhappiness. Overgeneralization is also evident in self-evaluations. A patient may infer that if she fails in one area, she is an abject failure as a person. Similarly, rejection by one person is viewed as a sign of social incompetence.

UNDERLYING ASSUMPTIONS

Beck and associates[7] have described underlying or silent assumptions that determine much of the depressed person's disturbed thinking. These may be distinguished from simple faulty beliefs in that underlying assumptions may not be readily identified or verbalized by the patient. The ideas that "shape is a valid frame of reference for inferring self-worth" and that "family members are infallible" are underlying assumptions typical of anorexia nervosa patients. These assumptions are often central to the anorexic patient's personal identity. Directly challenging them is usually not advisable since this may be interpreted as a personal attack and may elicit despair or rage, which could seriously damage the therapeutic relationship.[43] A particular class of underlying assumptions is relevant to self-concept deficits common in anorexia nervosa and bulimia.

SELF-CONCEPT DEFICITS

A detailed presentation of the cognitive basis for self-concept deficits in anorexia nervosa is beyond the focus of this chapter and has been elaborated elsewhere.[44,50,63] In earlier reports Bemis and I have distinguished two components of self-concept: *self-esteem* and *self-awareness*. Whereas self-esteem relates to attribution of one's own value or worth, self-awareness is defined as the ability to identify and accurately respond to inner experiences.[44] Deficits in self-esteem and self-awareness have formed the cornerstone of the etiological speculations of many prominent theorists.* Modification of the cognitive aspects of "self-concept" is a complex task that must be distinguished from changing simple beliefs and attitudes. Although some cognitive theorists may be reluctant to consider such global aspects of "personality" as amenable to cognitive restructuring because they seem so far removed from traditional behaviorism, there is a growing interest in applying cognitive methods to more complex problems.[63,81,82]

* See references 3, 16, 17, 21, 26, 27, 60, 80, 100, 102, and 104.

One guideline for improving self-esteem involves challenging the anorexic patient's tendency to construe her self-worth by idealized standards or by comparisons with others.[44] In therapy, more emphasis is placed upon self-validation through the pursuit of self-defined goals and the experience of pleasure rather than exclusive reliance upon external performance standards. This is an idea that is completely foreign to most patients. They are exceptionally "outcome-oriented" and rarely experience pleasure from the process of engaging in an activity. Many are terrified or feel guilty at the prospect of hedonic experience. This is often concealed by a supercilious facade of disinterest but almost invariably reflects a genuine incapacity. An essential aspect of psychotherapy is the gradual modification of the cognitive appraisal systems and underlying assumptions related to self-esteem.[44]

The deficits in self-awareness have been best captured by Bruch,[16] who has provided valuable clinical examples of patients' sense of "not knowing how they feel" (p. 338). This inner confusion is often related to distorted beliefs *about* feelings or bodily sensations.[44] They may relate to physiological needs or emotional states and represent a conflict between the inner experience and the *belief* about its *appropriateness, acceptability, justification,* or *legitimacy.* The principles for facilitating self-awareness are similar to those for improving self-esteem and may be broken down into interrelated steps as follows:

1. Identification of emotions, sensations, and thoughts.
2. Identification of distorted attitudes *about* these experiences.
3. Gradual correction of these erroneous convictions by cognitive methods that will be outlined later.
4. Practice in responding to previously avoided experiences.
5. Reinforcement of the patient's independent expression of previously avoided emotions, sensations, and thoughts.

The anorexic patient's misperceptions, faulty reasoning, and erroneous beliefs about her body must be identified and labeled without undermining her confidence that she can think for herself. Thus the treatment must proceed very gradually in correcting distortions and confirming authentic expressions of inner state, according to the methods outlined elsewhere.[44,50,63]

Basic Cognitive Techniques

In this section specific interventions will be described that have been derived from Beck and other cognitive theorists but adapted to anorexia nervosa.[43,44,50] The order of presentation does not reflect a particular sequence of application since cognitive methods may be interwoven and applied as errors in thinking emerge in therapy.

ARTICULATION OF BELIEFS

The mere articulation of beliefs may lead to belief change. One anorexic patient reported that hearing herself repeatedly verbalize her negative stereotype of obesity was an important factor in belief change because it was inconsistent with her attitudes toward other minority groups.

OPERATIONALIZING BELIEFS

The precise definition of an idiosyncratic construct may lead to more realistic thinking. A patient's observation that she reflexively defines favorable attributes such as achievement, fulfillment, popularity, and competence in terms of weight status may lead to questioning the validity of these inferences.

DECENTERING

Evaluating a belief from a different perspective may foster more realistic attitudes. Despite "feeling fat," patients often evaluate others of a similar weight as "too thin." This recognition combined with other convergent observations over many months may lead to the gradual erosion of unrealistic beliefs about weight. Through other examples of decentering, patients can appreciate that their own standards are far more stringent and unforgiving than those they apply to others. The use of analogies and similes is another means of correcting this distorted frame of reference. For example, a patient who feared weight gain because it meant losing her "identity as an anorexic" found it helpful to think of relinquishing her disorder as analogous to surrendering a treasure of counterfeit money.

DECATASTROPHIZING

Originally proposed by Ellis,[30] the technique of decatastrophizing may be used to challenge anxiety resulting from the arbitrary definition of negative consequences as intolerable despite evidence to the contrary.

For example, the implicit assumption that performing one less sit-up would have disastrous consequences may be explored by the question "What would be the worst thing that could really happen?"

CHALLENGING THE "SHOULDS"

The extreme thinking indicated by dichotomous reasoning, magnification, and overgeneralization is often reflected by the "moralistic" use of the words *should, must,* or *ought*.[6,30,68] Many of the anorexic patient's internal imperatives about food, weight, and performance are framed by these words,[44] and detailed analysis usually reveals the errors in reasoning.

CHALLENGING BELIEFS THROUGH BEHAVIORAL EXERCISES

The interdependence between cognitive and behavioral change is so fundamental that it is somewhat misleading to consider them separately. Particularly in the areas of food and weight, behavior change is an important vehicle for modifying both attitudes and emotions. As it is fruitless to expect the elevator phobic to make progress by simply talking in the therapist's office, it is unrealistic to assume that food and weight fears can be overcome without approaching these "phobic objects." Interweaving specific graded behavioral exercises with cognitive methods is a fundamental part of anorexia nervosa therapy.

PROSPECTIVE HYPOTHESIS TESTING

The technique of prospective hypothesis testing is particularly well suited for use with behavioral exercises since it involves generating specific predictors that may be tested through behavioral experiments. For example, a patient may assume that reduced exercise will have a major impact on weight. The consequences of a moratorium on exercise may be evaluated objectively and can be used to disconfirm the fear. If a client is self-conscious about eating a dessert because she assumes others will view her as gluttonous, she might conduct an informal poll to determine people's attitudes about dessert. However, if experiments involve obtaining feedback from others, the patient must be prepared to interpret negative results in a nondestructive manner.[43]

REATTRIBUTION TECHNIQUES

Patients with anorexia nervosa often misperceive amounts of food eaten, hunger versus satiety, and their body size. They then make self-defeating decisions based on their erroneous judgments. Rather than directly modifying these refractory misperceptions, my associates and I recommend altering *interpretations* of these experiences.[43,44,46,50] Since misperceptions in these areas characterize anorexia nervosa, it is helpful to attribute them to the disorder and emphasize that subjective experience is unreliable. This approach is opposite the general therapeutic goal of promoting trust in the validity and reliability of internal experiences; however, we have found that patients are so confused about body shape and eating that perceptions in these areas must be temporarily replaced by "non-self-defeating" rules for conduct.

PALLIATIVE TECHNIQUES

When reasoning ability is impaired because of intense anxiety, patients may be taught the palliative techniques of "distraction" or "parroting" to suppress or override the urge to engage in destructive behavior.[44] Both methods involve "changing the cognitive channel" rather than challenging beliefs with more sophisticated cognitive techniques. For example, patients who are overwhelmed by the urge to vomit after eating may interrupt the process by rehearsing prearranged "coping phrases" such as "I need to have the food stay down to encourage the gradual return of normal satiety feelings." Going for a walk or talking to someone on the telephone immediately after eating may provide potent enough distraction to allay the urge to vomit. These techniques presuppose the patient's commitment to the goals of therapy.[44]

CHALLENGING CULTURAL VALUES REGARDING SHAPE

In the past several decades, women have been victims of a tragic set of standards for thinness, which have placed them under intense pressure to diet. These and other cultural changes affecting women may be responsible for the dramatic increases in anorexia nervosa and bulimia.[53] Recent popular books[11,23] and research studies[58] may be recommended to assist patients in challenging social norms that encourage dieting in pursuit of a progressively more unrealistic standard of physical attractiveness.

Some more recent patients are more entrenched in their disorder in response to a favorable social connotation that anorexia nervosa has acquired. Anorexia nervosa has been glamorized by the media through its association with positive attributes such as upper-class affiliation, intelligence, perfectionism, self-discipline, and fitness. It has been the topic of popular novels, television dramas, and accounts of heroic battles waged against it by media personalities. Bruch[19] referred to a new generation of "me-too" cases resulting from social contagion. In these cases, cognitive therapy must encourage the patient to reattribute the disorder to failure rather than success and focus on the self-concept deficits that have led to the patient's identification with the illness.

The actual process of cognitive therapy closely conforms to that outlined by Beck and his colleagues.[6] Although the process is not simple or linear, it may be summarized by the following steps:

1. Teach the patient to monitor her thinking or heighten awareness of thinking. This involves extracting the essential or core aspects of dysfunctional beliefs. Beliefs must be articulated, clarified, and operationalized in order to determine their consequences.
2. Help the patient to recognize the connection between certain dysfunctional thoughts and maladaptive behaviors and emotions.
3. Examine with the patient the evidence for the validity of particular beliefs. The implications of certain attitudes or assumptions should be followed to their logical conclusion.
4. Teach the patient to gradually substitute more realistic interpretations based on the evidence.
5. Ultimately modify underlying assumptions that are fundamental determinants of dysfunctional beliefs.

Bulimia

There is growing recognition that bulimia occurs in patients who present at a normal weight,[25,64,96] with obesity,[29,61] and with anorexia nervosa.[42] There are several important theoretical and practical reasons for including a discussion of bulimia in a chapter on anorexia nervosa. First, since many anorexia nervosa patients also display bulimia, a brief outline of the management of binging and purging is warranted. Moreover, the same patients may move between the syndromes of anorexia nervosa and bulimia at different times.[109] Second, these syndromes are closely related theoretically, and the trend toward considering them separate disorders may be misleading. Although normal-weight bulimic patients may be clearly distinguished from patients with the bulimic subtype of anorexia nervosa,[1,75] the distinction between syndromes has been overstated; several recent studies have found that both groups present with similar clinical and psychometric features.[36,51,52,92] Bulimic patients report attitudes toward food, weight, and body shape similar to those in restricting anorexia nervosa. These parallel thinking patterns suggest that cognitive principles recommended for anorexia nervosa also may be applied to bulimic patients who are not emaciated.[33,44] To these must be added specific strategies aimed at controlling binging, vomiting, and purgative abuse.

Factors that cause and maintain bulimia are not uniform across individuals. Although many exhibit core personality disturbances found in anorexia nervosa, some appear free of primary psychopathology.* Russell[100] originally conceptualized bulimia as a self-perpetuating cycle involving both psychological and physiological mechanisms. Because these mechanisms have had direct implications for treatment, an adapted and abbreviated version of his model will be reviewed. First, shape dissatis-

* See references 32, 33, 36, 51, 52, 75, and 92.

faction, usually (but not necessarily) accompanied by low self-esteem and in some cases by more severe personality disturbances, leads to an organized system of beliefs aimed at strict dieting and weight loss. Second, weight loss and a sustained "suboptimal" weight produce physiological changes reflected by increased hunger, food preoccupations, and bouts of overeating, all of which are designed to return the organism to a "healthy weight"[100] or a constitutionally determined "set point" for body weight.[91] Third, cognitive and/or emotional factors determine whether binge eating will be "triggered" or prevented. For example, the slightest transgression from rigidly prescribed dieting leads the patient to conclude that she might as well give in to the urge to eat since perfect self-control has been "blown."* Emotional distress may interfere with the cognitive self-control required to sustain dieting in the presence of intense hunger. Alternatively, binging and vomiting may provide relief from unpleasant feelings.[70,106] Fourth, the reliance on vomiting perpetuates the disorder through several interacting processes. For one thing, it intensifies hunger by keeping weight at a reduced level.[100] It also allows the starving individual to surrender to her voracious appetite while mitigating aversive consequences such as fear of weight gain, guilt about consuming forbidden food, and acute gastric discomfort.[50,99] Occasionally, vomiting may be maintained by positive contingencies such as attention from family members or pleasurable sensations of eating.[50,105] These four interacting mechanisms are not the only factors contributing to this heterogeneous syndrome;[14,69,97] however, they form the basis for cognitive and behavioral recommendations in its management.

A number of cognitive-behavioral approaches have been advocated to break the cycle of binging and purging. Some multifaceted programs combine cognitive-behavioral principles with other methods designed to address a range of problem areas. Others with more limited scope focus only on the target symptoms of binging and vomiting. Many techniques are derived from cognitive and behavioral programs for obesity.[37,83,108] Most cognitive strategies are consistent with longstanding inpatient treatment programs for anorexia nervosa and bulimia, which encourage patients to consume previously avoided foods in reasonable quantities.[27,100,101] Similarly, the structure and support of the hospital have been used to help patients refrain from vomiting after meals.[2,27,80,107] Similar recommendations have been made by many cognitively oriented authors. Most of these have been described earlier and may be summarized as follows.

1. *Gradual exposure and attitude change to "forbidden" foods.*†
2. *Challenging dysfunctional attitudes related to body shape.*‡
3. *Information and education.*§

* See references 34, 50, 83, 94, and 95.
† See references 31, 34, 43, 44, 50, 58, 65, 78, 79, 88, 94, 98, 99, 111, 113, and 115.
‡ See references 31, 34, 43, 44, 65, 77, 78, 79, 94, and 115.
§ See references 34, 58, 78, 88, 94, and 115.

4. *Self-control.*[31,34,62,112]
5. *Self-monitoring.* Monitoring of food intake, episodes of binging and vom-
    iting, emotions, or thoughts have been used as measures of change as well
    as means of identifying factors that trigger symptomatic behavior. Data
    from self-monitoring may be used in the functional analysis of the binging
    and purging sequence.[41] Although emotional and situational factors trigger
    binge-eating, this must be understood within the context of dieting or
    weight suppression. Bulimia is an unlikely pattern among highly stressed,
    anxious, or depressed individuals who have not been dieting.
6. *Stimulus control.* Avoiding foods or situations that trigger binging or vom-
    iting has been advocated.[34,78,94,112] Patients are encouraged to engage in
    activities that are incompatible with symptomatic behavior. Cognitive
    stimulus-control strategies such as thought stopping, delay, and distraction
    also may be effective.*
7. *Developing or strengthening social skills.* Several broad-spectrum cognitive
    approaches emphasize the need to become more assertive, independent,
    and effective socially. Training in interpersonal problem solving has been
    proposed in some instances.†

Several writers suggest that bulimic patients' motivation to receive
treatment may be contrasted with the resistance and denial of anorexia
nervosa.[33,35,75] However, the bulimic patient's motivation may quickly
fade with the recognition that treatment must go beyond control of binging and vomiting. Bulimic patients are often as intransigent as their restricting anorexic counterparts in relinquishing "ego-syntonic" symptoms
such as dieting and, in many cases, the steadfast pursuit of a suboptimal
weight.[100] Some patients are so committed to maintaining a suboptimal
body weight that they would rather continue to struggle with bulimia,
vomiting, and all of their pernicious consequences than to gain weight.
Although not articulated, some bulimic patients essentially request to be
converted to what could be characterized as the restricting subtype of
anorexia nervosa (i.e., submenstrual weight and rigidly controlled eating).
Fairburn and Cooper[35] found that a majority of their bulimic sample
actually *prefer* a weight consistent with a diagnosis of anorexia nervosa.
Those who prefer a somewhat higher weight may be no more realistic
since many bulimic patients have a history of obesity[51,76] and may have
begun their dieting at a higher than average "set point" for body weight.[91]
Therefore, the goals of treatment must not be defined exclusively in terms
of self-control over binging and vomiting without emphasizing the likelihood that abnormal cravings for food will persist as long as the patient
remains at a suboptimal weight.[100] Certain therapeutic programs that focus
on exercise, self-control, and weight control[72] may inadvertently collude
with the bulimic patient's desire to assume an inappropriate body weight
through unrealistic dieting. If Nisbett's[91] argument is correct and the
probability of binge eating increases with weight loss, then many "normal-

---

* See references 34, 44, 62, 77, 79, 88, and 94.
† See references 34, 50, 65, 76, 77, 78, 79, 88, 94, and 115.

weight" bulimic patients should be offered therapeutic support for the decision to accept their "healthy weight," which may be statistically above average.

COURSE AND DURATION OF TREATMENT

Fairburn's[31,33] approach tends to be time-limited, lasting between four and six months with a different focus in each of the three stages. However, Fairburn[33] does indicate that the duration must be tailored to individual patients. There is remarkable variability in the course and duration of treatment across patients with bulimia, which makes it difficult or even misleading to specify uniform stages to the treatment process. For some patients, treatment is straightforward and limited to "track-one" issues outlined earlier. Control of binging and vomiting is achieved with behavioral methods that interrupt dieting. The educational aspects of treatment are effective in discouraging vomiting and purgative abuse. The cognitive component is to modify unrealistic attitudes about shape and to challenge cultural values that have led to dieting. For these patients, treatment may be brief and highly successful. For others, many with a history of anorexia nervosa, multiple treatment failures, and extremely chaotic eating patterns, their disorder may be complicated by profound psychosocial disturbances. Norman and Herzog[92] have reported on a sample of bulimic patients who demonstrate a greater level of persistent social maladjustment than normal, alcoholic, and schizophrenic women. These patients may require brief hospitalization, and the course of cognitive therapy is variable. Track-one principles may have to be applied over many months or reinstituted when eating patterns deteriorate. Cognitive therapy must focus not only on intransigent assumptions related to eating and shape but also on self-concept deficits, depressive thinking, poor impulse control, and pervasive interpersonal fears. Although brief therapy should be the aim, some patients require cognitive therapy of longer duration.

Thus differences in patient populations may be a major factor accounting for conflicting opinions about treatment course and duration. As Long and Cordle[77] have observed, optimistic reports have been largely based on college samples, where severe psychological disturbance may be less typical.* Some programs only admit patients who agree to comply with the treatment protocol,[75] which includes abstinence from vomiting.[88] Less auspicious reports come from some centers that treat anorexia nervosa.[27,80,100] With the increased media coverage over the last several years, it has become apparent that a larger proportion of patients referred to our treatment center are self-referrals rather than professional referrals with multiple treatment failures.

Despite these cautions, we share the opinions of others who view attitude change as a prerequisite for complete recovery for most patients

* See references 12, 24, 76, 89, and 98.

with anorexia nervosa and who consider cognitive-behavioral treatment as a valuable method for achieving this end. The effectiveness of cognitive-behavioral treatment has been supported by several case reports[62,76,77] and by an uncontrolled trial with a small number of cases.[31] These preliminary reports are encouraging and must be followed by more systematic evaluation of the active components in treatment, predictors of outcome, and durability of change.

Summary

This chapter presents a cognitive approach to anorexia nervosa that emphasizes the derivation of the symptom pattern from faulty thinking and dysfunctional beliefs. A cognitive-behavioral therapy is proposed that relies heavily on Beck's model but is adapted to meet the special needs of the anorexia nervosa patient. Specific recommendations are made for developing motivation for treatment, fostering a sound therapeutic relationship, normalizing eating, monitoring weight, and seeking medical consultation. A key ingredient is an awareness of the relationship between the physical and psychological aspects of the disorder. Common reasoning errors are presented and specific cognitive-behavioral methods are described with examples. Because of the close overlap between the syndromes of anorexia nervosa and bulimia, principles are proposed for dealing with binge eating. The conclusion reached is that attitude change is an important element in recovery and that cognitive-behavioral therapy has promise as a valuable treatment strategy for anorexia nervosa.

REFERENCES

1. American Psychiatric Association. 1980. *Diagnostic and statistical manual of mental disorders,* 3rd ed. Washington, D.C.: American Psychiatric Association.

2. Andersen, A. E. 1979. Anorexia nervosa: Diagnosis and treatment. *Weekly Psychiatric Update Series* 3:1–8.

3. ———. 1983. Anorexia nervosa and bulimia: A spectrum of eating disorders. *Journal of Adolescent Health Care* 4:15–21.

4. ———. 1984. Anorexia nervosa and bulimia: Biological and sociocultural aspects. In *Nutrition and behavior,* ed. J. R. Galler, pp. 305–338. New York: Plenum Press.

5. Beck, A. T. 1970. Role of fantasies in psychotherapy and psychopathology. *Journal of Nervous and Mental Disease* 150:3–17.

6. ———. 1976. *Cognitive therapy and the emotional disorders.* New York: International Universities Press.

7. Beck, A. T., Rush, A. J., Shaw, B. F., and Emery, G. 1979. *Cognitive therapy of depression: A treatment manual.* New York: Guilford Press.

8. Bemis, K. M. 1978. Current approaches to the etiology and treatment of anorexia nervosa. *Psychological Bulletin* 85:593–617.

9. ————. 1983. A comparison of functional relationships in anorexia nervosa and phobia. In *Anorexia nervosa: Recent developments,* ed. P. L. Darby, P. E. Garfinkel, D. M. Garner, and D. V. Coscina, pp. 403–416. New York: Alan R. Liss.

10. Ben-Tovim, D. I., Hunter, M., and Crisp, A. H. 1977. Discrimination and evaluation of shape and size in anorexia nervosa: An exploratory study. *Research Communications in Psychology, Psychiatry and Behavior* 2:241–257.

11. Bennett, W. B., and Gurin, J. 1982. *The dieter's dilemma: Eating less and weighing more.* New York: Basic Books.

12. Boskind-Lodahl, M., and White, W. C. 1978. The definition and treatment of bulimarexia in college women—a pilot study. *Journal of the American College Health Association* 2:27.

13. Boskind-White, M., and White, W. C. 1973. *Bulimarexia: The binge / purge cycle.* New York: Basic Books.

14. Brotman, A. W., Herzog, D. B., and Woods, S. W. 1984. Antidepressant treatment of bulimia: The relationship between binging and depressive symptomatology. *Journal of Clinical Psychiatry* 45:10–13.

15. Bruch, H. 1962. Perceptual and conceptual disturbances in anorexia nervosa. *Psychosomatic Medicine* 24:187–194.

16. ————. 1973. *Eating disorders: Obesity, anorexia nervosa, and the person within.* New York: Basic Books.

17. ————. *The golden cage: The enigma of anorexia nervosa.* Cambridge, Mass.: Harvard University Press.

18. ————. 1980. Anorexia nervosa: Therapy and theory. *American Journal of Psychiatry* 139:1531–1538.

19. ————. 1985. Four decades of eating disorders. In *Handbook of psychotherapy for anorexia nervosa and bulimia,* ed. D. M. Garner and P. E. Garfinkel, pp. 7–18. New York: Guilford Press.

20. Button, E. J. 1983. Construing the anorexic. In *Applications of personal construct theory,* ed. J. Adam-Webber and J. Marcuso, pp. 305–329. Toronto: Academic Press.

21. Casper, R. C. 1982. Treatment principles in anorexia nervosa. *Adolescent Psychiatry* 10:86–100.

22. Casper, R. C., and Davis, J. M. 1977. On the course of anorexia nervosa. *American Journal of Psychiatry* 134:974–978.

23. Chernin, K. 1981. *The obsession: Reflections on the tyranny of slenderness.* New York: Harper & Row.

24. Coffman, D. A. 1984. A clinically derived treatment model for the binge-purge syndrome. In *Binge-eating: Theory, Research and Treatment,* ed. R. C. Hawkins, W. Fremouw, and P. F. Clement, pp. 211–224. New York: Springer.

25. Cooper, P. J., and Fairburn, C. G. 1983. Binge-eating and self-induced vomiting in the community: A preliminary study. *British Journal of Psychiatry* 142:139–144.

26. Crisp, A. H. 1965. Clinical and therapeutic aspects of anorexia nervosa: A study of 30 cases. *Journal of Psychosomatic Research* 9:67–78.

27. ————. 1980. *Anorexia nervosa: Let me be.* London: Academic Press.

28. Dally, P. J. 1979. *Anorexia nervosa.* London: Heinemann.

29. Edelman, B. 1981. Binge eating in normal weight and overweight individuals. *Psychological Reports* 49:739–746.

30. Ellis, A. 1962. *Reason and emotion in psychotherapy.* Secaucus, N.J.: Lyle Stuart.

31. Fairburn, C. G. 1981. A cognitive-behavioral approach to the management of bulimia. *Psychological Medicine* 141:631–633.

32. ————. 1982. *Binge-eating and bulimia nervosa.* London: Smith, Kline & French Publications.

33. ————. 1983. The place of a cognitive-behavioral approach in the management of bulimia. In *Anorexia nervosa: Recent developments,* ed. P. L. Darby, P. E. Garfinkel, D. M. Garner, and D. V. Coscina, pp. 393–402. New York: Alan R. Liss.

34. ————. 1985. Cognitive-behavioral treatment for bulimia. In *Handbook of psychotherapy for anorexia nervosa and bulimia,* ed. D. M. Garner and P. E. Garfinkel, pp. 160–192. New York: Guilford Press.

35. Fairburn, C. G., and Cooper, P. J. 1982. Self-induced vomiting and bulimia nervosa: An undetected problem. *British Medical Journal* 284:1153–1155.

36. ———. 1984. The clinical features of bulimia nervosa. *British Journal of Psychiatry* 144:238–246.

37. Ferguson, J. F. 1975. *Learning to eat: Behavior modification for weight control.* Palo Alto, Calif.: Bull Publishing.

38. Frank, J. D. 1973. *Persuasion and healing.* Baltimore: Johns Hopkins University Press.

39. Fransella, F., and Button, E. J. 1983. The "construing" of self and body size in relation to maintenance of weight gain in anorexia nervosa. In *Anorexia nervosa: Recent developments,* ed. P. L. Darby, P. E. Garfinkel, D. M. Garner, and D. V. Coscina, pp. 107–116. New York: Alan R. Liss.

40. Fransella, F., and Crisp, A. H. 1979. Comparisons of weight concepts in groups of neurotic, normal and anorexic females. *British Journal of Psychiatry* 134:79–86.

41. Fremouw, W. J., and Heyneman, N. E. 1984. A functional analysis of binge episodes. In *Binge-eating: Theory, research and treatment,* ed. R. C. Hawkins, W. J. Fremouw, and P. F. Clement, pp. 254–263. New York: Springer.

42. Garfinkel, P. E., and Garner, D. M. 1982. *Anorexia nervosa: A multidimensional perspective.* New York: Brunner/Mazel.

43. Garner, D. M., and Bemis, K. M. 1982. A cognitive-behavioral approach to anorexia nervosa. *Cognitive Therapy and Research* 6:123–150.

44. ———. 1985. Cognitive therapy for anorexia nervosa. In *Handbook of psychotherapy for anorexia nervosa and bulimia,* ed. D. M. Garner and P. E. Garfinkel, pp. 107–146. New York: Guilford Press.

45. Garner, D. M., and Garfinkel, P. E. 1980. Socio-cultural factors in the development of anorexia nervosa. *Psychological Medicine* 10:649–656.

46. ———. 1981. Body image in anorexia nervosa: Measurement, theory and clinical implications. *International Journal of Psychiatric Medicine* 11:263–284.

47. ———. 1985. *Handbook of psychotherapy for anorexia nervosa and bulimia.* New York: Guilford Press.

48. Garner, D. M., and Isaacs, P. 1985. The psychology of anorexia nervosa and bulimia. In *Psychiatric update,* vol. 4, ed. R. E. Hales and A. J. Francis, pp. 503–515. Washington, D.C.: American Psychiatric Press.

49. Garner, D. M., and Olmsted, M. P. 1984. *The eating disorder inventory manual.* Odessa, Fla.: Psychological Assessment Resources.

50. Garner, D. M., Garfinkel, P. E., and Bemis, K. M. 1982. A multidimensional psychotherapy for anorexia nervosa. *International Journal of Eating Disorders* 1:3–46.

51. Garner, D. M., Garfinkel, P. E., and O'Shaughnessy, M. 1983. Clinical and psychometric comparisons between bulimia in anorexia nervosa and bulimia in normal-weight women. In *Understanding anorexia nervosa and bulimia: Report of the fourth Ross Conference on Medical Research,* pp. 6–13. Columbus, Ohio: Ross Laboratories.

52. ———. 1985. The validity of the distinction between bulimia with and without anorexia nervosa. *American Journal of Psychiatry* 142:581–587.

53. Garner, D. M., Garfinkel, P. E., and Olmsted, M. P. 1983. An overview of the socio-cultural factors in the development of anorexia nervosa. In *Anorexia nervosa: Recent developments,* ed. P. L. Darby, P. E. Garfinkel, D. M. Garner, and D. V. Coscina, pp. 65–82. New York: Alan R. Liss.

54. Garner, D. M., Olmsted, M. P., and Polivy, J. 1983. Development and validation of a multidimensional eating disorder inventory for anorexia nervosa and bulimia. *International Journal of Eating Disorders* 2:15–34.

55. ———. 1983. The eating disorder inventory: A measure of the cognitive/behavioral dimensions of anorexia nervosa and bulimia. In *Anorexia nervosa: Recent developments,* ed. P. L. Darby, P. E. Garfinkel, D. M. Garner, and D. V. Coscina, pp. 173–184. New York: Alan R. Liss.

56. Garner, D. M., Olmsted, M. P., Bohr, Y., and Garfinkel, P. E. 1982. The eating attitudes test: Psychometric features and clinical correlates. *Psychological Medicine* 12:871–878.

57. Garner, D. M., Olmsted, M. P., Polivy, J., and Garfinkel, P. E. 1984. Comparison between weight-preoccupied women and anorexia nervosa. *Psychosomatic Medicine* 46:255–266.

58. Garner, D. M., et al. 1985. Psychoeducational principles in the treatment of bulimia and anorexia nervosa. In *Handbook of psychotherapy for anorexia nervosa and bulimia,* ed. D. M. Garner and P. E. Garfinkel, pp. 513–572. New York: Guilford Press.

59. Goldfried, M. R. 1971. Systematic desensitization as training in self-control. *Journal of Consulting and Clinical Psychology* 37:228–234.

60. Goodsitt, A. 1985. Self psychology and the treatment of anorexia nervosa. In *Handbook of treatment for anorexia nervosa and bulimia,* ed. D. M. Garner and P. E. Garfinkel, pp. 55–82. New York: Guilford Press.

61. Gormally, J., Black, S., Daston, S., and Rardin, D. 1982. Assessment of binge eating severity among obese persons. *Addictive Behaviors* 7:47–55.

62. Grinc, G. A. 1982. A cognitive-behavioral model for the treatment of chronic vomiting. *Journal of Behavioral Medicine* 5:135–141.

63. Guidano, V. F., and Liotti, G. 1983. *Cognitive processes and emotional disorders: A structured approach to psychotherapy.* New York: Guilford Press.

64. Halmi, K. A., Falk, J. R., and Schwartz, E. 1981. Binge-eating and vomiting: A survey of a college population. *Psychological Medicine* 11:697–706.

65. Hawkins, R. C., and Clement, P. F. 1984. Binge-eating: Measurement problems and a conceptual model. In *Binge-eating: Theory, research and treatment,* ed. R. C. Hawkins, W. Fremouw, and P. F. Clement, pp. 229–253. New York: Springer.

66. Hawkins, R. C., Fremouw, W., and Clement, P. F., eds. 1984. *Binge-eating: Theory, research and treatment.* New York: Springer.

67. Hollon, S. D., and Bemis, K. M. 1981. Self-report and the assessment of cognitive functions. In *Behavioral assessment: A practical handbook,* ed. M. Hersen and A. S. Bellack, pp. 125–174. New York: Pergamon Press.

68. Horney, K. 1950. *Neurosis and human growth: The struggle towards self-realization.* New York: Norton.

69. Hudson, J. I., Pope, H. G., Jonas, J. M., and Yurgelun-Todd, D. 1983. Family history study of anorexia nervosa and bulimia. *British Journal of Psychiatry* 142:133–138.

70. Johnson, C. L., and Larson, R. 1982. Bulimia: An analysis of moods and behavior. *Psychosomatic Medicine* 44:333–345.

71. Johnson, C. L., Conners, M., and Stuckey, M. 1983. Short-term group treatment for bulimia. *International Journal of Eating Disorders* 2:199–208.

72. Johnson, W. G., Schlundt, D. G., Kelley, M. L., and Ruggiero, L. 1984. Exposure with response prevention and energy regulation in the treatment of bulimia. *International Journal of Eating Disorders* 3:37–46.

73. Keesey, R. E. 1980. A set point analysis of the regulation of body weight. In *Obesity,* ed. A. J. Stunkard, pp. 144–165. Philadelphia: W. B. Saunders.

74. Keys, A., et al. 1950. *The biology of human starvation.* Minneapolis: University of Minnesota Press.

75. Lacey, J. H. 1982. The bulimic syndrome at normal body weight—reflections on pathogenesis and clinical features. *International Journal of Eating Disorders* 2:59–62.

76. Linden, W. 1980. Multicomponent behavior therapy in a case of compulsive binge-eating followed by vomiting. *Journal of Behavior Therapy and Experimental Psychiatry* 11:297–300.

77. Long, G. C., and Cordle, C. J. 1982. Psychological treatment of binge eating and self-induced vomiting. *British Journal of Medical Psychology* 55:139–145.

78. Loro, A. 1984. Binge-eating: A cognitive-behavioral treatment approach. In *Binge-eating: Theory, research and treatment,* ed. R. C. Hawkins, W. Fremouw, and P. F. Clement, pp. 183–210. New York: Springer.

79. Loro, A., and Orleans, C. S. 1981. Binge-eating in obesity: Preliminary findings and guidelines for behavioral analysis and treatment. *Addictive Behaviors* 6:155–166.

80. Lucas, A. R., Duncan, J. W., and Pienx, V. 1976. The treatment of anorexia nervosa. *American Journal of Psychiatry* 133:1034–1038.

81. Mahoney, M. J. 1974. *Cognition and behavior modification.* Cambridge, Mass.: Ballinger.

82. ———. 1980. Psychotherapy and the structure of personal revolutions. In *Psychotherapy process,* ed. M. J. Mahoney, pp. 157–180. New York: Plenum Press.

83. Mahoney, M. J., and Mahoney, K. 1976. *Permanent weight control.* New York: Norton.

84. Maloney, M. J., Brunner, R., Winget, C., and Farrell, M. 1983. Hyperalimentation as a research model for studying the cognitive, behavioral and emotional effects of starvation and nutritional rehabilitation. In *Anorexia nervosa: Recent developments,* ed. P. L. Darby, P. E. Garfinkel, D. M. Garner, and D. V. Coscina, pp. 311–321. New York: Alan R. Liss.

85. Marmor, J. 1976. Common operational factors in diverse approaches to behavior change. In *What makes behavior change possible,* ed. A. Burton, pp. 3–12. New York: Brunner/Mazel.

86. Meichenbaum, D. 1974. *Therapist manual for cognitive behavior modification.* Waterloo, Ontario, Canada: University of Waterloo Press.

87. Mitchell, J. E., et al. 1983. Electrolyte and other physiological abnormalities in patients with bulimia. *Psychological Medicine* 13:273–278.

88. Mitchell, J. E., et al. 1985. Intensive outpatient group treatment for bulimia. In *Handbook of psychotherapy for anorexia nervosa and bulimia,* ed. D. M. Garner and P. E. Garfinkel, pp. 240–253. New York: Guilford Press.

89. Mizes, J. S., and Lohr, J. M. 1983. The treatment of bulimia (binge-eating and self-induced vomiting): A quasi-experimental investigation of the effects of stimulus narrowing, self-reinforcement, and self-control relaxation. *International Journal of Eating Disorders* 2: 59–65.

90. Mrosovsky, N., and Powley, T. L. 1977. Set points for body weight and fat. *Behavioral Biology* 20:205–223.

91. Nisbett, R. E. 1972. Eating behavior and obesity in men and animals. *Advances in Psychosomatic Medicine* 7:173–193.

92. Norman, D. K., and Herzog, D. B. 1983. Bulimia, anorexia nervosa and anorexia nervosa with bulimia: A comparative analysis of MMPI profiles. *International Journal of Eating Disorders* 2:43–52.

93. Olmsted, M. P., and Garner, D. M. In press. The significance of self-induced vomiting as a weight control method among college women. *International Journal of Eating Disorders.*

94. Orleans, C. T., and Barnett, L. R. 1984. Bulimarexia: Guidelines for behavioral assessment and treatment. In *Binge-eating: Theory, research and treatment,* ed. R. C. Hawkins, W. Fremouw, and P. F. Clement, pp. 144–182. New York: Springer.

95. Polivy, J., Herman, C. P., Olmsted, M. P., and Jazwinski, C. 1984. Restraint and binge eating. In *Binge-eating: Theory, research and treatment,* ed. R. C. Hawkins, W. Fremouw, and P. F. Clement, pp. 104–122. New York: Springer.

96. Pyle, R., et al. 1983. The incidence of bulimia in freshman college students. *International Journal of Eating Disorders* 2:75–85.

97. Rau, J. H., and Green, R. S. 1984. Neurological factors affecting binge eating: Body over mind. In *Binge eating: Theory, research and treatment,* ed. R. C. Hawkins, W. Fremouw, and P. F. Clement, pp. 123–143. New York: Springer.

98. Rosen, J., and Leitenberg, H. 1982. Bulimia nervosa: Treatment with exposure and response prevention. *Behavior Therapy* 13:118–124.

99. ———. 1985. Exposure plus response prevention treatment of bulimia. In *Handbook of psychotherapy for anorexia nervosa and bulimia,* ed. D. M. Garner and P. E. Garfinkel, pp. 193–209. New York: Guilford Press.

100. Russell, G. F. M. 1979. Bulimia nervosa: An ominous variant of anorexia nervosa? *Psychological Medicine* 9:429–448.

101. ———. 1981. The current treatment of anorexia nervosa. *British Journal of Psychiatry* 138:164–166.

102. Selvini-Palazzoli, M. 1978. *Self-starvation: From individual to family therapy in the treatment of anorexia nervosa.* New York: Jason Aronson.

103. Silverman, J. A. 1983. Medical consequences of starvation: The malnutrition of anorexia nervosa: Caveat medicus. In *Anorexia nervosa: Recent developments,* ed. P. L. Darby, P. E. Garfinkel, D. M. Garner, and D. V. Coscina, pp. 293–300. New York: Alan R. Liss.

104. Slade, P. D. 1982. Towards a functional analysis of anorexia nervosa and bulimia. *British Journal of Clinical Psychology* 21:167–179.

105. Stoller, J. 1982. Erotic vomiting. *Archives of Sexual Behavior* 11:361–365.

106. Strober, M. 1981. The significance of bulimia in anorexia nervosa: An exploration of possible etiological factors. *International Journal of Eating Disorders* 1:28–43.

107. ———. 1984. Stressful life events associated with bulimia in anorexia nervosa: Empirical findings and theoretical speculations. *International Journal of Eating Disorders* 3: 3–16.

108. Stuart, R. B. 1975. Behavioral control of overeating. *Behavior Therapy and Research* 5:357–365.

109. Vandereycken, W., and Pierloot, R. 1983. Long term outcome research in anorexia nervosa: The problem of patient selection and follow-up duration. *International Journal of Eating Disorders* 2:237–242.

110. Welch, G. J. 1979. The treatment of compulsive vomiting and obsessive thoughts through graduated response delay, response prevention and cognitive correction. *Journal of Behavior Therapy and Experimental Psychiatry* 10:77–82.

111. White, W. C., and Boskind-White, M. 1984. An experimental behavioral treatment

program for bulimarexic women. In *Binge-eating: Theory, research and treatment,* ed. R. C. Hawkins, W. Fremouw, and P. F. Clement, pp. 77–103. New York: Springer.

112. Wilson, G. T. 1984. Toward the understanding and treatment of binge eating. In *Binge-eating: Theory, research and treatment,* ed. R. C. Hawkins, W. Fremouw, and P. F. Clement, pp. 264–289. New York: Springer.

113. Wooley, O. W., and Wooley, S. C. 1982. The Beverly Hills eating disorder: The mass marketing of anorexia nervosa (editorial). *International Journal of Eating Disorders* 1: 57–69.

114. Wooley, O. W., Wooley, S. C., and Dyrenforth, S. R. 1979. Obesity and women. II. A neglected feminist topic. *Women's Studies International Quarterly* 2:81–92.

115. Wooley, S. C., and Wooley, O. W. 1985. Intensive outpatient and residential treatment for bulimia. In *Handbook of psychotherapy for anorexia nervosa and bulimia,* ed. D. M. Garner and P. E. Garfinkel, pp. 391–430. New York: Guilford Press.

17

Anorexia Nervosa: The Therapeutic Task

Hilde Bruch

Anorexia nervosa was first described a little more than one hundred years ago. The emphasis was on "nervous" factors that were presented in terms of the psychology of their time. In 1914 autopsy findings on certain cases of cachectic women prompted the theory of pituitary origin, and this opinion dominated the field for the next three or four decades. During the 1930s it was recognized that the diagnostic criteria of a psychogenic form of anorexia nervosa were decidedly different from those of cachexia of pituitary origin.

The Psychoanalytic View

Psychoanalysis played an important role in the understanding of psychological factors, but it presented its principal theoretical assumptions as fixed knowledge, the way many topics were presented as definite at that time. Anorexia nervosa was viewed as a form of conversion hysteria and as symbolically expressing repudiation of sexuality, specifically of oral impregnation fantasies. This view dominated the field during the 1940s and 1950s, and it has not yet completely departed. I looked eagerly for such fantasies in my first anorexic patient, and when I did not find them

This chapter is an unfinished draft that Dr. Bruch was working on for this book when she died on December 15, 1984. The chapter is published essentially unchanged in memoriam.

I reassured myself that she had not stayed long enough at the clinic for them to be discovered. I was sure that they were there somewhere. The literature revealed that even experienced analysts would offer similar explanations if they failed to expose these specific psychodynamics, so firmly established was the belief of their existence.

At that time classical psychoanalysis was considered the treatment of choice, though some analysts acknowledged quite early that psychoanalysis was rather ineffective and that the mental disturbance from which these patients suffered was more severe than those observed in neurosis. Psychoanalysis and anorexia nervosa have undergone many changes since 1940. By 1960 I had studied what I considered a sufficient number of cases to formulate my observations and new conceptions. The chief new finding was that anorexia nervosa is related to developmental deficits and only secondarily to sexual conflicts. In addition to the severe weight loss and the amenorrhea, characteristic symptoms include severe body-image disturbances and disturbances in the accuracy of the perception or cognitive interpretation of stimuli arising in the body. The most important of these is the failure to accurately recognize hunger and appetite. The third outstanding feature is a paralyzing sense of ineffectiveness, which pervades all thinking and activity of anorexic patients.

It is this form, the primary anorexia nervosa, that has been steadily increasing since the late 1950s. No reliable figures are available about the actual frequency. One might speak of an epidemic, though the contagion does not appear to be of an organic nature but seems to be related to psychosociological factors.

The Therapist's Conflict

The therapist is caught in a ambivalent role that involves encouraging greater autonomy and freedom in the patient while at the same time improving the food intake and weight gain. If there has been previous treatment—and this is the case more likely than not—the patient has been guided and directed to handle certain underlying unconscious problems; she has been told what she was thinking and what she felt. While acknowledging this, the new therapist is caught from the very beginning in this contradictory role of recognizing the unreality, perhaps deliberate but also unconscious thinking and acting, that needs to be clarified so that the patient can grow beyond this confusion. This needs to be done without making the patient feel deceitful or dishonest. Her early experiences have been so distorted that to a large extent she is unable to see facts realistically.

Twenty years ago there were few professionals, even among physicians, with special knowledge of metabolic disorders who had extensive experience with anorexic patients; nor had teachers, nurses, or others concerned with problems of adolescent health seen young people with the condition. In contrast, anorexia nervosa and other eating disturbances are recognized today as serious and not uncommon health problems that seem to occur with increasing frequency.

Primary Anorexia Nervosa

This increase was accompanied by efforts to formulate the biological and psychological factors that made anorexia nervosa a specific, describable disorder. The basic features have been discussed so widely that I shall give here only a brief sketch of the condition of self-starvation named anorexia nervosa. A specific form, named Primary Anorexia Nervosa, in contrast to unspecific forms of psychological undernutrition, was formulated in the early 1960s. The illness expressed itself in inner distress against which the victims feel helpless and which they try to correct or camouflage by starvation with the intent to change their size and body shape.

The increase in the occurrence of primary anorexia nervosa in the past twenty years has been so large that the illness is on the way to becoming commonplace. It also appears as if the picture of primary anorexia nervosa is less well defined. Many features are unrecognized or overlooked through the matter-of-factness with which the occurrence of anorexia nervosa has been studied. In spite of the active attention that has been given to it, primary anorexia nervosa has several features which have never been acknowledged as characteristic for it. One may conceive of the development of primary anorexia nervosa as representing an effort to correct or camouflage the underlying deficits in self-awareness. Control over food intake, body size, and configuration gives the anorexic patient a sense of identity or selfhood, and the increase appears to be related to the growing demands that women's liberation made on young girls, even those whose early life experiences had not prepared them for outstanding achievement in the business or professional world. It looks as if during the 1950s and 1960s the demand for special achievement was still recognized as a desire to be "different" in a very special way. In other words, avoiding the commonplace, the average, the not-special was the leading psychological motivation. The goal of anorexic patients during that period was to be unique, someone for whom there was no comparison.

"Me-Too" Anorexia

One feature of the modern anorexic patient points to the search for specialness as having been confused with the pursuit of slenderness in the compulsive drive to be recognized as successful. But this is no longer a unique achievement; the modern anorexic patient is preoccupied with how much or how little she weighs compared to her peers. It is this form of imitation anorexia for which I propose the "me-too" label. The search for thinness in which these modern teenagers engage, with the goal of being like everybody else, appears to make them the opposite of the original inventors, who wanted to be unique. The compliant "me-too" anorexic patients recover by following a "program," and they and their parents take part in self-help groups. The genuine primary anorexic patient continues to be an isolated original inventor and, in her claiming to be unique, becomes upset when she meets one of the other anorexics who seem to get the glory without having denied themselves in the way the true anorexic does. "Me-too" anorexia is still a developing condition.

Characteristics of Anorexia

Primary anorexia nervosa affects mainly adolescent girls and young women from educated and prosperous homes; it occurs only rarely in males, usually in prepuberty, and not at all in families haunted by poverty. An important new finding is that patients with primary anorexia nervosa do not suffer from loss of appetite; on the contrary, they are frantically preoccupied with food and eating. In this way they resemble other starving people. Relentless pursuit of thinness seems to be the outstanding symptom, and in this pursuit they deliberately, seemingly willfully, restrict their food intake and overexercise. These girls are panicky with fear that they might lose control over their eating; when they do, they will gorge themselves, often eating unbelievably large amounts; this is followed by vomiting.

The Therapeutic Task

Anorexic patients have been found to be uncertain in identifying hunger or satiety, and they use eating, or refusal to eat, for the pseudosolution of personality difficulties and problems of living. With changes in the theoretical construction of underlying forces, treatment requirements are also expressed differently. The goal is to help a patient with the cruel self-damnation that she tries to hide but which is one of the more important experiences. One important step during treatment is to help the patient develop a sense of competence in areas of functioning where she has been deprived of adequate early confirmation and validation.

This requires from the therapist a change in the conventional attitude. His or her task is not to confront the patient with the underlying hostile feelings and aggressive fantasies; these will come out soon enough, if the whole behavior of the patient is approached. But focusing on them in a negative way undermines the therapeutic alliance and avoids considering the whole life experiences. The therapist needs to be a mentor, a guide who is observant and perceptive and who helps the patient develop her undeveloped aptitudes, the expression of self-initiated behavior, so that she can become an active participant in the treatment process. Thus she can become eventually capable of living her life as a self-directed, competent individual who can enjoy her body and realistic living.

This formulation of the therapeutic task is the outcome of many years of examining and reexamining why certain treatment approaches had failed to help patients become more competent. By being tuned in to the slightest distortion in their sense of reality the therapist can instigate, without being judgmental, necessary reevaluations. I conceive of treatment as a process in which the patient's own abilities are evoked or brought into her awareness.

These patients suffer from an overriding, all-pervasive sense of ineffectiveness, of not being in control of their body and its functions, of mistrusting as pretense or fraud any thoughts or feelings originating within themselves. To these patients "interpretations" as they are used in traditional psychotherapy represent in a painful way the reexperience of being told what they feel and think. Their sense of inadequacy is thus confirmed, and this interferes with the development of true self-awareness and trust in their own abilities. The therapeutic task is to encourage the anorexic patient in her search for autonomy and self-directed identity in the setting of a new intimate interpersonal relationship where what she has to say is listened to and made the object of exploration.

18

Inpatient and Outpatient Treatment of Anorexia Nervosa

Arnold E. Andersen

Introduction

This chapter describes a comprehensive treatment program for inpatients and outpatients with anorexia nervosa. The treatment is based on my and my associates' experience with several hundred patients on the Phipps Psychiatric Service of The Johns Hopkins Hospital and a review of historical principles. It is intended to be a pragmatic guide to treatment.

We believe that anorexia nervosa is a psychological illness with profound biological and social consequences. It occurs only in societies that value thinness despite abundant food. Anorexia nervosa is a temporarily effective pseudosolution to a profound internal or external crisis that may occur during development, as noted by Bruch[5] and Crisp,[6] or in adult life.[2]

In order to deal with the psychological aspects of anorexia nervosa, much work must first be done for the nutritional rehabilitation and medical care of the patient. Only after the anorexic illness is resolved can the patient continue progress through the developmental stages described by Erikson.[7] The end products of these stages are separation, individuation, the capacity for intimacy, and the fulfillment of meaningful contributions to family and society.

Inpatient and outpatient treatment deal with similar problems that vary in severity and chronicity. Outpatient treatment can be successful only when one or more hours of therapy a week, without the structure and support of a hospital, can counteract the individual and societal factors that promote starvation to deal with profound psychological needs.

Diagnosis

Diagnosis is usually not a problem when a patient manifests self-induced starvation, fear of fatness, and an abnormality of reproductive hormone function.[19] The criteria presented by the third edition of the *Diagnostic and Statistical Manual of Mental Disorders*[1] are adequate in most cases. The last decade has witnessed the growth of specific criteria for diagnosis, in contrast to the former method, which involved eliminating all medical causes of weight loss. However, some special cases exist: (1) males, (2) onset during obesity, (3) mild weight loss of less than 25 percent of original body weight, and (4) inadvertent weight loss.

Males tend to be mildly overweight (approximately 125 percent of Ideal Body Weight) before dieting, in contrast to females who *feel* overweight but are within the normal range. Males have been omitted from the diagnosis of anorexia nervosa because certain psychodynamic or diagnostic formulations excluded them on a theoretical basis. The diagnosis can and should be made confidently in males using the same criteria in women, with the exception that testosterone, not estrogen, is decreased.

Female patients who begin dieting when heavier than normal may not become obviously thin even when amenorrheic and may not be afflicted with perceptual distortion and the other classical symptoms, because they began with a high "set point." They should not be excluded from diagnosis. A patient may be severely distressed and require treatment even though weight loss has been less than the 25 percent of initial body weight typically required for diagnosis. Diagnosis is appropriately made on the basis of psychopathology even though the formal weight-loss criteria may not be quite fulfilled.

Finally, some patients deny dieting as the cause of their weight loss. An anorexic illness can be launched by inadvertent weight loss—for example, from a flulike illness or trauma to the jaw—and only then proceed to classical symptoms.

TABLE 18.1

Criteria for Inpatient Treatment of Anorexia Nervosa

1. Significant weight loss.
2. Metabolic abnormalities, especially hypokalemic alkalosis from bulimic complications.
3. Lowered mood; thoughts or intents of suicide.
4. Nonresponsiveness to outpatient treatment.
5. Demoralized, nonfunctioning family.
6. Lack of outpatient facilities.

Inpatient Treatment

THE DECISION TO ADMIT

The decision to admit may be difficult. Referral for inpatient treatment may be seen as a failure of outpatient therapy and may be perceived to indicate an ominous prognosis. The decision to admit often provokes in the patient fears and fantasies about the nature of the treatment program. The usual fear is that of excessive weight gain. The patient and family may believe that cure will be easy. Admission is usually best presented as a practical necessity during which the patient and family should plan to work intensely to gain the maximal benefit from the experience.

INDICATIONS FOR ADMISSION (SEE TABLE 18.1)

Substantial Weight Loss. Substantial weight loss is the most common cause for admission. The medical consequences of weight loss depend on both its severity and rapidity. The most damaging situation results from total starvation. Dangerously low weight, seemingly too low to support life, can be attained in a slow, chronic fashion with surprisingly few ill effects, a fact that the patient will use to avoid admission. The most common medical symptoms are difficulty in concentration, coldness, lowering of pulse and blood pressure, and weakness despite hyperactivity. Because most patients take a daily vitamin and eat some protein, neuropathies occur infrequently and kwashiorkor is seldom seen.

Low Serum Potassium and Other Serious Medical Problems Secondary to Bingeing and Purging. Anorexia nervosa may be associated with bulimic complications in 40 percent of cases. Repeated purging, whether by vomiting, laxatives, or diuretics, causes hypokalemic alkalosis, with occasional severe cardiac arrhythmia in addition to the frequently noted bradycardia from weight loss. Most of the other symptoms of purging, such as the esophageal and gastric distress and parotid gland swelling, are uncomfortable rather than dangerous. The low potassium, however, is one reason thought to be responsible for death in acute cases of anorexia nervosa, the others being starvation and suicide. Purging with Ipecac, which contains emetine, has been reported to cause cardiomyopathy, a condition my associates and I have seen several times.

Psychological Distress and Behavioral Problems. Depression with suicidal thoughts is a painful psychological symptom that may necessitate hospitalization even if weight loss is not severe. While depression can often be treated in an outpatient clinic, the combination of depression and low weight is usually best treated in the hospital.

Persistent thoughts about food and weight can be so intrusive that normal thinking is not possible. A variety of behavioral problems can also lead to admission, especially relentless exercising and provocative behavior that the family cannot handle.

Lack of Response to Outpatient Treatment. Some patients do not respond to months or even years of well-organized outpatient treatment. They may be improved by a structured inpatient program. If a patient is admitted because of lack of response to outpatient treatment, the staff should not criticize the referring therapist or the patient, but rather see the admission as a practical necessity reflecting the tenacity of the symptoms.

Demoralized, Non-Functioning Family. Families are often emotionally and physically exhausted from months of frustration resulting from attempts to manage the patient's problem behaviors. Many have stayed up long nights with depressed patients, guarded food, or attempted to physically stop severe exercisers. Usually they blame themselves. The parental marital relationship is frequently strained through exhaustion, reduced time to communicate, and confusion or disagreement about how to manage the problem. Families are at various times frightened, angry, or apathetic toward the patient.

Lack of Experienced Outpatient Treatment Teams. Well-trained and experienced professionals can work with more severe cases as outpatients. In some areas, however, there are few experienced personnel, so inpatient treatment either locally or in a more distant center may be necessary.

PROCEDURES PRIOR TO ADMISSION

All patients, especially adolescents, should be involved in the decision to seek admission. There are times, however, when treatment must begin despite reservations by the patient. Encourage patients to identify something that they would personally like to get from treatment. A parent or referring doctor may be distressed by the low weight, but the patient may seek something else, like better social skills or improved self-esteem.

Pauker and I[3] have described various impediments that foster the considerable delay between the onset of an eating disorder and referral for treatment. In addition to patient-related factors, there are several reasons why parents may delay in getting treatment. They may not recognize the seriousness of the disorder, sometimes sharing the values that have been carried to an extreme in the ill child. These families emphasize thinness and self-control and view performance and productivity as the way to judge a person. Other parents may recognize the problem but be fearful of intervention. They may feel they cannot cope with the rebellion and defiance of the child in response to their demands for normal eating. Attending to one child may make parents feel they are neglecting the others. They may also be worried that family relationships will come to light and be criticized. Finally, some parents who attempt to treat the disorder on their own view professional help as an indication of personal failure.

A Preadmission Tour. A tour prior to admission helps decrease fears and fantasies of patients and families. They benefit from a detailed explanation of the program and from meeting staff and patients. A preadmission orientation also decreases the chances of the patient leaving the hospital against medical advice. Vandereycken and Pierloot have studied the reasons for dropouts from treatment.[21] Patients considering admission can speak privately with current inpatients to ask personal questions. We require prospective patients to sign a brief statement of willingness to participate in all phases of the program. Very few decline admission after a tour. They often feel more motivated, are less fearful, and are realistically optimistic.

If an anorexic patient does refuse treatment but is not critically ill, a period of reflection is helpful to prepare the patient to make a firm commitment. If a patient is very ill and refuses treatment, a court order or psychiatric commitment may be necessary. Many patients will voluntarily enter the hospital if they know the alternative is a court order or commitment.

Setting of Mutual Goals and Expectations. Mutual goals and expectations should be discussed openly before admission. Staff expectations include the following: the patient will eat all prescribed foods; will not use laxatives or diuretics or induce vomiting; will not use drugs or alcohol; will stay in the hospital as long as needed; and will participate in all aspects of the program. The family is expected to participate in weekly family sessions. All research procedures are described separately and in detail, and the patient is given an opportunity for participation after informed consent.

It is essential that staff avoid promises about the exact length of treatment, the number of calories to be prescribed, or the weight goals. Patients remember these even though they were tentatively stated and deal with them as if they were facts, becoming frightened or resentful if later changes are made.

STAGE OF TREATMENT

There are four stages in our treatment program. The rate of transition through each stage differs between patients. Movement from one stage to another is gradual but uneven, in that a patient may be at a later stage for some treatment goals and an earlier stage for others. Some goals are accomplished in one or two stages (nutritional rehabilitation), but others are carried throughout the program (comprehensive psychotherapy). The following account is intended as a description of this process. In practice, the stages are modified by individual patient needs. Hedblom, Hubbard, and I[12] describe the program in detail.

Stage One: Nutritional Rehabilitation. This first stage involves treatment of starvation, malnutrition, and medical problems by intensive, twenty-four-hour, one-to-one nursing care and careful medical supervision. Diet and exercise are prescribed "like medicine" and carried out under close supervision. A nurse sits with the patient during meals, encouraging the patient to eat and ensuring that food is not discarded. The patient is expected to eat regular, balanced meals and snacks planned by the dietitian. Patients may not choose their own menus, but a maximum of three disliked foods are allowed for exclusion.

Allowing patients to choose menus at this stage creates anxiety and aggravates fears about food, eating, and weight. Vegetarian diets are not allowed unless related to a religious commitment established well before the illness. Learning sound nutritional habits is emphasized, and minimizing struggles around food issues is encouraged. Food should be used only for nutritional purposes and to regain overall health. Staff members emphasize time and time again that the patient will not be permitted to become overweight, a fact based on years of treatment experience. The patient is observed while sleeping at night and when in the bathroom, with some provision of privacy. Walking around the day-room is the only exercise permitted. With continued encouragement and one-to-one management, tube feedings or other mechanical devices have proven unnecessary. Close, firm nursing encouragement has been effective with almost three hundred inpatients.

There are several approaches to setting the desired weight gain. In general, we try to achieve a healthy body weight that is slightly under the mean for age and sex. We use the 1983 Metropolitan Life Tables[17] or the nomograms described by Frisch and McArthur[9] for the required weight for at least a 50 percent chance of return of periods. For older, previously weight-stable patients we choose the lower range on The Metropolitan Life Chart for a given height and frame size (with appropriate age correction) as a reasonable compromise, unless they were stable at a higher or lower weight. For adolescents we use the weight indicated by Frisch and McArthur for a 50 percent chance of *return* of menstrual periods, but occasionally use the 25 percent figure for small frames. It should be noted that the weight for return of periods is at least several pounds higher than the weight to begin cycles during normal development. For younger patients with primary amenorrhea, weights may be chosen from pediatric scales.

Selecting weight from a chart is not entirely satisfactory; some attention should be given to the weight at which the patient functioned well prior to illness. Our average anorexic patient weighed about 10 percent above a matched population at the onset of dieting. Although we have compromised in our treatment by setting a "thin/normal" weight as a goal, it is sensible to set the goal at slightly *above* the mean-matched population weight since many of these patients will be biologically normal only when slightly above average in weight. Few patients accept this sound biological reasoning in practice, although they may agree in theory.

Where insurance coverage or other factors dictate a short treatment period, moderate weight gain (85 to 90 percent of normal) may have to be accepted as the goal with close follow-up in an outpatient program. Anything less than 85 percent of a mean-matched population weight at discharge is too low. A *range* for the goal weight rather than a single point should be set so that patients can fluctuate comfortably within this 3- to 5-pound range. Other factors include bone structure, but in practice very few patients are extremely petite or very larged boned, so usually the weights for average build can be used. Anorexic patients usually ask that charts for petite figures be consulted, quite out of proportion to the statistical occurrence of this type of body frame.

A weight goal is not set when the patient enters the hospital but after several weeks of treatment. It is made as a staff decision. Occasionally the nursing staff will comment that a patient nearing the goal looks plump or chubby. Staff members need to discuss whether this observation is realistic so that, if the body size would predispose the patient to teasing, the weight goal may be modified somewhat. Since we do not tell patients their weight goal until they are in the middle of the desired range, any goal changes can be made by staff members without producing fears of fatness or distrust that comes from a perceived breaking of promises about a given weight. Our "track record" of discharging people in a thin-normal range has been so well established that we feel comfortable asking patients to accept our weight range and to be notified about it only when they are in the middle of it. They find that the weight set by the staff has always been slightly below average for height and age, and this information is passed on to new patients.

Keys and associates[14] in their historic monograph on experimental starvation, noted that nutritional rehabilitation can take place at a rate of about 5,000 calories a day producing a gain of three to five pounds a week without adverse medical consequences. Our first hundred patients gained 2.17 pounds per week. Recently, the rate of weight gain has been increased to about 3 pounds per week, a brisker pace that allows more time for maintenance prior to discharge. Calories are increased by 500 to 750 a week until a maximum of 3,500 to 5,000 per day is achieved. The exact number will depend on the rate of weight gain, the size of the patient, and the presence of discomfort. One-half mg lorazepam an hour before meals may be used for a few weeks if necessary to decrease anxiety around mealtime, but only about 50 percent of patients require this medication. We explain that it helps promote relaxation but does not cause hunger.

The dietitian plays an essential role in relating to both patient and staff. The dietitian takes a complete history from patients when they enter the hospital, and then does not discuss any aspect of treatment with patients until the maintenance stage. Every day, however, the dietitian is present at staff rounds to aid with decisions about the dietary program. If the dietitian and patients interact directly during nutritional rehabilitation, patients make endless requests for changes in menu. During the maintenance phase, the dietitian again becomes active with patients regarding learning to choose balanced meals in a variety of settings.

A graduated exercise program is introduced within a week or two after admission. This must be adjusted to the physical status of the patient. It is a source of encouragement for patients to begin stretching and walking soon after admission. Weight gain will be better distributed if there is appropriate exercise. Compulsive exercise is discouraged, and strenuous exercise such as aerobics does not occur until later in treatment, close to discharge.

During nutritional rehabilitation, the person supervising the meals makes final decisions. Endless discussion about the contents of the tray are not allowed. Signs of staff disagreements are carefully noted and discussed in staff meetings. The theme is consistent, supportive, empathetic supervision that encourages normal eating patterns and insight into the fear of fatness and pursuit of thinness. An increase in weight does not automatically produce normal eating patterns. Specific teaching about nutrition and normal eating are vitally important.

The use of medicines to stimulate appetite is fundamentally misdirected. Our practice has been not to prescribe psychotropic medications (except occasional antianxiety agents), such as antidepressants, until weight and eating are normal and intensive psychotherapy is progressing. If the patient still meets the criteria for major depressive illness despite attaining normal weight, then antidepressants are prescribed. About 15 percent of bulimic patients and about 7 percent of anorexic patients have received antidepressants in our series of more than 180 patients. Reports in the literature are not sufficiently convincing to suggest the use of antidepressants for all anorexic patients, especially prior to weight gain and intensive psychotherapy.

In our program we have had a consistent weight gain of close to 25 pounds per patient. There have been no deaths and no cases of congestive heart failure. One patient developed gastric dilatation, which was successfully treated. Transient pedal edema and nonspecific gastrointestinal discomfort occurred often but always responded to conservative treatment. Patients are told about these symptoms in advance and recognize them when they occur. Patients dependent on laxatives are tapered off over a two-week period, with special attention given by the staff to prescribing diets with a high fiber content.

During their follow-up interviews we have questioned former patients about their feelings toward the nutritional rehabilitation. Most describe the one-to-one supervision as difficult because of the lack of privacy. They felt, however, that it was an essential part of the program in that it prevented them from avoiding weight gain through various tricks. The

TABLE 18.2

Factors Contributing to the Psychopathology of Patients with Anorexia Nervosa

1. Psychological consequences of starvation: inability to experience pleasure, restricted affect, preoccupation with thoughts of food, accentuation of preexisting personality features, decreased mental concentration, social isolation.
2. Central dynamic conflict: the purpose anorexia nervosa serves in the individual's life.
3. Cardinal symptoms of anorexia nervosa: fear of fatness, pursuit of thinness, severe perceptual distortion (if present).
4. Predisposing personality features: obsessional, histrionic, borderline.
5. Consequences of chronic illness: prolonged dependence; immaturity; change in, or lack of progression in, social role.
6. Associated psychiatric syndromes: depressive illness, obsessive-compulsive disorders, alcoholism (in anorexics with bulimic features).
7. Misbeliefs learned from family, peers, and society that thinness leads to happiness and effectiveness.

combination of support and supervision is helpful during this stage of treatment.

Other alternatives to refeeding have been attempted—for example, behavior modification. Systematic behavioral programs were described by Halmi, Powers, and Cunningham[11] and by Garfinkel, Garner, and Moldofsky.[10] These treatments induce weight gain by using principles of operant conditioning. Healthy behavior is rewarded with privileges, praise, and decreasing aversive situations such as restriction of mobility or the use of nasogastric feeding.

Some principles of behavioral treatment are implicit in virtually all programs. Behavioral methods differ from general programs by systematically structuring the method of weight change with specification of the exact weight that must be gained to achieve defined progressive privileges. This approach can be carried out in general medical or pediatric units as well as in psychiatric facilities. It generally produces weight gain but has been criticized by Bruch[4] for producing external compliance without internal change in attitude. Patients may "eat their way out of the hospital."

Stage Two: Intensive Psychotherapy. This stage includes an individualized program of psychotherapy. As nutritional rehabilitation progresses, patients' concentration and judgment have improved and personality traits and interactive style have emerged. Patients are asked to look beyond their symptoms to understand themselves and their families. This stage is begun only after patients have gained sufficient weight to concentrate and think clearly. Their ability to profit further is related to their psychological-mindedness, their commitment to understanding personality assets and vulnerabilities, and their acknowledgment of the nonnutritional role food has served. Increased weight precipitates concern with appearance, and issues about sexuality may emerge. The following are some sources of psychological symptoms. An appreciation of these multiple sources of psychopathology allows for more specific treatments to be carried out during this phase of hospitalization. These sources are summarized in table 18.2.

STARVATION. Many nonspecific symptoms such as difficulty in concentration, loss of emotional expressivity, and preoccupation with food result from starvation rather than from the psychopathology of the illness. Social isolation and immature self-centeredness often result from starvation.

PERSONALITY. Many patients have perfectionistic, self-critical, and obsessional personality traits prior to the illness. These features are accentuated during weight loss. In general, they are above-average in intelligence although not extremely gifted. Often there is repugnance toward sexual development.[15] They may have been praised as model children by their families for their compliant behavior and good grades in school. Associated with the perfectionistic personality is an all-or-none reasoning and the setting of unattainable goals. There is an interaction between starvation and the pre-illness personality. Many personality features are amplified or caricatured during starvation. Hence firm diagnosis of personality disorders should not be made while the patient is starved or while the patient is a young teenager and still developing.

THE ANOREXIC ILLNESS. The illness itself contributes to psychological symptomatology. The cardinal features are the fear of fatness and the closely allied pursuit of thinness. Perceptual distortion is frequently present but not unique to anorexia nervosa.

CENTRAL DYNAMIC CONFLICT. Underlying the symptoms of anorexia is a *central dynamic conflict* that the illness helps resolve. Therefore, a *dynamic formulation* is an essential part of psychological treatment. The dynamic formulation conceptualizes the central purpose the eating disorder serves in view of the patient's personal history, psychological defenses, and maturational stresses.

Bruch[5] and Crisp[6] both give similar conceptualizations of anorexia nervosa that are broad enough to accommodate most patients in an individualized manner. For example, Crisp's concept of anorexia nervosa is that it occurs when the individual's defenses and coping skills are overwhelmed by maturational crises. The breadth of the concept allows application to older patients. A middle-aged male faced with children going off to college, the dissolution of a marriage, or increased demands at work is facing crises as threatening to him as the maturational demands of adolescence. We have treated numerous older people who have developed anorexia as a result of attempting to increase their sense of effectiveness and control in settings of challenge and change.

PSYCHOLOGICAL CONSEQUENCES. There are psychological *consequences* from any chronic illness. The "sick role" legitimizes dependency needs and can be used to try to accomplish fundamental goals such as keeping together parents who otherwise might separate.

Individual psychotherapy for anorexia nervosa begins in the same way for most of these patients, but is then quickly individualized. Initially, all patients need support and reassurance. They need to know that staff members understand their symptoms and appreciate their fears. Empathy for their struggle against perceptual distortion and fear of fatness is essential. The therapist needs to appreciate the mourning that occurs as patients give up the fantasy that thinness will solve their problems; this appreciation will help create a bond between therapist and patient.

Effective individual psychotherapy will avoid either a purely supportive approach or a passive interpretive approach. Several recent approaches to psychotherapy, especially cognitive therapy, can be learned by therapists of diverse backgrounds in a reasonable time. The choice of a particular method of psychotherapy will depend on the qualities the patient brings to treatment. Age, capacity for insight, and psychological maturity are all factors that predispose toward a more dynamic psychotherapy. Typically, psychotherapy progresses from supportive to cognitive to dynamic approaches as progress is made.

Goals for treatment should be identified early so that progress toward them can be measured. A central goal for psychotherapy is to help patients deal directly with life's challenges rather than indirectly through the "pseudosolution" of anorexia nervosa. Patients try to cope with various crises that threaten to overwhelm them by developing their illness; the goals patients seek are usually *normal* developmental goals, such as improved self-esteem, but the solution they choose is inherently unsatisfactory. Because of their perfectionistic qualities, these patients cling to this overinvested solution of thinness to life's demands for change; accepting a more open-ended, ambiguous search for maturity and developing personal effectiveness mean having to learn more mature patterns of coping with the stages of development and the challenges they present.

Patients are encouraged to alter their intellectualized approach toward life and to increase awareness and comfort with emotions. Anorexic patients usually show significant alexithymia.[20] They demonstrate immaturity of feelings, fear of identifying them, and general inaccuracy in or paucity of the words they use to express emotions. They may look and sound angry, frightened, or depressed, and yet maintain they are perfectly normal in mood when asked about their feelings. Giving patients a safe environment in which to identify, express, and accept feelings is an essential goal of treatment.

Group therapy is an effective and valuable adjunct to individual and family therapy. As with individual therapy, extreme approaches to groups should be avoided. The most effective leadership is provided by a combination of male and female therapists who are active but not dominant facilitators of group process. A group can provide support and honest feedback. Patients often say that they experience acceptance for the first time and do not feel odd when they are in a group of others with similar symptoms. In our program we use two ninety-minute sessions a week that focus on identification and acceptance of feelings and emotions. Patients also benefit from work on assertiveness and anger management.

Much has been written about family dynamics in anorexia nervosa and approaches to family therapy. The most important guideline here is to deal with families empirically rather than theoretically. Hedblom, Hubbard, and Andersen[12] noted that many anorexic families fit the model of an emotionally reactive, overly close family. But others are distant emotionally, and still others show no psychopathology at all. Our family therapy begins by reviewing the nature of the illness and giving support for the family's efforts. Issues concerning the whole family are identified. These usually include communication skills within the entire family as well as between parents and the patient.

Stage Three: Maintenance. This stage is the last phase of inpatient treatment, during which decisions about eating and other activities are gradually returned to the patient. The goal is for the patient to assume more control over choices regarding food, weight, and exercise and to internalize the structure of the program so that inner controls will persist. This can be done in a systematic and successful manner for several reasons. Patients are better able to make decisions and take responsibility after starvation and abnormal eating patterns are improved. They are now more competent to make choices concerning food and weight and, most important, about life in general.

Several practical exercises take place during this stage. Choosing appropriate-sized "healthy" clothing is a difficult but important task. Nurses shop with patients for attractive clothing appropriate to age, weight, and personal taste, and encourage them to discard old clothing.

The nutritionist reenters at this point and works closely with the patient. During this final phase of treatment, support is given for healthy behavior; perceptual distortion and fear of fatness are confronted. Patients gradually learn to practice healthy eating patterns even though they *feel* slightly overweight. They learn to trust the scale and comments about their appearance from healthy, sensible, normal-weight peers. They develop a justified skepticism about their distorted perception and learn to act in a healthy manner even when misperceptions occur.

A major goal of the maintenance phase is to set up an effective follow-up program. This is more difficult when patients come from a distance and when there is either no therapist available or a therapist who is not acquainted with current methods of treatment.

Stage Four: Discharge and Follow-up. This stage will often take several years. Most patients are improved but not cured at discharge. The first several days are difficult for most patients even if they are well prepared for the transition. Perfectionistic attitudes tempt them to abandon effective weight control when they make a single mistake. We help patients to structure their time, to plan their meals, and to practice their assertiveness and relaxation techniques. They keep records of foods eaten and the accompanying feelings, so that follow-up outpatient therapy can begin with actual daily experiences and then move on to psychodynamic issues as appropriate.

While anorexia nervosa may present life-threatening symptoms, it often responds to well-planned treatment. We believe that many patients eventually become more effective people than they might have been had they never had the illness, even though this is a difficult route to maturity. Many are talented people with considerable potential, especially if the

TABLE 18.3
Best, Worst, and Average Outcome After Inpatient Treatment
for Anorexia Nervosa

	Best Outcome	Average Outcome	Worst Outcome
Number of patients	11	90	14
Age in years at admission	18.1	22	25.4
Sex	11 F	85 F; 5 M	13 F; 1 M
Years of illness	2.3	4.65	4.7
Number of previous hospitalizations	0.8	1.5	3
Percent of ideal body weight on admission	77%	72.6%	63.6%
Percent of food-restricting anorexia nervosa	73%	59%	36%
Months of follow-up	41	33	43
Percent of ideal body weight at follow-up	106%	88.8%	68.3%

energy once directed toward starvation can be redirected toward healthy goals. What a source of energy their perseverance potentially offers for health!

The partial response of some patients during hospitalization and the tendency for about 30 percent of patients to relapse after discharge remind us that much remains to be discovered about the causes and treatment of anorexia nervosa. There is considerable hope for developing more enduring treatment responses. As a general rule, the probability of good outcome is proportional to the health of the patient's premorbid personality, the lack of serious family psychopathology, and the acuteness of the illness. Vigorous treatment emphasizing early nutritional rehabilitation has decreased the death rate from previous reports of 10 to 15 percent to less than 1 to 2 percent.

Table 18.3 summarizes our long-term outcome from inpatient treatment by comparing the best, worst, and average results of treatment. Our best outcome occurred with patients who were younger, less chronically ill, had fewer previous hospitalizations, and had reached a less severely lowered weight on admission. This group contained a higher percentage of food-restricting patients than the worst-outcome group, which had a substantially greater number of individuals with bulimic complications.

Outpatient Treatment of Anorexia Nervosa

OVERVIEW

Some patients meeting the criteria for anorexia nervosa can benefit from outpatient treatment, especially those who are able to think clearly and are not totally preoccupied with thoughts of food. Outpatients generally are acutely rather than chronically ill, although there are exceptions, and they are more motivated than most inpatients to seek treatment. Ideally the family will be available to participate and the patient will be relatively free of serious personality disorder, especially borderline features.

As with inpatient treatment, it is important for the therapist and patient to agree on goals, including the number of sessions before inpatient treatment will be recommended. Patients must be able to implement the components of therapy in their own lives despite several hindering factors: the lack of guaranteed structure between sessions, the inner drive for thinness, and societal pressure for thinness.

STAGES OF TREATMENT

The stages of outpatient therapy are similar to those for inpatients but there is more overlap and the stages must sometimes be carried on simultaneously. For example, intensive psychotherapy generally begins immediately, as does nutritional rehabilitation. Psychotherapy should not precede nutritional work, however. Treatment that is limited solely to an insight-oriented dynamic psychotherapy without attention to nutritional rehabilitation usually is not effective. Therapists may feel conflicted about their role in structuring and directing a nutritional program. They may feel this is incompatible with the formation of a transference relationship required for the dynamic psychotherapy. This is largely a theoretical worry and in practice need not interfere with psychodynamic work. Collaboration with a nutritionist in setting up a dietary program may be helpful but is not necessary. The maintenance phase of outpatient treatment for anorexia varies in length from several months to several years.

UNIQUE FEATURES OF OUTPATIENT TREATMENT

Each of our outpatients keeps a daily record on 3-by-5-inch cards of the following information: time of day when food is eaten, location, the exact contents of the meal or snack, binging or purging, and a few words or a sentence about any feelings experienced around the meal. The emphasis is on recording exact feelings such as anger, disappointment, feeling stuck or bored, rather than psychological interpretations. Patients bring these records to sessions. After a weigh-in, the session focuses initially on a review of the food diary. There is an implicit accountability from this record keeping. The record keeping itself may have a therapeutic effect in organizing a patient's meals. Generally, however, the benefit comes from a joint review by therapist and patient. During the first part of the session, attention is focused on the content of the cards and whether the patient was able to meet the goals set for the week. Initially the patient is unable to make many associations between feelings, events, and eating. Eventually a pattern emerges that links these items. For example, a student may recognize that the comment "I feel fat" or "I feel bloated" occurred regularly on evenings before examinations and was associated with reduced food intake.

We have found it helpful to have patients respond at home, when on their cards they write the statement "I feel fat," by crossing out the word fat and substituting any word that does not relate to food or calories. This approach begins to deal with alexithymia by helping them get beyond the global emotionality expressed in those words. Many of these patients are unable to attach labels to feelings and instead use "I feel fat" for virtually all kinds of dysphoria. By first recording "I feel fat" and then making substitutions with words having specific emotional content, the patient begins discovery of real mood states and can link these feelings to past experiences. This is a long but productive process. Eventually patients begin making these connections on their own.

Another feature differentiating outpatient from inpatient therapy is the need to plan the time between sessions. Good inpatient programs are usually highly structured, and decisions are made by the patient only late in the program. Life for an outpatient is different. It often alternates between busy, hectic hours and times of being bored and unstructured. One goal of therapy is to plan a moderately paced, well-structured day with few hours that do not have a specific purpose. The purpose can be as simple as relaxing around a swimming pool, but needs to be chosen in advance. Patients have a tendency to feel fat or to binge during idle hours or times of frantic activity from self-imposed, excessively demanding schedules.

The rate of weight increase is more moderate with outpatients because they are not as severely starved and there are no supporting staff. One to 1½ pounds a week is usually adequate, although a gain of 2 pounds can be achieved with a motivated outpatient. Patients need to be reassured they will not be allowed to gain too much weight. An agreement regarding specific consequences for a lack of sufficient weight gain may be helpful.

Although outpatients have less structure than inpatients, there are some compensating benefits. They have access to some beneficial real-life activities not available to the inpatient. These include work or school, which may be sources of self-esteem, self-help groups, the presence of a family, and the knowledge they are progressing through their own efforts.

A typical session will begin with a cordial greeting of the patient followed by a weighing with the patient's back toward the scale. It is best for outpatients not to weigh themselves at home, although exceptions may be made. The focus then turns to the nutritional records that, as noted earlier, become a source of information about eating, emotions, and the starting point for the therapy. It helps to go from feelings noted on the records to what they remind the patient of in the past and when similar feelings were experienced previously. During early sessions, much time is spent on nutritional rehabilitation, record keeping, the structure of time, and practical issues in medical care. As the patient approaches a healthy weight, more time is spent in dynamic psychotherapy. Recently, Marziali has verified Malan's concept that progress in psychotherapy is related to the frequency of interpretation of transference emotions.[16] We find that timely interpretations of transference are useful for the treatment of anorexia nervosa. These interpretations should not be symbolic or abstract, but very much related to the vital relationships in the patient's life.

Special Situations Encountered in Outpatient Treatment

Individuals with bulimic complications require techniques that deal with both anorexia and bulimia. This may involve the use of antidepressant medication[18,22] or a cognitive-behavioral program for identifying and confronting the urges to binge.[8,13] We find this combination of symptoms—low weight plus bulimic behavior—the hardest situation to treat on an outpatient basis.

Older patients may not wish to or may be unable to come into the hospital. They may have had bad experiences with previous hospitalizations, have demanding professions, lack insurance coverage, or have other valid reasons. Our experience is that about half of these patients have done well and half have done poorly in outpatient treatment.

ATYPICAL ANOREXIA NERVOSA

This term is used for individuals who have the psychopathological features of anorexia nervosa but have not met the criteria for sufficient weight loss. They essentially have mild anorexia nervosa and should be treated as such. They often do well in short-term treatment because the more chronic symptoms have not appeared or become fixed.

Outpatient treatment can occasionally be quite successful, especially with mild cases of acute onset occurring in individuals with good personalities and family structures. One positive feature of outpatient treatment is that the difficult transition from inpatient to outpatient status is not necessary. The negative side is that one often settles for inadequate comprehensive goals such as chronic underweight because the patient demonstrates "insight." Truly effective insight leads to weight gain. Multiple specific goals need to be agreed on as well as the length of time for specified weight gain to occur in order for the patient not to be referred for inpatient treatment. This is never used as a threat, however, but is a practical necessity.

Conclusion

The treatment of anorexia nervosa is a stimulating, often frustrating, but rewarding experience. A therapist has the opportunity to deal comprehensively with a problem growing from an interaction of sociocultural norms, individual personality, and family dynamics that leads to life-threatening medical symptoms. Every aspect of this illness has the potential for substantial improvement. While total cure is seldom achieved quickly, adequate daily functioning and significant psychological growth can be attained. The most gratifying part of treatment comes when the individual resumes age-appropriate developmental tasks and goes on to a mature, well-balanced life. The goal is a sound mind in a sound body that can live sanely in a society preoccupied with dieting. Successful treatment brings great satisfaction both to the afflicted patient and to the therapist who works as a partner with the patient.

REFERENCES

1. American Psychiatric Association. 1980. *Diagnostic and statistical manual for mental disorders,* 3rd ed. Washington, D.C.: American Psychiatric Association.
2. Andersen, A. E., and Mickalide, A. D. 1963. Anorexia nervosa in the male: An underdiagnosed disorder. *Psychosomatics* 24:1066–1075.

3. Andersen, A. E., and Pauker, N. E. 1985. Outpatient treatment of anorexia nervosa. In A. E. Anderson, *Practical comprehensive treatment of anorexia nervosa,* pp. 98–101. Baltimore: Johns Hopkins University Press.

4. Bruch, H. 1974. Perils of behavior modification in treatment of anorexia nervosa. *Journal of the American Medical Association* 230:1419–1422.

5. ——. 1978. *The golden cage.* Cambridge, Mass.: Harvard University Press.

6. Crisp, A. H. 1980. *Anorexia nervosa: Let me be.* London: Academic Press.

7. Erikson, E. 1963. *Child and society.* New York: Norton.

8. Fairburn, C. G. 1983. The place of a cognitive behavioral approach in the management of bulimia. In *Neurology and neurobiology,* vol. 3. *Anorexia nervosa: Recent developments in research,* ed. P. Darby, P. Garfinkel, D. Garner, and D. P. Coscina, pp. 393–402. New York: Alan R. Liss.

9. Frisch, R. E., and McArthur, J. W. 1974. Menstrual cycles: Fatness as a determinant of minimum weight for height necessary for their maintenance or onset. *Science* 198:949–951.

10. Garfinkel, P. E., Garner, D. M., and Moldofsky, H. 1977. The role of behavior modification in the treatment of anorexia nervosa. *Journal of Pediatric Psychology* 2:113–121.

11. Halmi, K. A., Powers, P., and Cunningham, S. 1975. Treatment of anorexia nervosa with behavior modification. *Archives of General Psychiatry* 32:93–96.

12. Hedblom, J. E., Hubbard, F. A., and Andersen, A. E. 1981. Anorexia nervosa: A multidisciplinary treatment program for patient and family. *Social Work in Health Care* 7: 67–86.

13. Johnson, C., Conners, M., and Stuckey, M. 1983. Short-term group treatment of bulimia. *International Journal of Eating Disorders* 2:199–208.

14. Keys, A., et al. 1950. *The biology of human starvation,* vol. 2. Minneapolis: University of Minnesota Press.

15. King, A. 1963. Primary and secondary anorexia nervosa syndromes. *British Journal of Psychiatry* 109:470–479.

16. Marziali, E. A. 1984. Prediction of outcome of brief psychotherapy from therapist interpretive interventions. *Archives of General Psychiatry* 41:301–304.

17. Metropolitan Life Insurance Company. 1983. *1983 Metropolitan height and weight tables for men and women.* New York: Metropolitan Life Insurance Company.

18. Pope, H. G., and Hudson, J. I. 1982. Treatment of bulimia with antidepressants. *Psychopharmacology* (Berlin) 78:176–179.

19. Russell, G. F. M., and Beardwood, C. J. 1968. The feeding disorders, with particular reference to anorexia nervosa and its associated gonadotropin changes. In *Endocrinology and human behaviour,* ed. Richard P. Michael, pp. 310–329. London: Oxford University Press.

20. Taylor, G. J. 1984. Alexithymia: Concept, measurement, and implications for treatment. *American Journal of Psychiatry* 141:725–732.

21. Vandereycken, W., and Pierloot, R. 1983. Drop-out during in-patient treatment of anorexia nervosa: A clinical study of 133 patients. *British Journal of Medical Psychology* 56: 145–156.

22. Walsh, B. T., et al. 1982. Treatment of bulimia with monoamine oxidase inhibitors. *American Journal of Psychiatry* 139:1629–1630.

PART III

BULIMIA

19

Bulimarexia: A Historical-Sociocultural Perspective

Marlene Boskind-White and William C. White, Jr.

The term *bulimarexia*[10] was introduced in 1976 to identify an aberrant behavior pattern observed in a large number of female students seeking treatment at Cornell University. At that time the second edition of the *Diagnostic and Statistical Manual of Mental Disorders* considered "bulimia" a rare disorder that involved binge eating with no reference to purging. As a result, most of the women had been labeled anorexic. This diagnosis seemed inappropriate for women whose weights were within normal ranges and who were not starving themselves. Rather, these women binged on copious quantities of food and purged themselves of the calories via forced vomiting, laxatives, diuretics, or constant dieting. "Bulimarexia" distinguishes the binge-purge syndrome from bulimia and anorexia nervosa. It reflects our view that binge-purge practices represent a tenacious habit, not a disease process. Binging and purging are learned behaviors that can be unlearned utilizing the principles of social learning theory. Bulimarexia was thus defined in terms of specific primary and secondary behaviors.[12] This definition is commensurate with the revised third edition of the *Diagnostic and Statistical Manual,* and the terms bulimia and bulimarexia have therefore come to be used interchangeably. Despite potential confusion, many continue to prefer the term bulimarexia because of their distaste for the disease model and its obvious implications for treatment.[3]

Historical Antecedents of Bulimarexia

The Venus figurines, which depict obese primitive women, were sculpted for reasons other than gluttony. Paleolithic humans existed almost exclusively on meat. Primitive women needed surplus fat to adapt to extremes of weather and to sustain them while their men went off to hunt. In fact, the most rotund figurines have been found in extremely cold climates.[4]

A woman's role was defined as bearer of children and preparer of food. Her body shape and size had significant bearing on her fertility and ability to bear children. She, like modern anorexic women, would cease menstruating if her weight dropped to starvation levels. As long as a woman's identity was bound to her role as mother, men desired her body to reflect a "mother earth" image of fertility, health, and the ability to survive; in short, moderate plumpness was the ideal.[4] Since women were preparers of food, this function entitled them to important social and religious status. Food was an integral part of religion, magic and witchcraft. Food-giving assuaged pain and despair and was an important function at hospitality rites.[37]

Today we find similar emphasis on obesity as a favorable trait among certain African tribes. The Banyankole of East Africa fatten their young women and restrict their exercise from the age of 8 in order to prepare them for marriage.[37] Men are considered good providers and their status is enhanced if their women are plump. In cultures where men and women were expected to do the same kinds of work, women's body types and shapes resembled those of men.[4]

Primitive humans were gluttons when feasts followed famines or during magical and religious rites. Gluttony was an appropriate and predictable response after days or months of hunger. Powdermaker[37] quotes a Trobriand Islander who, in anticipating a feast, declares: "We shall be glad, we shall eat until we vomit" (p. 76).

As other cultures developed, new ideal traits were incorporated. Egyptian women were considered attractive and desirable to men if they were young, slender, and bedecked with jewelry.[6] The Greeks envied the Cretes for having drugs that permitted them to stay slim while eating as much as they wanted. They emphasized slimness, beauty, and seductiveness in their wives and daughters and dressed them in revealing garments. However, Greek goddesses such as Venus and Diana were glorified as "mother earth" with protruding abdomens and powerful, well-proportioned bodies. The Romans frowned on obesity as much as the Greeks. Beuf, Dglugash, and Eininger[6] point out that

> it seems that Roman women had to suffer as much as, if not more than, modern teenagers to keep slim. They were literally starved to make them thin as reeds. The Romans were also known for the invention of the vomitorium which permitted them to relieve themselves after gorging, a method of weight

control which we find revived by contemporary American college women. (P. 13)

During the Dark Ages and the Renaissance, robust women were viewed as ideal, as evidenced by Botticelli's Venus replete with rounded hips and belly. Raphael, Rembrandt, and Leonardo da Vinci portrayed women with large, statuesque bodies. During this period, however, a new trend emerged. Although Rubens painted pink nudes with fat buttocks and hips, his "Portrait of Wife" emphasized her tight bodice and delicate waist. Peasant women were still peasant women, however, and a robust fleshiness remained the ideal. Brueghel's women dance "The Wedding Dance" with swollen bellies and heavy hips while men literally burst their britches. Scenes of gluttony depict great vitality and joy, and it is easy to surmise that women enjoyed eating as much as men.

In the 1700s artists continued to emphasize fat among peasant women; however, there was a renewed emphasis on still smaller waists among the upper classes. Daumier's "Washerwoman" is solid and matronly while Hogarth's "The Graham Children," with their tiny, diminutive waists, appear to be holding their breath. The tightened bodice created still another desired effect in women—that of exaggerated breasts. Gainsborough's "The Dutchess of Devonshire" literally spills over her strained bodice. Necklines became lower and more seductive. Lace-layered breasts, cinched waists, and petticoats and bows created an hourglass shape. Fatness was not yet a sin and plump women were still desirable. Guy de Maupassant[16] described such a woman:

> the woman, one of the so-called ladies of the night, was famous for a precocious rotundity and it earned her the nickname Boule de Suef [Ball of Fat]. She was petite, round and soft as goose fat, her fingers were pudgy and squeezed at the joints like strings of little pork sausages; her skin was taut and shiny and she had enormous breasts that threatened to burst through her dress, but she was very appetizing and much sought after because her youthful freshness gave men such pleasure. . . . (P. 86)

During the next two centuries, however, fatness in the female form became increasingly viewed as bourgeois, a characteristic of the lower classes. Beuf and her colleagues[6] connect the proliferation of anorexia to historical eras that stressed slimness: "In the early 1930's following the 'flapper era' when slenderness was stylish and old established sex roles were being questioned, came the first 'outbreak' of the disorder. From that time until the present the incidence has increased but with a dramatic acceleration in the past ten years following the introduction of extremely thin models like 'Twiggy' " (p. 19). They conducted a longitudinal content analysis of fashion advertisements in women's magazines in the United States and Europe and found that until the 1920s full-figured womanhood was glorified.[6] Models were matronly and would be considered fat by today's standards. In the late 1920s, as clothing became more revealing, models became younger and slimmer. World Wars I and II further emphasized woman's attractiveness. This was the era of the "sex goddess." Rita Hayworth and Betty Grable revealed their ample breasts and long legs to the accompanying leers, cheers, and tears of servicemen. These were mature, full-figured women, and fashion thrived upon their seductiveness.

The sixties and early seventies, however, gave rise to a much slimmer, long-legged, teenage nymphet heralded by the arrival of "Twiggy" in 1966. Exaggerated youthfulness and wide-eyed innocent asexuality were personified by this child-model. She looked like a preadolescent, the most prominent age group at that time in the United States. Older women did not challenge the fashion world's teenage notions and embraced youthfulness and slimness. Many described it as the childhood they felt they had been denied. This was a significant occurrence for, historically, women of past generations had resisted such contagion. For example, during the "flapper" era, the majority of old women tolerated this youthful exuberance until a more conservative style of dress and figure made its inevitable reappearance.

In the sixties "old age" in women had become seriously devalued. Cosmetic surgery increased. The new insecurity of the times, contrasted with the youthful baby boom, began to create an insidious form of anxiety among older women who had begun to starve themselves in an attempt to dress and look like their teenage daughters. A recent survey of America's most beautiful women serves to corroborate this obsession with thinness.[21]

Sociocultural Factors in Bulimarexia

In the early 1900s unrealistic societal expectations regarding women's bodies intensified confusion and conflict among young women. Accounts of anorexia nervosa soon emerged. Janet's[25] case of the adolescent girl "Nadia" underlined the toxicity of excessive dieting, appetite suppression, and occasional episodes of gorging followed by terrible pangs of conscience and obsessive thinking about food. Nadia was unmarried and 27 years old. She had been referred to Janet five years previously with a diagnosis of hysteria. Her daily diet consisted of two small portions of bouillon, 1 egg yolk, 1 teaspoon of vinegar, and a cup of tea. The major precipitant was the fear of being fat. Janet was aware that Nadia was not a true anorexic because she suffered from a gluttonous compulsion, greedily devouring everything in sight. He connected Nadia's fear of obesity to her rejection of her obese mother. Feeling that she was attempting to conceal her sex and appear masculine, Janet inferred that she wanted to remain a child and thereby reject her femininity.

During the next few years psychoanalysts[53] attempted to explain anorexia in psychosexual terms centering on unconscious conflicts about sexuality, pregnancy wishes (bulimia), and fear of oral impregnation. Fear of eating was seen as fear of impregnation or penis fear. Food was symbolic of mother's milk, oral masturbation, or oral insemination. Thus the conflict "to eat or not to eat" and the resulting guilt and shame that ensued when control was abandoned and food was consumed were considered primary to the dynamics of anorexia. Wulff[53] proposed a psychoanalytic interpretation of bulimia that suggested it was a syndrome in its own right. There was, however, a strong commitment to traditional interpretation and no mention of purging. Omitting or ignoring purgative practices as part of bulimia persisted until 1976.[10]

A departure from the psychoanalytic interpretation of bulimia was the exceptionally rich and detailed case study of Ellen West.[7] After her suicide, Ellen's diaries provided insight regarding her tormented bulimarexic life style. As a child Ellen was lively, defiant, and headstrong. In adolescence her poems reflected a passion and great exuberance for life along with yearnings for power, knowledge, and prestige. In a poem written at seventeen, she expressed the ardent desire to be a boy, for then she would "be a soldier, fear no foe, and die joyously, sword in hand"[7] (p. 239). However, the independence she experienced as a child was deemed unsuitable by her parents, who began to control every aspect of her life. Forced to reject a suitor she loved, she was sent to Sicily to recover and forget. Once there she gained weight and was mercilessly teased by friends. Mortified, she began to fast and endure exhausting hikes, losing weight compulsively and horrifying her family. The rest of her life was characterized by extreme cycles of gorging and purging in which massive use of laxatives, dramatic vomiting, and violent diarrhea were quite common. To Ellen, fat was synonymous with aging and ugliness, whereas slimness reflected youth, attractiveness, and desirability.

Lindner's classic "Case of Laura" in *The Fifty Minute Hour*[27] is also historically significant. His intriguing analysis of Laura's dynamics focused on episodes of depression during which she would be seized by an overwhelming compulsion to gorge. Purging was, however, minimized, and Lindner interpreted Laura's excessive eating as a substitute for her sexual hunger for her father and her wish to be impregnated by him. *The Fifty Minute Hour* was widely read, and this articulate account of Laura's plight played a significant role in reinforcing a traditional approach to the understanding and treatment of bulimia. Treatment involved abandoning her "hatred of femininity" and learning to accept and adopt a passive, accommodating and classically feminine role orientation. What Lindner's Laura "really wanted" was to become pregnant. He observed her desperate desire for a man and presupposed that healthy resolution involved attracting one and becoming pregnant.

In Bliss and Branch's book[8] on anorexia nervosa, patients who vomited were common. In 1973 Bruch[14] published her classic work on eating disorders but did not consider bulimia a prevalent and distinct syndrome.

Her description of "thin-fat people" closely resembles the bulimarexic client; however, these individuals were described as formerly obese individuals who were desperately striving to remain slim via constant fasting, dieting, and to a lesser extent, purging.

Upon publishing our initial findings regarding the binge-purge syndrome,[10,11,12] we received hundreds of letters from women struggling with bulimarexia and scores of inquiries from professionals alarmed at seeing such women. There was little doubt that the syndrome was prevalent and that detection and treatment programs were desperately needed. Soon others began to share their work. In Great Britain, Palmer[34] referred to bulimia as the "dietary chaos syndrome," and Russell[42] introduced the term bulimia nervosa. During the last decade, a myriad of articles in the popular media have informed people about bulimarexia. *Glamour* magazine recently conducted a national survey of women's attitudes regarding their bodies and food. Of the 33,000 women polled, 41 percent were moderately or extremely unhappy with their bodies. Significantly, 30 percent were below recently established weight expectation norms. The majority (80 percent) felt that they had to be slim to be attractive to men. The survey revealed that 18 percent of the respondents admitted that they used laxatives or diuretics for weight loss while 15 percent relied on forced vomiting as a major weight-control strategy. Despite the fact that many women currently binge and purge daily and have never been anorexic, controversy continues as to whether bulimia is a unique, separate disorder. We consider this a moot point but agree with Orleans and Barnett[33] who suggest that "binge-purge practices and their affective and behavioral correlates require more careful study in their own right, as problems that can contribute to a serious eating disorder for excessively weight conscious individuals in obese, normal-weight and anorexic populations" (p. 145).

Alcoholism and manic-depressive illness among family members have been cited as preponderant among bulimic individuals.[21] Traumatic loss prior to the onset of symptoms was first noted in anorexia and recently in bulimia.[21,26,46] During the past ten years of applied research we have treated hundreds of bulimarexic clients and are convinced that such women are more different than they are similar.[13,49] Specific causative factors that may prove diagnostically relevant must await more controlled, well-designed studies. Before accurate and comparable data can be meaningful, appropriate population base rates must first be obtained. Wilson's recent review[52] underlines the potential futility of studies that search to uncover the definitive personality: ". . . the futile and wasteful quest for the alcoholic personality . . . should serve as a sobering reminder of the inherent limitations of such a research strategy . . . the data base is still too thin and clinical samples too small to permit broad generalizations. Moreover trait descriptions explain little and are not particularly useful for directing therapy" (p. 267).

Characteristics that seem pathognomonic of a syndrome must be carefully documented and researched before they are acknowledged as relevant. Over the years women participating in our group therapy programs have consistently described themselves as feeling dependent, helpless, and inadequate on a variety of psychological inventories including the 16PF, California Psychological Inventory, and Minnesota Multiphasic Personality Inventory.[12,50] The majority have also consistently embraced stereotypic, conventional views of femininity and bodily perfection.[12,13,50] Comparable results have also been cited by Norman and Herzog[31] and Orleans and Barnett.[33] Moreover, such findings are consistent with feedback we have received from over one hundred professionals currently treating bulimarexic women. Awareness of the bulimic woman's passive-dependent style and her oversubscription to a traditional female role orientation as well as her obvious obsession with her body has been crucial to the formulation of our treatment program. Much of our therapy is therefore devoted to role redefinition, risk-taking, and participant modeling.[51] Such techniques were spontaneously cited as most helpful by a majority of our clients in a recent long-range follow-up treatment evaluation.[49] As prime examples of Bem's "feminine women,"[4] most bulimic persons appear paralyzed by the fear of embarrassment or the threat of negative evaluation. Addressing this inability or unwillingness to reformulate socialization rituals that encourage passivity and dependency among bulimarexic clients is important to the success of treatment programs today.

Physiological Factors and Bulimarexia

The earliest systematic studies of diet-induced binging[19] were based on observations of male volunteers who reached 74 percent of their normal body weight via starvation. Most of these men became depressed, irritable, lethargic, and obsessed with eating. The majority lost their sex drive. After being refed to prior weight levels, subjects began to binge, eating as much as they could hold despite the unlimited availability of food. Comparable results have been cited by Wardle.[48] Bennett and Gurin's "set point theory"[5] is based on the contention that the human body is not meant to remain below a certain critical point. When such restrictions occur the body reacts adaptively. Polivy and her associates[35] attribute such a response to a decrease in insulin. These results have also been observed in the refeeding of anorexic clients.[18] Nevertheless, in their recent extensive review of the literature on restrained eating, Polivy and colleagues[35] concluded that although physiological factors are relevant, the major impact must be attributed to cognitive factors because restricted subjects were consistently ruled by an irrational fear that food would not be available or that they would somehow be deprived of the opportunity to eat. Consequently they ate more food than they were prepared to cope with, typically making themselves ill.

Such studies raise a number of relevant questions. Would results have been similar had the subjects been women? This is particularly interesting since women are genetically programmed to need more fat than men. Abdominal fat presumably protects the fetus during pregnancy, and the loss of fat in anorexia presumably leads to amenorrhea. Poor nutritional status in bulimic clients in itself (without significant weight loss) has the same impact. Osteoporosis (bone loss) has been linked to amenorrhea in groups of female anorexic and bulimic clients and female athletes.[22] Replacing fat with muscle in women may also lead to health problems. Active, exercising women need twice the daily dosage of riboflavin required by men to perform comparable tasks.[2] The impact of rapid, sustained weight loss on future childbearing has yet to be determined.

Current research by Dr. Orland Wooley and Dr. Susan Wooley, co-directors of the Eating Disorders Clinic at the University of Cincinnati College of Medicine, suggests that dieting *in itself* may be dangerous for slim women. Their analysis of responses from 5,000 of 33,000 women who responded to their survey conducted by *Glamour* magazine in 1984 revealed that, unlike obese women, slender women tend to start hating their bodies only after they begin to diet—casually at first, then violently. The Wooleys suggest that it may be appropriate to give (slim) women the warning, "Caution, dieting may be hazardous to your health," since this body dissatisfaction then may progress to anorexia or bulimia.* Research regarding the long-term physiological implications of anorexia, bulimarexia, dieting, and even compulsive exercising is obviously needed.

During the course of our work, we treated a small group of chronic bulimarexic clients who struggled with a number of significant problems, one of which was food binging. Some were addicted to drugs or alcohol. Most were unproductive, their lives chaotic. Some may be biochemically and/or neurologically impaired. Rau and Green's research[39,40,41] suggested that some bulimic clients demonstrate irregular electroencephalograms. They report successful intervention with anticonvulsant medication. Other researchers, however, failed to confirm their results.[29]

Pope and colleagues[36] recently conducted a double-blind, placebo-controlled study of the impact of imipramine hydrochloride on twenty-two mildly bulimic women whom they selected from a population of seventy potential subjects. Within a few days three subjects were dropped from the study because of severe side effects. Nine women were actually treated with imipramine. Most of these subjects reported curtailing their binging by more than 50 percent. However, inspection of the selection criteria revealed that subjects were binging at least twice a week and had purged at least once during the preceding month. By most standards, these subjects seem to have been barely bulimic. Even more relevant is

* The Wooleys' research is cited in the *Ithaca Journal* (Ithaca, N.Y.),[27] August 1985, and was presented by Susan Wooley at the 1985 annual meeting of the American Psychological Association.

the fact that there were no significant differences between treatment and control groups with regard to self-control with food. Attempts at "medicating away" a psychosocial behavioral pattern may serve to reinforce drug dependency among a population that has already demonstrated its vulnerability in that regard. This concern is further stimulated by the fact that over 70 percent of all tranquilizers and antidepressant prescriptions are written for women.[43] Such a practice is demeaning to women and reinforces those toxic behaviors that initiate and maintain binging and purging. Outcome research involving more seriously impaired subjects over longer follow-up intervals has revealed at least comparable, if not more impressive, results.[13,50] In addition, over the years we have treated scores of bulimarexic clients who have found imipramine and other antidepressant drugs of little value in the long run. Further research will be necessary to establish whether pharmacotherapy is of value, even with a small number of bulimic individuals.

Current Considerations

Pilot work utilizing short-term group therapy[12,13,49,50] has stimulated a great deal of interest among university and college mental health practitioners struggling with the large number of women seeking treatment. As a result, many colleges and universities utilize a short-term group treatment model to provide an appropriate milieu for bulimarexic clients.[32,38,44] Others have begun therapy programs based upon a sociocultural perspective and contemporary, eclectic, cognitive-behavioral intervention strategies.[15,28,30]

Self-help groups and the network established by National Anorexia Aid Societies are also helpful. These groups, when led or supervised by trained therapists in conjunction with women who have overcome this disorder, are often quite effective. Role models who willingly share concrete suggestions and strategies from their struggles and success experiences are often invaluable. Through such consciousness-raising experiences, many women have gained a more balanced perspective about their bodies and the aspects of today's socialization rituals that encourage women to adopt such behavioral patterns. For many women, however, the new consciousness has exaggerated feelings of helplessness and hopelessness. Unprepared to create new roles, they embrace youthfulness and slimness in order to feel needed and secure. The diet industry has therefore evolved into a multibillion-dollar enterprise. The pursuit of youth and beauty, however, is hardly a panacea, for rarely do expectations regarding that romantic "happily-ever-after" life ever materialize. Bart[1] studied a large contingent of middle-class women in psychiatric hospitals who subscribed to the role of traditional housewives, living through their children. When their children left home, they became depressed and were eventually institutionalized. Young agoraphobic clients and women in the prime of life with performance anxieties are being denied privileges, status, and power. Their energy is being consumed by fear, guilt, shame, denial, and avoidance.

The 1970s produced strange paradoxes. On the one hand, membership in women's movements increased dramatically. Centers were created to protect and counsel rape victims and battered wives. Organizations and lobbying efforts examined children's books, party platforms, and sex-role stereotyping. The Bipartisan National Women's Political Caucus was formed in 1971. Women were exerting control. Female models and leaders emerged from all walks of life. There was a proliferation of writing, art, poetry, and films by women for women. Such efforts promised broader role definitions for women. On the other hand, however, our nation was experiencing the impact of inflation, high rates of unemployment, and cuts in government spending for social programs. Confrontational feminism faded into moderation. A conservative government threatened to repeal abortion programs, and the Equal Rights Amendment was mortally wounded.

In 1972 Zelnik and Kantner[54] discovered that three-quarters of the 15- to 19-year-old unmarried, sexually active young women they studied used no contraception. Two uniquely feminine disorders, anorexia nervosa and bulimarexia, were widespread. What happened in the 1970s to account for such paradoxes?

While many families were intent on being liberated and nonsexist, Fagot[18] points out that girls and boys were still being treated very differently by their parents. Girls were encouraged to ask for help while boys were reinforced for handling things themselves. Block,[9] in an excellent review of most of the research on contemporary socialization rituals, reached similar conclusions. From a very early age girls were encouraged to be passive and dependent while boys were pressured to achieve. Perhaps the most revealing and disturbing study of the decade was the highly publicized work of Matina Horner,[23] which underscored the fact that college women in general shared a well-established tendency to fear and avoid success. Many bright, capable women believed that men would be threatened by their success. In the 1950s women dropped out of college to marry. In the 1960s they completed their undergraduate work and married soon thereafter. In the 1970s there was an unprecedented prolongation of education. Men were attending graduate school and avoiding early marriages. Abortion prevented "shotgun" or desperate marriages. For women, attending college had provided a sense of security, especially since most felt marriage would follow. Suddenly, however, women were expected to do something with their education. They could no longer hide behind a fear of success nor protestations of unequal opportunities. Men were expecting women to become economic partners. They were no longer expected to be the "sole breadwinner" but were asking for help in hopes of capitalizing on the new career opportunities now available to women. Discrimination suits were starting to have an impact. Universities, businesses, and industry were actively recruiting women. Ehrenreich and English[17] exploded the myth that "you've come a long way, baby" by pointing out that women were experiencing an ambiguous and frustrating form of liberation: "after the old dependency came the new insecurity of shifting relationships. A competitive work world, unstable marriages—an insecurity from which no woman could count herself 'safe' and settled. There was a sense of being adrift, but now there was no one to turn to . . ." (p. 196). Women were alone and on their own more than ever before. They had been socialized to be passive, fragile, and frightened of competitiveness and were therefore unprepared to take care of themselves psychologically and economically.

The renewed emphasis on unrealistic slimness drew many of these vulnerable women into the current insidious self-preoccupation with their bodies. In the 1980s many women continue to pursue a "bionic life style" with regard to a career, motherhood, and wifehood. Sensitive to criticism, pain, and confrontation, they expect to compete with men in the workplace. Feminist slogans such as "Do it on your own" create further pressure. A plethora of "shoulds" continue to nurture the pursuit of perfectionism we have attempted to expose as pathognomonic of bulimarexia. Such unrealistic pressures to achieve and perform are not consonant with the closed, rigidly defined role definitions and learned helplessness upon which modern-day women are being nurtured.

In 1937 Karen Horney hypothesized that the behavioral impoverishment of women, as reflected by phobias and compulsivity, was closely related to their desperate desire to maintain neurotic attachments to men.[24] Almost forty years later Horner[23] reiterated the fact that women continue to entertain the fear of success. By 1973 the negative attitudes expressed by aspiring women in Horner's 1964 survey increased from 65 to 88.2 percent.

Many of the same cultural pressures underlying eating disorders today were quite evident in the lives of the women presented earlier in this chapter. Nadia, Ellen West, and Laura were young, unmarried, and locked into rigidly conventional roles. In the final analysis, they came to value their appearance above all else.

Thus a major factor in the treatment of bulimarexia involves establishing a comfortable balance between the desire to be feminine and the necessity to become competent and autonomous. A broader-based concept of feminism is required for today's growing girls. This new consciousness must offer alternatives to passivity and dependency. Role models are obviously crucial. Characteristics leading to healthy survival in today's unstable times can no longer be labeled exclusively masculine. The ability to cope with stress must be nurtured in both sexes from infancy onward. Protecting young girls from pain will only serve to reinforce psychological and behavioral impoverishment. Preventive programs are crucial. If the toxic chain reaction of the terror of fat, fad diets, and eating disorders is to be broken, it is essential for the public to be properly informed regarding the dangers inherent in severe caloric deprivation. The media and fashion industry must take responsibility and introduce models who are womanly and fit rather than emaciated and unhealthy. Only then will women, young and old, begin to value themselves enough to reject inappropriate roles and implement more effective coping strategies with respect to food.

REFERENCES

1. Bart, P. 1976. The loneliness of the long distance mother. In *Women: A feminist perspective,* ed. Jo Freeman, pp. 156–170. Palo Alto, Calif.: Mayfield.

2. Belko, A. Z., et al. 1983. Effects of exercise on riboflavin requirements of young women. *American Journal of Clinical Nutrition* 37:509–517.

3. Beller, H. S. 1977. *Fat and thin.* New York: McGraw-Hill.

4. Bem, S. 1976. Probing the promise of androgyny. In *Beyond sex-role stereotypes,* ed. A. G. Kaplan and J. P. Bean, pp. 64–66. Boston: Little, Brown.

5. Bennett, W., and Gurin, J. 1982. *The dieter's dilemma.* New York: Basic Books.

6. Beuf, A., Dglugash, R., and Eininger, E. 1976. Anorexia nervosa—a sociocultural approach. Manuscript, University of Pennsylvania.

7. Binswanger, L. 1957. The case of Ellen West. In *Existence,* ed. R. May, pp. 236–262. New York: Basic Books.

8. Bliss, E. L., and Branch, C. H. 1960. *Anorexia nervosa: Its history, psychology and biology.* New York: Paul B. Hoeber.

9. Block, J. H. 1973. Conceptions of sex-roles: Some cross cultural and longitudinal perspectives. *American Psychologist* 29:512–529.

10. Boskind-Lodahl, M. 1976. Cinderella's step-sisters: A feminist perspective on anorexia nervosa and bulimia. *Signs: Journal of Women in Culture and Society* 2:342–356.

11. Boskind-Lodahl, M., and Sirlin, J. 1977. The gorging-purging syndrome. *Psychology Today* 2:50–56.

12. Boskind-Lodahl, M., and White, W. C. 1978. The definition and treatment of bulimarexia in college women—a pilot study. *Journal of the American College Health Association* 2:27–29.

13. Boskind-White, M., and White, W. C. 1983. *Bulimarexia: The binge-purge cycle.* New York: W. W. Norton.

14. Bruch, H. 1973. *Eating disorders: Obesity, anorexia and the person within.* New York: Basic Books.

15. Coffman, D. A. 1984. A clinically derived treatment model for the binge-purge syndrome. In *The binge-purge syndrome: Diagnosis, treatment and research,* ed. R. C. Hawkins, W. J. Fremouw, and P. F. Clement, pp. 211–224. New York: Springer.

16. de Maupassant, G. Boule de suef. In *Fat,* ed. K. Reed, pp. 104–144. Indianapolis: Bobbs-Merrill.

17. Ehrenreich, B., and English, D. 1979. *For her own good: 150 years of the experts' advice to women.* New York: Anchor Books.

18. Fagot, B. I. 1978. The influence of sex of child on parental reactions to toddler children. *Child Development* 49:459–465.

19. Franklin, J. S., Schiele, B. C., Brozek, J., and Keys, A. 1948. Observations on human behavior in experimental starvation and rehabilitation. *Journal of Clinical Psychology* 4:28–45.

20. Garfinkel, R. E., and Garner, D. M. 1982. *Anorexia nervosa: A multidimensional perspective.* New York: Brunner/Mazel.

21. Garner, D. M., Garfinkel, P. E., Schwartz, D. M., and Thompson, M. G. 1980. Cultural expectations of thinness in women. *Psychological Reports* 47:483–491.

22. Hale, E. 1983. Doctors link bone loss, menstrual ills. *Ithaca Journal* (March 11):23.
23. Horner, M. S. 1970. Femininity and successful achievement: A basic inconsistency. In *Feminine personality and conflict,* ed. J. M. Bardwick, E. Douvan, M. S. Horner, and D. Guttmen, pp. 45–75. Belmont, Calif.: Brooks/Cole.
24. Horney, K. 1937. *The neurotic personality of our time.* New York: W. W. Norton.
25. Janet, P. 1957. Les obsessions et la psychastenic. In *Existence,* ed. R. May, pp. 480–495. New York: Basic Books.
26. Kalucy, R. C., Crisp, A. H., and Harding, B. 1977. A study of 56 families with anorexia nervosa. *British Journal of Medical Psychology* 50:381–395.
27. Linder, R. 1955. The case of Laura. In *The fifty minute hour.* New York: Holt, Rinehart.
28. Loro, A. D. 1984. Binge-eating: A cognitive-behavioral treatment approach. In *The binge-purge syndrome: Diagnosis, treatment and research,* ed. R. C. Hawkins, W. J. Fremouw, and P. F. Clement, pp. 197–211. New York: Springer.
29. Mitchell, J. E., Hosfield, W., and Pyle, R. L. 1983. EEG findings on patients with the bulimia syndrome. *International Journal of Eating Disorders* 3:17–23.
30. Moyer, D. L. 1982. A group therapy format for bulimarexic women. Paper presented at the Western Psychological Association meetings, Sacramento, Calif., April 8.
31. Norman, D. K., and Herzog, D. B. 1983. Bulimia, anorexia nervosa and anorexia nervosa with bulimia. A comparative analysis of MMPI profiles. *International Journal of Eating Disorders* 2:43–52.
32. Oberwald, R. E. 1984. Psychosocial study of college women in group therapy for eating disorders. Paper presented at the 62nd Annual Meeting of the American College Health Association, Atlanta, Ga., April 25.
33. Orleans, C. T., and Barnett, L. R. 1984. Bulimarexia: Guidelines for behavioral assessment and treatment. In *The binge-purge syndrome: Diagnosis, treatment and research,* ed. R. C. Hawkins, W. J. Fremouw, and P. F. Clement, pp. 144–156. New York: Springer.
34. Palmer, R. L. 1979. The dietary chaos syndrome: A useful new term? *British Journal of Medical Psychology* 52:187–190.
35. Polivy, J., Herman, C. P., Olmstead, M. P., and Jazwinski, C. 1984. Restraint and binge-eating. In *The binge-purge syndrome: Diagnosis, treatment and research,* ed. R. C. Hawkins, W. J. Fremouw, and P. F. Clement, pp. 104–121. New York: Springer.
36. Pope, H. G., Hudson, J. I., Jonas, J. M., and Yurgelun-Todd, M. S. 1983. Bulimia treatment with imipramine: A placebo-controlled, double-blind study. *American Journal of Psychiatry* 140:554–558.
37. Powdermaker, H. 1973. An anthropological approach to the problem of obesity. In *The psychology of obesity,* ed. N. Kiell, pp. 75–83. Springfield, Ill.: Charles C Thomas.
38. Preston, P. 1984. A unified approach to the problem of eating disorders on campus: Prevention, treatment, support and followup. Paper presented at the 62nd Annual Meeting of the American College Health Association, Atlanta, Ga., April 25.
39. Rau, J. H., and Green, R. S. 1975. Compulsive eating: A neuropsychologic approach to certain eating disorders. *Comprehensive Psychiatry* 16:223–231.
40. ———. Soft neurological correlates of compulsive eating. *Journal of Nervous and Mental Disease* 166:435–437.
41. ———. 1984. Neurological factors affecting binge-eating—body over mind. In *The binge-purge syndrome: Diagnosis, treatment and research,* ed. R. C. Hawkins, W. J. Fremouw, and P. F. Clement, pp. 123–143. New York: Springer.
42. Russell, G. 1979. Bulimia-nervosa: An ominous variant of anorexia nervosa. *Psychological Medicine* 9:419–448.
43. Scarf, M. 1979. The more sorrowful sex. *Psychology Today* 11:45–89.
44. Simon, T. B. 1984. Eating concerns among college students: A short-term approach. Paper presented at the 62nd Annual Meeting of the American College Health Association, Atlanta, Ga., April 25.
45. Stordy, B. J., Marks, V., Kalucy, R. S., and Crisp, A. H. 1977. Weight gain, thermic effect of glucose and resting metabolic rate during recovery from anorexia nervosa. *American Journal of Clinical Nutrition* 88:262–266.
46. Strober, J. 1981. The significance of bulimia in juvenile anorexia nervosa: An exploration of possible etiologic factors. *International Journal of Eating Disorders* 1:28–43.
47. Ullmann, L., and Krasner, L. 1965. *Case studies in behavior modification.* New York: Holt, Rinehart.
48. Wardle, J. 1980. Dietary restraint and binge-eating. *Behavior Analyst* 4:201–209.
49. White, W. C. 1985. Bulimarexia: Intervention strategies and outcome considerations.

In *Eating disorders: Research, theory and treatment,* ed. S. Emmett. New York: Brunner/Mazel.

50. White, W. C., and Boskind-White, M. 1981. An experiential-behavioral approach to the treatment of bulimarexia. *Psychotherapy: Theory, research and treatment* 18:501–507.

51. ———. 1984. Experiential-behavioral treatment program for bulimarexic women. In *The binge-purge syndrome: Diagnosis, treatment and research,* ed. R. C. Hawkins, W. J. Fremouw, and P. F. Clement, pp. 77–103. New York: Springer.

52. Wilson, G. T. 1984. Toward the understanding and treatment of binge-eating. In *The binge-purge syndrome: Diagnosis, treatment and research,* ed. R. C. Hawkins, W. J. Fremouw, and P. F. Clement, pp. 264–280. New York: Springer.

53. Wulff, M. 1945. Ueber einen interissaten oralen symptomenkomplex und seine beziehung zur sucht. In *The psychoanalytic theory of neuroses,* ed. O. Fenichel, pp. 483–491. New York: Norton.

54. Zelnik, M., and Kantner, J. F. 1972. The probability of pre-marital intercourse. *Social Science Research* 1:335–371.

20

Bulimia: Theories of Etiology

W. Stewart Agras and Betty G. Kirkley

The recent emergence of bulimia as a well-defined and prevalent syndrome[1,6] has led to much speculation and investigation regarding its etiology. While binge eating is often found in obesity and anorexia nervosa, this chapter will focus on bulimia proper, as defined in the third edition of the *Diagnostic and Statistical Manual of Mental Disorders (DSM-III)*. Theories of the disorder's causation have ranged from the purely socio-behavioral to the purely biological. While there is some empirical evidence for both views, neither has emerged as the definitive explanation of why so many young women binge eat, induce vomiting, and/or abuse purgatives. This chapter reviews the evidence for both sociobehavioral and biological theories of etiology and discusses possible avenues for interaction between the two viewpoints.

Sociobehavioral Theories

From a sociobehavioral perspective, bulimia may be viewed as a deficit in self-regulation that has its inception in an extreme desire for thinness. According to this model, the young woman's desire to lose weight and be thin leads her to restrain her eating by dieting. This pattern of restrained eating may result in a state of real or perceived deprivation that inevitably leads to a breakdown in restraint and often to overeating. According to the model, excessive or binge eating may be viewed as the paradoxical result of a thin ideal and excessive dietary restraint.

DESIRE FOR THINNESS

Sociobehavioral explanations for bulimia are based on the assumption that many young women desire to be thinner. Furthermore, the differentially higher incidence of bulimia among females as compared to males requires that the desire for thinness and the resulting dietary restraint be more prevalent among young women than their male peers. These assumptions have generally been supported by data.

A pattern of young women being dissatisfied with their bodies has been repeatedly documented. In 1969 the interviews of Dwyer and associates[8] with high-school students revealed that 80 percent of the senior women, but less than 20 percent of their male classmates, wanted to lose weight. Consistent with their stated attitudes, 30 percent of the females but only 6 percent of the males were dieting. These findings were replicated in 1971 with a sample of Swedish adolescents.[25] In this study, Nylander found that the majority of female adolescents "felt fat" while their male peers seldom expressed such feelings. Furthermore, the girls' body dissatisfaction increased with age, with 50 percent of the 14-year-old and 70 percent of the 18-year-old girls indicating that they "felt fat."

A reanalysis of the National Health Survey data on adolescent weight confirmed the findings that a much higher percentage of young women than young men desire to be thinner.[7] These data shed light on the factors associated with this difference. The push for thinness was particularly strong in young women in upper socioeconomic groups, presumably because of the girls' tendency to negatively evaluate the increase in body fat that is a result of normal sexual maturation. The desire for thinness among females increased with each stage of sexual maturation. The majority of girls who had reached physical maturity desired to be thinner. In contrast, sexual maturation in males is accompanied by an increase in muscle mass and no increase in the desire for thinness.

The dissatisfaction most young women feel with their bodies may be partially due to societal pressures for thinness, pressures that seem to have been increasing in recent years. The measurement of subtle societal attitudes is difficult, but Garner and Garfinkel[13] have attempted to quantify what they perceive as an increasing pressure on young women for thinness. They collected data from *Playboy* magazine, Miss America pageants, and popular women's magazines. Over the last twenty years both *Playboy* centerfolds and Miss America contestants have become thinner relative to their peers. Their percent of average weight for age, height, and sex has decreased significantly since 1960. During that time the centerfolds' bust measurements became smaller, waists larger, and hips smaller, suggesting that the trend was away from the traditional hourglass figure and toward

FIGURE 20.1

Preferred female body shape from 1900 to 1983 as depicted in three popular women's magazines (Ladies' Home Journal, Good Housekeeping, *and* Harper's Bazaar*).*
Larger ratios indicate straighter figures.

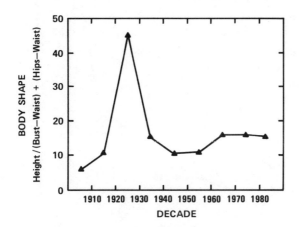

a more androgynous figure. In contrast to the ideal, however, actuarial data indicate that the typical American woman between the ages of 17 and 24 has become 5 to 6 pounds heavier during the last twenty years.[2]

The evidence that there is increasing pressure on young women to be thinner is supported if one looks at magazines from 1900 to 1983. A systematic examination and measurement of pictures in three popular women's magazines (*Ladies' Home Journal, Good Housekeeping,* and *Harper's Bazaar*) revealed that preference for a more androgynous body style, characterized by a smaller bust and hips relative to waist measurement, emerged during the 1960s and 1970s (see figure 20.1). This is in marked contrast to the hourglass figures popular during the early and midcentury and supports the findings of Garner and Garfinkel. The only departure from this trend was seen in the 1920s, when fashion dictated an absolutely straight silhouette.

The straight silhouette of the 1920s, however, appears to have been achieved by different methods (e.g., binding of the breasts and dress style) from those used today. A sample of the contents pages of these magazines indicated that not a single diet article was printed in the 1920s. Diet articles began to appear at a rate of approximately 0.1 per issue during the 1930s and 1940s and became quite frequent in the 1950s (0.5 per issue), 1960s (0.5 per issue), and 1970s (0.4 per issue). Interestingly, the first four years of the 1980s indicate a still greater emphasis on dieting in the popular press (1.25 diet articles per issue) (see figure 20.2). These rates would undoubtedly have been higher if fashion magazines had been sampled, but the relatively recent origin of such magazines made long-term comparisons impossible. It appears that in previous decades the desired body shape was achieved through fashion without dependence on

FIGURE 20.2

Number of diet articles printed (broken line) in three women's magazines (Ladies' Home Journal, Good Housekeeping, *and* Harper's Bazaar) *and preferred female body shape (solid line) from 1900 to 1983.*

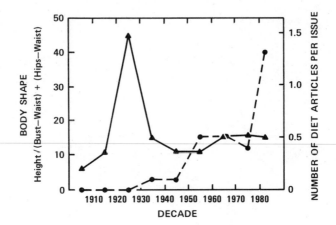

dieting. Since the 1960s the push for a more androgynous body style has been accompanied by an increasing emphasis on weight loss.

Not surprisingly, the number of articles discussing bulimia reported in two major medical journals (*Journal of the American Medical Association* and *American Journal of Psychiatry*) also began to increase in the 1960s. The first article on binge eating or self-induced vomiting appeared in the 1920s. Controlling for the number of pages in the journals, the number of such articles increased by approximately 100 percent each decade through the 1950s but remained small. The 1960s saw the largest increase in articles devoted to bulimia, with a 250-percent increase. This trend leveled off in the 1970s, with a 60-percent increase. Thus the period from 1930 to 1980 saw a dramatic increase in the number of medical articles discussing binge eating and/or self-induced vomiting, with the largest increase occurring in the 1960s. While no causal conclusions can be drawn from these data, they do support the idea that the 1960s was marked by an increasing pressure on young women to achieve a thin, somewhat androgynous body style, which was quantitatively different from the pressures they had faced previously, with the suggestion that they achieve this by dieting. Simultaneously, bulimia came to the attention and became a growing concern of the medical community.

ONSET OF BINGE EATING

Young women who eventually become bulimic may be particularly vulnerable to social pressures toward thinness due to a tendency to be slightly heavier than their peers. Fairburn and Cooper[10] surveyed 499 bulimic women recruited through a popular women's magazine. The mean age of onset of binge eating was 18.4 years, an age that corresponds with the highest rates of body dissatisfaction and dieting.[7,8,25] Furthermore, 45.2 percent of the bulimic women reported a highest weight since menarche that was more than 115 percent of the matched population mean weight, and 29.7 percent had weighed more than 120 percent of the mean. Similarly, in our own clinic the mean age of onset of bulimia for seventy-six women seeking treatment was 19.3 years. Their highest weight, a mean of 146.9 lb, tended to occur in late adolescence ($\bar{x}$ = 17.9 years) and prior to onset of bulimia. These findings are consistent with the clinical observation that many bulimic patients are slightly overweight before the onset of their disorder, tending first to restrict their food intake and then to binge and purge. These findings and observations have led to the notion that binge eating may be paradoxically associated with the push for thinness and excessive dieting so common among older adolescent girls.

An association between dieting and episodes of overeating has repeatedly been shown in the experimental literature. In a classic study, Herman and Mack[15] compared the consumption patterns of restrained eaters (steady dieters) and unrestrained eaters. The individuals were asked to rate three flavors of ice cream after consuming a preload of zero to two milkshakes. Unrestrained eaters decreased their consumption of ice cream as the size of their preload increased. In contrast, the restrained eaters' consumption of ice cream increased after eating a preload, and those who had two milkshakes ate substantially more than those who had only one. Herman and Mack provided a cognitive explanation for this phenomenon by attributing the counterproductive overeating to a collapse in motivation caused by the mandatory preload. Since the dieter had been forced to break her diet rules or calorie limits with the preload, she was left with no short-term reason to continue dietary restraint, so disinhibition occurred and overeating ensued. Bulimic patients often have rigid dietary rules that lead to avoidance of certain foods, typically those believed to be fattening.[9] For example, bulimic individuals often believe that they should never eat sweets or starches, and the consumption of even small quantities of such foods may lead to feelings of failure, loss of control, and binge eating.

Realizing that there were possible alternative explanations for the overeating among restrained eaters, Polivy[26] attempted to separate cognitive and physiological explanations for the phenomenon. To differentiate the roles of biological and cognitive factors, Polivy fed half the subjects a high-calorie preload and half an equivalent-tasting low-calorie preload. Within each condition, half were told that the preload was high in calories and half were told that it was low in calories. The restrained eaters who ate a high-calorie preload subsequently ate 20 percent more than those who had eaten a low-calorie preload, suggesting that the high-calorie preload may have stimulated hunger. However, an even larger effect was found for the cognitive manipulation. The restrained eaters who believed they had eaten a high-calorie preload ate 61 percent more than those who believed that the preload was low in calories. While a physiological explanation cannot be rejected, the cognitive explanation of disinhibition (breaking of food rules) appears to be more powerful. Interestingly, the only difference Polivy found between males and females was that females tended to score higher on the restraint scale. This further supports the notion that the high rate of bulimia among women is due to their higher incidence of dieting and not to intrinsic differences between the sexes. However, the lack of research and clinical reports about bulimia in males makes these conclusions tenuous.

There is evidence to suggest that bulimic individuals exhibit negative emotional states and may be particularly vulnerable to binge eating when anxious or dysphoric.[20] Similar relationships may exist among restrained eaters. Several studies suggest that restrained eaters are hyperemotional and overreact to environmental stimuli.[16,17,27] A study conducted by Herman and Polivy[16] sheds light on the relationship between these negative emotions and the disinhibition found among restrained eaters. Restrained eaters ate more when made anxious, while unrestrained eaters ate less. The authors suggested that anxiety may disrupt the cognitively mediated self-control processes involved in dietary restraint and thus lead to increased consumption of normally avoided foods.

Herman and Polivy's research may provide a laboratory model for the symptoms found in bulimia. Bulimic patients do score extremely high on the restraint scale. According to this model, the young woman who restrains her eating in a quest for thinness places herself in a chronically stressful, frustrating state that may increase her irritability and reactivity to environmental stimuli. The presence of negative emotions or the breaking of rigid dietary intake rules leads to disinhibition of cognitively mediated self-control over eating, and binge eating of "forbidden foods" occurs. This proposed relationship between dietary restraint and binge eating has been documented among obese binge eaters.[23]

This cognitive disinhibition may be exacerbated by the physiological effects of restraint and deprivation. Experiments with animals show that taste responsiveness is partially a function of biological state. Cabanac and his associates[3,4] demonstrated that sweet tastes are preferred when an animal is deprived and are avoided when the animal is sated. This phenomenon has also been demonstrated in animals at abnormally low body weight given access to food.[24] Thus both acute and chronic energy deprivation appear to enhance the preference for sweet-tasting foods in laboratory animals. Rodin, Slochower, and Fleming[30] found an increased preference for, and consumption of, sweet foods among people who completed a weight-loss program. Individuals who chronically restrain their eating in an effort to maintain a low body weight may paradoxically increase their desire for sweets. While this mechanism has not been demonstrated to play a role in bulimia, it provides a possible explanation for what many bulimics describe as "a craving for sweets."

ONSET OF VOMITING OR PURGATIVE ABUSE

Fairburn and Cooper[10] found that the onset of self-induced vomiting began almost one year after the onset of binge eating. When they began vomiting, bulimic individuals were an average of 19.3 years old, and 83 percent were attempting to lose weight. The majority (52.7 percent) reported that vomiting was their own idea, but 26.6 percent first got the idea from the media and 17.4 percent from other people. This suggests that self-induced vomiting and laxative abuse begin as means of weight control in the context of binge eating. Fairburn[9] has developed a treatment for bulimia that focuses on building up healthy eating patterns, in the belief that vomiting will cease if the individual learns realistic methods of weight control.

Rosen and Leitenberg[31] contend that vomiting becomes the central driving force in bulimia regardless of etiology. Individuals with a morbid fear of weight gain become anxious when eating large quantities of high-calorie foods, and vomiting reduces this anxiety and fear. Once the individual discovers that vomiting decreases the anxiety, her fears no longer inhibit overeating and binging is likely to continue or worsen. Conceptually, they view vomiting as "an escape-avoidance response reinforced by anxiety reduction, similar in function to compulsive hand washing and checking rituals in obsessive-compulsive neuroses" (p. 117). Consistent with this hypothesis, Leitenberg and colleagues[22] developed a treatment for bulimia based on prevention of the vomiting response. The bulimic patient is encouraged to eat binge food in the laboratory and to remain with the therapist until the desire to purge dissipates. They found that in persons receiving a response-prevention treatment for bulimia, the reported anxiety level and urge to vomit increased as eating progressed but gradually declined after eating if vomiting was prevented.

Both Fairburn[9] and Rosen and Leitenberg[31] believe that vomiting is initially a response to a morbid fear of weight gain and the discomfort that results from eating. There are, however, at least two possible conceptualizations for the role vomiting plays in maintaining the bulimic syndrome. Rosen and Leitenberg[31] view vomiting as the key component that reinforces binge eating through anxiety reduction. However, a model based strictly on the restrained eating hypothesis would suggest that the primary role of vomiting in maintaining bulimia lies in the return of the individual to a state of hunger and deprivation, which contributes to further binge eating. It is possible that both factors play a role.

Biological Theories

The most prominent biological theory of etiology links bulimia to affective disorder. The first evidence for this theory came from the clinical observation that many bulimic patients were depressed. In support of these clinical observations, a number of studies have reported a high prevalence of depression or dysphoria among bulimic patients. Johnson and Larson[20] investigated the daily moods and behavior of fifteen bulimic individuals using the Experience Sampling Method. To obtain representative reports, an electronic pager was used to signal the participants to fill out self-reports of their current mood and behavior. The bulimic participants reported significantly more dysphoric and widely fluctuating moods than did normal controls and, overall, they reported being sadder, lonelier, weaker, more irritable, passive, and constrained. These negative feelings were prominent just prior to and during binge episodes. Following a purge, the bulimic respondents reported decreased anger, increased feelings of control, adequacy, and alertness, but overall they continued to feel more dysphoria than their normal levels. These findings led Johnson and Larson[20] to conclude that bulimic persons may be experiencing "an agitated depressive state which is marked by frequent mood fluctuations" (p. 348) and that they may use food and overeating in an attempt to modulate their dysphoric and fluctuating moods.

Pyle and colleagues[29] found that individuals with more severe forms of bulimia (i.e., more frequent binging and the presence of vomiting or laxative use) had previously sought treatment for depression significantly more often than the less severe bulimic individuals who did not vomit or use laxatives. The authors suggested that there might be a link between primary affective disorders and the development of the more severe symptoms of bulimia, but also acknowledged that this group might tend to seek treatment more often.

Thus there is ample evidence that bulimic patients have a high rate of dysphoria and that it is associated with the more severe forms of the disorder. The causal link in this association, however, is not clear. A genetic predisposition toward major affective disorder may be linked with a biochemical disturbance of appetite that makes some young women vulnerable to developing bulimia. Alternatively, severe depression may increase risk for the development of bulimia, perhaps interacting with dietary restriction in the same way as anxiety. Finally, the loss of control that accompanies this disorder may make bulimic individuals prone to dysphoria. At least two reports[21,32] indicate that dysphoria reported by bulimic persons significantly decreases following cognitive-behavioral treatment. The resulting decrease in bulimic symptoms suggests that the latter explanation may be correct.

In an attempt to delineate the relationship between bulimia and depression or dysphoria, several investigators have determined the prevalence of major affective disorder among bulimic patients and their first-degree relatives. Hudson[18] found that six of ten bulimic persons showed some form of *DSM-III* major or minor affective disorder. Five of the ten had abnormal dexamethasone suppression test (DST) results. This incidence is significantly higher than that found among normal controls (4 percent) and patients with other psychiatric disorders (3 percent)[5] but is not significantly different from the rate found for patients with major depression (52 percent). Although controversial, the DST is thought by some to be a specific marker for major depressive disorder with melancholia. Gwirtsman and colleagues[14] replicated the high incidence of abnormal DST results among bulimic patients. They found that twelve of eighteen (67 percent) bulimic patients had clearly abnormal DSTs, and three (17 percent) had borderline abnormal tests.

Interviews with the ten bulimic patients studied by Hudson, Laffer, and Pope[18] revealed that 15 percent of their forty-six first-degree relatives had probable or possible major depression, 4 percent had alcohol dependence, and 2 percent each displayed cyclothymic disorder, agoraphobia, or possible bulimia. In a more extensive family study, Hudson and his colleagues again found a high rate of affective disorder in the families of bulimic individuals.[19] They studied fourteen women with anorexia nervosa, fifty-five with bulimia who had never had anorexia nervosa, and twenty who had both disorders at some time in their life. Comparison groups were thirty-three patients meeting *DSM-III* criteria for bipolar disorder, thirty-nine with schizophrenia, and fifteen with a diagnosis of borderline personality disorder. Detailed psychiatric information was obtained on first-degree relatives. This information was obtained through nonblind interviews with family members when possible (twenty-nine of fifty-five bulimic patients) and otherwise through interviews with the patient. Among the 251 first-degree relatives of the 55 bulimic patients, 41 (16 percent) had a major affective disorder. The morbid risk for affective disorder in first-degree relatives did not differ significantly between bulimia and bipolar disorder but was significantly lower in the other comparison psychiatric groups. Clearly, limited conclusions can be drawn from the interviews conducted in this study, but the results suggest a high incidence of major affective disorder in the families of bulimic individuals. Although environmental explanations for these findings cannot be ruled out, Hudson and associates[19] conclude that "genetics offer the most likely explanation" (p. 137).

In a further test of their theory linking bulimia and major affective disorder, Pope, Hudson, and coworkers[28] conducted a placebo-controlled, double-blind study of imipramine hydrochloride, which is typically used as an antidepressant. After six weeks of treatment the group receiving

imipramine reported a 70-percent reduction in binge eating, while the
placebo group reported virtually no change. The authors cited these findings as further support for the "growing evidence . . . that bulimia may
represent a form of affective disorder" (p. 558).

BULIMIA AS A METABOLIC DISTURBANCE

Wurtman and Wurtman have proposed a somewhat different biological theory to explain the etiology of excessive carbohydrate intake, a
theory that has particular relevance to bulimia.* They suggest that some
individuals are "carbohydrate cravers." This abnormal desire for carbohydrate is attributed to a "disturbance in the mechanism through which
the brain learns about the composition of the last meal" (p. 83). This
feedback mechanism is based primarily on the concentration of the
neurotransmitter serotonin. If breakfast contains primarily carbohydrate
with little protein, changes occur in plasma amino acid levels that raise
the level of the nutrient tryptophan in the brain. The production of serotonin, a product of tryptophan, is then accelerated.[11,12] These neurotransmitter changes predispose the individual to consume more protein
and less carbohydrate at the next meal. The action of this regulatory
mechanism has been demonstrated in rats. By feeding rats a carbohydrate-
rich premeal[34] or by administering a drug that enhances serotonin-
mediated neurotransmission,[33] rats can be manipulated to increase the
protein/carbohydrate ratio of the next meal.

If individuals do have disturbances in this metabolic feedback mechanism that causes them to crave carbohydrate, they have limited choices.[35]
They may eat regular meals supplemented by multiple carbohydrate
snacks and become obese, or they may maintain a normal weight by restricting their mealtime food intake or increasing their energy output.
Bulimic individuals may have found yet another option by restricting
mealtime intake and inducing vomiting after carbohydrate binges.

Conclusions

There is evidence to support both a sociobehavioral and a biological explanation for the etiology of bulimia, and at present a biopsychosocial
model that incorporates both perspectives seems most promising. It is
possible that each theory explains the disorder in some subset of bulimic
patients, or that the two forces interact together to produce bulimia.

Certain biological conditions may prove to be risk factors for what is

* See references 11, 12, 33, 34, and 35.

otherwise a learned behavior pattern. For example, within the current social context that encourages extreme thinness among young women, some may be prone to extreme dietary restraint and may be vulnerable to binge eating. This might include those who have a genetic or behavioral predisposition toward obesity, those with a faulty serotonergic carbohydrate feedback mechanism, or those with a tendency toward dysphoria or affective disorder. Those with a faulty carbohydrate feedback mechanism or another predisposition toward obesity would need extreme dietary restraint to stay thin. This restraint could lead to binge eating. Individuals with a tendency toward affective disorder would have two vulnerabilities to bulimia, since negative emotions disinhibit the cognitive controls involved in dieting and since binge eating may become a means of attempting to deal with fluctuating, negative emotions. No matter what factor predisposes a person toward dietary restraint and binge eating, the very act of binging is likely to lead to weight gain and a search for more stringent weight-control methods. For some, vomiting or laxative abuse provides the mechanism for avoiding weight gain and the resulting anxiety.

Despite the short history of research on bulimia, data suggest several theoretical approaches. A number of these approaches, both biological and sociobehavioral, are promising, but they are tentative. The evidence to support them is encouraging but limited and is often obtained with inadequate methods. Thus the elaboration and further testing of these theories represents a fertile realm for inquiry by both biological and behavioral scientists.

REFERENCES

1. American Psychiatric Association. 1980. *Diagnostic and statistical manual of mental disorders*, 3rd ed. Washington, D.C.: American Psychiatric Association.

2. Bureau of the Census. 1983. *Statistical abstract of the United States*. Washington, D.C.: U.S. Government Printing Office.

3. Cabanac, M. 1971. Physiological role of pleasure. *Science* 173:1103–1107.

4. Cabanac, M., and Duclaux, R. 1970. Obesity: Absence of satiety aversion to sucrose. *Science* 168:496–497.

5. Carroll, B. J., et al. 1981. A specific laboratory test for the diagnosis of melancholia: Standardization, validation, and clinical utility. *Archives of General Psychiatry* 38:15–22.

6. Casper, R. C. 1983. On the emergence of bulimia nervosa as a syndrome. *International Journal of Eating Disorders* 2:3–16.

7. Dornbusch, S. M., et al. 1983. The desire to be thin among adolescent females as a form of conspicuous consumption: An empirical test in a national sample. Manuscript.

8. Dwyer, J. T., Feldman, J. J., Seltzer, C. C., and Mayer, J. 1969. Body image in adolescents: Attitudes toward weight and perception of appearance. *American Journal of Clinical Nutrition* 20:1045–1056.

9. Fairburn, C. G. 1981. A cognitive behavioral approach to the treatment of bulimia. *Psychological Medicine* 11:707–711.

10. Fairburn, C. G., and Cooper, P. J. 1982. Self-induced vomiting and bulimia nervosa: An undetected problem. *British Medical Journal* 284:1153–1155.

11. Fernstrom, J. D., and Wurtman, R. J. 1971. Brain serotonin content: Increase following ingestion of carbohydrate diet. *Science* 174:1023–1025.

12. ———. 1972. Brain serotonin content: Physiological regulation by plasma neutral amino acids. *Science* 178:414–416.

13. Garner, D. M., Garfinkel, P. E., Schwartz, D., and Thompson, M. 1980. Cultural expectation of thinness in women. *Psychological Reports* 47:483–491.

14. Gwirtsman, H. E., Roy-Byrne, P., Yager, J., and Gerner, R. H. 1983. Neuroendocrine abnormalities in bulimia. *American Journal of Psychiatry* 140:559–563.

15. Herman, C. P., and Mack, D. 1975. Restrained and unrestrained eating. *Journal of Personality* 43:647–660.

16. Herman, C. P., and Polivy, J. 1975. Anxiety, restraint, and eating behavior. *Journal of Abnormal Psychology* 84:666–672.

17. Herman, C. P., Polivy, J., Pliner, P., and Threlkeld, J. 1978. Distractibility in dieters and nondieters: An alternative view of "externality." *Journal of Personality and Social Psychology* 36:536–548.

18. Hudson, J. I., Laffer, P. S., and Pope, H. G. 1982. Bulimia related to affective disorder by family history and response to the dexamethasone suppression test. *American Journal of Psychiatry* 139:685–687.

19. Hudson, J. I., Pope, H. G., Jonas, J. M., and Yurgelun-Todd, D. 1983. Family history study of anorexia nervosa and bulimia. *British Journal of Psychiatry* 142:133–138.

20. Johnson, C., and Larson, R. 1982. Bulimia: An analysis of moods and behavior. *Psychosomatic Medicine* 44:341–351.

21. Kirkley, B. G., Schneider, J. A., Agras, W. S., and Bachman, J. A. 1985. A comparison of two group treatments for bulimia. *Journal of Consulting and Clinical Psychology* 53:43–48.

22. Leitenberg, H., Gross, J., Peterson, J., and Rosen, J. C. 1984. Analysis of an anxiety model and the process of change during exposure plus response prevention treatment of bulimia nervosa. *Behavior Therapy* 15:3–20.

23. Marcus, M., and Wing, R. R. 1984. Binge eating and dietary restraint. Paper presented at the annual meeting of the Society for Behavioral Medicine, Philadelphia.

24. Mook, D. G., and Cseh, C. L. 1981. Release of feeding by the sweet taste in rats: The influence of body weight. *Appetite* 2:15–34.

25. Nylander, I. 1971. The feeling of being fat and dieting in a school population: Epidemiologic, interview investigation. *Acta Sociomedica Scandinavica* 3:17–26.

26. Polivy, J. 1976. Perception of calories and regulation of intake in restrained and unrestrained subjects. *Addictive Behaviors* 1:237–243.

27. Polivy, J., Herman, C. P., and Warsh, S. 1978. Internal and external components of emotionality in restrained and unrestrained eaters. *Journal of Abnormal Psychology* 87:497–504.

28. Pope, H. G., Hudson, J. J., Jonas, J. M., and Yurgelun-Todd, D. 1983. Bulimia treated with imipramine: A placebo-controlled double-blind study. *American Journal of Psychiatry* 140:554–558.

29. Pyle, R. L., et al. 1983. The incidence of bulimia in freshman college students. *International Journal of Eating Disorders* 2:75–85.

30. Rodin, J., Slochower, J., and Fleming, B. 1977. The effects of degree of obesity, age of onset, and energy deficit on external responsiveness. *Journal of Comparative Physiology and Psychology* 91:586–597.

31. Rosen, J. C., and Leitenberg, H. 1982. Bulimia nervosa: Treatment with exposure and response prevention. *Behavior Therapy* 13:117–124.

32. Schneider, J. A., and Agras, W. S. 1985. A cognitive behavioral group treatment of bulimia. *British Journal of Psychiatry* 146:66–69.

33. Wurtman, J. J., and Wurtman, R. J. 1979. Drugs that enhance central serotoninergic transmission diminish elective carbohydrate consumption by rats. *Life Science* 24:895–904.

34. Wurtman, J. J., Moses, P. L., and Wurtman, R. J. 1983. Prior carbohydrate consumption affects the amount of carbohydrate that rats choose to eat. *Journal of Nutrition* 113:70–78.

35. Wurtman, R. J., and Wurtman, J. J. 1984. Nutrients, neurotransmitter synthesis, and the control of food intake. In *Eating and its disorders*, ed. A. J. Stunkard and E. Stellar, pp. 77–86. New York: Raven Press.

21

Bulimia: Medical and Physiological Aspects

James E. Mitchell

The eating disorder bulimia is characterized by binge eating as well as by self-induced vomiting and/or laxative abuse. The medical problems associated with bulimia differ somewhat from those of anorexia nervosa, although there is considerable overlap. While many of the medical complications of anorexia nervosa result from emaciation, most of those seen in bulimic patients result from specific behaviors such as binge eating, self-induced vomiting, laxative abuse, and diuretic abuse. Such complications are also seen in the subgroup of anorexia nervosa patients who engage in these behaviors but are not present in typical restrictor anorexic patients (those who restrict food intake as opposed to periodically binging and vomiting).

Although usually considered more medically benign than anorexia nervosa, bulimia can have serious medical consequences. This chapter offers an overview of the signs and symptoms of bulimia and a discussion of the specific problems by organ systems.

Signs and Symptoms of Bulimia

In contrast to anorexia nervosa, almost no systematic work has been published on the signs and symptoms reported by patients with bulimia. These patients frequently complain of constipation, bloating, and abdominal pain, and many report feeling weak and lethargic. In my experience, many also report irregular menses, although prolonged amenorrhea appears to be uncommon.

There is usually little evidence on physical examination to indicate the severity of the problem. There may be evidence of dehydration if the patient significantly restricts fluid intake or loses fluid through vomiting or laxative or diuretic abuse. In some patients, particularly those who abuse laxatives, peripheral edema may be present.[28] Some patients may have maceration or callouses on their fingers caused by using their fingers to stimulate the gag reflex.[37] Some may have swelling of the salivary glands.[17] Beyond these findings, signs and symptoms are fairly uncommon. Therefore, it is often difficult to make the diagnosis of bulimia on the basis of routine history or physical examination unless the patient volunteers the problem.

Medical Complications by Organ System

RENAL COMPLICATIONS

Routine laboratory screening of patients with nonanorexic bulimia usually reveals normal renal function or, at most, an elevated blood-urea-nitrogen level, indicating dehydration[26] (see table 21.1). However, it is possible that the dehydration resulting from laxative abuse, diuretic abuse, or vomiting, particularly when associated with hypokalemia, might predispose to more severe renal problems.[21,28,48] Riemenschneider and Bohle[36] reported renal biopsy results in patients with hypokalemia and hyponatremia from a variety of causes including laxative abuse, diuretic abuse, anorexia nervosa, or chronic vomiting. Biopsy results indicated interstitial fibrosis and other changes felt to be secondary to low potassium nephropathy, which can result in a diminution in renal function. Although renal biopsies or renal functioning have not been thoroughly investigated in patients with bulimia, it can be anticipated that chronic bulimia might increase the risk for such renal disease. This is an area in need of further research.

GASTROINTESTINAL COMPLICATIONS

Elevated serum amylase levels are common in patients with bulimia.[8,26] The elevations are usually moderate and infrequently exceed two times normal values. The amylase elevations may be salivary in origin since salivary gland swelling is common in these patients. However, a pancreatic source has not been excluded. Rampling[30] has reported a patient hospitalized for episodes of acute pancreatitis following eating binges. He was able to correlate the episodes of pancreatitis to episodes of bulimic be-

TABLE 21.1

Laboratory Abnormalities and Medical Complications of Bulimia

Renal Complications	*Hematological Abnormalities*
Dehydration	Bleeding tendency
Hypokalemic nephropathy	
	Neurological Abnormalities
Gastrointestinal Complications	Electroencephalogram abnormalities
Gastric dilatation	
Sialodenosis	*Endocrine Abnormalities*
Amylase elevations	Blunted thyroid-stimulating hormone
Pancreatitis	response to thyroid-releasing
	hormone
Electrolyte Abnormalities	Pathological growth hormone response
Hyperuricemia	to TRH, glucose
Hypokalemia	Prolactin elevations
Alkalosis	Dexamethasone suppression test
Acidosis	nonsuppression
Laxative Abuse Complications	*Dental Problems*
Hyperuremia	Caries
Hypocalcemia	Enamel erosion
Tetany	
Osteomalacia	
Clubbing	
Skin pigmentation	
Hypomagnesemia	
Fluid retention	
Malabsorption syndromes	
Protein losing enteropathy	
Cathartic colon	

havior. Further studies should be undertaken on the fractionation of amylase to differentiate its possible sources.

Sialodenosis, or swelling of the salivary glands, has been documented both in patients with anorexia nervosa and in patients with nonanorexic bulimia.[4,17,40] The clinical picture is usually one of painless swelling in the salivary glands; the parotid glands are most commonly affected, but other salivary glands may be involved as well.[2] Levin and associates[17] reported one case of a biopsy finding of normal tissue. Walsh and associates[44] reported biopsies that showed asymptomatic noninflammatory enlargement in most cases with evidence of scattered inflammatory cells in one case. The pathophysiology of this complication is unclear. The problem has been variously attributed to high carbohydrate intake, alkalosis, and the malnutrition seen in some patients.[2,17]

Saul, in his review of cases of spontaneous rupture of the stomach, reported the case of a normal-weight individual with a history of anorexia nervosa who overate excessively and developed gastric infarction and perforation of the stomach that resulted in shock and death.[38] My associates and I also reported a case of gastric dilatation in a patient of normal weight with bulimia that was managed successfully without surgery.[24] These reports indicate gastric dilatation is a possible complication of bulimia as well as anorexia nervosa.

The superior mesenteric artery syndrome should be considered in the differential diagnosis of bulimia.[1] This condition, which presents with vomiting and abdominal pain, can have either an acute or a chronic course. The chronic form may present with weight loss and may mimic anorexia nervosa if the amount of weight lost is severe.[41] The syndrome involves compression of the third portion of the duodenum by the superior mesenteric neurovascular bundle. The problem is a mechanical one and creates an intermittent obstruction of the duodenum, which may be positional. The condition can sometimes be managed supportively but may require surgical intervention.

ELECTROLYTE ABNORMALITIES

Fluid loss commonly accompanies bulimic behaviors, particularly vomiting, laxative abuse, and diuretic abuse. Disturbances in electrolytes usually accompany these fluid changes, and electrolyte abnormalities are commonly seen on routine screening in patients with bulimia.[26] In one series of 168 patients with bulimia or atypical eating disorder, most of whom were self-inducing vomiting and/or abusing laxatives, 82 demonstrated some electrolyte abnormality. The commonly encountered changes included metabolic alkalosis (27.4 percent), hypochloremia (23.8 percent), and hypokalemia (13.7 percent).[26] Patients who reported vomiting at least daily were significantly more likely to manifest metabolic alkalosis. Metabolic acidosis was also described in a few patients; possible causes were fasting-induced acidosis or acidosis secondary to acute diarrhea from laxative abuse.

The pathophysiology of these electrolyte abnormalities is complex but can be understood on the basis of the attendant behaviors.[5,15] Vomiting, laxative abuse, and diuretic abuse cause volume depletion as well as the loss of sodium, potassium, and a net loss of hydrogen ion. The resultant volume contraction causes aldosterone secretion, which promotes further potassium loss through renal excretion. The lack of chloride, in the presence of volume depletion, limits the kidney's ability to excrete bicarbonate since bicarbonate is the only anion other than chloride that can directly accompany sodium reabsorption to any significant degree. However, with volume contraction, sodium reabsorption predominates and bicarbonate must also be reabsorbed. This worsens the alkalosis. Also, hydrogen is exchanged out of the cells for potassium to compensate for the alkalosis. The movement of potassium into the cells exacerbates the hypokalemia. The overall pattern is one of hypochloremia, hypokalemia, and alkalosis, or some variant of this pattern.

The electrolyte abnormalities represent one complication of bulimia that may require emergency treatment and/or periodic monitoring. In extreme cases of hypokalemia, intravenous potassium supplementation may be necessary. In most cases supplemental oral potassium will suffice.

It is unclear what clinical significance these electrolyte abnormalities may have for most patients. The alkalosis and potassium deficiency may cause some of the weakness, tiredness, and constipation seen in these patients and may also contribute to depression.[45]

HEMATOLOGICAL AND IMMUNOLOGICAL ABNORMALITIES

A single case report of a patient with bulimia who demonstrated a bleeding tendency has been published.[27] The patient was found to have a deficiency of vitamin K–dependent coagulation factors. The presumed mechanism was inadequate intake of foods containing vitamin K.

NEUROLOGICAL ABNORMALITIES

There has been considerable interest in possible neurophysiological dysfunction in patients with bulimia or related eating problems. Rau, Green, and their colleagues have published extensively in this area. Their work centers on the hypothesis that patients with compulsive eating problems may have electroencephalographic (EEG) abnormalities reflecting neurophysiological dysfunction.[31,32,33] In summarizing their studies, these authors reported that 64.4 percent of a series of seventy-nine patients had abnormal EEG's. The abnormalities most commonly encountered were paroxysmal dysrhythmias, particularly the 14- and 6-spike pattern. This pattern is also present in some normal subjects,[18,19] and the clinical significance is unclear.[4,6,20,43] My associates and I reported the EEG results of twenty-five patients with bulimia.[23] Twenty-one of the twenty-five tracings were normal when read twice by electroencephalographers blind to diagnosis. The question of EEG abnormalities in bulimia deserves further study.

There have been several reports of bulimic symptoms in patients with a variety of primary neurological problems. These reports have included Huntington's chorea,[47] as a postictal phenomenon,[35] following lobotomy[10] or amygdalectomy,[39] and central nervous system tumors.[16,34] The reports underscore the importance of careful neurological assessment of patients who present with disordered eating patterns.

ENDOCRINE ABNORMALITIES

Endocrine function is an important area to investigate in patients with bulimia. First, the endocrine system is clearly involved in weight regulation, appetite, and metabolism. Second, neuroendocrine control mechanisms can be evaluated as an indirect way of examining brain function, providing a "window" on the hypothalamus, an area of the brain important in both eating behavior and neuroendocrine control. Bulimic individuals offer a unique opportunity to study neuroendocrine control mechanisms in eating-disorder patients since weight loss is not the overriding factor as it is in anorexia nervosa. Neuroendocrine studies are just now being undertaken in several centers. Existing studies suggest the possibility of some neuroendocrine dysfunction in these patients.[8,22] Several different areas have been studied.

Routine thyroid function tests including triiodothyronine (T_3) and thyroxine (T_4) are normal in most patients with bulimia, and available data suggest that these patients are euthyroid. However, thyroid regulation may be dysfunctional in some patients. Gwirtsman and associates[8] reported results of thyroid-releasing hormone (TRH) stimulation studies in patients with bulimia and found that eight of ten patients had blunted thyroid-stimulating hormone (TSH) responses (a change in TSH of less than 5) following TRH administration. My associates and I reported normal TSH responsiveness to TRH in five of six normal-weight subjects with bulimia.[22] It is of note that Gwirtsman and associates[8] also reported an inappropriate increase in growth hormone (GH) in two of three patients following TRH administration.

Little work has been done on prolactin regulation in these patients. One study found elevated fasting prolactin levels in three of six normal-weight bulimic subjects, with five of six subjects demonstrating normal prolactin responsiveness to TRH stimulation.[22] Results of GH studies indicate paradoxical GH increases following glucose administration in three of six patients with bulimia,[22] a pattern that has been described in anorexia nervosa patients. These regulatory changes in GH and prolactin are of unknown clinical significance but are interesting since they suggest hypothalamic dysregulation.

There have been some interesting reports regarding the problem of bulimia in patients with diabetes mellitus.[9,12] It appears that some patients with diabetes may purposely run high plasma glucose levels as a means to "purge" by promoting glucose loss through the kidneys. This lack of diabetic control poses long-term hazards for these patients.

As with anorexia nervosa, there appears to be a high rate of dexamethasone nonsuppression in patients with bulimia. Several series of patients have been reported who had a high rate of nonsuppression: 56 percent of nine patients reported by Hudson and associates in 1982[13]; 47 percent of forty-seven patients reported by Hudson and associates in 1983[14]; 67 percent of eighteen patients reported by Gwirtsman and associates in 1982[8]; and 50 percent of twenty-eight patients reported by my associates and me.[25] Cortisol secretory patterns have not been reported.

Gwirtsman and associates[7] have reported three cases of bulimia in males. Two of the three were nonsuppressors on the dexamethasone suppression test, and one showed a blunted TSH response to TRH. Very little work has been reported regarding male bulimic patients.

DENTAL PROBLEMS

Dental problems are quite common in bulimic patients and appear to be attributable to the abnormal behaviors involved, particularly vomiting and high carbohydrate intake. In published reports, two major types of dental pathology are described: rapidly developing dental caries, presumably related to the high carbohydrate intake, and erosion of the enamel, a dental condition that develops secondary to chronic regurgitation. Decalcification of the lingual, palatal, and posterior occlusal surfaces of the teeth is usually described. This pattern of decalcification differentiates this condition from acid ingestion since the distribution indicates that the acid is coming from the back of the mouth. The clinical appearance is fairly characteristic.[11,42]

LAXATIVE ABUSE COMPLICATIONS

Increased attention is being given to the problem of laxative abuse as a complicating pattern in bulimia. Although much of the literature on laxative abuse has been in general medical journals,[37] clinicians who work with eating disorders are encountering patients who abuse laxatives as one of their problems. The percentage of bulimic patients who abused laxatives in one large series was approximately 40 percent.[26] For this reason, many of the complications described in patients with laxative abuse in the general medical literature may soon be found in patients with bulimia or anorexia nervosa who abuse laxatives. Many patients with bulimia who abuse laxatives may use them on a daily basis in quantities many times larger than the recommended dosage. Possible complications[3,28,29] of laxative abuse include:

1. *Gastrointestinal complications:* Nausea, vomiting, weight loss, malabsorption syndromes, protein-losing gastroenteropathy, cathartic colon (where the colon ceases to function adequately).
2. *Nongastrointestinal complications:* Fluid and electrolyte abnormalities (as described previously), hyperuricemia, hypocalcemia (which can be accompanied by tetany and osteomalacia), and hypomagnesemia. Pigmentation of the skin and digital clubbing have also been described.
3. *Laxative withdrawal complications:* Fluid retention, which can be dramatic, causing weight increases in excess of 10 pounds, and constipation.

Summary and Conclusions

This review of medical complications should be considered preliminary since much less is known about bulimia than about anorexia nervosa. Judging from our experience to date, the description of further problems can be anticipated.

As with anorexia nervosa, a careful physical examination and laboratory assessment are indicated for each patient. Careful attention on physical examination should be given to the state of hydration, oral hygiene, and the vital signs. Consideration should always be given to the possibility of a primary neurological lesion.

Routine screening laboratory work also appears indicated. Of particular importance are screening determinations of serum electrolytes, serum calcium, renal function tests, and plasma glucose. A routine screening battery including these elements should be part of every diagnostic evaluation. Electrolytes may need to be followed while patients are in therapy. Some centers routinely do more detailed neurological assessment including skull films with visual fields and/or computerized-axial-tomography scan. Certainly a careful neurological assessment on physical examination is indicated.

REFERENCES

1. Akin, J. T., Jr., Gray, S. W., and Skandelakis, J. E. 1976. Vascular compression of the duodenum: Presentation of ten cases and review of the literature. *Surgery* 79:515–522.

2. Anders, D., Harms, D., Kriens, O., and Schmidt, H. 1975. Zur frage der sialadenose als sekundarer organmanifestation der anorexia nervosa–beobachtungen en einem 13 jahrigen knaben. *Klinische Padiatric* 187:156–162.

3. Cummings, J. 1974. Progress report: Laxative abuse. *Gut* 15:758–766.

4. Dawson, J., and Jones, C. 1977. Vomiting-induced hypolalemic alkalosis and parotid swelling. *Practitioner* 218:267–268.

5. Gabow, P. 1976. Disorders of potassium metabolism. In *Renal and electrolyte disorders,* ed. R. Schrier, pp. 143–165. Boston: Little, Brown.

6. Gibbs, E. L., and Gibbs, F. A. 1951. Electroencephalographic evidence of thalamic and hypothalamic epilepsy. *Neurology* 1:136–144.

7. Gwirtsman, H. E., Roy-Byrne, P., Lerner, L., and Yager, J. 1984. Bulimia in men: Report of three cases with neuroendocrine findings. *Journal of Clinical Psychiatry* 45:78–81.

8. Gwirtsman, H. E., Roy-Byrne, P., Yager, J., and Gerner, R. H. 1983. Neuroendocrine abnormalities in bulimia. *American Journal of Psychiatry* 140:559–563.

9. Hillard, J. R., Lobo, M. C., and Keeling, R. P. 1983. Bulimia and diabetes: A potentially life-threatening combination. *Psychosomatics* 24:292–295.

10. Hofstatter, L., Smolik, E. A., and Busch, A. K. 1945. Prefrontal lobotomy in treatment of chronic psychoses with special reference to section of the orbital areas only. *Archives of Neurology and Psychiatry* 53:125–130.

11. House, R. C., et al. 1981. Perimolysis: Unveiling the surreptitious vomiter. *Oral Surgery* 51:152–155.

12. Hudson, J. I., Hudson, M. S., and Wentworth, S. M. 1983. Self-induced glycosuria. A novel method of purging in bulimia. *Journal of the American Medical Association* 249:2501.

13. Hudson, J. I., Laffer, P. S., and Pope, H. G. 1982. Bulimia related to affective disorder by family history and response to the dexamethasone suppression test. *American Journal of Psychiatry* 139:685–687.

14. Hudson, J. I., Pope, H. G., and Jonas, J. M. 1983. Hypothalamic-pituitary-adrenal axis: Hyperactivity in bulimia. *Psychiatric Research* 8:111–117.

15. Kaehny, W. O. 1976. Pathogenesis and management of metabolic acidosis and alkalosis. In *Renal and electrolyte disorders,* ed. R. Schrier, pp. 79–120. Boston: Little, Brown.

16. Kirschbaum, W. R. 1951. Excessive hunger as a symptom of cerebral origin. *Journal of Nervous and Mental Disease* 113:95–114.

17. Levin, P. A., et al. 1980. Benign parotid enlargement in bulimia. *Annals of Internal Medicine* 93:827–829.

18. Lombroso, C. T., et al. 1966. Ctenoids in healthy youths. *Neurology* (Minneapolis) 16:1152–1158.

19. Long, M. T., and Johnson, L. C. 1968. Fourteen- and six-per-second positive spikes in a nonclinical male population. *Neurology* 18:714–716.

20. Maulsby, R. L. 1979. EEG patterns in uncertain diagnostic significance. In *Current practice of clinical electroencephalography,* ed. D. W. Klass and D. D. Daily, pp. 220–224. New York: Raven Press.

21. Mitchell, J. E. 1983. Medical complications of anorexia nervosa and bulimia. *Psychiatric Medicine* 1:229–256.

22. Mitchell, J. E., and Bantle, J. P. 1983. Metabolic and endocrine investigations in women of normal weight with the bulimia syndrome. *Biological Psychiatry* 18:355–365.

23. Mitchell, J. E., Hosfield, W., and Pyle, R. L. 1983. EEG findings in patients with the bulimia syndrome. *International Journal of Eating Disorders* 2:17–23.

24. Mitchell, J. E., Pyle, R. L., and Miner, R. A. 1982. Gastric dilatation as a complication of bulimia. *Psychosomatics* 23:96–97.

25. Mitchell, J. E., Hatsukami, D., Pyle, R., and Boutacoff, L. 1984. The dexamethasone suppression test in bulimia. *Journal of Clinical Psychiatry* 45:508–511.

26. Mitchell, J. E., et al. 1983. Electrolyte and other physiological abnormalities in patients with bulimia. *Psychological Medicine* 13:273–278.

27. Niiya, K., et al. 1983. Bulimia nervosa complicated by deficiency of vitamin K-dependent coagulation factors. *Journal of the American Medical Association* 250:792–793.

28. Oster, J. R., Materson, B. J., and Rogers, A. I. 1980. Laxative abuse syndrome. *American Journal of Gastroenterology* 74:451–458.

29. Pietrusko, R. G. 1977. Use and abuse of laxatives. *American Journal of Hospital Pharmacology* 34:291–300.

30. Rampling, D. 1982. Acute pancreatitis in anorexia nervosa. *Medical Journal of Australia* 2:194–195.

31. Rau, J. H., and Green, R. S. 1975. Compulsive eating: A neuropsychological approach to certain eating disorders. *Comprehensive Psychiatry* 16:223–231.

32. ———. 1978. Soft neurological correlates of compulsive eaters. *Journal of Nervous and Mental Disease* 166:435–437.

33. Rau, J. H., Struve, F. A., and Green, R. S. 1979. Electroencephalographic correlates of compulsive eating. *Clinical Electroencephalography* 10:180–189.

34. Reeves, A. G., and Plum, F. 1969. Hyperphagia, rage, and dementia accompanying a ventromedial hypothalamic neoplasm. *Archives of Neurology* 20:616–624.

35. Remick, R. A., Jones, M. W., and Campos, P. E. 1980. Postictal bulimia. *Journal of Clinical Psychiatry* 41:256.

36. Riemenschneider, T., and Bohle, A. 1983. Morphologic aspects of low-potassium and low-sodium nephropathy. *Clinical Nephrology* 19:271–279.

37. Russell, G. 1979. Bulimia nervosa: An ominous variant of anorexia nervosa. *Psychological Medicine* 9:429–488.

38. Saul, S. H., Dekker, A., and Watson, C. G. 1981. Acute gastric dilatation with infarction and perforation. *Gut* 22:978–983.

39. Sawa, M., Ueki, Y., Arita, M., and Harada, T. 1954. Preliminary report on the amygdaloidectomy on the psychotic patients, with interpretation of oral-emotional manifestation in schizophrenics. *Folia Psychiatrica et Neurologica Japonica* 7:309–329.

40. Simon, D., Laudenbach, P., Lebovici, M., and Mauvais-Jarvis, P. 1979. Parotidomegalie au cours des dysorexies mentales. *Nouvelle Presse Medicale* 9:2399–2402.

41. Sours, J. A., and Vorhaus, L. J. 1981. Superior mesenteric syndrome in anorexia nervosa: A case report. *American Journal of Psychiatry* 138:519–520.

42. Stege, P., Visco-Dangler, L., and Rye, L. 1982. Anorexia nervosa: Review including oral and dental manifestations. *Journal of the American Dental Association* 104:548–552.

43. Struve, F. A., and Ramsey, P. R. 1977. Concerning the 14 and 6 per second positive spike cases in post traumatic and medical-legal EEGs reported by Gibbs and Gibbs. A statistical commentary. *Clinical Electroencephalography* 8:203–205.

44. Walsh, B. T., Croft, C. B., and Katz, J. A. 1981–82. Anorexia nervosa and salivary gland enlargement. *International Journal of Psychiatry in Medicine* 11:255–261.

45. Webb, W. L., and Gehi, M. 1981. Electrolyte and fluid imbalance: Neuropsychiatric manifestations. *Psychosomatics* 22:199–202.

46. Wegner, J. T., and Struve, F. A. 1977. Incidence of the 14 and 16 per second

positive spike pattern in an adult clinical population: an empirical note. *Journal of Nervous and Mental Disease* 164:340–345.

47. Whittier, J. R. 1976. Asphyxiation, bulimia, and insulin levels in Huntington disease (chorea). *Journal of the American Medical Association* 235:1423–1424.

48. Wigley, R. D. 1960. Potassium deficiency in anorexia nervosa, with reference to renal tubular vacuolation. *British Medical Journal* 2:110–113.

22

The Clinical Features and Maintenance of Bulimia Nervosa

Christopher G. Fairburn, Zafra Cooper,
and Peter J. Cooper

This chapter aims to describe the clinical features of bulimia nervosa and to examine the factors maintaining the disorder. The condition denoted by this term[43] has attracted other names, including bulimarexia,[5] the dietary chaos syndrome,[36] the abnormal normal weight control syndrome,[11] and bulimia, the term used in the third edition of the *Diagnostic and Statistical Manual of Mental Disorders (DSM-III)*.[2] These terms refer to essentially the same disorder. We prefer the term bulimia nervosa, since it emphasizes the important similarities between this condition and anorexia nervosa, and it avoids the ambiguities that result from using the word bulimia to refer to both the overeating associated with this disorder and the full clinical syndrome itself.

We are grateful to Marianne O'Connor for preparing the manuscript. Part of this chapter is based on research funded by the Medical Research Council of the United Kingdom. C. G. F. is a Wellcome Trust Senior Lecturer.

TABLE 22.1

Clinical Characteristics of Three Series of Patients with Bulimia or Bulimia Nervosa

	Russell[43] (N = 30)	Pyle, Mitchell and Eckert[41] (N = 34)	Fairburn and Cooper[19] (N = 35)
Diagnosis	Bulimia nervosa	Bulimia	Bulimia nervosa
Age (years)	—	24 (19–51)[a]	23.5 ± 4.4[b]
Age at onset of bulimia or self-induced vomiting (years)	21.2 ± 6.5[b]	18 (11–45)[a]	19.7 ± 4.2[b] (bulimia) 20.0 ± 3.7[b] (vomiting)
Self-induced vomiting at least daily (%)	—	47.1	74.3
Use of purgatives for weight control (%)	43.3	52.9	31.4
History of anorexia nervosa: applying narrow criteria (%) applying broad criteria (%)	56.7 80.0	29.4 47.1	25.7 34.3
Weight as % matched population mean weight	—	—	97.3 ± 10.3[b]

[a] Median and range.
[b] Mean and standard deviation.

The Clinical Features of Bulimia Nervosa

There has been little systematic research into the clinical features of bulimia nervosa. Four patient series have been described,[19,27,41,43] and there have been several general descriptions of the disorder.[14,15,33,34] However, any attempt to compare these series and clinical descriptions is complicated by the application of differing diagnostic criteria and the infrequent use of established assessment instruments. Nevertheless, from these accounts a relatively clear picture of the clinical features of bulimia nervosa emerges. Table 22.1 summarizes the principal characteristics of three patient series.

DEMOGRAPHIC CHARACTERISTICS

Bulimia nervosa is almost exclusively confined to women. The majority of patients are in their twenties and about a quarter are married. The social class distribution is similar to that of anorexia nervosa, with most patients coming from upper socioeconomic groups.

EATING HABITS

Although most patients with bulimia nervosa complain of having lost control over eating, their eating habits vary considerably. Usually episodes of overeating alternate with attempts to diet. In their more extreme form the bulimic episodes are relatively uniform in character. Almost invariably they occur in secret. Sometimes they are precipitated by unpleasant events, or by feelings of depression, anxiety, boredom, or loneliness. Often they follow the breaking of rigid and restrictive dietary rules. Occasionally they are planned. During such episodes food tends to be eaten rapidly with relatively little attention being paid to its taste or texture, and in general it comprises those items patients are attempting to exclude from their diet. Thus it usually consists of energy-rich food the patient considers "fattening," "forbidden," or "dangerous." The total quantity eaten varies markedly, 5,000 to 10,000 calories per episode not being uncommon. The amount of liquid consumed also varies: if self-induced vomiting is to follow, a large volume may be drunk in order to facilitate regurgitation. Bulimic episodes are usually terminated by self-induced vomiting, straightforward physical exhaustion, painful abdominal distension, interruption by others, or running out of food supplies. Afterward there is often a period of drowsiness and subsequent feelings of depression, guilt, and self-disgust. However, the initial stages of the bulimic episode are not necessarily unpleasant since there is a release from the rigors and monotony of strict dieting, a distraction from current problems, and a temporary decline in any feelings of depression and anxiety.

It is important to distinguish mere overeating from a bulimic episode. Most patients can readily make this distinction.[1] For an episode of eating to be regarded as bulimic it should fulfill two necessary conditions: first, the person should regard the quantity of food eaten as excessive; and second, it should be experienced as outside voluntary control.[14,15] What is of primary importance therefore is not the absolute quantity of food consumed but rather how the episode is experienced. The duration of the episode is also unimportant. While many episodes do last less than two hours, as required by the *DSM-III* diagnostic criteria,[2] others may last longer.[1,35] Neither is the eating necessarily inconspicuous, again a requirement of the *DSM-III* definition.

Patients vary in their frequency of bulimic episodes. Some report having several episodes a day, whereas others only occasionally lose control. In general, bulimic episodes are most likely to occur during periods of unstructured time—for example, in the evening and during weekends. A minority overeat at night. Between these episodes most patients attempt to follow strict dietary regimes involving the exclusion of all potentially, "fattening" food, and some impose a daily calorie limit, often in the region of 1,000 calories. Such patients may find it impossible to eat without calorie-counting.

Although patients with bulimia nervosa have poor control over their eating, there is no compelling evidence to suggest that this is due to any disturbance of the physiological mechanisms controlling food intake. They do not describe excessive hunger. Indeed, the majority report that they rarely feel hungry and that physiologically determined hunger does not influence when they eat. Clinical experience indicates that normal hunger sensations gradually return once a pattern of regular eating has been established.[17] This suggests that the irregular eating of these patients may have secondary effects on physiological hunger. Regarding satiety, many report feeling full after eating relatively small amounts of food. Such feelings of fullness are especially likely to develop after eating foods regarded as fattening, suggesting that this reaction may be largely cognitive in nature. Patients report that during bulimic episodes the urge to eat is so strong that they continue eating despite feelings of fullness. Overall, it appears that the eating of patients with bulimia nervosa is predominantly governed by psychological rather than physiological factors, although this has yet to be systematically investigated.

A minority of patients with bulimia nervosa practice certain unusual eating habits. For example, some chew food and then spit it out, while others engage in habitual rumination. The rumination usually begins shortly after eating and consists of the repeated regurgitation of food, which is then chewed, then reswallowed or spat out. Some patients regard rumination as an innocuous habit, while others view it with shame and self-disgust.[20]

METHODS OF WEIGHT CONTROL

The majority of patients with bulimia nervosa have a body weight within the normal range.[19] Nevertheless, they are highly concerned about their shape and weight. Their poor control over eating is therefore a source of great distress. Accordingly, they engage in various practices designed either to counteract the potentially "fattening" consequences of overeating or to promote weight loss in general. These include the extreme dieting mentioned earlier, self-induced vomiting, the taking of purgatives or diuretics, and excessive exercising.

Self-induced Vomiting. Most patients with bulimia nervosa practice self-induced vomiting. Usually this occurs during or immediately after each bulimic episode, although some patients vomit each time they eat. The frequency of vomiting therefore varies and may be as often as ten or more times daily. If it is foreseen that there will be no opportunity to vomit, overeating is usually resisted.

Self-induced vomiting is performed as soon as possible after eating in order to minimize the absorption of food. Patients become extremely distressed if, having overeaten, they are prevented from vomiting. In the majority of cases vomiting is achieved by stimulating the gag reflex, although some patients can vomit voluntarily without any mechanical aid. A minority engage in elaborate procedures to ensure they have vomited up everything they have eaten. For example, some eat a colored "marker" food at the beginning of the bulimic episode and continue vomiting until it reappears in their vomitus. Others drink and regurgitate copious quantities of water until their vomitus is free from all signs of food.

Self-induced vomiting tends to be highly secret and is an additional source of guilt and self-disgust. Most patients go to great lengths to conceal the habit. It is not uncommon for patients to report having vomited daily for many years without ever having been detected.

Self-induced vomiting is not only potentially harmful, it is also habit-forming. In the very short term it relieves the abdominal discomfort that results from overeating, it reduces anxiety, and it lessens the patient's fear of gaining weight. However, in the long term it seems to encourage overeating, partly because patients think that by vomiting they will avoid absorbing what they have eaten and partly because they discover it is easier to vomit when their stomach is full. As a result, a vicious cycle is gradually established with patients becoming progressively more reliant on vomiting to compensate for their mounting food intake.

Purgative Abuse. Purgative abuse is less common among bulimia nervosa patients than is self-induced vomiting. This is probably for two reasons: first, purgatives tend to be viewed as a less effective means of compensating for having overeaten, and second, the aftereffects are unpleasant. Nevertheless, these drugs are widely taken and, like self-induced vomiting, their use can be habit-forming. Not only is there a rewarding loss of weight shortly afterward, but patients who use purgatives on a frequent and regular basis find that if they stop taking these drugs their weight actually increases, probably as a result of water retention. Such patients therefore continue to take purgatives in order to avoid this weight gain.

The manner in which purgatives are consumed varies. Some patients take them only after episodes of overeating. Others take them as a routine weight-control measure. The number taken on each occasion also varies and may be as high as one hundred or more a day.

Other Methods of Weight Control. Some patients with bulimia nervosa exercise as a means of weight control. Such exercising tends not to be as rigorous as that practiced by patients with anorexia nervosa. It is used to promote weight loss in general rather than being a means of compensating for having overeaten.

Various other methods of weight control are encountered. For example, appetite suppressants or thyroid preparations may be taken. Some diabetic patients who have bulimia nervosa manipulate their illness in order to lose weight,[28,45] and women with bulimia nervosa who have young babies may continue breast-feeding for inordinate lengths of time in order to perpetuate energy loss through lactation.

ATTITUDES TO SHAPE AND WEIGHT

Perhaps the most striking feature of bulimia nervosa is the intensity and prominence of these patients' concerns with their shape and weight. These concerns are similar to those present in anorexia nervosa and are peculiar to these two disorders and their variants. With reference to anorexia nervosa, they have been characterized as a "morbid fear of fatness,"[42] "a pursuit of thinness,"[6] and a "weight phobia."[10] Given the strength of these concerns and their likely importance in the maintenance of both bulimia nervosa and anorexia nervosa, it is surprising that they have been the subject of so little research. In part this must be attributed to the difficulties inherent in their assessment.[16]

Only one study has attempted to measure the attitudes to shape and weight of patients with bulimia nervosa. In this study[19] a semistructured interview was used to identify four psychopathological features, each of which was defined operationally. These features were a morbid fear of fatness, extreme sensitivity to weight gain, pathological pursuit of weight loss, and body-image disparagement. It was found that the most prominent feature was a morbid fear of fatness, which was judged to be present to a marked degree in 86 percent of the patient sample. Over half (55 percent) exhibited extreme sensitivity to weight gain, but only a quarter had pathological pursuit of weight loss (23 percent) or body-image disparagement (29 percent).

The finding that a morbid fear of fatness and sensitivity to weight gain were the most prominent psychopathological features is consistent with clinical observations.[15] Because of their poor control over eating, the great majority of patients with bulimia nervosa feel in constant danger of gaining weight and becoming fat. This concern finds expression in their weighing. Some patients weigh themselves many times a day. These patients feel most unsettled if they are unable to do so and they may go to extreme lengths to prevent this from occurring—by taking, for example, bathroom scales with them on holiday. Other patients react in the opposite fashion and actively avoid weighing while nevertheless remaining extremely concerned about their shape. The finding that pathological pursuit of thinness was only present in a minority is also consistent with clinical observations.[15] The wish to become extremely thin is not often present in bulimia nervosa. Indeed, the mean desired weight of patients with bulimia nervosa is no different from that of women in the community.[19] However, it is common for patients with bulimia nervosa to set themselves a relatively inflexible desired weight.

Concerns about body shape are at least as salient as those centering on body weight, if not more so. These concerns focus on the appearance of the patient's stomach, hips, bottom, and thighs. Some patients assess their shape on the basis of the tightness of their clothes, some scrutinize themselves in mirrors, and a minority measure parts of their body. However, a proportion find their appearance so unsightly and distressing that they actively avoid any situation in which they might see themselves. These patients dress and undress in the dark, avoid communal changing rooms, and may even bathe or shower clothed.

Patients with bulimia nervosa react strongly to changes in their shape and weight. Even small changes may result in marked alterations in their mood and behavior. For example, weight loss may elevate mood, heighten self-confidence, and increase determination to diet.

Accompanying the concerns over shape and weight are certain strongly held values that are extreme forms of widely held attitudes. They concern the importance of having an attractive appearance and the desirability of self-control.

ATTITUDES TO FOOD AND EATING

Most patients with bulimia nervosa have strong views about food and eating. For example, the majority regard a variety of foods as "bad" and "fattening," and many are convinced that if they eat meals or snacks without vomiting, they will gain weight. Some of these attitudes may be attributed to years of reading slimming magazines and diet books.

MENTAL STATE

The majority of patients with bulimia nervosa present with a variety of neurotic symptoms. Depressive features are particularly prominent, and partly for this reason it has been suggested that bulimia nervosa is a form of affective disorder.[29] The depressive symptoms include depressed mood, pathological guilt, self-depreciation, hopelessness, and lack of self-confidence.[19] Thoughts of suicide are found in a minority although few are a true suicide risk. One study found that on an established measure of depression, the total score of these patients was similar to that of patients with major depressive disorder.[8]

Detailed analysis of the neurotic symptoms of patients with bulimia nervosa indicates that the similarities between these patients and those with depression are superficial. Several of the "depressive symptoms" of bulimia nervosa are idiosyncratic in character and quite different from the equivalent symptoms of depressed patients, and the interrelationship between the neurotic symptoms of bulimia nervosa is quite different from that found in depression.[8] It appears that many of the depressive symptoms are secondary to the eating disorder itself rather than being of primary significance. This view is supported by the finding that in the majority of cases these symptoms resolve in response to measures that enhance control over eating. However, it must be added that a minority of patients with bulimia nervosa appear to have a coexisting affective disorder and, in addition to treatment for their eating problem, they require antidepressant medication.[17] Unfortunately, at initial assessment it is difficult to distinguish this group from the remainder. "Biological" symptoms of depression are not a useful guide since appetite, weight, energy, and gastrointestinal function are all directly affected by the eating disorder itself. In clinical practice, therefore, the decision that the patient has a coexisting affective disorder often cannot be made for some weeks.

Like the depressive symptoms, most of the anxiety symptoms of these patients may be regarded as secondary to the eating disorder itself rather than being of primary significance. For example, the situational anxiety experienced by almost two-thirds of bulimia nervosa patients is usually related to social eating or being seen in public when "feeling fat."[8] Other neurotic symptoms are found, including irritability, lability of mood, and brief periods of elation during which there may be ideomotor pressure. True obsessional and compulsive symptoms are not common, and it is not appropriate to use the term "compulsive eating" to describe bulimic episodes. Body-shape misperception of the type found in anorexia nervosa is rarely encountered. Concentration impairment is common, with these patients being preoccupied with thoughts of food and eating and with concerns about their shape and weight.

OTHER CLINICAL FEATURES

Certain other clinical features merit comment. These patients tend to be more outgoing and socially accomplished than patients with anorexia nervosa. However, they appear to be equally industrious, perfectionistic, and achievement-oriented. Certain styles of thinking are common, such as dichotomous reasoning and overgeneralization. Their significance will be discussed later in the chapter. A minority of these patients abuse alcohol or drugs and some are prone to parasuicidal behavior. Stealing is found in about a third of these patients, and almost invariably it involves shoplifting food. Stealing, like the secrecy and deceit associated with years of bulimia and vomiting, is another source of guilt and self-condemnation.

THE ONSET AND DEVELOPMENT OF THE EATING PROBLEM

There has been little research into the development of bulimia nervosa. No childhood predisposing factors have been identified. The disorder usually begins in late adolescence. Often it appears to start with attempts to diet. In a proportion of cases this dieting is a response to being genuinely overweight.[19] Sometimes it appears to have been provoked by the physical changes that accompany puberty. In about a third of the patients, the dieting results in substantial weight loss and the development of anorexia nervosa. Subsequently, control over eating breaks down, episodic bulimia becomes established, and weight increases to within the normal range. In the majority of cases, however, weight loss is not marked and the diagnostic criteria for anorexia nervosa are never met. Such patients closely resemble those who have a history of anorexia nervosa,[19] although it is not yet known whether the two groups have a different natural history or response to treatment.

The presentation of bulimia nervosa is usually delayed. Patients often report having overeaten and vomited for several years. This delay in presentation is not because patients do not want help.[18] Rather it stems from the guilt and shame that accompany the disorder and, in many cases, the assumption that it is not treatable. Until recently, doctors may have contributed to the delay since it was not widely recognized that people with a normal body weight might nevertheless have a significant eating disorder.

Although there have been no satisfactory studies of the families of these patients, preliminary research has revealed two factors that may predispose to the development of the condition. The first is a family history of affective disorder. Four studies have found a high prevalence of affective disorder among these patients' first-degree relatives,[19,27,30,41] and one found the prevalence rate to be similar to that found among the relatives of patients with bipolar affective disorder.[30] The second possible predisposing factor is a family history of obesity. Such a history has been found in three patient series.[19,27,41]

ATTITUDE TO TREATMENT

Unlike patients with anorexia nervosa, those with bulimia nervosa are aware they have an eating problem and are eager to receive help. They are especially distressed by their loss of control over eating, which is not only unpleasant in its own right but also incompatible with both their desire for self-control and their fear of becoming fat. Because of the preeminence of their concern with control over eating, patients with bulimia nervosa comply poorly with treatments that do not address this issue. Many see themselves as having no difficulties other than their eating problem. Indeed, some are adamant that in all other aspects they are reasonably well adjusted. During treatment, however, it often emerges that their problems are not so encapsulated, other difficulties being masked by their preoccupation with food and eating and with their shape and weight. For example, dysphoric mood states are often not recognized as such, but instead are interpreted as "feeling fat."

The Maintenance of Bulimia Nervosa

Two different theoretical frameworks for understanding bulimia nervosa have been proposed: the condition has been regarded as a form of affective disorder, and it has been viewed in cognitive behavioral terms.

Four lines of evidence have been used to argue that bulimia nervosa is a form of affective disorder, or at least closely related to such disorders.[29] First, as mentioned earlier, it has been reported that the prevalence of major affective disorder among the first-degree relatives of patients with bulimia nervosa is similar to that among the relatives of patients with bipolar affective disorder.[30] This finding requires confirmation. Second, as noted, depressive symptoms are common in bulimia nervosa and their severity is similar to that of patients with major depressive disorder.[19] However, it is not clear whether the mood disturbance is of primary significance, whether it represents a secondary response to the eating disorder itself, or whether it is an independent co-existing phenomenon. Third, there have been several reports that bulimia nervosa patients respond to antidepressant drugs.[38,39,46] This suggests that the mood disturbance may be of primary significance; however, the findings of the two controlled studies of antidepressants are conflicting.[40,44] Fourth, it has been reported that approximately 50 percent of patients with bulimia nervosa have abnormal dexamethasone suppression test (DST) results.[24,31] Since it is claimed that the DST constitutes a specific laboratory test for the diagnosis of melancholia,[7] this finding would seem to support the suggestion that bulimia nervosa is closely related to the affective disorders. However, the interpretation of the DST findings is complicated by recent evidence indicating that the test is less specific than was thought.[9] Furthermore, preliminary research suggests that the test may be highly sensitive to weight loss,[4,13,32] a finding that clearly complicates its use in patients with eating disorders.

It is worth noting that the view that bulimia nervosa is a form of affective disorder does not account for the specific features of the condition. In contrast, the cognitive-behavioral view directly addresses this issue, although it does not account for the development of the disorder. In the remainder of this chapter a cognitive-behavioral analysis of bulimia nervosa is presented in an attempt to provide a conceptual framework for further psychological and physiological research.

A COGNITIVE-BEHAVIORAL CONCEPTUALIZATION OF THE MAINTENANCE OF BULIMIA NERVOSA

The cognitive-behavioral conceptualization of bulimia nervosa regards these patients' *attitudes* toward their shape and weight as central to the maintenance of the disorder. These overvalued ideas are peculiar to bulimia nervosa and anorexia nervosa and have been recognized by clinicians of widely different theoretical orientations.[6,10,42,47] Given their presence, most other aspects of these conditions become comprehensible. Thus, given the belief that shape and weight are of fundamental importance and that both must be kept under strict control, frequent weighing, sensitivity to changes in shape and weight, extreme dieting, self-induced vomiting and purgative abuse, and abnormal attitudes to food and eating all become intelligible. Even the apparently paradoxical episodes of bulimia may be understood in cognitive terms. It may therefore be argued, largely on *a priori* grounds, that these overvalued ideas are not simply symptomatic of the disorder but that they are of primary importance in its maintenance. Clearly this view has important implications for management. In particular, it suggests that change in these attitudes is likely to be a prerequisite for full and lasting recovery.[16,17]

The beliefs and values of patients with bulimia nervosa are relatively uniform in character. Patients tend to evaluate their self-worth in terms of their shape and weight: they view fatness as odious and reprehensible; they see thinness as attractive and desirable; and they positively value the maintenance of self-control. Such attitudes may be regarded as implicit unarticulated rules by which patients assign meaning and value to their experiences. These rules determine the way they organize their experiences and perceptions, the goals they set themselves, and their evaluation of themselves and their behavior. Patients are not necessarily aware of their presence or influence since they are so much a part of their conceptual scheme that they are usually unable to identify and question them. Typical examples include:

> "To be fat is to be a failure, unattractive, and unhappy."
> "To be thin is to be successful, attractive, and happy."
> "To exert self-control is a sign of strength and discipline."

It is apparent that such attitudes are not dissimilar to widely held views. Indeed, they are likely to be reinforced by prevailing social values—for example, the current fashion for slimness. Nevertheless, they are dysfunctional since they are rigid and extreme and are imbued with great personal significance.

The absolute and exaggerated nature of these beliefs and values reflects the operation of certain *dysfunctional styles of reasoning*. These are similar to those described in depression.[3] They include dichotomous thinking, overgeneralization, and errors of attribution. Examples include the belief that foods can be categorized as "fattening" or "nonfattening," the belief that minor dietary indiscretions are indicative of a complete absence of self-control, and the belief that success and failure are determined largely by appearance. Just as patients tend to be unaware of the presence and influence of their beliefs and values, so they are also unable to recognize these styles of reasoning.

The beliefs and values of these patients exert their influence through direct expression as *thoughts*. These thoughts constitute a habitual pattern of thinking. To the individual they seem plausible and are taken to be factual representations of reality. They are believed precisely because they are habitual, and their validity is not assessed.

The presence of unexamined thoughts expressing the extreme importance of shape and weight explains the maintenance of much of these patients' *behavior*. Frequent weighing is the most obvious direct consequence. Weighing clearly provides an objective means of monitoring body weight. It immediately alerts the patient to the possible need for corrective action. The actual frequency of weighing is likely to reflect the degree of concern with weight. Those patients who actively avoid weighing do so not because of lack of concern about their shape or weight, but because of the intense distress weighing causes them. Other means of gauging body shape, such as the assessment of the tightness of clothing, serve the same function as weighing. Such measures are also directly attributable to these patients' dysfunctional beliefs and values and their mediating thoughts. By evaluating their self-worth in terms of their shape and weight, patients are provided with a simple and immediate measure of their strengths and weaknesses.

The dysfunctional thoughts concerning shape and weight also account for the habitual use of purgatives and exercise for weight control. Both practices are self-perpetuating. The weight loss that occurs shortly after taking purgatives reinforces the behavior, as does the weight gain that may follow their discontinuation. Exercising may also be self-maintaining since it not only results in additional calorie expenditure, it also serves as a distraction from current problems and may elevate mood.

The principal way these patients attempt to control their shape and weight is by reducing their food intake. Again, this may be directly attributed to thoughts concerning shape and weight. It results in a selective avoidance of "fattening" food, an attempt to adhere to a strict dietary regime, preoccupation with food and eating, and, in some patients, calorie-counting. Despite these efforts, patients with bulimia nervosa do not succeed in maintaining control over their eating. Instead, their attempts to limit their food intake are disrupted by bouts of overeating. These episodes, paradoxical in the context of the patients' attitudes, are one of the main features of this condition as well as the "bulimic" form of anorexia nervosa. They present two related problems for this cognitive-behavioral analysis. First, it might be predicted that patients' fear of weight gain and fatness would simply lead to constant dieting, with success reinforcing further dieting. This is the situation in the "restricting" form of anorexia nervosa. Second, it might also be predicted that if, for some reason, patients fail to adhere to their dietary regime, they would simply recommence dieting. Clearly the clinical features of bulimia nervosa are not consistent with either of these predictions. Patients do not successfully adhere to their dietary regimes, and when they do "fail," rather than minimizing the indiscretion, they go to the other extreme and overeat.

Two principal explanations have been proposed to account for the episodes of bulimia. Both assume that they are secondary to these patients' extreme attempts to restrict their food intake. The first explanation postulates a cognitive link between the dieting and the overeating. According to this view, these patients' eating is governed by psychological rather than physiological factors, and it is their dieting that leads to and maintains the overeating. The intense concern with shape and weight leads patients to adopt extreme dietary rules that are impossible to obey, particularly at times of stress. The inevitable minor deviations from these strictures are viewed as catastrophic and evidence of weakness, reflecting the patients' tendency to think in dichotomous terms. The result is a temporary abandonment of all self-control. Once such control has been relinquished, other factors actively encourage overeating. These have been described earlier, and they include the pleasure that results from eating "naughty but nice" (*sic*) foods, distraction from current problems, and a temporary alleviation of feelings of depression and anxiety. In addition, overeating may be encouraged by physiological pressures to eat.

There is little direct evidence to support an association between dieting and episodes of bulimia. If the development of the disorder is considered, a period of intense dieting usually precedes the onset of bulimic episodes. This observation is clearly consistent with the association, but the support it provides is weak. The same is true of the clinical observation that episodes of bulimia almost never occur in the absence of extreme dieting. It has been suggested that certain experimental work supports the existence of a cognitive link between dieting and overeating.[37] This work has shown that under laboratory conditions, "dieters" eat more than "nondieters" following the consumption of food they *believe* to have had a high calorie content. This phenomenon has been termed "counterregulation." It has been suggested that dieters are able to maintain control so long as they believe their diet to be intact, but that they become "disinhibited" once they believe they have broken their dietary rules. However, care is needed when interpreting the findings of these laboratory studies. All the investigations are compromised by the use of an unsatisfactory measure of dietary restraint. The Revised Restraint Scale[26] cannot be regarded as an acceptable measure of dieting in this context since it includes certain items that create problems of circularity. Furthermore, it is not clear whether counterregulation is equivalent to the overeating of patients with bulimia nervosa.

Despite the paucity of supporting evidence, the cognitive explanation for the putative association between dieting and overeating has gained a remarkable degree of acceptance. This is probably because it is credible to clinicians. Patients with bulimia nervosa describe abandoning their controls after breaking their rules. Furthermore, it is clear that episodes of bulimia are particularly likely to occur at times when patients are anxious or depressed, mood states that have been shown to interfere with "dietary restraint."[23,25] Thus the laboratory studies, with all their limitations, have the benefit of considerable face validity.

The alternative explanation for a link between dieting and overeating is physiological rather than cognitive. This explanation can be incorporated within this cognitive-behavioral analysis of the maintenance of bulimia nervosa. It proposes that it is the particular type of diet of these patients that leads to the bulimic episodes. This proposal is almost entirely based on research using laboratory animals. Such research indicates that dietary manipulations can influence the entry of tryptophan into the brain and thereby affect serotonin (5HT) synthesis.[21,22] It also suggests that changes in brain 5HT may influence animals' choice of food. For example, drugs thought to enhance brain 5HT transmission diminish carbohydrate consumption relative to protein.[48] Such observations have led to the suggestion that carbohydrate-poor, protein-rich diets of the type consumed by extreme dieters may lead to diminished brain 5HT synthesis, which in turn may result in a strong urge to eat carbohydrate.[50] This proposal is highly speculative. Many of the animal studies have used diets of unusual composition: indeed, the dietary manipulations could be regarded as pharmacological rather than physiological. They have also involved food deprivation and feeding at unnatural times. Therefore, their relevance to normal circumstances is questionable.[12] Furthermore, it is far from clear whether it is justifiable extrapolating such findings from animals to humans. However, it must be acknowledged that the eating habits of patients with bulimia nervosa are grossly disturbed and therefore it is conceivable that they might have secondary effects on brain function. The only relevant study on humans examined the effects of low doses of the anorectic agent fenfluramine on the food intake of a small number of overweight subjects who reported "carbohydrate craving."[49] Fenfluramine, which enhances 5HT transmission, was found to reduce carbohydrate intake although it was not possible to assess its effect on protein consumption. The significance of this study to our understanding of bulimia nervosa is not clear.

Whatever the mechanisms responsible for episodes of bulimia, they are distressing to patients and are seen as evidence of poor self-control. The breaking of their dietary rules is intolerable, given the premium they place on self-control, and the associated risk of weight gain activates their fear of becoming fat. Consequently, they attempt to compensate for these episodes. Almost all renew their determination to diet, thereby possibly increasing their vulnerability to further episodes of overeating; many induce vomiting; and some take purgatives. As discussed earlier, the vomiting encourages yet further overeating and thus another vicious circle is established.

This cognitive-behavioral analysis does not account for the important observation that some patients with overvalued ideas concerning their shape and weight successfully maintain control over eating (i.e., "restricting" anorexic patients), whereas others experience episodes of bulimia (i.e., "bulimic" anorexic patients and patients with bulimia nervosa). Comparison of "bulimic" and "restricting" anorexic patients suggests that three factors may influence vulnerability to episodes of bulimia: a family history of obesity, a family history of affective disorder, and the influence of certain personality traits.[15] The relative importance of these factors and their mechanism of action is not known.

CONCLUSION

Although the conceptualization of bulimia nervosa as an affective disorder has been contrasted with a cognitive-behavioral analysis, the two views are not necessarily incompatible. The former is primarily concerned with the etiology of the disorder, whereas the latter deals exclusively with its maintenance. Both accounts require further study and their interrelationship merits particular attention.

REFERENCES

1. Abraham, S. F., and Beumont, P. J. V. 1982. How patients describe bulimia or binge-eating. *Psychological Medicine* 12:625–635.
2. American Psychiatric Association. 1980. *Diagnostic and statistical manual of mental disorders,* 3rd ed. Washington, D.C.: American Psychiatric Association.
3. Beck, A. T., Rush, A. J., Shaw, B. F., and Emery, G. 1979. *Cognitive therapy of depression: A treatment manual.* New York: Guilford Press.
4. Berger, M., et al. 1983. Influence of weight loss on the dexamethasone suppression test. *Archives of General Psychiatry* 40:585–586.
5. Boskind-Lodahl, M. 1976. Cinderella's stepsisters: A feminist perspective on anorexia nervosa and bulimia. *Signs: Journal of Women in Culture and Society* 2:342–356.
6. Bruch, H. 1973. *Eating disorders: Obesity, anorexia nervosa, and the person within.* New York: Basic Books.
7. Carroll, B. J. 1982. The dexamethasone suppression test for melancholia. *British Journal of Psychiatry* 140:292–304.
8. Cooper, P. J., and Fairburn, C. G. In press. The depressive symptoms of bulimia nervosa. *British Journal of Psychiatry.*
9. Coppen, A., et al. 1983. Dexamethasone suppression test in depression and other psychiatric illness. *British Journal of Psychiatry* 142:498–504.
10. Crisp, A. H. 1967. The possible significance of some behavioural correlates of weight and carbohydrate intake. *Journal of Psychosomatic Research* 11:117–131.
11. ———. 1981. Anorexia nervosa at normal body weight!—The abnormal normal weight control syndrome. *International Journal of Psychiatry in Medicine* 11:203–233.
12. Curzon, G. In press. Effect of food intake on brain transmitter amine precursors and amine synthesis. In *Psychopharmacology of food,* ed. M. W. Sandler and T. Silverstone. London: Oxford University Press.
13. Edelstein, C. K., Roy-Byrne, P., Fawzy, F. I., and Dornfield, L. 1983. Effects of weight loss on the dexamethasone suppression test. *American Journal of Psychiatry* 140:338–341.
14. Fairburn, C. G. 1982. Binge-eating and bulimia nervosa. *Smith, Kline and French Publication* 1:1–20.
15. ———. 1983. Bulimia nervosa. *British Journal of Hospital Medicine* 29:537–542.
16. ———. 1984. Bulimia: Its epidemiology and management. In *Eating and its disorders,* ed. A. J. Stunkard and E. Stellar, pp. 235–258. New York: Raven Press.
17. ———. 1984. A cognitive behavioural treatment for bulimia. In *Handbook of psychotherapy for anorexia nervosa and bulimia,* ed. D. M. Garner and P. E. Garfinkel, pp. 160–192. New York: Guilford Press.
18. Fairburn, C. G., and Cooper, P. J. 1982. Self-induced vomiting and bulimia nervosa: An undetected problem. *British Medical Journal* 284:1153–1155.
19. ———. 1984. The clinical features of bulimia nervosa. *British Journal of Psychiatry* 144:238–246.
20. ———. 1984. Rumination in bulimia nervosa. *British Medical Journal* 288:826–827.
21. Fernstrom, J. D., and Wurtman, R. J. 1971. Brain serotonin content: Increase following ingestion of carbohydrate diet. *Science* 174:1023–1025.
22. ———. 1972. Brain serotonin content: Physiological regulation by plasma neutral amino acids. *Science* 178:414–416.
23. Frost, R. O., Goolkasian, G. A., Ely, R. J., and Blanchard, F. A. 1982. Depression, restraint and eating behavior. *Behavior Research and Therapy* 20:113–121.
24. Gwirtsman, H. E., Roy-Byrne, P., Yager, J., and Gerner, R. H. 1983. Neuroendocrine

abnormalities in bulimia. *American Journal of Psychiatry* 140:559–563.

25. Herman, C. P., and Polivy, J. 1975. Anxiety, restraint and eating behavior. *Journal of Abnormal Psychology* 84:666–672.

26. Herman, C. P., et al. 1978. Distractibility in dieters and nondieters: An alternative view of "externality." *Journal of Personality and Social Psychology* 36:536–548.

27. Herzog, D. B. 1982. Bulimia: The secretive syndrome. *Psychosomatics* 23:481–484.

28. Hudson, J. I., Hudson, M. S., and Wentworth, S. M. 1983. Self-induced glycosuria: A novel method of purging in bulimia. *Journal of the American Medical Association* 249:2501.

29. Hudson, J. I., Pope, H. G., and Jonas, J. M. 1984. Treatment of bulimia with antidepressants: Theoretical considerations and clinical findings. In *Eating and its disorders*, ed. A. J. Stunkard and E. Stellar, pp. 259–273. New York: Raven Press.

30. Hudson, J. I., Pope, H. G., Jonas, J. M., and Yurgelun-Todd, D. 1983. Family history study of anorexia nervosa and bulimia. *British Journal of Psychiatry* 142:133–138, 428–429.

31. Hudson, J. I., et al. 1983. Hypothalamic-pituitary-adrenal axis hyperactivity in bulimia. *Psychiatry Research* 8:111–117.

32. Kline, M. D., and Beeber, A. R. 1983. Weight loss and the dexamethasone suppression test. *Archives of General Psychiatry* 40:1034–1035.

33. Lacey, J. H. 1982. The bulimic syndrome at normal body weight: Reflections on pathogenesis and clinical features. *International Journal of Eating Disorders* 1:59–66.

34. Mitchell, J. E., and Pyle, R. L. 1982. The bulimic syndrome in normal weight individuals: A review. *International Journal of Eating Disorders* 1:61–73.

35. Mitchell, J. E., Pyle, R. L., and Eckert, E. D. 1981. Frequency and duration of binge-eating episodes in patients with bulimia. *American Journal of Psychiatry* 138:835–836.

36. Palmer, R. L. 1979. The dietary chaos syndrome: A useful new term? *British Journal of Medical Psychology* 55:187–190.

37. Polivy, J., Herman, C. P., Jazwinski, C., and Olmsted, M. P. 1984. Restraint and binge-eating. In *Binge eating: Theory, research and treatment*, ed. R. C. Hawkins, W. J. Fremouw, and P. Clement, pp. 104–122. New York: Springer.

38. Pope, H. G., and Hudson, J. I. 1982. Treatment of bulimia with antidepressants. *Psychopharmacology* 78:176–179.

39. Pope, H. G., Hudson, J. I., and Jonas, J. M. 1983. Antidepressant treatment of bulimia: Preliminary experience and practical recommendations. *Journal of Clinical Psychopharmacology* 3:274–281.

40. Pope, H. G., Hudson, J. I., Jonas, J. M., and Yorgelun-Todd, D. 1983. Bulimia treated with imipramine: A placebo-controlled, double-blind study. *American Journal of Psychiatry* 140:554–558.

41. Pyle, R. L., Mitchell, J. E., and Eckert, E. D. 1981. Bulimia: A report of 34 cases. *Journal of Clinical Psychiatry* 42:60–64.

42. Russell, G. F. M. 1970. Anorexia nervosa: Its identity as an illness and its treatment. In *Modern trends in psychological medicine*, vol. 2, ed. J. H. Price, pp. 131–164. London: Butterworth.

43. ———. 1979. Bulimia nervosa: An ominous variant of anorexia nervosa. *Psychological Medicine* 9:429–448.

44. Sabine, E. J., et al. 1983. Bulimia nervosa: A placebo controlled double-blind therapeutic trial of mianserin. *British Journal of Clinical Pharmacology* 15(Suppl.):195–202.

45. Szmukler, G. I., and Russell, G. F. M. 1983. Diabetes mellitus, anorexia nervosa and bulimia. *British Journal of Psychiatry* 142:305–308.

46. Walsh, B. T., et al. 1982. Treatment of bulimia with monoamine oxidase inhibitors. *American Journal of Psychiatry* 139:1629–1630.

47. Wilson, C. P., Hogan, C. C., and Mintz, I. L. 1983. *Fear of being fat.* New York: Jason Aronson.

48. Wurtman, J. J., and Wurtman, R. J. 1979. Drugs that enhance central serotinergic transmission diminish elective carbohydrate consumption by rats. *Life Sciences* 24:895–904.

49. Wurtman, J. J., et al. 1981. Carbohydrate craving in obese people: Suppression by treatments affecting serotinergic transmission. *International Journal of Eating Disorders* 1:2–14.

50. Wurtman, R. J. 1983. Behavioural effects of nutrients. *Lancet* 1:1145–1147.

23

Assessment of Bulimia:
A Multidimensional Model

Craig Johnson and Darryl L. Pure

Introduction

The increase in the incidence of eating disorders[25,39,57] has created a need for more specialized and sophisticated assessment procedures. This need arises in part from a growing awareness that as the incidence increases, so does the heterogeneity of the clinical characteristics and etiological factors associated with the patient population. Consequently, consensus is emerging that effective treatment is being facilitated by thorough assessments of the biological, familial, sociocultural, and psychological factors that contribute to the onset and perpetuation of the disorder.

This chapter presents a comprehensive conceptual model for investigating how various milieu factors interface with the symptomatic behavior of bulimia. Figure 23.1 outlines the areas that will be discussed. The discussion of each of these areas will focus on our current understanding of how each is specifically related to eating disorders.

Overall Philosophy of the Assessment Interview

In a previous article regarding the initial consultation,[32] detailed recommendations were made for structuring the clinical interview. One aspect of the overall philosophy of the initial assessment merits repeating.

This work was supported by the George and Tina Barr Foundation. The authors would like to thank Mary Connors, Ph.D., for her assistance with this manuscript.

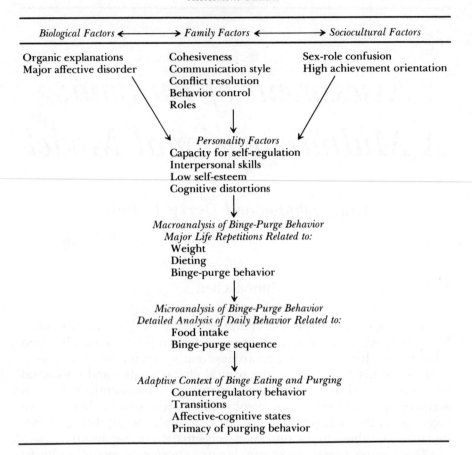

FIGURE 23.1

Assessment Outline

Among our clinicians in the Eating Disorders Program at North-western University we attempt to establish an overall frame of reference, which we refer to as the adaptive context. We consider anorexia nervosa and bulimia to be multidetermined disorders that affect a wide range of patients and that the symptoms are adaptations to a variety of biological, intrapsychic, familial, and sociocultural issues. Anorexia nervosa and bulimia reflect desperate attempts to adapt to difficult circumstances. The chances of establishing a collaborative relationship with the patient will be enhanced if this perspective is maintained.

Assessment Instruments

During the assessment process patients are asked to complete a series of questionnaires. Selecting appropriate instruments not only facilitates treatment recommendations but creates a data base that allows for the evaluation of treatment effectiveness. Foremost is to acquire background information about the symptomatic eating behavior. We recommend a standardized intake form such as the Diagnostic Survey for Eating Disorders (DSED) (see figure 23.2).

The DSED focuses on various aspects of anorexia nervosa and bulimia. It is divided into eight sections that provide information on demographic factors, weight history and body image, dieting behavior, binge eating and purging behavior, related behaviors, menstruation and sexual functioning, medical and psychiatric history for patient and family, and life adjustment. The survey can be used as a self-report instrument or as a guide for a semistructured interview. We also use the Eating Disorders Inventory (EDI)[20] which is a scaled instrument measuring eating attitudes and behaviors. In addition to specific instruments related to eating behavior, scales measuring psychiatric symptoms, family environment, personality, and social adjustment are included.

Biological Factors

Comprehensive assessment should include medical evaluation to rule out organic explanations for the abnormal eating behavior. Physical examinations along with standard laboratory tests such as multiple channel chemistry analysis, complete blood count, and urinalysis should be routine procedures. Although there are often medical side effects associated with bulimia (including electrolyte abnormalities, dehydration, edema, parotid gland enlargement, dental decay, anemia, gastrointestinal problems, and menstrual difficulties[1,14,26,48]), to date there has not emerged any consistent endocrine finding of etiological significance.

Much attention has been focused recently on the nature and extent of depression found among bulimic patients. Several investigations* have indicated that bulimic patients manifest affective instability, which has led to speculation that bulimia may simply be a variant of a biogenetically

* See references 21, 29, 36, 56, and 58.

FIGURE 23.2
Diagnostic Survey for Eating Disorders—Revised

INSTRUCTIONS: This questionnaire covers several eating problems that may or may not apply to you. You may find it difficult to answer some questions if your eating pattern is irregular or has changed recently. Please read each question carefully and choose the answer that **best** describes your situation **most of the time**. Also, please feel free to write remarks in the margins if this will clarify your answer. Thank you.

Card 1

(Column)

Name

Social Security Number   (1–9)

Current Address

Permanent Address

Telephone   (Day)   (Night)

Date   (10–15)

Code   (16–21)

Identifying and Demographic Information

Card 1
(Column)

Sex   Male ———₁   Female ———₂   (22)

Age ————————   (23–24)

Race (check one).

   Caucasian ———₁   Black ———₂   Oriental ———₃   Hispanic ———₄

   Other (Specify) ———   (25)

Your present religious affiliation (check one).

   Protestant ———₁   Catholic ———₂   Jewish ———₃

   No Affiliation ———₄   Other (Specify) ———   (26)

Card 1
(Column)

Religious affiliation of your family of origin (check one).

Protestant _____₁   Catholic _____₂   Jewish _____₃

No Affiliation _____₄   Other (Specify) _____   (27)

Marital status (check one).

Single _____₁   Married _____₂   Separated _____₃

Divorced _____₄   Widowed _____₅   (28)

Current occupation _____   (29)

Father's occupation _____   (30)

Mother's occupation _____   (31)

Spouse's occupation _____   (32)

Present primary role (check one).

Wage earner _____₁   Housewife/husband _____₂   Student _____₃

Other (Specify) _____   (33)

Current living arrangement (check one).   (34)

With parents or relatives	_____₁
Dorm or shared apartment with friend	_____₂
Conjugal (intimate relationship with one other person including spouse, boyfriend, girlfriend, etc.)	_____₃
Alone	_____₄

Highest level of education (check one for each person).   (35–38)

	Self	Father	Mother	Spouse
Completed post-graduate training	1———	———	———	———
Some post-graduate training	2———	———	———	———
Completed college, received four year academic degree	3———	———	———	———
Some college, but didn't receive four year academic degree	4———	———	———	———

Card 1
(Column)

	Self	Father	Mother	Spouse
Completed high school; may have attended or completed trade school or attended other non-academic training requiring high school completion	5———	———	———	———
Some high school	6———	———	———	———
Some grammar school	7———	———	———	———
No schooling	8———	———	———	———

Is your mother currently living?   Yes ———₁ No ———₂   (39)

Mother's age ———   (40–41)

What category best describes your mother's weight? (Circle one.)
(If no longer living, best described your mother's weight.)   (42)

1	2	3	4	5
very underweight	underweight	normal weight	overweight	very overweight

How preoccupied with food or weight is (was) your mother? (Circle one.)   (43)

1	2	3	4	5
not at all	somewhat	moderately	very much	extremely

Is your father currently living?   Yes ———₁ No ———₂   (44)

Father's age ———   (45–46)

What category best describes your father's weight? (Circle one.)
(If no longer living, best described your father's weight.)   (47)

1	2	3	4	5
very underweight	underweight	normal weight	overweight	very overweight

How preoccupied with food or weight is (was) your father? (Circle one.)   (48)

1	2	3	4	5
not at all	somewhat	moderately	very much	extremely

Number of brothers ———   (49–50)

Number of sisters ———   (51–52)

Do you have a twin brother or sister?   Yes ———₁ No ———₂   (53)

How many of your siblings are overweight?   ———   (54–55)

How many of your siblings are underweight?   ———   (56–57)

	Weight History			

<table>
<tr><td></td><td></td><td></td><td></td><td>Card 1
(Column)</td></tr>
<tr><td>Current weight</td><td>_____ lbs.</td><td></td><td></td><td>(58–60)</td></tr>
<tr><td>Current height</td><td>_____ inches</td><td></td><td></td><td>(61–62)</td></tr>
<tr><td>Desired weight</td><td>_____ lbs.</td><td></td><td></td><td>(63–65)</td></tr>
</table>

Adult Years

<table>
<tr><td>Highest adult weight
since age 18</td><td>_____ lbs.</td><td>at age _____</td><td></td><td>(66–70)</td></tr>
<tr><td>Lowest adult weight
since age 18</td><td>_____ lbs.</td><td>at age _____</td><td></td><td>(71–75)</td></tr>
<tr><td>How long did you
remain at your
lowest adult weight?</td><td>_____ days</td><td>_____ weeks</td><td>_____ months</td><td>(76–79)
(80) = 1
Card 2</td></tr>
</table>

Adolescent Years (Column)

<table>
<tr><td>Highest weight
between ages 12–18</td><td>_____ lbs.</td><td>at age _____</td><td></td><td>(22–26)</td></tr>
<tr><td>Lowest weight
between ages 12–18</td><td>_____ lbs.</td><td>at age _____</td><td>_____ inches</td><td>(27–33)</td></tr>
</table>

Using the scale below, please select the number which indicates your perception of your weight during the following years:

1	2	3	4	5
extremely thin	somewhat thin	normal weight	somewhat overweight	extremely overweight

6–12 years old _____   (34)

12–18 years old _____   (35)

18–30 years old _____   (36)

30 and over _____   (37)

As a child were you teased about your weight? (Check yes or no.)

Underweight	Yes _____₁ No _____₂	(38)
Overweight	Yes _____₁ No _____₂	(39)
No weight problems as a child	Yes _____₁ No _____₂	(40)

To what extent were you teased? (Circle one.)

1	2	3	4	5	(41)
never	rarely	sometimes	often	always	

Are you in an occupation that requires you to maintain a certain weight?

Yes _____₁   No _____₂   (42)

Are you in a food-related occupation?   Yes ——— ₁ No ——— ₂   (43)

Has there ever been a time when your feelings about yourself or your social
life changed substantially as a result of weight changes? (Check one.)   (44)

    Yes, <u>improved</u> when <u>lost</u> weight   ———₁

    Yes, <u>improved</u> when <u>gained</u> weight   ———₂

    Yes, <u>worse</u> when <u>lost</u> weight   ———₃

    Yes, <u>worse</u> when <u>gained</u> weight   ———₄

    No change   ———₅

How satisfied are you with the way your body is proportioned? (Check one.)   (45)

1	2	3	4	5
not at all satisfied	slightly satisfied	moderately satisfied	very satisfied	extremely satisfied

Please indicate on the scales below how you feel about the different areas of your body.
(Circle one.)

	Strongly Positive	Moderately Positive	Neutral	Moderately Negative	Strongly Negative	
Face	1	2	3	4	5	(46)
Arms	1	2	3	4	5	(47)
Shoulders	1	2	3	4	5	(48)
Breasts	1	2	3	4	5	(49)
Stomach	1	2	3	4	5	(50)
Buttocks	1	2	3	4	5	(51)
Thighs	1	2	3	4	5	(52)

At your current weight, how fat do you feel? (Circle one.)   (53)

1	2	3	4	5
not at all fat	somewhat fat	moderately fat	very much fat	extremely fat

During the past month, on the average, how many times have you weighed
yourself or measured your body size? ——— number of times/per week.   (54–55)

Using the scale below, please indicate the intensity of your feelings while you   (56–75)
are in the <u>process</u> of <u>gaining</u> weight.   (80) = 2

1	2	3	4	5
not at all	somewhat	moderately	very much	extremely

Card 2
(Column)

Independent _____   Confused about my thoughts/
                            feelings _____

Not sexual _____   Calm _____

Being my own person _____ Special _____

Helpless _____   Strong _____

Confused about who I am _____   Unsuccessful _____

Popular _____   Childlike _____

Self-assured _____   Rebellious _____

Sexually appealing _____   In control _____

Alone _____   Living up to others' expectations _____

Abandoned _____   Empty _____

Using the scale below, please indicate the intensity of your feelings while you are in the <u>process</u> of <u>losing</u> <u>weight</u>.

Card 3
(Column)
(22–41)

1	2	3	4	5
not at all	somewhat	moderately	very much	extremely

Independent _____   Confused about my thoughts/
                            feelings _____

Not sexual _____   Calm _____

Being my own person _____ Special _____

Helpless _____   Strong _____

Confused about who I am _____   Unsuccessful _____

Popular _____   Childlike _____

Self-assured _____   Empty _____

Abandoned _____   Rebellious _____

Sexually appealing _____   In control _____

Alone _____   Living up to others' expectations _____

Dieting Behavior

Have you ever been on a diet?   (42)

Yes _____₁   No _____₂

At what age did you begin to restrict your food intake due to concern over your body size?

(43–44)

———— years old

In your first year of dieting, how many times did you start a diet?

(45–47)

———— number of times

Over the last year how often have you begun a diet?

(48–50)

———— number of times

Using the scale below, please indicate how often you use the following behaviors as a way to diet.

(51–58)

1	2	3	4	5
never	rarely	sometimes	often	always

Skip meals ————   Reduce portions ————

Completely fast ————   Go on fad diets ————

Restrict carbohydrates ————   Reduce calories ————

Restrict fats ————   Diet camps/spas ————

Please indicate which physical symptoms you have experienced since the onset of your eating problems.

(59–73)
(80) = 3

	Yes$_1$	No$_2$		Yes$_1$	No$_2$
Sore throat	——	——	Water/fluid retention	——	——
Weakness/ tiredness	——	——	Dental problems	——	——
Seizures	——	——	Hair loss	——	——
Feeling bloated	——	——	Growth of fine downy hair	——	——
Stomach pains	——	——			
Feeling cold	——	——	Overly sensitive to noise, light, or touch	——	——
Dizziness	——	——			
Redness of eyes	——	——	Muscle spasms	——	——
Swollen glands (e.g., under jaw)	——	——	Other (specify) ————————		

Using the scale below, please indicate how often the following people have encouraged you to diet.

(22–31)

1	2	3	4	5
never	rarely	sometimes	often	always

Boyfriend _____   Sister _____

Girlfriend _____   Employer _____

Mother _____   Teacher/coach _____

Father _____   Child _____

Brother _____   Doctor _____

Using the scale below, indicate how characteristic the following statement is of you. "I have an intense fear of becoming fat, which does not lessen as I lose weight." (Circle one.)   (32)

1	2	3	4	5
not at all characteristic	somewhat characteristic	moderately characteristic	very characteristic	extremely characteristic

---

Binge Eating Behavior

Have you ever had an episode of eating a large amount of food in a short space of time (an eating binge)?   (33)

Yes _____₁ No _____₂

Please circle on the scales below, how characteristic the following symptoms are of your eating binge.

	Never	Rarely	Sometimes	Often	Always	
I consume a large amount of food during a binge	1	2	3	4	5	(34)
I eat very rapidly	1	2	3	4	5	(35)
I feel out of control when I eat	1	2	3	4	5	(36)
I feel miserable or annoyed after a binge	1	2	3	4	5	(37)
I get uncontrollable urges to eat and eat until I feel physically ill	1	2	3	4	5	(38)
I binge eat alone	1	2	3	4	5	(39)
I binge eat with others	1	2	3	4	5	(40)

Card 4
(Column)

How long does a binge episode usually last? (Check one.)   (41)

    Less than one hour   _____₁

    1–2 hours   _____₂

    More than 2 hours   _____₃

Using the scale below, please indicate how likely you are to binge eat during
these times/at these places.   (42–51)

1	2	3	4	5
never	rarely	sometimes	often	always

8–12 am _____	8–12 midnight _____	Car _____
12–4 pm _____	After midnight _____	Party _____
4–8 pm _____	Work _____	Restaurant _____
	Home _____	Other (specify) _____

How old were you when you began binge eating?   (52–53)

    _____ years old

How long did you have a problem with binge eating?   (54–57)

    _____ days   _____ months   _____ years

What is the longest period you have had without binge eating since the onset
of the problem?   (58–60)

    _____ days   _____ months   _____ years

Using the scale below, please indicate the degree to which the following   (61–72)
circumstances have helped you to not binge eat for that period of time.   (80) = 4

1	2	3	4	5	6
not at all helpful	somewhat helpful	helpful	very helpful	extremely helpful	not applicable

Began dieting _____   Started exercising _____

Sought professional help _____   Began romantic relationship _____

Left romantic relationship _____   Developed illness _____

Left home _____   Divorce _____

Marriage _____   Pregnancy _____

Work _____   Vacation _____

Other: Please specify _____

Using the scale below, please indicate how nervous you feel when eating the following foods.

1	2	3	4	5
never	rarely	sometimes	often	always

Bread/cereal/pasta _____   Eggs _____

Dairy products
(cheese, yogurt) _____   Fruit _____

Meat _____   Snacks _____

Fish _____   Sweets _____

Poultry _____   Vegetables _____

Using the scale below, please indicate how often you eat the following foods when <u>not</u> binging.

(32–41)

1	2	3	4	5
never	rarely	sometimes	often	always

Bread/cereal/pasta _____   Eggs _____

Dairy products
(cheese, yogurt) _____   Fruit _____

Meat _____   Snacks _____

Fish _____   Sweets _____

Poultry _____   Vegetables _____

Using the list below, please check which events, either positive or negative, preceded or coincided with the onset of your eating problems. (Check all that apply.)

(42–54)

	Yes_1	No_2		Yes_1	No_2
Death of significant other	____	____	Illness or injury to family member or significant other	____	____
Teasing about appearance	____	____	Problems in romantic relationship	____	____
Marriage	____	____	Family problems	____	____
Leaving home	____	____	Prolonged period of dieting	____	____
Illness or injury to family	____	____	Pregnancy	____	____
Failure at school or work	____	____	Work transition	____	____
Difficult sexual experience	____	____	Other (Please specify)	_____	

Card 5
(Column)

(55–70)
(80) = 5

Using the scale below, please select the number which indicates the intensity of each of the following feelings <u>before</u> a binge.

1	2	3	4	5
extremely intense	very intense	moderately intense	slightly intense	not at all intense

Calm _____   Bored _____

Empty _____   Frustrated _____

Confused _____   Panicked _____

Excited _____   Relieved _____

Angry _____   Guilty _____

Spaced out _____   Depressed _____

Inadequate _____   Nervous _____

Disgusted _____   Other (Please
                                specify) _____
Lonely _____

Using the scale below, please state the number which indicates the intensity of each of the following feelings <u>after</u> a binge.

Card 6
(Column)
(22–37)

1	2	3	4	5
extremely intense	very intense	moderately intense	slightly intense	not at all intense

Calm _____   Bored _____

Empty _____   Frustrated _____

Confused _____   Panicked _____

Excited _____   Relieved _____

Angry _____   Guilty _____

Spaced out _____   Depressed _____

Inadequate _____   Nervous _____

Disgusted _____   Other (Please
                                specify) _____
Lonely _____

Have you noticed a relationship between the frequency of your binge eating and your menstrual cycle?   (38)

Yes _____₁ No _____₂

If yes, please indicate when during your cycle you feel most vulnerable to binge eat. (Check one.) (39)

During menstruation ——1

11–14 days prior to menstruation ——2

7–10 days prior to menstruation ——3

3–6 days prior to menstruation ——4

1–2 days prior to menstruation ——5

After menstruation ——6

How uncomfortable are you with your binge eating behavior? (Circle one.) (40)

1	2	3	4	5
extremely uncomfortable	very uncomfortable	uncomfortable	somewhat uncomfortable	not at all uncomfortable

How willing would you be to gain 10 pounds in exchange for not binge eating anymore? (Circle one.) (41)

1	2	3	4	5
extremely willing	very willing	willing	somewhat willing	not at all willing

---

Purging Behavior

Have you ever vomited (or spit out food) after eating in order to get rid of the food? (42)

Yes ——1   No ——2

How old were you when you induced vomiting (or spit out food) for the first time? (43–44)

—— years old

How long have you been using self-induced vomiting (or spitting out food)? (45–48)

—— days —— months —— years

If you have ever tried to induce vomiting (or spitting out food) but decided to discontinue, please indicate the reasons for this. (49–52)

	Yes$_1$	No$_2$
Physically unable to induce vomiting	——	——
Afraid of choking	——	——
Too unpleasant	——	——

	Yes₁	No₂

Concerned about my health   _____   _____

Other (Please specify) _____

Have you ever used laxatives to control your weight or "get rid of food?"   (53)

Yes _____₁   No _____₂

How old were you when you first took laxatives for weight control?   (54–55)

_____ years

How long have you been using laxatives for weight control?   (56–59)

_____ days   _____ months   _____ years

What is the average number of laxatives that you use?   (60–62)

per day _____   or per week _____

Using the scale below, please select the number which indicates the intensity   (63–78)
of each of the following feelings <u>before</u> a purge.   (80) = 6

1	2	3	4	5
extremely intense	very intense	intense	slightly intense	not at all intense

Calm _____   Bored _____

Empty _____   Frustrated _____

Confused _____   Panicked _____

Excited _____   Relieved _____

Angry _____   Guilty _____

Spaced out _____   Depressed _____

Inadequate _____   Nervous _____

Disgusted _____   Other (Please specify) _____

Lonely _____

Using the scale below, please select the number which indicates the intensity of   Card 7
each of the following feelings <u>after</u> a purge.   (Column)
                                                                                      (22–37)

1	2	3	4	5
extremely intense	very intense	intense	slightly intense	not at all intense

Calm _____   Bored _____

Empty _____   Frustrated _____

Confused _____   Panicked _____

Excited _____   Relieved _____

Angry _____   Guilty _____

Spaced out _____   Depressed _____

Inadequate _____   Nervous _____

Disgusted _____   Other (Please
specify) _____

Lonely _____

Over the last month, what has been the average number of times you have
engaged in the following behaviors per week?

	Average number per week	
Binge eating	_____	(38–40)
Vomiting	_____	(41–43)
Use of laxatives	_____	(44–45)
Use of diet pills	_____	(46–47)
Use of enemas	_____	(48–49)
Fasting (skipping meals for an entire day)	_____	(50–52)

Over the past month, what has been average number of days per week that you have not
engaged in the following behaviors?

	Average number per week	
Binge eating	_____	(53)
Vomiting	_____	(54)
Use of laxatives	_____	(55)
Use of diet pills	_____	(56)
Use of enemas	_____	(57)
Fasting (skipping meals for an entire day)	_____	(58)

Over the past month, on the average, how many times per week have you
been able to eat a regular meal and not compensate in some way (i.e., fasting,
vomiting, using diuretics, laxatives, exercise)?   (59–60)

_____ number of times per week.

Exercise

			Card 7
			(Column)

How many minutes a day do you currently exercise (including going on walks, riding bicycle, etc.)?   (61–63)

———— minutes.

Have you ever been involved in serious training in any of the following activities? (Check as many as are applicable.)

	Yes$_1$	No$_2$	
Distance running	————	————	(64)
Weight lifting	————	————	(65)
Dancing	————	————	(66)
Gymnastics	————	————	(67)
Wrestling	————	————	(68)
Swimming	————	————	(69)
Modeling	————	————	(70)
Tennis	————	————	(71)
Other (Specify)	————————————————————		
	————————————————————		

Other Behavior

Do you feel that you have or have ever had an alcohol or drug abuse problem? (Circle one.)   (72)

1	2	3	4	5
not at all	somewhat	moderate	very much	extremely

Please indicate how frequently you have used the following substances since the onset of your eating problem.

Alcohol (Specify type)	Amount	Daily$_5$	Weekly$_4$	Monthly$_3$	Less than monthly$_2$	Never$_1$	
————————	————	————	————	————	————	————	(73)
Amphetamines (uppers)	————	————	————	————	————	————	(74)
Barbiturates (downers)	————	————	————	————	————	————	(75)
Hallucinogens	————	————	————	————	————	————	(76)

Marijuana   _____ _____ _____ _____ _____ _____ (77)

Tranquilizers _____ _____ _____ _____ _____ _____ (78)

Cocaine   _____ _____ _____ _____ _____ _____ (79)

Cigarettes   none_____1   0 to ½ pack/day _____2
1 pack/day _____3   more than 1 pack/day _____4   (22)

Have you ever made a suicide attempt? (Check one.)   (23)

    No   _____1

    Yes, 1–2 times   _____2

    Yes, 3–5 times   _____3

    Yes, more than 5 times   _____4

Have you ever tried to physically hurt yourself (i.e., cut yourself, hit yourself
with the intent to hurt, burn yourself with cigarettes)? (Check one.)   (24)

    No   _____1

    Yes, 1–2 times   _____2

    Yes, 3–5 times   _____3

    Yes, more than 5 times   _____4

Have you ever stolen items related to eating or weight (i.e., laxatives, food,
etc.)? (Check one.)   (25)

    No   _____1

    Yes, 1–2 times   _____2

    Yes, 3–5 times   _____3

    Yes, more than 5 times   _____4

Have you ever stolen other types of items? (Check one.)   (26)

    No   _____1

    Yes, 1–2 times   _____2

    Yes, 3–5 times   _____3

    Yes, more than 5 times   _____4

Sexual History

Have you ever engaged in sexual intercourse?   (27)

    Yes _____1   No _____2

Card 8
(Column)

If your answer is yes, at what age did you first engage in sexual intercourse?   (28–29)

Age _____

Have you ever engaged in masturbation?   (30)

Yes _____₁   No _____₂

If your answer is <u>yes</u> at what age did you first engage in masturbation?   (31–32)

Age _____

Please indicate on the line below your interest in sex <u>before the onset</u> of your
eating problem. (Circle one.)   (33)

1	2	3	4	5
not interested	somewhat interested	interested	very interested	extremely interested

Please indicate on the scale below whether there has been a change in your
sexual interest <u>since the onset</u> of your eating problem. (Circle one.)   (34)

1	2	3	4	5
not interested	somewhat interested	interested	very interested	extremely interested

How satisfied are you with the quality of your current sexual activity?
(Circle one.)   (35)

1	2	3	4	5
not at all satisfied	somewhat satisfied	satisfied	very satisfied	extremely satisfied

Please check your sexual preference. (Check one.)   (36)

Exclusively heterosexual   _____₁

Primarily heterosexual, some
homosexual   _____₂

Bisexual   _____₃

Primarily homosexual, some
heterosexual   _____₄

Exclusively homosexual   _____₅

Asexual (no sexual preference)   _____₆

Autosexual (prefer masturbation to
sexual relations with others)   _____₇

Menstrual History

How old were you when you first started menstruating? (If you have never
had your period, please mark 00.)   (37–38)

_____ years old

Do you have menstrual periods now? (Check one.)

    Yes, regularly each month   ———₁

    Yes, but I skip a month once in a while   ———₂

    Yes, but not very often (for example, once in six months)   ———₃

    No, I have not had a period in at least the last six months   ———₄

How long has it been since you last menstruated? (If you regularly
menstruate, please mark 00.)   (40–41)

    ——— months

How much did you weigh when you stopped menstruating?   (42–44)

    ——— lbs.

Medical and Psychiatric History

Have you had any serious medical difficulties?   (45)

    Yes ———₁   No ———₂

Are you currently on any medications?   Yes ———₁   No ———₂   (46)

    If yes, please identify ———————————————————————

Have you ever taken psychiatric medications?   Yes ———₁   No ———₂   (47)

    If yes, please identify ———————————————————————

Have you ever been hospitalized for eating or emotional problems?   (48)

    Yes ———₁   No ———₂

If yes, then complete the following:

	Most recent	Second prior	Third prior	Fourth prior	
Date admitted	———	———	———	———	
Date discharged	———	———	———	———	
Duration (months)	———	———	———	———	(49–64)
Age	———	———	———	———	(65–72)
Primary reason for admission*	———	———	———	———	(73–76)

* Use number code: 1 = bulimia; 2 = anorexia nervosa; 3 = chemical dependency;
4 = depression; 5 = psychotic disorder other than depression; 6 = other

Have you ever been treated as an outpatient for eating or emotional problems
(i.e., a logically continuous series of treatments)?   (77)

    Yes ———₁   No ———₂   (80) = 8

If yes, then complete the following:

	Most recent	Second prior	Third prior	Fourth prior	
Date began	——	——	——	——	
Date last visit of series	——	——	——	——	
Duration (months)	——	——	——	——	(22–37)
Age	——	——	——	——	(38–45)
Primary reason for treatment*	——	——	——	——	(46–49)

* Use number code: 1 = bulimia; 2 = anorexia nervosa; 3 = chemical dependency;
4 = depression; 5 = psychotic disorder other than depression; 6 = other.

	Most recent	Second prior	Third prior	Fourth prior	
Please indicate the types of treatment you have been involved in†	——	——	——	——	(50–61)

† Use code number: 1 = individual psychotherapy; 2 = group psychotherapy;
3 = psychiatric medications.

Please circle on the scale below how frequently you experience the following symptoms:

	Never	Rarely	Sometimes	Often	Always	
Extreme sadness	1	2	3	4	5	(62)
Anxiety	1	2	3	4	5	(63)
Difficulty getting up in the morning	1	2	3	4	5	(64)
Crying episodes	1	2	3	4	5	(65)
Irritability	1	2	3	4	5	(66)
Tiredness	1	2	3	4	5	(67)
Difficulty falling asleep	1	2	3	4	5	(68)
Wide mood fluctuation	1	2	3	4	5	(69)

Life Adjustment

Please circle on the scale below the quality of your relationship with each of the following persons:

Card 9 (Column)

	Terrible	Poor	Fair	Good	Excel-lent	Not applicable	
Mother	1	2	3	4	5	9	(70)
Father	1	2	3	4	5	9	(71)
Spouse/significant other	1	2	3	4	5	9	(72)
Male friends	1	2	3	4	5	9	(73)
Female friends	1	2	3	4	5	9	(74)
Children (if applicable)	1	2	3	4	5	9	(75) (80) = 9

Card 10 (Column)

Please circle on the scale below how much your eating problems interfere with the following areas:

	Never	Rarely	Sometimes	Often	Always	
Work/school	1	2	3	4	5	(22)
Daily activities (other than work)	1	2	3	4	5	(23)
Thoughts	1	2	3	4	5	(24)
Feelings about myself	1	2	3	4	5	(25)
Personal relationships	1	2	3	4	5	(26)

Over the past month, on the average, what percentage of your time each day have you been preoccupied with thoughts of food, weight, and/or eating? (Circle one.)

(27–29)
(79–80) = 10

0%	10%	20%	30%	40%	50%	60%	70%	80%	90%	100%

Not at all　　　　　　　　　Half the time　　　　　　　　All the time

Family History

Have any of your first degree relatives had any of the following problems?   Card 11
(First degree relatives include children, brothers, sisters, parents.)   (Column)

	Number of persons	Relationship to you (e.g. sister)	Require Outpatient Care? (If yes, check below)	Require Hospital-ization? (If yes, check below)	
Ulcers	22–23	24–28	29	30	
Colitis	31–32	33–37	38	39	
Asthma	40–41	42–46	47	48	
Depression	49–50	51–55	56	57	
Manic-depressive	58–59	60–64	65	66	
Schizophrenia	67–68	69–73	74	75	(79–80) = 11
Paranoid thinking	Card 12 22–23	24–28	29	30	
Hallucinations	31–32	33–37	38	39	
Obesity	40–41	42–46	47	48	
Alcohol	49–50	51–55	56	57	
Drug abuse	58–59	60–64	65	66	
Severe anxiety	67–68	69 73	74	75	(79–80) = 12
Phobias	Card 13 22–23	24–28	29	30	
Bulimia	31–32	33–37	38	39	
Anorexia nervosa	40–41	42–46	47	48	
Suicide attempts	49–50	51–55	56	57	(79–80) = 13

NOTE: Johnson, C., "Initial Consultation for Patients with Bulimia and Anorexia Nervosa," in *Handbook of Psychotherapy for Anorexia Nervosa and Bulimia,* ed. D. Garner and P. Garfinkel, New York: Guilford Press, pp. 19–51.

mediated affective disorder. Several converging pieces of evidence have been offered in support of this hypothesis.

The first line of evidence is related to preliminary findings that have indicated that a large number of bulimic patients report symptoms characteristic of unipolar and bipolar illness. These symptoms include a persistence of low and highly variable mood states, low frustration tolerance, anxiety, and suicidal ideation. These early reports suggest that bulimic patients present with vegetative symptoms similar to patients with major depression, but the etiology of the depressive experience remains unclear. The depressive symptoms may be physiological effects from weight loss or fluctuations in nutritional status, or psychological effects from repeated exposure to a pattern of thoughts and behavior that results in feelings of helplessness, shame, guilt, and ineffectiveness.

The most compelling evidence for the depression hypothesis comes from family studies, which indicate a high incidence of major affective disorder among first- and second-degree relatives of bulimic patients. Using the family-history method among a sample of seventy-five patients with bulimia, Hudson and his colleagues[28,30] found that 53 percent had first-degree relatives with major affective disorder. Likewise, substance-abuse disorder was highly prevalent (in 45 of 350 relatives). Results further indicate that the morbid risk factor for affective disorder in relatives was 28 percent, which was similar to that found in families of patients with bipolar disorder.

Strober and his colleagues[62,63] found strikingly similar results among anorexic patients who manifested bulimic symptoms. Their findings indicated a 20-percent morbid risk factor for affective disorder in the bulimic families. They also noted that 18 percent of first- and second-degree relatives reported histories of alcoholism.

There has also been a preliminary attempt to identify biological markers that are associated with depression and bulimia. Although consistent markers of affective disorders have not been isolated, two that are under consideration are suggestive of major depression among bulimic patients. The dexamethasone suppression test and the thyroid-releasing hormone stimulating test have been found positive in bulimic patients with the same frequency as in patients with major depression and much more frequently than would be expected in normal control populations.[24,28] Sleep architecture research has also recently indicated that a subgroup of bulimic patients at normal weight (with previous histories of anorexia nervosa) displayed sleep disturbance (shortened rapid-eye-movement latency) characteristic of patients with affective disorders.[41]

Finally, support for this hypothesis comes from early findings regarding the effectiveness of antidepressant pharmacotherapy. Both open trials and double-blind placebo studies of tricyclic and monoamine oxidase inhibitor treatment have resulted in significant improvement in frequency of bulimic symptoms.*

* See references 7, 37, 40, 47, 54, 55, 59, and 66.

Although further research is necessary to substantiate the prevalence of affective disorders among bulimic patients, it seems safe to assume that at least a subgroup of these patients will have major depressions that respond to antidepressant pharmacotherapy. Consequently, assessment should include careful inquiry about vegetative symptoms associated with major depression, family histories of major depression, and, if possible, laboratory tests investigating biological markers associated with primary affective disorder.

Family Assessment

Exploration of family issues is important for several reasons. It is necessary to rule out whether the patient's symptomatic behavior serves some adaptive function within the family system. Second, delineation of structural and communication style within the family should influence the treatment approach. For example, active and directive modes of therapy would be indicated for patients from disengaged and chaotic families, and a more nondirective treatment would be indicated for patients from enmeshed and overprotective families.

Few studies have evaluated the family environment among bulimic patients. Those that do exist consistently find families that are disengaged, chaotic, and highly conflicted. They also appear to manifest indirect patterns of communication; are less supportive, orderly, and organized; are less intellectually and recreationally oriented; and have high achievement expectations.* In light of these preliminary findings, it is important to assess the nature of the family environment during the initial consultation. The following categories provide guidelines for assessing the family milieu.

COHESIVENESS

"Cohesiveness" refers to the quantity and quality of involvement within the family system. Assessing cohesiveness is important because either underinvolvement or overinvolvement among family members can result in self-regulatory deficits. A crucial factor affecting cohesiveness is the nature of the boundaries that exist among different family members. "Boundaries" refer to the rules that govern interpersonal issues such as distance versus intimacy and autonomy versus symbiosis. Weak, porous boundaries among family members usually result in enmeshed family systems, which are characterized by extreme forms of proximity and intensity

* See references 19, 31, 34, 51, 62, and 63.

in family interaction. There is usually a high degree of overprotectiveness, which results in poor differentiation and an incapacity for independent self-regulation. Bulimic patients from enmeshed family systems are often quite phobic and dependent. The food-related behavior is often a desperate attempt to self-regulate in the absence of external caretakers.

Disengaged families represent the opposite end of a continuum of boundaries and cohesiveness. Within disengaged families, boundaries are overdefined and insensitive, which results in a lack of feeling of "connectedness" or meaningful involvement with others. Bulimic patients from disengaged families are often withdrawn and have had to develop autonomy prematurely. The regulatory deficits these patients experience result from *under-* rather than *over*involvement.

COMMUNICATION STYLE

"Communication style" refers to how the family exchanges information. Are messages directly and clearly expressed with appropriate affect, or are they displaced and affectively impoverished? Several characteristic communication problems within families of eating-disorder patients should be investigated during the assessment: disqualification and disconfirmation in which patients learn that expression of their thoughts and feelings is inaccurate or not valued; shifting of focus, a narcissistically oriented communication style that results in individuals withdrawing from efforts to communicate because it is an empty or disorganizing experience; and finally, double-binding, which occurs when a patient is given mutually exclusive messages. This type of communication often results in anxious conflict and feelings of being paralyzed and hopeless.

Problems in communications such as these often result in individuals having difficulty identifying and clearly articulating internal states. This is a characteristic of many bulimic patients. Consequently, assessment must explore the extent to which communication style had contributed to this type of difficulty.

CONFLICT RESOLUTION

Many eating-disordered patients come from family systems where they have not been given adequate tools to navigate interpersonal and intrapsychic conflict. It is important to assess whether patients have learned to openly acknowledge and accurately identify conflicts or whether they have learned to deny, avoid, and displace dysphoric events in an effort to maintain family homeostasis. It is also important to assess whether the patient has been criticized, rejected, or personally attacked as a result of expressing conflict. Many feel intimidated and nonassertive around conflicts and resolve conflictual issues through food-related behavior.

BEHAVIOR CONTROL

It is useful to identify the family patterns for rewarding and punishing behavior. Does the family have clearly stated rules and are punishments logical consequences for rules that are broken? Are rules rigidly enforced, thus contributing to a type of all-or-none thinking characteristic of eating-disordered patients, or are rules absent and chaotic, resulting in less sense of internal control and subsequent vulnerability to impulsive behavior? Finally, does the family system warmly compliment adequate performance, thus facilitating self-esteem, or does it criticize all efforts, thus undermining positive self-regard?

ROLES

"Roles" refer to patterns of behavior by which individuals fulfill family functions. It is important to assess whether the patient serves a specific role and what the demands of the role include. More specifically, is the role developmentally and structurally appropriate, and is the role rigid or flexible? Are the demands overadequate or underadequate? To what extent does the role mesh with other family members' needs, and how satisfied is the individual with the role?

When assessing roles it is important to identify what the developmental challenges are for each family member, particularly the patient and the parents. The age of greatest risk for developing eating disorders is adolescence and young adulthood, a time when most parents confront midlife issues. Many conflicts and pathological resolutions can emerge in the family system during this interface between adolescence and midlife transition.[35] Separation fears that are shared by both parents and child can be resolved by the child's assumption of a "sick role," thus binding the child into the family system. Many patients are pressured to maintain a certain appearance (thinness) to narcissistically gratify the parents, or to achieve at a high level and thus compensate for parental frustration over their own limited opportunities or successes. This latter role delegation is particularly important to assess because young females have been exposed to multiple and often contradictory role expectations, which will be discussed more fully in the next section.

Sociocultural Milieu

Several investigators have proposed a sociocultural explanation for the increased incidence of anorexia nervosa and bulimia over the last two decades.[16,17,61] The suggestion is that the selective increase of eating disorders among young women almost exclusively stems from changing role expectations and an emphasis on thinness for this group.

Research has indicated that over the last two decades, the sociocultural milieu for young women has become progressively unstable, which has precipitated substantial identity confusion among this age group.[3,18,44,53] Garner and Garfinkel[17] review evidence that shifting cultural norms for contemporary young women have forced them to face multiple, ambiguous, and often contradictory role expectations. These role expectations include accommodating more traditional feminine expectations such as physical attractiveness and domesticity, incorporating more modern standards for vocational and personal achievement, and taking advantage of increased opportunity for self-definition and autonomy. Garner and Garfinkel[17] suggest that "while the wider range of choices available to contemporary women may provide personal freedom for those that are psychologically robust it may be overwhelming for the field-dependent adolescent who lacks internal structure" (p. 14). Furthermore, amid this milieu of high achievement orientation and cultural confusion regarding how to express the drive to achieve, it appears that the pursuit of thinness (weight loss through restrictive dieting) has emerged in the culture as one vehicle by which young women can compete among themselves and demonstrate self-control.

In fact, the accomplishment of thinness has become a very highly valued achievement that secures respect and envy among women in this culture. Conversely, the absence of weight control, leading to even moderate overweight, leads culturally to social discrimination, isolation, and low self-esteem.[68] Consequently, amid a backdrop of confusing cultural expectations and high achievement expectations, the pursuit of thinness emerges as one very concrete activity that young women can engage in that results in consistently favorable social responses which enhance self-esteem.

Several issues related to sociocultural pressures are important to assess. Does the patient have a clearly defined set of values, goals, and role identity? Are the role demands that accompany the goals compatible or are they contradictory? Does the patient feel pressure to achieve either for herself or for other family members? Is the patient prepared for the demands inherent in her goals? To what extent has the patient's drive for thinness and body image been influenced by the broader social network or even by job requirements requiring body size maintenance? Finally, to what extent does the patient feel that thinness contributes to her social status and self-esteem?

Personality Factors

As depicted in figure 23.1, biological, familial, and sociocultural factors combine to influence the bulimic individual's personality (affects, cognitions, and behaviors) in many ways. While there is no single personality profile indicative of bulimia, research and clinical experience suggest several consistent patterns to which the therapist needs to be alert.

CAPACITY FOR SELF-REGULATION

Several factors predispose bulimic patients to affective variability that results in anxiety and vulnerability to impulsive behaviors. The intensity and pervasiveness of the anxiety and impulsive behavior offer significant clues about the patients' capacity for self-regulation. Self-regulatory deficits among bulimic patients range from mild to severe difficulties.[22,64] In mild cases the anxiety and impulsiveness are circumscribed to food-related behavior. These patients appear to have sufficient ego strength to benefit from brief psychoeducational and insight-oriented approaches that focus on self-monitoring skills and alternative coping strategies.[10] Among patients with more severe self-regulatory difficulties, the anxiety is extremely disorganizing and the impulsive behavior is expressed in a variety of ways, such as shoplifting of nonfood items, multiple substance abuse, and self-mutilatory behavior.[9,13] This latter subgroup may have borderline personality organizations. Among these patients the food-related problems are often secondary to more pervasive ego deficits.[12,32,65]

Several authors suggest that many eating-disordered patients have significant difficulties identifying and articulating internal states.[8,52] Self-regulation would be difficult if this were the case. Consequently, during the interview it is useful to observe how quickly and precisely patients are able to talk about their feelings.

INTERPERSONAL SKILLS

Bulimic individuals have been noted to have difficulty in interpersonal situations. They often feel alienated, self-conscious, and have difficulty expressing strong affects and asserting themselves.* They also report impaired social adjustment in areas of work, social and leisure activities, and family and marital functioning.[33,50]

While some bulimic persons may have interpersonal difficulties due to skill deficits, most are knowledgeable about proper interpersonal responses but inhibit themselves. Most bulimic patients appear to be exquisitely sensitive to the reactions of other people and fear angering them. Rather than risk anger or rejection, bulimic patients will often inhibit

* See references 6, 10, 38, 49, 56, and 60.

their own responses. The end result is avoidance of others and dissatisfaction with relationships.

Consequently, the assessment must cover both the quality and quantity of the patient's social skills. If the skills are present, is the patient using them effectively and if not, what is preventing this?

LOW SELF-ESTEEM

Frequently, bulimic patients complain of having low self-esteem.[10,12,36,45] Feelings of inadequacy, helplessness, ineffectiveness, guilt, and self-doubt are often expressions of this.

During the initial interview it is important to assess whether self-esteem problems predated the onset of the food problems. Many bulimic patients pursue thinness to enhance self-esteem. For a subgroup of patients weight loss does enhance self-esteem. Unfortunately, the maintenance of the self-esteem remains tied to the low body weight, which, for many, can only be accomplished through persistent purging behavior. Frequent use of purging behavior, however, often results in increased binge eating. This occurs because the normal negative consequences of overeating (painful fullness, nausea, weight gain) are removed, which in turn fuels unrestrained eating.

Paradoxically, as the patients become more restrained, they feel more out of control, which leads to social withdrawal and lower self-esteem, thus exacerbating the original self-esteem problems. This subgroup of patients resists challenges to their eating style because weight gain would disrupt social adjustment and self-esteem. It is also important to note that a different subgroup of bulimic patients have either exacerbated self-esteem problems or developed low self-esteem as a result of repeated experiences of failure in attaining thinness (failed dieters).

Many bulimic patients rely on the opinions of others to evaluate their self-worth. They will overaccommodate to the needs of others and ignore their own needs in an effort to gain approval. This reliance on others lowers self-esteem because patients feel they lack self-directedness, and their vigilance concerning others' reactions to them makes them particularly sensitive to rejection and vulnerable to criticism. Interestingly, there are also patients who experience low self-esteem around dependency needs that are in conflict with self-expectations to be independent. Within the current cultural context, a subgroup of young women in particular appears to interpret any longing for attachment or interdependency as weakness and failure in self-reliance.

COGNITIVE DISTORTIONS

As noted by Beck,[4] Ellis,[11] and others, self-esteem is not static and relates to the way people think about themselves and the world around them. According to this view, low self-esteem is the result of cognitive errors that "filter" the patient's experience and color it in a negative way. Recent research[15] and clinical experience have noted several cognitive errors that are common among eating-disordered patients.

Perfectionism. Similar to many depressive patients, bulimic patients often hold themselves to standards that they would never apply to another individual. Evaluating self-worth in relation to their accomplishments, they constantly strive for relativistic perfection that can never be satisfied, because the bulimic individual "could have done a bit better."

Failing to satisfy their perfectionism in other spheres, bulimic persons turn to dieting. For the bulimic person who is searching for an external criterion by which to judge herself, thinness seems ideal as it is a goal for which success is measured by an objective number. Initially, dissatisfaction with performance in many spheres is assuaged by successful dieting. Later the weight loss loses its reinforcing value as the patient again feels dissatisfied with her performance in other pursuits. This increases body dissatisfaction and, in turn, dieting, which eventually becomes too restrictive to maintain. At this point, binging and purging begin, which heighten the bulimic patient's dissatisfaction with her performance and lead to even more perfectionistic standards of performance.

Negative Filter. Many bulimic patients engage in the cognitive distortion Beck[4] termed the "negative filter." They fail to consider their accomplishments while disproportionately attending to their failures. They doom themselves to never meeting their perfectionistic standards because they discount evidence of success.

Dichotomous Thinking. Related to the negative filter is the bulimic person's tendency to classify events in all-or-nothing categories. The world is divided into categories consisting of pairs of polar opposites. An event thus fits one extreme or, by definition, it must fit the opposite extreme. This sort of thinking applies not only to food but often to other aspects of the patient's life such as studies, success, self-confidence, social approval, and so forth.

As noted by Marlatt and Gordon,[46] dichotomous thinking often co-exists with perfectionism. In addition to striving for perfection, any performance less than the best possible is viewed as total failure. This combination of cognitive errors often precipitates a binge from what begins as an episode of unplanned or uncontrolled eating. The scenario runs as follows: Seeking to control her weight, the bulimic individual diets. As a perfectionist, however, only rigid adherence to the diet is acceptable. This is violated by the episode of unplanned eating. The bulimic person will define the episode as a complete failure equivalent to even the largest binge. As the "sin" has already been committed, the bulimic individual decides that she must purge and is therefore free to eat whatever she wants.

Personalization. Bulimic people often believe they are the center of everyone's attention. They may interpret other people's behavior as reflecting judgments being made about them and may take the most innocuous behaviors as evidence of scorn and derision. This places patients in a bind as any attention from another person is assumed to contain derogatory intent while the same is true of a lack of attention. Personalization appears to be both a grandiose desire for attention and an intense self-hatred perpetuated by negative interpretations.

Fear of Alienating Others. Bulimic individuals often fear alienating significant others. They appear to ascribe to Ellis's first irrational idea[11]—they must have love and approval from all of the people they find significant. This interferes with a bulimic person's ability to assert her own desires for fear that this will anger or alienate others. Also, many bulimic individuals have families who define parental pleasure as primary to the child's pleasure, so the patients feel that their own pleasure is selfish and bad. Not wishing to incur the wrath of the parents, these patients avoid pleasing themselves and feel guilty if they do.

This avoidance of pleasure and the guilt that it produces is intimately associated with binging. Bulimic patients often report feeling tightly controlled—as though they were walking a tightrope—in their attempts to keep other people happy. Binging creates pleasurable discontrol that allows indulgence and freedom from the control of other people.

Superstitious Thinking. Superstitious thinking consists of assuming that two unrelated events are related or that an outcome must follow an event even though the two are not associated. Bulimic patients may believe, for example, that eating any amount of a "forbidden" food will result in a 10-pound weight gain, though they only consumed a few calories. Another example is the assumption that carbohydrates are fattening, irrespective of the amount ingested.

Bulimic individuals may also believe that they are responsible for the feelings of other people. Believing their actions cause rather than influence other's affects, these patients must constantly guess how other people feel about events and adapt their behavior in order to keep harmony.

A corollary of this cognitive error is the belief that external events cause people to feel as they do. Thus a bulimic individual believes that her low self-esteem is the result of what she ate or how her clothes fit. During assessment it is important to estimate how strongly the patient adheres to this belief and to focus treatment on separating the notion of causality from antecedent or contiguous events.

Cognitive Narrowing and Cognitive Diffusing. The cognitive style of bulimic patients is often diffuse and chaotic. Such patients often feel out of control and fragmented, especially when under stress. They use binging to refocus or narrow their field of cognitive concern. Bingeing is one behavior that is under their control and is a predictable and reliable way to create a specific affective and cognitive state. Due to its highly ritualized and repetitive nature, a binge can be used to organize thoughts and behavior.

Other bulimic patients are overcontrolled and obsessive. They use binging to be out of control and impulsive. These patients often report binging as a "letting go" or "spacing out" experience where they invest food with the power to overcome them and make them impulsive.

Assessment of Binge/Purge Behavior: Macroanalysis

The macroanalysis of binging and purging takes a long-range perspective on the behavior. The interviewer attempts to identify long-range patterns or major life repetitions that have influenced the patient's behavior at a more global level. This is opposed to the day-to-day patterns identified during the microanalysis. It is useful to establish when weight concerns, dieting, and binge eating began developmentally. The overall task is to assess, historically, how much weight concerns and body dissatisfaction affected self-esteem/life adjustment and what functional adaptation dieting and binge eating has served.

WEIGHT HISTORY

Initially inquiry is made into the patient's highest and lowest weight since age 13. If the patient has experienced cyclical patterns of weight fluctuations, it is useful to attempt to correlate them with specific life events, such as major transitions, separation or losses, family problems, or recurring illness. Inquiring about such correlates of weight change can help the patient begin thinking psychologically about the relationship among food, weight, body-related behavior, and life events.

Weight information about childhood and early adolescence is often unreliable. Consequently, the assessment of early years often focuses on how much emphasis family and peers placed on thinness, dieting, appearance, and what influence this had on self-concept and beliefs about self-control, social acceptance, and so forth. We also inquire whether the patient was teased about her weight. It is important to establish the extent of the teasing, the context, the content, who specifically was doing the teasing, and its impact on the patient.

DIETING HISTORY

Early onset and frequency of dieting are associated with the development of bulimia.[39] During the assessment, the interviewer should determine when the patient first began dieting, what prompted the decision to diet, whether there was a particular source of encouragement to diet, and to what extent a specific belief system has evolved around the process of dieting.

BINGE-EATING HISTORY

At the macrolevel the task is to determine when binge eating began, the precipitating circumstances, and whether fluctuations in symptoms correlate with recurring life events.

The mean age of onset for binge eating among bulimic patients is 18 years, the average duration of illness is five and one-half years, and purging behavior usually begins one year after the onset of binge eating.[38,56] The most commonly cited precipitant is a prolonged period of restrictive dieting.[38,56] Also cited are traumatic events such as loss or separation, interpersonal and job conflict, and difficulty handling emotions such as sexuality, anger, loneliness, and depression. Consequently, the greatest risk for onset among this patient population (18-year-old, predominantly Caucasian, upper-class, college-bound females) occurs at a time when separation and identity formation issues are at a peak.

It is also useful to inquire about the longest time the patient has been binge-free since the onset of her difficulties, what her life circumstances were during these periods, and what her affective response was to the symptom-free period. Patients often report symptom-free periods that correspond to vacations, leaving home, starting or ending a relationship, or good or difficult times at work. Similarly some patients find symptom-free periods frustrating, difficult, anxiety provoking, and depressing, while others report them to be happy, tension-free times. This information also shows the successful and unsuccessful strategies the patient has employed to cope with the binge eating.

Microassessment

The microanalysis focuses on the typography of the food-related behavior and the function it serves on a daily basis. The emphasis is on a detailed assessment of daily food intake, daily activities, frequency, duration and time of day the binge-purge sequence occurs, and the affects and cognitions associated with the sequence. This is often facilitated by having the patient carry a time-sampling diary (see figure 23.3), which is filled out four times per day for at least one week.

ANALYSIS OF CURRENT EATING AND DIETING BEHAVIOR

During the initial evaluation it is important to gather information about the patient's current eating and dieting habits. We have found it useful to ask patients to record their daily food intake over a one-week period. Patients may under- or overestimate the amounts and variety of food they eat. Frequently, bulimic patients alternate binging with severely restrictive dieting or fasting. Such physiological deprivation and psychological self-denial lead to intense hunger, fatigue, heightened feelings of self-denial, and difficulties in mental concentration: symptoms that are

FIGURE 23.3

Self Monitoring Form

Date: _____ Time: _____ AM/PM

What were you thinking about? _____

_____

Where are you? _____

_____

What was the **main** thing you were doing? _____

	Not at All	Somewhat	Quite	Very
How much choice did you have in selecting this activity?	+ --- + --- + --- + --- + --- + --- + --- + --- + --- +
Did you feel in control of your activity?	+ --- + --- + --- + --- + --- + --- + --- + --- + --- +
How guilty did you feel?	+ --- + --- + --- + --- + --- + --- + --- + --- + --- +
How vulnerable did you feel?	+ --- + --- + --- + --- + --- + --- + --- + --- + --- +
How self-conscious were you?	+ --- + --- + --- + --- + --- + --- + --- + --- + --- +
How much were you concentrating?	+ --- + --- + --- + --- + --- + --- + --- + --- + --- +
How satisfied did you feel with yourself?	+ --- + --- + --- + --- + --- + --- + --- + --- + --- +
	0 1 2 3 4 5 6 7 8 9

Describe your mood:

	Very	Quite	Some	Neither	Some	Quite	Very	
Alert	0	o	•	−	•	o	0	Drowsy
Happy	0	o	•	−	•	o	0	Sad
Irritable	0	o	•	−	•	o	0	Cheerful
Strong	0	o	•	−	•	o	0	Weak
Angry	0	o	•	−	•	o	0	Friendly
Active	0	o	•	−	•	o	0	Passive
Lonely	0	o	•	−	•	o	0	Sociable
Adequate	0	o	•	−	•	o	0	Inadequate
Free	0	o	•	−	•	o	0	Constrained
Excited	0	o	•	−	•	o	0	Bored
Proud	0	o	•	−	•	o	0	Ashamed
Confused	0	o	•	−	•	o	0	Clear
Tense	0	o	•	−	•	o	0	Relaxed
Fat	0	o	•	−	•	o	0	Thin

Describe your physical state:

	None	Slight	Moderate	Severe
Hungry	+ -- + -- + -- + -- + -- + -- + -- + -- + -- + --
Tired, slowed down	+ -- + -- + -- + -- + -- + -- + -- + -- + -- + --
Aches and pains	+ -- + -- + -- + -- + -- + -- + -- + -- + -- + --

Who were you with?

( ) Alone
( ) Brother(s), sister(s)
( ) Mother
( ) Father
( ) Strangers
( ) Coworkers

( ) Friend(s):
    Number _____
    ( ) Male
    ( ) Female
    ( ) Other(s): _____

Describe how you feel about one of the persons you are with. (If alone and thinking about someone, describe feelings about that person):

	Very	Middle	Very	
Close to	+ --- + --- + --- + --- + --- + --- + --- + --- + --- +			Distant from
Inferior to	+ --- + --- + --- + --- + --- + --- + --- + --- + --- +			Superior to
Friendly toward	+ --- + --- + --- + --- + --- + --- + --- + --- + --- +			Angry with
In control of	+ --- + --- + --- + --- + --- + --- + --- + --- + --- +			Controlled by

(Identify the person you are referring to: _____)

	Not at All	Somewhat	Quite	Very
How preoccupied were you with eating?	+ --- + --- + --- + --- + --- + --- + --- + --- + --- +			
Do you feel your eating has been out of control since the last report?	+ --- + --- + --- + --- + --- + --- + --- + --- + --- +			
How confident did you feel that you could resist the urge to binge eat?	+ --- + --- + --- + --- + --- + --- + --- + --- + --- +			
	0 1 2 3 4 5 6 7 8 9			

Indicate your alcohol intake since the last report:

Beer	*Wine*	*Liquor*
Number of Units	Number of Units	Number of Units
_____ cans (12 oz.)	_____ glasses (10 oz.)	_____ shots (1½ oz.)
_____ bottles (12 oz.)	_____ fifths (26 oz.)	_____ drinks (1½ oz.)
_____ glasses (10 oz.)	_____ quarts (32 oz.)	_____ pints (16 oz.)
		_____ fifths (26 oz.)
		_____ quarts (32 oz.)

Indicate your food intake since the last report:

Type	Quantity
_____	_____
_____	_____
_____	_____
_____	_____

How many times have you binged since the last report? _____

How many times have you purged since the last report? _____

associated with specific food cravings or an increased tendency to binge.*
Consequently, it is important to determine if the binge eating is a coun-
terregulatory reaction to either physiological deprivation or the psychological experience of repeated restrained eating.

We also inquire about foods that are avoided. To identify superstitious
thinking the patient has about nutrition, we ask why these are avoided.
Bulimic individuals often have mistaken beliefs about what calories are,
how food is digested, what the function of adipose tissue is, how weight
is gained, and how fad diets work.

TIME PATTERNS AND ALTERNATIVE BEHAVIORS

It is particularly important to investigate whether there is a specific
time pattern to the binge eating. Most bulimic individuals have difficulty
with food during the evening hours when they are alone and in unstructured situations.[43] Other time patterns, however, may emerge. Some patients, for example, binge only at work, while others binge following family
engagements or other social events. Since unstructured time is difficult
for these patients, it is also useful to assess whether they have activities,
interests, and hobbies that might help with "free time." Some patients
have skill deficits that can be remediated with directive, educational interventions. Others have adequate repertoires of leisure behaviors, but
when alone they lack either the internal organization or motivation to
involve themselves in the activities. This type of difficulty usually indicates
significant self-regulatory deficits as described earlier.

TRANSITIONS

Many bulimic patients have difficulty making transitions from one
context to another. Entering home in the evening hours after working,
going to sleep at day's end, and entering a social relationship after being
alone are all situations that require the use of different internal resources.
For many patients, it appears that the act of binge eating becomes a ritualized event that facilitates the process of transitioning. It is useful to
investigate whether the sequence has unwittingly emerged as an adaptation
to this difficulty.

AFFECTIVE AND COGNITIVE STATES

Bulimic patients binge eat and purge in response to a variety of affective and cognitive states. The microanalysis can evaluate whether there
is a pattern to the patient's thoughts and feelings before, during, and
after a binge-purge sequence. The following are characteristic experiences
associated with the eating behavior.

* See references 23, 27, 42, 46, and 53.

Diffuse Dysphoria. Bulimic patients often experience highly variable mood states that often do not appear to be related to specific events. These include anxiety, panic, depression, boredom, irritability, and euphoria. Throughout the day the variability, range, and seeming nonpredictability of the different mood states may become overwhelming and disorganizing for the patient. The concrete and repetitive act of binging and purging serves an integrating function by reliably creating a predictable affective and cognitive state through the sequence. When overwhelmed by diffuse and variable mood states, the binging and purging becomes both an explanation of the dysphoria ("I am feeling bad because I have binged") and a mechanism for regulating the dysphoria ("I feel relieved after I have binged").

Impulse Expression. Many bulimic patients have difficulty expressing affective states. Anger and sexuality often create conflict. Prohibitions against the expression of these feelings generate significant frustration that threatens impulse barriers. Since binging and purging do not carry significant moral, legal, or interpersonal consequences, they can emerge as an effective mechanism to impulsively discharge these feelings. Likewise, more obsessive, overcontrolled patients use binge eating to be temporarily out of control or have the phenomenological experience of "letting go" or "spacing out." These patients experience controlled discontrol. They invest food (an inanimate object that has no volition and can have only as much power as they grant it) with the power to overcome them and make them become impulsive. This allows relief from an overcontrolled psychological world, without having to take responsibility for the impulsive episodes.

Self-Nurturance. Some bulimic individuals are tormented by profound guilt and deny themselves pleasurable or self-enhancing activities. They are self-sacrificing and their continuous efforts to care for others often leave them feeling depleted and exhausted. Binge eating (with the attendant attribution that the event was externally determined) can serve as a mechanism for giving to oneself.

Some bulimic patients experience a basic mistrust of others that prevents them from receiving emotional support from the outside. Consequently they will invest food and binge eating with the ability to soothe, comfort, and gratify them. They will often project onto the food humanlike qualities that allow them the illusion of receiving emotional supplies from a source other than themselves. The fact that food (an inanimate object) can behave only as they desire allows them to simultaneously refuel and yet be protected from the potential disappointment in human relationships.

Oppositionality. Binge eating can also express oppositionality. For patients who feel restrained by others, binge eating can become an expression of "acting out" or defiance. This is particularly true of bulimic individuals raised in families where weight control and dieting were emphasized. The act of binge eating is a statement of protest and autonomy.

Whatever specific adaptation binge eating serves, once an episode has ended, the patients generally feel guilt, shame, disgust, and fear of being discovered. These feelings combine in a sense of panic about weight gain, which would be an observable indication that they are out of control, disorganized, undisciplined, greedy, and so forth. Consequently, evacuation techniques such as self-induced vomiting, laxative abuse, and enemas become mechanisms for undoing the binge eating.

MICROANALYSIS OF PURGING

In the third edition of the *Diagnostic and Statistical Manual of Mental Disorders,*[2] purging is one of several criteria that contribute to the diagnosis of bulimia, but is neither necessary nor sufficient for the diagnosis to be made. Most bulimic individuals, however, do purge by self-induced vomiting, diuretic abuse, or laxative abuse. Given the objective nature of these methods, it is often easier to define purging than it is to define binging.

The assessment of purging behavior begins by inquiring if the patient engages in the practice and what means of evacuation she uses. While most use self-induced vomiting, it is not unusual for patients to use several evacuation strategies. Each method has its own risks, with some that are commonly shared. All three, for example, have been associated with hypovolemia, electrolyte imbalances, hypertrophy of the juxtaglomerular apparatus, and rebound edema once the behavior has stopped. Laxatives also damage the intestinal mucosa, though their effects appear reversible.[1,14,26,48]

HYPER- AND HYPOREACTIVITY OF THE GAG REFLEX

Self-induced vomiting is associated with two other problems that merit inquiry. Some patients report that after they have used self-induced vomiting for a period of time, they have found it increasingly easy to regurgitate. Such patients often report that merely the intent to purge or a tightening of their abdominal muscles is sufficient to result in emesis. In others, the sensation of food in the stomach is sufficient to start a gag reflex. This may be the result of classical conditioning in which thoughts about purging or the sensation of a full stomach serve as the conditioned stimulus, the conditioned response for which is emesis. Treatment of such patients is complicated as it requires them to cease vomiting in response to the conditioned stimulus, which may necessitate their swallowing down vomitus.

Other patients who have persistently used self-induced vomiting have found it increasingly difficult to trigger their gag reflex. Such attenuation of the gag reflex may be dangerous because increasingly strong stimuli must be used to trigger it, and because the likelihood of accidental aspiration of food or vomitus increases. Some patients who lose their gag reflex present at area hospitals to have their stomachs pumped to avoid rupture, or have even resorted to the use of ipecac—a dangerous practice due to its cardiotoxicity in the event it does not trigger emesis.

ANTECEDENTS OF PURGING

The microanalysis of purging requires a detailed inquiry into the topography of the purging behavior, its onset, precipitants, duration, and frequency. Similarly, it is important to ask whether every binge is followed by a purge or if each purge is occasioned by a binge. Some patients purge only following binges, while others purge also following normal meals. Other patients report that only some binges are followed by purges, which requires the interviewer to attempt to identify any associations between certain binge episodes and purging. It must also be determined whether the client eats to occasion a purge. Some initial work at our clinic suggests that purging is sometimes more tension-regulating than binge eating. Clinical experience confirms this notion. Though most bulimic patients begin to binge eat without purging, within approximately one year they feel sufficiently out of control to start purging. Once they begin purging, it appears that a transformation takes place whereby the binging, which began as a tension reducer, becomes more of a tension producer. Eventually the binging no longer reduces dysphoric feelings, but instead exacerbates them, and it is the act of purging that restores a sense of control and reduces feelings such as anger, guilt, and loss of control. As is the case with binge eating, it is important to determine the antecedents and consequences of purging. We have found it useful to inquire about the time of day purging occurs; who was present before, during, and after the purge; and what thoughts and feelings the person had before, during, and after the purge.

THE ADAPTIVE CONTEXT OF PURGING

Like binge eating, purging can serve a variety of adaptive functions, some of which may become more important than the actual act of binge eating. As with binge eating, the act of purging can serve as a mechanism for tension regulation. This is particularly true of aggressive feelings. Vomiting can be a violent act, and the physical process of vomiting can be cathartic around aggressive feelings. For patients who feel especially guilty and self-critical about binge eating, the purging can serve as self-punishment and an act of undoing or penitence that pays for the crime of impulse expression. It allows the oppositional patient to get away with something without "getting caught" or having to pay the price of her overeating. For more borderline patients, purging (primarily laxative abuse) appears to serve an integrating function similar to other forms of self-mutilatory behavior. The intense pain created by the persistent diarrhea appears to make them feel alive and in touch with reality. For patients who have become involved with dieting for social approval, it keeps them thin while avoiding biological impass that continued calorie restriction provokes. Most important, overall, purging becomes highly reinforcing because it provides a mechanism whereby the binge eating can increasingly serve the adaptive functions mentioned earlier without the consequence of excessive weight gain. Essentially it gives the patients carte blanche to use the binge eating in any compensatory way desired without immediately apparent consequences.

As with binge eating, it is important to inquire about the longest period of abstinence from purging, including precipitants, its effect on the binging, and the patient's level of discomfort. At the same time, it is useful to inquire about the methods patients have used to abstain and about those methods that have proved unsuccessful.

It is also important to explore the patient's understanding of what purging accomplishes. Most bulimic patients believe that purging is necessary to reduce their weight and works by preventing calorie absorption. While this is true of emesis, it is not true of either laxatives or diuretics. Though laxatives do not control calorie absorption,[5] many bulimic individuals believe otherwise. More seriously, many laxative-abusing bulimic patients have peculiar and idiosyncratic beliefs about them that may indicate of a more serious cognitive impairment. Similarly, though diuretic abusers seem to understand that the medications do not effect calorie absorption, they often have mistaken notions as to the importance of weight.

Summary Comments

This chapter presents a multifactorial model for assessing disturbed eating behavior. Data were reviewed regarding the biological, familial, sociocultural, and personality factors thought to be associated with the onset of bulimia. Clinical impressions and recommendations were offered about how to assess the specific adaptations that the pursuit of thinness and binge eating may serve for individuals.

Clearly, sophisticated assessment procedures should serve a vital function in comprehensive treatment programs. It is our hope that the information in this chapter will facilitate effective assessment that will in turn improve treatment outcome.

REFERENCES

1. Ahola, S. J. 1982. Unexplained parotid enlargement: A clue to occult bulimia. *Connecticut Medical Journal* 46:185–186.

2. American Psychiatric Association. 1980. *Diagnostic and statistical manual of mental disorders*, 3rd ed. Washington, D.C.: American Psychiatric Association.

3. Bardwick, J. 1971. *Psychology of women: A study of bio-cultural conflicts.* New York: Harper & Row.

4. Beck, A. 1976. *Cognitive therapy and the emotional disorders.* New York: International Universities Press.

5. Bo-Linn, G., Sant Ana, C., Morawski, S., and Fortran, J. 1983. Purging and calorie absorption in bulimic patients and normal women. *Annals of Internal Medicine* 99:14–17.

6. Boskind-Lodahl, M. 1976. Cinderella's stepsisters: A feminist perspective on anorexia nervosa and bulimia. *Signs: Journal of Women in Culture and Society* 2:342–356.

7. Brotman, A., Herzog, P., and Woods, S. 1984. Antidepressant treatment of bulimia: The relationship between binging and depressive symptomatology. *Journal of Clinical Psychiatry* 45:7–9.

8. Bruch, H. 1973. *Eating disorders: Obesity, anorexia nervosa, and the person within.* New York: Basic Books.

9. Casper, R. C., et al. 1980. Bulimia: Its incidence and clinical significance in patients with anorexia nervosa. *Archives of General Psychiatry* 37:1030–1035.

10. Connors, M., Johnson, C., and Stuckey, M. 1984. Treatment of bulimia with brief psychoeducational group therapy. *American Journal of Psychiatry* 141:1512–1516.

11. Ellis, A. 1962. *Reason and emotion in psychotherapy.* New York: Lyle Stuart.

12. Garfinkel, P. E., and Garner, D. M. 1982. *Anorexia nervosa: A multidimensional perspective.* New York: Brunner/Mazel.

13. Garfinkel, P. E., Moldofsky, H., and Garner, D. M. 1980. The heterogeneity of anorexia nervosa: Bulimia as a distinct subgroup. *Archives of General Psychiatry* 37:1036–1040.

14. Garlo, L., and Randel, A. 1981. Chronic vomiting and its effect on the primary dentition. *Journal of Dentistry for Children* 48:383–384.

15. Garner, D. M., and Bemis, K. M. 1982. A cognitive behavioral approach to anorexia nervosa. *Cognitive Therapy and Research* 6:1–27.

16. Garner, D. M., and Garfinkel, P. E. 1978. Socio-cultural factors in anorexia nervosa. *Lancet* 2:674.

17. ———. 1980. Socio-cultural factors in the development of anorexia nervosa. *Psychological Medicine* 9:695–709.

18. Garner, D. M., Garfinkel, P. E., and Olmsted, M. P. 1983. An overview of socio-cultural factors in the development of anorexia nervosa. In *Anorexia nervosa: Recent developments in research*, ed. P. Darby et al., pp. 65–82. New York: Alan R. Liss.

19. Garner, D. M., Garfinkel, P. E., and O'Shaughnessy, M. 1983. Clinical and psychometric comparison between bulimia and anorexia and bulimia in normal-weight women. *Report of the Fourth Ross Conference on Medical Research*: 6–11.

20. Garner, D. M., Olmsted, M. P., and Polivy, J. 1983. Development and validation of a multidimensional eating disorder inventory for anorexia nervosa and bulimia. *International Journal of Eating Disorders* 2:15–33.

21. Glassman, A. H., and Walsh, B. T. 1983. Link between bulimia and depression unclear. *Journal of Clinical Psychopharmacology* 3:203.

22. Goodsitt, A. 1983. Self-regulatory disturbances in eating disorders. *International Journal of Eating Disorders* 2:51–60.

23. Gormally, J., Black, S., Daston, S., and Rardin, D. 1982. The assessment of binge eating among obese persons. *Addictive Behaviors* 7:47–52.

24. Gwirtsman, H. E., et al. 1983. Neuroendocrine abnormalities in bulimia. *American Journal of Psychiatry* 140:559–563.

25. Halmi, K. A., Falk, J. R., and Schwartz, E. 1981. Binge eating and vomiting: A survey of a college population. *Psychological Medicine* 11:697–706.

26. Haslwer, J. 1982. Parotid enlargement a presenting symptom in anorexia nervosa. *Oral Surgery, Oral Medicine, and Oral Pathology* 53:567–573.

27. Hawkins, R. C., II, and Clement, P. F. 1980. Development and construct validation of a self report measure of binge eating tendencies. *Addictive Behaviors* 5:219–226.

28. Hudson, J. I., Laffer, P. S., and Pope, H. G., Jr. 1982. Bulimia related to affective disorder by family and response to the dexamethasone suppression test. *American Journal of Psychiatry* 139:5.

29. Hudson, J. I., Pope, H. G., Jr., and Jonas, J. M. In press. Phenomenologic relationship of eating disorders or major affective disorder. *Psychiatric Research*.

30. Hudson, J. I., Pope, H. G., Jr., Jonas, J. M., and Yurgelun-Todd, D. 1983. Family history study of anorexia nervosa and bulimia. *British Journal of Psychiatry* 142:133–138.

31. Humphrey, L. In press. Family relations in bulimic, anorexic, and non-distressed families. *American Journal of Psychiatry*.

32. Johnson, C. 1985. The initial consultation for patients with bulimia and anorexia nervosa. In *Handbook of psychotherapy for anorexia nervosa and bulimia*, ed. D. M. Garner and P. E. Garfinkel, pp. 19–51. New York: Guilford Press.

33. Johnson, C., and Berndt, D. J. 1983. Preliminary investigation of bulimia and life adjustment. *American Journal of Psychiatry* 140:6.

34. Johnson, C., and Flach, R. A. In press. Family characteristics of bulimic and normal women—a comparative study. *American Journal of Psychiatry*.

35. Johnson, C., and Irvin, F. 1983. Depressive potentials: Interface between adolescence and midlife transition. In *Children of depressed parents*, ed. H. Morrison, pp. 115–137. New York: Grune & Stratton.

36. Johnson, C., and Larson, R. 1982. Bulimia: An analysis of moods and behavior. *Psychosomatic Medicine* 44:333–345.

37. Johnson, C., Stuckey, M., and Mitchell, J. 1983. Psychopharmacological treatment of anorexia nervosa and bulimia: Review and synthesis. *Journal of Nervous and Mental Disease* 171:524–534.

38. Johnson, C., Stuckey, M. K., Lewis, L. D., and Schwartz, D. 1982. Bulimia: A descriptive survey of 316 cases. *International Journal of Eating Disorders* 1:1–15.

39. Johnson, C., et al. 1984. Incidence and correlates of bulimic behavior in a female high school population. *Journal of Youth and Adolescence* 13:15–26.

40. Jonas, J. M., Pope, H. G., Jr., and Hudson, J. I. 1983. Treatment of bulimia with MAO inhibitors. *Journal of Clinical Psychopharmacology* 3:59–60.

41. Katz, J. L., et al. 1984. Is there a relationship between eating disorders and affective disorders? New evidence from sleep recordings. *American Journal of Psychiatry* 141:753–759.

42. Keys, A., et al. 1950. *The biology of human starvation*. Minneapolis: University of Minnesota Press.

43. Larson, R., and Johnson, C. L. In press. Disturbed patterns of solitude among bulimic patients. *Addictive Behaviors*.

44. Lewis, L., and Johnson, C. In press. A comparison of sex role orientation between women with bulimia and normal controls. *International Journal of Eating Disorders*.

45. Love, S., Ollendick, T., Johnson, C., and Schlesinger, S. 1985. A preliminary report of the prediction of bulimic behaviors: A social learning analysis. *Bulletin of the Society of Psychologists in Addictive Behaviors* 4:93–101.

46. Marlatt, G. A., and Gordon, J. 1980. Determinants of relapse. Implications for the maintenance of behavior change. In *Behavioral medicine: Changing health lifestyles*, ed. P. Davidson and S. Davidson, pp. 31–51. New York: Brunner/Mazel.

47. Mendels, J. 1983. Eating disorders and antidepressants. *Journal of Clinical Psychopharmacology* 3:59.

48. Mitchell, J., and Bantle, J. 1983. Metabolic and endocrine investigations in women of normal weight with the bulimia syndrome. *Biological Psychiatry* 18:355–365.

49. Norman, D. K., and Herzog, D. B. 1983. Bulimia, anorexia nervosa, and anorexia nervosa with bulimia: A comparative analysis of MMPI profiles. *International Journal of Eating Disorders* 2:43–52.

50. ———. 1984. Persistent social maladjustment in bulimia: A one-year follow-up. *American Journal of Psychiatry* 141:444–446.

51. Ordman, A. M., and Kirschenbaum, D. S. 1984. Bulimia: Assessment of eating, psychological and familial characteristics. Unpublished manuscript.

52. Palazzoli, M. S. 1974. *Self-starvation*. Trans. A. Pomerans. London: Chaucer.

53. Polivy, J., Herman, P., Olmsted, M. and Jazwinski, C. 1984. Restraint and binge eating. In *The binge-purge syndrome*, ed. R. Hawkins, W. Fremouw, and P. Clement, pp. 104–122. New York: Springer.

54. Pope, H. G., Jr., and Hudson, J. I. 1982. Treatment of bulimia with antidepressants. *Psychopharmacology* 78:176–179.

55. Pope, H. G., Hudson, J. I., Jonas, J. M., and Yorgelun-Todd, D. 1983. Bulimia treated with imipramine: A placebo-controlled, double-blind study. *American Journal of Psychiatry* 140:554–558.

56. Pyle, R. L., Mitchell, J. E., and Eckert, E. D. 1981. Bulimia: A report of 34 cases. *Journal of Clinical Psychiatry* 42:60–64.

57. Pyle, R. L., et al. 1983. The incidence of bulimia in freshman college students. *International Journal of Eating Disorders* 2:75–85.

58. Russell, G. 1979. Bulimia nervosa: An ominous variant of anorexia nervosa. *Psychological Medicine* 9:429–448.

59. Sabine, E. J., et al. 1983. Bulimia nervosa: A placebo-controlled therapeutic trial of mianserin. *British Journal of Clinical Pharmacology* 15(Supplement):195–202.

60. Schneider, J. A., and Agras, W. S. 1985. A cognitive behavioral group treatment of bulimia. *British Journal of Psychiatry* (Jan.):66–69.

61. Schwartz, D. M., Thompson, M. G., and Johnson, C. 1982. Anorexia nervosa and bulimia: The socio-cultural context. *International Journal of Eating Disorders* 1:23–25.

62. Strober, M., 1981. The significance of bulimia in juvenile anorexia nervosa: An exploration of possible etiological factors. *International Journal of Eating Disorders* 1:28–43.

63. Strober, M., Salkin, B., Burroughs, J., and Morrell, W. 1982. Validity of the bulimia-restricter distinction in anorexia nervosa. Parental personality characteristics and family psychiatric morbidity. *Journal of Nervous and Mental Disease* 170:345–351.

64. Sugarman, A., Quinlan, D., and Devenis, L. 1981. Anorexia nervosa as a defense against anaclitic depression. *International Journal of Eating Disorders* 1:44–61.

65. Swift, W. J., and Stern, S. 1982. The psychodynamic diversity of anorexia nervosa. *International Journal of Eating Disorders* 2:17–33.

66. Walsh, T., et al. 1982. A treatment of bulimia with monoamine oxidase inhibitors. *American Journal of Psychiatry* 139:1629–1630.

67. Wardle, J., and Beinart, H. 1981. Binge eating: A theoretical review. *British Journal of Clinical Psychology* 20:97–109.

68. Wooley, S., and Wooley, O. 1979. Obesity and women—I. A closer look at the facts. *Women's Studies International Quarterly* 2:69–79.

24

Cognitive-Behavioral and Pharmacological Therapies for Bulimia

G. Terence Wilson

The upsurge of interest in the nature and treatment of bulimia has been recent and sudden. It was only a few years ago that the *Diagnostic and Statistical Manual of Mental Disorders* (*DSM-III*) of the American Psychiatric Association[1] included bulimia as an eating disorder that is distinct from anorexia nervosa, obesity, or any known physical disorder. Prior to that, little attention had been focused on bulimia as an independent psychiatric disorder.[6,40] Only now are controlled treatment studies beginning to appear. Indeed, there are only a handful of reports of even an uncontrolled clinical series of patients. The treatment literature has consisted of isolated clinical reports of mainly single case studies (*AB* designs), together with the usual speculation, based on a loose mixture of clinical experience and theoretical analysis. In this chapter my purpose is to summarize and critique both uncontrolled clinical reports and controlled studies on the treatment of bulimia and to discuss some of the more important clinical strategies that have been proposed.

Cognitive-Behavioral Treatments

Virtually the full array of psychological therapies are used to treat bulimic individuals. This chapter concentrates on cognitive-behavioral methods because they have been most thoroughly evaluated and show distinct promise. Even within the loosely defined context of a cognitive-behavioral approach, a broad spectrum of treatment methods have been used. As is invariably the case in the psychological therapies, however, evaluation of cognitive-behavioral methods for bulimia have been confined to a narrower, more clearly delineated set of procedures.

UNCONTROLLED CLINICAL REPORTS

Multifaceted Treatment Programs. Fairburn[9] reported the individual treatment of eleven women with bulimia nervosa. He noted that the "treatment proved acceptable to all 11 patients, even though 3 had earlier rejected in-patient care along the lines conventionally used in anorexia nervosa. None of the patients dropped out, but patient 2 moved home after 3 months in treatment" (p. 709). The issue of acceptability of treatment is emphasized in the conclusions drawn in this chapter. Nine patients reduced their frequency of bouts of overeating and vomiting to less than once a month. This marked improvement was maintained in the seven patients who were followed for an average length of 9.6 months. Anxiety and depression decreased as did dysfunctional attitudes concerning shape and weight. Body weight did not change. Fairburn[11] has since reported that "subsequent experience with over 50 patients has confirmed that the majority of patients do indeed benefit from this cognitive behavioural approach with most remaining well and requiring no further treatment" (p. 161).

Fairburn's report[9] is a good example of the value of a systematic albeit experimentally uncontrolled clinical trial. As Barlow[3] emphasized, the necessary criteria for an informative clinical series of patients are clear specification of the sample, detailed description of treatment methods so as to allow replication, and comprehensive and discriminating outcome measures. In subsequent papers, Fairburn[10,11] described his treatment approach in even greater detail. This typical problem-oriented, present-focused approach in which the therapist actively provides information, advice, and support and which requires a good working relationship between therapist and patient has three stages: In the first, the

> main emphasis is on establishing some degree of control over eating and the techniques used are largely behavioural. In the second, treatment is more cognitively-oriented with particular stress being placed on the identification and modification of dysfunctional thoughts, beliefs and values. In the final stage the focus is on the maintenance of change. (P. 166)[11]

Initially treatment is intensive (two or three sessions weekly), with gradual thinning of this schedule to roughly once every two weeks during
stage 3.

The self-control and cognitive restructuring strategies that characterize this approach are standard fare in the behavior therapy literature
and need not be described here. Suffice it to emphasize a few aspects that
focus directly on body weight and eating. Most bulimic patients (and, by
definition, all patients with bulimia nervosa) fear weight gain. Fairburn[11]
urges patients to

> accept a weight range of approximately six pounds in magnitude. This weight
> range should not extend below 85 percent of her standard weight since at
> such a weight she will be liable to experience the physiological and psychological
> sequelae of starvation which may tend to worsen the eating problem. The
> patient should also be advised against choosing a weight range which neces-
> sitates anything more than moderate dietary restriction since restraint of this
> type is prone to encourage overeating. In practice, it is best that she postpone
> deciding upon a specific weight range until she has regained control over
> eating since only then will she be able to gauge the amount she can eat in
> order to keep her weight relatively stable. (P. 171)

In stage 1 patients are directed to eat three meals a day plus one or two
snacks to establish a stable pattern of eating.

A noteworthy feature of the program, occurring in stage 2, is what
Fairburn[9] termed exposure treatment:

> Typically, the patient avoids eating certain foods, usually those which she
> views as "fattening"; as a result, when she eats these foods she feels a failure,
> abandons all controls, and starts a bout of overeating. By encouraging the
> patient to introduce gradually "banned" foods into her diet their significance
> diminishes. The avoidance of other situations, for example, going out for a
> meal, may be tackled in a similar fashion. (P. 709)

In marked contrast to approaches to be discussed later, Fairburn[11] advises
that

> Vomiting does not need to be tackled since in the great majority of cases it
> ceases once the patient has stopped overeating. Nevertheless patients should
> be instructed to choose meals and snacks which they are prepared not to
> vomit. . . . if the patient feels tempted to vomit after a particular meal or
> snack, she should engage in a distracting activity for the following hour or
> so. (P. 174)

In the third phase, patients are provided with specific guidelines for
maintaining their improvement. These instructions emphasize prudent
behavioral planning and the use of self-control strategies. Among these
guidelines is one that is clearly similar to Marlatt's relapse prevention
model,[27] although not identified as such. Patients are advised that "one
failure does not justify a succession of failures. Note your successes, how-

ever modest, on your monitoring sheets"[10] (p. 255). And elsewhere Fairburn[11] prepares patients for future difficulties by informing them that occasional setbacks are to be expected. This systematic focus on maintenance is important, particularly since substance abuse disorders are characterized by high relapse rates.

Schneider and Agras[46] treated thirteen bulimic patients in groups that met weekly for four months. The treatment was an adaptation of Fairburn's,[9] with an explicit emphasis on "interpersonal problem solving related to deficient assertive skills" as well as a formal training in progressive relaxation. Schneider and Agras[46] state that "more attention was focused on actual vomiting behaviors and rituals surrounding them" but it is unclear what was done.

At posttreatment, vomiting had decreased from an average of 24 times a week to 2.2 times. Notably, a 33-percent reduction in vomiting occurred in the first week. Seven patients ceased vomiting, and there were significant changes in attitudes toward eating, depression, and assertiveness. Body weight did not change. A six-month follow-up on eleven of the patients showed a mean vomiting frequency of 3.8 times a week. Five patients were not vomiting, whereas three had relapsed. These results are not as encouraging as Fairburn's.[9] In commenting on this difference, Schneider and Agras[46] point to the greater severity of the problem in their sample, a shorter treatment program, and the lack of a maintenance component.

White and Boskind-White[52] treated fourteen bulimic patients with a modification of the Boskind-Lodahl and White[6] program (see below) which consisted of five consecutive five-hour group sessions. The change included a greater emphasis on interpersonal skills and the introduction of a male therapist "to underscore the importance of interpersonal risk taking in a heterosexual context" (p. 99).[53] This change was made to reflect the authors' review of their clinical experience in treating bulimic patients, that "in the final analysis, one overriding prognostic indicator emerged: Sustained progress appeared to be contingent upon initiating, maintaining, and enhancing the quality of their interpersonal relationships, particularly with men" (p. 98). Subjects showed increases in assertiveness and independence during the course of therapy. However, details of rates of binge eating and vomiting at posttreatment and follow-up were not reported. Three women had ceased binging at a one-year follow-up (no data on vomiting are provided). Another seven had "attenuated their binging frequency to less than five times a month during the last six months" (p. 100). All of these seven subjects had vomited less than five times during the same six-month period. The remaining four women reported little change.

Other clinical reports have been limited largely to the treatment of a single patient. Most have used some combination of behavioral self-control strategies, cognitive restructuring, dietary intervention, and relaxation training. Overall, the results have been positive,[22,23] although Mizes and Lohr[30] found only temporary improvement.

Exposure and Reponse Prevention Methods. There is now broad agreement that exposure and response prevention (ERP) is the most effective approach in treating phobic and obsessive-compulsive disorders.[4,25,38] These methods have been extended recently to addictive disorders such as alcoholism.[39] Since bulimia is obviously a form of substance abuse and has been conceptualized as a form of obsessive-compulsive disorder,[42,55,58] it is not surprising that ERP has been used.

In 1979 Welch[50] described the treatment with response delay and prevention of obsessive-compulsive vomiting in a 28-year-old woman. In many ways this patient met the criteria for bulimia nervosa, although her obsession about being viewed as repulsively fat by others had overtones of anorexia nervosa. A graduated response delay procedure was used in which the patient agreed to wait increasing amounts of time before engaging in each step of the response chain that culminated in vomiting. One minute at each step was the starting point. After eight weeks her vomiting, which occurred roughly four times a day prior to treatment, had ceased. At an eleven-month follow-up, there was no sign of relapse. Meyer[28] had previously described the use of a similar response delay procedure to overcome excessive eating in an overweight woman. Although not emphasized by the authors, response delay was one aspect of the multicomponent treatment programs of Linden,[22] Long and Cordle,[23] and Schneider and Agras.[46]

Rosen and Leitenberg[42] drew an explicit analogy between the conceptualization and treatment of obsessive-compulsive disorders and bulimia, and applied ERP in a comparable manner. As these authors put it:

> In bulimia nervosa, binge eating and self-induced vomiting seem linked in a vicious circle by anxiety. As in anorexia nervosa there is a morbid fear of weight gain. Eating elicits this anxiety (binging [sic] dramatically so); vomiting reduces it. Once an individual has learned that vomiting following food intake leads to anxiety reduction, rational fears no longer inhibit overeating. Thus the driving force of this disorder may be vomiting, not binging; binging might not occur if the person could not vomit afterwards. (In fact some patients report that the only reason they binge is to make it physically easier to vomit.*) By analogy to obsessive-compulsive disorders, the best way to extinguish these fears of weight gain and of uncontrolled eating behavior may be to attack the problem not from the binging side but instead from the vomiting side, through an exposure plus response prevention model of intervention. (P. 118)

The subject in this study was a 21-year-old woman who binged at least once a day and vomited several times daily. The procedure, using a multiple baseline design across three different foods, required the subject during each session to eat to the point where she would typically vomit. Therapy involved eighteen sessions, six for each food type. The subject's anxiety attendant on binge eating habituated across treatment sessions,

---

* Fairburn[11] has also observed that once bulimic individuals begin to vomit they binge more frequently, believing that they can "put right" the likely weight-related consequences of the binge. They also discover that it is easier to vomit after eating a lot, thereby increasing the size of the binge.

even though she ate increasingly more food. This suggests a progressive extinction (exposure) effect and mimics what has been found in obsessive-compulsive disorders. The multiple baseline design showed that it was only when a particular food type was targeted with ERP that anxiety and amount eaten changed, providing further evidence of a treatment-specific effect. The subject's binge eating and vomiting had decreased to 1.25 times a day at posttreatment. During the eighteen treatment sessions the subject was not instructed to implement response prevention procedures at home. With instructions to do this, she stopped vomiting completely forty-four days after treatment sessions had ended. She vomited only once during a ten-month follow-up.

Leitenberg, Gross, Peterson, and Rosen[21] extended this ERP procedure with five female bulimic patients. The food choices during the eighteen sessions were designed to elicit maximal anxiety. In each session the therapist tried to focus the subject's attention on whatever anxiety-eliciting thoughts and feelings were experienced. These centered around "negative body image, sensations of feeling full, gross, fat, wanting to vomit, fears of weight gain and binge-eating in public, and relationship issues with spouses, parents, friends and coworkers including themes of anger, loss, and rejection" (p. 7). Subjects were instructed not to vomit following the treatment session, but were not told to refrain from vomiting between sessions.

Leitenberg and associates[21] elaborated on what the subjects "discovered" during these treatment sessions:

1. In the absence of planned vomiting they do not have an uncontrollable craving to consume huge amounts of food; instead they have an obsessive craving to be slim, to eat as little as possible, to not gain weight; 2. Physical sensations of immediate weight gain and feelings of gross changes in bodily appearance (particularly stomach, thighs, and buttocks) following consumption of normal or even less than normal amounts of food are distorted, and these feelings are capable of being relieved without recourse to vomiting; 3. They are able to eat certain foods without "having to" vomit afterwards; 4. The anxiety they experience after eating forbidden foods is not as overwhelming as they first thought it would be and is capable of diminishing to tolerable levels even if they do not vomit; 5. Their desire to maintain a strict diet and their criteria of "bad" foods, "having eaten too much," "having blown it" are distorted and serve to trigger the impulse to eat even more and to vomit afterwards. 6. The obsessive desire to achieve a "perfect" slim body usually stems from a complex mix of disturbed family relationships, low self-esteem and associated fears of rejection and abandonment, a variety of guilt feelings, and cultural values and stereotyped beliefs about appropriate feminine appearance and behavior. (P. 7)

In-session eating triggered anxiety initially, which then declined over the course of the session. Both anxiety and the urge to eat habituated across sessions, although the amount of food eaten tended to increase. At posttreatment two subjects had stopped vomiting and maintained this improvement at the six-month follow-up. One subject showed no improvement, despite an additional eight treatment sessions that focused on response prevention at home. The remaining two subjects were vomiting less than once a day at the six-month follow-up. The four subjects who benefited from treatment either maintained or increased the amount of daily calories they digested relative to the calories vomited. They did not compensate for the decrease in vomiting by starving themselves. One subject did not change in weight, whereas the remaining four gained 10, 6, 9, and 1 pounds respectively. Improvement on self-report measures of depression, self-esteem, and attitudes toward eating also occurred.

Giles, Young, and Young[14] treated a series of thirty-four bulimic patients with an ERP procedure. Twenty patients showed a reduction of 80 to 100 percent in binge frequency; two showed a 50 to 79 percent reduction. This improvement was maintained at a mean follow-up of sixty-seven weeks (range = 26 to 82). Six patients dropped out, and six did not respond to this form of treatment.

CONTROLLED OUTCOME STUDIES

Between-Group Designs. Kirkley, Schneider, Agras, and Bachman[18] assigned twenty-eight female bulimic patients to either a cognitive-behavioral treatment or a nondirective control group, matching them on vomiting frequency. Treatment consisted of sixteen weekly group sessions, lasting ninety minutes, and led by two pairs of Ph.D clinical psychologists. The cognitive-behavioral treatment was that used by Schneider and Agras[46] as summarized earlier. Both groups graphed vomiting frequency and kept records of the circumstances associated with eating and vomiting. The nondirective control group discussed their food choices, eating frequency, eating rate, binge patterns, vomiting rituals, the role of stress in their bulimia, and ideas about forbidden foods but were not instructed how to alter these behaviors. Emphasis was placed on self-discovery, understanding one's bulimia, and self-disclosure.

Patients rated both treatments as highly (and equally) credible, so any differences between groups were not due to placebo effects. Moreover, both groups thought that their treatments would help them in overcoming bulimia. Five patients dropped out of the control group and one out of the cognitive-behavioral group. The cognitive-behavioral treatment produced significantly greater reductions in binge eating and vomiting. The mean frequencies of vomiting for the two groups at pretreatment were 13.6 and 13.0 respectively. At posttreatment the comparable figures were 0.62 and 4.0 respectively. Only the change in the cognitive-behavioral group was statistically significant. This superiority of the cognitive-behavioral treatment occurred despite the greater attrition, which favored the control condition. Both treatments showed significant reductions in depression, anxiety, and cognitions associated with eating disorders.

The superiority of the cognitive-behavioral treatment at posttreatment had largely disappeared at a three-month follow-up. Although five patients had ceased binge eating and vomiting compared to only one in the control treatment, 23 percent of the cognitive-behavioral group and only 11 percent of the control group had relapsed. At follow-up, 77 percent and 78 percent of each group showed decreased vomiting frequencies of at least 60 percent (an arbitrary cutoff). The lack of difference between the two treatments is disappointing, especially in view of the brief follow-up.

Lee and Rush[20] randomly assigned thirty female bulimic patients to either a cognitive-behavioral treatment or a waiting-list control group. The patients met twice weekly for six weeks. The treatment initially emphasized relaxation training as a substitute for binge eating and as a means of coping with the negative affect that triggered binges. Thereafter, group discussion was aimed at identifying and altering dysfunctional thoughts about eating and weight. Homework (unspecified) "was simultaneously used to shape normal eating behavior" (p. 8).

Four subjects dropped out of treatment, although outcome results are based on an N of 14 in both groups. At posttreatment, the mean frequency of binge eating per week had decreased from 12.5 to 3.7. The waiting-list control group showed no change. Ten of fourteen subjects were arbitrarily classified as treatment responders because they had decreased their binge eating by at least 50 percent. Only three of fourteen subjects in the waiting-list group could be so classified. Only four treated subjects and one control subject were abstinent at posttreatment. Pretreatment binge frequency was unrelated to treatment response.

Treatment produced a reduction in vomiting from 13 to 4.2 times a week, with the waiting-list group unchanged. Seven of the treated and one of the control subjects were treatment responders (using the 50-percent cutoff). Only two of the treated subjects had ceased vomiting. The greater the frequency of purging at pretreatment, the greater was the response to treatment. A three- to four-month follow-up showed that the treated subjects maintained their improvement on both binges and vomiting. Treated subjects had significant reductions in depression at posttreatment, which were maintained at follow-up.

As Lee and Rush[20] note, the lack of control for attention-placebo factors makes it impossible to attribute changes to the treatment package itself. Furthermore, the treatment and assessment were done by one person. The results themselves are modest; only 6 percent of subjects ceased to both binge and vomit. Some subjects continued to purge even when they no longer binged. Lee and Rush offer their clinical impression that "irrational attitudes towards body weight and shape were very difficult to alter" (p. 17).

Boskind-Lodahl and White[6] compared group therapy to a waiting-list control group with twenty-six women who had been binging and purging daily for at least three years. Subjects were assigned to these groups in the order that they entered the authors' clinic on eating disorders. Treatment was administered by female cotherapists for eleven two-hour sessions. A six-hour marathon session was held midway through therapy to identify group members' needs for the second half of treatment. The therapy consisted of specific behavioral techniques (e.g., self-monitoring, goal-setting, contracting, and the development of coping skills) within an experientially based group imbued with a feminist perspective. The waiting-list group was offered guided discussion of feminist issues and food-related problems. After four months they were offered treatment.

Methodological inadequacies preclude unequivocal interpretation of this study. These include inadequate outcome measures and the absence of information on attrition rates or compliance with treatment instructions. Another limitation is that Boskind-Lodahl and White[6] did not report the frequencies of binge eating or purging at pre- or posttreatment. The only information they provide is that at a three-month follow-up, "four members of the treatment group had stopped binging and purging, while six others reported binges that were less frequent and of shorter duration. In contrast, only one of the control-group members had curtailed her binging behavior to any extent" (p. 98).[53] Another problem is that the obvious comparison between the treatment and control conditions at posttreatment is not reported. Since it is not stated how many of the waiting-list control group entered subsequent treatment, this comparison cannot be easily interpreted. Finally, at a "follow-up over the next several months," (i.e., after the first three-month follow-up), five of the ten women who had initially shown a reduction in their binge eating/purging "had reverted to extreme binge-purge behaviors once again" (p. 98). White and Boskind-White[52] claim that their treatment produced improved body image, based only on increased participation in sports and social activities. Even without emphasizing the preliminary nature of this pilot study, the effects of this treatment approach on the eating disorder were modest.

Lacey[19] assigned thirty bulimic patients alternately to a ten-week treatment program or a waiting-list control group. Subjects in the control group subsequently received the same treatment program. All subjects met the *DSM-III* criteria for bulimia as well as Russell's[44] for bulimia nervosa. Their ages ranged from 21 to 37 years, their weight fell in the average range, and their mean frequency of binge eating and vomiting per day were 3.3 and 3.8 respectively. Treatment consisted of ten weekly meetings lasting half a day, and blending individual with group sessions. Lacey describes the treatment as eclectic, drawing on "behavioural, cognitive, and counselling techniques to bring structure and order to a chaotic eating pattern, but then it shifts gear as treatment progresses to provide psychodynamically orientated therapy" (p. 1612). The behavioral techniques featured a written therapeutic contract specifying, *inter alia*, that the subject would maintain her present weight, eat three meals a day, regulate amount of carbohydrates eaten, and cease binge/vomiting episodes in progressive stages. Demanding self-monitoring required subjects to record binge/purge episodes, thoughts and feelings, and explanations of why they were binging at a particular moment. Individual and group therapy sessions focused on delineation of emotional and social factors associated with bulimia and "new ways of dealing with their feelings and interpersonal difficulties" (p. 1610).

The results are remarkable, particularly in view of the brief treatment with no apparent maintenance component. No subject in the waiting-list condition showed any change. None of the treatment subjects dropped out, and twenty-four stopped binge eating and vomiting. An additional four subjects became abstinent within four weeks after treatment, and the remaining two showed significant reductions in binging and vomiting. A follow-up "up to two years" indicated that twenty patients maintained their abstinence, with one pursuing additional psychotherapy. Eight patients experienced occasional bulimic episodes, but had improved from four episodes a day to three a year. Two sought therapy toward the end of the follow-up period. Of the remaining two subjects, one did not attend follow-up and the other was hospitalized.

There is no obvious accounting for the unprecedented success of this program. All the therapeutic components have been represented in other treatment programs, although not in precisely the same package. It would be important to know how well subjects complied with the exacting self-monitoring requirements and how this was related to treatment outcome. How did the therapists cope with issues of noncompliance? The patients do not seem atypical compared to other studies reviewed here; in fact, their bulimia nervosa seemed severe. In another atypical result, Lacey reported that tension, anger, and depression followed "giving up the symptoms of bulimia nervosa" (p. 1612). Not only have other studies failed to find this relationship, they have shown the opposite, with depression decreasing as bulimia decreases.* And if a depression had been unmasked at the end of treatment, it is curious that no additional treatment was needed or prescribed and that the patients showed such unparalleled maintenance of therapeutic gains despite their depression.

SINGLE-CASE EXPERIMENTAL DESIGNS

Several single-case (*AB*) designs were reviewed in the section on uncontrolled studies. The two studies included in this section used crossover designs and focused on exposure and response prevention.

Rossiter and I[43] compared cognitive restructuring (CR) to ERP in a crossover design in four cases. Of the three clients treated with CR, none reduced binge eating or vomiting. Of the three clients who received ERP (one client dropped out after CR treatment before the crossover), two stopped binge/vomiting episodes by posttreatment and one showed a modest reduction from pretreatment. A one-year follow-up showed little change in these results, although one of the abstinent clients had binged six times and vomited twice during follow-up.

The obvious limitations of this study, including relatively brief CR and only four clients, call for caution in interpreting these data. Nev-

---

* See references 14, 18, 19, 20, 44, and 57.

ertheless, ERP seems significantly more effective than the verbal CR procedure. Qualifying the clinical feasibility of ERP is the finding that one client initially refused to participate in this treatment for fear of weight gain. After a period of supportive therapy and CR, she agreed to ERP and stopped binge eating and vomiting. A second client temporarily stopped attending sessions because of her reluctance to participate in ERP, again out of fear of weight gain. Special efforts had to be made to overcome this resistance. Finally, it is our unconfirmed impression that the client who dropped out of treatment following CR was reacting, in part, to the prospect of ERP treatment. ERP is often perceived as a threatening method, which might limit its acceptability to clients and necessitate alternative therapeutic strategies for overcoming client resistance.

Johnson, Schlundt, Kelley, and Ruggiero[17] compared ERP to a treatment derived from a conceptualization of bulimia as a breakdown in weight control through appropriate food intake and exercise (energy balance [EB]). The goal of the latter treatment was to prevent binge eating by teaching subjects proper eating habits, appropriate nutrition, and aerobic exercise to regulate their energy balance and thus achieve a desirable weight. The principal techniques were those commonly used for obesity, including scheduled eating, stimulus control, modification of eating habits, increased exercise, cognitive restructuring, and self-reward.

Three subjects received ERP followed by a cross-over to EB, and three the reverse order. The two treatments were evaluated in a multiple-baseline design across subjects. ERP was designed to reduce the frequency of vomiting while EB was designed to reduce the number of food intakes. Different therapists administered each treatment, although overall, all three therapists conducted both treatments with different subjects.

Of the subjects who received ERP as the first treatment, subject 1 showed an increase in vomiting from less than once per day per week during baseline to 1.5 times a day over the six ERP sessions. After five sessions of EB treatment, vomiting ceased. Subject 2, who vomited less than once a day during baseline, stopped during five sessions of ERP but resumed purging during EB treatment. Her posttreatment level was twice a week. Subject 3 reduced her rate of vomiting across six sessions of ERP treatment from twice a day to two to three times a week. Her posttreatment level was also twice a week. Among those subjects who received EB treatment first, subject 4 did not vomit at all at pretreatment. Subject 5 decreased vomiting twice a day to approximately once a day at the end of six EB sessions, then dropped out after a single ERP session. Subject 6 reduced her rate of vomiting from twelve times a day during baseline to seven times daily after six sessions of EB. Under ERP her rate dropped initially to three times a day, but by the end of six sessions her rate was increasing steadily.

It is difficult to conclude much about the effects of either treatment on vomiting or binge eating. (Binge-eating data are not summarized here since they appear to be as equivocal as the purge data.) Nor was the authors' objective of identifying target-specific effects achieved. Johnson and associates[17] stress that compliance with self-monitoring was a major problem, and they based their data partly on subjects' reports during interviews. Second, the data are difficult to interpret because both treatments had inconsistent effects and the results were modest. Using a multiple baseline across subjects design, Cullari and Redmon[8] treated three bulimic patients with a combination of self-monitoring, goal-setting, reinforcement, and dietary instructions. The dietary instructions involved information to eliminate sugar, start an exercise program, and go on the Pritikin diet. The subjects' ages were 29, 32, and 30 years respectively. Although all self-induced vomiting on occasion, only subject 1 always purged in response to a binge. Subject 1 had a mean frequency of binging of at least once a day; subject 2, five times a week; and subject 3, nine times a week. Surprisingly, all subjects showed zero binge/purge episodes after only seven weekly sessions of treatment. Remarkably, after brief but stable baselines, all subjects decreased their frequency of binge/purging to close to zero after a single session, an unprecedented finding that the authors do not address. Follow-ups ranging from four to seven weeks indicated maintenance of treatment effects.

Wilson and associates[24] compared a verbal CR treatment to CR combined with exposure and vomit prevention (CR/EVP). The latter proved to be significantly more effective than the former in reducing binging and vomiting, although the two treatments were equally credible and met with similar patient compliance. At one-year follow-up the patients treated with CR/EVP were completely abstinent. CR/EVP also produced significantly greater changes on several measures of psychopathology. Patients' prior lowest weights as adolescents were significantly related to treatment outcome.

Summary. The small number of controlled studies, involving differences in patient samples, treatment type and length, and outcome measures, not to mention various methodological shortcomings, provides far too meager a data base from which to draw firm conclusions about therapeutic efficacy. The best controlled study to date, by Kirkley and associates,[18] provides good evidence of the initial efficacy of a broad-spectrum cognitive-behavioral approach but raises concern about long-term treatment-specific effects. The results of a combination of CR and ERP used by my associates and me[57] are encouraging, rivaling Fairburn's[9] success rates achieved with individual therapy of longer duration. However, the small sample size currently precludes generalization to other (e.g., older) populations. Nevertheless, the Wilson et al.[57] study, taken in conjunction with the results of Rossiter and Wilson's[43] results and the encouraging clinical reports of Leitenberg and others,[21] indicates that ERP may be an efficient and effective form of treatment.

Pharmacological Treatments

PHENYTOIN

In 1974 Green and Rau[15] described the treatment of bulimia with phenytoin (Dilantin). However, a subsequent controlled study of this drug did not support a consistent or specific therapeutic effect.[51] More recently, Rau and Green[41] argued that the drug is effective only for a subset of bulimic patients whose problem is neurological rather than functional. Further analysis of this treatment must await controlled research that addresses the conceptual and diagnostic issues Rau and Green[41] have raised in reaffirming their clinical experience that phenytoin produces marked improvement in some bulimic patients.

ANTIDEPRESSANT MEDICATION

The major pharmacological approach to the treatment of bulimia today is the use of antidepressant drugs.

Uncontrolled Reports. Using tricyclics, Pope and Hudson[34] reported that six of eight consecutive cases of bulimia showed a moderate to marked decrease in binging within three weeks and maintained this improvement at a two- to six-month follow-up. Pope, Hudson, and Jonas[35] reported the results of an expanded sample of sixty-five bulimic patients. These authors included only those patients who had adequate trials of medication, namely, plasma levels of tricyclics and lithium in the established ranges for at least four weeks and platelet monoamine oxidase inhibition of at least 80 percent for at least four weeks. In several cases more than one antidepressant drug was administered. Overall, of forty-nine patients treated with tricyclics (mainly imipramine hydrochloride), ten showed remission; fifteen, marked improvement; twelve, moderate improvement; and twelve, no improvement. Remission was defined as cessation of binges for one month or more. However, the authors comment that "more than half of the remitted patients still report an occasional binge, or even a cluster of several binges, at times of unusual stresses, although such episodes may be months apart" (p. 275). Marked and moderate improvement was defined by reductions of 75 and 50 percent respectively in binging.

Pope, Hudson, and Jonas[35] interpret these clinical results cautiously, pointing out their limitations. Details of the patient sample are not presented, making it difficult to compare these findings with others. It is unclear whether all patients both binged and vomited. Nor is it known at what point the patients' response to treatment was evaluated. Presumably, most evaluations were made while patients were on medication. The authors observe that "many of our patients have periodically experienced brief relapses of bulimic symptoms in spite of a good overall response to medication. Some have even experienced a major relapse in which the drug's effect seemed to vanish entirely" (p. 279). In most of these cases they claim that sequential trials of two or more antidepressant drugs with careful monitoring of plasma or platelet levels, as the case may be, produced a positive response. The real value of this report is in the clinical guidelines it provides for treating bulimic patients with drugs.

Stewart and associates[48] treated twelve bulimic individuals with monoamine oxidase inhibitors (MAOIs). All patients met *DSM-III* criteria for bulimia, but whether they binged and vomited was not reported. Three patients also met *DSM-III* criteria for anorexia nervosa and five patients had past histories of anorexia nervosa. Six of the twelve patients met *DSM-III* criteria for major depression, and four patients had had an episode of major depression in the past. Ten of the twelve patients showed a rapid decrease in the binge frequency, from an average of fourteen binges per week to just over one binge per week. Eight virtually ceased binging. At a median follow-up of nine months, six of the initial ten responders to treatment had maintained their improvement. Of these patients, five continued on medication. Three patients relapsed within two to three months despite continuing MAOI treatment.

Brotman, Herzog, and Woods[7] conducted a retrospective study of twenty-two bulimic patients meeting *DSM-II* criteria. As in other drug studies, separate rates of binge eating and vomiting are not reported. Seventeen (77 percent) subjects met the criteria for affective disorder. They excluded another twenty-five patients because they did not "take medication in therapeutic doses for a sufficient time" (p. 7). Other unspecified patients were excluded on various grounds, such as previous treatment with antidepressants, noncompliance, and reluctance to take medication. Blood levels were not obtained.

Mean frequency of weekly binges are reported only for the thirteen subjects who were classified as responders, namely, a 50-percent reduction in binges. During a three-month follow-up, five of the initial treatment responders relapsed while taking their medication, and another relapsed on stopping the medication. Brotman, Herzog, and Woods[7] identified five (23 percent) subjects who were "true responders"; these patients did not binge during a six-month follow-up. All continued on medication, however, and three of these five "required more than one trial of medication before responding" (p. 8). Other theoretically relevant findings were that reduction of depression often did not eliminate binging, while reduction in binging was not necessarily accompanied by a decrease in depression. Patients with a positive family history for affective disorders did not show a better response to drug treatment. Particularly in view of the subject selection criteria, the results are extremely modest.

Controlled Studies. In a double-blind study, Pope, Hudson, and Jonas[35] randomly assigned twenty-two bulimic patients to treatment with either imipramine or placebo. Patients previously treated with antidepressant drugs or who had significant suicidal thoughts were excluded from the study. None had anorexia nervosa. Nineteen subjects completed the six-week treatment; two imipramine subjects were taken off the drug because of side effects, and one placebo subject withdrew from the study.

Subjects treated with imipramine showed a decrease in binging at posttreatment of 70 percent—a reduction in mean weekly frequency of 7.49. The therapeutic effect occurred at the two- to four-week interval. The placebo group did not improve. Using the same categories as described in the Pope and associates report,[36] four of the imipramine subjects showed marked and four moderate improvement. Although Pope and coworkers[36] emphasize that it is mandatory to obtain plasma levels to ensure adequate treatment with tricyclics, it is unclear whether plasma levels were measured in Pope, Hudson, and Jonas's study.[35]

Imipramine also decreased preoccupation with food and increased subjective global improvement. Reductions in binging were correlated with reductions in depression. Of the original twenty-two patients, twenty received a complete trial of at least one antidepressant medication. At a one- to eight-month follow-up, eighteen of these (90 percent) continued to report a moderate or marked reduction in binge eating with antidepressant treatment. Seven subjects (35 percent) ceased binge eating at follow-up.

In another double-blind study of the treatment of bulimia, Walsh and associates[49] randomly assigned patients to either a phenelzine sulfate or placebo treatment for eight weeks. Applicants to the program were screened out if they were acutely suicidal, had a recent history of suicide attempts or drug or alcohol abuse, or were deemed unable to adhere to a tyramine-free diet. Of an initial sample of thirty-five patients, twenty were included in the data analysis. The other fifteen were excluded because they were placebo responders (in the first two weeks), were unable to adhere to the diet, failed to keep appointments, or did not meet the prospectively determined criterion of taking at least 60 mg per day of phenelzine or the equivalent dose of a placebo for two weeks. Of these twenty subjects, only fifteen completed the full eight-week course of treatment. In interpreting the results, the selectivity of the patients whose data are analyzed in this study must be borne in mind.

At posttreatment, the treated group reported significantly fewer binges per week. Five of the nine phenelzine-treated patients ceased binging entirely and the other four reduced their binge frequency by at least 50 percent; none of the eleven placebo-treated patients stopped binge eating and only two reduced their binge frequency by 50 percent or more.

Follow-up data on eight of the treated patients, at intervals ranging from three to fifteen months, indicated that of five patients who discontinued phenelzine, three relapsed and two maintained abstinence. Of the other three who continued to take the drug, two maintained improvement and one showed partial relapse. Information on seven of the placebo patients subsequently given phenelzine showed that three improved markedly and three received no benefit.

Sabine and coworkers[45] randomly assigned fifty patients with bulimia nervosa in an eight-week double-blind trial of mianserin hydrochloride or placebo. Six subjects from the mianserin and eight from the placebo group dropped out, although these dropouts did not differ on any measure from subjects who completed the study. Both groups showed significant improvement on questionnaire measures of attitude toward eating and binging, depression, and anxiety. But the "number of days per week the subjects reported binging and vomiting did not change throughout the eight week period, for either group" (p. 199S). Weight was unaffected. Blood levels of the drug were not reported.

Why Do Antidepressants Work? Pope, Hudson, and Jonas[35] hypothesize that bulimia is a form of affective disorder that is responsive to antidepressants. The evidence, however, seems inconsistent with this view. Both Brotman, Herzog, and Woods[7] and Walsh and associates[49] found that bulimic patients who respond favorably to antidepressant drugs were often less depressed than those who failed to respond. Sabine and coworkers[45] reported that increases in dysphoric mood were associated with increases in binge/purge episodes and comparable across both the mianserin and placebo groups. They suggest that "bulimia is not a manifestation of an underlying affective disorder as such but that mood changes are more likely to be a secondary part of the syndrome" (p. 200S). Pope, Hudson, and Jonas's appeal[35] to their correlation between reductions in depression and binging could indicate that the latter causes the former. Consistent with Russell's earlier observations,[44] Fairburn and Cooper,[12] in their detailed study of bulimia nervosa, found that in all but two of their thirty-five subjects, "depressive symptoms were judged to be secondary to the eating disorder" (p. 244). Then, of course, the success of psychological treatments directed at the eating disorder in decreasing both binge/purge episodes and depression constitutes still further evidence against the affective disorder theory.

Walsh and associates[49] have proposed an alternative mechanism for the effects of antidepressant drugs, suggesting that they reduce the anxiety or tension that often precedes binge eating. As investigators in the area of anxiety disorders have pointed out,[26,59] both the tricyclics and the MAOIs have antianxiety as well as antidepressant effects.*

Summary. These studies indicate an effect on bulimia of antidepressant drugs, especially the MAOIs, although the mechanism of action is unknown. However, these effects might be modest in many patients and raise questions about long-term maintenance of improvement. Furthermore, in practice, drug treatment is not appropriate for many bulimic patients for several reasons, including lack of compliance.

---

* A parallel between the treatment of anxiety disorders and bulimia might be noted. The mechanism of action of imipramine in the treatment of anxiety disorders is also unknown. Suggestions that it achieves its effects through the reduction of depression seem implausible; the alternative view has been proposed that it decreases anxiety/panic directly,[47,59] although there is little direct support for such a notion.[54]

Evaluation of Treatment Effects

Little purpose is served by belaboring the litany of methodological short-comings in the studies described here. It goes without saying that future studies need superior methodological controls. Kirkley and associates' investigation[18] was the only one to include an attention-placebo control condition; specification of treatment quality and compliance rates; multiple measures of process and outcome; and longer, more informative follow-ups. Here I discuss what can be said, albeit tentatively, on the basis of existing evidence. One point should be made, however. The basic outcome measure in the treatment of bulimia is frequency of binge/purge episodes. Two methods have typically been used to secure this information: clients' written records of their binging and vomiting (self-monitoring) and their responses at intake to assessors' inquiries about such behavior. My co-workers and I[57] found that the latter yielded much higher frequencies than the former, perhaps because of the well-known reactive effect of self-monitoring. Using one or the other of these data sources as the pre-treatment level will influence the extent of change that is observed. Both types of data should be collected and reported.

Systematic evaluation of treatment outcome is best guided by Paul's question[32]: "What treatment, by whom, is most effective with this individual with that specific problem under which set of circumstances?" (p. 111). Nothing new can be said about who is best qualified to treat bulimic patients, other than to note the frequent emphasis on the importance of a good therapeutic relationship. And given the severity and complexity of diverse problems bulimic individuals often present, experienced clinical judgment is required in their treatment. The emphasis here, then, is on what methods seem effective with which patients.

WHAT TREATMENT METHODS ARE MOST EFFECTIVE?

The evidence for specific treatment effects of psychological therapies is meager. The multicomponent cognitive-behavioral treatment programs of Fairburn,[11] Kirkley and others,[18] and Lacey[19] appear to be the most promising psychological approaches, but definitive conclusions are not possible. Can particular methods with specific treatment effects be identified? Although the answer to this question must be tentative, several observations can be made.

Cognitive Restructuring. Cognitive restructuring is a prominent component of many of the treatment programs reviewed here.* The rationale

* See references 11, 18, 20, 46, and 57.

for using cognitive restructuring seems clear. Fremouw and Heyneman*,[13] reported that overweight bulimic patients, relative to nonbulimic control subjects, showed a distinguishable cognitive style. They evaluated themselves more negatively following a failure experience and they were more dichotomous or extreme in their evaluative style. Cognitive restructuring approaches such as Beck's cognitive therapy[5] are predicated, in part, on presumed cognitive dysfunctions of this kind.

Different conceptualizations of bulimia have emphasized the primary importance of cognitive factors. Polivy, Herman, Olmsted, and Jazwinski[33] suggested that their fundamentally cognitive theory of eating restraint applies to bulimic persons. Extrapolating from their model, they have argued that

> If the cognitive (diet quota) boundary could be made more flexible, so that it bends rather than breaks under caloric pressure, it could prevent further consumption following lapses. One way to do this might be to encourage dieters to eat small amounts of "forbidden" foods and to accept occasional "splurges" as treats instead of unforgivable (no turning back now) disasters. . . . This restructuring of both cognitive and eating patterns would allow the cognitive diet boundary to remain more often unbreached and also would serve to reduce the dichotomy inherent in "diet" thinking. (P. 120)

This suggested treatment strategy was the basis of Fairburn's treatment.[11]

Assuming that cognitive change of the sort envisaged by Fairburn[11] and Polivy and associates[33] is the focus of treatment, the question is how best to do this. Suffice it to say that behavioral procedures are the most effective means of producing changes in cognitive processes.[2] This point has been amply documented in the treatment of phobic disorders. Several studies have shown that primarily verbal or symbolic methods have proved ineffective, whereas performance-based procedures have produce significant changes in behavior and cognitive processes.[54] There would seem to be no reason to expect other than the same pattern in the treatment of bulimia.

Both Rossiter and I[43,55] note some of the clinical limitations of using a strictly cognitive procedure with bulimic individuals. Some patients find that the cognitive methods do not prevent the binge/purge, and some fail to implement cognitive strategies that have proved effective at other times. In the latter cases it seems as though clients have decided to binge/purge before they have challenged their dysfunctional thoughts. One of my clients described this phenomenon as the hand being quicker than the mind. Of course, this does not always occur, and rational challenging of dysfunctional thoughts may often prove effective. I have suggested that when there is an anticipatory awareness of the binge, cognitive self-

---

* Note that while Fremouw and Heyneman report that these subjects met the *DSM-III* criteria for bulimia, they were overweight and apparently did not self-induce vomiting. Therefore they could not be said to have presented with bulimia nervosa. Whether or not these workers' findings apply to persons suffering from true bulimia nervosa remains to be shown, although clinical experience would certainly support such a generalization.

control strategies are most likely to be effective. A lack of awareness, or "automatic" binge eating, may require alternative approaches.

Extrapolating from theoretical analyses of the interaction between cognition and emotion, I hypothesized[55] that binges or purges might be likened to primary affective reactions. The implications of such reasoning have been spelled out by Rachman[37]:

> If it is true that our affective reactions are instantaneous and automatic and that they are determined by stimulus characteristics that are extremely difficult to identify, then our attempts at self-understanding and indeed of therapeutic insight are bound to be unsatisfactory; particularly as they so often rely largely or entirely on cognitive analyses and the verbal mode . . . Repeated attempts to trace connections between an affective reaction and specific cognitions may in time give way to alternative tactics in which the therapist and patient strive to find more direct and appropriate techniques for modifying the affective reaction within the affective system rather than across the border from the cognitive system. (Pp. 286–287)

Exposure and response prevention methods, as discussed next, fit the bill of the "direct and appropriate" techniques to which Rachman referred.

In Fairburn's program,[11] behavioral procedures are used to achieve the cognitive changes deemed critical to eliminating bulimia. Examples include the instructions to patients to introduce "forbidden" foods into their diet and to weigh themselves only once a week. Both instructions are designed to disconfirm rigid and dysfunctional cognitions about obsessive concern with dieting and the putative effects of eating in a more normal fashion. Fairburn notes that as clients follow these behavioral instructions their dysfunctional cognitions decline and no "formal 'cognitive restructuring'" is required. It is my clinical experience that encouraging some clients to comply with behavioral interventions such as these is a difficult matter. Cognitive restructuring may be invaluable not so much as a means of stopping binge/purges directly but in preparing clients for the use of behavioral procedures and facilitating compliance with exposure and response prevention.

EXPOSURE AND RESPONSE PREVENTION

The reasons for using exposure and/or response prevention are persuasive. Conceptually, the anxiety disorder model of bulimia,[17,21] in which purging is a form of compulsive behavior, clearly dictates the use of these procedures to interrupt the negative reinforcing value of vomiting. Empirically, the early results have been encouraging. There are, however, a number of issues that require comment.

First, the analogy to obsessive-compulsive disorders, while obviously useful, is imperfect. Compulsive handwashers, for example, can be assured that if they refrain from washing their hands after deliberately touching a "contaminated" object, no adverse consequence will follow. Disconfirmation of clients' fear of contamination is unequivocal. The same cannot be said of persons with bulimia nervosa. In their case, engaging in a binge and then refraining from vomiting *may* result in the dreaded outcome— weight gain. The fear, conflict, and resistance this breeds must be addressed.

Rossiter and I[43] have documented the resistance some clients show to exposure and response prevention. Overcoming this resistance requires a good therapeutic relationship in which the therapist is seen as credible and trustworthy and provides a careful explanation of rationale and intensive cognitive restructuring devoted to attitudes and fears about weight control. An important aspect of the latter is helping clients define self-worth in terms other than physical appearance and moving toward acceptance of their body shape and weight. Inevitably clients must cope better with societal pressures to look slim regardless of biological boundaries on eating and weight management. Although the treatment details are beyond the scope of this chapter, the following observations provide an illustration of the cognitive-behavioral approach we follow.

Influenced by Beck's cognitive therapy,[5] we frame the exposure and response prevention sessions as a behavioral experiment, the outcome of which clients must discover for themselves. We emphasize to each client that whereas most of our clients do not gain weight, there is no guarantee that she will not. In the event that she does gain weight, we can teach her healthier, more sensible and effective methods for weight control. This candor is helpful in overcoming reluctance to participate. It is also useful to inform clients that self-induced vomiting does not eliminate all ingested calories. This is one reason that clients do not always gain weight when they cease the binge/purge cycle. Bulimic individuals often believe that they will gain weight by eating normally if they do not purge. We stress that their previous mode of weight regulation is dangerous and that there is no choice other than an alternative life style.

A second point is that ERP can be applied at different stages in the sequence of events, ranging from the initial urge to binge to the final act of self-induced vomiting. Rosen and Leitenberg[42] have argued that since it is vomiting that is the "driving force" behind bulimia nervosa, the behavioral chain is most effectively extinguished by preventing the negative reinforcement of vomiting. This view has been disputed.[29] Were ERP to be used in a more strictly analogous manner to its use with either alcoholism[39] or obsessive-compulsive disorders,[38] the bulimic person would be exposed to cues that elicit binge eating, and the eating would be prevented. This procedure was used by O'Neill[31] and by Rossiter and me[43]; we refer to it as binge prevention. The relative merits of these different versions of ERP remain to be established. An advantage of the binge-prevention procedure is the possibility that it is more acceptable to some clients who refuse the more demanding and threatening vomit-prevention version. A disadvantage is that it is sometimes difficult to identify cues that reliably elicit craving to binge that can then be systematically presented in therapy sessions. This is so when the precipitants of craving are situationally specific emotional or interpersonal events rather than simple ingestion of a "forbidden fruit."

Another version of exposure and response prevention is the response delay method.[50] In most studies this method is combined with other techniques[11,18] so its independent efficacy is unknown. Here again, either the binge eating or the vomiting could be systematically delayed, although the most common usage centers on the latter. This procedure can complement in-session use of ERP and may prove useful in clients who decline structured ERP sessions.

Finally, the principles embodied in exposure and response prevention procedures are clearly evident in Fairburn's program[11] for stopping binge eating. Among these are the instructions to eat three times a day with a snack and to include fattening foods during these meals. Functionally, this amounts to a more graduated application of the principles of the clients' home environment (what could be referred to as self-exposure instructions in the agoraphobia treatment literature). Whether adding therapist-directed in-session trials of self-exposure instructions is necessary cannot be decided at this time, although it is an issue that needs to be resolved. One of the relevant issues in this comparison will be the acceptability of the treatments to clients, together with the related question of compliance. Fairburn[11] reports that his clients have been reluctant to follow his behavioral instructions, which is certainly consistent with my own experience, but he does not specify how this recalcitrance is overcome other than by "insisting" on the necessity of clients overcoming dietary restraint.

Self-Control. Basic self-control procedures such as self-monitoring and self-evaluation are a common denominator of cognitive-behavioral treatments. Although several programs emphasize additional components, such as stimulus control of eating, their incremental value cannot be determined. It might be remembered that after more than fifteen years of research on the behavioral treatment of obesity, it is still uncertain that a method such as stimulus control adds much to core strategies of self-monitoring and evaluation.[31]

Relaxation Training. Mizes[29] has identified relaxation training as one of the effective treatment components. However, as discussed previously, the evidence for this method is too slim for much to be said. Given its record with the anxiety disorders,[25] it would be surprising if relaxation training were shown to add anything to methods such as exposure and cognitive restructuring.

Interpersonal Issues and Assertion Training. Clinical reports typically stress the interpersonal problems of bulimic individuals.[24,29,52] Yet systematic research aimed at specifying the nature of bulimic persons' social and sexual relationships, and relating any such difficulties to treatment outcome, is lacking. Even Fairburn and Cooper's detailed account[12] of the clinical features of bulimia nervosa does not describe social/sexual adjustment; it is unclear whether it was assessed. At this point, it cannot be said whether interpersonal problems are the cause, concomitant, or consequence of bulimia. Available data indicate that modification of interpersonal problems is not necessary in order to overcome bulimia.

To reiterate, the relatively few studies just reviewed do not permit anything but tentative inferences. Nevertheless, it cannot pass unnoticed that some of the studies with the best outcome apparently paid little explicit attention to interpersonal issues.[11,35] This observation must be coupled with the modest impact on binge eating and vomiting of White and Boskind-White's program,[52] which was largely predicated upon increasing independence and assertiveness, and was quite successful in this regard. This pattern of findings suggests that increasing assertiveness (overcoming interpersonal difficulties?) does not necessarily affect binge eating and vomiting. I reported anecdotal findings that are consistent with this picture.[55] Furthermore, it is clear that successfully targeting binge/purge episodes may also result in a concomitant increase in assertiveness.[43]

Pharmacotherapy. Until the necessary studies are completed, serious comparisons between antidepressant and cognitive-behavioral treatments cannot be made. Given the present unsatisfactory state of research findings, cognitive-behavioral treatments appear to be no less effective than pharmacological methods. Advocacy of antidepressant medication must also be tempered by the following findings.

First, it is unknown how many bulimic patients refuse treatment with antidepressant drugs. There are references to this problem in the emerging literature, and experience with anxiety disorders suggests that this will occur.[54] The same literature also indicates that the dropout rate will be higher for drug than for cognitive-behavioral treatment. This remains to be determined.

Second, antidepressants are associated with unpleasant side effects that contribute to the dropout rate. Pope et al.[35] and Walsh and coworkers[49] prudently emphasize the need for clinical caution in prescribing these drugs for patients with eating disorders. Their collective experience, however, suggests that informed usage does not carry unacceptable risks. Nor do the antidepressants seem to increase patients' weight.

Third, as in the anxiety disorders, the problem of relapse looms large when drugs are withdrawn. Existing follow-ups have been relatively brief and yet very few patients have maintained their improvement when taken off their medication. How long can bulimic individuals be continued on these often potent and potentially dangerous drugs? These critical issues relating to relapse have not been adequately addressed.

WHAT PROBLEMS IN WHICH PATIENTS?

At present this crucial question cannot be answered. Existing data do not permit identification of patient characteristics that influence treatment outcome. One of the few variables that has been related to outcome has been depression at pretreatment. Surprisingly, it has been unrelated to either pharmacological or cognitive-behavioral treatment effects. Other factors that need to be examined for prognostic potential are other types of coexisting psychopathology in addition to depression; patients' weight histories (Fairburn and Cooper[12] concluded that a previous diagnosis of anorexia nervosa should not exclude patients from the diagnosis of bulimia nervosa, but does such a history affect treatment outcome?); and family history of eating disorder/weight problems and affective disorder. Fairburn[10] draws a useful distinction between the general use of the term bulimia and the more specific syndrome of bulimia nervosa. Whereas virtually all patients who meet the diagnostic criteria for the latter also fulfill the criteria for the former, the converse does not necessarily hold. Much of the research just described concentrated on bulimia nervosa. Will therapeutic procedures that may be effective with bulimia be appropriate for bulimia nervosa? Can normal-weight and obese bulimic patients be treated the same way? These questions illustrate the importance of accurate diagnosis and careful description of patient samples in future outcome research. Fairburn has also shown how different definitions, sampling procedures, and the method and scope of assessment have resulted in conflicting findings. Inconsistency of this kind will greatly complicate evaluation of treatment effects.

Although the nature of bulimic disorders is not the focus of this chapter, a closing comment is in order. The often effective management of clinical disorders, the etiology of which is not fully understood, is one of the realities of contemporary clinical practice. Ultimately, however, the treatment of bulimic syndromes is inescapably linked to an adequate analysis of its etiology and maintenance. It would seem undeniable that different conceptualizations of the nature of bulimic syndromes would call for different treatments. Whether bulimia is viewed as a symptom of a neurological disorder,[41] as a form of affective disorder,[16] as rooted in the physiology of the regulation of food intake and the conditioning of anxiety reduction,[58] or as a product of dysfunctional cognitions[33] would seem to have decisive consequences for the choice of treatment techniques. In this regard, the results of the different methods discussed here have important implications for understanding the nature of bulimia. Although it would be a logical error to infer etiology from the modification of a problem, the outcome of different treatments can constitute powerful tests of some of the predictions of different theories of bulimia.

REFERENCES

1. American Psychiatric Association. 1980. *Diagnostic and statistical manual of mental disorders*, 3rd ed. Washington, D.C.: American Psychiatric Association.

2. Bandura, A. 1977. Self-efficacy: Toward a unifying theory of behavioral change. *Psychological Review* 84:191–215.

3. Barlow, D. H. 1980. Behavior therapy: The next decade. *Behavior Therapy* 11: 315–328.

4. Barlow, D. H., and Wolfe, B. 1981. Behavioral approaches to anxiety disorders: A report on the NIHM-SUNY, Albany Research Conference. *Journal of Consulting and Clinical Psychology* 49:448–454.

5. Beck, A. T. 1976. *Cognitive therapy and the emotional disorders.* New York: International Universities Press.

6. Boskind-Lodahl, M., and White, W. C. 1978. The definition and treatment of bulimarexia in college women—a pilot study. *Journal of the American College Health Association* 27:2.

7. Brotman, A. W., Herzog, D. B., and Woods, S. W. 1984. Antidepressant treatment of bulimia: The relationship between binging and depressive symptomatology. *Journal of Clinical Psychiatry* 45:7–9.

8. Cullari, S., and Redmon, W. K. 1983. Treatment of bulimarexia through behavior therapy and diet modification. *The Behavior Therapist* 6:165–167.

9. Fairburn, C. G. 1981. A cognitive behavioral approach to the treatment of bulimia. *Psychological Medicine* 11:707–711.

10. ———. Bulimia: Its epidemiology and management. In *Eating and its disorders*, ed. A. J. Stunkard and E. Stellar, pp. 235–258. New York: Raven Press.

11. ———. 1984. A cognitive-behavioural treatment of bulimia. In *Handbook of psychotherapy for anorexia nervosa and bulimia*, ed. D. M. Garner and P. E. Garfinkel, pp. 160–192. New York: Guilford Press.

12. Fairburn, C. G., and Cooper, P. J. 1984. The clinical features of bulimia nervosa. *British Journal of Psychiatry* 144:238–246.

13. Fremouw, W. J., and Heyneman, N. E. 1983. Cognitive styles and bulimia. *The Behavior Therapist* 6:143–144.

14. Giles, T. R., Young, R. R., and Young, D. E. In press. Behavioral treatment of severe bulimia. *Behavior Therapy*.

15. Green, R. S., and Rau, J. H. 1974. Treatment of compulsive eating disturbances with anti-convulsant medication. *American Journal of Psychiatry* 131:428–432.

16. Hudson, J. I., Pope, H. G., and Jonas, J. M. 1984. Treatment of bulimia with antidepressants: Theoretical considerations and clinical findings. In *Eating and its disorders*, ed. A. J. Stunkard and E. Stellar, pp. 259–274. New York: Raven Press.

17. Johnson, W. G., Schlundt, D. G., Kelley, M. L., and Ruggiero, L. 1984. Exposure with response prevention and energy regulation in the treatment of bulimia. *International Journal of Eating Disorders* 3:37–46.

18. Kirkley, B. G., Schneider, J. A., Agras, W. S., and Bachman, J. A. 1985. A comparison of two group treatments for bulimia. *Journal of Consulting and Clinical Psychology* 53:43–48.

19. Lacey, J. H. 1983. Bulimia nervosa, binge eating, and psychogenic vomiting: A controlled treatment study and long term outcome. *British Medical Journal* 286:1609–1613.

20. Lee, N. F., and Rush, A. J. n.d. Cognitive-behavioral group therapy for bulimia. Manuscript. University of Texas Health Science Center, Dallas.

21. Leitenberg, H., Gross, J., Peterson, J., and Rosen, J. C. 1984. Analysis of an anxiety model and the process of change during exposure plus response prevention treatment of bulimia nervosa. *Behavior Therapy* 15:3–20.

22. Linden, W. 1980. Multi-component behavior therapy in a case of compulsive binge-eating followed by vomiting. *Journal of Behavior Therapy and Experimental Psychiatry* 11:297–300.

23. Long, C. G., and Cordle, C. J. 1982. Psychological treatment of binge eating and self-induced vomiting. *British Journal of Medical Psychology* 55:139–145.

24. Loro, A. D. 1984. Binge eating: A cognitive behavioral treatment approach. In *The binge-purge syndrome: Treatment, research and theory*, ed. R. C. Hawkins, W. J. Fremouw, and P. F. Clement, pp. 183–210. New York: Springer.

25. Marks, I. M. 1981. *Cure and care of the neuroses.* New York: John Wiley & Sons.

26. Marks, M., et al. 1983. Imipramine and brief therapist-aided exposure in agoraphobics having self-exposure homework. *Archives of General Psychiatry* 40:153–162.

27. Marlatt, G. A. 1985. Relapse prevention: Theoretical rationale and overview of the model. In *Relapse prevention*, ed. G. A. Marlatt and J. Gordon, pp. 3–70. New York: Guilford Press.

28. Meyer, R. G. 1973. Delay therapy: Two case reports. *Behavior Therapy* 4:709–711.

29. Mizes, J. S. In press. Bulimia: A review of its symptomatology and treatment. *Advances in Behaviour Research and Therapy*.

30. Mizes, J. S., and Lohr, J. M. 1983. The treatment of bulimic (binge-eating and self-induced vomiting): A quasi-experimental investigation of the effects of stimulus narrowing, self-reinforcement, and self-control relaxation. *International Journal of Eating Disorders* 2: 59–65.

31. O'Neil, G. W. 1982. A systematic desensitization approach to bulimia. Paper presented at the Association for Advancement of Behavior Therapy, Los Angeles, Calif.

32. Paul, G. L. 1967. Outcome research in psychotherapy. *Journal of Consulting Psychology* 31:109–118.

33. Polivy, J., Herman, C. P., Olmsted, M., and Jazwinski, C. 1984. Restraint and binge eating. In *The binge-purge syndrome: Treatment, research and theory*, ed. R. C. Hawkins, W. J. Fremouw, and P. Clement, pp. 104–122. New York: Springer.

34. Pope, H. G., and Hudson, J. 1982. Treatment of bulimia with antidepressants. *Psychopharmacology* 78:167–169.

35. Pope, H. G., Hudson, J. I., and Jonas, J. M. 1983. Antidepressant treatment of bulimia: Preliminary experience and practical recommendations. *Journal of Clinical Psychopharmacology* 3:274–281.

36. Pope, H. G., Hudson, J. I., Jonas, J. M., and Yurgelun-Todd, D. 1983. Bulimia treated with imipramine: A placebo-controlled, double-blind study. *American Journal of Psychiatry* 140:554–558.

37. Rachman, S. 1981. The primacy of affect: Some theoretical implications. *Behaviour Research and Therapy* 19:279–290.

38. Rachman, S., and Hodgson, R. 1980. *Obsessions and compulsions.* Englewood Cliffs, N.J.: Prentice-Hall.

39. Rankin, H., Hodgson, R., and Stockwell, T. 1983. Cue exposure and response prevention with alcoholics: A controlled trial. *Behaviour Research and Therapy* 21:435–446.

40. Rau, J., and Green, R. S. 1975. Compulsive eating: A neuropsychologic approach to certain eating disorders. *Comparative Psychiatry* 16:223–231.

41. ———. 1984. Neurological factors affecting binge eating: Body over mind. In *The binge purge syndrome: Treatment, research and theory*, ed. R. C. Hawkins, W. H. Fremouw, and P. F. Clement, pp. 123–143. New York: Springer.

42. Rosen, J. C., and Leitenberg, H. 1982. Bulimia nervosa: Treatment with exposure and response prevention. *Behavior Therapy* 13:117–124.

43. Rossiter, E., and Wilson, G. T. 1984. Cognitive restructuring and response prevention in the treatment of bulimia nervosa. *Behavior and Research Therapy* 23:349–360.

44. Russell, G. 1979. Bulimia nervosa: An ominous variant of anorexia nervosa. *Psychological Medicine* 9:429–448.

45. Sabine, E. J., et al. 1983. Bulimia nervosa: A placebo controlled double-blind therapeutic trial of mianserin. *British Journal of Clinical Pharmacology* 15(Supplement):195–202.

46. Schneider, J. A., and Agras, W. S. In press. A cognitive behavioral group treatment of bulimia. *British Journal of Psychiatry.*

47. Sheehan, D. V. 1982. Current concepts in psychiatry. *New England Journal of Medicine* 307:156–158.

48. Stewart, J. W., et al. 1984. An open trial of MAO inhibitors in bulimia. *Journal of Clinical Psychiatry* 45:217–219.

49. Walsh, T. B., et al. In press. Treatment of bulimia with phenelzine: A double-blind placebo-controlled study. *Archives of General Psychiatry.*

50. Welch, G. J. 1979. The treatment of compulsive vomiting and obsessive thoughts through gradual response delay, response prevention and cognitive correction. *Journal of Behavior Therapy and Experimental Psychiatry* 10:77–82.

51. Wermuth, B., Davis, K., and Hollister, L. 1977. Phenytoin treatment of the binge-eating syndrome. *American Journal of Psychiatry* 134:1249–1253.

52. White, W. C., and Boskind-White, M. 1981. An experiential-behavioral approach to the treatment of bulimarexia. *Psychotherapy: Theory, Research and Practice* 18:501–507.

53. ———. 1984. An experiential-behavioral treatment program for bulimarexic women. In *The binge-purge syndrome: Treatment, research and theory*, ed. R. C. Hawkins, W. J. Fremouw, and P. F. Clement, pp. 77–103. New York: Springer.

54. Wilson, G. T. 1984. Fear reduction methods and the treatment of anxiety disorders. In *Annual review of behavior therapy: Theory and practice*, vol. 9, ed. G. T. Wilson, C. M. Franks, K. Brownell, and P. Kendall, pp. 95–131. New York: Guilford Press.

55. ———. 1984. Towards an understanding of binge eating. In *The binge-purge syndrome: Treatment, research and theory*, ed. R. C. Hawkins, W. J. Fremouw, and P. F. Clement, pp. 264–289. New York: Springer.

56. Wilson, G. T., and Brownell, K. D. 1980. Behavior therapy for obesity: An evaluation of treatment outcome. *Advances in Behaviour Research and Therapy* 3:49–86.

57. Wilson, G. T., Rossiter, E., Kleifield, E., and Lindholm, L. In press. Cognitive-behavioral treatment of bulimia nervosa: A controlled evaluation. *Behavior Research and Therapy.*

58. Wooley, S. C., and Wooley, O. W. 1981. Overeating as substance abuse. In *Advances in substance abuse*, vol. 2, ed. N. K. Mello, pp. 41–67. Greenwich, Conn.: JAI Press.

59. Zitrin, C. M., Klein, D. E., Woerner, M. G., and Ross, D. C. 1983. Treatment of phobias. *Archives of General Psychiatry* 40:125–138.

25

Intensive Treatment of Bulimia and Body-Image Disturbance

Susan C. Wooley and Ann Kearney-Cooke

Introduction

In this chapter we will propose a theory of bulimia that links its increase to changing role expectations for women and the cultural meanings of thinness. We will also describe a new treatment program that, in addition to providing concrete assistance with eating, addresses issues of female development believed to be related to bulimia. Using intensive group, individual, family, and body-image therapy, women are helped to explore and resolve conflicts around separation and the passage into the adult female role, to reconstruct their individual histories of body-image development, and to gain a sense of emotional connectedness to others.

Although central to eating disorders, body-image disturbances have generally proven refractory to treatment. Concerning, as they do, images and sensory memories, body-image problems do not readily lend themselves to verbal articulation. This has led us to develop new techniques employing imagery, art, and movement to explore and rework the symbolic and expressive meanings of body size and to integrate issues of body-image development within the larger context of psychological development.[22]

The proposed theory represents a generalization to which there are

The authors wish to acknowledge the contributions of Wayne Wooley, Ph.D., Kay Debs, Ph.D., Karen Lewis, ACSW, and Lynn Pierson, Ph.D., to the development of the concepts and therapeutic techniques described in this chapter.

doubtless many exceptions. But it has proven useful as an organizing framework that cuts across personality styles and suggests therapeutic interventions for women with varying degrees of eating disturbances, with character structures ranging from rigid and compulsive to disorganized and impulsive, and including those with borderline and narcissistic personality disorders. Obviously it is not a complete theory of all these disturbances, but it provides a common point of departure, from which further therapeutic interventions may be undertaken. The views described owe much to the theories and observations of others working in this field.

Understanding Bulimia

We regard bulimia as a disorder of maturation, a breakdown in the final stages of transition to adulthood, whose rising incidence in women seems attributable to problematic changes in cultural expectations of women's bodies and social roles. The three most prominent risk factors appear to be early dieting, early body-image disturbance, and conflict-engendering constructions of the adult female role.

Anorexia nervosa has long been conceptualized as a developmental crisis in which the child and her family cannot tolerate her passage into sexual maturity.[2,3] In comparison to bulimia, anorexia nervosa has a low and relatively stable incidence[10,14] and occurs in the context of a well-known family constellation, characterized by abnormally close ties, emotional enmeshment, and minimal autonomy.[2,3,12] Cases of anorexia nervosa have been reported in the medical literature for centuries, suggesting that its occurrence is less dependent on cultural shifts in preferred body type or women's roles and may be largely a function of family pathology.

Bulimia, by contrast, is a new syndrome. While bulimic symptoms are often a late phase of anorexia nervosa, the current epidemic is not composed of such patients. Surveys suggest the prevalence of bulimia (of mild to extreme severity) to be as high as 15 percent in college-age women,[12] whereas the prevalence of anorexia nervosa, in any age group, is no more than 1 percent.[10] Some bulimic women, in their initial dieting efforts, briefly meet the weight-loss criterion for diagnosis of anorexia; some approach it; some never get close, although virtually all cases of bulimia begin with weight-loss diets.[21]

The increasing incidence is demonstrated by the results of a survey, prepared by the staff of the Eating Disorders Clinic and published in *Glamour* magazine.[20] This survey, which drew 33,000 responses, showed that in the 15- to 35-year age range, the relationship between age and the reported use of vomiting as a weight-loss technique (now or in the past) was inverse and linear. Only 7.6 percent of women over 30 had ever used vomiting to control weight compared to almost 20 percent of women under 20.

It is our belief that while anorexia nervosa represents severe problems surrounding the passage *into* adolescence, bulimia reflects problems in passage *out of adolescence* and into independent adulthood. The anorexic individual appears to stumble on the first steps of transition to adulthood—the development of sexuality and the transfer of energy and interest from the family to peers. The bulimic individual usually negotiates these early phases successfully, often becoming sexually and socially active, but falters later in the establishment of intimacy and authenticity in peer relationships and in the separation from her family. She seems to know the steps but cannot dance. The barriers to further development are often more subtle than those found in anorexia and more difficult to identify.

These maturational difficulties appear to stem largely from two cultural changes. First is the increasing preference for a lean body type in women. Today's young women are not the first generation to be exposed to this bias, but they are the first to be exposed to it in childhood and to be raised by mothers rejecting of their own bodies and concerned about the size of their daughter's body from the moment of birth. This is a heritage of anxiety and self-loathing. Women reaching maturity have not had even the respite of childhood from concerns about body size and eating, and may approach puberty with a long history of negative body image, a problem that is intensified during adolescence. Relationships may be used to combat a sense of physical inadequacy. But the underlying insecurity prevents young bulimic women from learning that real thoughts and feelings are acceptable.

Second, this is the first generation of women expected to live a life different from their mother's—a life, instead, like their father's. This change in women's role is probably not independent of the change in preferred body type for women, the more masculine physique better reflecting the increasing emulation of traditionally male values of autonomy, achievement, and self-discipline. Recurrent associations to fat and thin, elicited in body-image therapy, have demonstrated the power of physical characteristics to connote role demands and have exposed an area of frequent conflict.[22] The ample female body is associated with a devalued demand for nurturance of others but also a much-longed-for connectedness. The thin body, on the other hand, connotes freedom from traditional role demands while also incurring isolation. The mother's social role and body type are ambivalently rejected, while the father's role and body type are ambivalently embraced. Either choice entails a cost.

The influence of the maternal attitudes on the daughter's body image is illustrated in the *Glamour* survey.[20] Daughters who reported that their mothers were critical of their bodies showed a poorer body image, a greater use of severe dieting practices, and a higher incidence of bulimia. Young females, preoccupied with their weight at increasingly early ages, diet with unprecedented frequency. Studies show that by age 18, 80 percent of females have started dieting.[13] A recent investigation revealed failure of normal growth in children who had covertly restricted their food intake to prevent obesity.[15]

Whether or not it is an intended message, a daughter learns from her mother (and the rest of the culture) that a woman's body is her life's work. Her happiness may depend on it. Her success in shaping her body is a matter of will. Daughters often interpret the bodily flaws of their mothers as evidence of inadequacy and assume that such flaws are the cause of all her discontent. Long before a daughter can test her own will against life's more substantive challenges—education, a career, the development of enduring relationships outside the family—she can test her ability to shape her body. In so doing, she enters into unspoken, sometimes unwanted competition with her mother, a process that has no happy outcome. To fail is to fear for herself; to succeed is to fear for her mother.

However, few people "win" in the struggle to conform to current fashion. As the standard of thinness becomes more stringent,[5] more young women diet and attempt to push themselves below their natural biological weights. Those who lose weight in spite of strong biological pressures meet new, unexpected problems. Research on the effects of prolonged semistarvation makes clear that binge eating is a normal, almost inevitable response.[8] Binges are either accepted as a temporary failure, leading to weight restoration, or are fought aggressively with purging, creating a vicious circle in which purging maintains a state of malnutrition sufficient to ensure binge eating, while binge eating necessitates purging.

The practice of binge purging is highly effective as a method of weight control and, unlike chronic restriction, is within the capability of most women. Not surprisingly, many women dabble in bulimia, although not all progress to chronic bulimia. For while it serves its intended purpose, it does so at great cost, requiring unusual financial resources, demanding a life of secrecy and isolation, perpetuating dependence on the family for money, companionship, emotional ties, and refuge.

We believe that bulimia becomes entrenched in those women for whom movement away from home represents an area of unresolved conflict, ultimately traceable to problems in the construction of womanhood. While this conflict is apparent in the bulimic woman's inordinate concerns for her mother and the confusion and loneliness that pervade her visions of the future, it is experienced primarily in bodily terms, in the conviction that mastery of eating and attainment of a correct body size will somehow ensure success and human connectedness. Her remarkable failure to learn from experience the futility of this course only emphasizes the difficulty she has in conceiving alternatives.

Admittedly, role confusion is ubiquitous in a period of such rapid social change. All young women arrive at the threshold of maturity required, to some degree, to reject the ways of their mothers and accept those of their fathers. Some seem able to articulate the conflicts between the masculine and feminine value systems with which they were raised and begin the process of achieving a personally acceptable integration. Bulimic women seem to have particular problems with this task. Most have failed even to understand it, some to progress in achieving a solution. While many explanations for this failure are possible, one factor may be an unusual polarization of parental traits.

In our experience, few mothers of bulimic women work outside the home. The few who do usually assist in the father's business, or work in such traditionally female areas as nursing or teaching. These mothers, often talented women, have devoted themselves to being wives and mothers and approach the "empty nest" empty themselves, depressed, confused, and ineffectual. Sometimes the mothers drink heavily, have relatively few friends, and are dependent on their bulimic daughter for emotional support and companionship. Sometimes the daughter is the mother's only confidante, with whom she shares the disappointments of her marriage. Sometimes the mother is silent about her problems, the daughter sensing but never understanding her unhappiness, finding her "unreal" and inaccessible.

The fathers of bulimic women often personify the old-fashioned man, self-made, independent, controlled, powerful, and successful. Their emotional distance forces the mother to rely on her children for companionship. Rather than being close-knit, these families sometimes seem to be on the verge of falling apart, and exploration may reveal that the daughter is attempting to keep her father emotionally attached to the family by one of several means.

She may hold his interest by realizing his social ambitions. Thus many bulimic women we have seen have been successful, even world-class, athletes, whose fathers were greatly identified with their achievements. She may coerce her father into the role of caretaker, often by returning home in a state of helplessness. One bulimic woman, unable to engender concern for herself, took her baby to her parents' house each morning so her father could play with him before he went to work. Some appear to use their own bodies as magnets, compensating for the mother's perceived unattractiveness to the father. Some have been their father's "favorite date," the one he took to business and social functions. Finally, virtually all hold the family together by creating a common concern, their illness, and in some cases through flagrantly disruptive behavior, a "common enemy" who draws attention away from other problems in the family.

While the anorexic woman's family is threatened by the increased autonomy attending the onset of adolescence, the bulimic woman often uses the autonomy and resources of adolescence to support and assist the family. Through her accomplishments, activities, sympathetic ear, and pleasing personality she meets the family's unexpressed needs. Her own conflicts become crippling only at the point that she must separate her own interests from those of the family. To go her own way is to abandon her mother, both literally, because she is no longer present as friend and confidante, and symbolically, in the sense that she has chosen to be like her father and to reject her mother's values. This may be to lose her entirely. Forced to choose between "victim" and "victimizer," she is stuck. Nor is she confident that she can make it in the world of men. As a result, she is often inordinately dependent on the social props learned from her mother and the surrounding culture: perfect appearance, an ingratiating manner, and a flawless facade. Unfortunately these go hand in hand with a lack of spontaneity, an inability to identify and express her own emotions or to take interpersonal risks.

Many of the problems of bulimic women can be understood within the context of this conflict in which autonomy and success are pitted against dependence and failure. It is the metaphor within which starvation and thinness come to symbolize strength, while eating and body fat come to symbolize failure. Nurturance, including nurturance of the self, is rejected as a symptom of weakness. The experienced conflict may lead to a distortion or exaggeration of the gap that exists between the patients and others, and organizes perceptions of others so that they are experienced as either so fragile or so powerful that real relationships become impossible.

Support for this view is found in an insightful study by Steiner-Adair[18] who related scores on the Eating Attitudes Tests (EAT) to adolescents' constructions of the adult female role. "Superwomen," who took as their own the new cultural model of the independent successful woman without recognizing the cultural pressures to do so, showed a 94-percent rate of EAT scores in the clinical range. "Wise women," who both recognized and separated themselves from this cultural prototype, maintaining the value of interdependence, showed no evidence of clinical eating disorders. Describing the "superwoman," Steiner-Adair states: "There is no integration or resolution of differences between attitudes for each sex. All that is uniquely female is annihilated in order to accommodate the cultural ideal image" (pp. 139–140). Of wise women: "In choosing an ideal image that supports their female development, these girls create a self-nourishing vision of adulthood" (p. 138). And, in summary: "The failure of some girls to identify prevailing cultural expectations of independence and success and to differentiate these expectations from their own values of care and connection may lead them to act out a conflict between these different values in self-destructive patterns of eating behavior" (p. 9).

Overview of Treatment

Opened in 1974, the Eating Disorders Clinic in the Psychiatry Department at the University of Cincinnati Medical College has treated several hundred bulimic women. In the Intensive Treatment Program for Bulimia, developed in 1983 to treat women from out of town and described here, six patients are accepted for each session. During their three-and-a-half-week stay, the patients are housed in a nearby hotel, coming to the

clinic for six to eight hours of therapy each weekday. They live in apart-
ments with kitchens and are responsible for their own meal preparation
and for managing their own affairs when therapy is not in session. Psychotic, alcoholic, or drug-dependent patients are not accepted. The only
other criterion is that the problems must be severe enough to warrant
intensive treatment. Arrangements for follow-up treatment in the patient's
hometown are made before entry into the program. It is not necessary
that the follow-up therapist have expertise in eating disorders, since the
patients leave with sufficient knowledge to deal with eating problems.

The first two days of the program are devoted to evaluation including a complete medical examination, whole-body calorimetry or oxygen consumption tests to determine caloric needs for weight maintenance, and psychological testing. Tests of disordered eating include the
EAT,[6] the Eating Disorders Inventory (EDI),[7] and the Revised Restraint
Scale.[19] Tests of self- and body-image include the Body Cathexis Scale,[17]
the Self Cathexis Scale,[17] and the Color-a-Person test, developed at the
Eating Disorders Clinic. Tests of general psychological functioning include
the Minnesota Multiphasic Personality Inventory and the Symptom
Checklist-90.[4]

The Color-a-Person test employs an outline drawing of a female body.
Patients color in the body, using five colored markers representing a
range of attitudes from highly positive to highly negative. This test allows
quantification of like/dislike of the whole body or body regions and lends
itself to qualitative interpretation since the renditions often indicate areas
of particular distress. For the patients it is a form of self-assessment that
begins the process of body-image therapy.

After the first two days, the program has a regular schedule that includes two educational seminars per week, a daily food group from 9:00
A.M. to 10:00 A.M., a daily process psychotherapy group from 10:15 to
12:00, body-image therapy meetings four days per week from 2:00 P.M.
to 4:00 P.M., and two to three sessions of individual therapy per week.
Families are asked to come at some time during the program for one or
more sessions of family therapy.

Management of Eating

EDUCATIONAL SEMINARS

The more patients understand about eating disorders, the more in-
telligently they can interpret and control their experience. A series of
seminars is designed to teach relevant facts and concepts.

Recovery from Bulimia. Patients are given the following framework.
The problem of bulimia is more a problem of what is not eaten than what

is. Most bulimic women are fearful of eating more than a semistarvation diet, unless they do so with the intent to purge. The hunger so created leads to binge eating. It is virtually impossible to overcome binge eating unless normal eating is restored. The reinstatement of normal eating requires overcoming a phobia. Like other phobias, exposure to the feared event must occur so anxiety can extinguish. Patients are told that the ingestion of larger meals or "forbidden" foods without intent to purge will lead to intense anxiety and that the endurance of this anxiety is crucial to cure.

Several factors produce exaggerated hunger in bulimia, all reversible with normal eating. One is an abnormality in "conditioned satiety,"[1,9] a process by which people learn to eat amounts of given foods, recognized by taste and texture, that in the past have met the body's needs. When purging occurs, only a fraction of the food consumed is digested, so that with repetition the conditioned satiety signal is delayed until a sufficient amount is eaten to meet nutritional needs despite purging. Until this is corrected by retention of food, eating normal amounts of foods formerly purged will be unsatisfying. It is probably for this reason that bulimic women feel safer eating only certain diet foods that they rarely, if ever, purge, while "binge" foods are hard to eat in moderation.

Since most bulimic women eat little except in binges, since most binges consist primarily of sweets, and since sugars are the nutrients likely to be absorbed in greatest quantity in the interval between initiation of a binge and purging, these patients live on diets extraordinarily high in sucrose. This may lead to abnormalities of insulin secretion that persist for some time after correction of diet, causing excessive hunger and occasional hypoglycemic panic attacks.

Finally, return to normal eating requires many physiological adjustments. Unaccustomed to a full range of foods, the body may have decreased its production of certain digestive enzymes. If the diet has been sparse, stomach-emptying time may have slowed. If laxatives have been used, the bowel may be sluggish. Both laxative abuse and vomiting will have replaced the normal function of the kidneys in excreting electrolytes and fluids.

Patients may experience feelings of "bloatedness," indigestion, cramping pain, gas, constipation, abnormalities in fluid regulation, sleep disturbances, hotness, and an array of symptoms accompanying reinstatement of hormonal activity and return of menses. Patients must be reassured that most or all of these problems are transient and self-correcting. Nonetheless, their aversiveness, especially to those addicted to sensations of emptiness and lightness, must be recognized as a real deterrent to behavior change and counteracted with symptomatic treatment and support.

Weight Regulation and Set Point. For every individual there appears to be a natural weight that can be maintained by spontaneous eating. This "set point" is probably primarily genetic, perhaps influenced by prenatal or early feeding, and is defended by physiological changes. If, through dieting, weight is pushed below the set point, two changes occur: Appetite increases and metabolic rate decreases. If weight rises above the set point, appetite decreases and metabolic rate increases.

One implication is that an unnaturally low body weight will require a permanently lowered intake and will produce chronic hunger, both factors that encourage bulimia and argue strongly for a realistic goal weight. A second implication is that there is a natural limit to weight gain. The rapid weight gain that normal eating may cause in a person below set point is likely to slow and stop with return to set point and restoration of normal metabolic rate.

Effects of Starvation. Research on semistarvation[8] is reviewed, emphasizing the impact on two areas of functioning. Physical effects include reduced metabolic rate, reduced work capacity, fatigue, loss of libido, hypothermia, lanugo, food cravings, and tendency to binge eat. Psychological effects include neurotic symptoms, especially depression, social withdrawal, peculiar eating habits, and food preoccupation. Patients are assigned reading materials and encouraged to reinterpret past and present symptoms attributable to food deprivation.

Feminist Views. The pressure to be "attractive" by meeting an increasingly stringent standard of thinness is directed almost exclusively to women and acts as a massive impediment to achievement and spontaneity. Having been taught not to "act" but to "appear," it is not surprising that as women gain entrance to the work world of men they become concerned with how to "look the part," emulating a hard, lean, male physique. The minimization of femaleness may be unconsciously encouraged by men for whom the entry of women into the workplace represents a disturbance. Ironically this denies women the same rights as men. Women's bodies require an irreducible minimum of fat tissue for reproduction, and this is an integral part of femaleness.

RETRAINING EATING BEHAVIOR

Most bulimic individuals require regular support and guidance as they undertake change. The anxiety produced by eating without purging often overwhelms them; the reinstatement of "control" is irresistibly comforting in the face of anxiety and bodily change. The modification of eating behavior is built around the daily discussion of eating records, which include time of eating, amount eaten, hunger level, anxiety before and after eating, guilt after eating, "bloat," and whether or not the food was purged. Most patients use the records as a diary, spontaneously recording moods, urges to binge, urges to purge, and the attempts made to curb these urges.

Discussion of eating records usually focuses on three issues. First is the move away from "dieting" and toward normal eating by ingesting larger quantities of food when not binging, increasing the variety of foods, and establishing a regular eating schedule. Second is an analysis of binges and purges. In contrast to usual outpatient treatment, in the intensive treatment program virtually all patients give up binge/purging as a daily, habitual behavior near the start of treatment. An occurrence of a binge and/or purge serves as an arrow pointing to specific physical and emotional states, areas of conflict, and distorted interpretation of bodily sensations. Third is the relationship of food intake to weight. Although spontaneous eating is easier to achieve without frequent weighing, patients are weighed daily so that the tendency to modify eating in response to weight change can be observed and challenged.

Even patients who acknowledge the need to gain weight typically revert to dieting upon the gain of even a pound and feel covert satisfaction with weight loss. Patients are encouraged to make food intake responsive to hunger rather than to minor weight fluctuations. The tendency to adjust eating to weight shifts must be noted and questioned again and again for it constitutes a powerful counterforce to improvement. It is usually not shared, being part of a private world in which the power to manipulate self-esteem through weight loss is closely guarded.

Treatment of eating requires therapeutic skill since many defenses will be employed to prevent change. Notable among these are the bland and impenetrable denial of hunger and food cravings, dependency and protestations of helplessness, overt or covert rage at the therapist for intrusion into a charged personal arena, and various transferences, sometimes an idealizing one that leads to compliance and the seeking of praise for "good" behavior without any real assimilation, and sometimes a negative one in which suggestions are experienced as humiliating criticism. The therapist must probe, confront, label, and interpret, without anger, the emotional responses that occur. Despite its concrete focus, the management of eating is as much a psychotherapy as any other.

Group Psychotherapy

The mission of psychotherapy is to discover and correct the developmental problems that have permitted bulimia to become a way of life. A young woman who embraces her present and future will not be trapped by bulimia. As stated earlier, we believe the problems center around passage into adulthood, including unresolved conflicts in parental identification, conviction that the family will be hurt if the patient leaves her "post," or paralyzing fears of bodily inadequacy.

Other causes of chronic bulimia include unresolved grief, traumatic neurosis in which bulimia is but one of several symptoms, and, with surprising frequency, history of sexual abuse leading to guilt and repetitive attempts at self-purification, with a repudiation of all pleasant sensual experience. Although certain common threads recur, each individual's history must be understood. Even our basic premise should be questioned, for we have occasionally seen longstanding bulimia dissolve with the simple transmission of basic information about eating, suggesting that in a few women it may be a habit that has been emotionally outgrown but not yet abandoned.

The core of the psychotherapy experience is the group, for here the patient will experience all her problems in relating to others. Memories, inhibitions, and tensions from the past will be evoked if not by the group as a whole, then by some member. Provided with symbolic parents and siblings, the patient's role within her family is recapitulated in an arena in which it can be identified and examined.

Bulimic individuals are well-socialized young women who have thoroughly assimilated the messages of the culture. Sensitive to external demands, they easily deceive therapists by surmising and providing what is wanted of them in the patient role. Bulimia groups are extraordinarily easy to conduct; effective ones are extraordinarily difficult to conduct, for bulimic women strive to make the therapist and other members feel at ease, discussing with enthusiasm any topic suggested to them, especially ones that pose little threat. Again and again, initial favorable responses to bulimic women are replaced by the recognition that they are not "real" in their interactions, their apparent warmth concealing grave difficulties in sustaining connection, avoidance of anger, and a preference for isolation.

The central task of therapy is to push patients outside their range of comfort into expression of meaningful emotion. The wracking process of dealing honestly with one another is the first step and requires frequent, confrontive interventions by therapists. Relating the intragroup experience to outside relationships, especially in the family, is the second step but must have immediacy and relevance for both the patient and the rest of the group, so that it fosters empathy and intimacy among members. Therapists, too, must expose themselves, becoming "real" to the patients.

The following six strategies for working on individual issues in a group have proven helpful: interrupting whitewashing, exploring ambivalence, exploring relationships, reenacting past events, dramatizing future events, and amplifying expression with movement.

The therapists must interrupt attempts at whitewashing of problems and rescuing of one patient by others. There is a fear of strong feeling, and unless the group adopts the value that discomfort is acceptable and useful, no real work will be done. The efforts of the therapist to block well-intentioned but derailing interventions of patients almost always causes some initial confusion and anger but is usually appreciated later. It is helpful for the group to see one patient do a difficult but productive piece of work early on and to experience the closeness and relief this brings.

Intense feelings can be missed when ambivalence results in qualified and contradictory statements ("I resent my mother; I am grateful to her").

The use of a Gestalt-style dialogue between the opposing halves, in which the patient must, for example, sit in one chair to express anger and another to express love, gives full voice to each feeling, usually revealing hidden intensity and permitting greater potential for resolution.

One example of dialogue concerned a patient who, though seemingly connected to the group, went out with local acquaintances almost every night, drinking heavily and taking drugs. Each day she described mixed feelings about her behavior. A debate between the part of her who wanted to stay with the group and the part who wanted to have a "good time" revealed loss and sorrow each time she left, as well as an angry assertion of her need to get away. She then uncovered her fear of letting her bad side be seen by people she cared about. We asked her to reveal that part by expressing to each member negative feelings she had experienced toward them and learning that she could still be accepted. Thereafter, she remained with the group.

Feelings toward family members are explored through dialogues with them. The patient may play both roles, or the therapist or another patient may enact the missing person. The therapist, in the role of parent or lover, may shift from the person's usual behavior to expression of what can be inferred about his/her underlying feelings, saying, for example, "You can't grow up; I will fall apart without you."

One example of such a dialogue was a daughter's inquiry of her mother whether she loved her, followed by a moving entry into her mother's feelings and an understanding of her own impediments to closeness. Several women have expressed their needs for greater separation from their mothers, confronting their fears of leaving their mothers with nothing. One woman was able to feel, for the first time, her rage and hurt as she described to her father the impact of a bout of friendly horseplay that veered suddenly into sexual fondling. "You made me hate my body," she said, weeping. "You made me hate the changes that caused this, and I lost you forever."

Past events may be explored by reenactments. Patients have reenacted everyday experiences of their childhood, such as family dinners; traumatic events such as rape, abortion, or their last contact with a dying family member; even events they have recently experienced as a group, such as the division of the check at a restaurant. They are encouraged to move beyond the event as it occurred to state what they actually felt and to show what they wanted to do.

The symbolic enactment of anticipated events can be helpful. One patient was able to begin to face the consequences of her recovery when the group portrayed her family as she envisioned it to be a year after her "cure," members flung to far corners of the globe. As she described the probable events, group members went to corners of the room, enacting, in monologue, their new life roles. Looking from first one to the other, she wept profusely as she felt the loss. Finally, after several minutes, she began to imagine when and where they might next meet. She said, "You know, maybe we will all be all right. Maybe this could be okay. I have to find a place for me now."

In an effort to help patients identify what they need, therapists may portray a healing event. As parents, for example, they may finish the unending and inconclusive fight about their daughter's condition and what it means, battling it out until they can achieve a consensus and commitment to work together. Or, again as parents, they may set clear limits for the child. What they are portraying is parents able to make their own relationship work without the child's intervention.

In some instances, emotional meanings can be further amplified with movement, to enhance symbolic impact. One patient disentangled the threads of resentment and pleading in a dialogue with her father by getting on her knees to beg and standing to express anger. The dramatization of her supplication fueled the anger that in turn so frightened her that she fell back on the floor. With each movement up and down the feelings became clearer and stronger till she wept and shouted with ease. Finally she said, "I don't feel as angry now, but I will never beg again."

In another instance, a young wife and mother who had experienced her husband as her rescuer and caretaker began slowly to recognize the extent of his dependency on her, but remained numb and flat. She described her feelings at the end of a work day when she would realize that she didn't want to go home but couldn't understand why. The feelings were at last released when the therapist, portraying her husband, lay on the floor pulling her leg and pleading for help while group members portraying her children tugged at her arms. As tears began to flow she said, "Yes, this is what I feel." She then realized the feeling was an extension of her feelings of responsibility for her physically ill mother and for her siblings during childhood.

The use of experiential techniques serves several goals. It permits intense exploration while maintaining a sense of "here and now," thus helping resolve the inevitable conflict in groups between discussions that include everyone and therapist-assisted work with individuals. Because all patients can be active participants, because the casting of historical or future events into the present is more compelling, and because issues are often shared ones, these experiences usually elicit intense emotion and promote group cohesion.

The program format, in which there are several therapy sessions each day, facilitates this kind of work, since it provides necessary support to enable greater risk taking and reduces the competition for attention that is an inescapable feature of weekly outpatient groups. With the next session only an hour away, leaving "unfinished business" is acceptable and even desirable, for patients are forced to stay with their tensions, something they rarely do. Daily staff meetings ensure continuity and maximize the integration of the therapeutic effort.

Family Therapy

The agenda of family therapy is to help the patient find a way to achieve necessary separation without the feared loss of all connection to her family. Sometimes this is done by creating an atmosphere in which she is free to state her own needs and feelings clearly, because others are doing so. Sometimes it involves facilitating communication between parents so that their daughter can step out of her role as mediator. Sometimes her guilt over leaving her mother is alleviated by discussion in which she is given permission to be different. When parents seem unable to respond to the daughter's emotional needs, therapists may foster a supportive alliance among the siblings.

In one session the therapist asked those members of the family who were usually outspoken to get on one side of the table and those who were reticent to get on the other side. The patient, her mother, and her father all chose the "reticent" side, while the patient's older sister, whom she envied and experienced as all-powerful, went to the "outspoken" side. Her brother went to an end of the table. The older sister began to cry, saying that, as usual, she felt alone and different. This precipitated a move to her side by the father who explained that he really felt he belonged there but hadn't wanted to leave his wife.

The patient then decided to join the "outspoken" side, explaining that that was where she wanted to be. Once there, she became acutely uncomfortable that her mother was alone. As the parents began to talk, the therapist instructed the patient to move back to her original place if she felt her parents couldn't handle things. The mother then told her daughter that she wanted her to be different and stronger than she; that, although she could never be outspoken herself, she was proud to have raised daughters who could be.

Another family, consisting of parents and several grown children, at first appeared united to help the patient with her "illness." When the therapist questioned their limitless loyalty ("I would cut off my arm to help her") and suggested that perhaps the patient was being "naughty," a variety of more honest responses began to emerge. The mother had always felt her daughter was selfish and willful. A brother expressed his rage, saying he would like to "choke that [sick] part of her." The father revealed that he had privately threatened to cut off her support if she did not complete the program and show evidence of improvement. The therapist pushed, asking the family members if they thought the father could really stick to his intentions.

Initially enraged by the apparent betrayal by the therapist, the patient later realized that she too was free to express anger and to pursue her own rather than her family's goals. She would no longer need to express resentment and autonomy by starving until she couldn't finish a term at the school of her parents' choosing, or by drinking in settings selected to embarrass her father. She saw that her mother, whom she had dismissed as irrational and overemotional, was stronger than she realized and experienced a longing to get to know her better. In order to keep the issues of autonomy and eating separate, she was asked by the therapist not to let her family know if she was eating well during the program.

In contrast to the consistent picture of pseudoharmony, family loyalty, and cohesion characterizing the families of anorexic patients, the families of bulimic women seem far more variable. Some resemble the anorexigenic family. But some have already undergone divorce and for others it appears imminent. There seems to be less cohesion and more conflict, a finding supported by early research data.[22] This helps to explain the frequency with which the bulimic daughter is caught up in an effort to hold the pieces together. Her disentanglement from the family may have repercussions that she must be helped to face. This fact only underscores the critical role of family therapy in the treatment of bulimic women.

Individual Therapy

Patients see an individual therapist for six to nine sessions. The individual sessions allow patients to reflect on their experiences in the other treatment modalities. The therapist seeks to clarify experiences that are confusing to the patient, to generalize experiences that are understood by the patient only in the narrow context of the specific group where they took place, and to bring preconscious reactions into awareness, thereby completing work begun in the group. For example, when one patient was surprised that group members found her cold and distant, she and her therapist examined the behaviors that led to her being perceived as uninterested in others, generalized this to prior occasions where she felt rejected, and confronted her denial that these perceptions of her were valid.

Family meetings are especially demanding and anxiety-provoking for most patients. In individual therapy the patient plans what she wants to say and anticipates the probable needs and responses of others. The individual therapist attends the meeting and later helps the patients to understand and integrate what occurred.

It is usually possible to develop a focus of psychotherapy that can be continued when the program ends. A productive focus usually concerns how a patient feels, and has always felt, about herself[11] and is related to her stage of development. Issues of separation-individuation, intimacy, and identity are of particular importance. It is useful to elicit feelings surrounding the end of the program and the loss of relationships with the staff and other patients. The therapist assumes an active stance in developing these issues and encourages the patient to continue her work when she leaves.

Body-Image Therapy

Body-image disturbance is of central importance in the bulimia syndrome. The goals of body-image treatment within this program are to reconstruct the development of body image; to correct distortions in body image; and to create a more positive body image, one where the body is no longer used as a vehicle of expression and a "battleground" but is accepted as a source of feelings and physical needs.

Women with eating disorders have difficulty discussing feelings about their bodies, despite their preoccupation with "bodily issues." They are comfortable calculating calories or discussing exercise programs, but not confronting disturbing feelings. They resist experiencing, describing, and understanding bodily perceptions. Even when they try, they find it hard to do with words. Expressive therapies, such as guided imagery, movement, and art, are useful in uncovering stored feelings and memories of bodily experience, because they deal with the stuff of which body image is made—images and physical sensations—and because their symbolic nature sufficiently obscures meaning to permit greater freedom of expression.

Guided imagery is especially powerful since body image is an image that patients have the potential to control. It is a fantasy-inducing process that combines deep muscle relaxation and the suggestion of images. This technique provides patients with a detailed picture of key relationships and developmental periods and events that have affected body image. The group provides a context for the revival of relevant emotion.

Many of the techniques used to explore and treat body-image disturbance have been described elsewhere.[3] This section will focus on three areas of exploration that have proven particularly important in reworking body image: incorporation of the changes of puberty, the influence of early sexual experiences, and the relationship of the mother's and daughter's body image.

TRANSITION OF PUBERTY

The way in which a woman incorporates into her body image the somatic changes of puberty plays a critical role in body cathexis. In an exercise designed to examine this, participants are asked to imagine how their bodies looked, moved, and felt before age 5, in first grade, in prepuberty, at menstruation, in adolescence, and the first time they left home. They are then asked to draw or sculpt the most salient image.

Memories surrounding the struggles of puberty, especially the onset of menstruation, have been clear in the minds of most bulimic patients, and most choose this as the subject of their art. The transformation into a woman's body was difficult and the changes were not welcomed. The onset of menstruation forces a girl to deal with the reality of being a female in whatever manner her own personal upbringing and culture define womanhood. Given the history of prejudice against females and the sexist tradition of viewing women in terms of their reproductive capacity, it is not surprising that achievement-oriented women, such as bulimic women, find menstruation—with its implied imperative to assume the female role—a time of conflict and depression.

Unable to identify with their mothers as mature female role models, the women often became frightened and more dependent. They were unsuccessful in their attempts to get close to their fathers who set stricter limits and distanced themselves from their daughters. Often they were identified with their fathers in childhood and experienced menarche as a time of loss. One woman remembered her father saying "She is a woman now" and instructing her brothers not to play with her any more. Another reported that her father, sensitized to the problems of incest where he worked, stopped touching her at all. As they began the separation-individuation process, they also became aware of increased levels of tension in the home and, withdrawing their energies from peer relationships, endeavored to care for their parents.

Instead of experiencing greater definition and acceptance of their bodies, bulimic patients experienced shame and loss of physical self-definition. Artistic renditions of menarche frequently suggest disgust for the normal female body, and many women remember this as the time they first experienced a wish to alter their body, to halt its transformation to one resembling their mother's, by hardening and strengthening it.

SEXUAL EXPERIENCES

To assist patients in understanding the impact of sexual experiences on body image, participants are asked to remember the following scenes: early sex play with peers; early sexual experiences with adults (including incest and pedophilia); masturbation; sexual encounters during adolescence; and recent sexual experiences. They visualize the actual settings where sexual experiences occurred and recall their feelings about their bodies and their eating habits at that time. When the imagery is concluded, they sculpt with clay the most salient image from the sequence. In response, many patients reexperience uncomfortable sexual experiences with significant adults and remember that at an early age they began to view their bodies and its functions as dirty, repulsive, and inadequate. They may recall the point at which they became obsessed with their bodies, making repeated efforts to "purify" or control them.

One woman sculpted herself as a 5-year-old child with a thin layer of clay draped over her head and a shell over her entire body. With great emotion she described for the first time an incestuous experience.

> My older brother came into my room and shut the door. He was talking to me and then told me to lie still. He put a towel over my head and began to touch my vagina. He told me to be quiet or I would get in trouble. I remember feeling something touching my vagina and wasn't sure why liquid came out of his penis. My vagina was wet. I was getting scared but began to feel numb. My grandmother called to him and he said, "Wait a minute." I thought he was gone so I took the towel off my head and saw him zipping up his pants. I didn't feel anything then. He left.
>
> The next image I had was when I was ten years old and my girlfriend and I were playing in the basement. He did the same thing to both of us. I felt dirty and ashamed of my body. I felt like I wanted to "clean my body out" and became interested in health foods and exercise. I wanted to purify my body and make it perfect. I started a diet and became obsessed with controlling my body. I wanted to make my body "sacred" but instead ended up bulimic.

By expressing this intense emotion and understanding the role it played in her bulimia, she stopped blaming her body and instead got angry at the perpetrator.

Another client who was depressed, drank heavily, and rejected help had an important breakthrough when she reexperienced the betrayal of her body during adolescence to fulfill the needs of her boyfriend. She described sexual acts with him that were abusive and many times physically painful to her. She would "tune out" her feelings by binging or getting drunk. Although she had referred to these experiences in other group and individual sessions, she had been unable to capture the associated affect or to connect it with her bulimia.

She wrote the following after working on these abusive experiences in the body-image group:

> I feel so much like screaming now. I can remember all the times I wanted to speak, all the time I was speechless while sentences were being said in my mind . . . And now I want to scream. I want to tell all those people they were wrong. I don't want to take it out on my body anymore. All the time I wished I could have said, "Get your fucking hands off me" and "How dare you?" . . . "What gives you the right?" And yet I sat there without speaking. Now I know I was right but I have to get over the past. I'm sick of silence. I want to say, "Mother fucker, I can feel. I'm a fucking person too. I can feel it all. I can feel more than you ever will." I won't betray my body anymore. . . .

Having initially told us that she couldn't stand to be touched, even by women, and did not know why, she now became openly affectionate to others in the program. Treatments developed to deal with the effects of sexual abuse, to be described in detail elsewhere, include reenactment of the event as it occurred, reenactment from a new position of power, examination of the ways in which the victim now victimizes herself, and a ritual developed to deal with residual shame. Most patients experience a progression of responses from blocking and denial, to rage, to shame, and finally, to self-acceptance.

MOTHER-DAUGHTER BODY IMAGE

Schilder[16] argues that it is primarily through identification with another person that an individual develops conscious and unconscious attitudes about his or her body. Because the mother is typically the primary focus of the daughter's identification, we developed an imagery and movement sequence to heighten awareness of the relationship between the mother's body image and daughter's body cathexis.

Each participant is asked to imagine the sequence of movements and feelings her mother experiences while getting ready for a social event. (Does she take a shower or bath? What parts of her body does she touch? What does she feel while dressing? Do her clothes fit? Does she use makeup? Does her mirror image please her?) She is then asked to picture her mother at the social event and observe her movements and gestures. (How does she use space? What does her body say to others?) Participants then move as they pictured their mothers moving in imagery. Finally they are asked to move in a way that captures feelings about their own bodies as they engage in the same sequence of events.

The theme of enmeshment between mother and daughter is a central one. One woman was struck by the similar style of movement and relating that she and her mother portrayed. During the imagery she saw her mother at a party standing with a drink in one hand and a cigarette in the other hand. She was aware of how tight and rigid her mother's position and movement were. She sensed that her mother did not feel good about her body and was ashamed of it. She felt uncomfortable when she realized that her own movements were similar to her mother's: She typically has a drink in one hand and is "grabbing" food with the other.

When the therapist asked what would happen if her mother relaxed and no longer held her body in such a tense, rigid manner, she replied that her mother would scream. She said her mother gave up everything for her family and is depressed most of the time. She suggested that both she and her mother utilize a tight posture to keep "feelings under control." Her fear was that the only thing they still have in common is a negative body image, which is portrayed through a rigid muscular armor. She expressed guilt that she has already achieved so much more than her mother. If she began to feel good about her body, what tie would remain?

Another client described her mother as someone who hated her own body and always talked about the need to lose weight. She and her mother had been dieting together since she was in the third grade. She described her mother as a "burden I carry on my back." The therapist then began to hang on the client's back and took on the role of the mother, saying "You must carry me, I can't do it myself." The client carried the therapist around the room until she got tired, gave up, and began to cry, saying: "No matter how much weight I lose you are still hanging on me. The weight loss doesn't take you away. I can't say no to you. I feel so responsible for you. But I can't take care of you anymore. You are too heavy for me to carry."

It became clear to this client that recovering from bulimia and beginning to feel good about her body had more to do with the relationship with her mother than her body shape. The issue wasn't losing more weight to feel in control but instead separating from her mother and establishing clear boundaries.

Other examples of the boundary diffusion between mother and daughter are portrayed through the following quotes from different women:

> My mother was thin until seven years ago. She began to drink a lot and gained a lot of weight. As she gained weight, I began to diet. I knew my thin body disturbed my mother. For some reason, I would undress in front of her on purpose. I hoped if I dieted and exercised enough that it would take the weight off my mother too.

> Every time I vomit, I vomit for my mother. Every time I lose a pound, I lose a pound for my mother.

> When I am with my mother my body image is like a stairway. I am long and winding and I don't know where I begin and where I end.

It is clear that for women struggling with bulimia, the need to control weight is motivated from a frightening sense that their bodies, as an aspect of self-organization, are out of control, easily invaded and intruded upon by significant others. Body-image treatment permits the realization that real control will not be found in weight loss.

CHANGING BODY IMAGE

The final stage of treatment is designed to impart a sense of the malleability of body image and to create a more positive body image. Participants summarize all they have learned about the development of their negative body image. They typically cite cultural influences, disturbing sexual experiences, cross-generational victimization between mother and daughter, and difficulties accepting the changes that occurred at puberty.

Clients who change their body image must go through a period of grieving a way of life, the central focus of which was a preoccupation with their body and dieting. Their daily routines must change. Relationships will be less predictable, and they must confront illusions about their bodies. They must, for example, relinquish the belief that thinness is power and look within to find power. They must face the losses that will occur when they begin to feel good about their bodies. Through guided imagery, participants are asked to imagine themselves with a positive body image and to become aware of the changes that might occur. One woman expressed the losses this way:

> I can see that it was easier for me to focus on the perfect body than what I wanted from life or why I was so depressed. This part of treatment is the most difficult part for me. I am no longer abusing my body till it's exhausted. But it doesn't always feel good. It's hard for me to figure out new goals in my life. My mother's main goal was to be a good physician's wife—which meant she had to look attractive and act nice. I'm not sure how you set new goals. At least the scale told me I was in control. For the first time I am experiencing the grieving process.

The therapists stress that grieving is a natural reaction to loss. Rituals are developed that help participants support each other as they begin to accept their bodily features with their inevitable limits and face the feelings of loss and powerlessness that obsession with their bodies has masked. They are assisted through the painful recognition that while their compulsive activities produced a temporary illusion of self, a well-formulated identity has not been achieved.

The final step in changing body image involves having patients first envision, then begin to move, dress, eat, and touch themselves as they would if they had a positive body image. One woman wrote the following of this change:

> I would move with certainty and dress as I want to portray myself. I would touch myself in a gentle, loving way. I would handle my sexuality in a [way] that is assertive and fun. I would stop blaming myself for the rape. . . . Something I have never been able to do till this program is take charge of my body. If someone says something I don't like I will very strongly defend my body— for it is my own.

THERAPY OUTCOME

Preliminary results of this treatment are encouraging. Table 25.1 shows psychological test data for a group of thirty-two consecutive patients completing the program. The Color-a-Person test was not used for the first two groups and data are available on only twenty patients. The results show a statistically significant improvement on all subscales of all tests. Of particular note are the substantial improvements on the drive for thinness, bulimia, and body dissatisfaction subscales of the Eating Disorders Inventory and on the Eating Attitudes Test.

One year follow-up data have been obtained from fifteen out of eighteen bulimic patients who have had sufficient time to reply.* One patient

* Data from two anorexic patients without bulimic symptoms are excluded due to noncomparability.

TABLE 25.1

Scores on Psychological Tests Immediately Before and After Treatment

	Pre-treatment	Post-treatment	p
Eating Disorders Inventory (N = 32)			
Drive for thinness	14.3	6.6	<.0001
Bulimia	10.7	2.5	<.0001
Body dissatisfaction	14.0	7.8	<.0001
Ineffectiveness	10.5	3.0	<.0001
Perfectionism	9.8	7.0	<.0001
Interpersonal distrust	5.8	3.2	<.0001
Lack of interoceptive awareness	12.1	4.8	<.0001
Maturity fears	3.0	0.9	<.0001
Revised Restraint Scale (N = 32)			
Cognitive restraint	13.7	12.0	<.05
Tendency toward disinhibition	12.9	9.2	<.0001
Perceived hunger	10.4	7.0	<.0001
Eating Attitudes Test (N = 32)	48.1	23.8	<.0001
Self-cathexis (N = 32)	145.9	177.9	<.0001
Body cathexis (N = 30)	138.6	161.5	<.0001
Color-a-Person Test (N = 20)			
Overall body dissatisfaction	3.4	2.8	<.0001
Stomach dissatisfaction	3.8	3.2	<.002
Hips dissatisfaction	3.9	3.3	<.003
Buttocks dissatisfaction	4.0	3.2	<.0005
Thighs dissatisfaction	4.0	3.1	<.0005
SCL-90 (N = 32)			
Somatization	0.77	0.58	<.02
Obsessive-compulsive	1.55	0.82	<.0001
Interpersonal sensitivity	1.80	1.12	<.0001
Depression	1.99	1.14	<.0001
Anxiety	1.66	1.15	<.0001
Anger-hostility	0.90	0.60	<.03
Phobic anxiety	0.61	0.32	<.002
Paranoid ideation	1.17	0.90	<.007
Psychoticism	1.25	0.55	<.0001
General symptomatic index	1.40	0.85	<.0001

informed us of her decision not to complete the posttests, one could not be located, and one has not replied. The patients in the follow-up group ranged from 18 to 31, with a mean age of 24.7. The duration of bulimia ranged from two to fifteen years, with a mean duration of 8.1 years. Based on duration and severity of bulimia alone, this would be classified as a group with relatively severe psychopathology. Three patients carried diagnoses of borderline personality disorder, and three more were regarded by prior therapists as having borderline features. Six of the fifteen had nonexistent or chaotic work histories and entered the program without any plan for future work or schooling. Only five could be said to have established a career line or to have any definite educational goal. Two were married, both with serious marital problems. One was divorced.

TABLE 25.2

*Scores on Psychological Tests Immediately Before Treatment,
After Treatment, and at One-year Follow-up*

	Pre-treatment	Post-treatment	Follow-up
Eating Disorders Inventory (N = 14)			
Drive for thinness	14.6	5.6	2.0
Bulimia	12.6	1.9	1.1
Body dissatisfaction	14.1	6.8	5.5
Ineffectiveness	9.4	3.5	1.8
Perfectionism	8.6	5.5	5.4
Interpersonal distrust	5.4	3.4	1.6
Lack of interoceptive awareness	11.5	5.3	1.9
Maturity fears	3.2	1.6	1.0
Revised Restraint Scale (N = 15)			
Cognitive restraint	13.1	11.4	8.9
Tendency toward disinhibition	14.3	9.1	7.5
Perceived hunger	11.6	7.3	5.3
Eating Attitudes Test (N = 15)	45.4	21.3	11.3
Self-cathexis (N = 14)	145.2	178.7	194.5
Body cathexis (N = 14)	145.1	166.3	171.3
SCL-90 (N = 13)			
Somatization	0.71	0.39	0.29
Obsessive-compulsive	1.57	0.80	0.83
Interpersonal sensitivity	1.77	1.03	0.80
Depression	2.03	1.11	0.84
Anxiety	1.86	1.05	0.79
Anger-hostility	0.96	0.46	0.53
Phobic anxiety	0.80	0.44	0.16
Paranoid ideation	1.06	0.95	0.58
Psychoticism	1.33	0.64	0.38
General symptomatic index	1.43	0.80	0.61

Table 25.2 shows test scores for the follow-up group before, immediately after, and one year after treatment. It is striking that not only was there no tendency toward regression, but that there was evidence of marked continuing improvement. With the exception of two subscales of the SCL-90 (both in a nonclinical range), scales of all tests showed further improvement. Figure 25.1 shows changes in binge/purge frequency, from the baseline period of the six months before treatment to the twelfth month of the follow-up period. During the targeted month, seven patients were entirely free of binge/purging, while the remainder showed reductions ranging from 63 to 94 percent, and averaging 85 percent. If the abstaining members are included, the group as a whole shows a slightly better than 91-percent reduction in binge/purge frequencies. Most of the women had some follow-up treatment, but the outcomes bear no obvious relationship to the type or amount of additional therapy.

It is becoming standard practice to use binge/purge frequencies, either at the end of treatment or at some follow-up interval, as the sole measure of success in treatment of bulimia, employing an arbitrary cut-off between

FIGURE 25.1

*Average Number of Binge / Purge Episodes Per Week for 15 Subjects in 6 Months
Before Treatment and in Month 12 of Follow-up Period*

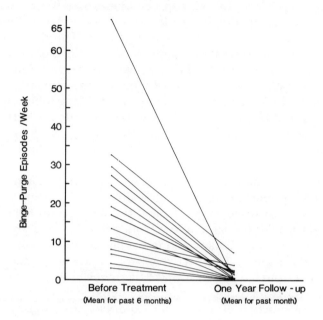

"successes" and "failures." We are concerned about this trend, which
can serve to minimize the important gains of women who, although continuing to binge/purge, show large reductions in bulimic behavior while
making important progress in other areas. Bulimic women are a heterogenous group. For many who suffer from multiple problems, the
achievement of total abstinence may rightfully be regarded as a secondary
or even remote goal.

   In our opinion, most of the nonabstainers benefited from therapy as
much or more as the abstainers. Although the one-year abstainers did
not differ from the rest of the group on initial binge/purge frequencies,
on the basis of this limited data they appear to have had a higher initial
level of general life adjustment. Thus, for example, of the five women
who entered treatment with an established career line or educational
goals, four were among the abstaining group at one-year follow-up. This
suggests that some simple indices of level of functioning may prove to be
important predictors of outcome, narrowly defined. But the group who
were still binge/purging actually reported somewhat larger gains in such
areas as feelings about themselves, relationships with friends, relationships
with family, and progress in educational and career goals. At one-year
follow-up, the number with an established career line or definite educational goals had more than doubled.

   Clearly the use of multiple criteria will make comparison of outcome among programs difficult. But unless the complexities are acknowledged, programs of sufficient scope and intensity to help more severely disturbed patients may not be offered. Worse yet, treatment centers may screen out disturbed patients in favor of well-adjusted ones whose success rates will undoubtedly appear superior. It would make sense to screen out these patients if they obtained no benefit from treatment. This does not, however, appear to be the case; they simply do not achieve perfect scores. Thus, for example, in month 12 the three women carrying diagnoses of borderline personality disorders showed binge/purge reductions of 100 percent (achieved by a gradual reduction throughout the follow-up year), 92.3 percent, and 86.5 percent. Although not total successes, these last two women clearly benefitted from treatment, having put in order lives of enormous chaos, marked by extreme self-destructive behavior.

It is interesting to look at patient ratings of the effectiveness of treatment components immediately after and one year after completion of therapy. The program components dealing directly with eating are rated somewhat lower with the passage of time, the food group falling from 6.7 to 5.8 and the educational seminars from 6.6 to 5.3 on a seven-point scale. By contrast, group therapy and individual therapy maintain their high ratings of 6.8 and 6.7 respectively, while body-image therapy increases its rating from 5.6 to 6.0. We take this to mean that the perceived value of the most psychologically oriented components of the program are not simply a function of a transient experience of intensity and involvement but are credited by patients, even after the passage of time, with being crucial to their success.

Conclusions

An epidemic of the proportions of bulimia in this decade, like the epidemic of hysteria in the nineteenth century, is inescapably telling of grave problems in the relationship of young women to the surrounding society. It may be decades more before these problems are, with the perspective of time, placed within their proper frame. But we believe that conceptualizations and treatments of bulimia must begin now to address the issues of female development that are inevitably implicated in a maturational breakdown of this magnitude.

We have described a theory that attempts to place the symptoms of bulimia within a comprehensive context and have developed treatments that allow women to explore the many layers of meaning embedded in their symptoms. These women must be helped not only to manage their eating but to find their places as women in a society that finds it equally difficult to give up what is uniquely female in the home or to value it when it is transposed to the work world of men.

Bulimia is not a mere fad, although like a fad it captures and expresses the aspirations of a large group of people. Nor is fat phobia the isolated creation of the fashion industry, although it is a fashion. Indeed, fat phobia may be woman phobia in its purest expression. Despite our own backgrounds in behavioral psychology and the physiology of eating disorders, we urge that bulimia not be "reduced" to a problem in energy expenditure and food intake, though understanding of these processes is essential. Nor do we believe that answers will be found in the conventional classifications of psychopathology even though groups of bulimic women, like any group, display a full range of psychological disorders.

The problem of bulimia is the problem of how we construct womanhood, a process in which physical appearance has historically played a central role. The treatment described here encompasses a broad agenda— to help women: accept their bodies while rejecting cultural prototypes; enjoy a sexuality that is self-respecting and empowering; preserve what is uniquely female while achieving broader spheres of influence than their mothers; maintain family ties while moving from the confines of the family home; and deepen their capacity for honest and satisfying human relationships. We believe we have achieved these goals to some limited degree, and hope that these goals become part of the treatment of all bulimic women.

REFERENCES

1. Booth, D. A. 1977. Satiety and appetite are conditioned reactions. *Psychosomatic Medicine* 39:76–81.
2. Bruch, H. 1973. *Eating disorders.* New York: Basic Books.
3. Crisp, A. H. 1965. Clinical and therapeutic aspects of anorexia nervosa: A study of 300 cases. *Psychosomatic Research* 9:67–78.
4. Derogatis, L. R. 1977. *SCL-90 R-Version I.* Baltimore: Johns Hopkins University.
5. Garner, D. M., and Garfinkel, P. E. 1980. Social-cultural factors in the development of anorexia nervosa. *Psychosomatic Medicine* 10:647–656.
6. Garner, D. M., and Garner, P. E. 1979. The eating attitudes test: An index of the symptoms of anorexia nervosa. *Psychological Medicine* 9:273–279.
7. Garner, D. M., Olmsted, M. P., and Polivy, J. 1983. Development and validation of a multidimensional eating disorder inventory for anorexia nervosa and bulimia. *International Journal of Eating Disorders* 2:15–34.
8. Keys, A., et al. 1950. *The biology of human starvation.* Minneapolis: University of Minnesota Press.
9. Le Magnen, J. 1971. Advances in studies on the physiological control and regulation of food intake. In *Progress in physiological psychology,* ed. E. Stellar and J. M. Sprague, pp. 203–261. New York: Academic Press.
10. Lucas, A. R., Beard, M., Kranz, J. S., and Kurtland, L. T. 1983. Epidemiology of anorexia nervosa and bulimia: Background of the Rochester project. *International Journal of Eating Disorders* 2:85–90.
11. Mann, J. 1981. The core of time-limited psychotherapy: Time and the central issue.

In *Forms of brief therapy*, ed. S. Budman, pp. 25–43. New York: Guilford Press.

12. Minuchin, S., Rosman, B., and Baker, L. 1978. *Psychosomatic families. Anorexia nervosa in context.* Cambridge, Mass.: Harvard University Press.

13. Nylander, I. 1971. The feeling of being fat and dieting in a school population. *Acta Sociomedica Scandinavica* 1:17–26.

14. Pope, H. G., Hudson, J. I., Yurgelen-Todd, D., and Hudson, M. S. 1984. Prevalence of anorexia nervosa and bulimia in three student populations. *International Journal of Eating Disorders* 3:45–51.

15. Pugliese, M. T., et al. 1983. Fear of obesity: A cause of short stature and delayed puberty. *New England Journal of Medicine* 309:513–518.

16. Schilder, P. 1950. *The image and appearance of the human body.* New York: International Universities Press.

17. Secord, P. F., and Jourard, S. M. 1953. The appraisal of body-cathexis: Body cathexis and the self. *Journal of Consulting Psychology* 17:343–347.

18. Steiner-Adair, C. 1984. The body politic: Normal female adolescent development and the development of eating disorders. Ph.D. diss., Graduate School of Education, Harvard University.

19. Stunkard, A. J. 1981. "Restrained eating": What it is and a new scale to measure it. In *The body weight regulatory system: Normal and disturbed mechanisms*, ed. L. A. Cioffi et al., pp. 243–251. New York: Raven Press.

20. 33,000 women tell how they really feel about their bodies. *Glamour*, February 1984.

21. Wooley, S. C., and Wooley, O. W. 1984. Should obesity be treated at all? In *Eating and its disorders*, ed. A. J. Stunkard and E. Stellar, pp. 185–192. New York: Raven Press.

22. ———. 1985. Intensive outpatient and residential treatment of bulimia. In *Handbook of treatment for anorexia nervosa and bulimia*, ed. D. Garner and P. Garfinkel, pp. 391–430. New York: Guilford Press.

The Eating Disorders: Summary and Integration

Kelly D. Brownell and John P. Foreyt

Has Our Mission Succeeded?

Our task of summarizing and integrating the chapters of this book is both exciting and challenging. A remarkable amount of information has been presented by the top people in the field. Individually, the chapters examine the important issues in obesity, anorexia, and bulimia. Collectively, what do they teach us?

The title of this volume captures our primary mission: the integration of physiology, psychology, and treatment. When we contacted prospective contributors for chapters, we were prepared to convince them of the conceptual and practical importance of this notion; little convincing was necessary. As is evident from the chapters, our contributors are expert in more than just the single area emphasized in their graduate or medical training. An interest in learning from other disciplines has spread among professionals in the eating disorders field and is reflected in the increasing tendency to assemble multidisciplinary teams for treatment. We hope this volume will foster this practice and that the product will be greater understanding of the physiological, psychological, and cultural causes of eating disorders, as well as their consequences, treatment, and prevention.

This notion of integration has obvious appeal to those involved with theory and research. We also wish to underscore the importance for practitioners. The treatment programs described in this volume consider the physiological, psychological, and cultural factors involved in the etiology and maintenance of the eating disorders. The implications for patient management are impressive. Numerous treatment issues arise from this perspective. For example: (1) How do exercise and food intake interact?

(2) At what stages of losing and gaining weight are patients most receptive to various treatments? (3) Are there common factors which promote or prevent relapse?

It was with these questions in mind that we sought chapters from experts involved in both research and clinical work. The clinical richness of the treatment chapters reflects our desire to take science full circle from theory to research to practical application and back to theory, where the cycle begins again. We hope this book will be valuable to practitioners and that the scientific basis for making treatment recommendations will be clear.

We are also pleased with the academic quality of the chapters. There is a focus on theory in many of the chapters. For both established and aspiring researchers, a number of important and intriguing research questions have been proposed. This strengthens our conviction that a volume of this type could help advance the field.

Common Themes

Several common themes arise from the chapters in this book. Each represents important developments in the study and treatment of eating disorders. We expect these will draw more attention in the future and may lead to major developments in the field. In addition, viewing each theme from the perspectives of the different eating disorders may help advance the field more rapidly than isolated work in each area.

PHYSIOLOGY OF WEIGHT CHANGE

Weight loss and gain provoke a series of physiological responses (see chapters by Bray, Garrow, Keesey, Björntorp, Mitchell, and Garner). The process of weight loss has been studied extensively in both obesity and anorexia. At first glance, the effects of weight loss in these two areas would seem much different because the anorexic starts at a normal weight and gradually becomes emaciated, while the obese person is simply attempting to achieve what they think is a normal weight. However, if one considers that the body may regulate its weight around a point or range (see especially chapters by Garrow and Keesey), weight loss in an anorexic and an obese person may provoke similar responses if they are regulating at different points. An obese person, for example, may weigh 40 pounds more than "ideal" weight, which may be determined by the size and number of fat cells (see Björntorp's chapter). Weight loss below this defended level could produce changes (e.g., decline in resting metabolism) similar to those that occur during weight loss in anorexia. There are differences as well as commonalities across the range of disorders, so there is potential merit for researchers in the obesity area to consider work on anorexia and bulimia and vice versa.

Little is known about the physiology of weight gain, even though this is important for all three of the eating disorders. Weight gain is a primary goal in the treatment of anorexia, the fear of weight gain promotes bulimia, and excessive weight gain is the defining characteristic of obesity. One could imagine that weight gain in bulimics and in presently or formerly obese persons, even if in response to psychological or environmental stimuli[10,11] might have similar physiological effects.

In this context, the issue of weight cycling arises. The majority of overweight persons lose and regain weight many times in a pattern labeled the "yo-yo syndrome." Obesity researchers have begun to study this in both animals and humans. The preliminary picture is that the organism responds to repeated bouts of weight loss and gain by increasing metabolic efficiency, thus creating a "dieting-induced obesity."[3] This impedes subsequent attempts to diet and facilitates weight regain (relapse). Repeated weight changes in bulimics have not been studied, but they may also have metabolic effects that make maintenance of normal weight more difficult. This could have psychological and environmental consequences which promote bulimic behavior, starting a maladaptive cycle of binging, purging, and metabolic changes. This issue may be best studied through a collective effort of researchers in each of the areas of anorexia, bulimia, and obesity.

THE PSYCHOLOGY AND PHYSIOLOGY OF RELAPSE

Relapse is endemic to the eating disorders, particularly to obesity and bulimia. Most obese persons regain lost weight, and even those who lose and keep the weight off usually do so only after many bouts of loss and regain. Viewed from the perspective of relapse, bulimia could be considered a disorder of frequent and repeated relapses. Bulimics establish self-imposed rules of food intake (see all chapters in Part III), the violation of which produces relapse (binge eating), sometimes followed by purging.

The frequent relapses that occur in bulimia may be important in their own right. Some degree of weight fluctuation takes place which may induce the metabolic efficiency described earlier. The great extremes of nutrient abundance and deprivation (binging and fasting) may produce psychological and physiological processes similar to those that occur in obese persons who lose weight on severe diets and then regain it by binge eating.

Relapse is important for theoretical as well as practical reasons,[4,9] and because of the possibility of similar processes occurring in persons with the various eating disorders, a good argument can be made for encouraging cooperation among researchers and clinicians in the various areas. The relapse issue has been studied more in the area of obesity than in the other two, and has received even more attention in the addictions field,[9] so the study of relapse presents another opportunity for interdisciplinary work.

BINGE EATING

Eating large amounts of food in a rapid fashion is another behavior which occurs across the eating disorders. It is central to the diagnosis of bulimia and occurs in a subgroup of anorexics. Many obese people eat in binges, with wide variations among individuals in the frequency and severity of the binges. This is another area in which research on a common issue may yield important information if studied from the various perspectives of obesity, anorexia, and bulimia.

Different theoretical models of binge eating suggest different treatments. In chapter 24, Wilson suggests that exposure and response prevention can halt the cycle of binging and purging, based on the theoretical notion that binge eating may be similar to an obsessive-compulsive pattern of behavior. The cognitive aspects of binge eating suggest a cognitive-behavioral approach (see chapter by Fairburn, Cooper, and Cooper). Another theory is that bulimia may be similar to or a side effect of affective disorders, suggesting that pharmacological methods may be helpful (see chapters by Agras and Kirkley, and Wilson). The fact that all these treatments appear to work for some patients suggests the possibility of different etiologies for the same symptoms. These theories and treatments draw largely from experience with anorexia and bulimia, but work on binge eating in obese patients may also be relevant.

SEX DIFFERENCES

The issue of sex differences, labeled sexual dimorphism by some, is increasingly becoming a focus of research in the health field.[1] The importance of the issue is apparent in fields such as the eating disorders, where a preponderance of sufferers are of one sex, or where the causes or consequences of a disorder are different for women and men. There is much to be learned from the eating disorders about these differences.

Anorexia and bulimia appear to exist almost exclusively in females, although cases in males are reported occasionally (see chapter by Szmukler and Russell). The prevailing sentiment is converging on social factors as a primary culprit. Chapters in this volume by Striegel-Moore and Rodin, Strober, Garner, Boskind-White and White, Fairburn et al., and Wooley and Kearney-Cooke underscore the importance of these factors. The combination of role conflicts, obsession with body shape, and other social pressures on women create the background against which certain personality and family patterns are manifested in disordered eating.

The question that arises, then, is: What can explain the low prevalence of eating disorders in men? Certainly many men have the personality factors and family background of anorexic women. These men may also have role conflicts about profession and family, and they live in a culture that exerts no small pressure on males to be thin. Are the differences between men and women in these factors sufficient to explain the imbalance in prevalence? Is it possible that physiological or psychological factors combine with culture to account for the variance?

Much work has been done on the physiological effects of starvation in anorexia, but most of the work, if not all, has been done with women. Keys and colleagues[6] studied starvation in men, but the subjects were normal weight volunteers without an eating disorder. There could be complex physiological differences in the way males and females respond to chronic energy restriction. It is possible, for example, that males have a stronger counter-response to deprivation than do females, so that hunger, satiety, metabolism, or other factors exert stronger pressure for weight restoration. Males who are potentially anorexic may encounter stronger resistance to the self-imposed starvation, so fewer males progress from the early signs to the chronic condition.

The preceding example is only hypothetical. We offer it to suggest that factors other than culture may be at work producing the high ratio of females to males in anorexia and bulimia. We feel that viewing these disorders with sex differences in mind may lead to new areas for research and suggest new possibilities for intervention.

Obesity is also an interesting disorder from the perspective of sex differences. The ratio of women to men is much closer with obesity than with anorexia or bulimia, yet 80 to 90 percent of individuals requesting treatment are women. This may be simply the reflection of a culture that puts more pressure on women to be thin. Yet there could be differences in metabolism, fat cell development, body fat distribution, macronutrient preference, or other factors that create different types of obesity for men and women. These types may differ in health risk, ease of remedy, psychological manifestations, and so forth.

One exciting new development in the obesity field is in the area of body fat distribution. Björntorp shows in chapter 4 that men tend to distribute weight in the upper body and women in the lower body. The same amount of fat in the upper body brings greater cardiovascular risk than in the lower body so that on the whole, men are at greater risk than their equally obese female counterparts. Leibel, Hirsch, and colleagues[7,8] have found differences in receptor activity in adipose tissue of the upper and lower body which may create differences between men and women in the danger of adiposity and the ease of weight loss.

The implications of this new development are not yet clear but could be far-ranging. Eventually, different dietary manipulations might be suggested for men and women, and if physiological or pharmacological treatments are developed, differences in adiposity of the upper and lower body may be a guiding factor in determining the nature of such treatments. They may also help explain sex differences in the preference for specific foods, the relationship between mood and food intake, the rate of eating, sensations in response to weight loss and gain, and so on.

Sex differences are being examined more closely in physiological and metabolic studies of obesity. We support this development and think the field would benefit from similar consideration of other aspects of obesity, as well as in the areas of anorexia and bulimia.

SOCIAL INFLUENCES

If there is one issue about which there is resounding agreement, it is the importance of social factors in the eating disorders. Nearly every chapter mentions these factors. The global picture that emerges is of a culture that socializes women to have intense concern for their body shape. The basic message to be thin is repeated through all channels of social influence, including the family, the schools, and the media. An interesting piece of evidence for this comes from the work of Garner (see chapter 16) and colleagues showing that *Playboy* centerfolds and Miss America contestants have become increasingly thin over the years and today are typically below ideal weight. The pressure to be thin, along with pressures to become an exemplary wife, mother, and working professional, combine to make women especially vulnerable to the eating disorders. The feminist perspective has helped in the understanding of the genesis and consequences of these factors (see chapters by Boskind-White and White, and Wooley and Kearney-Cooke).

The most common response to these pressures is dieting. The chapters in the bulimia section, along with other articles,[10,11] show that dieting creates a psychological and perhaps physiological environment in which binge eating is the natural outcome. This in turn increases the need for dieting, resulting in a vicious cycle. Purging is becoming an increasingly common component of this cycle.

The focus on these social factors has led to several advances in treatment. Programs like those outlined by Boskind-White and White, and by Wooley and Kearney-Cooke (see chapters 19 and 25) focus on reshaping body image, understanding the effects of social factors, and resolving role conflicts. It is too early to know how much these will contribute to a remedy for bulimia and anorexia when used alone or in combination with other approaches, because controlled trials have not yet been done. At the very least, the clinical consensus that exists in some quarters supports the need for further investigation.

There is increasing emphasis on dieting among teenage girls. The frequency of dieting in this group is alarming (again, see Wooley and Kearney-Cooke). The link between such behavior and the development of anorexia and bulimia is becoming more clear.

There is also concern over the effects of chronic dieting on growth and development. Dieting during childhood and adolescence imposes calorie restriction at a time when the body needs energy for normal growth. The issue involves not only calorie restriction, but the nutritional adequacy of the diet (see chapter by Nicholas and Dwyer). It would seem crucial for diets to be designed and monitored with great care so that maximum nutrition is provided in the small amount eaten. Of course, this is not done with most self-imposed diets, or when people follow the guidance of "experts" who write popular diet books (again, see Nicholas and Dwyer). Some would even claim that dieting is contraindicated for *any* child, except for those whose obesity poses a great risk, and even then, weight maintenance may be the best course to allow height to "catch up."

Epstein's chapter on obese children (see chapter 8) provides evidence that a carefully monitored diet for obese children does not seem to compromise growth. Epstein and his colleagues were the first group to evaluate this important issue in a systematic fashion. Still, little is known about the effects of dieting on non-obese children, particularly when the calorie levels and nutrient balance are not monitored. If the dieting-induced obesity described earlier[3] occurs, more severe restriction will be needed to maintain weight as the number of diets increases, which may exacerbate the problem of inadequate nutrition. This may be one of the most compelling issues to emerge from research and clinical work on the eating disorders, so we add our voices to the chorus of professionals in calling for more studies in this area.

The social issues surrounding obesity appear quite different from those for anorexia and bulimia. Stunkard outlines these in chapter 11. Factors such as socioeconomic status, ethnicity, religious affiliation, and geographic residence show strong associations with the prevalence of obesity. These demographic factors have received more attention in the obesity area than have cultural demands for a specific body shape. This is yet another area where research across the eating disorders may be useful.

The obesity field, as Stunkard notes, is an example in which realization of the importance of social factors has influenced treatment. Attempts have been made to involve spouses of dieters in the treatment process,[2] programs have begun in the schools (see Epstein's chapter), and macro-social programs have been tested at worksites and in entire communities (see Stunkard's chapter). These have great promise and may provide new ideas for social interventions in anorexia and bulimia.

TREATMENT

The notion of integration, which we hope is the cornerstone of this book, is evident in the chapters dealing with treatment. In the obesity section, for example, Nicholas and Dwyer (chapter 6) have written about nutrition, Stern and Lowney (chapter 7) about exercise, Brownell and Wadden (chapter 9) about behavioral approaches, and Blackburn and colleagues (chapter 10) about very-low-calories diets. In each case the importance of a comprehensive, multicomponent program is emphasized, and the authors note that the specific focus of their chapter is only part of the overall management of obesity.

We welcome this trend toward involving many disciplines in the study and treatment of the eating disorders, and feel it may at some point exert its influence on professional training. The professional trained in a single discipline, whether it is nutrition, exercise physiology, psychology, medicine, etc., will develop only part of the necessary expertise. This suggests a need for postgraduate training in centers that specialize in the eating disorders. A few such centers exist, but there has been no coordinated effort to establish training programs. Such an effort would be important to the advancement of the field.

Treatment Components. Several factors are mentioned time and time again in the chapters on treatment. We will note these only briefly because the chapters contain detailed information. The interaction of these factors, however, is an issue to which we would like to draw attention. These may form a most fruitful area for research.

Nutrition is a concern in all of the eating disorders. In the obesity area, there is growing realization that diet may be quite important beyond the need to "eat balanced meals." The craving for certain foods may be involved in the etiology of obesity. The chemical properties of some foods trigger physiological reactions that influence hunger and satiety, which may in turn precipitate binge eating, weight gain, and relapse. The binge eating issue is central to anorexia and bulimia, and we may be moving toward the day when we know that different types of bulimia, anorexia, or obesity may be created by dietary practices and that specific diets will be indicated in treatment.

Exercise is the second factor of obvious importance due to its role in energy balance and weight regulation. Hypoactivity is one factor often related to obesity and hyperactivity is common in anorexia. The physiological and psychological aspects of exercise have been studied most thoroughly in the obesity area (see chapter by Stern and Lowney) and deserve more attention in anorexia and bulimia.

A fascinating area for further research is the interaction of diet and exercise. The chapter by Stern and Lowney cites research showing that access to an exercise wheel can help rats prevent the obesity produced by exposure to a high-fat diet. Exercise may shift the preference for specific nutrients that in turn may increase or decrease the body's capacity for further exercise. Mood changes produced by certain foods may affect the desire to exercise; conversely, certain types or amounts of exercise may provoke the desire for specific nutrients.

Another aspect of treatment common to the three eating disorders is cognitive intervention. This seems particularly important in restructuring attitudes and cognitive tendencies that set the stage for relapse. The popularity of "cognitive-behavioral" treatment is due in part to the concept that cognitive processes are central to behavior, that they can be studied and measured, and that cognitive change is a necessary part of most treatments. The role of cognitive factors and specific treatment strategies is discussed in detail by Striegel-Moore and Rodin, and Brownell and Wadden in the obesity section; by Garfinkel and Kaplan, Garner, and Andersen in the anorexia section; and by Boskind-White and White, Agras and Kirkley, Fairburn et al., Wilson, and Wooley and Kearney-Cooke in the bulimia section.

Behavioral procedures have become the backbone of most treatments for the eating disorders. This has been the case for years in treatment for obesity. Psychoanalytic approaches have given way to other treatments in the anorexia area, and aside from the occasional use of antidepressant medication, behavioral and cognitive methods are the preferred treatment for bulimia. These methods are typically used with various combinations of family therapy, group support, medical management, and so forth. The behavioral approaches have focused attention on self-control strategies for behavior change and on the systematic evaluation and modification of behavioral and cognitive patterns. There is also a growing emphasis on long-term results.

Most treatment programs for the eating disorders consider the factors mentioned above (nutrition, exercise, cognitive and behavioral methods). There is great variation, however, in the quality of the material and education in these areas. A behavioral program, for example, may note the importance of exercise without doing justice to its actual role in treatment. This points to the need for integrated programs staffed by professionals from various disciplines to coordinate training, research, and treatment.

Is Obesity an Eating Disorder?

Our final issue relates to the basic philosophy of what constitutes an eating disorder. The recent trend has been to acknowledge anorexia nervosa and bulimia as "eating disorders" while excluding obesity. Books on the eating disorders generally do not consider obesity, conferences on the eating disorders are likely to follow the same course, and centers for the treatment of eating disorders are not always equipped to deal with obesity. Professionals and the public tend to discuss anorexia and bulimia as similar disorders while obesity is considered much different. This is an important and, in our opinion, unfortunate shift in direction for the field.

WHY ANOREXIA AND BULIMIA BUT NOT OBESITY?

There are several reasons for this trend. First, while anorexia and bulimia are considered a product of environmental, cultural, and psychological influences, obesity is more likely to include physiological factors in its origin. Certainly anorexia and bulimia have physiological components that are important in the course of these disorders, but few believe that physiological processes are crucial to their etiology. This is not the case with obesity (see chapters by Bray, Garrow, Keesey, and Björntorp). Obesity also has important cultural and psychological causes and consequences (see chapters by Striegel-Moore and Rodin, and Stunkard), but the physiology cannot be denied.

Perhaps because anorexia and bulimia share some features and etiological components, there is great overlap among scientists working in the two areas. Some renowned scientists, formerly known for their work in anorexia are now studying bulimia; examples are Garfinkel (chapter 14), Garner (chapter 16), and Halmi.[5] It is less common for scientists who have studied obesity to move to bulimia, although the work of G. Terence Wilson (see chapter 24) is an exception.

Anorexia nervosa and bulimia share many clinical characteristics and some aspects of treatment. They have some psychological manifestations in common and, to some extent, the treatment for bulimia has been adapted from anorexia programs. It is natural, therefore, for researchers and clinicians in these two areas to have a great deal of contact. This is a positive situation, but we propose that there is much to be gained from adding obesity to the group of disorders involved in this interactive process.

OBESITY AS AN EATING DISORDER

There are arguments both for and against classifying obesity as an eating disorder. It is true that many obese persons have disordered eating; if nothing else, the binge eating that is often associated with obesity constitutes an eating disorder. Such a label, however, has important implications.

Considering obesity an eating disorder implies that it is not a disorder of another sort, say a metabolic disorder or a genetic disorder. Such an inference may lead researchers and clinicians to focus on one aspect of the disorder (eating) and pay less attention to important physiological factors. It may also contribute to "blaming the victim" because most people feel that eating is a matter of personal control.

The most compelling reason to include obesity when considering the eating disorders is the likelihood that research and clinical work in each area will benefit all three. This occurs already in the areas of anorexia and bulimia, but there is less overlap between either of these with the area of obesity. We hope this situation will change and that books, conferences, newsletters, and any other forum in which clinical and research information is exchanged will include obesity as well as anorexia and bulimia. We recognize that obesity may not be an eating disorder per se, and that there are disadvantages in this label, but feel the interactions such an approach might facilitiate may be a more important consideration.

Concluding Remarks

The eating disorders field is advancing rapidly and we hope this volume will contribute to its progress. We thank our contributors for their hard work, innovation, and stimulation. We have learned a great deal from their chapters and if our readers learn as much, we will consider our efforts in assembling this book worthwhile. We hope our readers agree that this truly is a handbook that integrates the physiology, psychology, and treatment of obesity, anorexia, and bulimia.

REFERENCES

1. Blechman, E., and Brownell, K. D., eds. 1986. *Behavioral medicine in women.* New York: Pergamon.
2. Brownell, K. D. 1982. Obesity: Understanding and preventing a serious, prevalent, and refractory disorder. *Journal of Consulting and Clinical Psychology* 50:820–840.
3. Brownell, K. D., Greenwood, M. R. C., Stellar, E., and Shrager, E. E. 1986. Dieting-induced obesity: An animal model of weight cycling. Paper submitted for publication.
4. Brownell, K. D., Marlatt, G. A., Lichtenstein, E., and Wilson, G. T. In press. Understanding and preventing relapse. *American Psychologist.*
5. Halmi, K. A., Falk, J. R., and Schwartz, E. 1981. Binge eating and vomiting: A survey of a college population. *Psychological Medicine* 11:697–706.
6. Keys, A., Brozek, J., Henschel, A., Mickelson, O., and Taylor, H. L. 1950. *The biology of human starvation* (2 vols.). Minneapolis: University of Minnesota Press.
7. Leibel, R. L., and Hirsch, J. 1985. A radioisotopic technique for analysis of free fatty acid reesterification in human adipose tissue. *American Journal of Physiology* 248: E140–E147.
8. Leibel, R. L. In press. A radioisotopic method for the measurement of free fatty acid turnover and adrenoreceptor responses in small fragments of human adipose tissue. *International Journal of Obesity.*
9. Marlatt, G. A., and Gordon, J., eds. 1985. *Relapse prevention.* New York: Guilford.
10. Polivy, J., and Herman, C. P. 1985. Dieting and binging: A causal analysis. *American Psychologist* 40:193–201.
11. Striegel-Moore, R., Silberstein, L., and Rodin, J. 1986. Toward an understanding of risk factors for bulimia. *American Psychologist* 41:246–263.

NAME INDEX

SUBJECT INDEX

Abnormal normal weight control syndrome, 389

Abortion, 362

Acanthosis nigricans, 27

Activity diary, 55–56

Adipocytes, *see* Fat cells

Adolescence: affective disorders in, 274; anorexia nervosa in, 234, 241, 270, 303, 331, 336; body dissatisfaction in, 368; bulimia in, 371, 396, 480; constructions of adult female role in, 481; family conflict in, 432; obesity in, *see* Adolescent obesity; schizophrenia in, 274; sociocultural pressures in, 133

Adolescent obesity: educational disadvantages of, 37; locus of control and, 102; treatment of, 165, 173, 175; very-low-calorie diet for, 204

Adrenal function: in anorexia nervosa, 257; in obesity, 32–33

Adrenocorticotropic hormone (ACTH), 33

Aerobic exercise: for obese children, 166, 172; weight-loss maintenance and, 191

Aerobic Nutrition (Mannerberg and Roth), 125, 136, 137

Affective disorders: anorexia nervosa and, 240, 270, 272–73; bulimia as, 374–76, 395, 397–98, 407, 429–30, 465

African tribes, 354

Aging, set point change with, 74

Agoraphobia, 362, 375

Alcoholics Anonymous, 218

Alcoholism: bulimia and, 269, 270, 360, 396; exposure and response prevention in treatment of, 454; treatment programs for, 193

Alexithymia, 343, 347

Alkalosis: hypokalemic, 252; metabolic, 254, 382; sialodenosis and, 381

Ambivalence, exploration of, 386–87

Amenorrhea: in affective disorders, 274; in anorexia nervosa, 237, 248, 255–57, 267, 277, 279, 283, 329, 334, 338, 360; in bulimia, 360, 380; in Simmonds' disease, 267; on very-low-calorie diet, 205

American Cancer Society Study, 11–12, 24

American Journal of Psychiatry, 370

Amherst, University of Massachusetts at, 126

Amygdalectomy, 383

Amylase elevations, 380–81

Androgynous body style, 369, 370

Android obesity, 20, 88

Androstenedione, 34

Anemia, 407

Animal obesities, 76–80

Anorexia nervosa: affective disorders and, 240, 270, 272–73; ambivalent role of therapist in treatment of, 329–30; assessment of, 406, 407; assessment of beliefs in, 310; attitudes to shape and weight in, 394; atypical, 349; biological models of, 242; bulimia in, *see* Bulimia; cardiopulmonary complications of, 253; central nervous system dysfunction in, 255; characteristics of, 331; classification of, 238–39; cognitive therapy for, 301–18; and continuum of weight-preoccupied women, 270–72; descriptive and psychopathological factors in, 237–38; diagnosis of, 334; diagnostic conceptualizations of, 266–80; diagnostic criteria for, 276–79; endocrine complications of, 255–57; epidemiology of, 240–42, 270–71; family systems models of, 243; fluid and electrolyte complications of, 255; gastrointestinal complications of, 250–52; hematological and immunological complications of, 253–54; heterogeneity of, 268–70; historical antecedents of, 231–37; hospitalization for, 309–10, 333, 335–45; hypothalamic regulation in, 257–58; hysteria and, 268, 274–75; incidence of, 241; laboratory abnormalities in, 249; long-term course of, 288–89; long-term physiological consequences of, 360; in males, 297, 334; as maturational crisis, 477, 478, 480; meal planning in treatment of, 308; medical complications of, 249; metabolic abnormalities in, 248–50; "me-too," 331; minimum weight for outpatient treatment of, 307; mortality rate for, 288–89; motivation for treatment of, 304–6; as nonspecific syndrome, 275–76; normalization of eating